AMERICAN LOCAL GOVERNMENT AND ADMINISTRATION

THE MACMILLAN COMPANY
NEW YORK · CHICAGO
DALLAS · ATLANTA · SAN FRANCISCO
LONDON · MANILA

BRETT-MACMILLAN LTD.
TORONTO

AMERICAN LOCAL
GOVERNMENT AND
ADMINISTRATION

HAROLD F. ALDERFER

*Head, Department of Political Science
and
Executive Secretary, Institute of Local Government
The Pennsylvania State University*

THE MACMILLAN COMPANY New York

6215

To My Mother and Father

PREFACE

This volume is designed to present a modern and over-all description of the entire field of American local government and administration. Thus it includes not only an account of urban and municipal local units but also of counties, townships, school districts and special districts as well. In these days of changing conditions, it is impossible to isolate one kind of local government unit from the rest and arrive at any real understanding of local government problems.

Neither can local government be considered without relating it to the state and the nation, and, therefore, this book deals in more than usual detail with federal-local and state-local relationships, especially as they have developed since World War II. For example, new data in the field of federal-local relationships have been made available in the publications of the Commission on Intergovernmental Relations of the national government which made its final report in June 1955, and this material is summarized in appropriate places throughout the volume. Emphasis in each chapter is given to illustrative material of recent date, and this includes bibliography.

We would like to acknowledge with deep appreciation the services of Professor Arthur W. Bromage of the Department of Political Science, University of Michigan, and Professor Russell M. Ross of the Department of Political Science, State University of Iowa, who read the manuscript and gave invaluable suggestions for its improvement. Also, we would like to acknowledge the competent work of Miss Elizabeth Smedley, technical consultant, Institute of Local Government, The Pennsylvania State University, who constructed two tables relating to home rule and to the types of municipal corporations, and the efforts of Miss Catherine Sgro of the Institute staff who aided in the preparation of the manuscript.

The author alone is to be held accountable for any defects of omission or commission.

Harold F. Alderfer

University Park, Pennsylvania

CONTENTS

17. THE PUBLIC SCHOOLS 627

AMERICAN LOCAL GOVERNMENT AND ADMINISTRATION

Chapter I

THE UNITS OF AMERICAN LOCAL GOVERNMENT

The American system of government is federal. The United States Constitution establishes a national government and recognizes the governments of the several states. To the national government, it delegates specific powers; and in the words of the Tenth Amendment, "the powers not delegated to the United States by the Constitution, nor prohibited by it to the states, are reserved to the states respectively, or to the people."

The establishment of local government not being delegated to the national government nor prohibited to the states is clearly within the sphere of state power. This power is exercised by the state legislatures except where the state constitutions restrict their powers. While each state has its own system of local government, there are many similarities. For the fundamental principles and institutions of local government are common throughout the United States. But there is a wide variety of forms and practices depending upon history, experience, and conditions. Thus, both stability and flexibility, so essential to governmental success anywhere and any time, are basic qualities of American local government as they are in the federal system of nation and states.

Broadly speaking, there are several major classes of local government. The first are the subdivisions of the state. State law specifically directs these units to do certain things for their inhabitants as agents of the state. Moreover, all the territory of the state is divided into such units to achieve uniformity of administration. The best example of this class is the county. In all states, except Louisiana where the comparable unit is called the parish, there are counties, and in all states every square mile is in some county with but very few exceptions. Likewise, in the 22 states in which townships or unincorporated towns exist as subdivisions within the counties, these come also within such classification.

Counties and townships were originally laid out by state legislatures to include all the territory involved; they were established without the solicitation or petition of the inhabitants; they were directed to carry out governmental rather than corporate powers. Thus, these units are considered by the courts in most of the states as quasi-corporations. The line, however, cannot always be clearly drawn. For example, there are some areas of the state in which the county has been consolidated with the city. In most states that have rural townships, incorporated places are separated and independent from the townships surrounding them. Local petition is necessary in some instances to establish new townships. All local units, not only counties and townships, are considered as agents of the state under certain circumstances. Nevertheless, counties and townships must be considered to be in a separate class of local government units.

Incorporated places or municipalities comprise a second group. These include cities, boroughs, villages, and incorporated towns. They are the units of government established especially for communities in which people live close together, under more or less urban conditions, although thousands of them contain less than 2,500 population which the United States census holds as the dividing line between urban and rural places. The governments of these units are designed to give their inhabitants such services as are necessary to urban life: police and fire protection, water supply and sewage disposal, streets and traffic control, for example. In the eyes of the law, these local units are known as municipal corporations for they are given full corporate powers and those of a local, rather than of a statewide, nature. Furthermore, they come into being only after petition on the part of people desiring such incorporation.

A third group of local units are the special districts which are created to carry on specific functions or projects. The most numerous of these is the school district, but there are many others: for example, water supply, road, drainage, irrigation, sewage, and mosquito eradication districts. These districts are called *ad hoc* (for this) because they are established for a particular, not general, purpose. The courts view them as quasi-corporations.

People usually live within the jurisdiction of more than one local government. They may live in a city, a county, a school district, and sewage district at the same time. Or they may live in a township, a county, and a school district. In a city which has combined with the county and which operates the school system, people may have only one local unit, but that is rare.

What Is a Local Unit?

Technically speaking, to be a local unit requires certain qualifications. The Bureau of the Census sets up three general criteria. *First, it must have existence as an organized entity.* To have this, it must have some form of organization and some corporate powers such as the right to sue and be sued, to make contracts, and to own property. *Second, it must have governmental character.* Its officers must be elected by the voters, or appointed by elective officials. It must account to the public for its activities. *Third, it must have substantial autonomy,* that is, considerable fiscal and administrative independence. This generally includes the right to determine its budget, to raise its revenues and to go into debt, subject only to state law and supervision.[1]

Professor William Anderson (University of Minnesota) clothes a true local government unit with the following elements: (1) *terri-*

---

[1] United States Department of Commerce, Bureau of the Census, *Governments in the United States in 1952*, State and Local Government Special Studies: No. 31, Washington, D. C. (1953), pp. 6–7.

tory, (2) *population*, (3) continuous *organization*, (4) separate *legal identity*, (5) *independence* from other local units, (6) *governmenetal powers and functions*, and (7) power to raise *revenue.*[2]

These definitions justly exclude a large number of national, state, and local districts such as federal reserve districts, forest protection districts, judicial districts, election districts, highway maintenance districts, and a whole host of other such governmental areas which do not have the basic characteristics of units of local government.

THE NUMBER OF LOCAL UNITS

There were 116,694 units of local government in the United States in 1952.[3] These included 3,049 counties, 16,778 municipalities, 17,202 townships, 67,442 school districts, and 12,319 special districts. Minnesota led all the states with 9,025; Rhode Island had the least with 89.

Counties

While the most inclusive local unit is the county, there are fifty-five areas in the United States in which counties are not independently organized or where county government is lacking.[4]

Texas has the largest number of counties—254—while Delaware has 3 and Rhode Island none. Sixty-seven counties in the United

---

[2] William Anderson, *The Units of Local Government in the United States,* Public Administration Service, No. 83 (1949), pp. 8–10.

[3] *Governments in the United States in 1952, op. cit.,* p. 1.

[4] *Ibid.,* p. 8. These include the county governments listed as cities, townships, or towns only: Counties of Bronx, Kings, New York, Queens, and Richmond, in the city of New York; the parishes of Baton Rouge and New Orleans, in Louisiana; the counties of Nantucket (town of Nantucket) and Suffolk (city of Boston) in Massachusetts; the county of Philadelphia; the county of San Francisco; the county of Denver; independent cities carrying out county functions: Baltimore, St. Louis (Missouri), and 28 Virginia cities; nine unorganized areas bearing county names in Rhode Island and South Dakota; and four federal areas: the District of Columbia, and the Yellowstone National Park in Idaho, Montana, and Wyoming.

States have 250,000 or more population and contain 46 million people, more than one-fourth of the total. Two hundred and fifty-four counties have less than 5,000 each and together aggregate 798,000. The average population served by a county government is 43,770 but Loving County, Texas, has only 227 people while Cook County (Chicago metropolitan area) has 4,508,792. Only one new county, Los Alamos in New Mexico, was created between 1942 and 1952.[5] The largest county in the United States is San Bernadino, California, with 20,175 square miles; the smallest is Arlington, Virginia, with 25 square miles.

Municipalities

Municipalities are incorporated places, those that function under the terms of a charter of incorporation provided either by a specific or general law of the legislature. They include cities, boroughs, villages, and incorporated towns. They are of all sizes. One hundred and six cities have populations of 100,000 or more, and these comprise almost half the population of the United States. But more than half of the municipalities have less than 1,000 population. From 1942 to 1952, the number of municipalities increased by 558.[6]

The New England Town

The traditional and most important local unit of government in the six New England states is the town. Except for areas in northern Maine and Vermont that are wild and virtually uninhabited, a net of town government covers the entire New England area.[7] The

---

[5] *Ibid.*, p. 2.
[6] *Ibid.*
[7] William S. Carpenter, *Problems in Service Levels* (1940), p. 108 fn. "A count of the different forms of local government in Maine in 1935 revealed the following: Cities, 20; Towns, 434; Organized plantations, 22; Wild land plantations, 41; Townships, 392. Total 909." The last three groups, totaling 455 units, may be considered as having little or no local government, coming under the direct administration of the state. Local governments in both Maine and Vermont may be deorganized and then are administered directly under state administration.

Bureau of the Census lists the New England states with 1,429 towns
and 204 municipalities. The New England town is not incorporated,
but as many of the towns in Massachusetts, Connecticut, and Rhode
Island are thickly populated it renders services to urban communities and from that standpoint has the powers of a municipality.
In the more northerly areas it is primarily a unit of rural government. However, villages and settlements within the town areas are
not separately incorporated as they are in some states, but are served
by the town government. This natural integration of the entire community into one political entity is one of the reasons for the present
vitality and strength of this old and respected American unit of
local government.

The Township

Townships are found in 16 states, almost entirely in the North
Central and Middle Atlantic regions.[8] They are rural counter-
parts to municipalities and carry on limited functions of government.
This unit of government is practically unknown in the southern and
trans-Mississippi states where from the beginning of settlement the
plantation and ranch type systems of agriculture prevailed. Large
waste areas and scanty population made subdivisions smaller than
the county unnecessary.

From central Ohio west within the Northwest Territory, the land
belonged to the United States before settlement and was laid out by
federal surveyors in geographical townships, six miles long and six

[8] The Bureau of the Census lists the following states as having townships in
1952: Illinois, Indiana, Kansas, Michigan, Minnesota, Missouri, Nebraska,
North Dakota, New York, New Jersey, Ohio, Pennsylvania, South Carolina
(only 2), South Dakota, Washington, and Wisconsin. Lane Lancaster, *Government in Rural America* (1952), states that "the township exists generally in
Indiana, Iowa, Kansas, Michigan, Minnesota, New Jersey, New York, Ohio,
Pennsylvania, and Wisconsin. It is found in parts of Illinois, Nebraska, Missouri,
and the Dakotas. In the number of other states administrative districts called
townships exist, but have no political organization of importance. In New York,
the term 'town' continues to be used." (p. 61 fn.) The Bureau of the Census
did not list Iowa because the county has absorbed "nearly all former township
functions," but lists 70 townships in the state of Washington.

miles wide. These congressional townships, as they were called, were usually taken as the district within which to establish a civil township. While there are many exceptions due to geographic features of the country and the establishment of independent municipalities, the midwest township is still generally an area of thirty-six square miles. Townships in the eastern part of the United States vary greatly in size and form. Established in the early days from social communities, they conform even today more accurately to natural neighborhoods.

Usually cities, boroughs, and villages are separated from townships upon their incorporation. Villages in New York and Michigan, however, remain part of the township. All or almost all the municipalities in Ohio, Nebraska, Indiana, and Illinois are parts of townships. But in all the states, the more compactly settled districts are organized into municipalities for the more urban purposes of government, leaving townships to deal almost entirely with rural problems.[9] There are some important exceptions to this. Seventy townships of the first class in Pennsylvania, which are required to have three hundred population per square mile, are local units within the metropolitan areas of Philadelphia, Pittsburgh, and other Pennsylvania cities. Many of them have large urban settlements requiring the urban services of an average city. The largest of these, Upper Darby, outside of Philadelphia, has a population of 85,000. These units are more like the urban New England town than rural townships. Likewise, townships that include cities, such as is the case in Indiana and Illinois, have large populations.

Most of the townships in the United States, however, are rural districts with small populations. While governmentally insignificant in comparison to cities and other incorporated places, the recent exodus from the central cities to their peripheries has given these townships a new importance.

[9] John A. Fairlie and Charles M. Kneier, *County Government and Administration* (1930), pp. 451–452.

NUMBER OF GOVERNMENTAL UNITS, BY STATE: 1952

This table includes all governmental units in the United States as defined by the United States Bureau of the Census. From "Governments in the United States in 1952" (State and Local Government Special Study No. 31) issued in 1953.

State	All Governmental Units [a]	Local Governments Except School Districts					School Districts [d]
		Total	Counties [b]	Municipalities	Townships and Towns [c]	Special Districts	
Alabama	548	439	67	302	——	70	108
Arizona	367	96	14	48	——	34	270
Arkansas	1,089	666	75	360	——	231	422
California	3,764	1,753	57	306	——	2,390	2,010
Colorado	1,953	600	62	241	——	297	1,352
Connecticut	363	359	8	33	152	166	3
Delaware	108	92	3	49	——	40	15
District of Columbia	2	2	—	1	——	1	—
Florida	617	549	67	294	——	188	67
Georgia	976	788	159	475	——	154	187
Idaho	938	632	44	193	——	395	305
Illinois	7,723	4,238	102	1,157	1,433	1,546	3,484
Indiana	3,050	1,934	92	540	1,009	293	1,115
Iowa	5,857	1,203	99	934	——	170	4,653
Kansas	6,933	2,948	105	605	1,514	724	3,984
Kentucky	796	563	120	313	——	130	232
Louisiana	489	421	62	215	——	144	67
Maine	664	659	16	42	473	128	4
Maryland	328	327	23	146	——	158	——
Massachusetts	584	583	12	39	312	220	——
Michigan	6,766	1,920	83	489	1,264	84	4,845
Minnesota	9,026	2,798	87	796	1,844	71	6,227
Mississippi	693	599	82	263	——	254	93
Missouri	7,002	2,110	114	781	329	886	4,891
Montana	1,598	310	56	121	——	133	1,287
Nebraska	7,981	1,588	93	533	477	485	6,392
Nevada	243	76	17	15	——	44	166
New Hampshire	551	322	10	12	222	78	228
New Jersey	1,151	669	21	334	233	81	481
New Mexico	289	182	32	72	——	78	106
New York	5,483	2,567	57	610	932	968	2,915
North Carolina	608	607	100	401	——	106	——
North Dakota	3,968	1,888	53	348	1,393	94	2,079
Ohio	3,936	2,470	88	904	1,338	140	1,465
Oklahoma	2,771	670	77	499	——	94	2,100
Oregon	1,723	651	36	208	——	407	1,071
Pennsylvania	5,156	2,649	66	990	1,564	29	2,506
Rhode Island	89	88	—	7	32	49	——
South Carolina	413	363	46	237	2	78	49
South Dakota	4,917	1,517	64	307	1,090	56	3,399
Tennessee	435	421	95	241	——	85	13
Texas	3,963	1,483	254	738	——	491	2,479
Utah	385	344	29	209	——	106	40
Vermont	414	393	14	71	238	70	20
Virginia	366	365	100	223	——	42	——
Washington	1,539	993	39	240	70	644	545
West Virginia	350	294	55	216	——	23	55
Wisconsin	7,258	1,959	71	534	1,281	73	5,298
Wyoming	519	200	23	86	——	91	318
Total	116,743	49,348	3,049	16,778	17,202	12,319	67,346

[a] Includes federal government and the 48 states.
[b] Excludes 54 areas corresponding to counties but having no organized county government.
[c] Includes "towns" in the 6 New England States, New York, and Wisconsin.
[d] Excludes local school systems operated as part of state, county, municipal, or township governments.

8

School Districts

In 1952, there were 67,442 school districts in the United States; in 1942, there were 108,579. This represents a reduction of thirty-eight per cent, an indication of the intensity of the movement in the last decade for consolidation of rural school districts. By 1954, the number was down to 59,631.

Nine states had more than 3,000 school districts, all were middle western states where the common school district is the basic pattern of organization. The common school district is found in twenty-seven states.[10]

In nine states, the town or township school district is in operation. In the six New England states, the school district is usually coterminous with the town. In Indiana, New Jersey, and Pennsylvania, except for independent city and borough districts, the township boundaries are also those of the school district. County or modified county systems are where the schools are organized on a county basis, with or without the urban independent districts. Twelve states, all southern except Utah, have countywide systems.[11]

Special Districts

If school districts were reduced in number during the 1942–52 decade, special districts increased: from 8,299 to 12,319, forty-eight per cent. Six states: Illinois, California, New York, Missouri, Kansas, and Washington had more than five hundred such special local units in 1952.

Special districts are usually created to carry out one particular

---

[10] The National Commission on School Reorganization, *Your School District* (1948), tables on pp. 258–261. The states are: Arizona, Arkansas, California, Colorado, Delaware, Idaho, Illinois, Iowa, Kansas, Michigan, Minnesota, Mississippi, Missouri, Montana, Nebraska, Nevada, New York, North Dakota, Ohio, Oklahoma, Oregon, South Carolina, South Dakota, Texas, Washington, Wisconsin, and Wyoming. For 1954 figures, see Bureau of the Census, *School Districts in the United States in 1954.*

[11] *Ibid.* The county unit states are Alabama, Florida, Georgia, Kentucky, Louisiana, Maryland, New Mexico, North Carolina, Tennessee, Utah, Virginia, West Virginia.

function or project. Many of these are financed by means of loans that are repaid from revenue derived from the project or function, but some special districts have the right to levy taxes. Over half of all the special districts are fire, drainage, and soil conservation districts.[12]

ARE THERE TOO MANY LOCAL UNITS?

The American system of local government has been severely criticized in recent years on the ground that there are too many local governments, that they overlap and duplicate each other, and that many are too small in population and too weak in financial resources to give their inhabitants efficient, modern services. "Oxcart" and (chronologically a little less damning) "horse-and-buggy" are the descriptions that have been applied alike to their size, form, and procedure. While we are here concerned mainly with size and numbers of local units, it must be pointed out that there are many small units governed very well and some large units poorly administered. But somewhere along the line a unit can be *too* small to be administered properly under normal conditions. Where that point is cannot be easily determined.

Size of Local Units and Functions

A municipality of five thousand may be capable of operating a water supply system in an efficient and economical manner. It could support an up-to-date plant with full-time and experienced employees from the revenue derived from reasonable water rates to the

----

[12] California has more than two thousand special districts. Among them are districts for fire protection, cemeteries, irrigation, lighting, sewer maintenance, mosquito and pest abatement, road supervision, sanitation, water, utility and many others. See Stanley Scott and John C. Bollens, *Special Districts in California Local Government,* Bureau of Public Administration, University of California (1949).

Pennsylvania has more than three hundred "municipal authorities." They are mostly for construction of school buildings, water supply, sewage disposal, parking, and airport facilities. *The Authority* (Spring Issue, 1953), p. 14. In addition, there are about five hundred "school building authorities," so established to take advantage of state loans.

inhabitants of the town and of the fringe area around it. On the other hand, it is too small for an effective public health program. Public health administration requires a wider jurisdiction to cope with communicable diseases, drainage problems, stream pollution, milk inspection, and other activities that require a high grade of technical skill and modern laboratory facilities. One full-time, trained public health administrator could hardly function in the many activities of the field with any great efficiency, nor could he be expected to confine his efforts wholly within the municipality. Health problems know no municipal boundary lines.

It is generally agreed that the one-room country school district is financially and administratively unable to give children an education that will give them an equal chance with those who have the opportunity to attend the more modern and specialized urban or consolidated schools. The large reduction of school districts during the past decade indicates a growing acceptance of the need to provide better facilities, better teaching, and a better system in rural education. But how far should consolidation go? Many educational authorities believe that each state should be redistricted so that complete schooling can be provided from kindergarten through senior high school.

A county of thirty thousand could keep at least one full-time official busy handling the various kinds of records gathered and kept by an ordinary county, but it would be too small to maintain a decent institution for the aged indigent. Even a township of a thousand people could well support a full-time official to act jointly as secretary of the board of township supervisors, the tax collector, the tax assessor, the school board secretary, and even the justice of the peace. He could be the representative of the county in all its ramified activities in the township. On the other hand, the township might well be rid of the function of rural road construction and maintenance. This could better be handled by the county which could afford modern road machinery and trained personnel.

Thus the size of the local unit is directly connected with its functions. Experience has taught that it is easier to legislate changes in functions than to abolish or consolidate established units of local government. In every state, there is a real need for an exhaustive study of governmental functions performed by all the classes of local government with the object of developing a more rational allocation than now exists.

Democracy and Local Units

Looking broadly at the American system of government, there is no doubt that only at the local level can the activity, interest, judgment, and support of the lay citizen be fully utilized. The hundreds of thousands of men and women who are elected by their fellow citizens to the governing bodies of our 117,000 cities, counties, boroughs, townships, villages, school, and special districts are the "pillars of their communities" and the "anchors of our democracy." They give balance to the state and national levels already heavily loaded with experts, career public servants, and professional politicians. The local officials are amateurs in government but they do represent the rank and file of American citizenry. Most of them serve with little or no compensation. They do so as a community service. Everything possible should be done to encourage the interest and efforts of these valuable and basic atoms of American democracy.

The size of local units has a distinct bearing upon the strengthening of "grass roots" democracy. Citizens who serve local governments want to be useful. They cannot utilize their utmost abilities in local units that are too small to grapple with the real community problems or that are too weak financially to obtain modern facilities. They do not want to waste their time batting their heads against the stone walls of legal restriction or getting lost in a labyrinth of local complexity that obtains in most states. Often frustrated local officials, despairing of action, encourage the state "to come in and help us." Small wonder it is that the state has been taking over many functions that are rightfully local. It can deal with a problem in larger areas of operation unimpeded by the procedural difficulties presented when working with multiple layers and segments of government—all autonomous, all independent.

An Ideal Size?

Is there an ideal size, both in population and area, for a local unit of government? Is there a range in which local units can best prosper? Plato and Aristotle speculated on the ideal size of a city, which in Greece at its "high time" was an independent and largely autonomous state. Plato said "so long as the city can grow without abandoning its unity, up to that point it may be allowed to grow, but not beyond it." [13] Patently, Plato was impressed by the dangers of large cities. He limited the ideal state to 5,040 persons. On the one hand, it should be large enough for self-sufficiency and a proper specialization of effort; on the other, it should allow a working integration between industry and agriculture, between town and county. Aristotle believed that a state became too large when politics could not be based on immediate personal contact. Of course, the Greek city state handled all governmental functions—it was a one-level government. He thought one ought literally to be able to see across its area.

But these ideal considerations had as little effect upon the reality of city growth in the Graeco-Roman world after Plato and Aristotle as they have had on the growth of American cities during the past hundred and fifty years. Local communities have never been built upon the specifications of philosophers, and it is as idle to speculate today on their ideal size as it was twenty-four centuries ago. Suffice to say, there are with us, large and small, and we must work with them and for them as we can.

Furthermore, a size proper one hundred years ago in rural and pioneer America is not adequate in these days of the automobile, airplane, and telephone. And what might be adequate now may not apply to a future age of rocket ships, H-bombs and bacteriological warfare. The flow of history, not the thoughts of philosophers, determines the kind of governmental arrangements we have. The trend of world events in the 20th century is toward dominance of supergovernments that are big, top-level, and all-powerful. In that kind

[13] *Republic*, IV, p. 423. Quoted from Charles Howard McIlwain, *The Growth of Political Thought in the West* (1932), pp. 10–13.

of world, small inadequate local units have not even the slightest chance of survival. While their shells may remain as an outward symbol of what once was, real power will have departed from them long since. Local government can survive in reality as well as in name only if its strength and its implements are modern enough to cope with the realities of the world about and in them.

Arthur C. Millspaugh in *Local Democracy and Crime Control* states that local units need to have a population of 25,000 or more to have a staff and keep it occupied, that they need a population of at least 20,000 to pay for services out of their own revenue. Below this figure costs per capita become exceedingly high. Likewise, there must be a maximum area so that in case of counties, for example, people can conveniently visit their county seat.

Practically speaking, there can be no arbitrary limit set on size of local units except in extreme cases. Many factors must be taken into consideration before judgment is rendered. *First,* there is local history and tradition. Has the local unit been in existence for a long time and does it have a historical significance to those who live in it? *Second,* do the inhabitants constitute a social community built along the boundary lines of the governing unit? *Third,* is the unit able to carry on efficiently the functions assigned to it by law and has it the necessary sources of revenue to finance them? *Fourth,* can the unit support adequately one full-time employee, adequately compensated? No local unit should be allowed to exist without one full-time employee. This should be the irreducible minimum.

This is not to say, however, that all units that do not now have one full-time employee should be doomed. Many that now have three, six and even ten part-time employees could undergo internal structural and functional reorganization so that the routine duties could be merged in the office of one man, a sort of manager, needing not too many technical qualifications. Such a functionary might also act as representative of other levels of government in his unit carrying out functions of a routine nature, for example, the licensing of hunters and fishermen and the collection of incidental revenues for the state. How stimulating it would be for the cause of good government and democracy to have in each local community at least one officer, a general public administrator, fully cognizant of local needs and conditions, yet constantly active in developing improved practices and techniques so necessary in modern government. How much better it would be than having the same functions performed by uninterested and untrained part-time officers or, worse still, by a number of roving field men, often the lowest paid in their organizations, sent out by the functional departments of the state and national governments!

Village and Hinterland Mergers

At present, there is a widespread feeling that rural townships in the 16 states where they exist should be greatly reduced in number. But very little is said about eliminating the large number of small, equally weak, incorporated towns, villages, and boroughs. There is every reason to believe that a union of such small incorporated places with the outlying rural townships is not only feasible but will become a modern necessity if local rural government is to be preserved. The problem of local services to the inevitable fringe of inhabitants outside incorporation boundaries has never been successfully solved except by the union exemplified so well by the New England town or by the more urban townships of Pennsylvania where rural and urban areas are joined in political community. The problems of finance, police, fire, zoning, and other functions would be much more easily solved by such an arrangement. One reason for the long life of the New England town government is its long-term success in both rural and urban regions. Most of the small incorporated places are the economic and social nucleus of a larger hinterland and government organization should accommodate itself to this relationship. The problem of providing equal services for equal tax rates for the rural and urban populations of these units could be met by differentiated tax rates or assessments, by the creation of service districts, or by direct payment for services rendered.

The Anderson Reduction Proposal

In concluding his classic study of local units in the United States, Professor Anderson suggests a radical reduction in the number of local units from the present 117,000 to 18,000. *First,* he would eliminate all separate school districts. Counties, cities, and larger incorporated places might administer local schools within their limits but there would be no separate corporations for school administration. *Second,* practically all other special districts would also disappear under the application of the same principle, namely, that there should be only one local government in each area. *Third,* townships in most of the middle western and middle Atlantic states would cease to exist as governing units, but, *fourth,* the towns in the New England states should remain largely as they are although a number of the smaller ones could be consolidated. *Fifth,* present municipalities, except many of the smallest, should remain as they are now. *Sixth,* in metropolitan areas there should be city-county consolidation and only one unit of government should handle all city, county, and school district functions. *Seventh,* in rural areas the county should be the main unit for the performance of all governmental functions including education and rural roads and that the number of counties should be reduced to the extent that the smaller and poorer ones would be consolidated with their stronger neighbors. As a result, there would be 200 city-counties, 2,100 counties, 15,000 incorporated places, and 500 miscellaneous units.[14]

Should Separate School Districts Be Abolished?

The independent school district is a product of the 19th century and Jacksonian democracy. When this agency was established, it was believed that education should be divorced from the regular governmental organizations not only to "keep it out of politics" but also so as to maintain professional standards. The general belief since then is that education really has been administered on a higher

[14] Anderson, *The Units of Local Government in the United States,* Public Administration Service, No. 83 (1949), pp. 35–37.

plane than the ordinary functions of local government. School directors are usually elected under much less political strain and stress. The superintendent of schools is, in fact, a trained manager and his staff has minimum qualifications that are higher than any group of local government employees.

On the other hand, it is pointed out by advocates of city and school district consolidation that such a move would result in the simplification of governmental machinery and the elimination of a great deal of duplication which would bring with it a possible reduction in costs. It would increase the interest of the teachers in municipal government which is now most unfortunately lacking as well as bring about an over-all local public finance program.

Henry and Kerwin say: "The observations made in the course of this survey do not indicate that the schools are subjected to greater political pressure in those areas in which school and municipal services are administered cooperatively than in the situations in which the school authorities administer the same functions independently." [15]

But without more evidence than is available, it would seem that the present normal arrangement of school districts independent from the municipal governments should not be generally undermined. The counties, which, according to the Anderson specifications, should administer rural education, are at present in no condition to perform the task of educational administration. Of all local structures the county is the most decentralized, and most "political."

In the rural, as well as the urban areas, joint activity between school districts and other local units, especially towards integration of effort to obtain a reasonable over-all local government revenue, expenditure, and debt program should be encouraged. This might be accomplished preliminarily by a mandatory annual meeting of the governing boards of the county, city, school district, and other taxing units within the county for the purpose of considering joint financial problems and evolving an over-all program of public finance.

[15] Nelson B. Henry and Jerome G. Kerwin, *Schools and City Government* (1938), pp. 96–97.

The National Commission on School District Organization declared that a comprehensive program of education can be offered at reasonable cost only where local administrative units are large enough to bring together in convenient centers sufficient numbers of children in each age group to justify employment of well-balanced staffs of teachers for both elementary and secondary schools. This can be done if the unit has at least 1,200 pupils between the ages of 6 and 18, and if possible, as many as 10,000. The minimum enrollment of 1,200 would require forty classroom teachers at the rate of one to every thirty pupils.[16]

Shall Special Districts Be Eliminated?

Although the total number of local units was reduced by almost forty thousand in the decade ending in 1952, the number of special districts, other than school, increased from 8,279 to 12,319. This in itself shows them to be useful institutions. They allow two or more local units to join together and form an organization to carry on a particular function such as water supply, sewage disposal, rubbish and garbage incineration without recourse to any drastic change in boundaries or structure of government. They allow municipalities to evade statutory and constitutional debt limitations and the legal complications that go with them. They can be financed with bond issues supported entirely by revenue from the project or function carried on by the special district or authority. They are designed to take utilities and other service out of "politics," because the governing bodies may be appointed by the local councils or other authorities rather than elected by the people. Flexible financing, independent operation and business-like management are more possible than under the regular municipal units of government, it is claimed.[17]

On the other hand, observers point out dangers and weaknesses. The already complex nature of local government is further com-

[16] National Commission on School District Reorganization, *Your School District* (1948), p. 131.

[17] Charles F. LeeDecker, "Special Districts in Pennsylvania," *Municipal Finance* (February, 1952), p. 110.

plicated by new and overlapping governmental units when the crying need is for simplification. This is especially true where the regularly established units of government already have the powers to do that which is given to the special district of authority. For example, in Pennsylvania there are many water and sewage authorities doing what cities, boroughs, and townships are empowered to do and actually do. Furthermore, authorities are not directly responsible to the voters even though their functions may be of utmost public importance. In addition, interest rates on revenue bonds are usually higher than ordinary municipal bonds, while failure to pay principal and interest charges might conceivably lead to the taking over of the utility or project by the bondholders themselves.[18]

Shall Townships Be Abolished?

Very few students of government will admit that the rural township has a promising future. In fact, most of them would be glad to see it abolished and are debating whether the county should be revitalized or if salvation lies in state centralization of local rural governmental functions. A comparative study of eleven Illinois counties with townships and seven without townships showed that the cost of government for general governmental purposes other than schools and highways in the counties without townships was $1.84 per capita while in the counties with townships it was $3.83. Official commissions of inquiry in Indiana and Michigan reported the township as a costly, unnecessary, and wasteful unit of government. Surveys in New York and Pennsylvania also pointed to the need for a smaller number of townships in order that better administration might be established.[19]

In its *Recommendations on Township Government* the committee on county government of the National Municipal League stated that

[18] Joseph E. McLean, "Use and Abuse of Authorities," *National Municipal Review* (October, 1953), pp. 438–444.
[19] Arthur W. Bromage, "Shall We Save the Township?" *National Municipal Review* (October, 1936), p. 585, et seq. Also see: Clyde F. Snider, "Twilight of the Townships," *National Municipal Review* (September, 1952), pp. 390–396; and Richard C. Spencer, "Iowa Townships Still Here?" *National Municipal Review* (September, 1952), pp. 397–399.

the township "is generally too small for the proper financial support
and efficient administration of governmental functions. Its governmental structure, like that of the county, is antiquated. On the other
hand, township government is defended as a training school of
democracy. No absolute solution of the problem is at hand and no
single solution will hold true for every state in which the township
exists." [20]

The objections to the township as indicated in this report are that
it is an unnecessary burden on the taxpayer, that it is not a good
unit for the administration of justice, health, or welfare. It is also
questioned as an efficient administrative unit for rural highway
maintenance and construction, assessment of property for taxation,
tax collection, and financial records.

The report proposes that the township be eliminated by several
methods: (1) by the gradual transfer of township functions to
county, city, or state; (2) by enacting legislation to permit individual townships to be deorganized or consolidated; (3) by the abolition of townships by county option, and (4) by constitutional
amendments permitting county home rule charters to set up optional
plans of county organization so that townships may transfer to the
county any of their powers.

In spite of all this, well settled rural communities should have
some form of local government. It may be that the township should
be larger or have different functions than it has now. But where it
has existed for a long time—in some states more than 200 years—it
cannot be abolished with a "flick of the pen." Many townships still
have historical continuity, social homogeneity, and political unity.
Because the West and South can do without them is no indication
that in New York and Pennsylvania they cannot be used to good
advantage. But townships might be united with the smaller independent villages and boroughs in a natural community as in New
England. However, even where there are small villages, there is
some conflict between the village and farm population. Farmers do
not want to pay for services given only to villages. Villagers see no

[20] "Recommendations on Township Government," *Supplement to the National
Municipal Review* (February, 1934), No. 2, p. 139.

reason to help pay for rural roads. Artificial fashioning of such communities out of presently independent villages and townships, it is granted, would be most difficult, even if desirable. The township might also have closer administrative ties to the county so as to develop sounder administration. But where the township has any vitality it should not be arbitrarily abolished for the sake of economies on paper that are hardly ever translated into savings for the taxpayers.

An improved form of township government was proposed for New Jersey by the Princeton Local Government Survey. It was based on four general principles: *First,* the four basic services—schools, roads, welfare, and health—were to be administered and supported on a communitywide basis, that is, for the entire township. *Second,* additional services such as police, fire, sewers, garbage removal, and lighting were to be supplied for districts within the townships and paid for entirely by the benefiting districts. *Third,* the township committee was to be chosen from election districts—one from each district. *Fourth,* special service districts would be established by the township committee on petition by and subject to referendum of the voters of the area affected. The township committee would approve all budgets of the special districts and might appoint an administrator resident in the districts to operate the special services.[21]

ACTUAL PROGRESS TOWARD CONSOLIDATION

With five exceptions,[22] all states have general legislation making possible consolidation or annexation of local units. Their application is usually optional on the part of the inhabitants of the local units concerned and may be restricted by conditions involving maximum or minimum areas, distances from county seats and other special factors depending upon the particular state law. Such procedure begins with a petition of voters, taxpayers, or property owners, followed by approval by popular election or by governing boards,

[21] Carpenter, *Problems in Service Levels* (1940), pp. 135–136.
[22] Connecticut, Delaware, Maine, Maryland and Rhode Island. Cited in Carpenter, *Problems in Service Levels* (1940), p. 69 fn.

courts, or other public bodies. The difference between consolidation
and annexation is that the former involves a combination of two or
more separate legal jurisdictions, whereas in the latter the legal
boundaries of one unit are extended to include additional area
within, or all of, an adjoining local unit. Of course, annexations go
on incessantly, chiefly between municipalities and townships. Consolidations have been confined largely to school districts.

County Consolidation

County consolidation was first undertaken in Tennessee in 1919
when two counties were merged. No other county consolidation was
effected in that state since then but in 1939 the legislature set up a
procedure for consolidation to encourage and simplify the process
by making state grants to each absorbing county for a period of five
years equal in amount to a tax rate of eight mills on the taxable
property of the county being absorbed in addition to a grant of
$50,000 to each county involved. Both grants are to be used to
reduce county indebtedness. In 1932, Georgia effected a consolidation of three counties with one in which Atlanta is situated. Although Georgia has more counties in proportion to its area than any
other state, there has been no further consolidation.

Only five consolidations in a half century is a strong indication
that the American people are not interested in having fewer counties. In geographic outline and number, the county set-up remains
practically the same as it was in 1900. There are a number of reasons
for lack of action along this line. County residents, especially east
of the Mississippi and south of the Mason-Dixon line, have an
intense pride and loyalty for their county name. This is especially
noteworthy in rural areas where generations of families have lived
in the same regions. Officeholders, usually the most politically active
segment of the population, are invariably against losing their offices
by such a method. Tradesmen in the county seat oppose a change of
status because of the loss of trade from those who come to the
county seat. So do newspapers which would lose "county printing"
a lucrative source of income. Richer counties will oppose consolida-

tion with poorer counties, believing that costs will rise and that they will have to subsidize the newcomers with increased services. This is especially true when rural areas are proposed to be merged with urban. All in all, county consolidation in the foreseeable future shows little promise.[23] As Professor Carpenter (Princeton University) says: "County consolidation, now dormant as an issue in American local politics, cannot be revived by homiletic reviews designed to tell people what is good for them."[24]

City-County Consolidation

City-county consolidation in populous urban areas has gained more headway than county consolidation. By such an arrangement, one government performs the functions of both city and county within the boundaries of that local unit.

Counties have no jurisdiction in Virginia cities. From colonial days, the English pattern of the county borough in which there was only one government was adopted. There is nothing in the state constitution or law that requires this arrangement; it is the result of adherence to custom. Today, twenty-eight cities in Virginia are without county government, city officers carrying out county functions.[25] Baltimore city was separated from Baltimore County in 1851, and like Virginia cities carries on county functions.

In 1854, the city and county of Philadelphia were made coterminous. The city council was made the tax levying and spending body for the consolidated government, the city treasurer and city controller acted for both units. All the other county officers were retained and subsequent court decisions held that these officials retained their county status, so the merger was incomplete and unsatisfactory. A state constitutional amendment passed in 1951 provided for more complete consolidation whereby city council has the right to merge county offices into the city organization. Enabling legislation passed in 1953 withheld from city council the

[23] Clyde F. Snider, "American County Government: A Mid-Century Review," *The American Political Science Review* (March, 1952), pp. 66–68.
[24] Carpenter, *op. cit.*, p. 76.
[25] John A. Rush, *The City-County Consolidated* (1941), pp. 193–206.

right to merge five county offices, which therefore still have an independent status.[26]

The city and county of San Francisco was established in 1856. After a long period of indecision on the part of the courts and the legislature as to the full meaning of this consolidation, a constitutional amendment in 1914 finally put to rest any doubts and today San Francisco has almost complete city-county consolidation.[27]

Under a provision in the state constitution of Missouri adopted in 1875, the city of St. Louis was separated from the county in which it was located. The city was not made a county but city officers performed county functions. As in San Francisco, the courts and the legislature refused to accede to complete consolidation, but great improvement in administration and finances nonetheless resulted.[28]

The city and county of Denver is the only example where complete consolidation existed from the first. It was created in 1902 by a state constitutional amendment and is considered as the best example of city-county consolidation in the United States. Only two of the seventeen county offices were kept. The work of the county officers was largely taken over by those of the city. The work of the sheriff was taken over by the police department and the city council took the place of the county commissioners.[29]

Five counties—New York, Kings, Richmond, Queens, and Bronx—were merged into Greater New York beginning in 1898. They still retain some functions regarding the administration of justice and elections. Finances have been completely merged with those of the city. So have charities and supervision over property and public works. Most of the county offices have been abolished.[30]

New York in 1730 was the first city with boundaries coterminous with the county. The second was New Orleans in 1805. There has

[26] Act 433 of the 1953 General Assembly, Commonwealth of Pennsylvania. The offices still independent and protected from action of the city council are: the district attorney, the sheriff, the city commissioners, the board of revision of taxes, and the registration commission.

[27] Rush, *op. cit.*, pp. 265–288.

[28] Fairlie and Kneier, *County Government and Administration*, (1930), pp. 512–513.

[29] *Ibid.*, pp. 515–516.

[30] Rush, *op. cit.*, p. 207.

been substantial governmental consolidation in New Orleans. For the city and parish there is but one clerk, one treasurer, one auditor, one legislative, and one administrative body. The coroner of the parish is the city physician. There are, however, some parish officers such as the sheriff, the tax collectors, the tax assessors, and the court.[31] Since 1942, Baton Rouge also has had city-parish consolidation.

URBAN COUNTIES (174 HAVE OVER 100,000 POPULATION)

(The First Five)

County	Population	No. of Local Nonschool Units	Units School Districts
Cook, Ill. (Chicago)	4,509,000	257	164
Los Angeles Calif.	4,152,000	80	117
Wayne, Mich. (Detroit)	2,435,000	47	59
Allegheny, Pa. (Pittsburgh)	1,515,000	130	116
Cuyahoga, Ohio (Cleveland)	1,390,000	68	32

From International City Managers' Association: *The Municipal Year Book 1955*, p. 123.

The consolidation of city and county functions of the city of Boston and the county of Suffolk began in 1821. Then the functions of the court of session of the county which corresponds to a county board were transferred to the city council and mayor where they are still exercised. The treasurer and auditor of the city act also for the county, all property is owned by the city, all expense paid by it. However, a large number of elective and appointive officers still operate within the county.[32]

In 1951, legislation gave partial consolidation to Atlanta and Fulton county. The city's boundaries are extended, overlapping functions eliminated. The county will carry on the health services of the area, while the city will handle police, fire, parks, and sanitation.

[31] *Ibid.*, pp. 229–238.
[32] Fairlie and Kneier, *op. cit.*, pp. 514–515.

City and county employees will be transferable.[33] The city and county of Honolulu were completely consolidated in 1907. And, of course, Washington, D. C. has only one local government operating within its boundaries.

One of the most interesting attempts to solve the city-county problem was the Pittsburgh plan for a new city-county unit called the "City of Pittsburgh" which was to include all the 122 cities, boroughs, and townships of the populous Allegheny county in a federated arrangement. This proposal had a long and checkered career beginning in 1923 with the appointment of a commission to investigate consolidation. It included two adoptions by the state's electorate as a constitutional amendment, state legislative approval, disapproval by the electorate of Allegheny county of the state enabling act because of a joker, and several major revisions. At present, it appears to be a dead issue. Provision for it still exists in the state constitution and can be revived by an enabling act and subsequent action on the part of the voters of Allegheny county. The consolidated city was to take over all county functions and specified municipal powers such as police, zoning, traffic control, smoke abatement, transportation, and certain public works and utilities. The municipalities were to retain some of their powers.[34]

City-county consolidation and city-county separation are not the same thing. In consolidation, the whole county with its rural areas and small municipalities becomes a city. Usually the people outside the city vote against any such plan. They are afraid of domination by political machines, of higher taxes, and of the obligations of city indebtedness. Separation is easier to achieve, has been more successful, but does not solve the metropolitan problem and the need for unified administration of urban services within the entire community.

A number of such consolidation and separation proposals in other cities suffered defeat because of the opposition of the rural areas of the state when a constitutional amendment was necessary, and the

---

[33] *National Municipal Review* (April, 1951), p. 215.
[34] H. Marie Dermitt, "Metropolitan Growing Pains in Allegheny County," *National Municipal Review* (September, 1940), pp. 579 et seq.

opposition of the suburbanites and officeholders who did not want to be taken in by the city. In 1913, the city-county committee of the American Political Science Association recommended that when a city attained a given population, it should automatically become a city-county with complete consolidation of functions and government. This is the plan of county boroughs in England numbering close to three hundred. In spite of the legal obstacles set up against the plan in those cities which have adopted some form of consolidation or separation, either complete or partial, success has been general. Government is simpler, more efficient, and less expensive—both in theory and in actual practice.

Municipalities

During the ten year period ending in 1952, there was an increase of 558 municipalities in the United States, about three per cent.[35] All but nine states gained, Texas leading by far with an increase of 103. The states in which the number remained the same or decreased were: Arkansas, Mississippi, North Carolina, Massachusetts, Rhode Island, Connecticut, Maine, Vermont, and Delaware.

The United States Census reported about 8,000 incorporated places in 1890, thus showing an increase of one hundred per cent to 16,000 in the past sixty years. The greatest period of increase was in the two decades before 1910, and since then it has tapered off.[36]

[35] *Governments in the United States in 1952, op. cit.* p. 2. The first classified enumeration and analysis of the units of local government in the United States was made by Professor William Anderson in 1932 and 1933 with the aid of a grant from the Social Science Research Council and the University of Minnesota. Revised as of 1941, Anderson noted that the changes in numbers of municipalities during the previous decade showed an over-all increase of 104, or less than one per cent. The greatest net decreases were in the ten southeastern states, the most consistent increases in the middle western states. The largest numerical increases were in Texas and Utah. Anderson points out the difficulty of an accurate count especially among the incorporated places that have less than one hundred population or are totally inactive. State records still record those units that ceased to function but which do not go through the legal process of dissolution. (See Anderson, *The Units of Local Government in the United States,* Public Administration Service, No. 83 [1949], pp. 3–5.) The first complete United States census enumeration of local units was in 1942, the second in 1952.

[36] *The Municipal Year Book 1936,* p. 132.

LOCAL GOVERNMENTS AND LOCAL
GOVERNMENTAL AGENCIES

New York City. The city of New York, the boroughs of Brooklyn, Bronx, Manhattan, Queens, and Richmond; counties of Bronx, Kings, New York, Queens, and Richmond; the city docks and piers; the New York City school system including Brooklyn College, City College, Hunter College, and Queens College; American Museum of Natural History Planetarium Authority; Brooklyn, New York, and Queens public libraries; New York City Housing Authority; New York City Parking Authority; New York City Transit Authority; Triborough Bridge and Tunnel Authority; Port of New York Authority.

Chicago. The city of Chicago including the Chicago Land Clearance Commission, the Chicago Public Library, the Housing and Redevelopment Coordinator, the Municipal Airport, and the Municipal Tuberculosis Sanatarium; Cook County including the Cook County Forest Preserve District and the health districts; the Chicago City School District; the Housing Authority of Chicago, the Chicago Park District; the Chicago Sanitary District; and the Chicago Transit Authority.

Philadelphia. The city of Philadelphia including Philadelphia county functions, the city piers, the municipal airport, the Philadelphia Institution District, the Philadelphia Parking Authority, the Philadelphia Redevelopment Authority; the Philadelphia School District; the Delaware River Port Authority; the Philadelphia Housing Authority.

Los Angeles. The City of Los Angeles including the Department of Water and Power, the Los Angeles Community Redevelopment Authority, the Los Angeles Coliseum, the Municipal Airport, the municipal improvement districts, the port facilities; Los Angeles County including the Air Pollution Control District of Los Angeles County, the Los Angeles County Flood Control District, the Los Angeles County Public Library, the Vehicle Parking District No. 1 of Los Angeles County, county improvement districts, and 258 fire protection, garbage disposal, lighting, lighting maintenance, park, recreation, parkway, sewer maintenance, and waterworks districts administered by the county board of supervisors; the Los Angeles City Elementary School Districts, the Los Angeles City High School District, the Los Angeles City Junior College District; the Los Angeles City Housing Authority, the Los Angeles County Sanitation Districts, and the Metropolitan Water District of Southern California.

From Bureau of the Census, *Local Government in Metropolitan Areas,* State and Local Government Special Studies, No. 36 (April 2, 1954).

Ninety-six million people live in municipalities in the United States. This represents sixty-four per cent of the total population. While there will probably be some increase of municipalities for some decades to come, it will be slight. Due to regional shifts in population especially in New England and the southern states, many small places will go out of business as incorporated places. Some states may make efforts to deorganize such places and revert them to the status of rural areas. But usually they will continue their legal but semi-dormant existence. In metropolitan areas there will be in the future more effort to consolidate incorporated places than to create new ones. However, the movement away from the metropolitan areas which may be more pronounced in the future will cause the incorporation of many places now small rural villages.

Rural Townships and New England Towns

In these categories, there was little change between 1942 and 1952. The Bureau of the Census excluded Iowa townships from its tabulations in 1952 for the reason that: "County governments there have absorbed substantially all the former township functions." [37] There were 1,608 Iowa townships in the 1942 count. Outside of these, there was a decrease of only 96. New England towns decreased from 1,442 to 1,429; rural townships in the fifteen states, outside of Iowa, decreased only 77.

In some states, townships may be deorganized under general law. In Minnesota, legislature in 1933 provided that any township, whenever its assessed valuation dropped below $50,000, or whenever its tax delinquency amounted to 50 per cent of its real estate, must be dissolved by action of the county board. In 1937, the legislature dropped the mandatory feature and left the matter to the discretion of the county boards. Referenda by the voters were also provided for before dissolution was effected and $40,000 was made the minimum assessed valuation for a township. Since general legislation on the subject was first adopted in 1931, at least 78 townships have

[37] *Governments of the United States in 1952, op. cit.,* p. 3.

been dissolved and their functions have been turned over to county authorities.

Illinois, Missouri, Nebraska, and Oklahoma also have deorganization legislation. Township government was never important in the governmental framework of these states. Many counties in these states are without townships. Townships may be dissolved on a countywide basis by popular vote. Counties then acquire the township functions.

In Oklahoma, townships were virtually eliminated through indirection by abolishing their rights to levy taxes for township purposes. Here, too, in 1935 the counties obtained township functions and townships have virtually ceased to exist. Indiana County commissioners may deorganize townships upon petition by a majority of freeholders; and without petition, if the township or part of the township lies in any city of 15,000 population. In North and South Dakota, townships may be deorganized upon petition, popular election, and action by the county supervisors in various combinations.

In Maine and Vermont, towns have been deorganized by special legislative act. In Maine there are 465 territorial units classed as wild lands which are directly in charge of the state. When towns cease to be municipal corporations in Vermont, the governor appoints a supervisor to carry on their management.[38]

Very little reduction will come from voluntary consolidation on the part of the townships or from wholesale abolition on a statewide scale. In some states, townships are constitutional units of government and the difficult process of constitutional amendment must be invoked. Township officers make up their lack of broad powers by being numerous and collectively are powerful influences in the legislatures. Rural dwellers also are sensitive about their declining influence in states that have been industrialized and urbanized since the turn of the century. Therefore, they rise in arms against any action by the state to eliminate their government. Possibly there will be reduction of townships in large forest areas that are wild and virtually uninhabited, and as in Maine and Vermont the townships in these areas may be deorganized and administered directly by the

[38] Carpenter, *Problems in Service Levels* (1940), pp. 99–116.

state. On the other hand, townships in highly urbanized areas have in reality changed from rural units of government to municipalities rendering urban services to their inhabitants with general satisfaction of all concerned.

However, if rural townships are to remain vital units of local government and if they are to function as the cradles of rural democracy for which they were originally established, they must be consolidated to such a size as to be able to render to their inhabitants services of government in a modern manner and at a reasonable cost. Otherwise they are certain to be eliminated or allowed to die on the vine.

School Districts

The most substantial reduction of local units in the United States has been in school districts. In 1942, the Bureau of the Census reported 108,579; in 1952, there were only 67,442. This represented a thirty-eight per cent decrease in a decade. Professor Anderson reported a decrease of 8,800 between 1933 and 1941, so the trend during the last twenty years has been sharply toward reduction. Seven states reduced their school districts two thousand or more during this ten-year period. They are: Arkansas, Illinois, Kansas, Missouri, New York, Oklahoma, and Texas. Even then, nine other states still had more than three thousand districts in 1952: Nebraska, Minnesota, Wisconsin, Missouri, Michigan, Iowa, Illinois, Kansas, and South Dakota. These reductions were almost entirely in the number of "one-room" school districts. But in 1952 there were still 44,393 school districts with less than fifty pupils enrolled.[39]

The movement to redistrict reached a new high in the period since 1940 when half the states passed legislation making this possible. Three general methods were used. The first allowed local action on the part of the various school districts themselves. At the other extreme was mandatory legislation setting up county units as in Florida and West Virginia. More popular and effective was a third arrangement whereby county boards of education or commit-

[39] *Governments in the United States in 1952, op. cit.,* p. 4.

tees could order redistricting with or without a vote of the people.
By this method, the county committee initiated the proposals for
new districts after intensive study and public hearings. A state
committee of educators was available for over-all technical advice,
and made available expert field workers for research if the county
committee needed such help. Each new district was established only
after a favorable vote on the part of the voters of the district. Twelve
states utilized this procedure.[40]

Reorganization of school districts has usually been accomplished
by active efforts on the part of professional educators and the state
departments of education. But also advantages were offered to local
units which reorganized. Among "helpful provisions" are included
state aid for transportation, state funds guaranteed to maintain a
minimum school program, penalization of small schools which do
not reorganize, and state aid for new school buildings. On the other
hand, it was found that continued state aid for "one-room" districts
discourages reorganization.[41]

Special Districts

While there has been expressed some doubt and criticism of the
trend to establish special *ad hoc* districts, they will increase in numbers as long as the need for them appears to exist. If municipalities
are to continue to be limited in their taxing powers, if the assessed
valuation of property subject to local taxation continues to remain
far under market value, if local indebtedness continues to be limited
in spite of the fact that new urban conditions have arisen, if legal
procedure continues to straitjacket local units in their financial activities, if fragmentation of local units in metropolitan areas is not
rectified, then special districts and municipal authorities will continue to be formed. If, in addition, these districts following the example of school districts, adopt modern administrative organization

---

[40] Kenneth E. McIntyre, "School Redistricting in the Forty-Eight States,"
School Board Journal (April, 1950), pp. 25–27.
[41] The Council of State Governments, *The Forty-Eight State School Systems*
(1949), pp. 63–64.

such as the manager plan or some modification of it and, because of this, turn in creditable "non-political" performances, then the regular local units may expect to have their powers and their operation even more circumscribed by these new units. And the way it looks, this is exactly what will happen. On the other hand, many of these special units were established only to float indebtedness and construct projects, and when this is accomplished they will deed the property back to the municipality they represent and go out of business. This is especially true with such agencies as school building authorities which were created to take advantage of financial inducements provided by the state to build consolidated school facilities as a joint district authority.

Cooperation among Local Units

Actual consolidation of local units admittedly has made little real progress except perhaps in school districts. Even here there have been a great many "jointures" in which the original school districts remain but join together to administer an enlarged school system with consolidated physical plants. But cooperation among local units for the administration of services to the people is on the increase and has taken on many forms. The need for such cooperation is a sign of the unrealistic nature of present local government boundaries. A natural metropolitan area, for example, many include a dozen or even a hundred local units each one of which may be too small to furnish a required urban service such as sewage disposal with the result that cooperation or joint action is necessary. State laws are generally most liberal in allowing such action. Local units may join with each other by contract or by administrative agreement to furnish police and fire protection. The smaller unit may contract with the larger unit to carry on such a function which the smaller local unit will pay for at a stipulated rate. Many central cities supply their smaller suburban neighbors with such services. Again, local units have power to join together in special districts or in authorities to provide such services as water supply, sewage dis-

posal, and other services which can be financed by revenue from the
services rendered. The governing body of such a district or authority represents each of the member local units.

A few examples illustrate actual developments in this field. The
Los Angeles metropolitan area is governed by more than four hundred taxing units and contains about four million people. Public
health constitutes a problem for all localities alike and it was natural
in this fast-growing region that some form of joint action would be
sought. Forty of the forty-five cities in this area contract with Los
Angeles county for their health services. The five cities that do not
contract with the county must also help pay for the cost of county
health administration as well as their own. A city desiring to have
the county health department enforce state health laws within its
limits is required to pass an ordinance. The county then performs
the services indefinitely without cost to the cities other than the
regular county tax rate. In addition, cities desiring the county to
enforce their local ordinances are required to contract each year
with the county for that purpose and pay the cost. Cost records are
kept on the basis of visitations and inspections. Cities desiring
rodent eradication programs must pay separately for this work. The
county also serves the unincorporated territories within the county
with health services but these are paid only through the regular
county tax rates. The delivery of public health services is largely
achieved through thirteen health centers situated throughout the
county and staffed with public health workers and equipped with
diagnostic and clinical facilities. Over 600 persons are employed.
The seven functional bureaus of the department are general administration, preventable diseases, maternal and child health, medical social service, public health nursing, laboratories, and sanitation.[42]

Counties in metropolitan areas provide many "municipal-type"
services to unincorporated places. In most states, planning and zoning are county functions; in a few states, libraries, sewage disposal,

[42] Margaret Morden and Richard Bigger, *Cooperative Health Administration
in Metropolitan Los Angeles,* Bureau of Governmental Research, University of
California, Los Angeles (1949).

police protection, and other such functions are provided in metropolitan areas. But municipalities supply most of the urban services required by the outlying unincorporated places. This is especially true as to water supply and fire protection, and to a more limited extent sewage disposal and police protection. Special districts supply these services to unincorporated areas in New York, Pennsylvania, and Texas.[43]

The incendiary bomb of World War II and now the atomic bomb has done for local governments what no amount of urging and exhortation by public administrators and political scientists has been able to do. It has motivated a spirit of cooperation between local units especially in the field of fire protection. Just as air attack would be directed against a region rather than a single municipality, so must fire defenses be organized to meet such a threat. The *Los Angeles* region offers a good illustration of the problem and ways of meeting it. In this area are forty-seven fire-fighting agencies, of which forty-four are municipal. The three other services are the county field divisions and fire protection districts, and the Federal Forest Service. The Mutual Aid Act passed by the California state legislature and signed by the governor in 1940 declared that in the event of national or local emergency any services performed, or expenditures made in connection therewith, by any public agency *whether within or without the territorial limits of such agency* "shall be deemed conclusively to be for the direct protection and benefit of the inhabitants and the property of such agency." Such services to outside areas shall be ordered by the chief administrative officer of the agency furnishing the service unless otherwise provided by the governing body. Ordinary methods of cooperation between fire-fighting agencies are by formal contract and by informal means. Such cooperation calls for mutual assistance between fire-fighting agencies and for assistance outside municipal boundaries.[44]

[43] Stanley Scott, Joseph D. Lubin, and Robert J. McNeill, *Public Services in Unincorporated Communities*, Bureau of Public Administration, University of California, Berkeley (1953), pp. 1–4.

[44] James R. Donoghue, *Intergovernmental Cooperation in Fire Protection in the Los Angeles Area*, University of California at Los Angeles (1943).

Although comparatively few positive achievements can be recorded in the field of cooperative public purchasing on the local level, this is a promising area of cooperation for the future. There are, however, some most successful enterprises in this field. The oldest and most successful of joint buying arrangements in metropolitan areas is the *Cincinnati* plan, which was established in the depression year of 1931, for joint purchasing for the city, the county, the board of education, the public library, and the University of Cincinnati. Each governmental agency has its own purchasing organization and the purchasing agents join together in the Coordinating Committee of Purchasing Agents of Hamilton County. This group discusses at weekly meetings the possibility of joint purchasing and ways and means to get the best results. The work of negotiating the joint contracts is divided among the agencies. In *Milwaukee,* the city, the county, the school board, the board of vocational education, the sewage commission, and the municipal auditorium make joint purchases. The work is done by the purchasing agency of the city of Milwaukee. The *Los Angeles* County Purchasing and Stores Department, in addition to serving the regular county departments, also operates as the central buying agency for some 225 special districts including school, lighting, fire protection, sewer, and flood control, as well as twenty-three of the smaller cities within the county. In Michigan, the *Michigan Municipal League* acts as the purchasing agent for well over a hundred of its member cities for such items as fire hose, ballot boxes, street signs, and other such items. As a result of this effort, prices on some items such as hose have been reduced. A number of other state leagues of municipalities have some experience in cooperative purchasing for cities. In a few states, local units may purchase on contracts negotiated by the state.[45]

Intermunicipal and interlocal cooperation is found in many other functions, among them recreation, libraries, personnel, hospitals, water supply, and sewage disposal. It is a field that is being intensively explored in metropolitan areas. It is one means by which the

---

[45] James D. Kitchen, *Cooperative Government Purchasing,* Bureau of Governmental Research, University of California, Los Angeles (1953).

present system of multi-unit regions can be made to answer the needs of the modern urban and suburban dweller.

The Transfer of Functions

Because consolidation of local units has been slow and difficult, there have been significant reallocations of local government functions since the turn of the 20th century. The states have taken huge bites out of spheres of government once entirely local in the fields of highways, relief, welfare, health, and education, to mention only those of major importance. This has been accomplished without making a public issue subject to widespread public discussion or legislative debate. Those responsible for this trend just quietly hacked away at legislatures getting a little every session. Then came the great depression of the thirties and local governments, relying almost entirely upon the property tax for their revenues, called for help. As a result, the state governments acquired tremendously increased responsibilities. This trend is still going on because the local governments are shackled in power and revenue, and in ability to do things that must be done for the modern citizens. Likewise, the need for broader areas of uniformity in almost every activity because of the automobile and the increased mobility of the population has been a factor leading to more state participation.

But the cases where the state has taken over local functions lock, stock and barrel, as for example in Pennsylvania where the entire administrative and financial responsibility for public assistance (outdoor relief) was taken from local governments and given to the state, or in North Carolina where the state assumed entire responsibility for schools and highways, are comparatively rare. The process has been rather along lines that lead to divided responsibility where, for example, the county may limp along doing a very poor job and the state steps in, assists with money but along with such assistance takes also the responsibility for supervision. Arthur C. Millspaugh says: "In spite of the steady progress in the knitting together of state and county agencies, division and confusion may be expected to reign so long as the idea persists that local governments, in the major administrative fields, must *direct* and *control* and the state merely *supervise* and *assist*." He continues by suggesting that it is the function of the state, in the major fields, to direct and control and the function of the local units to supervise and assist. The unit that has the capacity for leadership and technical proficiency can work most effectively in its own organization, and to divide the administration and financing with local units always reduces efficiency and raises costs.[46] While this may be good logic and may apply in many cases, it must not be forgotten that state administration is not always economical or efficient; in fact, a great many well-equipped local units do a better job on the spot than can mediocre state departments by remote control and district management, especially where state employees are on a patronage basis.

Nevertheless, there is need for a basic reallocation of functions in the light of modern conditions. Some now held by the county, township, and city might well go to the state, some that the state now administers could be administered by local units with proper size, modern equipment, and adequate finances. The determination of what is a state and what a local function is the job of the state legislatures which should direct commissions to study and recommend such a program. It would help immeasurably to reduce the present chaos and confusion. For example, the county, not the township, is the ideal unit for the construction and maintenance of rural, secondary roads in an automobile age. But the county must be given the administrative and financial possibilities of doing a good job. If townships were consolidated into large units which would include small villages and towns, it could provide adequate police and fire protection. But it would need modern organization and better finances.

What of the Future?

For the immediate future, action to reduce the number of local units in the United States will continue as far as school districts and

[46] Arthur C. Millspaugh, *Local Democracy and Crime Control* (1936), pp. 179–215.

rural townships are concerned. The one-room rural school and its administrative common school district are both on their way out. Americans have made up their minds that rural children should and can get the same advantages as those in the city and town. Hard roads and bus transportation have made the consolidated school possible; state aid augmenting local real estate taxes has made the change economically attractive.

While the rural townships may not be legislated out of existence, their powers and responsibilities will continue to be limited so much that they may exist in name only. If there comes a time when substantial governmental savings will have to be made on the local level, the township will feel the pinch. The example of Iowa and Oklahoma in giving to the county the functions of the rural township will no doubt be invoked in other states. Townships can save themselves only if they are large enough or if they consolidate to become large enough to be able to carry on local rural governmental functions with effectiveness and reasonable economy. It is all very well to talk about democracy on a small scale as being grassroots, but when the units are so small that they have little power or reason to exist, who will want the offices? The New England town and the urban township will, however, continue to be a vital and useful local unit of government.

As for counties, even if many are too small to be efficient, little or no consolidation can be expected. They are simply too deeply etched in American life to be uprooted, consolidated or federated. The county we will have with us always. For that matter, it has been a basic Anglo-American institution that extends back to the Norman invasion of England almost nine hundred years ago. If improvement in the county is hoped for, it must come through internal reorganization.

Incorporated places or municipalities will continue to increase on a flattened curve scale. Many small municipalities should merge with their rural hinterland and form strong and vigorous rural community units of local government. This has happened in the case of consolidated and joint school districts. If there is little or no problem between the farm and town dwellers in relation to school administration, there should not be in other aspects of government either, given the correct organization. But we expect very little activity along this line.

Far more hopeful and far more necessary is the consolidation or federation of smaller municipalities in metropolitan areas contiguous or close to the borders of a city. In order to assure the kind of government such urban communities need, something must and will be done. Unfortunately, the correct solutions are not yet available, and we will discuss the alternatives in a later chapter.

Professor Carpenter puts the matter sanely when he says: "The methods of action whereby self-government, effective service areas, and tax-paying capacity can be brought together in a nice poise and balance are well-known. They depend for their success less upon the formulation of political theories than upon the intelligent application of experience gained in the conduct of local government since the early colonial days." He points out that this may require reallocation of major services to other units of government, cooperation of different units of government through interjurisdictional agreements for the conduct of services beyond the reach of a single locality, and a wider use of the special district in rural districts possessing urban concentrations. These steps, he feels, are but preliminary ones for the later partitioning of states into more serviceable units of local government.[47]

In the same vein writes Professor Lane Lancaster of the University of Nebraska. He agrees that consolidation is difficult, hopes for increased cooperation between local units, points out the need for internal reorganization of local units, and sees the necessity for a reallocation of functions to meet the modern needs.[48]

[47] Carpenter, *Problems in Service Levels* (1940), pp. 138–139.
[48] Lancaster, *Government in Rural America* (1952), pp. 336–360.

State	Types of Municipal Corporations	Minimum Requirements to Incorporate
Alabama	CITIES: over 2,000 population (sometimes classified according to population in particular acts relating to specific subjects) TOWNS: under 2,000 population	100 population
Arizona	CITIES: over 3,000 population TOWNS: under 3,000 population	500 population
Arkansas	CITIES: 1st class: over 4,000 population 2nd class: 1,750–4,000 population county seats under 1,750 TOWNS: under 1,750 population	At least 20 registered voters
California	CITIES: 1st to 4th class: a number of special classes, based upon 1920 population, covering cities over 20,000. All are now home rule cities 5th class: 8,000–20,000 6th class: 3,300–8,000	
Colorado	CITIES: 1st class: 40:000 population and over 2nd class: 2,000–40,000 TOWNS: under 2,000 population	Petition must be signed by 75 electors who are landowners (40 in counties under 5,000).
Connecticut	CITIES } BOROUGHS } all created by special act	
Delaware	CITIES } TOWNS } all created by special act	
Florida	CITIES: 300 or more registered voters TOWNS: under 300 registered voters	150 freeholders and registered voters

* Prepared by Elizabeth Smedley, Institute of Local Government, The Pennsylvania State University.

State	Types of Municipal Corporations	Minimum Requirements to Incorporate
Georgia	CITIES: incorporated by special act TOWNS: incorporated by special act or by application to superior court	25 voters
Idaho	CITIES: 1st class: 15,000 or more population 2nd class: 1,000–15,000 population VILLAGES: under 1,000 population cities of 2nd class under 1,500 may revert to villages	125 population
Illinois	CITIES: over 1,000 population VILLAGES: under 1,000 population TOWNS: created by special charter	1,000 population not more than 4 square mile area 100 population not more than 2 square mile area, no part more than 1 mile from the boundary of a municipality
Indiana	CITIES: 1st class: 250,000 or over population 2nd class: 35,000–50,000 3rd class: 20,000–35,000 4th class: 10,000–20,000 5th class: 2,000–10,000 TOWNS: under 2,000 population	2,000 population 250 population, not less than 1 person to 4 acres
Iowa	CITIES: 2,000 or more population TOWNS: under 2,000 population	Not within limits of city or town. Petition must be signed by at least 25 qualified electors.
Kansas	CITIES: 1st class: 15,000 or more population 2nd class: 2,000–15,000 3rd class: under 2,000 population and incorporated county seat towns	100 population (40 population if located in county of 52,000–60,000 and there is no incorporated city within 2 miles)

State	Types of Municipal Corporations	Minimum Requirements to Incorporate
Kentucky	CITIES: 1st class: 100,000 or more population 2nd class: 20,000–100,000 population 3rd class: 8,000–20,000 population 4th class: cities and towns: 3,000–8,000 population 5th class cities and towns: 1,000–3,000 population 6th class towns: less than 1,000 population	125 inhabitants Boundaries at time of incorporation no more than ½ mile in either direction, the form being square
Louisiana	CITIES: 5,000 or more population TOWNS: 1,000–5,000 population VILLAGES: under 1,000 population	150 population
Maine	CITIES: created by special act	
Maryland	CITIES: created by special act (Baltimore home rule) TOWNS: created by special act	
Massachusetts	CITIES: created by special act	12,000 population
Michigan	CITIES: 4th class: 3,000–10,000 population or cities with population under 10,000 incorporated prior to 1895, or county seat villages under 3,000 population home rule: 2,000 population or more 5th class: 750–2,000 population VILLAGES: other incorporated places	Not less than 500 persons per square mile Area not less than ¾ square mile, resident population 250 or more (except in Upper Peninsula)

State	Types of Municipal Corporations	Minimum Requirements to Incorporate
Minnesota	CITIES: 1st class: over 50,000 population 2nd class: 20,000–50,000 3rd class: 10,000–20,000 4th class: 10,000 or less VILLAGES: 100–10,000 population BOROUGHS: (Belle Plaine, created by special act)	Resident population of 100 and plotted land
Mississippi	CITIES: 2,000 population or more TOWNS: 300–2,000 population VILLAGES: 100–300 population (no new villages to be created after 1950)	
Missouri	CITIES: 1st class: 65,000 population or more and electing to become 1st class 2nd class: 27,500–99,000 and electing to become 2nd class 3rd class: 3,000–29,999 4th class: 500–2,999; towns under special act with population less than 500 electing to be 4th class; villages with more than 200 electors electing to become 4th class	
Montana	CITIES: 1st class: 10,000 or more population 2nd class: 5,000–9,999 3rd class: 1,000–4,999 TOWNS: 300–999 and places 1,000–2,499, by resolution of council	
Nebraska	CITIES: metropolitan: 150,000 or more population primary: 40,000–149,999 1st class: 5,001–40,000 2nd class: 1,001–5,000 VILLAGES: 100–1,000; county seat towns under 100, and 2nd class cities under 5,000 population reverting to village status	

State	Types of Municipal Corporations	Minimum Requirements to Incorporate
Nevada	CITIES: 1st class: over 20,000 population 2nd class: 5,000–19,999 3rd class: under 5,000	250 persons casting ballots at last general election
New Hampshire	CITIES: created by special act	
New Jersey	CITIES: created by special acts prior to 1882. Thereafter by successive general acts: 1st class: over 150,000 population 2nd class: 12,000–150,000 3rd class: under 12,000 4th class: seaside or summer resort cities on Atlantic ocean BOROUGHS: created by special acts TOWNS: created by special acts prior to 1888, thereafter by general act VILLAGES: created by special act (only one remains in existence)	
New Mexico	CITIES: 3,000 population and more TOWNS: 1,500 population VILLAGES: under 1,500 population	At least 150 population; at least 40 acres; no more than 4 square miles, no two outer boundaries more than 8 miles apart
New York	CITIES: created by special act VILLAGES: 1st class: 5,000 or more population 2nd class: 3,000–5,000 3rd class: 1,000–3,000 4th class: under 1,000	At least 500 population May not be in a city or incorporated village. Maximum area of 3 square miles or comprises entire boundaries of a water, lighting, fire or school district, or entire town or 2 school districts

State	Types of Municipal Corporations	Minimum Requirements to Incorporate
North Carolina	CITIES ⎫ TOWNS ⎬ no distinction	50 or more inhabitants, at least 25 freeholders or homesteaders and at least 25 voters; assessed valuation at least $25,000
North Dakota	CITIES: 200 population or more VILLAGES: 100 population or more	Maximum area 4 square miles
Ohio	CITIES: 5,000 population or more VILLAGES: under 5,000 population	Must be plotted (except if located on an island) Petition of at least 30 electors. Limits not unusually large or small
Oklahoma	CITIES: over 2,000 population TOWNS: other incorporated places	2,000 or more population and plotted. Surveyed and plotted
Oregon	CITIES: 150 or more people	150 or more population
Pennsylvania	CITIES: 1st class: 1,000,000 or more population 2nd class: 500,000–999,999 2nd class A: 135,000–499,999 3rd class: under 135,000 BOROUGHS: municipalities incorporated as such TOWNS: Bloomsburg; incorporated by special act	10,000 population
Rhode Island	CITIES ⎫ TOWNS ⎬ incorporated by special act	
South Carolina	CITIES ⎫ TOWNS ⎬ Incorporated by Secretary of State following petition	At least 1,000 population At least 100 population

State	Types of Municipal Corporations	Minimum Requirements to Incorporate
South Dakota	CITIES: Municipalities of 1st class, 5,000 or more population Municipalities of 2nd class, 500–5,000 population TOWNS: Municipalities of 3rd class under 500 population	
Tennessee	CITIES } TOWNS } Specially incorporated	At least 100 residents and real estate worth at least $5,000.
Texas	CITIES: TOWNS OR VILLAGES: under 10,000 population	At least 200 population
Utah	CITIES: 1st class: 90,000 or more population 2nd class: 15,000–90,000 3rd class: under 15,000 TOWNS: 100–7,000 population	800 population 100 population
Vermont	CITIES: all created by special act VILLAGES:	30 or more houses
Virginia	CITIES: 1st class: over 10,000 population 2nd class: 5,000–10,000 population and those under 5,000 previously incorporated TOWNS: 300–5,000 population	300 population, area not excessive
Washington	CITIES: 1st class: over 20,000 population 2nd class: 10,000–20,000 3rd class: 1,500–10,000 Unclassified: operating under special charter and not reorganized TOWNS: 4th class: 300–1,500 population	At least 300 inhabitants

State	Types of Municipal Corporations	Minimum Requirements to Incorporate
West Virginia	CITIES: Class I: over 50,000 Class II: 10,000–50,000 Class III: 2,000–10,000 TOWNS } VILLAGES } Class IV	At least 100 inhabitants. Territory urban in character. Not within any incorporated municipality Not less than 500 inhabitants per square mile, provided the area does not include an amount of territory disproportionate to the number of inhabitants thereof
Wisconsin	CITIES: 1st class: 150,000 and over 2nd class: 39,000–150,000 3rd class: 10,000–39,000 4th class: under 10,000 VILLAGES: all others	Village over 1,000 population. Any area with 1,500 population containing an incorporated village Resident population at least 150, not more than ¼ square mile or for places under 200 population if over ½ square mile, population at least 200; at least 400 population to the square mile otherwise. No village may be incorporated in a resort or tourist area where ½ or more of the area is owned by nonresidents not qualified to vote in the state or township
Wyoming	CITIES: 1st class: over 4,000 population TOWNS: under 4,000 population	Resident population at least 150 and not more than 3 square miles in area

TEN SUBJECTS FOR FURTHER STUDY

1. In the state where you live, should the number of local units be reduced?
2. Township government in the Middle West.
3. Consolidation and jointures of school districts since 1945.
4. City-county separation in Virginia.
5. City-county consolidation in Denver.
6. Local government units in Maine.
7. The boroughs and counties in the city of New York.
8. Special districts in California.
9. Municipal authorities in Pennsylvania.
10. The Michigan Municipal League as a purchasing agent for Michigan cities.

REFERENCES

John A. Bailey, "Three Boroughs Build Streets Jointly," *The American City,* October 1953, p. 96.

Frederick L. Bird, *A Study of the Port of New York Authority* (New York, 1949).

John C. Bollens, "They All Want to Stay Out; San Francisco City-County Presses Hard Against Its Borders but Efforts for Consolidation with San Mateo County Fail," *National Municipal Review,* June 1948.

William S. Carpenter, "Deorganization in Maine," *American Political Science Review,* December 1938, pp. 1139–1142.

Bureau of the Census, *Local Government Structure in the United States* (Washington, 1954).

O. K. Cope and M. D. Tarshes, "Consolidation of City-County Health Functions in San Diego," *Public Administration Review,* Summer 1954, pp. 170–179.

James W. Drury, "Townships Lose Ground," *National Municipal Review,* January 1955, pp. 10–13.

Mayo Fesler, "Denver Consolidation a Shining Light," *National Municipal Review,* June 1940, pp. 380–384.

William C. Harvard, *Municipal Annexation in Florida* (Gainesville, 1954).

Lynwood M. Holland, "Atlanta Pioneers in Merger: City Area Tripled and Services Are Divided with County in Award-Winning Movement to Solve Metropolitan Problem," *National Municipal Review,* April 1952.

Charles F. LeeDecker, "Special Districts in Pennsylvania," *Municipal Finance,* February 1952, pp. 103–110.

John W. Manning, "County Consolidation in Tennessee," *American Political Science Review*, August 1928, pp. 733–735.

Joseph E. McLean, "Use and Abuse of Authorities," *National Municipal Review*, October 1953, pp. 438–444.

James E. Pate, "Virginia Counties Turn Cities," *National Municipal Review*, September 1952, pp. 387–389.

Kirk H. Porter, "A Plague of Special Districts," *National Municipal Review*, November 1933, pp. 544–547.

Raymond B. Pinchbeck, "City-County Separation in Virginia," *National Municipal Review*, July 1940, pp. 467–472.

John Andrew Rush, *The City-County Consolidated* (Los Angeles, 1941).

Edward W. Weidner, "Some Comparative Experience in Adjusting Local Units and Areas," *American Political Science Review*, August 1948, pp. 730–745.

Max R. White, "Town and City Consolidation in Connecticut," *American Political Science Review*, June 1942, pp. 492–502.

Chapter 2

HISTORICAL FOUNDATIONS

The roots of American local government reach far down through the ages. A glance at the very names of local units and their officials shows their antiquity and hardiness. Although their functions may have changed during the centuries, they retain at least a nucleus of their original power and purpose. Local governments, both in Europe and in the United States, have often had a longer continuous existence than their national and state contemporaries. Medieval cities were flourishing and prosperous several centuries before the nation states of France, Italy, Spain, England and Germany came into existence, and were virtually independent entities after they shook themselves free from the feudal ties to which their land was originally bound.

Ancient Lineage

Interesting examples of ancient lineage abound. The sheriff who now acts as a peace officer and court official in the American county is encountered in England as early as the 9th century as the Anglo-Saxon shire-reeve. Originally the stewart of the royal estates and chief representative of the Crown in a local district, he had gradually increased in power until he was chief executive of the shire court. After the Norman Conquest in 1066, he became the King's representative in military affairs, the police magistrate and the peace officer as well. Because of his growing power, he became unpopular with the people and even suspected by the kings themselves with the result that he was slowly demoted to ministerial officer of the county court, conservator of the peace and returning officer in elections.[1] Today, this is his status in American counties. With the rise of the state police, he is now losing his role as a major local police officer in rural areas which he already lost in urban areas with the rise of the city police departments during the 19th century. For more than a thousand years under feudal, monarchical and democratic systems of government, the sheriff continued as an important local official.

Take the lowly American constable who today is fast on his way to extinction. He still acts as a local peace officer and a cog in the minor judiciary. He has had even greater prominence and a longer genealogy than the sheriff. He was once the *comes stabuli,* or count of the stable, in the heyday of the Eastern Roman or Byzantine empire which had its capital in the great city of Constantinople. He is mentioned in the Theodosian Code, 438 A.D., and given the importance of a marshal. His responsibility was to supply the Byzantine army with horses. Once head groom of the imperial Roman stables, he later became principal officer of the household of Frankish kings, and later of the great French feudal units. He was a field marshal and commander of armies—all before the word was taken into the English language. The early English usages were simply taken over from the French after the Norman Conquest. The Lord High Constable was once the chief functionary of the English royal household, the manager of its feudal estates. As a local peace officer, he is found as High Constable of the hundred as early as 1285, originally empowered to raise military levies, and as a petty constable of the parish or township as early as 1328.[2]

The prothonotary, which in Pennsylvania and Delaware is the clerk of the court of common pleas (civil), has an equally ancient lineage. This name is derived from the late Latin *prothonotarius* (*proto,* principal *notarius, clerk*); he was the principal notary of the

---

[1] Fairlie and Kneier, *County Government and Administration* (1930), pp. 4–6.
[2] *A New English Dictionary on Historical Principles,* edited by James A. H. Murray, 10 vols. (1888). Consult this magnificent work for derivations and historical changes in the names of various local units and officers.

emperors in the Byzantine court at Constantinople as early as 400 A.D. Later, the office became common throughout Europe. There were protonotaries apostolic, a college of twelve prelates, whose function was to register papal acts in the Vatican. The office is found in England as early as 1460.

The coroner, whose chief modern function is to hold inquests over dead bodies believed to have met death by violence, was originally the *custos placitorum coronae,* or guardian of the pleas of the Crown. In early France, he was an important officer of the royal household and was charged with maintaining the rights of the private property of the Crown. His title was popularly abbreviated to "crowner" and then to coroner. The office was first instituted in England in 1194. In his descent in importance he was also a royal officer in a county or municipality, but was reduced to his present status many centuries ago. In many states, he is giving way to the medical or health officer of the municipality or local unit. His days also seem numbered but he has had a long and eventful life.

The office of mayor (from the Latin *major*) is found many centuries ago in the Frankish mayor of the palace, the prime minister or major domo of the Merovingian kings. From this office came the Carolingian line of kings, the greatest of whom was Charlemagne, who began his reign in 768.

Other officials of American local government can trace their ancestry back through England, into France before the Norman Conquest, into the historical abysses of the Frankish kingdoms, and finally back into imperial and republican Rome. The title of treasurer came from the late Latin *thesaurius* common in root form in all Romanic areas; controller (*controlleur*) and commissioner (*commissionaire*) are of ancient French vintage and of Latin foundation. Auditor (*audire*, to hear) also of old French origin, goes back to the time when financial accounts were orally vouched for. Surrogate (*surrogare*, to deputize), now the county officer who probates wills in New York state, was once a deputy of an ecclesiastic judge who presumably probated wills and was guardian of orphans in the days when the church exercised such temporal jurisdiction.

The same journey back may be followed with the names of the

local units themselves. The county, brought to the colonies from England, took the place of the shire there some centuries after the Norman invasion. It was not a common expression for that unit before the 15th century. The periodical meeting of the court under the sheriff in that district, once known as the shire moot (Anglo-Saxon) became finally the county court. The origin of the name "county" was the Latin *comitatus,* a body of companions or more officially, a retinue or escort. In early French times the *contè* became the territory which was the domain of the count, and at this time, the term entered the English language.

"City" also has French-Latin lingual antecedents. Derived from the Latin *civitas,* the name given to Gaulish urban areas, it denotes a body of citizens or a community rather than the locus or place which was *urbs.* Only in later times did it acquire the meaning it has now. All Anglo-Saxon towns were *burhs* (boroughs) and the term *citè,* which came with the Normans, applied only to the larger places, mostly to the cathedral towns which were the seat of the episcopal sees. Even now boroughs are the basic English urban unit; those which are cities have acquired that title as an added honor which does not bring with it a different government organization as it does in the United States. The term "municipality" has Latin roots both in language and fact. Roman cities were called *municipia.* They were "free" cities united to Rome in sovereignty only, keeping their own laws, liberties, and magistrates. It is derived from *munus,* duty, and *capire,* to take.

Pre-Norman England also left its mark on American local government. In the Saxon era the town was called a *burh* or *burg.* The term is of Teutonic origin from *beorgon,* to protect. In similar forms it is found in Germany (burg), Scotland (burgh), and Denmark (borg). There was even a late Latin *burgus.* It is said that in the term by-law, the prefix is of Scandinavian usage meaning "town," and therefore our by-laws were once "town-laws." The *burh* denoted a walled town, a fortified place. It was governed by a "moot" or court presided over by a "reeve" who represented the king.

The township in ancient England was an organized self-acting group of families exercising common proprietorship over a definite area and forming the basic unit of early society. "Ascending in the analysis of the Anglo-Saxon state," says Sir F. Palgrave in his *English Commonwealth*, "the first and primary element appears the community, which, in England during the Saxon period, was denominated the town or township." Above the township was the hundred, and above the hundred was the shire. The township, compounded from *tun*, town, and *scipe*, ship, stemmed either from the Teutonic *mark* or the late Roman *villa* (diminutive of the Latin *vicus* meaning village or a small group of inhabitants living in an unfortified area). It was a social and economic, rather than a political, district: a small rural community composed mostly of peasants, whose local affairs were managed by an assembly of inhabitants who elected a town-reeve, a tithing man, a constable and representatives to the court of the hundred and shire.

The hundred was an early Anglo-Saxon unit with judicial powers and was composed of several townships. A monthly court, composed of individual landlords and representatives of the constituent townships, was held. Gradually, the hundred disappeared as an administrative unit, and much of its judicial power was absorbed by the manorial courts. By the 17th century, the high constable, who was elected by the court of quarter sessions, was its only officer. However, the hundred must not have disappeared altogether for it was mentioned in colonial Maine and Virginia; it was an important local unit in colonial Maryland, and it still exists in Delaware in place of the township.

THE ENGLISH BACKGROUND

American local government rests solidly upon English foundations. During the six centuries from the Norman Conquest until the founding of the English colonies along the Atlantic seaboard, English local government institutions slowly matured into the well-developed system it was when transplanted on American soil.

The Evolution of the County

As noted before, the county in Early England was called the shire. Its sphere of action in Anglo-Saxon times was the administration of justice through the agency of a court. Its executive officers were an ealdorman, a shire-reeve and a bishop. After the Norman Conquest, the ealdorman and bishop disappeared in active county administration, and the sheriff became supreme as the king's representative. Still another county officer, the lord-lieutenant, came into the picture and was given power over the local militia. By the 17th century, the sheriff and lord-lieutenant were head officers of the county and still powerful. They were chosen by the Crown, selected from a list of three nominated by the Privy Council. They held a court for small civil claims, presided over the county court for the election of members to Parliament, and for the royal court meeting in semi-annual assizes in their districts. They summoned jurors, executed judgments of the court and had charge of the local jail. These duties are generally the scope of duties of the American sheriff today.

The rise of the justices of the peace in English local government dates back to 1349 when Edward III appointed them with executive police powers, to fix wages and prices at the scale in force before the Black Death. Although this did not work out as a permanent arrangement, the office thus created began its long and important career. The functions of justices were slowly combined with those of officials who were charged with keeping of the peace. This officer fulfilled, say Thompson and Johnson, medieval historians, "the fondest hopes of any medieval ruler. He was appointed and dismissed by the king; he was unpaid; he was chosen from the lesser landlords who possessed enough property to be held responsible and yet not enough to escape punishment, while the office carried enough honor and social prestige to make the best seek it." [3]

Other local officers—sheriffs, coroners, constables, and bailiffs—became servants of the justices and often their nominees. The justices at their quarter sessions also constituted the fiscal board of

[3] James Westfall Thompson and Edgar Nathaniel Johnson, *An Introduction to Medieval Europe* (1937), p. 326.

the shire or county, and this agency assessed, levied and expended county funds, maintained county roads and bridges, prisons and public buildings. Later they began to be charged with investigations in criminal cases, they administered a great mass of statutory police legislation including laws against vagabonds and beggars, for the regulation of wages, on apprenticeship and prices, and for the licensing of beer-houses and trades. After the Reformation, they enforced the ecclesiastical laws against papists and nonconformists and were given important powers over the parish in reference to poor relief, police, highways, and local taxation. The justice of the peace was truly "the state's man-of-all work."

By the 17th century, five or six hundred pages of legal textbooks were needed to enumerate the duties of the justice of the peace, acting singly or jointly. The justices of the whole county, gathered together, acted as a court of quarter sessions. This was a court of criminal jurisdiction for all crimes except the most petty, on one hand, and the most serious, on the other. It was also the administrative board for the county charged with supervision over roads, bridges, county property and tax levy. The justices of the peace of 17th century England were transplanted to American soil and exercised almost the same functions in colonial times. In fact, today their position remains practically unchanged in most of the southern states.[4]

The Parish and Manor

Later, after the organization of the church, parishes were established, usually coterminous with the township. This unit was given management over the ecclesiastical affairs of the community under the management of the assembly of inhabitants known as the vestry. Officers included the rector (after the break with Rome), church wardens, and overseers of the poor.

After the Norman Conquest, another unit of local administration, the manor, came into existence. "Manorialism, the characteristic medieval system of cultivating the soil by the labor of a village

[4] Fairlie and Kneier, *County Government and Administration* (1930), pp. 6–9.

community, from the political and economic points of view is definitely a part of feudalism," say Thompson and Johnson.[5] The manor was the local unit of feudal government; in the manorial court, the landowner enforced his feudal rights over his subjects, the peasantry. The lord had officials such as the steward and bailiff with powers in manorial government, but there were also officers selected by the village, such as the general supervisor called the reeve.

Thus, three primary units of local rural government—township, parish and manor—are found in rural England from the Norman invasion until the 17th century when English colonists first made permanent settlements in America. They existed together in varying combinations and relationships. Sometimes, they overlapped in jurisdiction; sometimes, one was completely supreme; and still other times, all three existed side by side. One represented ancient Anglo-Saxon England, one the medieval church and the other Norman feudalism. At the beginning of the 17th century, these local units were so closely interwoven that they were often used as synonymous terms for the same unit.

The most active officer was the constable, chosen in some places by the steward or lord of the manor, in others by the court leet of the manor, in still others, by the vestry or by the justices of the peace.

The English Boroughs and Their Charters

William the Conqueror gave a new charter and special protection to the City of London in 1066. As other boroughs grew in importance and size, they too demanded charters of local freedom from the king. By the middle of the 12th century, most boroughs had charters. During the Crusades, King Richard (1189–99) needing money for his forays into the Near East, sold charters to the burghers, who were becoming increasingly wealthy with the growth of trade and commerce. So did King John (1199–1216), and other barons gave similar liberties to urban areas which could not develop in the straitjacket of rural feudalism.

[5] Thompson and Johnson, *op. cit.,* p. 326.

These charters enumerated certain privileges of the townsmen and in return the king obtained the support of the towns against rival barons. While in the beginning, these liberties were not uniform, toward the 15th century the charters became more standardized. *First,* they contained the right to have the status of a corporation, that is, to be an independent municipality. This was not granted until after 1350; early grants of rights were given to the inhabitants as individuals, not to the borough as a legal entity. *Second,* financial concessions were given. Thus, the sheriff would not come to collect taxes from individuals but the borough was empowered to raise annually a lump sum known as *firma burgi* in lieu of these taxes. There were also commercial privileges such as the right to operate markets and other such ventures, freedom from road tolls and the like. *Third,* charters granted the right to the burghers to choose some of their own officers. In this manner, common councils came into being alongside the executive officers once appointed solely by king or feudal lord. These councils gradually became oligarchic, the same members being elected from year to year. The guilds that they represented grew in importance and exclusiveness while the freemen, who in the beginning of municipal existence had the right to vote, were narrowed down to a small percentage of the population. In short, the once free community became a close corporation. The aldermen, as the chief figures in the corporation were called, governed the borough. The name alderman stems from the Anglo-Saxon *ealdorman* meaning head man. As early as 750, he was the representative of the king in a district or county; in 1130 we find him head man of the guild and since the guilds ran the borough by 1200, aldermen were the chief members of the corporation. They were its magistrates, next in importance to the mayor.[6]

The rise of English boroughs to power and glory had its counterpart in Europe. The springtime of Western culture was between 1200 and 1500. Town life flourished in Italy, France, south Germany, Spain and in the Low countries, as well as in England. These were

[6] William Munro Bennett, *The Government of European Cities* (1927), pp. 3–9.

the days when the great cathedrals were built in all the glory of their Gothic architecture; when the peerless Italian masters painted for the ruling families and the churches of Florence, Venice, Milan, Pisa, Naples and the other members of the brilliant galaxy of the independent Italian "renaissance" cities; and when along the Rhine, Albrecht Durer and others wrought their magic. New forms developed in literature, science, politics and commerce. New wealth was created; new worlds explored. A new life came into existence. The world was once again going some place. No one can see those old cities even as they are now without realizing the beauty, the solidity, the vitality they once must have had. And it was in this time that the municipal corporation as we know it came into its own. American local urban government today draws its fundamental features from the boroughs of England of this colorful period.

Control by the Crown

A significant feature of English local government as it developed up to the 17th century was the control that the Crown exercised over it. There were, however, elements in the situation that restrained national power. One was the ancient democracy of Anglo-Saxon times still expressed in assemblies of inhabitants such as the parish vestry, the hundreds court, the manor court leet, the borough corporation, and the shire or county court, even when the latter were made up of the justices of the peace appointed by the Crown. Although the national government chose most of the executive officers of the local units, the choice of some (such as the church wardens and the select committee of the parish, and many administrative officials of the boroughs) was by these bodies of local inhabitants. That these bodies represented not all the people but the upper economic and social classes does not change the situation. They represented the most organized, vocal and independent elements of the communities. Likewise, the executive officers appointed by the Crown were not mere rootless functionaries of the national government but in most cases sprang from the rural and urban gentry, the propertied classes, whose loyalties were local rather than national in character. Direct elections of officials by the people as a whole, of course, did not exist at the time; that came during the early 19th century democratic movement in America.[7]

LOCAL GOVERNMENT IN THE COLONIES

Thus, when the first American colonies began their political life, the county, the township or parish, and the borough were thriving institutions of English local government. Manors and hundreds had not yet disappeared but were less important. Many present day officers such as the justice of the peace, the sheriff, the alderman, the coroner, the constable, and the mayor had long been important cogs in the local government machinery. On the other hand, many that then existed have since gone the way of all flesh. Such was the destiny of the beadle, the sexton, the hayward, the ale-conner, the way-warden, the questman, the sidesman, the escheator, and a host of others.

This system of local government, transplanted to America with the English colonists, was entirely English. Changes in early America came as a result of conditions in a new country and not from the influence of any other national groups. The Dutch, Swedish, French, and Spanish colonists that settled in the original thirteen colonies left no lasting impression on local government institutions. Colonial local government, however, while following the general English pattern, differed in the various sections because of varied geographic conditions and the influence of the people who first settled there.

The New England Town

In New England, the unincorporated town developed in primary importance. It had the elements of a parish and manor, and traces

[7] Fairlie and Kneier, *op. cit.* See Chapter 1, "Local Institutions in England," for an excellent outline of English local government through the 17th century.

a part of its lineage to them. These towns were composed mostly of groups of landowners who belonged to a particular church congregation that was Puritan in character.

The functions of the town included poor relief, road building and maintenance, public schools, militia organization, business regulation, land recording, and criminal and civil justice. It also served as the unit of representation in the colonial assembly. While the lawmaking body of the province legislated much uniformity into the system, essentially these towns were quite independent and sometimes thought of themselves collectively as a federation of towns rather than as a commonwealth.

The nucleus of town government was the town meeting, an annual event of great importance. This body of freeholders or of all the inhabitants elected the town officers, each of whom were given specific duties and who reported directly to it. It levied taxes, made appropriations and passed by-laws. "This meeting," say Fairlie and Kneier, "reassembled the assembly of freeholders and tenants in the manorial courts, without the presence of the lord's stewart." It was more democratic than the parish vestry for the presence of small freeholders and the leveling effect of the Congregational Church organization made it so, even though toward the close of the colonial period the "first families" exercised general leadership.[8]

The chief executive body of the town meeting were known as selectmen, elected by the town meeting. They acted for the freeholders between meetings under their general instructions. They had charge of the common lands, handled the finance and had some judicial powers. A constable was responsible for law and order; a town clerk was in charge of records; and a treasurer, a tax collector, a surveyor, a fence viewer, overseers of the poor, criers and other officers carried out their special duties throughout the year.

While the town developed into the basic local unit, New England colonies had counties but to them were delegated mainly judicial duties. But in Massachusetts, for example, town by-laws were often approved by the county justices meeting in quarterly court; repre-

---

[8] *Ibid.*, p. 15. See John F. Sly, *Town Government in Massachusetts* (1930), for a detailed description of the New England town, past and present.

sentatives from towns met at the county seat to equalize taxes; the county was the militia district; and officers such as the county treasurer, clerk, chief militia officer, and recorder came into being. Still the county played a minor role in local government there as it does today.

The Middle Atlantic County-Township Combination

In the Middle Atlantic colonies (New York, Pennsylvania, New Jersey, and Delaware) original settlements of the Dutch and Swedes yielded no permanent impressions on local government. In New York, there evolved an elective county board of town supervisors consisting of a freeholder from each town (township) which supervised, levied, and assessed taxes for county purposes. The town had been recognized as the basis of local government in New York by the Duke of Yorke's Laws after the English conquest of New Netherlands in 1664. Town officers included the constable and overseers elected by freeholders in a town meeting. This new county board gradually took over the administrative powers of the justices of the peace, leaving them at the end of the colonial period mainly judicial in their jurisdiction. A similar development took place in New Jersey.

In Pennsylvania, Penn organized his proprietary colony in 1682. In the absence of strong township government, there evolved a vigorous county government. First, assessors were appointed to assist the justices of the peace in tax matters. In 1724, three county commissioners, elected at large by the county freeholders, took their places in tax assessment and gradually developed into the chief county administrative authority. Many states to the west adopted this original American institution as territorial expansion proceeded. County offices such as the sheriff, prothonotary, clerk of the court, and coroner were transplanted from England, others such as the district attorney, recorder of deeds, and register of wills developed from comparable provincial offices decentralized to the county level. Still others, such as the auditors and treasurer were new and incident to the expanding needs of the colonial county administration.

Most of these were appointed by the governor, but some by the county court of justices or the county commissioners. It was not until after the Revolution that they were elected by the people as they are at present.

The important feature in the Middle Atlantic states was the evolution of a county board to administer county affairs and thus take away administrative responsibilities from the county courts of justices. Here begins a "separation of powers" preceding those recognized in the later state and national constitutions. Likewise, the township in these states had somewhat the status of a subdivision of the county rather than as an independent unit of government as in New England.[9]

The Southern County

Local government in the southern colonies differed from that in New England with its emphasis on the town and from the Middle Atlantic county-township combination. Here the county early became the chief unit of local rural government. In Virginia, the original plantations and hundreds first became parishes organized with a vestry, churchwardens and minister. But in 1634, the colony was divided into eight shires or counties with a sheriff, lieutenant, coroner, and justices of the peace, all appointed by the governor upon the recommendation of the justices, who usually were aristocratic planters. Parish government dwindled in importance and demands for town government were not heeded. Tobacco raising and the general agricultural development on the large plantation made the county the logical basis for local government.

Maryland began its existence with manors and hundreds under proprietary rule but as a royal colony, counties and parishes were established. At the time of the Revolution, its local government

[9] See E. L. R. Gould, *Local Government in Pennsylvania* (Johns Hopkins Studies in Historical and Political Science, I, Baltimore, 1883); George E. Howard, *An Introduction to the Local Constitutional History of the United States* (Johns Hopkins Studies in Historical and Political Science, I, Baltimore, 1889); H. L. Osgood, *The American Colonies in the Seventeenth Century* (3 vols., New York, 1904–1907).

favored that of Virginia. In the royal colonies of the Carolinas which were not settled until the 18th century, counties were also the important units of local government. There were, however, parishes in South Carolina for ecclesiastical purposes and poor relief. Counties were not organized in Georgia until after the Revolution; parishes there were the only active units. They also were established for ecclesiastic and poor relief purposes.

Justices of the peace, sitting in quarterly sessions, were, in the South generally, the nucleus of county administration. They were both judicial and administrative officials, and are still so today.[10]

Colonial Municipal Incorporations

During the century and a half of colonial existence, local government in America was confined largely to that of county and town or township. There were very few incorporated municipalities; only twenty-three municipal charters were granted and seven of these were short-lived and unimportant. The more important colonial boroughs were: New York, Philadelphia, Albany (N. Y.), Westchester (N. Y.), Chester (Pa.), Annapolis (Md.), Perth Amboy (N. J.), Bristol (Pa.), Williamsburg (Va.), New Brunswick (N. J.), Burlington (N. J.), Norfolk (Va.), Wilmington (Del.), Elizabeth (N. J.), Lancaster (Pa.), and Wilmington (N. C.).[11]

The organization of these municipal corporations adhered closely to the form of the English borough at the close of the 17th century. The charters were granted by the Crown through the royal governor or proprietor, although they were occasionally amended by the colonial assemblies. Government was in the hands of a mayor, recorder, aldermen, and common councilmen sitting together in one council. The first three officials had, in addition, the judicial powers of a justice of the peace, which in the case of the mayor and aldermen to this day usually adhere to the office.

While most of the English boroughs had at this time self-per-

[10] Fairlie and Kneier, *County Government and Administration* (1930), pp. 13–14, 21–22.

[11] Thomas H. Reed, *Municipal Government in the United States* (1934), pp. 60–61.

petuating governing bodies, only three, Annapolis, Norfolk, and Philadelphia, had such charter provisions in the colonies. In the rest, the aldermen and common councilmen were elected by the freeholders on a ward basis. The mayor was usually appointed by the governor, but in the "close corporations" by the council. He presided but had few rights other than those held by his colleagues. He was not an executive officer in the sense that "strong mayors" are today. It was his responsibility to see that the by-laws and ordinances were executed. What little administrative work there was came under the supervision of council committees.

There were only five municipalities in 1760 with more than 8,000 population. Philadelphia led with 18,000; New York, Boston, Charleston, and Newport followed. The corporation was more a business enterprise than a governmental unit. Most of the revenue came from the operation of such public utilities as markets, docks and ferries, and from regulation and inspection of businesses such as bakeries. There was no public lighting, water supply, rubbish and sewage disposal, or street cleaning. Only a few streets were paved; night watches were only sometimes furnished at public expense. The original borough ordinances did not provide the power to tax and this power was only sparingly given them by colonial legislatures by the time of the Revolution.[12]

Restricted Suffrage

In England there was no general and free suffrage at the close of the 17th century. The county franchise since 1430 had been given only to "forty-shilling freeholders"; that is, those who had property netting annually this amount above charges. The same condition existed in the colonies. The power to vote for local officers, at first given to freeholders and not always on the condition of landownership, was by the 18th century narrowly restricted to those who owned land above a minimum expressed either in income therefrom, value of, or in terms of acreage. As town life developed, the alter-

[12] William Bennett Munro, *Municipal Government and Administration* (1927), Vol. 1, pp. 85–91.

native of owning personal property was introduced. Tax payment as an additional alternative was first adopted in South Carolina in 1759 and in Pennsylvania in 1776. Besides, there were religious and moral qualifications including church membership in force for a time in the New England colonies.

Fifty-acre freeholds were requisite for suffrage at the close of the colonial period in Delaware, Georgia, Maryland, North Carolina, Pennsylvania, and Virginia, the latter with an alternative of twenty-five acres and a house twelve feet square. New Jersey required a hundred acre freehold with an alternative of fifty pounds personalty and some land; South Carolina had a hundred acre freehold or, as an alternative, a settled plantation. Connecticut and Massachusetts required a forty-shilling freehold or a freehold worth forty pounds for suffrage. New Hampshire required one worth fifty pounds; New York and Rhode Island, one worth forty pounds.

Personal property as an alternate to real property was recognized in five states: Pennsylvania (fifty pounds); Delaware, Maryland, Connecticut, and Massachusetts (forty pounds); and South Carolina by a tax payment of ten shillings. This alternative was made in the interest of the town dweller. In addition, certain boroughs and towns allowed all freeholders and inhabitant householders to vote, while others required only some personal property.

Only a fraction of the population, both in town and county, could meet these qualifications, especially as the eastern seaboard became more settled. It has been estimated by Professor A. E. McKinley (Reed College) in a study of the suffrage franchise in the colonies that only 2 per cent of the population was qualified to vote in Philadelphia; 8 per cent in rural Pennsylvania; 9 per cent in Rhode Island; and 16 per cent in Massachusetts. About 8 per cent of the population actually voted in New York and about 3½ per cent during the decade before the Revolution in Boston. Poor communications, large election districts, and absence of party organizations were also contributing factors in making elections an affair for a small minority of the population.[13]

[13] Edward McChesney Sait, *American Parties and Elections* (1939), pp. 18–22.

Characteristics of Colonial Local Government

Local government and its administration in the colonial period was rudimentary. The wilderness had to be made safe and habitable. People were concerned with getting enough to eat and a roof over their heads. Economic organization was decentralized; self-sufficiency of individual establishments and communities was characteristic.[14] It is not surprising, therefore, that its pattern continued in the English design without any sudden or abrupt break. There was neither time nor inclination to invent political gadgets. Certain changes, however, were inevitable. Boroughs tended to lose their "close" corporation status. The freeholders gradually became an electorate. Suffrage was broadened because land was more available than in England; alternatives to property ownership resulted in further democratization. Elective county officers to handle financial administration challenged the supremacy of the justices courts in administration—foretelling the coming era of division of power. In conclusion, local government showed a spirit of independence of the English Crown and a reliance upon the colonial assembly rather than the governor.

THE IMPACT OF JACKSONIAN DEMOCRACY

The period from the Revolution to the Civil War is characterized by the application of the principles of democracy to all American institutions. Local government felt the full impact of this irresistible movement. Starting slowly, it gained impetus with the settlement of the land west of the Alleghenies so that by the 1850's most of the state constitutions contained a great number of changes in local government directly attributable to the application of the spirit of Jacksonian democracy.

[14] For a lively, authentic, and detailed account of life in the six largest colonial towns, see Carl Bridenbaugh, *Cities in the Wilderness (1625–1724)* (1938).

The Importance of Elections

The first and cardinal principle of this new ideology was that government should be close to the people. Frequent elections of *all* officials was considered necessary to keep government from becoming a burden and a tyrant. This tendency actually started in the colonial period, received impetus when the governors lost their power of appointment after the Revolution, and was in full swing by 1830. By 1860, justices of the peace, sheriffs, coroners, county commissioners, and most of the major county and township officers were elected. Moreover, the terms of the majority of elective officers were for one and two years. It was the same in incorporated towns, boroughs, and cities. Mayors were no longer appointed by the governor, but elected by the people. So were councilmen and an increasing number of special administrative officers. The "long ballot" was now an established fact.

Abolition of Property Qualifications for Voting

Along with the increasing emphasis on elections came the abolition of suffrage restrictions relating to property. By 1860 free, white manhood suffrage was the rule in all the states except a few in the East which still required tax payment. Only three states, excepting the thirteen original ones (Ohio, Louisiana, and Mississippi), entered the Union with restrictions based on property or its equivalent and these were removed before the Civil War.[15]

Division of Powers

Changes in structure, while gradual and piecemeal, flowed inevitably from the needs of this period of democracy, decentralization, and territorial expansion. The national and state governments, broken down by the application of Montesquieu's theory of the division of power into separate legislative, executive, and judicial units, set the fashion for local governments. In the county, the Pennsylvania pattern of a small, administrative board of county

[15] Sait, *op. cit.*, p. 16 fn.

commissioners elected at large was adopted in most of the original and newly formed states, but several of the northwestern states, Michigan and Wisconsin notably, followed the New York system of a large county board of township supervisors. Justices of the peace sitting as a county court were deprived of their administrative powers and left with only judicial ones. In most of the southern states, however, these justices kept their judicial and administrative duties intact.

Separation of powers was carried to extreme lengths by election of county "row" officers responsible to no superior officer or agency. Offices such as the district attorney, once entirely a state office, were decentralized as county offices and made independent of the original state office. Township officials were made elective and had little official relation with county government.

Changes in Municipal Government

Municipal government also underwent great changes in this period. Charters were no longer granted by the governor but by the state legislature. These charters came into the status of ordinary law for now they could be granted, except in case of municipal corporations, and amended without the consent of the inhabitants of the municipality. The era of state legislative control had arrived.

Municipal governments also felt the application of the division of powers theory. The once compact council made up of the mayor, recorder, aldermen, and common councilmen began to break up. The mayor, although elective, was given few administrative powers. But he had veto power as a check on the council from which body he gradually withdrew. By 1850, he had even lost the power of presiding over council except on rare and special occasions.

Along with the mayor, special administrative officers were also elected by the voters. Up to this time, officers such as the assessor, tax collector, and constable were appointed by action of the council. Now they and new officers—such as street commissioner, fire chief, engineer, marshal, treasurer, auditors, solicitor, and attorney—became elective.

In many of the larger eastern cities, council itself divided into two houses. The original division between aldermen and common councilmen were used to introduce bicameralism in municipal government. In the West and in all the smaller municipalities, however, council remained unicameral. The number of councilmen tended to increase with the establishment of new wards, election at large being a later development. Council, in spite of its loss of exclusive appointive power, was still the dominant branch of government in the city because of its finance power and the lack of centralized administration.

Another tendency which appeared by the end of this period was the establishment of special elective boards for the administration of special new functions such as education, water supply, lighting, health, sewerage—in fact, most of these new functions involving public works were divorced from councilman control which, during this period, had been found wanting.

Legislative Control

After the Revolution, the state legislature became all-powerful in state government and began to exercise more and more control over local government. As cities grew in size and wealth, there were franchises to be granted, lucrative jobs to be created, new activities to be undertaken. Soon legislatures were passing hundreds of special or local laws regulating specific cities, counties, and other local units. They established salaries and minutely organized departments; they created new offices and boards but did not integrate them with the already established administration. Interest groups and individuals desiring favors, jobs, franchises, revenge, or new powers lobbied at the state capital through their local representatives. Local governments were hamstrung, especially those in the rapidly growing cities; they had no opportunity to develop a sound administrative organization.

The Rise of Political Parties

With the increase of elective offices in local government, party activity and organization came into its own. Local officers in England, both those appointed by the Crown and those elected by local governing bodies, had been drawn largely from the upper classes. They served unpaid but were rewarded by the prestige and honor which the offices brought. Such was also the case in the colonies but with the elimination of the Tories during the Revolution this situation gradually changed. The democratic wave did not really break down all class barriers in local government until the time of Andrew Jackson when the frontier and the rising industrial areas began to be important enough to demand and receive a political hearing.

Political parties were organized to secure control of these newly elective positions and other rewards made available by control of the government. Anyone was eligible for office provided he obtained enough votes; the rich, the few, and the well-born had to take a back seat. "To the victor belongs the spoils," said Senator Marcy in 1832 and this expression has epitomized since then government by unrestrained party control. This development had important consequences and represented a significant alteration of a centuries-old condition of affairs in Western history. Political office was now within the reach of all white males despite differences in economic and social class. Professional competence, however, was not yet recognized as a qualification except perhaps in the case of solicitors and an occasional engineer.

THE DARK AGES OF AMERICAN LOCAL GOVERNMENT

The period from the end of the Civil War to 1900 has been termed by Professor Munro (Harvard University) as the "dark ages of American municipal history." The forces released by the democratic wave in the first half of the century, blending with the increasing growth of cities and industry, the waves of new immigration, and materialism of all American thought and activity, culminated in unrestrained fury upon American local government.

The Politician and the Businessman

The last citadel of aristocratic control has been stormed when the southern planter took his place alongside of the "first families" of Beacon Hill, the Hudson Valley, and Philadelphia in the limbo of forgotten gentlemen. The "politician" was now coming into his own. Parallel in his rise to glory was the coming of the great business and industrial tycoon who was building railroads, steel industries, commercial houses, and banks. Both of these newcomers were getting a good grip upon the rapidly increasing material resources of a United States. They had need of one another. The politician needed the contributions of the newly wealthy businessman to carry on his political campaigns; the businessman could use the politician in getting contracts for the building of public works and the control of public utilities at a time when cities and towns were expanding to meet the demands of the new industrialization.

The new immigrant groups that had come over in great numbers before the Civil War and settled in the growing cities were by 1870 in a position of political leadership in most of the cities. It was they who fashioned the first great urban political machines. In anything that had in it some phase of municipal politics, party organization, office holding, police and fire administration, or contracting business, these newer citizens developed colorful leaders in political command in most of the American cities during this hectic period of growth. While the notorious Tweed and Croker machines in New York are the best known, each city had its comparable organization and the names of James McManes of the Philadelphia Gas Ring of Philadelphia, "Honest George" Cox of Cincinnati, and many others emulated and sometimes outshown the New York City organization. There was a great deal of graft, which that mythical New York observer, Mr. Dooley, classified as "honest and dishonest." Honest graft consisted of rewards obtained by having a "stand-in" with the controlling forces and was gained without committing an overt illegal act; dishonest graft involved fraud in the administration of the government and was frowned upon by expert politicians as unnecessary is those days of plenty.

But in those times of unexampled growth of cities, industries, markets, natural resources, population, and standard of living, Americans were not squeamish. And cities were built, streets paved, water and other utilities furnished—even though often at exorbitant cost. There was need for quick action, and the decentralized local government was incapable of achieving it without the liaison offices of the informal political boss which the increased power of the enfranchised masses raised to power. The political leaders did make government work; they took care of the unfortunate, and furnished the urban dwellers with the necessities of their existence. There were indeed no precedents for this in American or English politics; for industrial America was something entirely new. There were no theories of urban government for a society under the impact of the twin 19th century forces: industrialism and democracy. And when "business was good" the most able and aggressive people were immersed in the challenging task of making the most of it. It is difficult to cast blame on politicians when businessmen suggested, aided, abetted, and profited by their machinations. Many politicians in those days were merely businessmen in politics who by their own confessions were not in the game "for their health." They built up organizations comparable to those in business. Some became very wealthy. They were successful when they "delivered the goods." It is better perhaps to view the latter half of the 19th century as a period when American city government was having the trials and tribulations of a healthy, virile, but undisciplined and neglected adolescent. Bad company, bad manners, and bad examples could not destroy its potential, adult idealism and usefulness, as we shall see.[16]

Local Legislation Abolished

There were, however, signs of reform and change already developing. The chaotic system of legislative control, whereby the

[16] Every student of American local government should read Lincoln Steffen's *Autobiography,* a greater part of which is devoted to his experiences and reflections as a "muckraker" of corruption in city government throughout the United States at the turn of the new century.

state legislatures would pass special and local acts for local governments at the instance of almost any influential individual, group, or party, using them as a football of politics or as fair game for commercial exploitation, went from bad to worse. State constitutions were changed and amended prohibiting such local legislation with the result that all local units of one class or kind received its legislation from general laws applying equally to all. This proved too extreme in the other direction for there were great ranges in the population of cities, towns, and other local units and therefore different needs. Almost immediately population classes were established by the legislatures for each kind of local unit and legislation was passed for each class. While such classification of local units was sometimes abused, it became a permanent procedure and was interpreted as constitutional by the courts. Ohio and Indiana led the parade of states in prohibiting special legislation as early as 1851 and many others followed during the next twenty years.

Home Rule Is Born

But the reaction against legislative interference did not stop with restrictions against local legislation. Constitutional provisions granting "home rule" to cities—that is, the power under certain restrictions to determine their own type of government—were first adopted in this period. Missouri, in 1875, was a pioneer. It adopted home rule for cities of 100,000 or over, with special provisions for St. Louis. Washington followed in 1889, California in 1896, and Minnesota in 1898. But while twenty-five states have adopted home rule provisions in their constitutions up through 1954 (six since 1930: Utah, New Mexico, West Virginia, New Jersey, Louisiana, and Rhode Island), this movement, once so promising, has not spread because of the growing complexity of state-local relations in fields of mutual interest.[17] Numerous other provisions to "freeze" conditions and arrangements of local government into stability outside the influence

[17] Joseph D. McGoldrick, *Law and Practice of Municipal Home Rule, 1916–1930*, Columbia University Press (1933). Also Rodney L. Mott, *Home Rule for America's Cities* (1949), pp. 60–62.

of state legislatures were embodied in the state constitutions. Such provisions dealt most often with classes of local units, types of officers, limits of indebtedness, and other financial safeguards.

Rise of the Mayor

The most important change in the structure of government in American cities between the Civil War and 1900 was the emergence of the American mayor as chief executive officer in charge of city administration. Gradually, in the larger cities, the power of appointment shifted away from the council, independent elected department heads were abolished, some independent boards were supplanted by departments under the mayor (although between 1865 and 1900 more boards were newly created than abolished), and his term was lengthened from two to four years. The "strong mayor" emerged by slow steps, not all consummated during this period, but the tendency toward a unified administration was marked. There was evidence of a need for more economy and efficiency than a city ruled by invisible government and a boss could provide. Council, however, still retained implements to restrain him by its power to appropriate money for expenditures and to pass upon his appointments and removals.

Changes in Council

The decline of the council from the dominant position it had in municipal government before the Civil War was gradual and incomplete, as we have seen. Its competitors for power were the state legislature, the mayor, other elective boards or administrative officers, and, lastly, the people. The legislature regulated in detail on the powers, restraints, procedures, and officers of local government. The mayor became chief administrative and executive officer, and other boards and officers took special powers which, when they lost them, went to the mayor. But it was not until the new century was well under way that the people, through initiative and the referendum, really challenged the powers of the council.

The bicameral system of council which developed in imitation of the federal model during the first part of the century now began to disappear. Some of the larger cities in the East kept it until the 20th century, but the newer western cities either never adopted it or shed it very quickly. New Orleans adopted it in 1852, abandoned it in 1870; Milwaukee adopted it in 1858 and abandoned it in 1874; Cincinnati adopted it in 1870, abandoned it in 1890. Detroit had it only from 1881 to 1887; New York from 1830 to 1873. Cleveland and Chicago never had a bicameral council.[18] As late as 1903 it is estimated that one-third of all cities over 25,000 had bicameral councils.

City councils had, during the 19th century, grown large in size. This was due to the fact that wards were made the basis of representation when members to council were made elective during the colonial and early national periods. As cities grew, more wards were created and democratic practice clung to the ward system. As a result many cities had large councils, too large for administrative efficiency. In 1885, New York had a lower house of 21; Chicago had a council of 36. Boston's two houses contained 85 members; Philadelphia's two houses had about a hundred. Baltimore's two houses had 30, St. Louis' two houses had 41, and Pittsburgh's two houses had 70. By the close of the century, it was apparent that any changes would be in the direction of single chambered councils, a smaller number, and election at large. Likewise, terms of councilmen tended to increase from one and two years to three and later to four. Councilmen, who originally received no compensation, by this time drew salaries in some of the larger cities.

Smaller Units Unaffected

In view of the decentralization of the internal organization of the old colonial borough into its component parts and the rise of an independent and potentially powerful executive officer in the person of the mayor in the later 19th century city, it is significant that in smaller municipalities, counties, townships, school districts and many

[18] Reed, *Municipal Government in the United States* (1934), pp. 81–82.

special districts, the governing body—that is, the council, the board of commissioners, the board of directors or the board of supervisors, whatever its particular name—remained more or less impervious to this tendency. In New England, the town continued its board of selectmen without a chief executive. The Pennsylvania borough, copied by many municipalities in the West, had a council with an elective burgess who had veto and judicial powers but very little administrative power. In other smaller municipalities, the mayor might merely be one of council, *prima inter pares,* but with little administrative power. In some cases, however, the mayor in imitation of the larger cities became the chief, if not the only, executive officer. In these municipalities, other elective administrative officers and boards were still common.

In counties and townships there was no semblance of a chief executive. In the county, the board of commissioners was flanked by a host of independent elective officers who kept the board from developing as the chief governing body. The township board, however, was not challenged to the degree that the county was but exercised dominant control. But even here, there were a number of independently elected officers such as the justice of the peace, constable, and tax collector. The form and structure of these units had fully developed by the turn of the century and froze as far as their essential features are concerned. The lighter impact of urban necessities on these rural units and the increased state administrative activity in their functions accounts for the static condition of their structure.

THE NEW AND BETTER CENTURY

The 20th century so far is one of reform and improvement in the government of American local units. In the beginning, a great wave of popular revulsion against the political machine was fanned into flame by muckrakers, "yellow" journalists, reform organizations, and political liberals. Lincoln Steffens' articles which ran in *McClure's Magazine,* and were later incorporated in a book *The Shame of the Cities,* published in 1904, cited names, incidents, and methods of political graft and corruption in a survey of a score of large American cities. Viscount Bryce, the great English observer of American government, had written in 1888: "There is no denying that the government of cities is the one conspicuous failure in the United States."

Beginnings of Reform

But now some people were bent on doing something about it. Municipal reform organizations, some of which had begun their existence in the latter part of the last century, now came into the limelight. Reform parties or cliques within parties opposed the regular slates. Here and there, reform groups "threw the rascals out," only to lose the next election when popular interest subsided. Offending corruptionists and grafters were hunted down and prosecuted in the courts. Some disappeared before the arm of the law was put on them. Through organizations of city clubs, reform groups, and community associations, opportunity was given the more fortunate economic groups to come back into the sphere of political activity from which they had practically disappeared during the last half of the 19th century. Reform politics became respectable, a duty of conscientious and intelligent citizens. Great and lasting good came from this movement. Even though it did not, in most cases, break up the political machine or eliminate corruption in city government, it created a barrier against the raw forces of greed. It showed what an aroused organized public could do, and it revealed the defects and weaknesses of American municipal government organization.[19]

In the opinion of many observers, the ills of city government stemmed largely from the complicated and disintegrated organization which allowed—even made necessary—invisible government and the boss. New laws effecting structural changes to bring about concentration of responsibility, simplification of machinery, and

[19] See Richard S. Childs, *Civic Victories, the Story of an Unfinished Revolution,* Harper & Brothers (1952). The story of civic reform during the past half century as reported by one of the leaders in the fight for better state and local government. Also Frank Mann Stewart, *A Half Century of Municipal Reform* (1950). This is a history of the National Municipal League.

increased democratic control were enacted. The elevation of the mayor to a position of chief executive, which had already begun before the turn of the century, seemed to fit the needs of the large city. Here it seemed necessary to create an officer within the government who could challenge the boss and the machine for control. For the boss and machine could thrive only when the government was decentralized. The mayor emerged as a leader of the people and the chief executive of the government rolled into one.

The Commission Form of Government for Cities

Two new forms of municipal government were introduced early in the 20th century; both received their major initial impetus to popular acclamation because of local disasters. The first was the commission form; the second, the city manager. Municipal government by commission was not entirely unknown in the United States before the Galveston flood in 1900. The carpet bagger government of New Orleans in 1870 had a mayor and seven administrators, each head of a department of government. Collectively, they were the council. (It was changed back in 1882 to the ordinary mayor-council form.) Washington, D. C., came under the government of a commission of three in 1874. Memphis, Tennessee, and Mobile, Alabama, used it as an emergency setup before 1900; and Sacramento, California, had used it.

But the flood of Galveston brought so much destruction and disaster that the people ignored the feeble efforts of its municipal government and turned to the "Deep Water Commission," which was a body of businessmen which had been working on methods of improving the harbor. They devised a government under the control of a commission of five, who originally were supposed to be appointed by the governor but because of opposition were elected by the people under the Act of 1903 setting up the commission. Not only was municipal power concentrated in the hands of these five men acting as a council but they individually were heads of specific departments. The latter characteristic is the difference between the commission plan and a board of county commissioners or a regular council system without an independent executive. The Galveston plan was an immediate success. Its commission started with nothing and after ten years had paid all current expenses, financed its share of the rebuilding, and was in good financial shape, considering the added burdens. It received national publicity through articles in *McClure's Magazine.*

Houston, Texas, adopted the above plan in 1905, in a modified form, with an elective mayor who had veto and appointive power but who was a member of the commission. Five Texas cities and one in Idaho followed in 1907, while in the same year the states of Iowa, Kansas, North Dakota, and South Dakota gave cities legislative permission to adopt this form of government. As adoptions increased, new devices were added to "make it safe for democracy."

The initiative and referendum, whereby the voters were given power to suggest by petition and to vote on ordinances without action on the part of the commission, and the simple referendum whereby ordinances passed by the commission could be by petition brought to a vote of the people before final enactment, were "improvements" designed to check the legislative power of this new body which had been given such concentrated authority. The recall was designed to return commissioners to private life by vote of the people before expiration of their term, if they acted contrary to public good.

Nonpartisan elections with nomination by petition were also added. Politics should not taint this new and precious form of government, the reformers vowed. These devices took away the suspicion of "un-American" concentration of power and provided popular checks and balances. The commission form plus these democratic safeguards was known as the "Des Moines Plan" because of the excellent publicity this Iowa city received upon its adoption.[20]

The spread of this new form was most rapid from 1909 until 1913. After that its rate of adoption began to decline because of the growing popularity of the city manager form. In 1954, 356 or 14.1 per cent of all cities over 5,000 population operated under the commission plan. But since New Orleans dropped it for the mayor coun-

[20] Reed, *Municipal Government in the United States* (1934), pp. 184–195.

cil plan in 1952, Washington, D. C., remains the only commission governed city over 500,000. Two hundred and sixty-one of the commission cities have a population between 5,000 and 25,000.[21] While commission governed cities are scattered in most states, the bulk of them are concentrated in New Jersey, Pennsylvania, Illinois, and in the southwestern part of the United States. In Pennsylvania, for example, the commission form of government is mandatory for all of its 47 cities of the third class which includes cities between 10,000 and 135,000.

The Coming of the City Manager

The commission plan emphasized concentration of responsibility in the hands of a few elected commissioners who were usually full-time, paid administrators as well as legislators. It was an antidote to the weak mayor-council form which was the characteristic form of 19th century American municipal government. The commission was likened to a board of managers so common in business and therefore popular as a means of getting "more business in government." The council-manager plan added thereto an administrative officer in whom rested the responsibility for carrying out the will of this board of managers who again became part-time legislators and policy makers, divesting their administrative duties. The manager was "hired and fired" by the commission or council, but while in office he was responsible for all administrative duties and the administrative employees under his direction. In effect, the plan is a counterpart in government to the organization in business of a corporation with a board of directors and a general manager.

Staunton, Virginia, in 1908 was the first city to hire a manager. He was Charles E. Ashburner, who later held similar posts in a number of larger cities. The next city in the limelight was Sumter, South Carolina, held by some to be the first city with a true council-manager plan, adopted in 1912. Dayton, Ohio, was considering the manager plan among others when the great flood struck it. Its adoption of it in 1913 and its immediate success, under the leader-

[21] *The Municipal Year Book 1955*, p. 57.

ship of John Patterson of the National Cash Register Company, made national news and gave the city manager its real start in American life. Colonel Henry M. Waite was its first manager and was to gain one of the first national reputations as a "public administrator" in local government.

The manager-council form spread rapidly. As of January 1, 1955, there were 1,260 cities (including cities, boroughs, towns, and townships) and 15 counties operating under manager government with standards approved by the International City Managers' Association. This is more than double what it was in 1940. Of cities over 5,000 in the United States in 1954, 764 or 30 per cent were governed under the council-manager form. States having the largest number of manager cities are California (120), Maine (121), Michigan (96), Texas (105), and Virginia (65). The population of all places under the manager plan totals more than 23 million. It has so far made little headway in counties. The fifteen manager counties are in California, Georgia, Maryland, Montana, New York, North Carolina, Tennessee, and Virginia.[22]

An increasing number of smaller municipalities, while not of approved manager status, have given certain key employees—such as engineers, secretaries, and superintendents—over-all responsibilities and these have gradually assumed direction of administration. Often these officers have powers almost comparable to managers without holding such status, designation, or title.[23]

Schools are uniformly governed under the general principles of the manager plan with an elected board of directors which hires a superintendent of schools or a supervising principal. This unit of government never had to go through a long period of decentralized internal organization. Teachers and superintendents were never elective public officials but always hired employees of the board of directors. In other special districts, the commission plan with a

---

[22] *Ibid.,* pp. 57, 501–527. The total figure of manager places includes 6 in Alaska, one in Puerto Rico, and 38 in Canada.

[23] See John C. Bollens, *Appointive Executive Local Government; the California Experience* (1952). Also Charles F. LeeDecker, *Manager Government in Pennsylvania Municipalities,* Institute of Local Government, Pennsylvania State University (1947).

managerial officer is usually in operation. There is no doubt that the manager idea has a firm and permanent hold in American local government.

Local Governments Needed Help

Before 1900, local governments were individually "on their own"; that is to say, no outside agencies looked after their needs or attempted to aid them in the administration of their duties. True, the state legislatures passed laws relating to their structure and powers but, when these laws were passed, the legislature forgot local governments until the next session. Likewise, while the courts kept them in line with their interpretations of law, this came only upon the institution of a particular court case. Local officers were elected from the ranks of the citizenry and their appointees were drawn from the same source. None, except perhaps solicitors and engineers, were required to have qualifications for particular positions—the people were supposed to elect "good" men and they, in turn, appoint qualified employees. But most of these officials had had no previous training or knowledge of local government work and what they learned depended entirely upon their intelligence and application. As the cities and towns grew, and more and complicated duties devolved upon them, the defects of a strictly amateur body of local government administrators became more and more apparent. They needed the stimulation of special knowledge, new techniques, and moral support if their administration was to be economical and efficient.

Personnel Progress

Since 1900 a great many aids to good local government have been made available. Some of these have been direct, many indirect. Perhaps the most important gain in this respect has been in the field of personnel. Civil service reform for local government dates back to the 1880's and its spread throughout the thousands of local units has been laborious, hesitant, and even now is incomplete. But the merit system (induction into and promotion upward on the part of employees in local government on the basis of ability) has been adopted in all large cities although it must be said without uniform success. Small municipalities, townships, and counties generally are still without the pale, but there is reason to hope for substantial gains in this direction in the future. Through the merit system, elective officers have been given a foundation on which to build a qualified personnel, and have been relieved of the embarrassment of making appointments on the basis of politics.

A more recent development for improving personnel has been in-service training. Some of the larger municipalities established training programs early in the century for certain of the more numerous classes of officers such as police and firemen, usually under the instruction of the chief or ranking officers. In the 1920's, a few of the state leagues of municipalities organized such training to be available for all municipalities within the state. New York and Virginia were especially notable in this regard. In 1936, the George-Deen Act, passed by the United States Congress, extended aid for vocational training to public service occupations and as a result many state departments of education have developed a series of training courses for a large variety of local officers under a system of federal-state subsidies. Colleges and universities have taken an increasing interest in such training.

Local Government Literature

Since 1900, also, an impressive literature on American municipal and local government has come into existence. Several monthly national magazines (*National Municipal Review, Public Management, The American City*) cover the field on current developments and improved administrative techniques. The *Municipal Year Book* and the *Municipal Index and Atlas* provide invaluable and authoritative information about officials, local units, departmental activities, equipment and methods. Innumerable books have been written on all phases of local government. The books are written by local officers, college professors, officials of state and national departments dealing with special phases of local government, and members and directors of staffs of private organizations working for improved local government. The exposés of political corruption, so popular in the early part of the century, were done mostly by journalists.

It cannot be said that the interest of the general public in local government has grown very much since the days of the muckrakers. An occasional scandal makes newspaper headlines, but newspaper coverage of local government still leaves much to be desired. Public reports by local officers have just recently begun to make progress in readability, simplicity, and attractiveness, but it must be recorded that public hearing on budgets, future plans, and other subjects are attended only sparsely except perhaps when a major increase in taxes or indebtedness is being proposed.

State Leagues of Municipalities

Most heartening has been the increase in the interest of local government officers in their own work. Realizing that the positions into which they have come require no small amount of knowledge, they have been more ready to make use of available technical information. Many have been taking correspondence courses, joining associations of officers, and utilizing information gathered by public and private advisory agencies.

One of the most important movements toward improved local government has been the rise of the state league of municipalities. The first effort on the part of municipalities to cooperate was in Indiana in 1891 and by 1900 leagues were formed in California, Indiana, Iowa, and Wisconsin. In 1952, there were 42 active state leagues representing a membership of 11,336 municipalities in the United States. Most of these leagues have headquarters at their state capitols and render year-round service to their membership. This usually includes legislative representation, periodical magazines, annual conventions, and information services. Some leagues have sponsored programs of in-service training for municipal officers and employees, centralized purchasing of specific items for municipal use, and have even set up personnel services through which smaller municipalities might have technical assistance that they could not otherwise obtain. A number of them have field agents who visit municipalities, find out their problems, and render information and advice. Any problem in which the member municipalities need assistance is considered as a possible league sphere of activity. In addition, union on the part of municipalities in the state makes their officials feel their true importance and the need to better administer their duties. It brings to them the realization of the high place their combined governments have in the American system of democracy.[24]

The national federation of these state leagues of municipalities is the American Municipal Association, founded in 1924. Its function is to assist the state leagues in their work by preparing information and research bulletins, by maintaining a comprehensive municipal information service, by providing consulting service on special problems and by representing the municipalities on the national scene. Its national headquarters are now in Washington D.C., but the research division is at "1313" in Chicago. One of the most important aspects of AMA activity is the work of the Washington office which keeps leagues informed of current developments and future possibilities of the national government in its ever increasing relationship with local government. Beginning with the great depression and continuing through the war days, this service has been an indispensable part of the program.

"1313"

A number of nationally organized groups of local and state officials are housed in a splendid building on the campus of the University of Chicago, a gift from the Spelman Fund. These associations have already made history in the movement to improve government in the United States at all levels. They include the International City Managers' Association, founded in 1914; the Municipal Finance Officers Association, founded in 1906; the American Public Works

[24] For a list of these leagues of municipalities, see *The Municipal Year Book 1955*, pp. 153–154.

Association, founded in 1894; the Civil Service Assembly, founded in 1906; the American Public Welfare Association, founded in 1930; the Council of State Governments, founded in 1933; the National Association of Housing Officials, founded in 1933; the American Society for Planning Officials, founded in 1934; the National Institute of Municipal Clerks, founded in 1947; the Public Administration Service, founded in 1933; the National Association of Assessing Officers, founded in 1934; the American Society for Public Administration, founded in 1939; and finally the Public Administration Clearing House, founded in 1931, which for many years under the leadership of its director, the well-known and energetic Louis Brownlow, exercised general supervision of "1313." All these groups have from time to time received substantial aid from the Spelman Fund whose sole object is to stimulate increased efforts towards better governmental administration.[25]

A Variety of Helpful Organizations

There are, of course, other important national organizations which have exerted much influence for good on local government in the United States. The National Municipal League located in New York City has, since its founding in 1894, been the most influential organization in the field of municipal reform. It has supported and encouraged such reforms as commission government, manager government, the short ballot, proportional representation, budgeting, civil service, and many others. The United States Conference of Mayors with headquarters in Washington has been influential in the recent development of national-local relations. The Government Research Association has built up an *esprit de corps* among the various municipal and other research agencies interested in the field of local, state, and national government. The American Political Science Association and other academic groups have contributed to this general movement for improvement through its meetings and the activities of its members.

While the urban municipalities are the most highly organized

[25] *Ibid.,* pp. 153–154.

groups of local units, counties, townships, and school districts have comparable national and state federations. Likewise, almost every large class of local officer and employee is similarly organized. Policemen and firemen, for example, have for many years been influential in obtaining legislation for the improvement of their conditions of work and have made great headway in the technical education and training of their membership. Their large membership in the various states has made them a power to be reckoned with at state capitols. The International Chiefs of Police Association has been a factor in the improvement of American police techniques and organization. Sheriffs, justices of the peace, tax collectors, tax assessors, recreation administrators, finance officers, school directors, sanitation engineers, solicitors and a host of other local officers have organizations in most states and many of them are nationally organized. Sometimes they are a part of the municipal or local government associations, sometimes they are independent. One and all have at least the popular "annual convention" where exchange of ideas, new information, and social amenities are merged in a most enjoyable and useful occasion. Most of them carry on state legislative activities and many of them have publications containing information for the good of the order.

Then, too, there are the civic associations and taxpayers organizations interested in economy and efficiency in local government. These organizations are supported by private contributions of interested laymen. Most large cities have had at some time a bureau of municipal research. The oldest of these was the New York Bureau founded in 1906, and which is now the Institute of Public Administration. The more important of these bureaus are found in Detroit, St. Louis, Kansas City, Rochester, and Minneapolis. Their primary object is to help city officers improve their administration and they make elaborate and special studies primarily for their benefit. A few cities have research organizations supported from public funds as, for example, Chicago and Boston. Taxpayers associations are sometimes organized on a state-wide scale with local organizations functioning in an integrated program. Such, for example, is the Pennsylvania Economy League with offices in Philadelphia, Pittsburgh, Harrisburg, and a number of county seats.

Certainly, one of the greatest differences between local government in the 20th century and that preceding has been the rise of such organizations, which are estimated to number about two thousand. No more can the local officer say that he can obtain no technical, administrative, or inspirational aids for the improvement of his work. He need only call and the services of experts are at hand. Such service has already been of immeasurable value; it continues to gain in influence.

Schools and Colleges Enter the Field

Educational institutions have recently awakened to their responsibilities in training future citizens for more intelligent participation in local government and for actual careers in its administration. Secondary schools all over the United States teach civics and problems of democracy to implement their students with a more adequate understanding of the governments under which they live. Study projects, field visits, and contacts with local officers often are a part of the instruction. If something better is still to be desired in this field, it is largely because of the overemphasis of national and state government at the expense of local government in the texts, and in the collegiate training of the teaching personnel.

Colleges are now "going strong" for increased instruction in public administration generally as a supplement to the regular courses in government. More of this is now directed to the field of local government than ever before. Students now can "major" in most of the larger colleges and universities in a curriculum that will prepare them for public service and public administration. Some universities have developed specific graduate courses as for example, Syracuse University, University of Michigan, University of Minnesota, University of Kansas, University of California, Harvard University, University of Pennsylvania, The Pennsylvania State University, University of Cincinnati, University of Southern California, American University, Wayne University, New York University, and perhaps a few others.[26] While most of these institutions have emphasized public administration on the state and national levels, local governments, especially in urban areas, have profited by such training. But the national and state governments have absorbed the lion's share of the annual crop of such students since 1933. One of the continuing problems is to find ways and means to get trained, career men and women in local governments. A grave danger exists for local governments because this young, trained, and able group is not fully utilized in their service.

The Development of State Administrative Control

Another 20th century feature is the development of state administrative control over an increasing number of functions of local government and the actual absorption by the state of many one-time local functions. While the 19th century was characterized by legislative interference in local matters, the worst features of this condition were practically eliminated by the adoption of constitutional amendments prohibiting special and local legislation. The development of state administrative control has been especially rapid in the field of education, rural highways, rural police, poor relief, welfare, local indebtedness, and local finances; but every field of local government has felt the impact of state government in recent years. In reality, state administrative control is merely a refinement of earlier legislative interference. State administrative departments work the year around and can, if they will, employ technical assistants. As the control of these state departments develops, they eventually take it upon themselves to introduce legislation relating to their activity and aspire to leadership in their field. That such control has been often beneficial cannot be denied, but its effect has not been uniformly wholesome especially when state departments are manned by personnel appointed for their political activity

[26] See George A. Graham, *Education for Public Administration* (Public Administration Service, Chicago, 1941) for the only detailed study of American college and university public administration training programs.

rather than for their capabilities. It must be stated, however, that greater advancement in state administrative control over the local government has been in the rural areas. Cities often have large and well staffed departments that need little aid from the outside. This state administrative control over local governments is not integrated even within the state government. There is often a lot of duplication —one arm of the state not knowing what the other one does.[27] Nevertheless, this trend will continue because of the ever increasing need for uniformity of administration so evident in the fields of highway, education, relief, and other such functions. Whether the state will ultimately act as an advisor to stimulate efficiency rather than an organization for direct administration of these functions is a problem for the future. It will take high morals, good technique, and good spirit to work out an ideal relationship between local units and the state government, which is at best a delicate governmental balance.

The National Government and Local Units

The modern age has also brought another new condition that is in itself foreboding and difficult to evaluate in terms of local government. This is the increasing activity on the part of the national government in local government affairs. Little of this existed before 1933, but the years of depression and war brought local governments directly under the influence of the ever growing Great Leviathan. Certain it is that the problems since 1933 demanded unified action and rightful subordination on the part of local governments, but there is danger to the very existence of local government in the situation. While state and national relations with local government will be discussed at length in a later chapter, it is important here to mention it as a phase of utmost importance in historical development. This tendency towards national and state control reached its height earlier in the European nations than in the United States. But what the future will be, no one can say.

[27] H. F. Alderfer, "Centralization in Pennsylvania," *National Municipal Review* (1938), pp. 189–196.

TEN SUBJECTS FOR FURTHER STUDY

1. The English borough in the 17th century.
2. The New England town in colonial days.
3. The Tweed Ring in New York City.
4. Boss Cox of Cincinnati.
5. Lincoln Steffens.
6. The rise and decline of the commission form of city government.
7. "1313" in Chicago.
8. Universities and college services to local government.
9. The league of municipalities in your state.
10. The doctrine of separation of powers as applied to American municipal government during the early 19th century.

REFERENCES

Charles A. Beard, "Teutonic Origins of Representative Government," *American Political Science Review,* February 1928, pp. 28–44.

Wyatt Winton Belcher, *The Economic Rivalry between St. Louis and Chicago, 1850–1880,* Columbia University Press (1947).

Richard Bigger and James D. Kitchen, *How the Cities Grew: A Century of Municipal Independence and Expansionism in Metropolitan Los Angeles,* Bureau of Governmental Research, University of California, 1952.

Carl Bridenbaugh, *Cities in Wilderness,* 1625–1742 (New York, 1938).

———, *Cities in Revolt: Urban Life in America, 1743–1776* (New York, 1955).

Bureau of the Census, *Historical Statistics on State and Local Government Finances 1902–1953* (Washington, 1955).

Henry S. Churchill, "What Kind of Cities Do We Want?" Chapter III in Coleman Woodbury, ed., *The Future of Cities and Urban Redevelopment* (Chicago, 1953).

Stanley H. Friedenbaum, *Origins of New Jersey Municipal Government,* Proceedings of the New Jersey Historical Society (January 1955).

Ernest S. Griffith, *History of American City Government—The Colonial Period* (New York, 1938).

Public Administration Clearing House, *Public Administration Organizations; a Directory—1954* (Chicago, 1954).

A. M. Schlesinger, *The Rise of the City* (New York, 1933).

Frederick Shaw, *The History of the New York City Legislature* (New York, 1954).

A. F. Weber, *The Growth of Cities in the Nineteenth Century* (New York, 1899).

Coleman Woodbury, "The Background and Prospects of Urban Redevelopment in the United States," Part V in Coleman Woodbury, ed., *The Future of Cities and Urban Redevelopment* (Chicago, 1953).

Chapter 3

POPULATION, GEOGRAPHY AND METROPOLITAN AREAS

One of the wonders of the modern world has been the settlement of the North American continent by the peoples of Europe and to a lesser extent by those from Asia and Africa. In less than four centuries, thousands of square miles of trackless wilderness and open prairie have been converted into what is now the richest and most favored region in the whole world. Continental United States alone had 150,000,000 people according to the 1950 census; in 1790, the date of the first decennial census, its population was just slightly under 4,000,000.

The rate of growth has been phenomenal. From 1790 to 1880, the increase ran well over thirty per cent each decade except one. But from 1880, the rate of increase declined until the 1930–40 decade when it was only 7 per cent. The increase from 1940 to 1950, however, rose to 14 per cent.

The rapid growth during the 19th century resulted from a combination of three factors: high fertility, declining mortality, and immigration. The birth rate, until recently, has been steadily decreasing. In 1800, for the white population it was estimated at 55 per 1,000; one hundred years later, it was 30 per 1,000, and by 1940, it dropped to 18. But in 1950, it had risen to 24 per thousand.

On the other hand, the mortality rate has also dropped. In Massachusetts in 1789, it was 27.8 per thousand. Since 1900, the rate has decreased 44 per cent. Thirty years ago, it was 13.5 per thousand. In 1952, it was 9.6 per thousand.

Until the inauguration of the quota system in 1921, immigration was an important factor in American population growth, reaching an all-time peak of almost nine million in the decade from 1900 to 1910. The quota system was based upon an annual immigration of 150,000. Therefore, since the second decade of this century, immigration has no longer been an important source of population increase.[1]

The 1950 census indicated the main currents of post-war migration in the United States. First, Americans are moving to town from rural areas in greater numbers than ever before. Second, a movement from the central city to the suburbs has been almost as great. Third, there has been heavy migration into the border states, especially to the Southwest.[2]

Urban Population

The growth of cities and urban places in the United States has been the most significant population trend during the 20th century. In 1790, there were only twenty-four places over 2,500 population; only two cities, Philadelphia and New York had more than 25,000 population. Only 5 per cent of the people, roughly 200,000 lived in urban places. By 1920, United States had become an urban nation— more than half the people lived in urban places. By 1950, sixty-four per cent of the population was urban—almost one hundred million out of a total population of one hundred and fifty million.

In 1950, New Jersey had the highest percentage of urban population—86.6 per cent. Other states with more than four out of five living in urban places included Massachusetts, Rhode Island, New York, California. Thirty states were more than half urban. The northeast section of the United States had four-fifths of its popula-

[1] Philip M. Hauser and Conrad Taeuber, "The Changing Population of the United States," *The Annals of the American Academy of Political and Social Sciences* (January, 1945), pp. 12–21.

[2] Roy V. Peel, "What the 1950 Census Means for Cities," *Public Management* (October, 1950), pp. 218–221.

GROWTH OF LARGEST UNITED STATES CITIES

Cities	1950	1900
New York, N. Y.	7,891,957	3,437,202
Chicago, Ill.	3,620,962	1,698,575
Philadelphia, Pa.	2,071,605	1,293,697
Los Angeles, Calif.	1,970,358	102,479
Detroit, Mich.	1,849,568	285,704
Baltimore, Md.	949,708	508,957
Cleveland, Ohio	914,808	381,768
St. Louis, Mo.	856,796	575,238
Washington, D. C.	802,178	278,718
Boston, Mass.	801,444	560,892
San Francisco, Calif.	775,357	342,782
Pittsburgh, Pa.	676,806	451,512
Milwaukee, Wis.	637,392	285,315
Houston, Texas	596,163	44,633
Buffalo, N. Y.	580,132	352,387
New Orleans, La.	570,445	287,104
Minneapolis, Minn.	521,718	202,718
Cincinnati, Ohio	503,998	325,902
Seattle, Wash.	467,591	80,671
Kansas City, Mo.	456,622	163,752

tion in urban territory, the South less than one-half. The Middle West and West were between sixty and seventy per cent urban. The most rural state was North Dakota—73.4 per cent.[3] Most of the southern states, especially Mississippi and Alabama were among the most rural.

[3] Howard G. Brunsman, "Urban Places and Population," *The Municipal Year Book 1955*, pp. 21–24.
The 1950 census defines urban territory as including (1) places of 2,500 inhabitants or more incorporated as cities, boroughs, and villages; (2) unincorporated places of 2,500 inhabitants or more outside an urban fringe; (3) towns of 2,500 inhabitants or more, except in New England, New York, or Wisconsin where "towns" are considered minor subdivisions of counties; and (4) the densely settled urban fringe, incorporated or unincorporated, around cities of 50,000 or more. The urban fringe must have a population density of 2,000 to the square mile, or 500 housing units per square mile, with at least 100 dwelling units in the area. All other territory is classified as rural.
The 1940 census defined urban areas as incorporated places of 2,500 or more plus 80 unincorporated places (towns in New England, townships in New Jersey and Pennsylvania) under special rulings. The 502 unincorporated places over 2,500 were not included. These had almost 3 million inhabitants in 1940.
Urbanized fringes for 157 cities defined as urban in 1950 by the Bureau of the Census with the aid of local authorities have about 9 million inhabitants. These areas were not listed as urban in 1940.

In 1950, there were 1,262 places of ten thousand or more population, and these had 74 million or 49.3 per cent of the total population. In 1940, the census listed 1,077 such places of which 997 of them were still in the same category in 1950. The places that were listed in both the censuses as urban places over 10,000 people had roughly the same percentage of total population in both 1940 and 1950—approximately 47 per cent of the total. In other words, these places gained in about the same ratio as the nation as a whole—about 14 per cent.

The most notable increases in population in urban places of 10,000 or more in population were in the South and West. In the South, 123 such places increased 25 per cent or more during the last decade. Annexation was responsible for some of this increase, especially in Texas where Dallas, Fort Worth, Houston, and San Antonio increased their areas ninety per cent or more. Eighty-one cities in the Pacific and mountain states, increased twenty-five per cent or more in population. In the Middle West, only 47 of 326 cities of 10,000 increased in population. In the Northeast, 77 out of 309, or one-fourth of the total, actually decreased in population. In Pennsylvania, for example, 47 out of 92 such cities lost population.

Of the cities over 100,000, San Diego, California, topped the list with an increase of 64 per cent in population during the last decade, with an increase of only 4 square miles of area. San Antonio was second with a 61 per cent increase in population but had a 96 per cent increase in area. Los Angeles, with less than one square mile of increase in area, increased 31 per cent in population.[4]

The change in population dominance is illustrated by listing the first fifteen cities in 1890 and in 1950. In 1890, they were in order of their population: New York, Chicago, Philadelphia, St. Louis, Boston, Baltimore, Pittsburgh, San Francisco, Cincinnati, Cleveland, Buffalo, New Orleans, Washington, Detroit, and Milwaukee. In 1950: New York, Chicago, Philadelphia, Los Angeles, Detroit, Baltimore, Cleveland, St. Louis, Washington, Boston, San Francisco,

---

[4] Albert G. Ballert, "The Rise and Decline of American Urban Centers during the 1940's," *Land Economics* (August, 1952), pp. 203–211.

Pittsburgh, Milwaukee, Houston, and Buffalo. In sixty years, New York went from two and a half to almost eight million; Chicago from one to three and a half million; Philadelphia from one to two million; Detroit from 200,000 to 1,850,000; Los Angeles from a relatively small town to fourth largest in the nation with almost two million people.

Nearly half the gain in population in continental United States between 1940 and 1950 was registered in the suburbs of the 168 standard metropolitan areas as delineated by the 1950 census. Out of the national gain of 19 million, the metropolitan areas gained 15 million; but the central cities gained only about 6 million, whereas the suburban regions increased about 9 million. In 1940, the increase of the suburban areas over 1930 was 17 per cent as compared with 35 per cent in 1950 over 1940.

Rural Population

Rural population in the United States has actually increased each decade since 1790; in 1950, under the new urban-rural definitions, 54 million people still lived in rural territory. But the rate of growth in comparison to the nation as a whole and urban areas in particular has steadily fallen. All during the 19th century, urban population increased at a greater rate than rural in each decade save one. Since 1900, however, the rate of increase of rural population was under ten per cent in each decade, while the urban increase went as high as forty per cent. Between 1940 and 1950, the rate of rural growth (7.9 per cent) was only about half of the national growth (14.5 per cent). Urban populaion, figured under the 1940 definition, increased 19.5 per cent. There were losses of rural population in 17 states.

Moreover, the census has divided the rural population into two classes; rural farm and rural nonfarm. Rural farm population is now only 15 per cent of the total population of the nation, while the rural nonfarm make up twenty per cent of the population. In other words, one out of every seven in the nation lives on the farm, the other "rural" people are those who live in rural places but are employed in villages, gasoline stations, motels, lumbering, mining, food processing, and other such pursuits.[5]

This change from a rural to urban society is due not only to the great expansion of other segments of our national life—manufacturing, government, education, commerce—but to increased agricultural productivity, tripled since 1870. In that year, more than half the workers were on farms; in 1950 only 13 per cent were needed. Today farming is so highly mechanized that the once common sight of horses hitched to a plow or harrow is almost a rarity. Farming is tending to be organized as a business with trained specialists for agricultural operation. Farm units are larger; rural mass production methods are used.

As a result, the old rural way of life is changing. Farm and city people are becoming more like each other. They see and hear the same TV and radio programs, read the same newspapers and magazines, their children go to the same consolidated schools, they have the same sensitivity as do industrial workers to economic ups and downs. Urbanism and industrialism have almost engulfed a once rural America.

Many people do not look forward to the disappearance of the rural community, the independent farmer, and the security of farm life. They believe the American farm was the backbone of our national culture since early beginnings and view the tendency toward urbanization as a factor that may undermine the stability of our national life. As far back as Thomas Jefferson there were statesmen and publicists who feared the coming of the Big City. However, time marched on. Man cannot turn back destiny. Perhaps the city, after all, can be "the hope of democracy" and country life will be more attractive with its modern comforts.

This transformation of rural life is highly significant in its relation to government. The national government has been more influential in rural life than either the states or the local units. National governmental agencies are concerned with soil conservation, parity

[5] Lane W. Lancaster, *Government in Rural America* (1952), pp. 2–6.

prices, rural electrification, rural road subsidies, agricultural research and education. States and local units have taken secondary roles.

Migration

Migration within the United States has increased in tempo and intensity with each passing decade. While there was a continuous movement westward to take possession of new lands during the 19th century, this was a rural area to rural area movement. This has now been overshadowed in the past several decades by the tremendous migration flow from country to city, and from city to suburbs. The east-west movement is still continuing—during the 1940–50 decade eighty to eighty-five per cent of the increase in Pacific Coast states came from migration, nearly all of which was internal. But comparatively few people went on farms. California now ranks with Pennsylvania and New Jersey in its proportion of urban population. Since 1900, the industrial cities of the Northeast and Middle West have drawn more and more workers from the South. On the other hand, the central cities are attracting a smaller and smaller proportion of the metropolitan increase. Satellite areas are getting an increasing share. Since 1950, about 2,000,000 college students have been considered by the census as residing in the towns and cities where the colleges were situated rather than in the places of their homes.

For the first time in 1940, the United States census took into consideration the migratory habits of the people when it tabulated those who migrated across a county or a large city boundary between 1935 and 1940. It was found that 15.7 million or 12 per cent of the 1940 population were migrants. About half of these lived in rural areas, half in urban. Of those who lived in urban areas, one-half came from within the state, others from outside the state. Very few of the cities over 100,000 in 1940 showed a net gain through migration. Migrants were heavily concentrated between the ages from fifteen to thirty-four. The highest ratios of old people are in New England and the Middle West from whence large numbers of young people have migrated to other places. In general migrants are better educated than nonmigrants. People with a college education show an unusually high degree of migration. Rural areas constantly lose educated people to the urban areas. Migration rates are higher in occupations requiring the most training. White collar workers are more migratory than hand workers. People generally move from areas of low earning power to those of higher earning power. Areas are low earning for several reasons: low ratio of natural resources to the population; lack of capital, technical resources and organization; mechanization leaving a large share of the population without work.[6] And, of course, automobiles, hard roads, luxury trailers and trailer camps have increased migration possibilities. So have great national disasters such as the Dust Bowl, floods, and severe unemployment.

GEOGRAPHY AND THE GROWTH OF AMERICAN CITIES

The actual historical origins of American cities are well known; it is possible to say how they came to be established and why they grew to their present size. Behind each city there is a set of factors that made it what it is today. There are definite reasons for its original location as well as for its growth. The eminent sociologist, Charles Cooley, formulated the "break in transportation" theory of city location. He said: "Population and wealth tend to collect wherever there is a break in transportation." [7] A break occurs wherever there is an interruption or stoppage of movement of goods sufficient to necessitate a transfer or storage. If the transfer is physical only, the break is a mechanical one; if there is a change in ownership, it is commercial. In either case or both, persons, equipment, and facilities are required and a town or city is in the making. Commercial cities are almost always located originally on the basis of transportation advantages.

Manufacturing cities, on the other hand, are influenced by other

[6] Warren S. Thompson, *Population Problems* (1953), pp. 294–314.
[7] Charles Horton Cooley, *Sociological Theory and Social Research* (1930). The chapter relating to the theory of transportation appeared first in 1904.

factors as well: nearness to raw materials and markets, the needs of its hinterland, access to power facilities, the labor market, and the industrial background of the region. Generally, no city is wholly commercial or manufacturing. Once established, a city grows in relation to its over-all attractiveness to people. Are there opportunities there for successful business ventures and productive industry, for good salaries and wages, for professional development? Further but actually secondary, does the city have decent housing, good schools, adequate community facilities? In short, is the city a good place in which to work and live?

Of the 992 cities in the United States with over 10,000 population, Victor Jones (Wesleyan University) classifies 32 per cent as manufacturing, 20 per cent as industrial, 34 per cent as retail, and 13 per cent in other categories.[8]

Our Five Largest Cities

New York City owes its preeminence largely to location with respect to water facilities. It has splendid harbor facilities that can take care of great numbers of ocean-going ships. Even more important, it was the first of the Atlantic seaboard cities to make permanent economic connection with the growing West. The Mohawk Valley is the only natural gap through the Appalachian mountain range that extends north and south from New England to the Gulf of Mexico. Enterprising New Yorkers dug the Erie Canal, which was opened in 1825, to connect the Hudson River with the Great Lakes. Thus, goods from Europe destined for the West and goods from the West marked for Europe quite naturally came to New York for reshipment to their ultimate destination. Later, the New York Central Railroad followed the same path. Around this impor-

[8] Victor Jones, "Economic Classification of Cities and Metropolitan Areas," *The Municipal Year Book 1953*, pp. 49–57. Manufacturing cities are defined as those in which manufacturing comprises 50 per cent of aggregate employment, and the retail trade 20 per cent or less; industrial cities have more than 50 per cent of the employed in manufacturing but more than 30 per cent in retail trade; retail cities have a greater number of employees in retail trades than in any other category, and manufacturing employment is less than 20 per cent.

tant commercial location, great manufacturing concerns concentrated so as to be as close as possible to national and international markets, and ancillary institutions flocked there to the growing metropolis. Basically, that is why New York, largest city in the world today, rose in population from 50,000 in 1790 to 8,000,000 in 1950. Its metropolitan area—also the largest in the world—is estimated at close to 13,000,000 people.

Chicago was settled in the early 1800's because it was in a favorable location between two great systems of water transportation—the Great Lakes and the Mississippi River and its tributaries. The Chicago River for many years was the connecting link and the Illinois-Michigan Canal became the permanent jointure. Even though the site of the future metropolis of the Middle West was swampy and disease laden, it was a natural site for a city because it was there that a break in transportation had to be made. Later when railroads came, Chicago was sought because it was located at the southernmost tip of Lake Michigan and all railroads connecting the Northwest to the East had to come around this point. In 1870 it forged ahead of St. Louis, its arch-rival, because it gained control of the transportation in the entire upper Mississippi river valley, the future breadbasket of the nation. Today, Chicago is the second largest city in the United States with a 1950 population of 3,620,000 and of 5,500,000 in the five-county metropolitan area. It is the nation's greatest railroad center with 22 live haul railroads and 13 switching and terminal companies. Every day 1,770 trains arrive and depart, carrying 66,000 passengers from other places and 300,000 local commuters. It is also the largest meat packing center, the center of the mail order business, a leader in lumber and steel, and the major grain exchange in the country.[9]

Many of the world's large cities are located not on the seacoast but on bays, gulfs, and estuaries of rivers. Commercial seaports are usually as far inland as possible in order that exporters and importers may take advantage of cheap water transportation, and because natural indentations afford superior harbor facilities and

[9] See W. A. Robson, *Great Cities of the World* (London, 1954).

protection from ocean storms. Such was the case with *Philadelphia* situated at the confluence of the Delaware and Schuylkill Rivers. Its own fine harbor and the added facilities of the Delaware River from Trenton, New Jersey, to the sea, make the Delaware River valley second only to the New York area in volume of annual shipping tonnage. Philadelphia sought unsuccessfully a water transportation route to the West in the early 19th century. Canals and rivers led to the Allegheny mountains of central Pennsylvania but there was no way through. Here the famous inclined plane was built to take freight over the mountains to the other side where other canals would connect with the Monongahela River and so with the Ohio and Mississippi river system. This was found to be expensive transportation and never seriously challenged the Erie Canal. By 1852 the Pennsylvania Railroad had made the crossing and connected Philadelphia with Chicago, but New York had already achieved her position as the first city of the land which she has never relinquished. However, Philadelphia, too, grew to be a great manufacturing center for textiles, leather, ship building, paper, chemicals, and steel and metal products. It is today the third largest city in the United States with over 2,000,000 population and about 3,700,000 in the metropolitan area. The recent location of the gigantic Fairless United States Steel plant within the Philadelphia metropolitan region using as raw material iron ore from new sources in eastern Canada, Cuba, and Venezuela attest to the advantageous position of Philadelphia in relation to water-borne freight.

Los Angeles in 1850 was a country town of 3,500; in 1900, it was a mere 100,000. By 1950 it had zoomed to the fourth largest city in the United States with almost 2,000,000 people in the city and 4,-367,000 in its metropolitan area. It is our fastest growing city. The basic and underlying cause of its phenomenal growth is its dry and sunny climate which attracted tourists and permanent residents by hundreds of thousands. The climate was also responsible for the development of the great aviation industry there. The movie industry concentrated in the Los Angeles area because out-of-door sets could be utilized and little time was lost on account of inclement

ECONOMIC CLASSIFICATION OF CITIES

Government Center. Fifteen per cent or more of people who live in the city and who are in the labor force are employed by a governmental unit.

Mining Town. Fifteen per cent or more of the resident labor force reported mining as an occupation.

Manufacturing City. Employment in manufacturing is at least 50 per cent of aggregate employment in manufacturing, trade, and service; employment in retail trade is less than 30 per cent of aggregate employment.

Industrial City. Employment in manufacturing totals more than 50 per cent as in manufacturing city but is balanced by retail trade employment of at least 30 per cent.

Diversified City. Employment in manufacturing is dominant but less than 50 per cent.

Diversified City. Employment in retail trade is dominant, but manufacturing is at least 20 per cent of aggregate employment.

Retail Trade Center. Employment in retail trade is greater than employment in manufacturing, service, or wholesale trade, and employment in manufacturing is less than 20 per cent.

Education Center. Enrollment in schools of collegiate rank within the city totals 20 per cent or more of city's population.

Transportation Center. Twenty-five per cent or more of people who live in the city and who are in the labor force reported transportation as an occupation.

Wholesale Trade Center. Employment in wholesale trade in the city totals at least 25 per cent of aggregate employment in manufacturing, trade, and service.

Resort or Retirement Town. Employment in manufacturing is less than 15 per cent and 10 per cent or more of the resident labor force is employed in restaurants and other eating places, hotels, or places of amusement and recreation.

Of the 18 cities of the United States over 500,000 population: Chicago, Detroit, Philadelphia, Cincinnati, Cleveland, Milwaukee, and St. Louis are manufacturing cities; New York, Los Angeles, Baltimore, Minneapolis, and Pittsburgh are diversified with manufacturing dominant; Boston, Houston, and New Orleans are diversified with retail trade dominant; Buffalo is an industrial city; San Francisco is a wholesale center; and Washington is a government center.

Of 922 cities over 10,000 population, 32 per cent are manufacturing, 20 per cent are industrial, 34 per cent are retail, and 14 per cent are other.

Of 992 cities over 10,000 population, 184 are central cities, 287 are suburban cities, and 521 are independent cities, the latter not located in a standard metropolitan area.

Of 1,219 cities over 10,000 population classified by metropolitan status, 56 per cent are employing cities to which people come to work, 18 per cent are dormitory from which people go to work in some other place, and 18 per cent are balanced.

From International City Managers' Association, *The Municipal Year Book 1955,* pp. 53–67.

weather. The demands of the climate developed a distinctive apparel industry ultimately supplying the needs of hot, dry regions in many parts of the world. Great oil producing wells give the region the largest oil refining industry in the West.

Detroit is the fifth largest city in the United States with a 1950 population of 1,849,000 and a metropolitan area numbering more than 3 million. In 1900 it had less than 300,000 people. In its beginnings it was primarily a lake port and because all Great Lakes traffic had to go through the Detroit river, it early became an important shipping and shipbuilding center. With the coming of the railroads, the Great Lakes lost some of their commercial importance and Detroit was no longer on the main route between New York and Chicago. The automobile industry gave Detroit its present manufacturing importance. In the early days the city was close to the hardwood forest and developed the woodworking industry, making carriages, wagons, and furniture. A number of master minds such as Ford, Haynes, and Olds who devoted their lives to transportation vehicles evolved the early horseless carriage, and from there the industry developed into its present gigantic proportions. Detroit's geographical advantages for this industry was considerably less than those of Toledo and Cleveland, but its early start in automobile manufacturing was decisive. Detroit is the world's number one automobile town; its present and future is tied up with the automotive industry.

Internal Structure

The American city has been called a "mosaic of cultural and social worlds." In its confines are the rich and the poor, the worker and the business man, "the butcher, the baker and the candlestick maker." There are all manner of races and creeds, all kinds of ways of making a living. At first glance, the city is a vast confusion, but examination will reveal order as well as disorder. The study of the spatial distribution of persons and institutions is called human ecology—a term borrowed from biology. The city is a patch work of ecological units; that is to say, people and institutions in cities are arranged in a pattern which, when studied closely, has some recognizable rhyme and reason.

In 1923, Professor Burgess (University of Chicago) set forth the theory of concentric zones to explain the urban pattern of living. Each, beginning with the central core and continuing outward toward the hinterland, has certain characteristics.[9]

The first and inner zone is the *central business district*. It includes skyscrapers, office buildings, department stores, specialized shops, hotels, restaurants, theaters, movies, and night clubs. It is an area of business organization, retail trade, light manufacturing, and commercialized recreation. It has high real estate values and a heavy concentration of transient population. Comparatively few people actually are residents of this area. Examples are the Chicago "Loop" and the Pittsburgh "Golden Triangle."

Around this inner core and in the path of business expansion is the *zone of transition*. It is heavily populated with persons of the lower income classes and is filled with slums, cheap rooming houses, and blighted areas. Parts of this zone were once quality residential areas but are now deteriorating. In it are the ghettos, the Little Italys, Chinatown, and the Negro belt and other racial enclaves. Here, too, the footloose, the unconventional, and the unfortunate congregate.

The third zone according to Burgess is that of *workingmen's homes*—not fancy but by no means slums. Industries and factories of all kinds are found here. The fourth zone is that of the *middle class dweller*, and the fifth is the *commuters zone*. This last is likely to be found outside the political boundries of the city in the area known as the urban fringe.

While the Burgess scheme is considered by some to be an oversimplification, and based specifically on the city of Chicago, the theory is validated in a general way by other studies and by observation. A main criticism is that the lower economic groups are not exclusively concentrated in the zone outside the central city.

[9] E. W. Burgess, "The Growth of the City," in Park, Burgess, and McKenzie, *The City*, p. 51.

They are found in all sections of the city—especially adjacent to industries and railroads. Another criticism points up the fact that population often pushes axially along main thoroughfares to constitute "prongs" in a starlike formation. On the other hand, Burgess showed conclusively as far as Chicago was concerned, that delinquency rates, percentage of foreign born, and poverty tend to decrease, and home ownership to increase, in passing from the central business area outward toward the hinterlands. This finding has been substantiated in other cities, too.

Significant ecological processes are constantly at work within and outside of American cities.[10] *Concentration* of population in modern times has been made possible by the factory, mass transportation, and the elevator. In many urban areas there is extreme population density. *Centralization,* the drawing together of institutions and activities for specific reasons, is manifested in the central business district, the focal point and control center of all commercial and business activities of the community. *Decentralization* is exemplified by the movement of people and institutions away from the central zones of the city. While there has been a decided decentralization of people, business, and industry since World War I, it has been mainly to the peripheral zones rather than to the outlying hinterlands. The National Resources Committee said in 1933: "There is no evidence of a marked dispersion of industry from the cities to the country."[11] However, since then many industries have moved into the suburbs and the trend is continuing. *Segregation* refers to the clustering in space of like persons and institutions whether racial, economic, or cultural. Segregation may be voluntary or involuntary. *Invasion* means the movement of one type of population or one type institution into an area previously inhabited by a different class. Business moves into residential districts, population moves toward the suburbs, racial groups move into areas inhabited by members of other races—these are examples of continual movement and change in

[10] Neel P. Gist and L. A. Halbert, *Urban Society* (1946), pp. 146–157.
[11] National Resources Committee, *Our Cities: Their Role in the National Economy* (1937), p. 38.

American cities. *Succession* occurs when the invasion is completely successful and an entirely new life prevails in an area. In some cases only the architectual survivals are reminders of a previous and different cultural life.

Great stretches of city blocks in the modern American city show where disorganization reigns supreme. There are areas of homeless men in which all family and community life has disappeared, sections where gangsters and criminal elements have defeated law and order, slums where there is no decent habitation, places where live the poor, the unfortunate, the failures, the sick, and the afflicted, the unwanted, and the people who never had a chance. With all its modern trappings and its great achievements, the American city has not yet solved all the problems of its people. There is still much to do in the future.

THE METROPOLITAN PROBLEM

The most important population shift within the United States during the 20th century has been the flow from central cities into suburban areas. In 1950, eighty-four million people lived in the 168 "standard metropolitan areas," and of these thirty-five million lived outside city borders. Between 1940 and 1950, population growth in the suburbs increased 36 per cent, in the central cities 14 per cent, and outside metropolitan areas only 6 per cent. Half the population gain in continental United States during this decade was in the suburbs.[12]

The reasons for this dramatic change are not hard to find. With the automobile and rapid transit facilities, people can live outside densely congested areas and still work in the central city. The urge to bring up a family in a home with a house and yard rather than in an apartment is much stronger in America than in Europe, and much more possible of fulfillment. There has been a frantic desire to get away from blighted areas, from excessive street traffic, from

[12] *The Municipal Year Book 1955*, pp. 27–30. For the 1950 population of individual standard metropolitan and urbanized areas, see Table II, pp. 31–36.

the noise and dirt of a big city into quiet, secluded and somewhat restricted neighborhoods that even the trials and tribulations of daily
commuting could not dull. Lower taxes also beckoned, and the feeling for community independence was strong. It is now "the thing" to
live in the suburbs, just as it was to live in the middle of the city
fifty years ago.

In Flint, Michigan, a survey showed that of the people who
moved from the city to the fringe areas 30 per cent wanted to own
a home, 27 per cent to get more elbow room and away from apartment life. In Milwaukee County, Wisconsin, 60 per cent of suburbanites questioned moved to more rural areas because they were
cleaner, less congested, and had lower taxes.[13] But it must not be
forgotten also that while the United States has been predominantly
urban in population since 1920, the boundaries of the cities and
larger towns did not expand with the growing population of the
community, so people just had to live outside city lines. There was
no room within.

What Is a Metropolitan Area?

This shift of population gave rise to a new term: the metropolitan
area. It is not a governmental unit or a legal entity; it is really a
sociological designation for an entire urbanized area including and
surrounding the central city core. As defined by the United States
Bureau of Census, it has precise meaning. A standard metropolitan
area contains one or more cities of 50,000 population or over. When
two cities of that size are within twenty miles of each other, they
are included in the same metropolitan area. Each metropolitan area
includes the entire county or counties containing the central city or
cities. Contiguous counties are included when they contain a certain
number or ratio of nonagricultural workers, and where at least
half the population resides in contiguous minor civil subdivisions with a population density of 150 per square mile, or where

[13] Betty Tableman, *Government Organization in Metropolitan Areas,* Institute
of Public Administration, University of Michigan (1951), pp. 6–7.

there is evidence of social and economic integration with the central city.[14]

The 168 standard metropolitan areas in continental United States, containing 84 million people in 1950, constituted 56 per cent of the total population. One-third of these metropolitan areas were in five states: Texas, Pennsylvania, Ohio, Massachusetts, and California; more than half in the East and Middle West.

Government Chaos in Metropolitan Areas

The movement outward from the cities has had dire consequences for central and fringe areas alike. Because land is cheaper and taxes lower across the borders, industries as well as residences gravitate

[14] United States Bureau of the Census, *1950 Census of Population, Preliminary Counts*, "Population of Standard Metropolitan Areas: April 1, 1950," Washington (1950). The contiguous counties are included if they meet the following criteria: (1) have 10,000 nonagricultural workers or 10 per cent of the nonagricultural in the standard metropolitan area, or have at least half of its population residing in contiguous minor civil divisions with a population density of 150 or more per square mile; (2) have nonagricultural workers constitute at least two-thirds of the total employed labor force of the county; (3) show evidence of social and economic integration with the central city such as, for example, having 15 per cent or more of the workers employed in the county containing the central city, having 25 per cent or more of the persons working in the county living in the county with the central city, having an average of four or more telephone calls per subscriber per month in the county containing the central city.

In New England, the standard metropolitan area is defined in terms of cities and towns, not counties. A population density of 150 persons per square mile, or 100 where evidences of strong integration are found, is the standard in those places.

In the censuses of 1920, 1930, and 1940 the metropolitan district, defined in 1940 as a central city or cities of at least 50,000 population plus surrounding local units with a population density of 150 per square mile, was the unit reported. The 1950 census makes possible broader statistical comparisons because more data are reported on a countywide basis.

The 1950 census also delineates the "urbanized area." It has a central city of 50,000 or more plus a "nearby and closely settled" fringe including incorporated places of 2,500 or more, or places of less that number providing they have 100 dwelling units or more with a density of 500 units per square mile, or territory devoted to industrial or other functions related to the central city, or territory within one and a half miles of the central urban area. There were 157 urbanized areas in 1950. See United States Bureau of Census, *ibid.*, "Population of Urbanized Areas: April 1, 1950," Washington (1951).

there. Commercial establishments follow. Stores spring up to meet the needs of the suburban population. Because they cannot provide easy access and free parking, the central cities lose a lot of trade.

Blighted areas bordering around the central business concentrations degenerate into slums and become problem areas for the city government. Buildings are fire hazards, health menaces, overcrowded. In such surroundings, crime rates are high. City government costs far more in such sections than revenue produced.

Every morning and evening the narrow thoroughfares are choked with traffic, the transit facilities crowded beyond capacity. The life of a commuter who rides from two to four hours each work day is not a happy one. The psychological impact, while yet unmeasured, is one with grave social overtones. The people who work in the city during the day, except when they pay a city wage or income tax, contribute little to the upkeep of city services.

Outside the city, the governmental services that urban life needs are in many places not available. In the unincorporated areas, rural township or county governments have neither tax resources, personnel, or organization to provide them. The small incorporated villages, boroughs, and cities cannot do the job. The householder's dream of low taxes and political independence often vanishes in the fervent quest for water, sewage facilities, police and fire protection, and adequate schools. In newly developed areas, new and costly buildings and installations are required. In some rich and restricted areas, taxpayers can afford to pay for the very best and often get better services than the central city could offer. But in the medium class districts and especially in the poor and ramshackle areas, the inhabitants are worse off than they would have been in the city. Unpaved streets, outdoor plumbing, health nuisances, hodge-podge and jerry built housing, overcrowded school rooms belie the promise of modern life.

In these 168 standard metropolitan areas, according to the United States Census, there were in 1952 16,210 local units: 256 counties, 2,328 townships, 3,164 municipalities, 2,598 special districts, and

7,864 school districts.[15] Ordinarily, there is little or no relationship between these units or with the central city. While telephone companies, department stores, milk distributing concerns, autobus companies, electric utilities, newspapers, and most all of the major economic and social organizations recognize the metropolitan area as *one* entity and organize their services on this basis, government is hopelessly splintered and fragmented. There is no feeling of political unity. Citizens living outside the city have no responsibility for electing city officials although what they do vitally affects their business inside the city. Suburbanites fight against wage and salary taxes levied by cities on income earned in the cities; they oppose expansion of the city by annexation. As a result much of the better brains and moral resources of the community are denied the city. This has been evidenced by the ease with which underworld elements have been able to entrench themselves within many of the larger municipalities.

The problems of metropolitan areas in the United States are further complicated by the fact that, according to the 1950 census, 336 cities straddle county lines. Multi-county cities occur most often in Illinois with 34, Georgia and Ohio with 24 each, Texas with 21, Wisconsin with 16, and Minnesota and Missouri with 14 each. Interestingly enough this condition is found most prevalent in rural, not urban states. Thus, it is not always possible to look to the county as the unit of government for metropolitan purposes.[16]

[15] In 1942, the 140 metropolitan districts contained 15,881 units of government. These included: 272 counties, 895 townships, 172 central cities, 1,623 suburban cities, 11,822 school districts, and 1,097 special districts. Fifty-three districts had more than a hundred local units; five, more than five hundred. Twenty-eight metropolitan districts overlaid two or more states. United States Bureau of the Census, *Governmental Units in the United States, 1942,* Washington, D. C. (1944).

Thirteen cities in metropolitan areas in 1948 were hosts to 29 municipalities completely or substantially surrounded or closed off by them. Among them were Boston, Cincinnati, Pittsburgh, Los Angeles, and Indianapolis. Richard R. Spencer, "Cities within Cities," *National Municipal Review* (May, 1948), pp. 256–258.

The Chicago urban region had in 1930, 1,642 governments: 15 counties, 204 cities and villages, 165 townships, 978 school districts, 280 special districts. Charles E. Merriam, Spencer D. Parratt, and Albert Lepawski, *The Government of the Metropolitan Region of Chicago,* University of Chicago (1933).

[16] *American Municipal Association,* Release of January 31, 1955.

In the fringe areas, there is no chance for adjustment between governmental needs and fiscal resources. A suburb made up largely of industrial workers without commercial and industrial property cannot maintain local services, especially in times of unemployment. On the other hand, a large industrial concern situated and paying taxes in a small municipality is not meeting its civic responsibilities because most of its workers live outside the borders. Its tax rate is ridiculously low in comparison to its place in the economic picture of the community at large. The Boston City Planning Board came to the conclusion that about 8 per cent of the gross area of the city pays the deficit incurred by the other 92 per cent. The business area downtown and about 10 per cent of the wealthier residential areas pay for the loss in industrial and the other residential districts.[17] Without taxes from industrial and commercial properties, the great majority of residential units outside the central city are unable to give their inhabitants ordinary urban services.

This condition of governmental chaos in metropolitan areas inevitably leads to increased activity of the state government in fields that rightfully belong to local government. But because there is no unified program within the area and inadequate financial resources, the inhabitants call upon the state for protection by the state police, state health services, and state-financed roads and streets. If the metropolitan area were a governmental unity, it would have the necessary resources to finance its own services. Thus, centralization of governmental power in the state continues to increase in scope and intensity. A depression like that of the thirties merely accelerates what is going on all the time because of the inadequacy of the local units of the fringe areas.

Solving the Metropolitan Problem

Only in recent years has it been recognized that an imaginative and forthright approach is needed to effect solutions worthy of the gigantic and complex metropolitan problem in America today. For a long time, annexation took care of the normal growth outside a

[17] Victor Jones, *Metropolitan Government*, Chicago (1942), p. 73.

city or town, but in recent decades active and passive resistance of the fringe dwellers slowed down this process. They left the city. They don't want to go back. They view with alarm the high tax rates, the bonded indebtedness, the political machinations, and the inadequacies of administration in the city. Sometimes these shortcomings are alleged rather than real in comparison to the condition on the fringe, but nevertheless annexation has ceased to be the complete answer to the metropolitan problem, whether or not it might be theoretically the best. Other methods are being put forward, some of them are being tried.

Annexation, however, is not dead. In fact, it is on the increase. During a four-year period in the late thirties, annexations were completed each year by an average of only forty-eight cities, but in 1952 four hundred and two cities made annexations.[18] Professor Bollens (University of California, Los Angeles) believes widespread recognition that the problems of the fringe ultimately become the problems of the adjoining city have caused many municipalities to give serious consideration to their solution by annexation. From recent experience, it has been found that four elements are required for successful use of annexation. First, annexation should be general, not selective. Wealthy sections already equipped with water and sewer facilities should not be the only areas sought by the central city; the poorly developed fringe must be improved for the general welfare of the whole community. Second, annexation should be undertaken before the area becomes extensively developed. Third, there should be sound financing and well-balanced over-all development; and fourth, the central city should accept leadership in the city-fringe community so that its own growth will not be unnaturally restricted.

Annexation is by no means always profitable to, or desired by, the central city. It is likely to pay out more in services and installations than it receives in taxes and other revenues, especially in the first few years. For example, the Municipal League of Seattle estimated that to annex an area with 40,000 inhabitants would bring in

[18] John C. Bollens, "Trends and Forecasts in Fringe Areas," *Public Management* (December, 1953), pp. 271–275.

$950,000 in revenue but would cost the city $1,250,000 at the rate of $30 per capita for seven basic city services—police, fire, streets, sanitation, parks, health, and library. The average home owner when he is brought into the city of Seattle will pay $30 to $40 less in taxes, $13.60 less for garbage collection, less for fire insurance premiums, fifty per cent less for water, but may have to pay special assessments for streets, sidewalks and sewers. Seattle has undergone extensive annexations since 1950. By 1954 it had added almost 100,000 to its population.

Toledo found that the imposition of a one per cent income tax on residents, and on nonresidents who worked in the city, made annexation more popular to the fringe because it kept real estate taxes down. If nonresidents living on the fringe have to pay city taxes, they might as well have other city advantages such as street lighting and cleaning, zoning, reduction in water rates, fire protection, lower insurance rates, reduced university fees, supervised recreation and other city services.

Pasadena, California, collects a "joining fee" for annexation at the rate of $100 for each 50 by 150 foot lot plus $250 an acre for water service and $1.25 per foot for water mains.

One of the largest annexations of the 20th century was completed in San Antonio, Texas, in 1952 when 80 square miles and 42,000 people were added to the city. From 1850 when the city was incorporated until 1940, the area remained at thirty-six square miles while the population had grown from 3,500 to 250,000. Piecemeal annexation from 1940 to 1952 increased the area to 74 square miles. A detailed study revealed that, because of the absence of zoning, substantial portions of the fringe area were substandard and even slum. Many parts of the outlying areas were without water and sewerage, and city services were strained to provide even partial service because there was no over-all program. In 90 Texas home-rule cities, annexation can be accomplished by an ordinance of the city providing the area is not incorporated.

Assurances were given by the city to outlying areas that there would be protection of residential property against encroachment, that every effort would be made to minimize congestion through zoning and off-street parking, that industrial areas would be extended, and that agricultural sections would be protected from premature subdivision. The annexation program, the city planning and zoning commission declared, would prevent incorporation of areas on the outside, would stop the extension of slum areas, would safeguard residential areas and home buyers with zoning and building regulations, would allow the provision of orderly traffic control, would improve all city services, and would provide an adequate flood control and housing program.[19]

In Pennsylvania there were 190 annexations of portions of contiguous units of local government by municipalities within the 1940–48 period. Without exception, these annexations were by petition of residents or freeholders of the fringe areas and, almost without exception, the annexations were for purposes of obtaining specific public services otherwise unavailable. Most of the annexations were of portions of rural, second class townships to boroughs or cities, almost all the properties being either residential, undeveloped, or tax exempt—very few industrial or commercial.[20]

Legal requirements in many states makes annexation a difficult procedure. As a rule, a majority vote is required from the area to be annexed and from the annexing city. Sometimes only an ordinance by the council of the annexing city and a petition of the majority of property holders in the annexed territory is required.

In Pennsylvania, portions of townships of the first class may not be annexed to contiguous local units unless the voters of the entire township vote favorably for such action. This makes annexation virtually impossible in these units and has resulted in having a number of second class townships eligible for first class status to elect change in class. In 1953, the annexation law for Pennsylvania second class townships was amended to provide for a judicial review if requested by petition. In Virginia considerable success has been reported by the use of a judicial commission of three to review

[19] John C. Bollens, "Metropolitan and Fringe Area Developments in 1952," *The Municipal Year 1953*, pp. 33–48.
[20] Lee C. Moore, *Annexation in Pennsylvania Municipalities*, unpublished thesis. Department of Political Science, Pennsylvania State University (1954).

annexation proceedings to make decision. This makes it impossible for a small, hostile minority to block the city expansion.

Rural townships which lose by annexation choice areas in which property values are high may suffer financially by annexation and are often left with areas without enough taxable resources to support required services for the rest of the population.

Where popular approval for annexation must be obtained, many cities have undertaken programs of information and education. The city of Milwaukee has a regular governmental department on annexation. States such as Texas and Virginia have had greatest success in annexation because of the more favorable legal provisions and thus their metropolitan areas have far below the average numbers of incorporated suburbs.

Annexation is feasible only in relation to unincorporated areas; where outlying areas are incorporated into villages, boroughs, or cities annexation or consolidation to the central city has been almost impossible. The suburban government provides some of the necessary services and local loyalties prevent any move to merge identity in the big city.[21] City-county consolidation and city-county separation have been discussed in Chapter I. The first is a partial solution to the metropolitan problem but the second evades it.

In Connecticut, town and city *consolidation* serves the purpose of county-city consolidation because the town in New England is more important than the county in both urban and rural areas. According to Max R. White (University of Connecticut), such consolidation eliminates duplication of corporate bodies and officials. One government provides the services necessary for both rural and urban areas. Separate taxing districts are established by which people of the entire district pay for over-all services, while only people in urban areas pay for urban services. Thus, urban and farming groups can come under one government. Between 1874 and 1942, such consolidation has occurred in 21 towns.[22]

[21] Tableman, *Government Organization in Metropolitan Areas,* Institute of Public Administration, University of Michigan (1951), pp. 11–13.
[22] Max R. White, "Town and City Consolidation in Connecticut," *American Political Science Review* (June, 1942), pp. 492–502.

Many municipalities provide services to their fringe areas. The most common are water supply and sewage disposal, but fire protection is also made available in many cases. The police radio facilities of central cities are often at the disposal of outlying local governments.[23]

Contracts may be made with the governments in the fringe but direct service may also be given to consumers. Usually costs of water and sewage disposal to outlying residents are higher than to those living within city boundaries. In the case of fire protection, charges are made upon the basis either of flat fee per call, or equipment hours used, or an annual fee for the area. In many places, especially where there are voluntary fire departments, service is given free. The merchants of the town who are active in these organizations feel that it is good public relations to render such service to those who are actually members of the over-all consumer community and who spend money in town.

The Toledo Master Plan recommends that water and sewer service be extended to areas expected to develop a population density of five to the acre, that the water system should be under city control, but a new special district should manage the sewers. But a growing number of cities are refusing requests for services outside their borders for several substantial reasons. The first is that unless there is a good system of cost accounting the city is liable to lose money and thus supply services at the expense of their own taxpayers. Second, if fringe dwellers are able to get the most important urban services, especially at a good rate, from the city, they do not want to become annexed. Thus, the natural growth of the political community is retarded.

Some cities do have governmental powers over adjoining territory. State laws have given them the right to exercise limited control in such matters as zoning, subdivision control, building regulations, and sanitation. The control usually extends from one to three miles

---

[23] Tableman, *op. cit.,* pp. 138–154. Appendix A contains detailed information on types of services rendered by cities outside their borders in metropolitan districts within the United States.

outside city lines and does not include the whole metropolitan area. This is, in effect, limited annexation. This, too, is not a permanent solution, merely a temporary expedient.

Alabama grants municipalities broad powers to provide governmental services to fringe areas. First, police and sanitary ordinances of the city may be enforced within three miles of corporate limits of cities of six thousand population and over, and within a mile and a half in those with less. This area is commonly designated "the police jurisdiction" and the police powers have been broadly construed by the courts. Second, the city is given the right to levy business licenses in this area at a rate not to exceed one-half the rate within the city. Third, cities may exercise control over subdivision plats within an area of five miles from corporate limits. Says Robert T. Daland (University of Alabama) of the Alabama experience: "Alabama's method of granting extensive police power, licensing power, planning supervision, and authority to provide municipal type service outside the city limits has by no means solved the fringe area problems of all Alabama cities. . . . To say this, however, is not to deny the usefulness of extraterritorial powers for cities. . . . First, they may be used by cities to solve fringe problems during a transitional period prior to annexation, preventing satellite incorporations, planning interests of the developing city. Secondly, they may be used by many of the small cities with comparatively small fringe area problems as a method of integrating the urban and suburban areas. Thirdly, they do not supplement, and may, in fact, conflict with the regulation of unincorporated areas of metropolitan communities in which other approaches to metropolitan integration are being tried." [24]

Special districts or municipal authorities have been created to provide specific governmental services in metropolitan areas. Such agencies are useful devices in that they can serve more than one local unit and can include, in fact, the entire metropolitan area. The

[24] Robert T. Daland, *Municipal Fringe Area Problem in Alabama,* Bureau of Public Administration, University of Alabama and the Alabama League of Municipalities (1953), p. 66.

popularity of the special district is shown by the growth in numbers in the decade since World War II.[25] The earliest use of the special district in the United States was in Philadelphia in 1790 when a board of prison inspectors, elected by the city and its suburbs, was established. Nine others dealing with such matters as poor relief, port developments, public health, police, and education had come into existence by 1850 but the city-county consolidation of 1854 liquidated them.[26] A similar development in the New York City area ended in consolidation in 1870. The oldest existing metropolitan district operation still functioning is in Boston where sewerage, park, and water districts, established between 1889 to 1895, were combined in the Metropolitan District Commission in 1919 which covers 43 cities and towns having an area of 472 square miles. Strictly speaking, this is not a local governmental unit because it is state-controlled, its five directors are appointed by the governor, and it receives appropriations from the state.

One of the largest metropolitan special districts is the Port of New York Authority, which was established in 1921 by interstate compact between New York and New Jersey. Within a twenty mile radius around the port of New York, it constructs and operates projects relating to port development, motor truck terminals, bridges, airports, railroad belt lines, and other area services. It has almost four thousand employees. It is financed from bond issues which are paid back from the revenues derived from the operation of the projects. Its board of twelve is appointed by the governors of both states, six by each.

The Cleveland Metropolitan Park District includes sixty cities and villages and seven townships having a total population of 1,600,000. It is financed largely by tax levies, and administers about 13,000 acres of land. Its directors are appointed by the court.

The Sanitary District of Chicago serves a population of about 4 million in 67 cities and villages, and parts of 16 townships, all in Cook county. It protects water supply from pollution, constructs

---

[25] See Chapter 1.
[26] Jones, *Metropolitan Government* (Chicago, 1942), pp. 91–99.

canals and sewers, and sewage treatment works. It also distributes electricity for its own use and for street lighting. It is financed by bond issues, tax levies, and revenues.

The Hartford County Metropolitan District provides water supply, sewage disposal, and regional planning for the city of Hartford and six adjacent towns in Connecticut. It has a board of directors of 23, one from each town, and fifteen at large of which eight are from Hartford and seven from the other towns. It is financed by bond issues, tax levies, service charges, and special assessments.

The Metropolitan Water District of Southern California (Los Angeles) serves a population of 3,500,000 in 13 cities, 2 water districts, and the San Diego County Water Authority.

The Los Angeles County Air Pollution Control District, established in 1947, covers four thousand square miles of territory, and was established after separate ordinances of Los Angeles city and county failed to correct the situation.

While water, sewerage, and parks are the most common services provided by these special districts, many others are provided. Most districts and authorities have only one function. These special districts or authorities are created by state law, by approval of the voters, by ordinance of the local governing bodies, or through action of the courts in various combinations depending upon state legislation and existing circumstances. They may be completely separate from other local units; they may be federations of existing local units; or they may be established for one local unit only.

The metropolitan district can give wide areas uniform and modern services because it can be made large enough for economical and efficient organization whereas small local units of the fringe area could not provide such services. From the political standpoint, it is easier to create a special district than to annex territory by the central city or to effect consolidation of existing local units. It makes possible also the financing of services from revenues of projects without raising tax rates. On the other hand, special districts add to the confusion of metropolitan government by creating yet another unit of government. It may lead to political irresponsibility because the directors are removed from popular control.[27]

Unincorporated areas outside municipal boundaries often choose to become municipalities so that they may furnish urban services. This, in fact, has been the common practice since the beginning of the century and has resulted in an excessive number of incorporated places in almost every metropolitan area in the United States. In Allegheny county, the area outside of Pittsburgh includes 122 cities, boroughs, and townships—all integral parts of Greater Pittsburgh. In the Cook county part of metropolitan Chicago, there were in 1938 a total of 358 separate governments including 89 cities and villages.

The presence of numerous incorporations in the fringe area does not help to solve the metropolitan problem because their residents and officials oppose consolidation and annexation to the central city for reasons of independence and loyalty, yet many of them are too small to render the urban services necessary for the area and quickly degenerate into low-grade municipalities. Another factor is political stratification. The central city may be under the control of a one party organization, so the residents of a community where the majority is with the other party are antagonistic to the idea of unity. Some cities, Cincinnati among them, actively oppose incorporation of fringe territories.

The county has provided urban governmental services to fringe dwellers in some places in spite of the fact that it was not established to render such municipal services as police and fire protection, water supply, sewerage and regulation of sanitation. This de-

---

[27] Tableman, *op. cit.* Appendix B contains brief but excellent descriptions of selected metropolitan special districts, pp. 155–167. Chapter 4 outlines the general pattern of organization and function.

See also Illinois Legislative Council, *Chicago Sanitary District,* Publication No. 114 (1953).

United States Bureau of the Census, *Special District Governments in the United States,* State and Local Government Special Studies, No. 33 (1954) states that the 12 largest special districts having 1,000 or more employees (total 42,878) received about 38 per cent of all special district revenue in 1952. The largest special district is the Chicago Transit Authority with 17,472 employees.

velopment has created a precarious situation in California. During
the decade between 1940 and 1950, California cities increased by 41
per cent, but the population of unincorporated places increased by
79 per cent. By 1950, the population of unincorporated areas in
Los Angeles county alone was 867,000, and in California as a whole
there were almost as many unincorporated communities of 10,000
or more as municipalities. Belvedere Gardens with 100,000 population is probably the largest unincorporated place in the United
States, if not the world.

The drift of industry to unincorporated places in California counties has been aided by the fact that building standards are less
vigorously enforced, that there are fewer subdivision regulations,
that sanitation standards are not as high as in the city, that cities sell
services to fringe areas that local government there cannot supply.
Furthermore, the county supplies important urban services which
the taxpayers of the whole county, including those of the central
city, must help to pay. Almost $1.50 out of $6.00 county tax goes for
streets, lighting, police protection, and library services for unincorporated places. This represents an enormous subsidy on the part
of counties to unincorporated areas and a double burden to the city
taxpayers. Naturally with such benefits industry as well as residents
do not want to be annexed to the central city.[28]

Counties in urban areas all over the United States are gradually
expanding their spheres of action. They are being empowered to
administer public health, zoning, planning, building regulation, and
other functions where it is desirable to have uniformity within the
entire community. But if the county is to be the government for the
whole metropolitan area, it must undergo drastic reorganization because its decentralized, headless structure is not conducive to modern efficiency. Almost everywhere the county is still "the dark continent of American politics."

In 1952, Atlanta, Georgia, and Fulton county entered into a unique
arrangement—part merger, part annexation—when the city tripled

[28] Richard Graves, "Fringe Areas Should Pay Their Own Way," *Public
Management* (February, 1952), pp. 30–33.

its geographical area and added almost a hundred thousand population. During the past thirty years, the city had increased 64 per cent in population while the suburban areas had increased 167 per cent. The county had been providing many urban services to the fringe areas which the city dwellers helped to pay. There was duplication between city and county. Under the new arrangement, the functions for the whole area—city and outside—were divided between the two governments. The city now handles police, fire, water, sewage, refuse, inspection, parks, library and auditorium, recreation, and airports. The county has been withdrawn from these functions, but was given all the health services, public welfare, the administration of justice, agriculture, and the offices of coroner, sheriff, and surveyor. Schools and public works are handled by a separate department of both city and county, but the city was given 39 additional schools to administer. Planning and zoning were set up as joint functions, while the housing authority and the metropolitan planning commission are jointly financed.[29]

Joint undertakings between contiguous local units of government including the central city and the county in such fields as purchasing, recreation, hospital construction and administration, public buildings, fire protection, sewage disposal, airport construction, regional planning, and even administration are common throughout the United States. In Cincinnati, the city, county and school district have joint purchasing of more than 150 commodities. In Pasadena, the county, city, and school district jointly administer recreation. The American Municipal Association has found thirty-four cases of joint city-county occupancy of public buildings. As early as 1870, the Brooklyn Bridge was financed jointly by New York and Brooklyn. Louisville has a joint city-county public health unit. Fire protection is a joint city-county function in Fulton county—Atlanta area in Georgia. There are many joint city-county airports. Usually there is joint financing according to use but a separate administrative agency for operation. The California Regional Planning Commis-

[29] Lynwood M. Holland, "Atlanta Pioneers in Merger," *National Municipal Review* (April, 1952), pp. 182–186.

sion, Los Angeles county, coordinates the work of 45 local planning agencies in the area.[30]

LOCAL GOVERNMENTS IN METROPOLITAN AREAS: 1952

Total metropolitan areas	168
1950 population	84,671,000
Number of local governments	16,210
Counties	256
Townships	2,328
Municipalities	3,164
Special Districts	2,598
School Districts	7,864

From International City Managers' Association: *The Municipal Year Book 1955*, p. 29.

Metropolitan federation is the most far-reaching suggestion to solve the governmental problem in metropolitan areas. Under such an arrangement a new local unit called the federated city would be established. It would be composed of the central city and the out-lying municipalities and local units of the whole area. The federated municipality would be given certain specific powers and functions, the local units would keep those functions which they could best administer. In most states, federation would require an enabling constitutional amendment because it is a totally new kind of local unit that does not come within the classification set forth in the constitution.

The idea of metropolitan federation is not new. The most important development in this field has been the London County Council and twenty-eight metropolitan boroughs. Proposals for a federated metropolis have been defeated in Pittsburgh, St. Louis, Miami, and Oakland during the past forty years, but the idea of federation of metropolitan government is steadily gaining ground. Professor Victor Jones (Wesleyan University), an authority on metropolitan problems, speaking about the ultimate solutions, says: "I doubt that any proposal has much chance of success unless it is based upon the

[30] Tableman, *Government Organization in Metropolitan Areas*, Institute of Public Administration, University of Michigan (1951), pp. 40–47. Also see Appendix A.

'federal principle' of allocating metropolitan functions to a metropolitan government and leaving other functions to less-than-metropolitan governments." [31]

The most important development of metropolitan government in the Western Hemisphere has been the establishment in 1954 of the Municipality of Metropolitan Toronto in which the city of Toronto and twelve suburban units of government were merged in a new governmental unit which will take over the supply and wholesale distribution of water to the local municipalities, operate trunk sewers and sewage treatment plants, establish a metropolitan roads system, develop a program of land-use planning and supervise local planning, and assume final authority for public transportation services. It has sole authority over new indebtedness for all units in the area of the new metropolis. The twelve suburban municipalities are separated from the county and its functions including administration of justice and some welfare responsibilities will be taken over by the new unit. Concurrently with its member units, the new municipality may undertake municipal housing and redevelopment, and also has power to develop parks and recreation areas. The local units will keep their remaining present functions.

The jurisdiction of the over-all government covers 245 square miles with a total population of 1,200,000—almost twice the number of Toronto proper. The Metropolitan Council has twenty-five members including the mayors or reeves of the suburban communities and twelve representatives from the city of Toronto including the mayor, two of the four elective controllers, and one of the two aldermen from the nine wards of the city. The chairman is appointed by the provincial government. In addition, there is also a metropolitan school board similarly elected.[32]

Thomas H. Reed, long time authority and practitioner in the field of metropolitan government, sees *little progress toward final solution*

[31] Victor Jones, "Local Government Organization in Metropolitan Areas: Its Relation to Urban Redevelopment," Part IV, *The Future of Cities and Urban Redevelopment,* edited by Coleman Woodbury, University of Chicago (1953), p. 605.

[32] Eric Hardy, "Metropolitan Area Merges," *National Municipal Review* (July, 1953), pp. 326–330.

of the metropolitan problem since 1925. It calls for drastic surgery on the present corpus of local government, he says. For a complete cure, many cities, counties, towns, and villages must be eliminated as entities and in their place must be one single urban government. The public has not yet adopted a realistic conception of the present-day city. It sees it as a compact and closely knit urban area, but in reality it is a sprawling macropolis of built-up and open spaces extending miles from the central core.

While there is little movement toward complete consolidation at present, Mr. Reed believes that palliatives should not be used for they prolong the ultimate solution and confuse the real problems. But there are steps to be taken short of complete consolidation as, for instance, the metropolitan federation which was adopted by Toronto, and functional consolidation giving increased powers to the county in zoning, building regulation, and planning. Above all, there is the need to foster a feeling of unity within the entire metropolitan area. That will ultimately bring about the urge to make the necessary improvements.[33]

It is all very well to suggest ways and means of getting more governmental unity in metropolitan areas. Experts and technicians may have plans, but plans need legislative, councilmanic, and electoral approval. This is hard to get for a number of reasons. First, very few people know "the metropolitan problem"—it is too complex to be explained in a few headlines and therefore it is passed over as ordinary political conversation and chit-chat. And because it is a problem known to "the few" any suggestions are suspected by "the many" as newfangled blueprints for the future by eggheads, dreamers, and idealists. Second, there are diverse interests involved —each suspecting the other of trying to "pull something." The suburbanites resent any plan for integration as a plot hatched up by the central city people to get the fringe dweller and his property under their control. On the other hand, the chambers of commerce and businessmen of the central city want a "big city" so that they can attract more business and industry on account of their higher place

[33] Thomas H. Reed, "Hope for 'Suburbanitis,'" *National Municipal Review* (December, 1950), pp. 542–553.

in the population charts. Labor groups are usually set against any plans of the industrial and business leaders even before they know what they are, and so have to have exceptionally good arguments to convince them. Political office-holders in suburban regions are generally against any integration because it may change their power and status in the governmental picture. Rural and small town leaders throughout the state will usually support them in the legislature. The real job necessary to develop actual integration in American metropolitan areas in the foreseeable future is education—either that or an overwhelming emergency in which metropolitan unity is so obviously necessary for survival that all can see and understand it. Like the threat of atomic attack.[34]

TEN SUBJECTS FOR FURTHER STUDY

1. Urban-rural population changes in your state since 1900.
2. The economic factors in the growth of the largest city in your state.
3. The standard metropolitan areas in your state: their population and local units.
4. Annexation in Texas.
5. A map of the areas or zones in your city showing the main industrial, business, and residential sections.
6. A detailed description of a blighted area in your city or town.
7. The metropolitan federation of Toronto.
8. The expanding suburbs.
9. The "police jurisdiction" in Alabama.
10. The Port of New York Authority.

REFERENCES

Harold F. Alderfer, "Organizing and Financing Metropolitan Government," *The Daily Bond Buyer*, Special Convention Issue, November 28, 1955, pp. 30–34.

Chester W. Bain, "Annexation: Virginia's Not-So-Judicial System," *Public Administration Review*, Autumn, 1955, pp. 251–262

A. W. Banister and R. J. Ellison, "Two Little Communities Build Joint Sewage-Treatment Systems," *The American City*, February 1952, pp. 102–103.

---

[34] Victor Jones, "Politics of Integration in Metropolitan Areas," *Annals of the American Academy of Political and Social Science* (January, 1940), pp. 161–167.

Donald J. Bogue, *Population Growth in Standard Metropolitan Areas, 1900–1950, with an Explanatory Analysis of Urbanized Areas* (Washington, 1953).

——, *Metropolitan Decentralization: A Study of Differential Growth,* University of Miami, August 1950.

John C. Bollens, "Metropolitan and Fringe Area Developments in 1954," *The Municipal Year Book 1954,* pp. 37–52.

Howard G. Brunsman, "Urban Places and Population," *The Municipal Year Book 1955,* pp. 21–26.

J. D. Carroll, Jr., "The Future of the Central Business District," *Public Management,* July 1953, pp. 150–153.

Charles R. Cherington, "Pattern for Greater Boston," *National Municipal League,* February 1949, pp. 68–72.

Weldon Cooper, *Metropolitan County: A Survey of Government in the Birmingham Area,* Bureau of Public Administration, University of Alabama, 1949.

Edwin A. Cottrell, "The Metropolitan Water District in Southern California," *American Political Science Review,* August 1932, pp. 695–697.

Edwin A. Cottrell and Helen L. Jones, *Characteristics of the Metropolis,* (Los Angeles, 1952).

——, *Metropolitan Los Angeles: Study in Integration,* 16 vols., Hays Foundation (Los Angeles, 1955).

Winston W. Crouch, "Extraterritoriality Powers of Cities as Factors in Government," *American Political Science Review,* April 1937, p. 286.

——, "Metropolitan Government in Toronto," *Public Administration,* Spring 1954, pp. 85–95.

Rowland A. Egger, "The Proposed Charter of the Federated 'City of Pittsburgh,'" *American Political Science Review,* August 1929, pp. 718–732.

——, "City-County Consolidation in Allegheny, Pennsylvania," *American Political Science Review,* February 1929, pp. 121–123.

Eric Hardy, "Toronto Federation Makes History," *The American City,* June 1953, pp. 83–84.

Melvin P. Hatcher, "How Kansas City, Missouri, Sells Water to Its Suburbs," *The American City,* May 1952, pp. 99–101.

Carl P. Herbert, "What Price Aid to Suburbs?" *National Municipal Review,* June 1946, pp. 280–283.

Judith Norvell Jamison, *Intergovernmental Cooperation in Public Personnel Administration in the Los Angeles Area,* Bureau of Governmental Research, University of California (Los Angeles, 1944).

G. Edward Janosik, "Suburban Balance of Power," *American Quarterly,* Summer, 1955, pp. 123–141.

Victor Jones, "Local Government Organization in Metropolitan Areas: Its Relation to Urban Redevelopment," Part IV in Coleman Woodbury, ed., *The Future of Cities and Urban Redevelopment* (Chicago, 1953).

Lane W. Lancaster, *Government in Rural American* (New York, 1952).

Christian L. Larsen and Robert H. Stoudemire, *Metropolitan Charleston,* University of South Carolina, Columbia, January 1949.

C. Arthur Lascelles, "Toronto Metropolitan Government," *The Daily Bond Buyer,* Convention Issue, November 28, 1955, pp. 30–36.

Russell W. Maddox, "Cities Step Over Line," *National Municipal Review,* February 1955, pp. 82–88.

Walter T. Martin, *The Rural-Urban Fringe* (University of Oregon, 1953).

Charles Edward Merriam, Spencer D. Parratt, and Albert Lepawsky, *The Government of the Metropolitan Region of Chicago,* (Chicago, 1933).

Ellis McCune, *Intergovernmental Cooperation in Recreation Administration in the Los Angeles Area,* Bureau of Governmental Research, University of California (Los Angeles, 1954).

National Municipal Review, "We're all in the Same Boat," July 1954, pp. 337–343, "Defense of Metropolitan Areas," September 1954, pp. 403–410 (East River Project conclusions).

William F. Ogburn, *Social Characteristics of Cities* (Chicago, 1937).

John A. Perkins, "The Government of 'Rurban' Areas," *American Political Science Review,* April 1943, pp. 306–313.

Public Administration Service, *The Government of Metropolitan Miami* (Chicago, 1954).

John Rannells, *The Core of the City* (New York, 1954).

Thomas H. Reed, "Changes Needed in Governmental Structure of Metropolitan Areas," *American City,* February 1953, p. 134.

———, "Hope for 'Suburbanitis' " *National Municipal Review,* December 1950, pp. 542–553.

———, "Progress in Metropolitan Integration," *Public Administration Review,* Winter 1949, pp. 1–10.

Beldon H. Schaffer, *Growing Suburbs and Town Finance,* Institute of Public Service, University of Connecticut (Storrs, Connecticut, 1954).

Wendell G. Shaeffer, "Miami Looks at the Problems of Metropolitan Government," *Public Administration Review,* Winter 1955, pp. 35–38.

Robert A. Sigafoos, "Municipal Finance and Metropolitan Areas," *Public Management,* June 1953, pp. 126–129.

Herbert A. Simon, *Fiscal Aspects of Metropolitan Consolidation,* Bureau of Public Administration, University of California (Berkeley, 1943).

William L. Slayton and Richard Dewey, "Urban Redevelopment and the Urbanite," Part III in Coleman Woodbury, ed., *The Future of Cities and Urban Redevelopment* (Chicago, 1953).

Richard C. Spencer, "Twenty-nine Cities within Cities," *National Municipal Review,* May 1948, pp. 256–258.

Paul Studenski, "New York Area Still Stymied," *National Municipal Review,* May 1954, pp. 235–239.

Paul Studenski and Others, *The Government of Metropolitan Areas* (New York, 1930).

Betty Tableman, *Governmental Organization in Metropolitan Areas,* University of Michigan Press (Ann Arbor, 1951).

————, "How Cities Can Lick the Fringe Problem," *Public Management,* March 1952, pp. 50–54.

Tax Institute, *Financing Metropolitan Government,* a symposium (Princeton, 1955).

The Municipal Year Book 1955, "Metropolitan and Urbanized Areas," pp. 27–36.

Warren S. Thompson, *Population Problems,* 3rd ed. ⟨New York, 1942).

Herman Walker, Jr. and Peter L. Hanson, "Local Government and Rainfall: The Problem of Local Government in the Northern Great Plains," *American Political Science Review,* December 1946, pp. 1113–1123.

Chapter 4

LOCAL GOVERNMENT
AND THE STATE

In the American system of government as established by the United States Constitution, local government is strictly a state affair. This is not to say that the national government is not concerned with the affairs of local units, for as we shall see there is an ever-increasing sphere of federal-local relations. But local government is not one of the functions delegated to the national government by the Constitution and therefore it belongs within the legal jurisdiction of the state. Local government owes its existence, obtains its powers and finds its limitations in three instruments of state law: the constitutions, the statutes, and the judicial decisions.

The State Constitutions

The basic law of the state is its constitution. In it are outlined those provisions relating to structure, powers, and procedures of government, both state and local, that the sovereign people believe to be important enough to be a part of the constitutional law of the state. The early constitutions were short and simple; they said little about local government. In the absence of constitutional guidance, legislatures were free to pass whatever laws they wished relating to cities, counties, and other local units. That they abused this privilege is attested by the restrictions on their power placed in the newer constitutions after the middle of the 19th century. Almost every state constitution today contains many provisions relating to local government.

These constitutional provisions can be divided into five classes. The first contains those that specifically provide for local government: its organization, powers, procedures, restrictions, and other details. For example, in Alabama, county and local indebtedness is limited; in Arizona, county officials are designated; in Arkansas, local tax levies are limited; in California, consolidation of local units is provided for; in Michigan, powers of municipalities are enumerated. Most constitutions now have some sections devoted to certain aspects of local government.

The second class are the unqualified denials of legislative power. For example, the Missouri constitution denies the legislature the right to lend credit to municipal corporations; the Pennsylvania constitution prohibits the general assembly from authorizing local units to become stockholders in any corporation.

The third category requires local action on or approval of legislation affecting local units. In Illinois, no law affecting the municipal government of the city of Chicago shall go into effect until ratified by the majority of legal voters of the city voting on the question. In New York, special city laws after passing both houses of the legislature must be submitted to the corporate authorities of the city directly concerned. Many constitutions provide for the election of local officials.

The fourth group are those provisions that prohibit the legislature from enacting special or local legislation. A special law is one that relates to a particular person or thing within a certain class. For instance, a law granting immunity from taxation to the First Methodist Church of Des Moines would be special legislation, while a law granting such immunity to all church organizations within the state of Iowa would be a general law. Similarly, a law establishing the commission form of government for the city of Fort Wayne would be a local law, while a law providing the commission form of government for all the cities of Indiana would be a general law. Special and local laws are deemed to be synonymous, the former applying to people, institutions, or things; the latter, to territory.

These constitutional provisions came as the result of the misuse by state legislatures of their power to pass special and local laws. At the instance of the elected representative of a district if he happened to be a member of the majority party in the legislature, that body would pass laws relating to the organization, powers, and procedures of individual local units. Special groups and individuals were thus able at times to get a stranglehold on the municipality, rip out elected officials and substitute state-appointed commissions, dispose of franchises for operating profitable public utilities, get control of the law enforcement machinery, and in short take advantage of the helplessness of local government for selfish ends. Local government became a shambles and so the people through constitutional means sought to control the legislatures and make order out of chaos.[1]

The fifth class of constitutional provisions relating to local government are those giving local government the right of self-government and home rule. Missouri became the first constitutional home rule state in 1875 when the constitution of Missouri gave to the city of St. Louis the power to frame and adopt its own charter. Since that time, a total of twenty-five state constitutions have made it possible for municipalities to adopt and amend their own charters.[2]

Constitutional Home Rule

The three main objectives of home rule, according to the American Municipal Association, are: (1) to prevent legislative inter-

[1] Typical prohibitions against local legislation are found in the Pennsylvania constitution. It provides that the "General Assembly shall not pass any local or special law" on the following subjects: liens, counties, cities, wards, boroughs, school districts, townships, names of places, ferries, bridges, cemeteries, county seats, incorporation of local units, elections, local offices, fees, management of schools, remission of fines, tax exemption, and creation of corporations. Constitution of Pennsylvania, Article III, section 7. (Adopted 1873.)

[2] Arizona (1912), California (1879), Colorado (1902), Louisiana (1946), Maryland (1915), Michigan (1908), Minnesota (1896), Missouri (1875), Nebraska (1912), New Mexico (1949), Nevada (1924), New Jersey (1947), New York (1923), Ohio (1912), Oklahoma (1907), Oregon (1906), Pennsylvania (1922), Rhode Island (1951), Tennessee (1953), Texas (1912), Utah (1932), Virginia (1902), Washington (1889), West Virginia (1937), Wisconsin (1924).

ference with local government; (2) to enable cities to adopt the kind of government they desire; and (3) to provide cities with sufficient powers to meet the increasing needs for local services.

Home rule means simply that local units are granted powers of self-government without interference from state law. But, of course, there is nothing like complete autonomy for local units. Home rule is a strictly relative matter.

First, the constitutions themselves define it in vague terms: to frame a charter for its own government (Missouri); the right to make and enforce all laws with respect to municipal affairs (California); all local and municipal affairs (Colorado); local concerns (Ohio); local affairs and government (Wisconsin); property, affairs, or government (New York); power to frame and adopt their own charters and to exercise the powers and authority of local government, subject to restrictions imposed by the legislature (Pennsylvania).

Second, home rule is never granted to all local units by state constitutions. Usually, it is applied only to municipalities—cities, boroughs, towns, villages—although six states have granted home rule to counties.[3] Quasi-municipal corporations such as park districts, port districts, school districts, "municipal authorities," and even townships are rarely granted powers of home rule. But not all municipalities in a home rule state are eligible: in Arizona and California, only those over 3,500 population; in Maryland, until 1954, only the city and county of Baltimore (now all cities and towns); in Washington, only cities over 20,000 population. But in states like Michigan, Minnesota, New Jersey, New York, North Carolina, Ohio, and Utah all municipalities are included.

Third, constitutional home rule provisions are not always self-executing or utilized to their fullest extent. They need enabling legislation on the part of the state legislature, and this is sometimes difficult to obtain.[4] In Pennsylvania, for example, home rule for cities was provided by amendment to the constitution in 1922, but it was

[3] California, Maryland, Texas, Ohio, Missouri, and Washington (as of 1952).
[4] In Michigan, Minnesota, Nevada, New Jersey, New York, Pennsylvania, South Carolina, Texas, Virginia, Washington, West Virginia, and Wisconsin.

not until 1949 that the first city, Philadelphia, was enabled to frame and adopt its own charter. Other cities are still operating under a strict state-controlled system. In Utah, no cities have made use of the home rule grant, and in both Missouri and Nebraska only three. According to Rodney L. Mott (Colgate University), in sixteen states which in 1949 had 3,654 cities eligible to frame their own charters only 646 or about one-sixth of the number were operating under home rule charters.[5] Opposition or lethargy is the characteristic attitude of many municipal officials when it comes to home rule for their communities for they are against any change in the structure of government under the impression that a change in the form of government may be directed against their own administration and they might lose their official position in case a change would be made. The fight for city home rule has been carried on largely by civic and reform groups rather than by local officials.

An example is West Virginia, the constitution of which contains a home rule provision but where municipalities do not actually enjoy home rule. Since 1937 cities of 2,000 in population have been free to draft, adopt, and amend charters. But the legislature passed an enabling law enumerating in considerable detail the powers of home rule cities. The constitution itself allows cities to pass only laws and ordinances "not inconsistent with the constitution or present or future laws of the state." In addition, many general laws, especially pertaining to fiscal affairs limit the power of home rule cities. The state courts have adhered to the "Dillon Rule"—that of strict interpretation of local powers. As a result, home rule in West Virginia "has yet to emerge from the realm of theory." [6]

Fourth, where home rule is granted to local units it is only in the field of "local affairs." But what are local affairs in contrast to those of state concern? This is a matter for judicial determination and the courts have been called to decide many cases. Michigan cities were forced to defend their powers in the state supreme court seventy

[5] Rodney L. Mott, *Home Rule for American Cities,* American Municipal Association (1949), p. 22. Michigan, Oregon, Texas, and California have the greatest number of home rule cities.

[6] Harold J. Shamberger, "Home Rule Still a Farce," *National Municipal Review* (November, 1954), pp. 523–525.

times between 1930 and 1949. Texas cities had more than one hundred cases during the same period of time.[7] There is no clear delineation between state and local powers; interpretation varies from state to state, from time to time. Professor McGoldrick (Columbia University), an accepted authority on home rule, classifies as examples of matters of state concern: education, courts, public utilities, and annexation. On the other hand, local matters could include subjects such as: forms of government, local officials, police, zoning, and the exercise of general police power, health, safety, and welfare of the residents. Subjects in which he indicates there is no consensus are: finance, taxation, indebtedness, special assessments, eminent domain, and claims.[8]

McQuillin compiles a more detailed list of local concern: street construction, liens for sidewalk construction, special assessments for improvements, maintenance of sewers and drains, parks and playgrounds, eminent domain, providing water, light, and other utilities, municipal officers, municipal taxes, forms of local government, salaries of employees.[9]

State affairs he defines as public matters concerning the people of the state at large in common with the inhabitants of a given community while local matters concern the people of a particular community alone. He lists as state matters: the administration of justice, the maintenance of a police force, fire protection, public health, sanitary regulations, conservation of resources, education, neglected or delinquent children, elections, public records, control of streets and traffic, public utility rates, conditions of work for municipal employees, boundaries, indebtedness, and taxation.[10]

California court decisions indicate that it is impossible to make any clear definition of the term municipal affairs. Examples of matters held to be of municipal interest are licensing, supply of utilities, fiscal management of city, enactment of zoning regulations, im-

---

[7] Mott, *op. cit.*, p. 28.

[8] Joseph D. McGoldrick, *Law and Practice of Municipal Home Rule, 1916–1930* (1933), pp. 319–351.

[9] Eugene McQuillin, *The Law of Municipal Corporations,* second edition (1940), Vol. 1, pp. 566–570.

[10] *Ibid.,* pp. 561–565.

provement of parks and boulevards, issuance of bonds, improvement of municipal buildings, hours and wages and working conditions of employees, regulations of fire and police departments, enactment of municipal ordinances and resolutions, violations of charter provisions or city ordinances, municipal elections, disposition of municipal funds, city streets, and city civil service systems. Matters held to be of statewide interest include city boundary line changes, tort liability of cities, public schools, and regulation of traffic.[11]

This difficulty of drawing the line between state and local affairs in home rule states has led Professor McGoldrick to predict even worse results than the present confusion. "It may be suggested," he says, "that if this is persisted in (distributing functions of government between state and local units in constitutional home rule states) it will ultimately all but destroy municipal home rule. The number of matters that can be assigned completely and exclusively to local discretion will ultimately prove few indeed. This will become more apparent as municipal functions develop. . . . If the courts are forced to deny all state control in order to permit local control of specific problems, it may be expected that more and more matters will be declared state concerns.

"One of the distinct handicaps which the home rule movement now faces is the absence of a mechanism for the handling of problems in which there is both state and local interest." [12]

In home rule states, communities desiring to take advantage of their right to frame and adopt their own charters usually resort to the following procedure:

1. A charter commission is elected by the voters.

2. The charter commission studies the problem, holds hearings and makes recommendations.

3. The charter commission drafts a charter. In the charter are the basic elements of city government: powers, organization, procedures and restrictions.

[11] Edith Foster Howard, *Home Rule for Municipalities,* Bureau of Public Administration (University of Tennessee, 1949). Letter from California League of Municipalities cited, pp. 3–4.

[12] Joseph D. McGoldrick, *Law and Practice of Municipal Home Rule, 1916–1930* (Columbia University Press, 1933), p. 317.

4. The charter is submitted to the electorate for vote.[13]

In 1953, the American Municipal Association, representing directly or through state leagues of municipalities more than 11,000 municipalities in the United States, proposed model constitutional provisions for home rule.[14] They were based on the following principles: (1) that the legislature should pass only general laws in relation to municipal corporations; (2) that only general laws should prevail in the case of incorporation, government, and boundaries of municipalities; (3) that the legislature should classify municipalities into not more than four classes based upon population; (4) that the legislature should provide optional plans of municipal organization and government, under which an authorized optional plan might be adopted or discarded by a majority vote of the qualified voters of the municipality voting thereon; (5) that the qualified voters should be empowered to adopt a home rule charter, proposed by the local legislative body or by a charter commission, and to amend and repeal it; (6) that home rule charter municipalities might exercise any power or function which the legislature has power to devolve upon a non-home rule charter municipality, or which is not denied them by statute; and (7) that state legislation requiring increased municipal expenditures should be approved by the legislative body of the municipal corporation in which it is to be effective, unless passed by two-thirds vote of each legislative chamber, or unless state grants sufficient to meet the costs are provided in the same legislature.

The AMA model constitutional provision for municipal home rule differs in some important respects from the provisions for home rule embodied in the Model State Constitution of the National Municipal League published in 1948. The NML model sets forth the powers of home rule municipalities in broad general terms to pass laws and ordinances relating to local affairs, property, and government with specific enumeration of certain powers within this

[13] See National Municipal League, *A Guide for Charter Commissions* (1947).
[14] American Municipal Association, *Model Constitutional Provisions for Municipal Home Rule*, The Committee on Home Rule (1953). Also see: Arthur W. Bromage, "Home Rule—NML Model," and Jefferson B. Fordham, "Home Rule—AMA Model," *National Municipal Review* (March, 1955), pp. 132–142.

field: to pass local police, sanitary, and other similar regulations; to levy, assess, and collect taxes, borrow money and issue bonds, levy and collect special assessments; to furnish all local public works, and to acquire certain public works; to maintain art institutes and other cultural institutions; to establish and alter streets; to acquire and operate public utilities; to issue nondebt revenue bonds; to organize and administer public schools; to provide for slum clearance, low cost housing, and rehabilitation. Such language seeks to create a self-executing *imperium in imperio*, that is, a sphere of power that legislatures cannot touch, and in case there is any conflict the courts must decide. The AMA model, on the other hand, provides that a home rule municipality "may exercise any power or perform any function which the legislature has power to devolve upon a non-home rule charter municipal corporation and which is not denied to that municipal corporation by its home rule charter, is not denied to all home rule charter municipal corporations by statute and is within such limitations as may be established by statute." Thus, there is a constitutional grant of substantive powers, which is effective without the aid of enabling legislation but is not beyond legislative control. In other words, the power is there unless the legislature clearly denies it to the municipality. However, the provisions do grant full autonomy to municipalities as to municipal executive, legislative, and administrative structure, organization, personnel, and procedure by making the charter provisions superior to statute.

While home rule has not proved the panacea some of its proponents promised, and granted that it has encountered many legal difficulties in the courts and political obstacles in the legislatures and even among city officials themselves, nevertheless it has proven better than the condition of absolute legislative supremacy over local units that still obtains in many states. A real home rule city has more choice in its governmental organization and more power over its officials and employees; it will likely have more powers to minister to the needs of its citizens than a non-home rule city; it will likely develop more efficient administration because it will not be tied as much to state restrictions; it will have a better city charter because this instrument will be adjusted to local conditions. In addition, home rule tends to liberalize the state legislature's attitude toward local government and considerably reduces its burden. Home rule strengthens the fabric of the whole body politic.

State Legislatures and Local Government

The classic statement on the legal relations between the legislature and local units was made in 1868 by Judge J. F. Dillon, adjudged by many as the nation's foremost authority on municipal law. He said: "Municipal corporations owe their origin to, and derive their rights wholly from, the legislature. It breathes into them the breath of life, without which they cannot exist. As it creates, so it may destroy. If it may destroy, it may abridge and control. Unless there is some constitutional limitation . . . the legislature might, by a single act, if we can suppose it capable of so great a folly and so great a wrong, sweep from existence all the municipal corporations of the state, and the corporation could not prevent it." [15]

But this sweeping statement was challenged by a no less famous jurist as early as 1871. Judge Cooley in a famous Michigan case said: "The state may mould local institutions according to its view of policy or expediency; but local government is a matter of right, and the state cannot take it away. It would be the boldest mockery to speak of a city as possessing municipal liberty where the state not only shaped its government but at its discretion sent in its own agents to administer it; or to call that system one of constitutional freedom under which it would be equally admissable to allow the people full control in their local affairs or no control at all." [16]

Judge Cooley went further by stating that the right of local self-government of municipalities is recognized by law as "of common law origin, and having no less than common law franchises" and that this is recognized in most of the state constitutions. As examples, he

[15] City of Clinton *v.* Cedar Rapids and Missouri Railroad Co., 24 Iowa 455 (1868).

[16] People *v.* Hurlburt, 24 Mich. 44 (1871).

points out that in some the bill of rights declares local government as belonging to the people, in others the counties and townships are established for local government, and cities given the power to adopt their own charters, and in many more the legislature is prohibited from passing local legislation.[17]

Following Judge Cooley and the Michigan courts, which consistently and valiantly stated the right of local self-government and checked any attempt on the part of the state to meddle, were other state courts, notably in Indiana, Kentucky, Iowa, Texas, Montana, and Florida. Several cases involved the power of the state to set up independent boards or commissions with powers in municipal functions such as police, fire, and streets, and providing for appointment of such a board by the legislature and governor. The right to choose local officers was recognized only as to those deemed to be performing strictly local functions, as distinguished from state functions in which the local unit acted as an agent of the state, but nevertheless such opinions punctured the state supremacy doctrine. While this doctrine still has not been disclaimed in some states, it is generally recognized, in the words of the Committee on State-Local Relations of the Council of State Governments, that: "The doctrine of inherent rights of local self-government has now lost even the small acceptance it once enjoyed." [18]

State supremacy, moreover, was recognized by the Supreme Court of the United States in several leading decisions. Mr. Justice Cardozo stated flatly that a municipal corporation "has no privileges or immunities under the Federal Constitution which it may invoke in opposition to the will of its creator." [19]

The Supreme Court of the United States made no distinction be-

[17] McQuillin, *The Law of Municipal Corporations*, second edition (1940), p. 551.

[18] The Council of State Governments, *State-Local Relations* (1946), p. 141.

[19] Williams *v.* Mayor and City Council of Baltimore, 289 U. S. 36 (1933). In Trenton *v.* New Jersey, 262 U. S. 182 (1923), the United States Supreme Court said that a municipality is merely a department of the state, a political subdivision created for the exercise of such governmental powers as may be entrusted to it. In Hunter *v.* City of Pittsburgh, 207 U. S. 161 (1907), the court held that in the absence of constitutional restrictions, the legislature may at its pleasure modify or withdraw any powers so entrusted to a city, hold such powers itself, or vest them in other agencies.

tween state or local powers in asserting legislative supremacy as far as the Constitution of the United States was concerned. However, certain state courts have ruled that property held by the municipality as a private corporation is protected from legislative interference. The supreme court of Massachusetts held that waterworks, markets, hospitals, cemeteries, libraries, and the system of parks of the city of Boston were established for public benefit yet declared that they are "held more like the property of a private corporation" and therefore protected in some degree from legislative interference.[20] While it is agreed that there might be some limits to legislative control of municipal corporations, the unsettled condition of the law makes it impossible to state these limits precisely. Any limitations involve a distinction between the governmental powers of the local units which are derived from the state and the local or proprietary powers which inhere in the corporation and community. But later cases, it must be admitted, recognize no other restrictions on the legislature than the constitutional provisions in a given state.

Urban Representation in State Legislatures

The present inequities in urban representation in state legislatures are too well known to be belabored here. Briefly, they take several forms: (1) constitutional provisions that each county have at least one member in the senate or house no matter what the population may be; (2) constitutional limitations on the number of members in the house or senate from any one county no matter how large its population; (3) refusal of the legislature to reapportion after census returns show major shifts in population.

According to the Council of State Governments, 17 states have constitutional provisions for the senate and 22 for the house which relate to minimum or maximum limits of representation for counties.[21] This is especially significant since the 1950 census shows that

[20] Mount Hope Cemetery *v.* Boston, 158 Mass. 509.
[21] The Council of State Governments, *The Book of the States, 1954–55,* pp. 116–118.

more than half the population of the United States dwells in 168
standard metropolitan areas which together comprise only 281, or
about 9 per cent of the 3,049 counties of the nation.[22] Furthermore,
census figures for eighteen of the largest agricultural states show
that all the population gains between 1940 and 1950 have been in
their urban areas, and that rural areas had relative or actual losses.

Legislative apportionment has been undertaken in twenty-one
states since 1950, presumably to adjust for changes in population.
Although no definitive study on this subject has yet been made, it
is doubtful whether such reapportionment has had much effect upon
urban representation since few, if any, of the constitutional restrictions have been lifted. Twelve additional states had their last reapportionment between 1940 and 1950; thus 15 state legislatures
have not been reapportioned before 1940.[23]

In Pennsylvania, for example, in 1953 the membership in the
house of representatives was increased from 208 to 210. According
to the 1950 census, 70 per cent of the state's population is urban in
character. While 31 of the 50 senators and 140 of the 210 members
of the house are from urban districts, on the basis of urban population there should be 35 senators and 148 representatives.[24] While
these inequities between urban population and urban representation
do not seem overwhelming, legislators in the urban areas outside
big cities line up along with the rural representatives against the
big cities, for they consider themselves "up-state" or "suburban"
instead of urban. Party alignment also has been a factor in that the
governments of the two largest Pennsylvania cities were at times
Democratic while the state itself and the majorities in both houses
of the general assembly were Republican.

In 1948, the United States Conference of Mayors made a study
which indicated that in the legislatures of 1947, the urban population, which then constituted 59 per cent of the total population, had
only 25 per cent of the legislators. And this group, it was estimated,

[22] Roy V. Peel, "Political Implications of the 1950 Census of Population,"
The Western Political Quarterly (December, 1950), pp. 615–619.

[23] *The Book of the States, 1945–55,* pp. 116–118.

[24] Legislators are considered urban if the majority of population in their
districts was considered urban according to the 1950 census.

paid 90 per cent of all taxes.[25] The situation is even more unbalanced now that, according to the 1950 census, 64 per cent of the nation's population is urban.

A survey of attitudes held by municipal officials throughout the United States showed that a majority felt that cities do not receive equal treatment with rural areas at the hands of the state legislatures, that rural areas receive more state financial assistance than cities, that there is hostility among legislators towards municipal problems, that governors and other state administrative officers are more sympathetic to rural areas than to cities, that cities are discriminated against in the tax structure of the states and that they do no receive a fair share of state revenues.[26]

These attitudes, of course, vary in intensity from state to state, but there seems to be greater antagonism on the part of the state legislatures toward the large cities than toward the smaller municipalities. Unfortunately, legislators who represent smaller municipalities and the urban fringe of larger cities often side against the large city, not realizing that only through municipal and urban unity can more consideration for urban problems be obtained. While strong state leagues of municipalities have influenced better treatment of municipalities by state governments (especially in California, Tennessee, Virginia, Wisconsin, Minnesota, Michigan, and New York), cities still consider themselves "stepchildren" in most states.

How Legislatures Control Local Units

After the Norman invasion in 1066, William the Conqueror granted to the City of London a municipal charter which confirmed its ancient borough privileges. But in 1100 his grandson, King Henry, granted the inhabitants a more elaborate charter with the right to choose their own sheriff, be exempt from various tolls, and be tried in their own courts. This *Carta civibus Londonarum* is basic in Anglo-Saxon municipal history. It set the pattern of municipal

[25] United States Conference of Mayors, *Government of the People, by the People, and for the People* (1948).
[26] Gordon E. Baker, "Cities Resent Stepchild Lot," *National Municipal Review* (September, 1953), pp. 387–392.

rights and liberties found in the English borough charters for the next six hundred years. The charters were granted by the king and gave the townsmen certain powers and privileges that resulted in some independence from the royal and feudal lords around them. In the charter the community was given the status of a corporation, immunities from certain royal taxes, commercial privileges, and the right to choose their own officials.

When the English people settled the American colonies, they brought along this concept of municipal organization. During the colonial era, municipal charters were granted to a number of towns: New York, Philadelphia, Annapolis, Williamsburg, Richmond, and others. In all cases, the charters were granted by the colonial governor or proprietor rather than the king. But they were never granted by the colonial assembly. This was a royal prerogative in England and colonial practice followed it. As the colonies grew, the communities found that these borough charters did not give them enough power to tax, so the colonial legislatures—the only agency with power to do so—gave them certain taxing powers.

After the Revolution, the power to grant charters was taken away from the governors and given to the legislatures which now reigned supreme. Governors had represented the royal yoke and as the colonists wanted to get rid of all evidences of royal power, governors in the early years of national existence were of secondary importance in state government. Now that the legislatures granted the charters, these were really laws so that charter and law became interchangeable terms. Thus charters were granted by special act of the legislature. But today, only a few states continue this practice.[27] Its rejection by forty-one states proves that it was found wanting.

But local government was controlled by special and local legislation for a long time after special charters were generally discarded. The abuse of special legislation for local units is illustrated by the New York statute of 1857 creating a metropolitan police district for New York City and its environs. Control over police was vested in

[27] Connecticut, Delaware, Maine, Massachusetts, New Hampshire, Rhode Island, and Vermont.

a commission appointed by the governor and state senate. Although residents of the city rioted in protest, state courts ruled the act valid.[28] Likewise, the legislature of Pennsylvania passed an act appointing commissioners to control the erection of a new municipal building for the city of Philadelphia. The act constituted this body a close and perpetual corporation empowered to fill vacancies. It was given unlimited power to create debts which had to be paid by compulsory tax levies on the part of the local authorities. The constitutionality of the act was sustained and the city was forced to furnish money for twenty years, as one judge phrased it, "upon an enormous pile which surpasses the town halls and cathedrals of the Middle Ages in extent, if not in grandeur."

Special legislation is still an important feature in state-local relations despite home rule charters, classification, and constitutional restrictions. In 1939, Maryland passed 309 acts relating to individual cities, counties, and towns. There are even a large number of salary rates for specific officials in specific localities. But there are a great number of laws affecting local units in states where general laws and classification of local units exist. In Pennsylvania, at recent sessions of the legislatures, one-half of the approximately twenty-five hundred bills introduced consisted of legislation on local government. It concerned powers, structure, organization, procedure, and specific functions for the various classifications of local units although none applied by name to a particular municipality or local unit.

The Report of the Committee on State-Local Relations of the Council of State Government points up many of the disadvantages of special and local legislation: (1) the burden of local legislation makes undue demands on the time and energy of members of the state legislature; (2) it accentuates the feeling of localism in state legislatures; (3) it encourages log-rolling among members; (4) legislators cannot take the time to understand each measure introduced; (5) it causes instability and confusion in local government; (6) local affairs are brought into the arena of statewide politics; and

[28] Council of State Governments, *State-Local Relations,* citing People *v.* Draper, 15 N. Y. 532 (1857), p. 144.

(7) it removes control of local government from the hands of local citizens where it belongs.[29]

About the middle of the 19th century, reaction against special legislation set in. The new constitutions prohibited the practice. This meant that the legislatures had to desist from legislating for individual local units such as Patton county, Jefferson city, Munhall borough, East Moon township, and Chippewa school district and instead had to pass laws only for all counties, all cities, all boroughs, all townships, or all school districts within the entire state regardless of their size, geographical location, financial status, or other differentiating factors. These are called general laws as distinguished from local or special laws. Obviously, the governmental problems and needs of a city like Chicago and an Illinois city with barely ten thousand population are bound to be different; the same can also be said about highly industrialized and urban counties in contrast with heavily forested and rural counties with a scattered population. Local government fell out of the frying pan into the fire.

Out of this dilemma there developed a new concept—*classification*. By this method, local units can be divided into groups on the basis of population and laws passed for the particular class only. Thus, there might be three classes of cities, ten classes of counties, four classes of school districts, and two classes of townships. The first classifications used often overlapped each other; they differed in population ranges for different purposes; there was almost as much confusion as under special legislation. But gradually order was fashioned, the courts approved the idea, and even some constitutions provided the number of classes there could be for each type of local subdivision. Classification was here to stay.

Out of the maze of court decisions in the various states, McQuillan summarizes his doctrine of classification.[30] Lawful classification of cities, and the same applies to all local units, must (1) be based on substantial distinctions making one class different from another; (2) must be germane to the purpose of the law; (3) must be based on

---

[29] Council of State Governments, *op. cit.*, pp. 146–148.
[30] McQuillin, *The Law of Municipal Corporations*, second edition, Vol. 1 (1940), p. 678.

existing circumstances, not future possibilities; (4) must apply equally to each member of the class; and (5) must be based upon the fact that the characteristics of each class are so different from another as reasonably to suggest the propriety of such classification.

In Pennsylvania, the courts have described classification as the "grouping together for purposes of legislation for communities or public bodies which by reason of similarity of situation, circumstances, requirements and conveniences will have their public interests best subserved by similar regulations." [31] Classification, however, may not evade the general intent of the state constitution prohibiting local legislation and be abused. For example, in Ohio there were eleven classes of cities, eight of which contained only one city, a condition which led the supreme court of that state in 1902 to declare the whole system of classification unconstitutional. But the fact that there is only one city in a class does not make the law a local one if all other standards are met.

A Pennsylvania court stated clearly the accepted principle guiding classification. "There can be no proper classification of cities or counties except by population. The moment we resort to geographical distributions we enter the domain of special legislation, for the reason that such classification operates upon certain cities or counties to the perpetual exclusion of all others." [32]

However, there are several instances in which the courts sustained geographical classification by other than population standards. In Minnesota, uniform airport control was provided for contiguous cities, and in New Jersey there is reference to counties that have fresh water lakes and cities bordering the ocean. But such classification is the exception. [33]

Some states have granted a considerable degree of home rule to local units by statute. [34] This granting of legislative home rule is promising, but it has several disadvantages. What the legislature gives, it can take away. Furthermore, legislative home rule does not

[31] Wheeler *v.* Philadelphia, 77 Pa. 338.
[32] Commonwealth ex rel. Fertig *v.* Patton, 88 Pa. 258 (1878).
[33] Jefferson B. Fordham, *Local Government Law* (1949), p. 62.
[34] Florida, Georgia, Iowa, Mississippi, North Carolina, South Carolina, and Connecticut.

hinder the passage of special laws in some states which have it, for example, North Carolina, South Carolina, and Florida. The best results, from the viewpoint of cities, have been found in Wisconsin where statutory home rule is backed up by a constitutional grant, and in those states, notably Oklahoma, Minnesota, New York, and Washington where the home rule statute is short and confers broad powers.[35]

A number of states allow municipalities or classes of municipalities the right to choose from among several standard forms of municipal organization.[36] The three most popular forms are: the mayor-council, the commission, and the council-manager forms, and usually these three or variations thereof are available for choice. Usually, a local referendum is used as the means of making the choice.

New Jersey offers an interesting example of recent legislation in its Optional Municipal Charter Law of 1950. New Jersey municipalities desiring to change their form of government are offered a wide variety of choices. Three basic plans are proposed: the mayor-council, the council-manager, and the small municipalities plan. Within each of the major divisions are several choices: six kinds of mayor-council forms, five council-manager options, and four variations in the small municipalities plan. The citizens of a community, by the election of a charter commission, may study the problem and recommend either one of the optional plans or a special charter designed to be more suitable to their local needs—the latter to be granted by the legislature. The electorate may, without the services of the charter commission, vote for one of the options by means of petition and referendum.[37]

Furthermore, as of January 1, 1955, approved council-manager

[35] Mott, *Home Rule for American Cities*, American Municipal Association (1949), p. 15.

[36] States allowing optional forms of municipal or local government are: Alabama, Arkansas, California, Colorado, Idaho, Illinois, Iowa, Kansas, Kentucky, Louisiana, Massachusetts, Minnesota, Mississippi, Nebraska, New Jersey, New Mexico, Nevada, North Carolina, North Dakota, Ohio, Oklahoma, South Carolina, South Dakota, Tennessee, Virginia, Washington, West Virginia, Wisconsin, Wyoming.

[37] Benjamin Baker, *Municipal Charter Revision in New Jersey*, Bureau of Government Research, Rutgers University (1953), p. 2.

municipalities are found in forty-five states, and in the three where there are none—Arkansas, Louisiana, and Indiana—either provisions allowing such a form have recently been adopted or initial steps towards adoption have been attempted.[38]

Greater freedom for local units with respect to structure and organization has been paralleled in the field of finance. As of September 1, 1953, the use of permissive local income taxes by local units was allowed in four states: Ohio, Pennsylvania, Kentucky and Missouri, and utilized in about 300 municipal and school districts (285 in Pennsylvania). Sales taxes are allowed local governments in six states: Alabama, California, Colorado, Louisiana, Mississippi and New York; and 193 local units, 165 in California, are using them. Admissions may be taxes in eleven states, cigarettes in eleven states, gasoline in seven states. These are almost entirely developments since World War II. The first local income tax was instituted in Philadelphia in 1939, however, and the first general sales tax in New York City in 1934.[39]

The Powers of Local Governments

All units of local government: cities, boroughs, towns, villages, counties, townships, school districts, and special districts are considered as agents of the state. They carry out governmental powers granted to them by act of state legislature. Therefore, they are governmental agencies of the state. But they also have corporate powers. In this regard they can be divided into two classes: municipal corporations and quasi-municipal corporations. In the first class are cities, boroughs, incorporated towns and villages—generally the more urban units of government; in the second are the counties, townships, school districts, and special districts.

A municipal corporation is a body politic and corporate established by state law. It possesses a legal existence; it has a name and a seal. It is given definite limits as to territory and the population

[38] *The Municipal Year Book 1955*, pp. 503–527.
[39] United States Treasury Department, *Overlapping Taxes in the United States*, prepared for the Commission on Intergovernmental Relations (January 1, 1954).

within its borders is under its jurisdiction as defined by law. As a corporation it has perpetual succession, the right to contract, to sue and be sued, to hold and dispose of property and thereby acquire rights and incur liabilities. Its characteristic feature is the right of self-government; it regulates the local or internal affairs of the area or district that is incorporated, through officers selected by the corporation, and shares in the civil government responsibilities of the state in its particular locality.

A quasi-municipal corporation is a local unit that may have a limited number of corporate powers given to it by law but is low in the scale of corporate existence. It is more a governmental agent of the state than it is a municipal corporation. The precise nature of a given unit of local government in this regard depends upon the statutes and judicial decisions in a particular state. One of the most important differences between a municipal corporation and a quasi-municipal corporation is that in the case of a municipal corporation the inhabitants of the territory have usually solicited by petition or otherwise the legislature or the courts to create a municipal corporation or give legal concurrent approval to its creation, whereas in the case of the quasi-municipal corporations such as the county and township the state created them without any such solicitation.

The general rule on local government powers is that local units of government, either municipal corporations or quasi-municipal corporations, possess no powers except those conferred upon them by state law. These are held to include those granted in express terms, those implied in powers expressly granted, and those essential to the declared objects and purposes of the municipality—those "not simply convenient, but those indispensable," as Judge Dillon expressed it. And, of course, these powers must conform to a higher law of nation and state. Judge Cooley's "reasonably strict interpretation" of these powers is generally accepted by the courts: "There is a principle of law that municipal powers are to be strictly interpreted; and it is a just and wise rule. Municipalities are to take nothing from the general sovereignty except what is expressly granted. But when a power is conferred which in its exercise concerns only the municipality, and can wrong or injure no one, there is not the slightest reason for any strict or literal interpretation with a view of narrowing its construction. . . . This is good sense, and it is the application of correct principles in municipal affairs." [40]

Municipal Liability for Torts

There are two kinds of powers given to local governments. The first class are governmental or public, those that the local unit carries on as an instrumentality of the state, as a local government organ of the state supplying community needs, conveniences, and comforts. The second are private or corporate, those exercised by the local unit as a municipal corporation.

These powers differ in two respects. When the local government acts in its governmental capacity, it acts as a sovereign. As a sovereign in Anglo-American legal theory can do no wrong, the local unit is not subject to private action in the courts for torts for harm done to persons through negligence of its officers and employees except when specifically made liable by state law. But acting as a private corporation it can be held for negligence of its officers and employees in much the same manner as an ordinary corporation or person. The second difference is that, while the legislative power of the state legislature extends to both governmental and private powers—that is, they can be exercised only when specifically granted by law—the exercise of private powers is not as strictly constructed, and courts have been inclined to interpert them less narrowly than governmental powers.

What are governmental and what corporate powers? According to Barnet Hodes, there are three tests to tell whether a municipal power is governmental or corporate. (1) Is the function one which a private individual would perform for a profit? (If so, it is corporate.) (2) Is the function performed by the local unit for the benefit of the citizens of the state at large or for the benefit of the citizens of a corporation? (If the latter, it is corporate.) (3) Is the function one imposed by the state as a duty upon the local unit?

[40] Port Huron *v.* McCall, 46 Mich. 565.

(If so, it is governmental.) Examination of the judicial decisions, however, shows no safe guide; all that can be done is to determine each case as it arises.[41] In Illinois, the court said: "The division of municipal functions into public and governmental on the one hand and private and corporate on the other is not well defined, but is vague and indefinite. . . . The reason and essence of the rule is clear and easy to be understood, but its application to specific cases is often of great difficulty." [42]

The difference between governmental and corporate powers has been the subject of thousands of court cases involving claims for damages against municipalities. As a general rule, the city is granted immunity against claims for damages for its acts done in its governmental capacity, that is, when it acts as an agent of the state. On the other hand, when acting in its proprietary or corporate capacity it is subject to all the liabilities of a corporation or person in private law.[43] In the case of quasi-municipal corporations—counties, townships, school districts, and special districts—the general rule is that they are not liable for torts unless action is allowed by statute. They are public agencies, and their duties are governmental. However, even here the line is not absolutely drawn. For example, they can be held liable for nuisances created by them.

The attitude of the various state courts dealing with such problems is not well defined. But generally speaking governmental functions of a municipality include schools, hospitals, workhouses, jails, poor houses, and fire, police, and health protection. In these fields damages for negligence of officials and employees may not be claimed. At the other extreme are functions such as water and light plants and other utilities, sewers, management of municipal property, and any business operated for profit. In these fields the

---

[41] Barnet Hodes, *Law and the Modern City* (1937), pp. 55–62.

[42] Roumbos *v.* City of Chicago, 332 Ill. 70 (1928).

[43] The State of South Carolina is an exception. A municipal corporation being an agency of the state for governmental purposes cannot be sued in tort, except where such action is allowed by statute. The distinction between governmental and private functions does not obtain in South Carolina. Here action is allowed by statute to any person who shall receive damages to his person or property (1) through a defect in any street, or (2) by reason of defect or mismanagement of anything under the control of the corporation. See McQuillin, *The Law of Municipal Corporations,* revised, Vol. 6, p. 1015.

municipality can generally be held liable for negligence. There is, of course, in every state a large middle ground in which decisions may vary from time to time and where there exists no judicial certainty.

Let a few examples of actual cases illustrate the general principles involved. In North Carolina, the operation of an incinerator for the disposal of garbage was held to be a governmental function; in Wisconsin, highway repair; in Georgia, operation of a traffic light at street intersections; in Colorado, the authorization of traffic markers; in Wisconsin, work on a project to raise railroad tracks. In Arkansas, the maintenance of a light plant the output of which was restricted to the lighting of streets and public places was held to be a governmental function, although it is generally agreed that where electricity is sold to consumers the municipality is acting in its corporate capacity. On the other hand, a garage maintained for maintenance and repair of city vehicles even though under the jurisdiction of the chief of police was held to be a corporate function in Oklahoma. The supply of water to the inhabitants has generally been considered a corporate function, except where it is supplied for public health and safety. The operation of a garbage truck was considered a corporate function in Florida, but the hauling of ashes and the collection of refuse governmental functions. While the operation of a fire department is considered a governmental function, a case occurred where a pedestrian knocked down by a stream of water coming from a defective fire hydrant was able to sue because it appeared that the defect was known for a long time and the city did nothing to repair it. In Denver, Colorado, a pedestrian tripped on a water hose where city employees were engaged in flushing a storm sewer. The city contended the flushing was done to protect the health of the citizens and therefore was governmental, but the court held it was cleaning the streets which was corporate and therefore the city was liable for damages.[44]

The cases cited indicate the absurdity of the situation from the viewpoint of the ordinary citizen. As Murray Seasongood, veteran

---

[44] These and hundreds of other cases are cited in McQuillin, *op. cit.*, revised, Vol. 6, in Chapter 53, "Municipal Liability for Torts."

Cincinnati municipal official and governmental student, said: "It is impossible to explain to one who has had a fractured skull that his mistake was in having the break result from a city fire truck rather than from a city-owned passenger bus or street railway or that, if the injury was from a city park vehicle, he was injured in the wrong state where park maintenance is treated as governmental." [45]

Is there any solution? Should municipal governments be considered entirely as corporations and therefore be liable for all torts? If so, it would increase the cases many times and create a hardship upon larger cities which would have thousands of cases. Should liability be defined by state statute? This is done in South Carolina and partially in some other states. Should municipalities like states and the nation be exempt from all suits for damages? But is not the victim of municipal negligence deserving of some redress? No real solution has been advanced so far; the problem remains unsolved, the status quo is unsatisfactory.

Judicial Review of Local Activities

A basic principle in the American system of government is that of judicial review. Says Dean Fordham (University of Pennsylvania Law School): "Judicial review of legislative, executive and administrative action is extensive and crucial at all levels of government, but we find it to be most detailed and most persuasive at the local level." [46] All local units must stay within the bounds of national and state law both as to substantive powers and as to procedure. They may be compelled to act or they may be restrained, and a large armory of judicially administered remedies and sanctions are available: writ of mandamus, prohibition, quo warranto, and certiorari, as well as civil liability for damages, equitable relief by injunction, declaratory judgments, and even criminal liability.

For example, if municipal officials spend more money than the

---

[45] Murray Seasongood, "Municipal Corporations: Objections to the Governmental or Proprietary Test," 22 *Virginia Law Review,* 910 (1936).

[46] Jefferson B. Fordham, *Local Government Law* (1949), p. 36.

law allows or spend it for some purpose not allowed by law, they may be surcharged, that is, obliged themselves to pay the amounts disallowed by the courts. However, the courts generally do not interfere with the exercise of discretionary powers, that is, those in which local officers are allowed by law to do or not to do, according to their own judgment, providing they have acted within the orbit of their lawful powers. Courts will not sit in review of proceedings of municipal officers and departments, especially those involving legislative discretion, in the absence of bad faith, fraud, arbitrary action, and abuse of power.

Again, the line between discretionary power and ministerial power is hard to define. Its position rests upon the discretion granted the city by state law to discharge or not to discharge a certain function. Where the duty is absolute, the city has no discretion, the duty is therefore ministerial, its discharge is required by law and does not depend upon the judgment of a municipal official. Municipal corporations are not liable for failure to perform, or for errors in performing, their discretionary powers, either legislative or judicial. But they are liable for neglect to perform, or for improper and unskillful performance of their ministerial duties. In the case of the construction of buildings and public works, for example, it is generally held that if errors are committed in the planning of the construction, this being a discretionary power no liability attaches. But if there are errors in the actual building—a ministerial power—which lead to damage, the city is liable. Even where a statute exempted cities from liability for injuries to persons caused by the negligent operation of an airport, as in Texas, the court held such an act unconstitutional.

State Administrative Supervision of Local Government

Constitutional and statutory provisions relating to local government are enforceable in the courts. Hundreds of decisions have been handed down in the field of local government by state courts, and these decisions provide both interpretation and enforcement of such provisions. But such control, basic though it is, is slow, cumbersome, and expensive. Court action must wait for a particular case to be brought up for adjudication. A citizen, person, or corporation, sometimes the state itself or a local government, must initiate proceedings. Many possible infractions of the constitution and law are never judicially examined. Furthermore, judicial control is largely negative in that its main interest is to keep local government within bounds of law, not in making it a positive force of government within the state.

In recent years another kind of state control has developed. Laws have been enacted giving state administrative departments and agencies power to (1) control certain phases of local government, (2) to advise with and provide technical assistance to local officials, and (3) to gather information and statistics about local government. The objectives of state administrative supervision are to (1) achieve uniformity throughout the state; (2) raise standards of local administration and practice; and (3) enforce provisions of law as directed by the legislature. However, it must be emphasized that administrative supervision does not supersede judicial control, it merely complements it in specified fields. By far the most substantial portion of local government law is not enforceable by state administrative agencies, and even the actions of the state agencies can be reviewed by the courts.

State administrative supervision is largely a 20th century development and is a part of the increasing centralization on the part of the states in relation to local government. State administrative agencies are stepping into fields once entirely local in character. They are carrying on many actual functions once local, and controlling the action of local governments in many other fields where they were once free to act. There are, of course, reasons for this trend. The automobile, big industry, and other modern developments have broken down barriers between communities. Modern economic and social problems are statewide, even nationwide, rather than local; many of them must be attacked from the vantage point of larger administrative areas than those of the locality. On the other hand, much of the increase of state control can be traced to the fact that local governments themselves have not been provided with modern tools to confront the problems that are facing them. Too many local units are too small to do a good job, too restricted in their power to raise revenue, too shackled by state law to adopt modern organization.

State supervision in the field of local government is not uniform as between states, nor even between functions within the same state. It is a result of haphazard legislation over a period of years. It is found most highly developed in education, highways, welfare, and finance. It assumes many forms: uniform reporting, establishment of standards, inspection, technical assistance, information service, and even, on occasion, direct control and substitute administration.

In education, most states have taken an active part in shaping the public school system which is administered by local school districts or local governments. They do this through state departments of education headed by a state board of education whose administrative officer is the state superintendent of education usually appointed by the governor but sometimes elected by the people. The duties of the state departments include: certification of teachers—to see that they have the required training; the supervision of teacher training programs—in state teachers' colleges and in private institutions of higher learning; determination of courses of study and adoption of textbooks; development of state educational policies and programs; supervision of school building plans—so that basic health features are included; stimulation and administration of special educational activities such as vocational education, adult education, consolidation of school districts, provision of public transportation, school libraries, interscholastic athletics, and school attendance.

In a few states, notably North Carolina, West Virginia, and Delaware, state centralization in education has reached extreme limits. In North Carolina in 1933 the state dissolved some twelve hundred local school districts, established county unit boards of education, and guaranteed from state funds the basic school program for eight months. The state prescribes textbooks and courses of study, allocates the number of teachers, passes on county school budgets, controls pupil transportation and certifies teachers. The local boards actually hire the teachers and may provide for additional facilities at local expense.

In West Virginia, too, local school districts were abolished and county units established in 1933. A state board of school finance passes upon local budgets and monthly reports, and supervises the entire financial process. In Delaware the state pays for the basic program and local school budgets must conform to the state regulations. But here local school districts have broad discretion in curriculum and school policy. As an example of a state in which local control and financial support is paramount, Massachusetts requires only a certain minimum core of courses to be taught and designates the length of term. Here cooperation between the state and local units is encouraged and the state department staff assists local units to improve their personnel and methods without recourse to regulation.[47]

The depression in the 1930's resulted in extensive changes in the fields of public welfare and relief which before that period were largely of local concern. Local units were not equipped or financially able to cope with large scale unemployment. Nor could they build modern institutions for the mentally handicapped and for other special wards of the state. Furthermore, the national government by the passage of the Federal Social Security Act of 1935 asserted national interest in employment security, old-age and survivors insurance, old-age assistance, aid to the blind, aid to dependent children, child welfare, and aid to the handicapped. While in many of these fields only the states and the national government are concerned, in others federal and state funds are channeled to local units for administration of special or categorical programs under strict financial supervision on the part of the state. The federal legislation designated the states as locally responsible and thereby state supervision over local units resulted. State welfare departments have taken over entire financial and administrative responsibility in a few states, as in Pennsylvania and Arizona, in the case of direct relief, but have strict supervisory powers over local units which participate in the financing of the services as is the case in most of

[47] Council of State Governments, *State-Local Relations*, pp. 14–20.

the states. The state supervision includes: the issuance and enforcement of regulations, the control of local personnel, the review of local decisions, the control of finances, and the use of reports and statewide statistics. It can be said that today the state is dominant in the field of public welfare.[48]

From the early 1900's through the early years of the depression there was a trend toward centralization of the administration of highways in the state governments. Complete responsibility for local roads was assumed by the state governments in North Carolina (1931), Virginia (1932), West Virginia (1933), and Delaware (1935). Since then the movement has been brought to a virtual standstill and emphasis has been placed on the development of a federal-state-local system of cooperation. There has been, however, a steady increase in state highway mileage—171 per cent, or 431,000 miles, from 1921 to 1946, but in the latter year 82 per cent of rural mileage, or 2,459,000 miles, in the United States was still under local control.[49]

Until recently, major highways and rural roads received the lion's share of state attention. Today the urban traffic problem is paramount; arterial street needs in cities are critical. While state aid for local roads, streets, and highways has increased since the beginning of the depression, the passage of the Federal Aid Highway Act of 1944, recognizing particularly the needs of urban areas and appropriating money specifically for urban streets was an event of utmost importance to cities. Highway design in congested areas with limited access facilities and major arterial street systems is of grave importance. The fact that federal as well as state funds are generally expended by state departments of highways, directs attention to the conclusion that state-local highway relationships must be enlarged, procedures must be modernized, cost sharing must be revised, and state department personnel must develop a better understanding of the involved urban problems incident to highway construction and planning.

---

[48] *Ibid.*, pp. 20–24.
[49] Norman Hebden and Wilbur S. Smith, *State-City Relationships in Highway Affairs* (1950), p. 11.

Administrative supervision and control of the state departments of highways over urban extensions of state highways, and over other streets where state aid is provided includes in various combinations: construction, maintenance, inspection, reports, advice and service, approval of plans, maintenance of minimum technical standards, local audits, and traffic control.

State aid and supervision in its various forms is especially necessary in the urban fringe of metropolitan areas because the small local units are not able to carry on the highway and street program needed for the urban region. Likewise, in rural areas where small townships attempt to handle the local road problem the state is taking more and more responsibility. The county is the ideal unit to construct and maintain rural roads. By and large, it can be said that state control increases where local units are not large and strong enough to provide the revenue and administrative personnel necessary to do a modern job.

One of the main fields of state supervision over local functions is in municipal and local finance. According to T. E. McMillan (University of Texas),[50] this takes various forms: supervision of municipal accounts (25 states), auditing of municipal accounts (30 states), financial reporting (23 states), budget supervision (32 states), and debt supervision (20 states). Only four states—Iowa, Massachusetts, New Mexico, and Tennessee—engage in all five types of supervision. Forty-one states have one or more types.

There is a great variation in the intensity, competence, and coverage of the supervision. In some states, it is available but not mandatory; in some, it applies to certain classes of local units only. Some supervisory state departments have well trained personnel; others have small and untrained staffs. In New Jersey, there is a department of local government; in North Carolina, a local government commission; in Pennsylvania, a bureau of municipal affairs; in New Hampshire, a division of municipal accounting is a part of the state tax commission; in Mississippi, the general department of audit is empowered to supervise municipal accounts; in Tennessee, the ex-

[50] T. E. McMillan, Jr., *State Supervision of Municipal Finance,* Institute of Public Affairs, University of Texas (1953).

tension service of the university operates a municipal technical advisory service, financed by state and local funds, which is offered free to municipalities.

The growth of state supervision has been slow indeed. This is illustrated by the fact that it has taken 65 years for only 21 states to undertake the supervision of municipal accounts. Wyoming, when it entered the Union in 1890, was the first. Seven states began state supervision between 1900 and 1910, three between 1911 and 1920, six between 1931 and 1940, four between 1941 and 1950, and none since 1950.

There has been substantial progress on the state level in about 15 states in modernizing local property tax assessment and bringing about full-value assessments.[51] These efforts have had three main objectives: (1) to provide increased local revenues; (2) to increase local debt limitations that are based upon assessed valuation; and (3) to establish more equitable bases for the return of state-collected taxes or state grants-in-aid. Even in these states, progress towards full-value, equitable assessment has been slow, for state-established market values are usually not accepted for local tax purposes, and local assessing agencies generally remain hostile to general reassessment, especially of rural property.

In North Carolina, the state agency for supervising local finance is the Local Government Commission composed of nine members, five appointed by the governor, and four state officials *ex-officio*.[52] The appointees of the governor hold office at his pleasure. One of these is required to have had some experience as a county commissioner and one as a city official. The executive committee of the commission are the *ex-officio* members and, as the whole commission meets only quarterly, this is a powerful body. There is a director, an assistant director and a small staff.

The commission's powers relate entirely to the financial affairs of all local units. The most important of these is the approval of bonds and tax anticipation notes, the marketing of bonds and notes, and

[51] Eugene A. Myers and Randall S. Stout, "Recent Trends in Property Tax Equalization," *National Tax Journal* (June, 1950), pp. 179–186.

[52] James W. Fesler, "North Carolina's Local Government Commission," *National Municipal Review* (June, 1941), pp. 327–334.

the negotiation of refinancing plans. During the depression there existed a chaotic debt situation in North Carolina local units—in 1933 half of the counties and cities were in a condition of default. There is practically unanimous opinion that the Local Government Commission performed an invaluable service in rehabilitating North Carolina municipal credit. Its efforts have received general approval throughout the state. In this case, a state commission, representing both the state and local units, provided a needed service with the minimum of expense and arbitrary action.

State supervision over local finance has developed most extensively in New Jersey where there is a division of local government in the state department of taxation and finance. Within the division is a local government board which assumes control of a local unit if it defaults on its debt, does not make tax payments due the state, develops a budget deficit, or has an excessive debt or tax delinquency. The regular staff of the division headed by the director administers all laws relating to local finance, offers advice and instruction to local officials, prepares financial statistics, provides a uniform accounting system for local governments, supervises audits for cities, and supervises local accounting and budgeting.[53]

Some states supervise local governments in other fields. In Massachusetts, the state Civil Service Commission has direct charge of merit examinations and general personnel work in all cities; in New York, the state Civil Service Commission renders technical and administrative services to cities on a reimbursable basis, and serves mandatory merit personnel systems in counties. Most states direct the state departments of health to supervise in some degree the work of local health boards and departments. In only a few states has state control over police and fire departments developed but in some, such as Pennsylvania and Texas, state police organizations have taken over the regulation of traffic along state highways, and over law and order in rural areas.

Another hopeful development in the field of state-local relations is the increasing activity of state universities and private institutions of higher learning in rendering technical assistance to local units of

[53] Council of State Governments, *State-Local Relations,* pp. 37–38.

government. Perhaps the outstanding example involving a new kind of arrangement is in Tennessee where the Municipal Technical Advisory Service of the extension services of the University of Tennessee offers free technical services to municipalities for the improvement of their accounting systems and annual financial reports. Likewise, this organization acts as a research arm of the Tennessee Municipal League. The service is supported by state funds and by contributions from the municipal share of state-collected taxes.

There are other states in which the state universities and private colleges are providing, either directly or through leagues of municipalities, services to local units such as in-service training programs, correspondence courses, meetings and conferences on municipal and local problems, research and magazine editing. Among these is Pennsylvania where there are three institutes of local government in three state-aided universities, Pittsburgh, Pennsylvania, and Pennsylvania State, and three colleges, Wilkes, Lafayette, and Franklin and Marshall, which are serving local governments in many ways. Likewise in Colorado, New Jersey, Michigan, Florida, Minnesota, Connecticut, Oregon, South Carolina, South Dakota, Texas, Washington, and other states, such university-local government relationships have blossomed in recent years.[54] This development is particularly helpful in states where league of municipality activity is limited and where state agencies are not active. In truth, the state university is an arm of the state and thus such university activity is, in reality, state-supported and state-inspired.

State supervision over local functions and local agencies cannot always be taken at face value; that is, what the law and the regulations provide is not always carried out. Words and phrases, coined long ago and found in every textbook—*requirements for reports, inspection by central government officials, clearing house for information, technical advice, administrative assistance, direct control*— are like beauty which is as beauty does. For example, financial reports may be received but never examined; and if not received, the penalty may not be imposed. Inspection is often cursory and apolo-

[54] Carl H. Chatters, *Relationships between Universities and Leagues of Municipalities,* American Municipal Association (1954).

getic. A clearing house for information sometimes means a straggling questionnaire or two, the results of which are promptly lost in the files. Technical advice from persons appointed for political reasons, whose former occupation was something far different from the subject of the advice, is not always received gratefully by local officials, and for that matter is not often forced upon them. Some state supervision is competent, but much of it is worthless—a sham and a delusion.

A report from Kansas carries this idea one step further.[55] "While it may be true technically," it concludes, "that the local governments are creatures of the state, in practice local governments are politically potent. Few changes that might affect local governments are made in highway organization in the state when local governments are opposed to the change." Many gestures of conciliation were made to local government as the state highway system was developing in Kansas: financial concessions, abandonment of annual reports from counties, compensation for highways taken over by the state, payment of state secondary road money for federal matching to counties and cities, ignoring state law requiring plans for bridges to be submitted to the state for approval, lack of actual state department power to regulate salaries of county engineers even when law so provides. Although the highway commission is one of the most powerful state agencies in Kansas, it must "tread softly" where local government is concerned.

State interest in local functions has a genuine place in a modern system of state-local relations. But the emphasis should not be on substitute administration and on taking over functions that are naturally local in character. Poor administration of such functions in certain local areas is in itself no good reason for the state to walk in; states themselves have been notoriously poor administrators on many an occasion, as the recent "little Hoover Commission" surveys have shown. In fact, many large cities have more modern administrative practices than most states. They have more merit appointments, more modern organization, and better administered line services.

[55] Government Research Center, *State-Local Relations in Kansas, the State Highway Commission,* University of Kansas (1954), pp. 73–76.

In the majority of states, political appointments are still the rule, administrative practice is fossilized, and departmental organization is confused and complicated.

State agencies dealing with local governments should view themselves as service agencies providing administrative, advisory, or technical services to local officials who cannot get them from any other source. State supervision should strive to maintain the minimum standards of local administration prescribed by the legislature, high levels of local performance, and high personnel standards. It should provide the best available technical aids through programs of in-service training, as a clearing house for information, and as an ever-ready consultant. Most local officials, it must be remembered, are amateurs; many full-time and career employees in local government have had little opportunity to study public administration or the phases of it most closely connected with their work. Generally speaking, state advisory and technical aid is welcomed by local officials—especially when it is competent, cooperative, and non-political, when acceptance of it is voluntary and not mandatory.

State supervision appears to be growing, if somewhat slowly. But in a great many instances when state departments are given supervisory powers over local units and local functions, the legislature does not provide enough money to do the job properly. Appropriations are not sufficient to maintain a competent, qualified staff. As a result, the state agency finds itself always behind in its work and local officials lose faith in the state and develop increased hostility toward state employees. Without question, the present standards of state supervision can stand a great deal of improvement.

How can this be done? First of all, each state should have a department of local government equal in rank to other cabinet departments. In this agency should be concentrated all basic information about local government in the state: personnel, organization, functions, finances, activities, and problems. This information should be made available at a minute's notice by the use of modern filing and classification systems. This department should be the agency to answer all inquiries about local government from any source.

Second, this department should furnish technical and advisory assistance in the field of finance, organization, and procedure through municipal experts visiting local units upon request.

Third, it should carry out legislative requirements relating to local standards. Where highly technical line services are required, the department should act as liaison between such departments as highways, education, health, and welfare. The department of local government should report on all local problems, record results, and follow up where necessary.

Fourth, it should act as a coordinating agency between local governments and the state: arrange meetings of local officials with state officials when mutual problems have to be ironed out, between different classes of local officials, between officials from different geographical sections of the state. It should work closely with leagues of municipalities and associations of local officials.

But such a department must be staffed with qualified persons having training or experience in public administration and local government, recruited through a merit system, adequately paid, and protected from the ravages of politics. Otherwise, a feeling of respect for it on the local level can never be developed. It must be the core of a state-local system of the future. Within it there should be established a commission of local government made up of representatives of the legislature, the state administration, and local government to advise with its staff at periodic meetings, prepare legislation for consideration, and hold hearings on local government problems.

State Financial Aid to Local Units

The forty-eight state governments paid $5 billion out of a total of $13½ billion general expenditures to their local governments in fiscal 1952.[56] This is three times the amount of state intergovernmental expenditures in 1942. However, the total proportion of all state general expenditures represented by intergovernmental payments

[56] Bureau of the Census, *State Payments to Local Governments in 1952*, State and Local Government Special Studies, No. 35, Washington, D. C. (1954).

dropped slightly from 39.1 per cent in 1942 to 36.8 per cent in 1952. Great variations existed in the states: from $5.45 per capita in New Hampshire to $73.67 in California.

The highest ten states, in which 40 per cent or more of general state expenditures in 1952 was intergovernmental, included Alabama, California, Colorado, New York, Wisconsin, Indiana, Kansas, Massachusetts, Michigan, Minnesota, and Ohio—six of which can be classed as midwestern. The lowest ten states, in which twenty per cent or less went for intergovernmental expenditures, were Connecticut, Maine, Montana, Nevada, New Hampshire, New Jersey, Rhode Island, South Dakota, North Dakota, and North Carolina.

The highest eleven states with respect to per capita intergovernmental expenditures in 1952—all $40 or more—included Alabama, Colorado, Kansas, Louisiana, Massachusetts, Michigan, New Mexico, New York, Washington, Wisconsin, and Wyoming. The lowest thirteen—all $20 per capita or less—include Connecticut, Illinois, Kentucky, Maine, Missouri, Montana, New Hampshire, New Jersey, North Carolina, Pennsylvania, Rhode Island, South Dakota, and Vermont.

IMPORTANCE OF GRANTS-IN-AID IN THE REVENUE AND
EXPENDITURES OF THE STATES AND IN THE REVENUES
OF LOCAL GOVERNMENTS
1953

(in millions)

Total general State revenue	$13,429
Total Federal grants to the States	$2,329
Per cent of State revenue from Federal grants	17.3
Total State Expenditures	$15,834
Total State payments to local governments	$5,044
Per cent of State expenditures as grants-in-aid	31.9
Total local revenues	$19,336
Local revenue from State grants	$5,044
Per cent of local revenue from State grants	26.1

Source: Bureau of the Census, *State Government Finance in 1953*.

Generalizations as to regional characteristics from such data must necessarily be vague. Within the past decade the increases in the ratio of intergovernmental expenditures to general state expenditures are to be found almost entirely in the South, the Far West and New England. High ratios of intergovernmental expenditures in 1952 centered in the Middle West, lowest ratios were mainly in the East. States with the highest per capita intergovernmental expenditures tended to be mostly in the Far West and states with the lowest in the East. In the South, the Far West, and New England, therefore, there seems to be the most ferment and extremism as to state intergovernmental expenditures.

The distribution of 1952 state intergovernmental expenditures by functions shows that of the total 50 per cent went for education, 19 per cent for public welfare, 14 per cent for highways, 3 per cent for health and hospitals, and 14 per cent for all other functions.

Of the total 1952 intergovernmental expenditures, 41 per cent went to school districts, 31 per cent to counties, 18 per cent to cities, 2 per cent to townships, and 8 per cent to other classes of local units.

There are two main categories of state aid: shared taxes, which are a portion of state-collected taxes given by state law to local units; and grants-in-aid, which are specified grants of state monies given local units usually but not always for specific purposes. Each state has its own system of sharing state revenues with local units. Distribution of the shared taxes is made on the basis of population, amount of local collections, property valuations or some other arbitrary basis and usually have no regard for need. Grants-in-aid may be distributed on the basis of local matching funds, wealth of the locality, population, or other formulae. Grants now exceed locally shared taxes in volume at least ten times. The present tendency is away from earmarking of specific revenue for particular purposes to broader grants for more inclusive or general purposes. There is also a trend towards equalization between the richer and poorer communities, especially with regard to educational grants.[57]

One of the most progressive systems for grants to local government is that of New York inaugurated in 1946. Briefly, the novel

[57] *Ibid.*, pp. 5–6.

features are these: (1) discontinuance of six state-collected taxes shared with local governments; (2) establishment in their place of annual per capita grants to all classes of municipalities ($6.75 per capita for cities, $3.55 for towns, and $3.00 for villages); (3) tapering off provisions so that the shift from shared-tax to per capita grants will not upset the financial balance in local units; (4) division of the state executive budget and the state general fund into two parts: local assistance and state purposes; (5) establishment of two reserve funds to help stabilize the state's revenues, the money to come from any excess of revenues in one year over a norm determined in advance for state and local expenditures.

This program did not aim to increase state aid, but to enable localities to count upon a fixed amount of money from the state regardless of the cyclical sensitivity of the state's tax system. It was the first state program to provide grants-in-aid for general governmental purposes. It blazed a new trail in financial relations between the state and its local units.[58] In 1952, New York returned $631 million to local units: $357 million to cities, $99 million to counties, $161 million to school districts, and $14 million to towns. The total was $41.99 per capita, of which 44 per cent was for education, 33 per cent for public welfare, 5 per cent for highways, 8 per cent for health and hospitals.[59]

In 1952, California returned to its local units $812 million, of which $384 million went to counties, $332 million to school districts, and $94 million to cities. The total per capita was $73.67, of which 42 per cent was for education, 34 per cent for public welfare, and 10 per cent for highways. The educational grants were on varied bases: daily attendance, an equalization formula, growth of school population, local budgets for salaries, and approved special programs. Highway grants were on the basis of motor vehicle registration, highway mileage, population, and local expenditures. Public welfare grants were allocated on the basis of local funds expended

[58] David M. Blank, "Reform of State-Local Fiscal Relations in New York," I and II, *National Tax Journal* (December, 1950), pp. 326–347; and (March, 1951) pp. 77–91.

[59] Bureau of the Census, *op. cit.*, pp. 48–50.

and the number of recipients of aid. Health grants were on the basis of local expenditures for each program.[60]

In Alabama in 1952, the sum total of $126 million was returned to local units, of which $59 million went to counties and $64 million to school districts, but only $4 million to cities. The total per capita was $41.58, of which 50 per cent went for education, 26 per cent for public welfare, 17 per cent for highways, and 4 per cent for health and hospitals. State funds for education were distributed locally on the basis of an equalization formula, school population, local expenditures, and approved local programs; for highways, on the basis of mileage, county expenditures, and flat rate to counties; for health, on the basis of local expenditures per patient; and general purpose grants, on the basis of local collections and population.[61]

Some observers have noted that there is not always a close connection between financial aid from the state to local units and state supervision of the function thus assisted. Supervision does not always follow the purse in state-local intergovernmental expenditures, often it is at a minimum or does not exist at all. Sometimes, it has actually been encouraged by the local administrators who need technical assistance not locally available. Sometimes, there is supervision when there are no state grants; sometimes, state grants are made without state supervision. There is no strict correlation. For example, the amount of state supervision over local education does not nearly match the millions of dollars pumped into local school districts by the state. State standards are usually the result of legislative influence of interest or occupational groups rather than state administrative agencies.

The Future in State-Local Relations

Americans have little conception of the magnitude, complexity, and significance of the present problems of state-local relations. Newspapers are rarely at ease with the subject, usually emphasizing the needs of certain groups, such as teachers, or of the urban area

[60] Bureau of the Census, *op. cit.*, pp. 16–18.
[61] *Ibid.*, pp. 13–14

which they serve. Legislators lack pertinent facts and figures that bear upon relevant legislation. All too little basic research has been done.[62]

First of all, there are conditions prevalent in American state-local relations that are obstacles to their satisfactory adjustment.

1. Urban population, urban places, and urban interests are inadequately represented in the state legislatures.

2. Progress toward municipal home rule and freedom of local units is painfully slow.

3. State administrative supervision over local units is inclined to be unimaginative and routine at its best, and entirely devoid of competence and understanding at its worst.

4. The opposition to modernization of local government structure and areas has left thousands of units poorly equipped to contend with increased demands especially, but not entirely, in urban industrialized areas.

5. There is a growing and unmistakable centralization of governmental power in the states, with the result that local governments are becoming more restricted, more supervised, and less flexible in their day-by-day work. In some states, notably in the South, local government is withering on the vine and the state is taking complete control.

But there is a brighter side too—indications that improvement is possible, in fact that it has already shown itself in a substantial way:

1. State aid to local units in the form of grants-in-aid or shared taxes is on the increase. Thus, municipalities and local units are strengthened financially with the result that they can carry out local

---

[62] Recent examples of excellent and helpful research in state-local relations are: Commonwealth of Kentucky, *State-City Relations* (1954), and *State-Local Fiscal Relations* (1952), Legislative Research Commission, Frankfort, Kentucky; University of Kansas, *State-Local Relations in Kansas, The State Highway Commission*, Special Report No. 60, prepared by Charles J. Hein, Government Research Center; J. E. Larson and H. J. Shamburger, *Intergovernmental Relations in West Virginia*, Publication No. 4, Bureau of Government Research (University of West Virginia, 1951); Commonwealth of Massachusetts, *Proceedings of the First Governor's Conference on State-County-Municipal Relations*, six pamphlets (1953).

functions which would ultimately be taken over by the state without such aid.

2. Some states have pioneered in the adoption of forward-looking measures, such as the Pennsylvania act giving local governments additional tax revenue sources, the New York plan of per capita grants-in-aid for general purposes, and the New Jersey legislation offering municipalities a number of different optional and modern forms of governmental organization.

3. The quality of municipal administration, through the spread of the council-manager and related forms of government, has been steadily rising. Thus, a strong argument for the state to take over local functions because local government cannot do the job is nullified.

4. There is now a growing awareness of the problems of state-local relations in the states as a result of the impetus given by the Federal Commission on Intergovernmental Relations. And a number of the universities and colleges have been lending assistance to state survey groups through research in this field.

State legislatures must modernize state agencies and procedures in order to develop sound state-local relations. But they must also strengthen local government. Both are doing more work than they ever did before; each needs the other. The state needs to be free from detailed legislative responsibility over local government; the local units need to be free from 19th century restrictions.

To fashion a workable system of state-local relations is not easy. Such a system would have doubtful validity if it were static—for the American governmental scene is dynamic under the hammer of an ever-changing world. Nor would it be useful if it presupposed uniformity throughout the states—for states differ from each other in many characteristics. Finally, it would be worthless altogether if it came merely from the mind of man and not through the experience of men. Nevertheless, it is necessary from time to time to restate, reintegrate and redraft general principles, most of which are already generally known, to guide future developments in the hope that order may finally prevail.

1. The state and its localities are one body politic—they are not

competing entities. Their chief governing body is the state legislature.

2. The state legislature must be made truly representative of the urban-rural composition of the state. Gross inequities must be rectified. This means that the growing urban population should have more adequate representation than exists now in most states.

3. The state legislatures must devolve upon the local units more freedom in organization, powers, and revenue than now exists in most states. This can be done through constitutional home rule, legislative home rule, the prohibition of special legislation in local affairs, optional laws relating to forms of government, or some combination of these appropriate to differing conditions in each state. The ultimate objective should be to give local units broad and discretionary powers in fields that are by nature local, and to free the legislature from the burden of the details of local government.

4. Concurrently, the legislature must accept responsibility for encouraging through permissive legislation the improvement of local government as to form and organization, administrative procedure, size of units, and quality of personnel. In short, it must provide the legal basis for action on the local front to achieve modern and efficient government.

5. The financial strength of the local units must be comparable to the functional load they must carry. When locally raised revenues are not sufficient, the state legislature must work out a system of state grants so as to stabilize local revenues and make them sufficient. These should be given to local units on the basis of need and in accordance with the fiscal capacity of the local unit.

6. State administrative supervision over local governments, where carried on with competence and understanding, with the emphasis upon technical and research assistance rather than upon control, where minimum standards of financial integrity and professional performance are enforced, has proved to be useful and welcome to local governments. Direction of supervision should be concentrated as far as possible in one department of local government with cabinet status. A local government commission representing the legislature, the state administration, and the local governments should

MUNICIPAL HOME RULE IN THE 48 STATES *

State or Territory	Constitutional Home Rule	Legislative Home Rule
Alabama		
Arizona	Cities over 3,500 population Art. XIII, sec. 2, 1912	1912
Arkansas		
California	1879—San Francisco 1887—cities over 10,000 1892—cities over 3,500 Art. XI, sec. 8	
Colorado	Denver charter set down in constitution Art. XX. People authorized to make, alter, or amend their charter or adopt a new one 1902 Cities and towns over 2,000 population 1902 am. 1912 Art. XX, sec. 6	
Connecticut		All cities, towns, and boroughs 1951
Delaware		
Florida		All cities and towns 1915
Georgia		All cities 1947 repealed and superseded 1951 (1951 act declared unconstitutional)
Idaho		
Illinois		
Iowa		Municipalities under special charters may amend and alter them
Indiana		
Kansas		
Kentucky		

* Prepared by Elizabeth Smedley, Institute of Local Government, The Pennsylvania State University.

State or Territory	Constitutional Home Rule	Legislative Home Rule
Louisiana	Baton Rouge (city—parish) 1946 Art. XIV, sec. 3a Shreveport 1948—Art. XIV, sec. 37 New Orleans 1950—Art. XIV, sec. 22 Any Municipality 1952—Art. XIV, sec. 40	
Maine		
Maryland	Baltimore 1915 Art. XI—A All municipalities 1954 Art. XI—E	
Massachusetts		
Michigan	Cities and villages 1908 Art. VIII, sec. 21	Cities over 2,000 population 1909
Minnesota	Cities and villages 1896 Art. IV, sec. 36	
Mississippi		Municipalities under special charters may amend and alter them
Missouri	Cities over 100,000—1875 Cities over 10,000—1920 Art. VI, sec. 19	Cities over 10,000—1946
Montana		
Nebraska	Cities over 5,000—1912 Art. XI, secs. 2–4 Cities over 100,000 may adopt existing charter as home rule charter, thereafter amend it. 1920 Art. XI, sec. 5	
Nevada	Cities and towns Art. VIII, sec. 8 1924	Cities and towns incorporated under general law 1907
New Hampshire		
New Jersey	All municipalities 1947 Art. IV, sec. VII (10)	
New Mexico	City-county combination over 50,000 1949 Art. X, sec. 4	Cities 1917

State or Territory	Constitutional Home Rule	Legislative Home Rule
New York	Cities 1923 Art. IX, sec. 12 Villages 5,000 or more, 1938 Art. IX, sec. 16	Cities 1924
North Carolina		Municipalities 1917
North Dakota		
Ohio	Municipalities 1912 Art. XVIII, sec. 3	
Oklahoma	Cities over 2,000 population 1907 Art. XVIII, sec. 3	
Oregon	Cities and towns, 1906 Art. XI, sec. 2	
Pennsylvania	Cities or cities of any particular class, 1922 Art. XV, sec. 1	Cities of 1st class (Philadelphia) 1949
Rhode Island	Cities and towns 1951, Art. XXVIII	Providence—1939
South Carolina		Cities and towns may amend charter articles of incorporation.
South Dakota		
Tennessee	Municipalities 1953, Art. XI, sec. 9	
Texas	Cities over 5,000 population 1912 Art. XI, sec. 5	1913
Utah	Cities and towns, 1932 Art. XI, sec. 5	
Vermont		
Virginia	Cities and towns, sec. 117c, 1902	
Washington	City 20,000 or more population Art. XI, sec. 10 1889	
West Virginia	Municipalities over 2,000 population Art. VI, sec. 39a, 1937	
Wisconsin	Cities and villages Art. XI, sec. 3 1924	Cities and villages 1925
Wyoming		

advise this department, the legislature, and local governments themselves on broad problems in the field of state-local relations.

TEN SUBJECTS FOR FURTHER STUDY

1. The provisions relating to local government in the constitution of your state.
2. The application of home rule, if any, in your state.
3. Ten judicial decisions by the courts in your state relating to the powers of local government.
4. Judge Dillon and Judge Cooley on local government and the state.
5. Urban and rural representation in your state legislature.
6. Special legislation in Maryland.
7. Classification of local units in New Jersey, Iowa, Florida, Washington, and in your state.
8. Ten judicial decisions by the courts in your state on municipal liability for torts.
9. State administration supervision in your state in the field of health.
10. State centralization in North Carolina.

REFERENCES

Benjamin Baker, "Cities on Their Own," *National Municipal Review*, April 1955, pp. 193–197.

A. C. Breckenridge, "The Mockery of Classification," *National Municipal Review*, November 1947, pp. 571–573.

Bureau of the Census, *State Payments to Local Governments in 1952* (Washington, 1954).

Charleton F. Chute, "How to get a New City Charter," *National Municipal League*, September 1951, pp. 403–410.

Council of State Governments, *State-Local Relations* (Chicago, 1946).

J. F. Dillon, *Commentaries on the Law of Municipal Corporations* (Boston, 1911).

Louis C. Dorweiler, Jr., "Minnesota Farmers Rule Cities," *National Municipal Review*, March 1946, pp. 115–120.

Rowland Egger, "In One Consent," *Public Administration Review*, Autumn 1950, pp. 262–269.

Bayard H. Faulkner, "New Road to Home Rule," *National Municipal Review*, April 1955, pp. 189–192.

Jefferson B. Fordham, *Local Government Law* (New York, 1949).

R. A. Gomez, Intergovernmental Relations in Highways (University of Minnesota, Minneapolis, 1950).

Clarence J. Hein, *State Administrative Supervision of Local Government Functions in Kansas,* University of Kansas (1955).

John P. Keith, "Home Rule—Texas Style," *National Municipal Review,* April 1955, pp. 184–188.

Wylie Kilpatrick, *State Supervision of Local Budgeting,* National Municipal League (New York, 1939).

———, *State Supervision of Local Finance,* Public Administration Service (Chicago, 1941).

David E. Lilienthal, "Big Government Not Inevitable," *National Municipal Review,* February 1947, pp. 65–71.

John H. Marion, "State Supervision in New Jersey over Municipalities in Unsound Financial Condition," *American Political Science Review,* June 1942, pp. 502–508.

H. L. McBain, *The Law and Practice of Municipal Home Rule* (New York, 1916).

Joseph D. McGoldrick, *The Law and Practice of Municipal Home Rule,* Columbia University (New York, 1933).

Dean E. McHenry, "Urban vs. Rural in California," *National Municipal Review,* July 1947, pp. 350–354, 388.

Eugene McQuillin, *The Law of Municipal Corporations,* 3rd Edition, Chicago, 1949.

Rodney L. Mott, *Home Rule for American's Cities,* American Municipal Association (Chicago, 1949).

———, "Strengthening Home Rule," *National Municipal Review,* April 1950, pp. 172–177.

Municipal Finance, May 1947, pp. 12–22, State and Provincial Services to Local Government; contents: "In the Province of Saskatchewan," by Louis Jacobs; "In the State of New Jersey," by Walter R. Darby; "In the Province of Quebec," by Maurice Turgeon; "In the State of Texas," by Stuart A. MacCorkle.

National Municipal Review, 1932. Ten articles on "What Municipal Home Rule Means Today." States covered: California, Minnesota, Michigan, Washington, Missouri, Ohio, Texas, Nebraska, Wisconsin, and New York.

Clark F. Norton, "Home Rule Fight Fails," *National Municipal Review,* May 1955, pp. 242–247.

James E. Pate, "State Supervision of Local Fiscal Officers in Virginia," *American Political Science Review,* November 1931, pp. 1004–1008.

O. W. Phelps, "Personal Liability of Councilmen for Official Acts," *Public Management,* March 1941, pp. 75–80.

M. H. Satterfield, "Counties in a Strait-Jacket," *National Municipal Review,* February 1948, pp. 81–85.

Charles W. Shull, "Reapportionment—A Chronic Problem," *National Municipal Review*, May 1940, p. 305.

Paul W. Wager, "State Centralization in North Carolina," *American Political Science Review*, November 1931, pp. 996–1003.

Harvey Walker, "Let Cities Manage Themselves," *National Municipal Review*, December 1947, pp. 625–630.

Schuyler C. Wallace, *State Administrative Supervision over Cities in the United States*, Columbia University (New York, 1928).

Chapter 5

THE FEDERAL GOVERNMENT AND LOCALITIES

There was a time when the federal government had almost nothing to do with the government of localities. But those days are gone forever. Today the government at Washington has many dealings with the local units, urban and rural. More than a hundred different services are available to local governments; more than forty federal grants-in-aid are channeled into the states and their local units. While the constitutional pattern of the American system has not changed—local government is still almost entirely within the legal jurisdiction of the states—the extra-legal, the informal, the cooperative methods of governmental action have grown to huge proportions. There are valid reasons for this. The two World Wars and the Great Depression had an overwhelming impact on 20th century American life. So great were the problems engendered that the national government was changed in a few decades from one of limited powers to a Great Leviathan. Furthermore, the continued nationalization of business and industry, the progress in transportation and communication, and the emergence of the United States as a world power forced a sometimes reluctant, sometimes aggressive federal government to greater and greater powers and responsibilities. Now that seventy per cent of all the people live in urban areas, the serious and basic problems of modern urban life—not able to be fully solved by the localities and states—call for help from Washington. Undernourished financially, the cities welcome federal assistance for housing, airports, sewage treatment works, work relief projects, civilian defense equipment, slum clearance, and other urban necessities. But rural areas, too, have felt the ever-increasing power of the federal government. School lunches, rural electrification, rural zoning, health projects, child welfare, agricultural extension, and other federally assisted programs impinge directly upon rural life.

The year 1932 can be designated as the turning point in federal-local governmental relations. First mention of the word "municipalities" in a federal statute was made in that year when Congress authorized the Reconstruction Finance Corporation to make loans to cities for self-liquidating public works projects.[1] Later, the Public Works Administration made possible the construction of hundreds of water works, sewage systems, streets, schools, municipal buildings, and local projects by making grants and loans to municipalities. The federal government granted outright thirty per cent of the cost of a project and loaned seventy per cent on approved projects. Thus, employment was stimulated and community development was enhanced. Another federal agency more concerned with immediate reduction of man unemployment was the Works Progress Administration. It employed four million in a vast program of public works in which the federal government furnished the labor and the local units most of the material and equipment.[2] Since the depression, the local government stake in the national government has increased in almost geometric proportions with each passing year. An indication of the trend is the fact that four of the most important national associations of local officials—the American Municipal Association, the United States Conference of Mayors, the National Association of County Officials, and the International Association of Chiefs of Police—maintain their main offices in Washington.

[1] Raymond S. Short, "Municipalities and the Federal Government," *The Annals of the American Academy of Political and Social Sciences* (January, 1940), pp. 44–53.

[2] Clarence C. Ludwig, "Cities and the National Government under the New Deal," *American Political Science Review* (August, 1935), pp. 640–648.

SOME CONSTITUTIONAL AND STATUTORY
RELATIONSHIPS

Local government must operate in conformity with the Constitution of the United States although relatively few of its provisions affect it. The Constitution prohibits states from passing laws "impairing the obligation of contracts."[3] A municipal ordinance or resolution, if it impairs a contract, is a law within the inhibition of the Constitution in this regard.[4] If the states are so prohibited, it stands to reason that they cannot authorize municipalities to impair contracts.

Furthermore, the Fourteenth Amendment provides that no state shall "deprive any person of life, liberty, or property, without due process of law." A municipal corporation such as a city has been adjudged by the courts as a person. Therefore, can a city be entitled to protection against the state from taking its property without due process of law? The courts have held that while a city is without such protection when it is acting as an agent of the state, when it is holding property for its own private purposes as a corporation it is to be regarded as a constituent of the state with the same rights as private persons, and therefore cannot be deprived of property without due process of law.[5] This distinction, one court held, was well founded, but "no exact or full enumeration can be made of the kinds of property which will fall within it, because in different states different kinds of property may be held . . . with different duties and obligations, so that a kind of property in one state might be held strictly for public uses, while in another state it might not be."[6] But it must be emphasized that the power of the state over the rights

---

[3] *Constitution of the United States.* Art. I, section 10.

[4] New Orleans Waterworks Co. *v.* Louisiana, 185 U. S. 336 (1903). But a mere breach of contract by the municipality raises no federal question under the contract clause.

[5] People ex rel. Park Commission *v.* Common Council of Detroit, 28 Michigan 227; New Orleans *v.* New Orleans Water Co., 142 U. S. 79. See also E. B. Schulz, "The Effect of the Contract Clause and the Fourteenth Amendment upon the Power of the States to Control Municipal Corporations," *36 Michigan Law Review,* 385 (1938).

[6] Mount Hope Cemetery *v.* Boston, 158 Massachusetts. 509.

and property of cities held and used for governmental purposes cannot be questioned, nor does the Fourteenth Amendment deprive the state of the power to determine the structure and powers of local government.[7]

Race Segregation in Schools

The provision also found in the Fourteenth Amendment that no state shall "deny to any person within its jurisdiction the equal protection of the law" received momentous significance on May 17, 1954, when the Supreme Court handed down its decision against race segregation in public schools. Lower federal courts had denied relief to plaintiffs who claimed that segregation deprived them of equal protection of the laws under the Fourteenth Amendment. They set forth the doctrine that "separate but equal" school facilities met the constitutional requirements which had been voiced by the Supreme Court in 1896 in regards to transportation facilities. In deciding the school segregation cases, the Supreme Court admitted that there were equal facilities and therefore the sole question was: "Does segregation of children in public schools solely on the basis of race, even though the physical facilities and other 'tangible' factors may be equal, deprive the children of the minority group of equal educational opportunities?" The court decided: "We conclude that in the field of public education the doctrine of 'Separate but Equal' has no place. Separate educational facilities are inherently unequal." This decision radically affects state and local educational organization in the southern states, and it will undoubtedly require some years to adjust to the pronouncement. Many of the seventeen states in which segregation was mandatory by state constitutional law had been making extraordinary efforts to provide Negro pupils with "equal facilities" in the hope that this would be finally acceptable in the eyes of the Supreme Court.

On May 31, 1955, the Supreme Court of the United States unani-

[7] See *Constitution of the United States,* Annotation of Cases Decided by the Supreme Court (1938), p. 775 wherein are mentioned Soliah *v.* Heskin, 222 U. S. 522 (1912), and Trenton *v.* New Jersey, 262 U. S. 182 (1923).

mously ruled to confirm the ban on segregation made in 1954 and ordered that white and Negro pupils be "integrated" throughout the country promptly—but with reasonable regard for the admitted difficulties. "Full implementation of these constitutional principles," the court said, "may require solutions of varied local school problems. School authorities have the primary responsibility for elucidating, assessing, and resolving these problems; courts will have to consider whether the action of the school authorities constitutes good faith implementation of the governing constitutional principles. Because of their proximity to local conditions and the possible need for further hearings, the courts which originally heard these cases can best perform this judicial appraisal. Accordingly, we believe it appropriate to remand the cases to those courts." (The courts that are meant are the United States district courts which had tried the cases originally.) Since the original decision of 1954, some states have already made progress toward integration, while those of the "deep South" stood firm on their traditional antagonism against desegregation. It is the considered opinion of observers that years of court litigation loom ahead before complete solutions will be obtained.

On November 7, 1955, the United States Supreme court in separate unanimous actions affirmed a decision holding racial segregation illegal in public parks and playgrounds and ordered Negroes admitted to public golf courses. This decision swept away whatever remained of the historic "separate but equal" doctrine applied to tax-supported facilities.

Immunity of Federal Property from State and Local Taxation

In a federal system of government, it is essential that one division does not seriously impede the work of another. This danger is apparent when two legally equal partners have the power to tax as in the American system. The question was raised early in the history of national development and decided by the Supreme Court in the case McCullogh *v.* Maryland in which Chief Justice Marshall said:

"That the power to tax involves the power to destroy" is a proposition "not to be denied." From this principle has come the doctrine that instrumentalities of the national government cannot be taxed by the state governments. Thus post offices, national armories, and other federal property are not subject to local real estate taxes. Nor can special assessments for improvements be imposed.[8] Until recently, this condition of affairs was of little consequence. But during World War II and thereafter, the gigantic defense efforts of the national government and the increase of federal property have taken large bites out of the local tax roll and so considerably reduced local revenues in defense areas. Furthermore, the new residents brought in have increased the cost of school, police and fire protection, health services, and local government as a whole. The federal government has sought to mitigate this impact on local units by providing payments in lieu of taxes, grants for community facilities, and other financial assistance but these actions have as yet been sporadic, specific, and temporary. While they were a help to many local governments, they did not provide the permanent adjustment which the changed conditions seem to require.

The United States Congress has given this problem serious consideration in recent years mainly through the Senate committee on governmental operations. Representatives of municipalities appearing before it in 1954 set forth the annual losses which their cities sustained by reason of the withdrawal of real and personal property used in the defense efforts from their tax rolls.[9]

The philosophy behind the proposed legislation to rectify this situation was stated in Senate Bill 2473 of the 83rd Congress as fol-

[8] United States *v.* County of Allegheny, 322 U. S. 174 (1944).

[9] Hearings before the Subcommittee on Legislative Program of the Committee on Governmental Operations, United States Senate, 83rd Congress on S. 2473 and H. R. 505, June 2 and 3, 1954, Washington (1954).

Also see: George Deming, "Tax Free United States Industrial Property a Problem," *National Municipal Review* (February, 1954), pp. 95–96. Losses were reported as follows: Dallas, Texas, $385,161; New Orleans, Louisiana, $225,000; Adrian, Michigan, $87,958; Detroit, Michigan, $257,318; Gary, Indiana, $180,000; San Francisco city and county, California, $3,135,000 and San Diego, California, $2,400,000.

lows: "Although the federal government is under no constitutional obligation to pay taxes or to contribute to the States or local governments any sums in lieu of taxes on account of property owned by the federal government, the Congress declares it as a policy of the United States in carrying out the national program of military security and defense to avoid insofar as feasible the impairment of the finances of State and local governments through acquisition, ownership or use of any defense production facility by the federal government or through requirements for State or local governmental services arising directly from federal ownership or use of any such facility."

Such ameliorative legislation would authorize the same ad valorem tax payments, or administratively determined tax payments reasonably related to ad valorem tax payments, that might be applicable to private property. In other words, municipalities and local units could tax or receive payments from federal property used in defense efforts at about the same rate as they get from ordinarily taxable property. Taxable property would include both real estate and raw materials used in production but not property of the Atomic Energy Commission and national stockpiles of war and defense materials. Thus is reflected the belief that defense production facilities are of national interest and benefit and that property tax costs should be borne by the nation. The committee estimated that the aggregate gross cost of property that might be subject to S. 2473 was $11.5 billion, of which $2.4 billion was in real estate, and $9.1 billion personal property, raw materials, and equipment. At an estimated average rate of 1 per cent, these taxes would cost the federal government from $115 to $127 million in fiscal 1954 if the legislation had gone into effect. While such legislation has not yet been enacted into law, there is no doubt that some measure for the relief of local units ultimately will be forthcoming. In 1948, the Reconstruction Finance Corporation law was amended to allow state and local ad valorem taxation on its real property and to allow local assessments for improvements, and so provided a precedent.[10]

[10] Public Law 548, 80th Congress, 2nd session.

AREA, IN ACRES, OF LANDS IN FEDERAL OWNERSHIP [a]

State	Total Land Area (Acres)	Federal Lands and Per Cent of Total	Federal Government Land (Acres)
Alabama	32,689,920	3.36	1,099,722
Arizona	72,691,200	69.43	50,471,920
Arkansas	33,744,000	8.98	3,031,431
California	100,353,920	45.74	45,900,157
Colorado	66,538,880	37.35	24,851,005
Connecticut	3,135,360	.50	15,714
Delaware	1,265,920	3.21	40,603
District of Columbia	39,040	33.41	13,043
Florida	34,727,680	8.21	2,851,207
Georgia	37,451,520	4.89	1,831,193
Idaho	52,997,120	64.69	34,285,000
Illinois	35,806,080	1.25	448,992
Indiana	23,171,200	1.45	336,952
Iowa	35,831,040	.29	105,310
Kansas	52,552,320	.61	323,118
Kentucky	25,669,760	3.69	946,131
Louisiana	28,913,280	3.64	1,053,161
Maine	19,865,600	.72	143,131
Maryland	6,327,680	3.63	229,392
Massachusetts	5,060,480	1.04	52,671
Michigan	36,494,080	7.42	2,709,428
Minnesota	51,205,760	7.46	3,819,665
Mississippi	30,348,800	4.89	1,484,713
Missouri	44,332,800	3.70	1,641,502
Montana	93,642,240	36.54	34,213,875
Nebraska	49,057,920	1.50	735,224
Nevada	70,273,280	84.71	59,526,959
New Hampshire	5,775,360	11.82	682,600
New Jersey	4,814,080	2.00	96,462
New Mexico	77,767,040	45.62	35,479,713
New York	30,674,560	1.17	358,214
North Carolina	31,450,880	6.13	1,927,562
North Dakota	44,834,560	5.91	2,651,898
Ohio	26,318,080	.98	259,156
Oklahoma	44,341,120	8.78	3,891,209
Oregon	61,664,000	52.72	32,510,870
Pennsylvania	28,828,800	2.05	590,522
Rhode Island	677,120	2.79	18,917
South Carolina	19,580,160	4.66	912,702
South Dakota	48,983,040	17.23	8,610,766
Tennessee	26,855,040	6.13	1,646,281
Texas	168,732,160	1.33	2,246,572
Utah	52,701,440	71.33	37,592,044
Vermont	5,937,920	11.69	694,184
Virginia	25,535,360	8.14	2,078,615
Washington	42,865,280	34.99	14,998,067
West Virginia	15,417,600	8.36	1,289,062
Wisconsin	35,017,600	6.41	2,243,003
Wyoming	62,403,840	51.61	32,207,086
State total	1,905,361,920	23.89	455,146,726

[a] Committee print, Committee on Public Lands, House (81st Cong., 1st sess.), November 15, 1949, serial No. 22.

From Commission on Intergovernmental Relations, *Payments in Lieu of Taxes and Shared Revenues* (June, 1955), p. 177.

In addition to defense activities, projects such as the Tennessee Valley Authority, national forests, conservation areas, and atomic energy commission activities have taken large chunks out of the local tax rolls. In Nevada, 87 per cent of all property is nationally owned, and in five other states over 50 per cent. According to an inventory report filed with the United States Senate committee on appropriations by General Services Administration, real property holdings of the United States, excluding the public domain such as national parks, national forests, other conservation uses and Indian tribal land, represent an acquisition cost of $30.2 billion. This is the sum total of all property acquired since 1789 and still in federal ownership on inventory day, December 31, 1953. The United States owns 455.1 million acres of land (including public domain), about 24 per cent of the nation's continental area (cost $2.2 billion excluding public domain); it owns 428,786 buildings (cost $14.4 billion); it owns $13.6 billion in structures and facilities for utilities, harbor installations, railroads, roads and bridges, and the like. One of the objectives listed in the inventory report include "the return of such properties to the tax rolls of state and local government," indicating that the United States government realizes the importance of federal property withdrawal from local taxes rolls.

A study committee report to the Commission on Intergovernmental Relations made the following recommendations:

1. Congress should not consent to payment of property taxes or any payments in lieu of property taxes (1) on federal property which, if privately owned and used, would by reason of its use be exempt from taxation under state law; (2) on federal property used for services to the local public such as post offices, court houses, airports; (3) on federal office buildings not associated with commercial and industrial activity and such institutions as hospitals, military installations, and prisons; (4) on federal property which shares its revenue with state and local governments; and (5) on stocks of strategic and critical materials, agricultural commodities, and other personal property not incidental to industrial and commercial activities. This immunity should not apply to special assessments.

2. The federal government should consent to nondiscriminatory state and local taxation on (1) properties acquired by the federal government to protect its financial interest in connection with loans and contracts, such payments to continue until the federal government has disposed of such property; (2) properties sold by the federal government under conditional sales contract or leased to taxable persons.

3. The federal government should make payments in lieu of property taxes (1) on commercial and industrial properties, (2) on properties held to serve primarily material or broad regional interests, and (3) rental housing other than low-rent housing. Payments in lieu should be equivalent to the amount of taxes assessable against the property if owned privately.

4. Taxes and payments in lieu of taxes should not be made for properties acquired by the federal government before September 8, 1939.

5. The federal government should consent to payments of special assessments to finance local improvements.[11]

Federal Taxation of Local Salaries

Until 1939, the salaries of state and local public officials and employees were exempt from the payment of federal income taxes. Then Congress included them and the Supreme Court upheld the legislation.[12] In 1943, the state and local governments were made unpaid federal tax collectors of their employees' income taxes by the passage of the income tax withholding plan. On the other hand,

[11] Commission on Intergovernmental Relations, *Payments in Lieu of Taxes and Shared Revenues* (June, 1955), pp. 6–12.

[12] In Graves *v.* New York ex rel. O'Keefe, 306 U. S. 466 (1939), the court said: "The theory, which once won a qualified approval, that a tax on income is legally or economically a tax on its source, is no longer tenable." The only possible immunity, the court continued, could come when and if the economic burden of the tax could be passed on to the national government tantamount to an interference in the performance of its duties. Helvering *v.* Gearhardt, 304 U. S. 405 (1938) in which it was held that salaries of the Port of New York Authority officials were subject to federal taxation was the first break in the precedent.

state and local income taxes can and are levied upon federal employees upon the same principle.

Immunity of Municipal Bonds

Municipal as well as state bonds, both principal and interest, are exempt from federal taxation, and United States government bonds cannot be taxed by the states. There have been some attempts to make the interest from municipal bonds taxable in regards to the federal income tax, but each time Congress considered such a change organized local government in the United States rose as one man and the measure was defeated. Proponents of such taxation claim that local government bonds are given a preference in the bond market and therefore local governments are stimulated to excess expenditures. Another argument is that this immunity allows wealthy persons to invest in municipal bonds just to evade federal taxation. Be that as it may, federal taxation in this case would work a hardship on local government which is already shackled by many limitations and restrictions. It is because of their municipal borrowing power and the attractiveness of the bonds that local governments can carry on activities that their citizens need. To restrict this further would generate more pressure on state and national governments for grants-in-aid or eventually lead them to take over more local functions. As long as statutory exemption exists, the Supreme Court will not deviate from the immunity rule laid down in Pollock *v.* Farmers' Loans and Trust Co., 157 U. S. 429 (1895). The federal government cannot tax the interest on bonds, it held, because it cannot tax the sources, that is, the bonds.

Social Security for Local Officials

By the 1950 amendments, social security under the terms of the old age and survivors insurance provisions of the Federal Social Security Act was extended to public employees not covered by a state or local retirement system. Under Public Law 761 of 1954, eligibility for coverage was provided for members of public retirement systems. Under the 1950 amendments, the only way members of a system could be covered was by dissolving the existing local retirement plan. Several states and many local units took advantage of this, but reestablished the local system to supplement social security benefits. Now it is no longer possible to dissolve the local retirement system for the purpose of substituting social security without the approval of members of the system. The 1954 amendments provide that a state may bring in members of a state or local retirement system, except policemen and firemen, under its old age and survivors insurance agreement if a referendum by secret written ballot is held among the members of a system and if a majority of those eligible to vote in the referendum approve coverage. Because of the special nature of their occupational duties, policemen and firemen who are members of local retirement systems remain ineligible for coverage. However, state legislation is necessary to make it possible for members of the existing retirement systems to participate in federal social security.

The benefits under social security include the *primary insurance benefit* payable beginning at age 65 and the attainment of a fully insured status. This is at the rate of 55 per cent of the first $110 of the average monthly wage, plus 20 per cent of all wages above that amount, up to a total maximum wage of $350 per month. The *minimum primary insurance benefit* is $30 per month, the *maximum* $108.50 per month. The *maximum family benefit,* for there are extra benefits for dependents, is $200 per month or 80 per cent of total monthly wages. *Widow's insurance benefit* is equal to 75 per cent of worker's primary insurance benefit. *Lump sum death benefit* is equal to three times worker's monthly primary insurance benefit, not to exceed $255. The *veterans pensions credit* is a wage credit of $160 a month for each month of World War II service. The *maximum salary measure* is $4,200 a year. The *rate* both for covered employee and employer from 1943 to 1959 is 2 per cent of salary. This rate increases up to 4 per cent for 1975 and thereafter.

Various methods may be used for adjusting a local retirement system with social security. The object of such integration would be to get full retirement benefits from the local system while at the same time taking advantage of the less expensive rate under social security.[13]

Federal Legal Restraints on Political Activity by Public Employees

Public employees, both state and local, who are engaged in work towards which the federal government contributed funds, are forbidden by the Hatch Act of 1939, as amended in 1940, to take part in political campaigns, solicit political contributions, interfere in elections in any number of ways, or disclose the names of any persons receiving public relief. This act, as regards state and local employees was upheld by the United States Supreme Court in 1947.[14] They are allowed, however, activity in local elections where minor officials are elected without party designation and in referenda in which policy matters are decided. Violation of this act on the part of federal officials means removal, but in case of state and local officers lighter penalties may be given.[15]

FEDERAL GRANTS-IN-AID TO LOCALITIES

Total federal grants to states and local units in 1953 reached almost $2.8 billion in 1953; in 1941, they were less than one-fourth that amount. Most of the forty-odd grants are made to the states, which in turn direct a small portion to cities and counties depending upon state arrangements. But some, too, go directly to local governments.

Total grants-in-aid average $17.28 per capita. Income payments per capita in 1952 averaged $1639. Federal grants-in-aid were therefore almost one per cent of income payments, still not a great factor in the national economy. Nevertheless, they are becoming a sizable

[13] Municipal Finance Officers Association, *Coordinating Local Retirement Systems with Federal Social Security,* Special Bulletin 1955A (1955).

[14] State of Oklahoma *v.* United States Civil Service Commission, 91 L. Ed. 537 (1947).

[15] Herbert W. Cornell, "Legal Restraints in Political Activity by Public Employees," *Public Management* (July, 1947), pp. 190–195.

portion of state budgets and constitute a growing element of national expenditure. The largest grants in 1953 were:

For old age assistance	$ 895,500,000	or	$5.61 per capita
For aid to dependent children	332,700,000	or	2.08 per capita
For highway construction	509,500,000	or	3.19 per capita
For unemployment compensation and employment service	195,100,000	or	1.23 per capita
In all others	826,000,000	or	5.17 per capita
Total 1953 [16]	2,758,000,000	or	17.28 per capita

Not all federal grants-in-aid programs vitally concern local government. For example, unemployment compensation and employment security are entirely federal-state in character. But it can safely be said that most of them have some direct or indirect effect. In some cases such as the grants made to combat diseases such as tuberculosis, cancer, venereal, and heart, the money is given to state departments of health but may in turn be given in part to county or city health departments for administration. This is true also of old age assistance, aid to dependent children, aid to the blind, aid to the permanently disabled, aid for maternal and child health, aid to crippled children, and aid for general health facilities. Some grants may be handled entirely on the state level (for example, those for mental health programs and for vocational rehabilitation) but the work done with the money relieves local participation. The regularly established local units are not utilized for some programs. Local offices of state departments of health, welfare, and highways are set up for these purposes. But state law in most cases determines the extent and character of local participation.

It is not the purpose here to examine the entire field of federal grants-in-aid because of the predominance of state interest. Yet so great is their significance to local government that they must be taken into consideration in any study of intergovernmental relations. The avowed purposes of grants-in-aid have been clearly

[16] Basic figures from the *Annual Report of the Secretary of the United States Treasury, 1953,* p. 584.

States ranked by fiscal year 1953 per capita income payments	Fiscal 1953 per capita income payments	Total grant payments (ALL programs) b	Highway construction	Employment security	National school lunch program (cash plus cost of comm.)	School construction and survey
United States	$1,616	$17.19 *	$3.22 *	$1.24 *	$0.82 *	$0.73 *
Delaware	2,256	15.52 36	6.79 10	1.16 21	.59 39	—
Nevada	2,201	51.19 1	27.88 1	2.73 1	.48 44	5.93 1
Connecticut	2,132	10.92 46	1.89 43	1.35 18	.47 46	1.08 17
District of Columbia	2,122	7.88 49	.80 49	.78 42	.33 49	—
New York	2,110	13.04 42	1.64 46	2.00 4	.48 44	.09 40
Illinois	2,038	13.75 40	3.12 32	1.00 29	.65 35	.34 31
New Jersey	2,035	8.84 48	1.89 43	1.78 9	.47 46	.24 33
California	2,008	21.29 18	2.63 38	1.60 12	.58 41	1.17 15
Ohio	1,942	12.47 43	2.69 36	1.02 26	.68 33	.37 30
Michigan	1,916	14.67 37	2.68 37	1.57 15	.60 38	.84 22
Washington	1,846	25.71 12	3.80 24	1.60 12	.80 26	3.44 2
Maryland	1,806	12.37 44	1.64 46	1.24 20	.53 42	2.10 7
Massachusetts	1,792	16.31 35	1.58 48	1.83 7	.61 37	.01 43
Pennsylvania	1,778	10.04 47	1.86 45	1.44 17	.53 42	.16 37
Indiana	1,751	11.81 45	3.25 29	.80 41	.59 39	.40 29
Oregon	1,718	17.85 29	5.60 15	1.45 16	.73 31	.50 27
Rhode Island	1,705	17.27 30	4.65 18	2.03 2	.47 46	.12 38
Wisconsin	1,694	14.51 38	4.51 19	.84 38	.67 34	.01 43
Montana	1,690	30.45 7	12.45 5	1.67 11	.64 36	1.09 16
Wyoming	1,654	32.74 5	16.30 2	1.99 5	.91 19	—
Colorado	1,652	32.85 4	6.72 11	1.06 24	.79 27	1.24 13
Missouri	1,631	23.68 15	3.56 25	.82 40	.83 24	.55 25
Kansas	1,590	21.79 17	6.24 13	.74 45	.81 25	.92 19
New Hampshire	1,586	16.73 33	4.24 22	1.73 10	.84 23	—
Nebraska	1,558	16.64 34	5.37 16	.70 46	.70 32	.18 36
Iowa	1,546	17.25 31	4.50 20	.63 48	.86 22	.21 34
Minnesota	1,524	18.34 27	4.67 17	1.01 27	1.00 15	.09 40
Arizona	1,488	25.96 11	7.23 9	1.82 8	.95 17	2.79 4
Utah	1,484	28.17 9	10.15 7	1.86 6	1.27 10	1.53 11
Texas	1,468	18.84 24	3.39 28	.88 35	.89 21	.93 18
Idaho	1,448	24.89 14	9.17 8	1.59 14	1.09 14	2.23 5
Vermont	1,382	21.06 19	6.39 12	2.02 3	.92 18	.26 32
Maine	1,364	18.09 28	5.62 14	1.10 22	.77 30	.07 42
Florida	1,352	17.02 32	2.08 42	.95 32	.79 27	.88 20
Virginia	1,350	13.17 41	3.25 29	.52 49	.91 19	2.01 9
New Mexico	1,337	30.68 6	11.29 6	1.34 19	1.30 9	3.21 3
Oklahoma	1,310	34.51 3	4.49 21	.93 33	1.23 12	1.28 12
South Dakota	1,296	28.93 8	13.69 4	.78 42	.79 27	.20 35
North Dakota	1,270	27.23 10	13.71 3	1.08 23	.97 16	.12 38
West Virginia	1,245	19.21 22	2.37 40	.70 46	1.14 13	—
Louisiana	1,240	34.94 2	2.76 35	.96 31	1.85 1	.64e 24
Georgia	1,162	23.31 16	3.53 27	.84 38	1.26 11	2.21 6
Tennessee	1,156	19.05 23	3.22 31	.88 35	1.43 6	.85 21
Kentucky	1,146	18.56 25	2.85 34	.78 42	1.33 8	.48 28
South Carolina	1,092	19.40 20	2.97 33	1.03 25	1.60 4	1.91 10
North Carolina	1,078	14.11 39	2.24 41	.88 35	1.42 7	.55 25
Alabama	1,021	18.44 26	2.51 39	.90 34	1.55 5	1.19 14
Arkansas	953	25.30 13	4.09 23	1.01 27	1.66 3	2.05 8
Mississippi	830	19.26 21	3.55 26	.98 30	1.68 2	.66 23

* Rank of States by per capita grant.
  a Per capita data computed by dividing total grants by Census Bureau 1953 estimates found in *Current Population Reports*, Series P-25, No. 110.
  b Total grant payments for all programs, $2,721,902,000.
  c Includes venereal disease control, tuberculosis control, general health assistance, mental health activities, cancer control, and heart disease control.

Maintenance and operation of schools		Public health service [c]		Hospital construction survey and planning		Children's Bureau grant [d]		Old age assistance		Aid to permanently and totally disabled		Aid to dependent children		Aid to the blind		Other grants	
$0.40	*	$0.20	*	$0.67	*	$0.19	*	$5.66	*	$0.37	*	$2.11	*	$0.21	*	$1.37	*
—		.27	15	.57	31	.50	4	1.46	45	.12	31	1.36	37	.25	13	2.45	4
2.48	1	.45	2	.42	38	.86	1	5.40	23	—		—		.04	49	4.52	1
.39	22	.15	42	.36	41	.18	35	2.54	43	—		1.19	44	.05	48	1.27	37
—		.34	5	.49	35	.42	7	1.24	49	.66	13	1.87	26	.12	34	.83	48
.05	45	.14	46	.31	45	.06	49	3.21	40	1.00	4	2.52	17	.14	28	1.40	33
.15	36	.16	37	.64	25	.09	46	4.34	37	.18	29	1.89	25	.18	24	1.01	45
.20	32	.14	46	.62	27	.08	48	1.44	47	.12	31	.63	48	.06	47	1.17	41
1.24	4	.13	49	.33	44	.09	46	9.02	6	—		2.92	8	.39	2	1.19	39
.25	29	.16	37	.59	28	.11	43	4.40	36	.26	25	.95	47	.20	21	.79	49
.13	38	.15	42	.41	39	.15	40	4.62	34	.09	34	2.30	20	.11	38	1.02	44
1.08	6	.15	42	.36	41	.19	33	9.31	5	.87	5	2.33	18	.13	31	1.65	24
.48	19	.20	29	.45	37	.30	21	1.45	46	.49	18	1.52	33	.07	45	1.90	15
.14	37	.15	42	.51	33	.13	42	7.76	10	.62	15	1.75	29	.14	28	1.08	43
.10	40	.16	37	.51	33	.11	43	1.99	44	.27	24	1.77	27	.26	11	.88	46
.18	34	.16	37	1.19	7	.11	43	2.95	41	—		1.18	45	.14	28	.86	47
.25	29	.17	34	.52	32	.18	35	4.75	32	.50	17	1.26	40	.09	43	1.85	17
.67	13	.17	34	.40	40	.26	27	4.24	38	.22	26	2.63	13	.09	43	1.32	36
.06	44	.14	46	.59	28	.19	33	4.46	35	.11	33	1.43	35	.13	31	1.37	34
.39	22	.26	19	.74	16	.50	4	6.22	16	.74	10	2.31	19	.32	6	3.12	3
.35	25	.32	8	1.11	10	.65	2	5.73	19	.64	14	1.31	38	.12	34	3.31	2
1.16	5	.21	26	.36	41	.28	24	15.01	3	1.16	2	2.78	11	.11	38	1.97	14
.20	32	.20	29	.46	36	.18	35	11.39	4	1.13	3	2.57	14	.22	17	1.57	30
1.32	3	.18	32	.65	23	.20	30	6.60	14	.53	16	1.23	42	.11	38	2.26	9
.60	15	.21	26	.16	48	.44	6	4.78	31	.05	36	1.70	30	.22	17	1.76	19
.49	18	.18	32	.67	21	.15	40	4.99	29	—		1.26	40	.20	21	1.75	20
.08	41	.17	34	.63	26	.21	29	6.66	13	—		1.53	32	.21	19	1.56	31
.02	47	.16	37	1.23	5	.20	30	6.32	15	—		1.68	31	.15	26	1.81	18
.84	10	.26	19	.88	13	.20	30	5.75	18	—		2.87	9	.30	8	2.07	11
1.01	8	0.22	24	0.58	30	0.41	9	5.12	25	0.86	7	2.67	12	0.12	34	2.37	7
.62	14	.22	24	.74	16	.18	35	8.35	7	—		1.15	46	.24	14	1.25	38
.40	21	.30	11	.05	49	.33	16	5.04	27	.47	19	1.95	24	.10	42	2.17	10
.12	39	.30	11	.67	21	.64	3	5.47	22	.20	27	1.48	34	.15	26	2.44	5
.36	24	.20	29	.21	47	.30	21	4.80	30	—		2.85	10	.21	19	1.60	28
.34	26	.28	14	.70	20	.18	35	6.73	12	—		2.56	16	.35	4	1.18	40
1.36	2	.21	26	.65	23	.26	27	1.25	48	.31	23	1.20	43	.12	34	1.12	42
.75	11	.27	15	.72	18	.38	12	4.69	33	.87	5	3.97	4	.18	24	1.71	22
1.07	7	.23	23	.31	46	.28	24	16.83	2	.67	12	5.10	2	.44	1	1.65	24
.70	12	.24	22	.81	14	.38	12	6.15	17	.19	28	2.57	14	.11	38	2.32	8
.31	28	.31	9	.71	19	.31	18	5.04	27	.46	20	1.76	28	.07	45	2.38	6
.03	46	.26	19	2.10	1	.33	16	3.85	39	.77	8	5.86	1	.19	23	1.61	27
.07	43	.34	5	1.18	8	.28	24	17.96	1	1.91	1	4.87	3	.26	11	1.86	16
.89	9	.36	3	1.00	11	.31	18	8.08	9	.33	22	2.18	22	.28	10	2.04	13
.08	41	.27	15	1.29	4	.34	15	5.62	20	—		3.15	7	.30	8	1.62	26
.54	16	.29	13	1.72	2	.36	14	5.07	26	—		3.46	5	.24	14	1.44	32
.44	20	.35	4	1.13	9	.29	23	5.33	24	.76	9	1.31	38	.23	16	2.05	12
.17	35	.27	15	1.21	6	.31	18	2.93	42	.44	21	1.98	23	.34	5	1.37	34
.34	26	.33	7	.97	12	.39	11	5.54	21	.72	11	2.27	21	.13	31	1.60	28
.50	17	.31	9	1.67	3	.42	7	8.17	8	.08	35	3.32	6	.32	6	1.70	23
.24	31	.47	1	.75	15	.40	10	6.88	11	.14	30	1.39	36	.38	3	1.74	21

[d] Includes maternal and child health services, services for crippled children and child welfare.
[e] Less than $0.01.
Source: Income payments from Department of Commerce, *Survey of Current Business*, August, 1954. All grant data from the *Annual Report of the Secretary of the Treasury*, 1953, except the school lunch program which is from the Department of Agriculture. From the Commission on Intergovernmental Relations, *Report to the President for Transmittal to the Congress*, pp. 303–304.

stated in a recent United States Senate report.[17] They were: (1) to inspire states and local units to action in fields that are of national interest but within state jurisdictions; (2) to provide financial and administrative support for programs of national interest; (3) to establish parity and equality as between states; and (4) to complement state and local revenues.

The attained objectives, according to the Hoover Commission report on federal-state relations, were: (1) the development of needed standards in many fields; (2) the stimulation of services which some states and local units could not or did not want to supply; (3) the development of a pattern for the division of responsibility between federal, state, and local governments in the administration and support of such functions; (4) the general improvement in state and local administration in the fields receiving assistance.

Weaknesses of the present system are many. Grant programs are largely piecemeal, uncoordinated, and unrelated. The more than forty federal aid programs are administered in many federal and state departments with little or no integration at either level. The legislation in Congress is formulated in various committees, advised and pressured by various interest groups, and supported by various governmental agencies and civic organizations. In the states there is little coordination and sometimes little interest except to get federal money. Federal grants have altered the pattern of state government by requiring money for matching for some activities that has led to neglect of other areas not assisted. They have removed large portions of discretionary power from the hands of state and local officials. In some states the fiscal effect of federal grants has been the relief of state and local financial responsibility. Both state and local governments have exerted less total tax effort because of federal grants. Likewise, although federal statutes have improved administrative practices in fields where aid was given, this effect has not been felt in departments not assisted. There is too much reliance

---

[17] *Intergovernmental Relationships between the United States and the States and Municipalities,* Report of the Subcommittee to Study Intergovernmental Relations, Committee on Expenditures of the Executive Departments, Senate Report No. 94, 82nd Congress, 1st Session (1951).

upon formulae, many of which are not actually significant; and therefore the programs tend to become inelastic and often wasteful.[18]

Some of the grants-in-aid programs are of special importance to local governments and these are herewith briefly discussed.

Civil Defense

The atomic age has made every large urban and industrial concentration a critical target area. Civil defense was organized to decrease vulnerability of such areas and to assist in the procurement, construction, and leasing of equipment, materials, and facilities to be used for civil defense purposes. The federal government pays up to 50 per cent of the cost of such items, and the state and localities match these grants. The allocation of federal funds to each state is on the basis of the urban population of the critical target areas as determined by the Federal Civil Defense Administration. Federal funds cannot be used for state or local personnel and administration expenses, for items of personal equipment, for fire fighting equipment, or for the procurement of land.[19]

State council of defense and local defense councils are responsible for evacuation plans in case of atomic attack, shelter programs, control centers, public information, and the training of civilian personnel. Local civilian agencies in metropolitan areas tend to include programs for the entire areas rather than for the central municipality alone.[20]

Low-Rent Public Housing

The federal low-rent housing program was originally established by the United States Housing Act of 1937 which authorized federal assistance to local communities to remedy unsafe and unsanitary

[18] See John E. Burton, "Grants-in-Aid: Good and Evil," *National Municipal Review* (January, 1950), pp. 11–13.

[19] The Federal Civil Defense Act of 1950 (P. L. 920, 81st Congress).

[20] American Municipal Association, *Status of Civil Defense in America's Largest Cities* (1954).

housing conditions and the acute shortage of decent dwellings for families of low income. This program can be undertaken in any locality which has set up in accordance with state enabling legislation a local housing authority to develop and own public housing projects. These housing projects are financed by the issuance of bonds which are exempt from federal income tax or from funds borrowed from the Public Housing Agency. The Public Housing Agency annual contribution to the local housing authority is equal to the level of debt service on the capital borrowings of the local authority for the project, reduced by the amount by which rents collected exceed current operating costs. In short, the federal government makes up the difference between revenues from rents and the over-all annual cost of the projects, including debt service. Municipalities and local units contribute to the project by exempting housing projects from all local taxation. While the law permits local authorities to make payments in lieu of taxes up to 10 per cent of the shelter rents, it is estimated that local contributions equal about half of the federal contributions.[21] As of December 31, 1952, there were 242,000 families living in low-rent public housing. About 38 per cent were families of veterans and servicemen. The 1954 Housing Act authorized assistance for 35,000 additional units which must be supplemented by slum clearance and urban renewal programs.

Slum Clearance and Urban Renewal

This program has for its purpose assistance to localities in clearing slums and blighted areas, and making them available for redevelopment. By the terms of the Housing Act of 1954, the term "urban renewal" describes the general objective and includes urban redevelopment, rehabilitation, and conservation. Thus it is broader than slum clearance and redevelopment and extends to assistance for

[21] United States Housing Act of 1937 (P. L. 412, 75th Congress), amended by the Housing Act of 1949 (P. L. 171, 81st Congress), and the Housing Act of 1954 (P. L. 560, 83rd Congress).

rehabilitation as well. Redevelopment includes the acquisition of slums in a given area through eminent domain, the clearance of slum structures, the replanning of the area for re-use, and the disposition of the cleared area to private developers who agree to develop in accordance with the community plan.

The emphasis in urban renewal is upon the improvement of the neighborhood and the installation of necessary public improvements such as lights, parks, streets, and playgrounds by the city government. Federal aid comes in the form of reimbursement of two-thirds of the loss on a public project whether it be slum clearance, redevelopment, or urban renewal on the assumption that any project entails a loss in public funds higher than the fair value of the cleared land. The locality makes up the other one-third, unless some state aid is forthcoming.

Localities applying for aid to the Housing and Home Finance Agency must present a workable plan which includes a general plan for the locality, adequate housing and building codes, adequate zoning ordinances, adequate machinery for enforcing the codes, a relocation program for those displaced, and a plan for eliminating or rehabilitating blighted areas. Local housing and redevelopment authorities, established and appointed by the local governments carry on the urban renewal projects, but it has been stated that municipalities themselves usually have the necessary authority and do not need new agencies and powers.[22]

Grants for Streets and Roads

Federal grants to states for highway purposes began in 1916 and have steadily increased since then. The present program is based upon the Federal Aid Highway Act of 1944 as amended by each succeeding Congress. It authorizes aid for four federal-aid road systems: (1) the primary system of major through highways;

---

[22] The Housing Act of 1954 was approved August 2, 1954, P. L. 560, 83rd Congress. See also William L. Slayton, "The States and Urban Renewal," *State Government* (October, 1954), pp. 203–204.

(2) the secondary system of feeder roads; (3) the urban system of arterial city streets; and (4) the interstate system, designating routes connecting metropolitan areas. Federal grants are made to state highway departments for fifty per cent of approved projects. The matching must be made within two years of the fiscal year of allocation but the money can be used at any time. The Bureau of Public Roads in the Department of Commerce administers this program. The objectives of the federal aid legislation are summarized as follows:

(1) to establish the pattern for a long range public highway program designed for national defense and to serve four major kinds of traffic: interstate, intercity or intrastate, rural-farm-to-market, and interurban;

(2) to recognize the state highway department as the exclusive legal representative of the state;

(3) to provide a more comprehensive rural road program;

(4) to assure continuous improvement of the road system by an annual program of projects;

(5) to designate "urban areas" predicated upon the characteristic urban quality of traffic which overflows municipal boundaries into suburban communities and to plan and develop arterial highways to serve such areas.

The Federal Aid Highway Act of 1954 was the biggest highway authorization bill up to that time in the nation's history. It increased the fiscal 1956 and 1957 money available for the federal-aid highway program from $550 million to $966 million. Federal contributions for urban road projects total $175 million a year on the national system of interstate highways "including extensions thereof through urban areas." The formula for distribution of the $966 million for each of the two years is 45 per cent for the federal aid primary system, 30 per cent for the federal aid secondary system, and 25 per cent for the federal aid urban system. Federal funds for the urban system may be used only on federal aid system roads in urban areas. Allocations for the secondary system may be spent in municipalities under 5,000 population not in urban areas and on urban projects in states with a density of 200 or more people per square mile. Federal funds are not to be used for maintenance or for toll roads.[23]

On January 27, 1955, President Eisenhower submitted to Congress "the grand plan" for improving the nation's highways for the period ending in 1965. Calling attention to the backlog of needs, anticipating population growth and increased density of population, citing the continuous increase in the number of motor vehicles and the tragic toll of traffic accidents, the President outlined a plan which would go a long way in overcoming the major deficiencies. A safe and efficient highway network, he declared, was essential to the economy, and to military and civil defense.[24] While this plan, involving a ten-year federal-state expenditure of $101 billion was not adopted by Congress, there is no doubt that some "big" national highway program will come into being in the near future. There is too much at stake in this atomic, motorized, industrial age to be satisfied with our highway system as it is now.

Airport Construction

The purpose of federal aid for airport construction is to develop a national airport system to serve both commercial and noncommercial aviation. The program started with a billion dollar, post-war airport construction program. The Federal Airport Act of 1946 authorized federal appropriations to aggregate $500 million to be matched locally. The program was to be extended until 1958. The National Civil Aeronautics Commission prepares a national program, indicating the projects deemed necessary and their geographic location. Grants are made only for projects listed in the plan and those in conformity with CAA regulations. Seventy-five per cent of the appropriations are allocated to states on the basis of population and area, the rest at the discretion of the administrators of the plan. Many of the airports aided are under the control of an "authority"

---

[23] The American Municipal Association, *The Federal Aid Highway Act of 1954,* Publication BJQ (1954).

[24] American Municipal Association, *A Ten-Year National Highway Program,* Special Information Bulletin (January 11, 1955).

having jurisdiction over a large metropolitan area, but municipalities, large and small, are eligible for these grants.

Federal Aid to Local Schools

Defense industrial and atomic production radically changed the population statistics in many communities—sometimes in a very short time. New plants sprang up overnight. Established plants were expanded to take care of government contracts. Workers and their families moved into the community and school population mushroomed. In order to assist such communities the federal government has granted funds for the purpose of school construction and school operation in "federally affected areas." Payments are authorized directly to local school districts where children live on federal property, where their parents are employed on federal property, and where the increased attendance results from activities of the United States whether carried on directly or through a contractor.[25]

Vocational education has been an object of extensive federal aid since 1917. Beginning with the Smith-Hughes Act of that year, grants for public school vocational courses have been provided in the fields of agriculture, home economics, trade and industry, and distributive occupations. Federal funds are used almost exclusively for salary and travel of teachers. The federal grant must be matched dollar for dollar, either by state or local funds. The federal agency administering the program is the Office of Education in the Department of Health, Education and Welfare.[26]

Since 1947, a national school lunch program has been in operation under the administration of the Department of Agriculture. Emergency agencies began to assist community school lunches in 1933; surplus food donations were initiated by the Department of Agriculture in 1935. The federal dollar must be matched by one dollar

[25] Financial aid for school construction, P. L. 815, 81st Congress; P. L. 246, 83rd Congress; P. L. 357, 83rd Congress.
Financial aid for school operation, P. L. 874, 81st Congress; as amended by P. L. 11, P. L. 170, and P. L. 248, 83rd Congress.
[26] Present acts in force are the Smith-Hughes Act of 1917 (P. L. 347, 64th Congress), and the Smith-Barden Act of 1946 (P. L. 586, 79th Congress).

and a half of local funds until 1955, by three dollars of local funds beginning in 1956. More than a half a million children are now served daily. This program provides the main outlet for surplus commodities purchased by the federal government to support farm prices.[27]

On February 8, 1955, President Eisenhower sent a message to Congress with a program for federal aid to education. He cited the fact that there was a deficit of more than 300,000 classrooms, "a legacy—in part—of the years of war and defense mobilization when construction had to be curtailed." Furthermore to keep up with mounting enrollments, the nation had to build at least 50,000 new classrooms a year and, still in addition, had to replace a large number that had become obsolete. The President said that fundamentally this was a job for the states and communities, but that the present emergency required quick and effective action. The President therefore recommended a program which would authorize the federal government, cooperating with the states, to purchase school bonds issued by local units which are handicapped selling their bonds at a reasonable rate of interest. The amount suggested to be made available for this purpose was $750,000,000 over a period of three years. A second recommendation was that the federal government should share with the states in establishing for state school building agencies a reserve fund equal to one year's payment on principal and interest. The state school building agency would issue its bonds through customary agencies, then build schools to lease to local school districts. Rentals would be sufficient to pay for the debt service. The President recommended federal participation to the point where $6 billion worth of new buildings could be built in the next three years. A third recommendation was for the payment of direct grants-in-aid by the federal government where tax and debt limits are so low as to make it impossible for the local school district to build the schools it needs. The sum of $200,000,000 was recommended for that part of the program. Finally, he recommended federal aid for state conferences on education.

While the amount of money recommended for these purposes is

[27] The National School Lunch Program Act (P. L. 396, 79th Congress, 1946).

small in comparison to the estimated need, the President's action constitutes a milestone in the development of federal aid for education. For many years, the question of federal participation in the education function has been debated but it appears that federal participation will increase rather than decrease.[28]

Grants for Hospitals

In 1946, the Hill-Burton Act authorized a comprehensive and national program for the construction of public health facilities, based upon an exhaustive survey in each state. Since then about half a billion dollars have been appropriated. At first state and local matching had to be at the rate of two dollars to one, but later this proportion was liberalized up to two-thirds of the cost to be paid for by federal funds depending upon standards set up by the Public Health Service which administers the program. The amounts allocated to each state are based upon population and per capita income.

Grants for Water Pollution Control

Under the Federal Water Pollution Control Act of 1948, the Public Health Service has been authorized to conduct surveys and research relating to the prevention and control of water pollution caused by industrial wastes. The health and economic well-being of every community depends upon adequate water supply. Water requirements of municipal areas have steadily increased because of increase of population while at the same time the amount of water suitable for municipal use has been decreasing as a result of pollution of streams from wastes discharged from city sewers and from factories.

Municipalities and industries have a major stake in our water resources and both are vitally interested in pollution abatement. However, construction of treatment facilities by municipalities and industries has not proceeded at a sufficiently rapid rate to keep pace with the growing pollution problem.

Construction of sewage treatment plants has lagged, due partly

[28] *New York Times* (February 9, 1955), p. 20.

to financing difficulties and partly to the fact that in comparison with other public facilities and services competing for municipal funds the direct benefits to the taxpayer are less readily apparent. The strictly limited tax resources and debt capacity of municipalities will not finance the required sewage disposal facilities, the need for which is estimated to exceed $3 billion in cost.

Some industries have been slow to approve the substantial capital outlays required for plant facilities which are not only usually non-productive, but in most states are subject to state and local tax. Failure of industry to construct such facilities might eventually require restriction of industrial production.

Passage of the federal Water Pollution Control Act in 1948 indicated that the federal government too has an interest in the pollution problem because of its jurisdiction over the nation's waterways and because of the benefits of pollution abatement to the public health. The act establishes the policy of federal responsibility for research and technical services, financial assistance to states and municipalities, and enforcement of interstate pollution controls.

Research being conducted under the authorization of the federal act is developing new knowledge which will aid municipalities in the more effective and efficient construction of treatment plants and in providing better and cheaper methods of treatment. This may ultimately result in great savings to the public.

Recommendations of the Commission on Intergovermental Relations

The importance of grants-in-aid, in fact of all intergovernmental relations, led to the establishment of the Commission on Inter-governmental Relations by President Eisenhower in September, 1953. After a year and a half of broad and detailed study, it presented a full and voluminous report.[29] The main conclusions are here summarized:

1. Leave to private initiative all the functions that citizens can

[29] The Commission on Intergovernmental Relations, A Report to the President for Transmittal to the Congress (June, 1955).

perform privately; use the level of government closest to the community for all public functions it can handle; utilize cooperative intergovernmental arrangements where appropriate to attain economic performance and popular approval; reserve national action for residual participation where state and local governments are not fully adequate, and for the continuing responsibilities that only the national government can undertake (p. 6).

2. Explore the possibilities of distributing surplus agricultural commodities through commercial rather than governmental channels (p. 164). (Local governments are concerned in this phase of federal grants in that surplus commodities are used in school lunches and are given to counties and other local units for their welfare institutions.)

3. Federal aid for airport construction should be continued on the present basis of national-state-local cost sharing (p. 170); and the present system of apportioning 75 per cent of federal aid among the states on the basis of area and population and distributing the remaining 25 per cent through the Civil Aeronautics Administrator's discretionary fund should be continued (p. 172).

4. Congress should amend the Federal Civil Defense Act to reallocate responsibility for civil defense from a primary state and local responsibility to a responsibility of the national government, with states and localities retaining an important supporting role; and to provide that the national government will be responsible for over-all planning and direction of the civil defense effort, development of civil defense policies and technical doctrine, and the stimulation of interstate cooperation; and that states and localities will be responsible for day-by-day planning operations and for the adaptation of national policies and doctrines to local situations (p. 180). Congress should liberalize the financial participation of the national government in state and critical target area civil defense costs (p. 182). The present practice of conducting civil defense relationships mainly from the national government through the states should be modified to allow direct relations between the national government and critical target cities and their support areas (p. 183). Federal agencies should obtain direct participation of state and local gov-

ernments in national planning aimed at reducing the vulnerability of our cities (pp. 183–184).

5. The accomplishments of the school lunch program are recognized and it is recommended that states take action to expand the program to include many schools and school children presently unable to participate. Federal assistance in the form of commodity donations should be continued as long as these stocks are held as surplus by the national government, but there should be a reduction and elimination of cash grants after a reasonable period of time, with the assumption by states, localities, and parents of full responsibility for the cash financing required (pp. 188–189).

6. Grants for school construction and operation in federally affected areas for such time as the need exists should be continued (p. 190).

7. Federal grants for vocational education should be made only in relation to subjects vested with a clear and special national interest (p. 191).

8. The responsibility for providing general public education should continue to rest squarely upon the states and their political subdivisions. A general program of federal aid to elementary and secondary education is not recommended. However, where financial need is clear, the national government might assist the states temporarily in providing school facilities but to avoid interference by the national government in educational processes or programs (p. 194).

9. The present federal-aid highway program should be continued and funds appropriated therefore should be increased and so allocated to give recognition to the national responsibility for highways of major importance to the national security, including special needs for civil defense, and to provide for accelerated improvement of highways in order to insure a balanced program to serve the needs of our expanding economy (p. 216). The expanded program should be financed substantially on a pay-as-you-go basis from increased motor fuel taxes (p. 219). Federal supervision accompanying highway grants-in-aid should be reduced (p. 219). Legislative provisions in the Hayden-Cartwright Act requiring the states to expend certain

amounts of specific taxes for highway purposes should be repealed (p. 220).

10. Responsibility for the initiation and administration of public housing, slum clearance, and urban renewal programs should rest with the states and local governments. States should supply guidance, and localities should take positive action to develop over-all city and metropolitan area plans; to adopt and administer local housing codes, and zoning, building, and planning regulations; and to coordinate neighborhood conservation plans. The states should assume increased responsibility for meeting housing needs which are beyond the combined resources of private initiative and the local units of government. Specifically, states should lend financial, technical, and professional assistance to localities on the basis of need; pass enabling legislation to encourage subdivisions to adopt by reference modern and uniform building, housing, and sanitary codes; to provide for the establishment of metropolitan planning agencies to assist in redefining city limits and in providing for the integrated design of new suburban areas; and to assume responsibility for the working out of interstate compacts where necessary with assistance and leadership from the national government where required (p. 227). The national government should continue, with certain modifications, technical and financial assistance to state and local governments for slum clearance and urban renewal, metropolitan area planning, and low-rent public housing (p. 228). Congress should provide that national technical and financial aid be administered on a state basis where the state establishes by law comprehensive programs of public housing and slum clearance including significant state aid (p. 228). National financial participation in the public housing program should continue to be in the form of annual contributions rather than one-time capital grants (p. 229). States and municipalities should give increased attention to unifying their community services through the creation of metropolitan planning authorities to deal with problems related to urban affairs; and the states should provide technical, professional, and financial assistance where the locality is unable to meet its own needs. The national government should provide leadership through research on

community design and layout and the dissemination of information of methods for achieving improvement in local planning. The federal 50–50 matching grants to states and municipalities for metropolitan area planning should be continued (pp. 231–232). In planning future slum clearance and public housing projects, all levels of government should give serious attention to the problem of urban decentralization for defense (p. 232).

11. Federal financial assistance for disaster relief should be extended to any state and its local governments only after the state has qualified for aid by passing legislation obligating itself and the local units to pay a proportionate share from state and local funds (p. 235).

12. Federal grants-in-aid to states for general health purposes and for specific categories should be continued for the purpose of encouraging improved measures for controlling diseases and the demonstration of new public health methods, but they should be tapered off and not continued indefinitely. Such grants should be aimed to support a national pattern of minimal standards of public health. Health grants should be allocated to states on the basis of a uniform formula, susceptible of flexible administration (pp. 251–252). Grants and loans for the construction of hospitals and other health facilities should be continued but state needs and the suitability of standards should be kept under continuing review (p. 252). Additional funds should be made available for research in the health sciences, but such research should be decentralized as far as possible to institutions and states equipped to do the research (pp. 253–254). Grants-in-aid funds should be continued to be used for in-service and graduate training of public health personnel of the state and local units (p. 254).

13. General assistance should continue to be financed by states and local units (p. 270). National contributions for old-age assistance should be decreased as total expenditures for such assistance are reduced (p. 271). Aid to dependent children, aid to the blind, aid to the permanently and totally disabled, and child welfare services should be continued, and federal funds should be made available for the support of needy children receiving foster care.

THE BROADENING SCOPE OF FEDERAL POLICY

The ever-broadening scope of federal policy, and therefore of federal activities, is not an isolated phenomenon of American life; it is an integral part of the change in the institutional fabric of the nation. The trend is toward nationalization—in the economy, in the government, and in society in general. The trend is also toward centralization of governmental power on the part of the national government, and of authority in the hands of the president, and of administrative activity by the executive departments and agencies. These trends have deep significance for local government, both urban and rural. In rural fields, the national government has from the very beginnings of national existence taken an active part; the majorities in both houses of Congress have reflected the 19th century ruralness of the nation. Only recently, however, has the national government brought its power to bear on the solution of urban problems and all signs point to increased national interest in the welfare of the urban majority of our population. Since the depression, many large cities have dealt directly with agencies of the national government rather than through state departments and this is bound to continue. As a result, the future may see on an informal, extra-legal basis not two entities (the national and state governments) but three units (the nation, the states, and the cities) in our American system of government. The constitutional and traditional relationships will be changed under the hammer of 20th century reality.

Federal Policy and Rural Local Government

Federal policy and activity have affected the people who live in rural areas from the very beginning of our national existence. All through the 19th century, the United States was a rural nation and therefore a great deal of our national interests in internal affairs was directed to the welfare of rural folk. In spite of the predominance of urban dwellers in the 20th century, the fact that each state has equality in the United States Senate has given rural areas much greater influence in molding national policy than their numbers and their comparatively advantageous conditions seemed to warrant. But one result of national activity in rural areas has been to retard the activities and the self-sufficiency of rural self-government. In most states, rural government—what there is of it—is no match for the federal and state governments in power, revenues, and administrative competence. Rural local government today has lost to a great extent whatever vigor it once had. The farmer and the nonfarm rural dweller look to the national and state governments for assistance, advice, and help—not to local government.

One of the more significant federal-local relations has been the federal land grant policy stemming from the Northwest Ordinance of 1785 in which was provided that section 16 of each township comprising 640 acres of land in the national domain should be set aside for maintenance of the public schools. From the national domain, contained in twenty-nine states, more than 77 million acres were granted to states for public school purposes.[30] This early federal policy has had a far-reaching effect on the scope and quality of rural education, especially in the middle western and western states, not only at the elementary and secondary levels but also in the work of the state colleges and universities in agriculture and related fields. The eastern and southern states in which there was little national domain from which revenues could be derived did not enjoy this advantage. Even today in such states as Minnesota where the constitution declares that land grants shall remain a "perpetual school fund" and the principal from such sales has not been disbursed but the income from the fund is available for schools on the basis of school population, the results of this policy are still being felt.

Another far-reaching federal policy was the establishment in 1933 by Congress of the Tennessee Valley Authority which covers seven south central states. This agency has undertaken a great regional improvement program that embraces planning, flood control,

[30] Robert L. Morlan, "Intergovernmental Relations in Education," *Intergovernmental Relations in the United States as Observed in the State of Minnesota,* University of Minnesota (1952), pp. 70–71.

irrigation, water supply, and power production. TVA has many relations with local governments in the area. It sells its power at wholesale price to cities and cooperatives which in turn sell to consumers. Ninety-two municipalities distribute power to 670,000 users. TVA cooperates in furnishing many other services to the local units: library service, health services, planning assistance, and flood control. A one-time commissioner, David E. Lilienthal, summing up the federal-local relationships in the TVA area for the first ten years of its existence, said: "It is notably true that local community government and functions are more vigorous. I know of no other place in the United States of which this can be said with equal basis of performance." [31]

Other examples of federal activity affecting rural life and government are: the Rural Electrification Act of 1936 which encourages rural electrification by local units, cooperatives, and private companies; the Soil Conservation and Domestic Allotment Act of 1936 whereby new voluntary local units of government—soil conservation districts—are established by a majority vote of those occupying land in the district; federal stimulation of rural zoning by local units; the Federal Real Estate Board of 1939 whereby loans to pay delinquent taxes on land were made available; the land grant colleges, agricultural extension service, and agricultural experiment stations which for many decades have pointed the way to improvement of agriculture and farm life in all its phases.

Many aspects of the Social Security Act of 1935 bring the federal government directly into rural areas: for example, through the United States Public Health Service which cooperates with local units in building up local public health programs; and the administration of funds for old age assistance, for the blind, for dependent children, and for the permanently disabled. The federal aid highway program of 1944 provided that thirty per cent of federal aid funds should go to the states for the improvement of secondary feeder roads. [32]

[31] David E. Lilienthal, *TVA—Democracy on the March* (1944), pp. 125–126.
[32] See Lane Lancaster, *Government in Rural America* (1952), pp. 1–20, 216, 275–281, 299–303.

Federal Policy to Improve Local Administration

The list of services rendered by federal agencies that help local government to do a better administrative job is long and still growing. They are furnished usually without charge to local governments and the public in general by a variety of federal agencies such as the Bureau of the Census, the Office of Education, the Federal Bureau of Investigation, the United States Public Health Service, the Housing and Home Finance Agency, the Bureau of Public Roads, the Federal Bureau of Public Assistance, and many others. These services include the collection and dissemination of information, long term research projects, the development of administrative and technical standards, the preparation of model laws and ordinances, demonstration projects, loan of personnel, inspection and field work, conferences with state and local officials, in-service training courses, loans and grants for planning, and many other devices that can help local officials. They have grown up as ancillary to the main functions of such agencies but as the work expanded local government was included in its orbit. These services indicate the growing field of cooperation between federal, state, and local levels that at its best makes for better government throughout the whole American system. At its worst, it can lead to greater and greater federal dominance to the end that local units take a minor role even in functions that are local in character. It is not so much that federal agencies want to be dominant, it is that by providing more and more services, local action is atrophied.[33]

The Federal Policy on Organized Crime

Until recently, the administration of criminal justice was almost entirely a state and local responsibility. This was not one of the functions delegated by the Constitution to the national government, so legally it came under the jurisdiction of the states. There were national enforcement agencies but they were concerned only with

[33] See *Urban Government,* Vol. 1 of the Supplementary Report of the Urbanism Committee to the National Resources Board (1939).

violations of special federal laws covering such crimes as smuggling, counterfeiting, and the infraction of postal laws. The great expansion of national functions naturally caused comparable expansion of its law enforcement powers and machinery. But over and above this, there have been important extensions of federal jurisdiction over general criminal offenses which aim at the control of crime itself. Congress derives such powers from its constitutional authority to control interstate commerce, to establish a postal system, and to collect taxes. Examples of such extended jurisdictions include the White Slave (Mann) Act of 1910, the Motor Vehicle Theft Act of 1919, the Kidnapping Law of 1932, the Stolen Property Act of 1934, the Fugitive Act against persons traveling interstate to avoid prosecution, and the National Firearms Act. Recent legislation against racketeering, communism, international spies and subversives, combined with its power to protect its great accession of properties in the defense effort, has enlarged the federal jurisdiction to impressive proportions. No longer can it be said that the enforcement of criminal justice is "almost entirely a state and local responsibility."

But the story does not end there. Congress has realized for several decades the need for national leadership to fight crime in all its phases. It not only established the Federal Bureau of Investigation in the Department of Justice but also gave to it all federal enforcement powers except those specifically delegated to some other federal agency. It also appropriated money to it so that it could develop into the great law enforcement agency that it now is. As it evolved to its present status, it took upon itself the leadership of all law enforcement units—federal, state and local—in the fight against organized crime in the United States. It made available its extensive informational, identification, technical, and expert facilities and personnel to state and local police departments by means of news releases, manuals, uniform crime reports and statistics, demonstrations, identification services, in-service training, research into crime, scientific analysis of evidence, loan of personnel, and numerous other means. It is perhaps no exaggeration to say that the FBI has become the best equipped, best manned, and best organized law enforcement agency in the world today. The G-men have become not only a legend in the crusade against crime, but they have been molded into a well trained, resourceful, and dedicated staff second to none.

Organized crime has become so deeply embedded in our life and institutions that national interest is definitely involved. The famous Senate committee of 1951, known as the Kefauver Committee, the hearings of which were televised brought to the American people as nothing had ever done before the enormity of organized crime and its undermining effects on American life.[34] The committee concluded the federal government does not have the responsibility for widespread gambling, for vice conditions, for citizens who influence the governments of the large cities to protect crime through political activity—these are state and local. It pointed out that their task was to control the crime wave and suggested ways to accomplish this: (1) Each state should create a statewide committee to investigate organized crime; (2) there should be grand jury investigations in places where there was open gambling and racketeering; (3) a survey of enforcement agencies should be made to achieve better integration; (4) racket squads should be organized; (5) criminal laws should be analyzed so that they could be strengthened; (6) licenses of places doing business in which gambling is practiced should be revoked; and (7) citizen crime committees should be organized.

The committee was especially impressed by the failure of local enforcement agencies to work together. This seemed to be most important in metropolitan areas where sometimes hundreds of departments operate independently of each other. The states have no centralized direction of crime fighting efforts. Therefore, because crime has national manifestations, the federal government must take a leading part in attempting to develop a unified and nationwide program to combat crime. Congress, the Department of Justice, the Federal Bureau of Investigation can supply the techniques of coor-

[34] *Third Interim Report of the Special Committee to Investigate Organized Crime in Interstate Commerce,* United States Senate Report 307, 82nd Congress, First Session, 1951. For pertinent excerpts, see *National Municipal Review* (July, 1951), pp. 354–358.

dination, and the "know-how" in ever-increasing ratio. The states and local units can carry the burden of the campaign in every locality of the nation.

Crime in its present stage within the United States shows a number of characteristics entirely new. It is a gang activity, loosely but effectively organized. The gangsters hold human life cheap, and play ruthlessly for big stakes. They are often better equipped than the local enforcement officers, they are swift to strike and to get away. Their operations are interstate, sometimes international. The reasons for the American gangster are complex, a combination of factors including the existence of great cities, large quantities of personal and liquid wealth, modern means of transportation, corrupt politics in some places, and decentralized crime administration.[35] As urbanism continues to absorb the nation, crime will continue to increase unless a modern, hard-hitting, unified, and large-scale attack is made upon it. The national government has already assumed the leadership, the states and local units are bound to follow.

Federal Policy on Metropolitan Areas

The metropolitan area is fast becoming the most significant urban unit as far as federal relations are concerned. Professor Daniel R. Grant (Vanderbilt University) has called attention to the fact that the federal government has already recognized the metropolitan area in a number of fields: the census, federal aid for advanced planning of public works, low rent housing, slum clearance, urban redevelopment, aid for urban streets and highways, airports, investigation of organized crime, and studies on the dispersion of industry to protect against atomic attack and to utilize atomic energy in the future. He further states that 23 of the 168 standard metropolitan areas cross state lines and thereby can be considered interstate communities; that 28 more border state lines; and that 43 million people live in these 51 standard metropolitan areas that have interstate

[35] Arthur C. Millspaugh, *Crime Control by the National Government,* The Brookings Institution (1937), pp. 8–9.

and therefore national significance. Professor Grant believes that the next step would be that all federal agencies uniformly recognize metropolitan areas in dealing with urban problems.[36]

What will be the effect of such a step on the development of municipal government? First, municipal authorities for metropolitan areas will be created and will be slanted towards making themselves available for federal loans or grants. Of course, such authorities have been in existence for years—housing and airport authorities are the most numerous. A good example, Pittsburgh's Urban Redevelopment Authority, which has never used tax monies, has paid off its original debt, has eighteen years of assured income for the future, and has been responsible for the investment of $100 million of private capital in the Pittsburgh area.

It may be also possible to establish *ad hoc* agencies such as urban street and highway authorities eligible to receive the federal aid available for urban streets and highways, civilian defense and defense planning authorities, and even public industrial development authorities which would work on the use of atomic power in urban areas. Under the influence of federal interest in urban areas progress is bound to be made towards achieving a workable metropolitan government no matter how deeply one feels about local autonomy and home rule. Many urban problems are already considered to be of national interest.

If the metropolitan area is to be recognized what about its government? Shall it be the municipal authority for special single purposes, for multi-utility purposes, for all purposes? Or shall it be a metropolitan federation of local units with specific powers granted to it by action of the governing bodies of the participating local units. There is no one answer at hand now. Each metropolitan area must develop as it can and out of further experience there will surely develop better guides than are now available. Much will depend upon the urgency of the problems, the financial condition of the local units, the kind of leadership for progressive changes that each area has.

[36] Daniel R. Grant, "Federal-Municipal Relationships and Metropolitan Integration," *Public Administration Review* (Autumn, 1954), pp. 259–267.

Federal Policy in the Atomic Age

Project East River, a government sponsored study of civil defense, has brought to the attention of the American people an awareness of the threat of atomic warfare. As cities and metropolitan areas are critical target areas, national defense and local government are merged solidly in an effort to reduce city vulnerability. This is a joint, long range and all-inclusive federal-local project.[37] The task of East River Project was to determine the optimum combination of nonmilitary measures necessary to reduce urban vulnerability in case of atomic attack and to provide for national defense. Interestingly enough, its conclusions point to the need for doing things that should be done for our cities even without the atomic menace.

The report stated that one of the basic hindrances to urban progress was that real estate taxes continued to be the main sources of urban revenue. Because of this, a one hundred per cent utilization of land sites was necessary. This meant that continued concentration of high property values in the central city was necessary if urban services were to be financed as they are now. This is a great deterrent to lower population densities so necessary to reduce vulnerability within an urban area for the real property taxes do not yield enough taxes to pay for the urban services required. Natural dispersion is therefore slowed down or blocked.

Another problem brought out by the report was that of worker transportation in relation to intensity of land use. Arterial and circumferential highways are too few; mass transportation is not geared to the need for efficient transportation so that little has been done so far to improve the home-to-work and the work-to-home ordeal.

[37] Joseph E. McLean, "Planning for Civil Defense," *National Municipal Review* (June, 1954), pp. 278–283. See also *Bulletin of the Atomic Scientists* (September, 1953); the entire issue is devoted to "Project East River—The Strategy of Civil Defense." Project East River is a work of ten volumes. Those most concerned with federal-local relationships are: II *Measures to Make Civil Defense Manageable*; II B *Federal Leadership to Reduce Urban Vulnerability*; and V *The Reduction of Urban Vulnerability*. The project was jointly undertaken by the Department of Defense, the Federal Civil Defense Administration, and the National Security Resources Board.

This is seen to have increasing psychological as well as physical impact on city life.

The need for the speedy elimination of slums around the central business area was emphasized both because they were most vulnerable and provided a fire hazard of extreme danger to the entire urban area and because their preservation hindered the development of the urban areas as a whole. The report stressed the need for urban surgery; to reduce atomic vulnerability, slums must go. In dealing with slums, cities have already possibilities for action under the Federal Housing legislation; in fact, area surveys and planning can be partially financed with federal funds under recent housing laws.

The detailed mapping of fire storm areas was another recommendation. A fire storm area is one in which inflammable buildings cover twenty per cent or more of the land in an area of at least one square mile.

East River Project concluded also that programs which would look forward to the better spacing of industry should be developed in order to provide better protection against atomic attack.

And finally, the provision of adequate local government for the entire metropolitan area to insure smooth administration of all local services in the interest of safety in case of attack was deemed of prime importance.

But there looms yet another set of urban problems growing out of the atomic age. Will the coming of atomic power for peacetime purposes basically change the American city? [38] Experts take for granted that atomic power will be available to industry at competitive prices. But it must be remembered that while a small amount of atomic material theoretically capable of supplying tens of thousands of kilowatt hours of electric energy can be transported to any place at little cost the supply of industrial energy requires a large capital investment for there is no inherent difference between arrangements to make use of heat from a nuclear reactor than from

[38] See Walter Isard and Vincent Whitney, *Atomic Power, an Economic and Social Analysis* (1952).

any everyday coal burning furnace. Large scale power plants, atomic shields, and complex and expensive machinery are required. Nuclear energy will be practically available to industry only when political and economic considerations justify the heavy capital investments required. Nuclear energy will be forced to compete with present power sources such as coal and hydroelectric. Atomic power can be used simultaneously with other power, but will take a dominant place only when other power is relatively high in cost or in danger of becoming exhausted.

The use of atomic power may theoretically allow industrial deconcentration but such a trend will be restricted by the fact that industries will need railroads, buildings, and other nonnuclear facilities that are already available in present industrial areas. In other words, while atomic energy will not move industry out in the country it may allow and stimulate further dispersion within an already built-up metropolitan industrial area. An industrial area that has high power costs but other locational advantages may get more industries because of cheaper atomic power.

Furthermore, it must be realized that power is not the deciding factor in the location of industry these days. Only in the electro-process group of industries is power of dominant cost importance. The proportion of fuel and purchased energy to value added by manufacture has never been higher than nine per cent (in 1907) in the United States. In 1947, this ratio was 4.5 per cent. The general decline in power costs during the 20th century did not bring with it great direct savings in production outlays and this cannot be counted on in the future. In short, atomic power probably will not revolutionize industry.

While it is true that both the technical knowledge and fissionable material necessary to operate a nuclear generating plant are transportable anywhere in the world, the same is not true of value systems and culture. Atomic power cannot be developed out of the context of its indigenous social organization. Atomic power can be best used within the culture that invented and developed it. Therefore, atomic power may even have the effect of concentrating industry even more than it is at present because it can develop best within a successful, modern industrial pattern. It may even intensify our present urban-industrial problems.

In summary, there is no real prospect that atomic power will disperse people uniformly, that new atomic cities will grow up out of wastelands except when subsidized by the national government for military purposes, that underdeveloped areas and nations will be changed overnight, or that industry as a whole will seek new loca-

---

FEDERAL-LOCAL CONTACTS IN ACTIVITIES DUE PRIMARILY TO FEDERAL INTEREST IN AN ACTIVITY

1. Street and highway construction
2. Flood control and prevention
3. Improvement of rivers, harbors, and waterways
4. Water-pollution control
5. Control of communicable diseases including tuberculosis and venereal
6. Services to crippled children
7. Health centers and clinics
8. Disaster relief
9. Civil defense
10. Housing, slum clearance, and urban redevelopment
11. School-lunch program
12. Special problems of federally impacted areas
13. Airports and air terminals
14. Distribution of electricity
15. Old age and survivors' insurance for local government employees
16. Hospital planning and construction
17. Suppression of crime
18. General welfare assistance
19. Categorical assistance under the Social Security Act
20. Vocational education
21. Vocational rehabilitation
22. Agricultural extension services
23. Soil conservation

From Commission on Intergovernmental Relations, *Local Government* (June, 1955), p. 15.

---

tions. Rather, industry will remain where it is now; there will be further growth of metropolitan areas, and further extension into the suburbs. Whatever dispersion of industry and people will be within a larger metropolitan area for the sake of more safety, less vulnerability, and more elbow room for living and working. Cities of a half a million, planners say, can be so rearranged industrially that the economy will be strengthened. The urban area can be divided into groups of semi-independent communities clustered around an urban center. Thus, the region will be less vulnerable to attack, and a higher degree of efficiency and better working conditions will result. What the American people must do to prepare for the atomic age, they ultimately had to do anyway if cities were to be preserved from dry rot. The atomic age is really accentuating municipal change that was already on its way, just as the advent of atomic energy was a logical step in the general development of Western science.

The important point relative to intergovernmental relations in the United States is that the federal government will, and must, consider the problems of American cities of national interest and must act accordingly. And this, no matter what previous ideas about the place of each level of government might have been. True statesmanship must seek ways to protect the cities on the one hand, and on the other, to preserve the American principles of government.

The Impact of Federal Aid on Local Government

A number of state studies were undertaken at the behest of the Commission on Intergovernmental Relations to determine the impact of federal grants-in-aid on state and local government structure, functions, and fiscal condition. The observations relating to local government are interesting and significant. *Connecticut*: Federal highway aid "has weakened the vitality of local government." [39] *Mississippi*: Federal grants-in-aid have resulted in "the transfer of authority from local to state officials." [40] *South Carolina*: Federal aid has had three principal influences upon local government. A number of former local functions have become state functions. "In all of the functions for which substantial portions of total cost are borne by

[39] Commission on Intergovernmental Relations, *The Administrative and Fiscal Impact of Federal Grants-in-Aid* (June, 1955), p. 5. Dr. W. Brooke Graves, Library of Congress, edited this volume which included summaries of survey reports made by Griffenhagen & Associates (Connecticut), J. L. Jacobs & Company (Kansas and Wyoming), Public Administration Service (Michigan), McKinsey and Company (Mississippi and Washington), and Governmental Affairs Institute (South Carolina).

[40] *Ibid.*, p. 47.

Federal grants the State has taken over total or almost total responsibility." Because rural county delegations in the state legislature exercise predominant power in state government, increased federal grants to states have increased the importance of rural interests in urban local government, generally to its disadvantage. Because of this, urban governments tend to turn directly to the federal government for assistance. Grants-in-aid have tended to "diminish the general stature of local government." [41]

Washington: "It is paradoxical in some instances to observe a shift in the administration of a function from local to State control when

---

ACTIVITIES DIVIDED BETWEEN FEDERAL, STATE, AND LOCAL GOVERNMENTS WITH EACH GOVERNMENT PAYING DIRECTLY ITS OWN COSTS

1. Police protection and law enforcement including
   a. Police records and statistics including identification
   b. Detention and custody of prisoners
   c. Police communications
   d. Prevention and investigation of crimes
   e. Probation and parole of prisoners
   f. Control of prostitution, liquor, and narcotics
   g. Fish and game protection
2. Maintenance of hospitals
   a. General hospitals
3. General libraries
4. Recreation facilities
   a. Forest parks and camps
   b. Monuments and historical sites

Commission on Intergovernmental Relations, *Local Government* (June, 1955), p. 19.

---

at the same time less Federal controls are requested. The public assistance program has gradually moved out almost entirely from local control to complete State administration and supervision. We were informed the elected county officials welcomed this change as they had been faced with continuing individual problems with little chance to do anything about them. They were faced with a state-wide plan and Federal-State regulations. Basically, the State de-

[41] *Ibid.*, pp. 70–72.

cided, that they could do a better job than could be performed by the individual counties. They eliminated, therefore, even the nominal control of the county commissioners over the program." [42]

Alabama: Complexities of finance under the federal grants system have caused the state to take over the preparation of county budgets for the county health departments. The result is that local health officers have nothing to do with the county health budgets and this had led to disillusionment on the part of long-time county health officers and deterioration of state-local relationships. [43]

Arkansas: "The attitude of Arkansas towards Federal grants-in-aid might be summed up by saying that the State is grateful that they have been made available, hopeful that they will be continued and increased, but fearful that they may be reduced or cut off." [44]

Colorado: "There seems to be no reason to impute a loss of initiative and inventiveness to local officials because of Federal grants-in-aid." On the other hand, federal grants brought them into full flowering in efforts to find more federal money. [45] *Delaware*: The housing authority in Wilmington dealing directly with the national government across city lines is a separate public agency whose members are appointed by the state and not subject to supervision by the mayor and council of the city of Wilmington. As a result, integration on the local level has become impossible and the outlook for metropolitan planning "when the authority for such is so splintered" is not bright. [46] *Florida*: "Most of the grant programs filled a vacuum which had been created by default of the local governments. These programs were centrally controlled from their inception."

[42] *Ibid.*, p. 90.
[43] Commission on Intergovernmental Relations, *The Impact of Federal Grants-in-Aid on Structure and Functions of State and Local Governments* (June, 1955), pp. 37–40. Dr. Roger H. Wells, Department of Political Science, Bryn Mawr College, was general editor of this volume. Dr. Coleman B. Ransone, Jr., made the Alabama report.
[44] *Ibid.*, pp. 59–60. Dr. Franklin M. Budge, Department of Government, University of Arkansas, made this report.
[45] *Ibid.*, pp. 73–74. Dr. Laird Dunbar, Department of Political Science, University of Colorado, made the Colorado report.
[46] *Ibid.*, pp. 91–92. Delaware report by Dr. Paul Dolan, Department of Political Science, University of Delaware.

Federal grants have led to introduction of forms of state supervision not previously used in the state.[47] *Idaho*: "As a whole, programs supported by Federal aid, were not formerly carried out in most local units and since most local units have reached their tax limits, they are glad to have the additional activities partially financed by the Federal Government."[48] *Illinois*: "Centralization in Illinois both in the transfer of functions from smaller to larger units and in increased supervision of smaller units by larger has gone on apace in Illinois and many would like to see it go further."[49]

Iowa: The public health programs which have expanded "never could have been extended without Federal aid." Municipal officials believe that the cities would get a more satisfactory share of highway funds if they could deal directly with the national government.[50] *Kentucky*: Federal grants have resulted in the taking over of the county functions, notably in the fields of welfare and highways, by the state and the increase of state supervision. Cities, too, have experienced a growth of state supervision in civil defense, public health, and airports because of federal grants. Direct federal aid to cities as in housing and slum clearance is made to semi-autonomous agencies and city officials have little control over them. Red-tape is as pronounced in direct federal programs as it is under state supervision.[51]

Massachusetts: Federal requirements in the social security law of 1939 led the general court in 1950 to provide a merit system for welfare agents, to sever boards of selectmen from public assistance administration and to write a new law authorizing towns to set up welfare districts. Thirty-one such districts have been formed and

[47] *Ibid.*, pp. 113–114. Florida report made by Dr. Vincent V. Thursby, Department of Political Science, Florida State University.

[48] *Ibid.*, pp. 133–134. Idaho report by Dr. Boyd A. Martin, Department of Social Sciences, University of Idaho.

[49] *Ibid.*, pp. 155–157. Illinois report made by Dr. Phillip Monypenny, Department of Political Science, University of Illinois.

[50] *Ibid.*, pp. 173–175. Iowa report made by Dr. Donald Bruce Johnson, Department of Political Science, State University of Iowa.

[51] *Ibid.*, pp. 189–191. The Kentucky report was made by Professor J. E. Reeves and Mrs. Glennalou Ryan, Department of Political Science, University of Kentucky.

they are primarily for the administration of the federal categories, but cities and towns may assign the general relief program to them.[52] *Nebraska*: "Some observers consider the most adverse effect of the Federal grant programs has been made on local governments and local attitudes. One close observer expressed deep concern that the Federal expansion of its bureaucracy has developed some ill will toward the governmental process. In his opinion, some elements of high-pressure salesmanship and an over-stimulation of local projects were demoralizing public affairs." [53] *New Hampshire*: "To meet the Federal grant requirements, New Hampshire has placed responsibility for the administration of welfare programs wholly at the state level, with the result that one major segment of public policy has been removed from the jurisdiction of towns and cities." [54]

OVERLAP IN FEDERAL, STATE, AND LOCAL RESEARCH, PLANNING AND RECORDS

1. Police records and statistics
2. Highway engineering and research
3. Water conservation and utilization
4. Pollution of lakes and streams
5. Health—in many phases
6. Educational research and statistics

From Commission on Intergovernmental Relations, *Local Government* (June, 1955), p. 19.

New Jersey: Local government is only negligibly affected by federal programs.[55]

New Mexico: "Forces were already at work which resulted in centralized state administration; Federal grants accentuated the trend

[52] *Ibid.*, pp. 212–216. Dr. Victoria Schuck, Department of Political Science, Mount Holyoke College, made the Massachusetts report.

[53] *Ibid.*, pp. 234–239. The Nebraska report was made by Dr. A. C. Breckenridge, Department of Political Science, University of Nebraska.

[54] *Ibid.*, pp. 262–268. Dr. Robert B. Dishman and Dr. David C. Knapp, Department of Government, University of New Hampshire, made this report.

[55] *Ibid.*, pp. 279–280. Ernest G. Miller, fellow in the Department of Politics, Princeton University, made the New Jersey report.

and hastened the process. . . . A shift back to city or county administration involves more risks than many citizens or organized groups are willing to take—reduced services, lower standards, increased costs and injection of local politics in administration.[56] *Ohio*: "Frankly, it must be said that county governments have come to depend increasingly upon Federal programs. As a result, county responsibility for public assistance and poor relief has been dissipated and county planning in these areas has been neglected."[57] *Oregon*: "While the Federal grant-in-aid programs have stimulated this trend toward central control by requiring a single point of contact within the State, an existing agency already active in the subject area has usually been available for this role. . . . Federal grants have served to accelerate, rather than initiate State activity. . . . In an overall sense, however, it is correct to say that Federal grants and Federal supervision have liberated, rather than constructed the energies of local officials. In general, Federal standards and suggestions, are accepted, consciously and explicitly, as representing goals that are desirable of themselves. There is little concern in Oregon that Federal grants have sapped the vitality of local government."[58]

Pennsylvania: "All parties interviewed agreed that there is little 'grass roots' discussion of or agitation for or against Federal aid."[59] *Rhode Island*: "The State has taken over many city and town roads in order to qualify for larger Federal highway grants."[60] *South Dakota*: "The reorganization of local government structures has been impeded through Federal grants. Governor Anderson expressed the idea that the State's taking over of responsibility of certain local functions has obviated much of the necessity for re-

[56] *Ibid.*, pp. 294–295. Dr. Charles Judah and Professor Dorothy I. Cline, Department of Government, University of New Mexico, made this report.
[57] *Ibid.*, pp. 308–311. Dr. Dayton E. Heckman, Department of Political Science, Ohio State University, made this report.
[58] *Ibid.*, pp. 327–328. Professor A. Freeman Holmer, Department of Political Science, Willamette University, made the Oregon report.
[59] *Ibid.*, pp. 345–346. The Pennsylvania report was made by Dr. John H. Ferguson and Dr. Charles F. LeeDecker, Department of Political Science, The Pennsylvania State University.
[60] *Ibid.*, pp. 360–361. Dr. Felix Rackow, Department of Political Science, Brown University, made the Rhode Island report.

organization." [61] *Tennessee*: "There are only two cases in Tennessee of State assumption of a program already in existence on a local level which took place to make it possible to receive Federal funds. These were highway construction and maintenance, and public welfare." [62] *Texas*: "There have been important shifts in state-local functional responsibilities in education, highways and welfare, but Federal aid has had little, if any influence on this trend." [63] *Utah*: "Federal grants-in-aid which funnel through State offices add to the concentration of power at the State level. . . . The local governments can much more easily demand recognition and sympathetic treatment from the State than they can from Washington." [64] *Vermont*: "It is generally conceded that pressures from the local governments would have been exerted, with but few exceptions, in the absence of Federal grants, and that expansion in State activity and State support would have been inevitable." [65] *Virginia*: "Federal aid to welfare led to the creation of welfare agencies in every county and independent city of Virginia. This was the requirement of the Federal law. Without this over-all plan, some counties probably would never have set up welfare agencies." [66] *West Virginia*: Cities and counties have cooperated to establish joint health departments and to construct airports stimulated by federal grants-in-aid.[67]

Dr. Roger Wells, editor of the volume containing the state reports cited above, concludes that "federal grants are far from being the sole factor affecting State-local relations." The situation varies from state to state. Some federal grants have led to new forms of state

[61] *Ibid.*, pp. 380–381. Mr. L. M. Carlson, Legislative Research Council, State of South Dakota, made this report.

[62] *Ibid.*, pp. 400–402. Dr. Avery Leiserson and Dr. Daniel Grant, Department of Political Science, Vanderbilt University, wrote this report.

[63] *Ibid.*, pp. 417–418. Dr. O. Douglas Weeks and Dr. Wilfred D. Webb, Department of Government, University of Texas, wrote this report.

[64] *Ibid.*, pp. 434–437. Dr. M. R. Merrill, Department of Political Science, Utah State Agricultural College, wrote this report.

[65] *Ibid.*, p. 456. Dr. Rolf N. B. Haugen, Department of Political Science, wrote the Vermont report.

[66] *Ibid.*, pp. 470–471. Dr. Spencer D. Albright, Department of Political Science, University of Richmond, and Mr. Jess H. Walters, University of California graduate student in political science, wrote the Virginia report.

[67] *Ibid.*, pp. 482–485. Dr. Mavis A. Mann, Department of Political Science, West Virginia University, wrote this report.

supervision. Federal grants have had little or no effect on reorganization of local government structure and organization. In general, Dr. Wells believes that "cooperative federalism" is working successfully and can be improved with more coordination at all levels.[68]

TEN SUBJECTS FOR FURTHER STUDY

1. The latest federal aid highway program.
2. Proposals for general federal aid to public schools.
3. Should municipal bonds be taxed?
4. Civil defense organization in your community.
5. Federally owned property in your city.
6. The Hatch Act as it relates to local government employees.
7. Local government and the TVA.
8. The FBI and local police.
9. The Kefauver investigation of crime.
10. The government of Washington, D. C.

REFERENCES

Committee on Government Operations, *Payments in Lieu of Taxes to States or Local Taxing Units* (Washington, 1953).

Commission on Intergovernmental Affairs, *The Impact of Federal Grants-in-Aid on Structure and Functions of State and Local Governments,* U. S. Printing Office (June 1955).

———, *Local Government,* U. S. Printing Office (June 1955).

———, *A Report to the President for Transmittal to the Congress,* U. S. Printing Office (June 1955).

———, *Twenty-five Federal Grants-in-Aid Programs,* U. S. Printing Office (June 1955).

Lawrence L. Durisch, "Local Government and the TVA Program," *Public Administration Review,* Summer 1941, pp. 326–334.

Joint Committee of the National Education Association and the American Teachers Association, *Legal Status of Segregated Schools* (Washington, 1954).

Wylie Kilpatrick, "Future Federal-State and Local Relations," *Municipal Finance,* November 1953.

———, "Neglected Aspects of Intergovernmental Fiscal Relations," *American Political Science Review,* June 1947, pp. 452–462.

Simeon E. Leland, "The Coordination of Federal, State and Local Fiscal Systems," *Municipal Finance,* August 1933, pp. 35–46.

[68] *Ibid.,* pp. 1–21.

C. C. Ludwig, "Cities and the National Government Under the New Deal," *American Political Science Review*, August 1935, pp. 640–648.

M. H. Satterfield, "TVA-State-Local Relationships," *American Political Science Review*, October 1946, pp. 935–947.

Earl C. Segrest and Arthur J. Misner, *The Impact of Federal Grants-in-Aid on California*, Bureau of Public Administration, University of California (Berkeley, 1954).

Harvey Walker, *Federal Limitations Upon Municipal Ordinance Making Power* (Columbus, 1929).

Chapter 6

THE PEOPLE AND
THEIR LOCAL GOVERNMENT

More than at any other level of American government, the people are sovereign in localities. They elect local officials, they vote on community policy in referenda, they run for and hold office, they watch carefully their local governments in action, and they organize community affairs. In short, local government in the United States is close to the people. Even in the large metropolis, John Q. Public has the ways and means to bring his citizenship to bear on City Hall.

This is not to say that all is well on the municipal front, or that it ever was. In fact, the worst abuses in American government have been perpetrated at the local level. Lord Bryce, a most astute English commentator on American political institutions, wrote in 1888: "There is no denying that the government of cities is the one conspicuous failure of the United States." [1] Most of the fast-growing urban areas have been continuously threatened or actually controlled by the "boss and the political machine" since the end of the Civil War, and many metropolitan areas are still plagued with frequent recurrences of boss-rule, underworld control, graft, and other diseases so common to the American local body politic. At the turn of this century, the county was aptly characterized as the "dark continent of American politics" it still is.

But, on the other hand, American local government has greatly

[1] James Bryce, *The American Commonwealth*, II, p. 281.

235

progressed during the first half of the 20th century. The boss has his back to the wall. Where he still holds forth, he often has to fight an aroused citizenry. In many places he has fallen and vanished from the political scene, and his place as political leader has been taken by an elective mayor, cooperating with a free and independent governing body, supported by wide-awake civic associations, and implemented with modern administrative staff and methods. Even in the largest cities where conditions were often the worst, the very need for economical and efficient service has brought about vast improvement. If the last half of the 19th century was discouraging, the first half of the 20th has proved tremendously promising to the cause of good local government in the United States.

For in the American system, the people have the tools to forge the chains of local well-being. In spite of the increase of the federal and state powers, local units still have broad fields of independent action. They can still cooperate with the higher levels of government on more or less equal terms. By their votes, the people can elect competent officials; by their interest, they can get good government; by their good will, they can bring to fruition the great promise of American life in their own communities.

It is not in every country that the common man still commands the scene: not where local government has been strangulated by overpowering strength at the national level, not where the privilege of free elections has been taken away from the people, not where the forces of evil have taken over the complex machinery of public service and democratic action. Modern history gives many examples where democracy has failed, some places even in our own land, but in America the people still can win if they work at it.

THE LOCAL ELECTION PROCESS

The American voters elect a host of local government officials. These include the chief executives and governing bodies of cities, towns, boroughs, villages; and of counties, townships, school districts, and special districts. In addition, such officials as assessors, tax collectors, justices of the peace, constables, auditors, controllers, treasurers, and many others are elective depending upon the constitution and law in each state.

The voters also have supreme power in the political parties. By means of the direct primary, they nominate party candidates for the elective offices and elect party officers.

But in addition to the power to nominate and elect officials, they have specific powers to vote upon policies to be adopted in their localities. This they do by means of referenda submitted to them for their vote by governing bodies, and by the initiative and referendum whereby policies can be adopted without action on the part of the local governing body. Again, the extent of their opportunities depends upon state law and their own use of them.

The Long Ballot

Comparatively few national and state officials are elected by the voters; on these levels the *short ballot* obtains. On the local level, it is different. Here the condition is aptly described as the *long ballot* for sometimes there are hundreds of names from which the local voter must make his choices. The inevitable result of the *long ballot* is that the rank and file of the voters feel inadequate to make good choices and therefore are inclined to vote the straight party ticket in elections, follow the party designations in primaries, or else do not vote at all. This allows both the party organization and the organized minorities to concentrate on their particular candidates who can win even though they may be far from the choice of the majority. Where there is a *long ballot*, a strong political organization is usually found—the one leads to the other. This does not necessarily mean that government will therefore be bad for party organization depends on conditions and persons. There are local party organizations that strive for good government, but there are more that are interested in political power and the material fruits of such power. The point is that where there is a *long ballot* the voter cannot do his best job. He does not know the candidates and cannot

tell what they stand for or might do in office. He is at the mercy of
those who try to guide him—the political leader, the civic leader, the
newspaper editor, the commentator on radio and TV, the neighbor. And a lot depends upon what his guides and mentors want.
It must be emphasized, however, that in commission and council
manager cities, the short ballot is in general use, for it was the long
ballot that was partly responsible for their development.

A few examples of the *long ballot* will show what the local voter
is up against. Spencer Albright (Richmond University) found that
in 1932 the average size of the election ballot where candidates were
listed in party columns was 565 square inches and contained 102
names and three referenda. In states where the candidates were
listed by offices, the average size was 349 square inches and contained 77 candidates and four referenda.[2]

In Pennsylvania the voters in Philadelphia elect 108 officials, most
of them every four years; in Pittsburgh, 83 officers; in cities of the
third class, 57 officers; in boroughs, 61 officers; and in townships,
between 56 and 59. The great majority of these are local judiciary,
county row officers, local governing bodies, and independent local
officials such as the tax collector and assessor.[3]

Watertown, Connecticut, is a town of about 11,000 people. The
voters elect a total of 56 town officers including three selectmen,
nine members on the board of education, three members of the
board of assessors, a town clerk, a town treasurer, six members of
the board of finance, a fire district committee, tax collector, three
members of the board of tax review, seven constables, eight justices
of the peace, one judge, four registrars of voters, one judge of probate, six grand jurors, a prosecutor and an assistant.[4]

In 1950, the Gallup poll asked 1,500 voters: "Could you tell me
the names of all the candidates you voted for in the recent election

[2] Spencer Albright, "How Does Your Ballot Grow," *Bulletin of the American
Legislators Association,* May 10, 1933.
[3] J. Tanger, H. F. Alderfer, and M. Nelson McGeary, *Pennsylvania Government,* The Pennsylvania State University (1950), p. 8.
[4] Richard S. Childs, *Civic Victories, the Story of An Unfinished Revolution*
(1952), p. 60. Mr. Childs believes Greenwich, Connecticut, holds a record
with 268 elective officers.

of November 7?" Seventy-six per cent replied that they could remember only the most important.[5]

People interested in the improvement of local government contend that a short ballot must replace the long one. But how short should the local ballot be? First of all, it should include the governing body of each local unit—the city council, the board of county commissioners, the board of school directors, the board of township supervisors, the trustees of special districts. How large should these bodies be? There are all sizes but the general trend has been toward reduction, the ideal number being from five to nine. Richard Childs, long-time short ballot advocate, states that where the voters have nine such offices to fill it "is just too many to elect at one time." The voters are prone to accept ready-made tickets, good or bad as the case may be. But with five running for office, Mr. Childs believes that the voters can exercise their own judgment.[6]

If a municipality has a chief executive officer such as the mayor, independent of the council, this official should also be elected, and in order to have an independent finance officer so should the controller. But there is no demonstrable reason for electing any other municipal officers. All others should be appointed by the chief executive officer or, where none exists, by the governing body. In council-manager municipalities, subordinate officials and employees should be appointed by the manager with the consent of the council, preferably on the basis of merit under civil service regulations.

It is in the county that the long ballot has been carried to extreme lengths. Here the board of commissioners or supervisors or judges as the case may be, which is the governing body of the county, exists side by side with a dozen or more elective "row" officers. In Pennsylvania, these include the controller or three auditors, the treasurer, the district attorney, the sheriff, the prothonotary, the clerk of the

[5] *Ibid.*, p. 12.
[6] Richard S. Childs, "We Must Keep Ballot Short," *National Municipal Review*, July, 1949. He examines four council-manager cities in which nine councilmen were elected: Fort Worth and Dallas, Texas, and Long Beach and Sacramento, California, and comes to the conclusion that even on nonpartisan tickets the tendency was to vote for tickets rather than for individuals. In 53 elections for 477 posts only two per cent of the seats went to "independents."

courts, the register of wills, the recorder of deeds, two jury commissioners, the surveyor, the coroner, the clerk of orphans' court, and one or more common pleas judges.[7] In California, elective county officers include, besides the board of supervisors, the assessor, auditor, clerk, coroner, district attorney, justice of the peace, public administrator, public defender, recorder, sheriff, superintendent of schools, surveyor, tax collector, and treasurer.[8] In many states, county and other officials have been made elective by the constitution so it proves next to impossible to change them to appointive officials, for they have extensive political influence. Being integral parts of the local political organizations, these officials make themselves felt in the legislature out of all proportion to their numbers and services. But it may safely be said that no lasting improvement in rural local government can come until county structure is modernized and the short ballot is established there. The long ballot stems from the days of Jacksonian democracy when American political ideology was based upon the premise that all officials performing important functions should be elective in order to keep the government close to the people. This principle was never applied to the national government. It is gradually disappearing in the states with the reorganization of state administration, and is also giving way in larger municipalities to the strong mayor, the commission, and the manager forms of government. But it yet remains in all its original strength in the American county. In many rural units and small towns, too, there are still numerous independent officers such as assessors, tax collectors, justices, constables, and street commissioners that are still elective, part-time officials. These, along with the county row offices, should be consolidated and appointed by the governing bodies of the local unit under which they operate.

In the case of local judicial officers, the case is not so simple. Where there is a court of record, election or appointment is not strictly a local problem and the tradition followed in each state

[7] J. Tanger, H. F. Alderfer, and M. Nelson McGeary, *op. cit.*, p. 194.
[8] John C. Bollens and Stanley Scott, *Local Government in California,* University of California (1952), p. 71.

should not be broken except on a statewide basis. As for the minor judiciary (the magistrates, the aldermen, and the justices of the peace—those who are elected by the people and paid by fees) the trend is toward gradual consolidation, better training and selection either through election upon sponsorship by the court, or actual appointment by the district court. But not much headway on these lines can be reported. The break will come first in the highly urbanized areas where much dissatisfaction with the present arrangements seems to exist.

The object of the shortening of the ballot is not having local government become undemocratic, but the very opposite. Democracy cannot work well when the constituent units—the people themselves—are given tasks they cannot do. Conditions in a democracy must be right, if democracy is to work in this complicated world.

Who Can Vote?

The extension of suffrage has been one of the most significant phenomena of American politics. In the colonies, voting was restricted to those who owned property and sometimes to those who belonged to the official church. A mere fraction of the population had the right to vote. After the Revolution, the trend toward universal suffrage began. First, free white men over twenty-one, then colored men, then women were included in the suffrage lists.

Today, voters must be twenty-one years of age or over (except in Georgia where the voting age is eighteen); they must be United States citizens; they must be residents in the state from six months to two years (usually one year); and they must be residents in the county or in the district in which they wish to cast their votes for a specified length of time (usually from one month to six).

There are no property qualifications (except to vote for bond issues and special assessments in six states).[9] Literacy tests

[9] The Council of State governments, *The Book of the States, 1954–55,* p. 80. The states are Michigan, Montana, Nevada, New Mexico, Texas, Utah. In South Carolina, ownership of property is the alternative to literacy.

are required in seventeen states, and poll tax receipts in five states.[10]

All states allow absentee voting on the part of military forces and armed forces personnel. Absentee voting on the part of citizens not in the armed forces is provided for in all but four states: Maryland, New Mexico, Pennsylvania, and South Carolina.

Election Administration

The conduct of elections, both primary and general, is governed by state law. The supervision of elections on a statewide basis is usually lodged in the office of the secretary of state or in a state election board. The responsibility for local administration of elections is given to a county or city election board, which is usually the board of county commissioners and sometimes the city council *ex officio*. It is this board that prints the ballots in the manner prescribed by state law, enters the names of the candidates submitted to them, designates and rents the polling places, buys and stores the voting machines, sets up the election machinery, receives the voting tabulations, and reports them to the state election office or the court. Costs of all elections are borne by the county or city.

The county or city is divided into election districts or precincts usually including several hundred voters. Each election district has a polling place which is manned by such election officers as are provided by law. These election officers include the judge of elections, the inspector of elections, the clerks, or whatever names the officers are given. These persons conduct the elections: identify the voters, give them ballots, see that the ballots are deposited in ballot boxes, man the voting machines, tabulate the votes, and make the return to the county or city election board. The local election officials are

[10] *Ibid.*, p. 80. States having literacy tests for voting are Arizona, California, Connecticut, Delaware, Georgia, Louisiana, Maine, Massachusetts, Mississippi, New Hampshire, New York, North Carolina, Oregon, South Carolina, Virginia, Washington, and Wyoming.

States having poll tax qualifications are Alabama, Arkansas, Mississippi, Texas, and Virginia.

chosen by the county or city election board, or are elected by the voters at the preceding election or primary. There is usually some division of the election officers between the two major parties. In addition, political parties and organized groups have the right to appoint election watchers whose duty it is to see that the election officers commit no frauds. According to the Model Election Administration System of the National Municipal League, the administration of registration and elections should be in one office and in cities or counties over 200,000 there should be a special office rather than an *ex officio* one, and this office should be under a single commissioner rather than an election board.[11]

Registration

Registration is the process of preparing a list of persons who meet the qualifications for voting. On election day the election officers in charge of voting in the polling places permit those persons to vote whose right to suffrage has been established. In the early days of the Republic when the nation was predominantly rural, the people knew their neighbors and whether or not they were eligible to vote. They still do in the small towns and rural areas. But as the urban areas grew, there was chance for fraud—for personation, for repeaters operating in gangs throughout the entire city, and for fraudulent voting lists. To combat those evils, registration was developed.

There are several kinds of registration: (1) *permanent*, where the voter is permanently enrolled on the voting lists, and *periodic*, where he is enrolled at regular intervals; (2) *personal*, where the voter must make his personal appearance to get on the voting list, and *nonpersonal* where the list is made up from information available; and (3) *compulsory*, where the voter's name must be on the list if he is to vote, and *noncompulsory*, where the voter may vote on election day by establishing his qualifications then and there.

[11] See Joseph P. Harris, *Election Administration in the United States,* The Brookings Institution (1934), for the most detailed analysis of voting practices in the several states.

Permanent registration has been adopted in forty-four states. In some of these, it applies only to cities. Periodic registration is used in fifteen states. Arkansas is the only state without any registration provisions.[12]

The Direct Primary

The great majority of local officials are elected on a party basis. Where they are, the party must nominate candidates to represent it in the election. As party organization developed in the United States, the process of nomination evolved from the informal to the legal, from the oligarchic to the democratic. In the early days, party candidates were chosen by self-appointed party leaders and active workers in caucus, that is, by getting together at a meeting and deciding who should run for what office. Once the choices were made, it was assumed that the party members would support them down the line. This informal caucus turned into a formal meeting in the early decades of the 19th century and came to be called the convention. Regularly chosen delegates made up the convention. There were conventions for every level of government—national, state, county, city, judicial district, township, and ward. These conventions were the accepted party instruments for the nomination of candidates and the election of party officials. But the impetus towards democracy did not relax, and as conventions came under the influence of the political machine and bosses the convention system gradually gave way to the direct primary.

The direct primary is really an election within the party using all the equipment, personnel, and procedure of a regular election. Primary elections are held in accordance to state law and conducted by the regular election officers at the regular polling places. They are held several months before the elections, often in September when the elections are in November, but in some states they are

---

[12] *The Book of the States, 1954–1955,* p. 81. Also see Joseph P. Harris, *Registration of Voters in the United States,* The Brookings Institution (1928), for detailed analyses of registration law and practices in the several states.

held in spring. Usually all legal parties polling a small percentage of the vote in the last regular election must use the primary to nominate their candidates and elect their party officers. Would-be candidates get on the ballot by petitions signed by a stated number of voters, and the winners automatically get on the election ballots. Other candidates not nominated by primary may obtain places on the election ballots by petition, and blank spaces are provided for "write-in" candidates in primaries as well as in general elections. In Detroit and its surrounding Wayne County, Michigan law allows candidates for nomination to get on the primary ballots by depositing a sum of money returnable if the candidate polls a certain percentage of the vote.

It has been held that the direct primary originated in Crawford County, Pennsylvania, as early as 1842.[13] It was not adopted extensively until several decades after the Civil War. It was then that the political machine reached its greatest strength in the convention and proceeded to make it do its will. The rank and file voter was helpless and revolted. It was the Populists, the Progressives, and the Liberals in both major parties who sought to abolish the convention in favor of the primary. In the 1890's it was first adopted as a state system in the Democratic party of South Carolina and Georgia; in the first decade of the 20th century it swept through the Middle West. By the end of World War I all but a few states had adopted it for statewide offices. By 1954, Connecticut was the only state without the direct primary, but fifteen states still combined the convention with the primary in some form.[14]

The direct primary has by no means eliminated party organization. As might have been expected, the party soon adjusted to its demands and again became or remained the dominant factor in local politics. The party organization put forward its own slate in the primaries and worked for its success. Not many independent

[13] James H. Booser, "Origin of the Direct Primary," *National Municipal Review*, 24 (1935), pp. 222–223.
[14] *The Book of the States, 1954–55,* p. 83. The states are Alabama, Arkansas, Delaware, Indiana, Georgia, Massachusetts, Iowa, Michigan, New Jersey, New Mexico, New York, South Dakota, Texas, Utah, and Virginia.

candidates ever defeated a well-organized party organization, for it
is the old story about one against many. But the primary provides a
method to beat the party organization if some candidate can arouse
the membership against it. The primary, therefore, provides a channel to blow off political steam. It also tends to make the political
organization more careful as to the candidates they choose. What
with radio and TV, a "dud" is a political liability to the party and
cannot expect support at the polls from the party members who are
not active party workers. The primary has proved its worth, and is
here to stay.

Several gadgets have been added to the direct primary in some
states. The *preprimary convention* allows the party organization to
put forward an "organization" slate in the primary. These candidates
so appear on the official primary ballot. In Rhode Island, the party
committee is allowed this privilege. In Colorado, each candidate
receiving twenty per cent or more of the preconvention vote is
placed on the primary ballot.

Eleven states, all in the South and all "one-party" states, use the
run-off primary.[15] In these states, nomination in the Democratic
primaries is tantamount to election, and it has been deemed necessary to allow the majority to exercise its will. Therefore, if no candidate receives the majority vote, the two highest are voted on in the
run-off primary held several weeks later. In other states, the candidate receiving a plurality, or the highest number of votes, is declared nominated. Many times, therefore, a minority candidate
represents the party in the election.

In ten states, voters receive the ballots of all parties and may vote
in whichever primary they wish. This is called the *open primary*.[16]
This has the tendency of destroying party responsibility for it allows
members of other parties to vote for weak candidates so that they
may be defeated in the coming elections. V. O. Key (Harvard University) believes that while the open primary may not increase party

[15] *Ibid.*, p. 83. The states are Alabama, Arkansas, Florida, Georgia, Louisiana,
Mississippi, North Carolina, Oklahoma, South Carolina, Texas, and Virginia.
[16] *Ibid.*, p. 83. The states are Arkansas, Idaho, Michigan, Minnesota, Mississippi, Rhode Island, South Carolina, Utah, Washington, Wisconsin.

responsibility it may "contribute to a sharper definition and determination of political issues." [17]

Another variation in the direct primary is "cross filing" or "double filing" by which a candidate may run for the nomination in more than one party. California makes greater use of this practice than any other state. In 1944, for example, eighty per cent of the eighty assemblymen and ninety per cent of the twenty senators elected to office were cross filers. Cross filing in California was adopted in 1913 and used primarily by the third-party Progressives. Since then, it has been used by virtually every major contender for partisan office in the state.[18] Since 1940, the large majority of election contests have been decided at the primary by the successful candidate getting the nomination of both parties. One of the principle effects of cross filing in California has been to aid incumbents in office of both major parties to be elected. Only a few other states permit cross filing in some form in the primaries: Maine, Vermont, Massachusetts, and Maryland. Cross filing is generally conceded to undermine party responsibility.

The *nonpartisan primary* is used in some states, mostly for local and judicial offices. Candidates do not run under any party label, the contests being entirely between individuals. In this system, there is only one primary open to all candidates for the office. The persons obtaining the first and second highest number of votes become candidates in the election, although in some states if the person receives a majority of all votes cast in the primary, he is declared elected. The nonpartisan primary does not necessarily eliminate partisan activity or influence. To win candidates usually must have some organized support, whatever name it goes under.

The National Municipal League recommends the primary to nominate candidates and elect party officers. In proposing its Model Primary Law it recommends that individual candidates should be

[17] V. O. Key, *Politics, Parties and Pressure Groups,* third edition (1952), pp. 422–423. In Washington the open primary is carried to its logical extreme. Voters can split their vote by voting for different offices in different party primaries.

[18] Evelyn Hazen, *Cross Filing in Primary Elections,* University of California (1951), p. 1.

allowed to file only for one party, thereby eliminating cross filing and multiple nominations. Party candidates, if chosen in preprimary conventions or in organization meetings, should be so designated on the primary ballots. The direct primary should be mandatory for all political parties polling ten per cent or more of the vote cast in the last preceding election. The candidate with the highest vote should win, but in one party states it would be advisable to have run-off primaries of the first two highest, if there is no majority.[19]

Nonpartisan Elections

One of the important local political developments in the United States has been the increase of nonpartisan elections. Arthur Bromage (University of Michigan) sees a distinct trend toward non-partisan primaries and elections in cities.[20] He found that in 1950, 81 per cent of cities over five thousand population that were governed under council-manager government had nonpartisan ballots. So also had 75 per cent of the commission cities, and 42 per cent of mayor-council cities.

Contrasting partisan and nonpartisan municipal elections, Professor Bromage states that in partisan municipal elections independents are debarred as councilmen, those who run in the primary are examined as to previous party activity and given support on that ground, old timers can be more easily put across, and minority parties have little or no chance for success. Furthermore, candidates with the "wrong" party labels do not win, and new ideas about the structure of city government have little support from party organizations. Party organizations look upon municipal elections as essential cogs in party operations. Richard S. Childs after questioning forty-eight cities covering more than five hundred elections found that in nonpartisan elections the politicians "did not throw their weight, officially or nonofficially, openly or covertly." [21]

[19] National Municipal League, *A Model Direct Primary Election System* (1951).
[20] Arthur W. Bromage, "Partisan Elections in Cities," *National Municipal Review* (May, 1951), pp. 250–253.
[21] Richard S. Childs, "500 'Nonpolitical' Elections," *National Municipal Review* (June, 1949), pp. 278–282.

Two great American political scientists disagreed about non-partisanship in local affairs. Charles E. Merriam (Chicago University) said: "The lines that divide men in national affairs do not run in the same direction in local questions, and the attempt to force them to do so has been a conspicuous failure in this country." [22] Charles A. Beard (Columbia University) said: "But I cannot be too emphatic when I say that not a single one of our really serious municipal questions—poverty, high cost of living, overcrowding, unemployment, low standards of life, physical degeneracy—can be solved, can even be approached by municipalities without the co-operation of the state and national governments, and the solution of these problems call for state and national parties." [23]

Attempts to Get More Precise Representation

Where, for example, a city council of five is elected at large, it is entirely possible for all five members to be elected from one party even if the winning party polls only a few more votes than the losing party. When this happens, the large minority of voters is unrepresented on the city council. This is considered undemocratic by some and ways to obtain minority representation have been explored and sometimes tried. *Limited voting* is a crude device toward this end. If three offices are to be filled, each voter is allowed to vote only for two. Thus, the minority party may be able to elect one of their candidates because it is assumed that they will concentrate on one while the majority party will try to elect two. Of course, this does not always work and sometimes the majority party can elect all three because it has overwhelming voting strength. Limited voting is used mainly where three or more of the same kind of offices are being filled: county commissions, city councilmen, and judges especially.

An interesting but bitterly opposed method to achieve more precise representation on councils, commissions and other elective bodies is the *Hare system of proportional representation*. The elector

[22] Charles E. Merriam, *Chicago, A More Intimate View of Urban Politics* (1929), p. 99.
[23] Charles A. Beard, "Politics and City Government," *National Municipal Review,* 6 (1917), pp. 201–206.

votes for as many offices as are to be filled, but he votes for his first, second, third, and so forth choices rather than casting votes for the number of persons needed to fill the offices. The quota necessary to elect a candidate is arrived at by dividing the total number of ballots cast by the number of offices to be filled, and then taking the next highest number. All those who have the quota of first choices are declared elected. Then the ballots with first choices that are surplus and not needed are taken and their votes for second choice are used. If still the number of candidates necessary are not elected, the ballots of the candidate receiving the lowest number of first choices are utilized for their second choices, and so on up the line until the requisite number are elected. While the voters' task in proportional representation is simple, the counting is most difficult and this has militated against wide acceptance of the plan. The National Municipal League has recommended proportional representation for the election of city councils because it provides for obtaining representation among parties or groups according to their voting strength, because it eliminates primaries—both party and nonpartisan —and because it encourages independence in voting. Its opponents charge that P. R. encourages splinter parties and breaks up the conventional two-party system, that it foments division on racial and religious lines, and that the counting procedure is too difficult. P. R. has had hard sledding in the United States. Beginning with Ashtabula, Ohio, in 1915, it has been used in twenty-two cities but by the end of 1952, it was still in service only in nine, the largest being Cincinnati, Ohio.[24]

There are several methods devised to make certain candidates are elected by a majority of votes. In the ordinary election, it is quite possible, and often happens that the candidate is elected by a

[24] Richard S. Childs, *Civic Victories*, Chapter 26, pp. 242–251. Belle Zeller and Hugh A. Bone, "The Repeal of P. R. in New York City—Ten Years in Retrospect," *American Political Science Review* (December, 1948), pp. 1127– 1148.

Cities using P. R. at the end of 1952: Cincinnati, and Hamilton, Ohio; Cambridge, Lowell, Worcester, Medford, Quincy, and Revere, Massachusetts; and Hopkins, Minnesota.

Cities having repealed P. R. by the end of 1952: Ashtabula, Ohio; Boulder, Colorado; Kalamazoo, Michigan; Sacramento, California; West Hartford, Con-

plurality of votes but not a majority. Thus, the minority is represented at the expense of the majority. As long as the two-party system predominates in American politics, this danger is not too great as far as elections are concerned. Minority parties will poll, as a rule, only a slight percentage of the total and not often affect the results. But in primaries pluralities are often the rule especially in three cornered races where the candidates are fairly evenly matched. In such cases, the winner does not represent a predominant segment of the party. Likewise where twelve candidates, for example, seek the same office, the result is ludicrous.

In one-party states in the South, a *run-off primary* has been adopted to insure majority elections. Another system is *preferential voting* in which the primary itself is not needed. The names of all candidates no matter what party or group they represent are listed and to the right are boxes for first, second, and third choices. The voter indicates his choices for the first three. The candidate with a majority of first choices is declared elected, but if no candidate has a majority then the candidates second choice ballots are added to his first, and the candidate with the majority of first and second choices is elected. If no one has the majority, the third choices are added, and the candidate with the highest total is declared elected.

None of these "more refined" methods of voting has taken great hold in American elections. The elector seems to be satisfied with the majority-plurality system which when supported by the two-party system has proven generally acceptable.

The Initiative, Referendum, and Recall

Brand Whitlock, famous reform mayor of Toledo, once said: "The cure for the ills of democracy is more democracy." Such was the

---

necticut; Cleveland and Toledo, Ohio; Wheeling, West Virginia; New York City, Yonkers, and Long Beach, New York; Coos Bay, Oregon; and Saugus, Massachusetts.

All P. R. adoptions were made by referendum of the people and all but two repeals by referendum. In West Hartford, the legislature of Connecticut banned its use, and in Sacramento it was declared unconstitutional by the courts.

hope on which the initiative, referendum, and recall, sometimes known as the "newer instruments of democracy," became popular. They came into the present American political system as a part of the late 19th century movement toward more democracy and home rule, but they were invented long before that time. Both the initiative in primitive form and the referendum were in use in colonial New England—in urban areas mostly—and later were applied to trade unions and in industrial spheres.[25] The recall was found in Swiss cantons as an integral part of their democratic organization.[26]

The initiative and referendum puts upon the electorate a portion of responsibility for determining legislative policy and assumes that the people should participate directly in the legislative process. While in many states, these instruments are used on a statewide basis for constitutional and statutory proposals, they are used most extensively in the local level. Today, every state except Delaware, Indiana, and Rhode Island permits one or both of these devices to be used in certain classes of cities, but the petition referendum has the wider acceptance.[27]

The local initiative is a device whereby a certain number of qualified voters may draft a municipal charter amendment or a municipal or local ordinance, and submit it sometimes to the city or local council for action and sometimes directly to the electorate itself. Before this can be done, a petition setting forth the suggested provision must be signed by a certain percentage of the qualified electorate and submitted to designated officials for checking. If the city council adopts the proposition when it is submitted, there is no need for an election, but in case it rejects it or has not the right to pass upon

[25] John G. Thompson, *Urbanization: Its Effects on Government and Society* (1927), p. 224.

[26] See William B. Munro, *The Initiative, Referendum and Recall* (1913).

[27] Winston W. Crouch, "The Initiative and Referendum in Cities," *American Political Science Review*, 1943, pp. 491–504. In 1897, Nebraska was the first state to pass a general enabling law permitting electors to use the initiative and petition referendum on municipal problems. In 1898, San Francisco and Vallejo in California established direct legislative procedures in their charters. After 1907 when Des Moines adopted the commission form of municipal government with the initiative and referendum as a check upon the commission, many other commission governed cities followed suit.

it, it is then submitted to the electorate, and a majority of those voting determines the issue.

The referendum is where the local electorate has the right to vote upon state laws as applied in localities, and municipal ordinances or charter provisions after they have been adopted by the city council. Some referenda are *compulsory*, for example those on municipal charters and amendments in home rule states, and those on bond issues. Such propositions, by terms of state law, must be submitted to the voters. Others are *by petition* wherein action of the local council or even the state legislature are not immediately effective and time is given for petitions to be circulated calling for a vote of the people on the action taken by the legislative body. If the council repeals its action, there need be no referendum, but if not and the number of signers to the petition is sufficient, then the proposition is submitted to the electorate and the majority decides. Sometimes, there are *advisory* referenda and city councils ask for a "straw vote" on particular issues, and they may or may not follow the result of the referendum. *Voluntary* referenda in which the governing body may ask for a vote on a proposition may be legally binding in some states. The subjects on which referenda are most frequently allowed include: the form and structure of local government, the selection of a corporate name for the unit of government, the selection of sites for the county seat or city hall, the designation of the area embraced by the local unit, proposals relating to taxation, expenditures and bond issues; and policy decisions on such "vexing" questions as local option on liquor sales, Sunday movies and commercial entertainment.[28]

The recall has to do with elective officials rather than legislation. With this instrument, they can be recalled from office before the expiration of their term. The proceedings are begun with a petition signed by a certain percentage of qualified voters, often as high as twenty-five per cent to discourage abuse, and continue with the recall election. When this occurs, the incumbent official runs again

---

[28] See Ellis Paxon Oberholtzer, *The Referendum in America* (1900) for the most detailed analysis of historical development and 19th century usages of the referendum.

and other candidates may run against him. The one with the highest number of votes wins. The first official recognition of the recall was in the Los Angeles charter of 1903. In spite of the fact that at least a thousand cities in thirty-eight states provide for some use of the recall, it has been used sparingly.[29]

These newer instruments of democracy were most popular the first twenty years of the present century when it was believed that better government would automatically result from greater participation on the part of the electorate. While they have not been adopted as enthusiastically since the end of World War I, neither have they been abolished where once they were implanted. In fact, they are considered to be an integral part of city government where the strong mayor, commission, and council-manager forms are used because they make possible popular checks of the exercise of concentrated authority in city council and on the part of other elected officials. These devices are valuable adjuncts to the arsenal of democracy not only for the times they are exercised by the electorate but also for the realization on the part of public officials that those instruments can be utilized when and if the public officials fail to meet the demands of the electorate. They are a standing reminder that the people are the masters of local government, and that regular elections of officials are not the only means available to express this mastery. These instruments appear to have increased the interest and knowledge of the voters in their government, and so have been educational in character. True, they make for a longer ballot when a short ballot is desirable, and they sometimes unduly increase the voters' burden. But they have not been abused to any great degree. The common sense of the common people has always been a bulwark against their abuse by selfish or minority interests.

The New England Town Meeting

No American political institution has received more antiquarian interest than the New England town meeting. It has been hailed as one of the three examples in world history, along with the Greek

[29] F. L. Bird and F. M. Ryan, *The Recall of Public Officers* (1930), p. 4.

city-state and the Swiss canton, of pure democracy. The town meeting of the New England town was in colonial history the sovereign body of adult male citizens meeting annually to govern the town. It debated on the needs of the town, adopted the annual budget, levied the taxes, reviewed the acts of the selectmen and other administrative officers, and elected them for the coming year. The supreme judicial court of Massachusetts described its political value as follows: "No small part of the capacity for honest and efficient local government manifested by the people of the Commonwealth has been due to the training of citizens in the forum of the town meeting. . . . The practical instruction of the citizen in affairs of government through the instrumentality of public meetings and fact-to-face discussions may be regarded quite as important as their amusement, edification, or assumed temporal advancement in ways heretofore expressly authorized by statute and held constitutional." [30]

The success of the town meeting was based upon the fact that the community it represented was closely knit in ideas, compact in physical arrangement, and homogeneous in population. It was the composite result of English traditions of democratic action, the form of church government, and the kind of land system which evolved in the New England colonies. Today in the more rural areas, the town meeting still is a working institution, but in the more urban and industrial areas, it has gradually broken down because the communities became too large, their populations became mixed with newcomers who had different governmental traditions, and the governmental problems became too complicated to be disposed of in open meetings of all the citizens. Here the representative or limited form of town meeting is used.

But the fact that the New England town meeting stood for the efficacy of public discussion in public affairs has continued to be basic in American local government. While only a few states in the Middle West have adopted the town meeting as a local institution, the idea that community affairs should be debated has led to the tradition of discussion rather than official directive in local affairs.

---

[30] Quoted in Lancaster, *Government in Rural America*, D. Van Nostrand Company, Inc. (1952), pp. 37–38, from Wheeler *v.* Lowell, 96 Mass. 220 (1907).

There are thousands of town meetings in American communities sponsored by service clubs, women's organizations, radio and television program arrangers, and even by the governments themselves. Discussion is still a foundation stone of American municipal action.

Ballots and Voting Machines

In the early days of the Republic, voting was vocal. Electors appeared before election officials and orally indicated their choice of candidates. Then came the system of ballots in which each party listed its candidates on separate ballots and gave them to electors who then cast them at the polls. Ballots were made with unusually bright colors or designs so that they would be easy to detect as they were put in the ballot box. Toward the middle of the 19th century, bribery and threats became such common methods of influencing elections that reformers began to cry for a secret ballot. The Australian ballot was introduced into the United States in 1880 when Kentucky adopted it for the municipal elections of Louisville. Today only South Carolina operates without some form of the Australian secret ballot.

There are several ballot forms that are widely used. The *party-column* ballot lists the candidates for all offices under party designations, most of them either making provision for straight-ticket voting or printing a party emblem at the head of the column. The *office-block ballot* lists the candidates by office so that electors must vote for each office rather than a straight party ticket. Pennsylvania, however, provides for a combination of office blocks and straight party voting. *Nonpartisan election ballots,* of course, have no party symbols. *Consolidated ballots* have all the elections on one ballot, while in some states *separate ballots* are used for sets of offices or propositions to be voted upon.[31] A slight majority of states have party type, consolidated ballots, although there are many variations in form.

In spite of the secrecy of the ballot, many ingenious ways have

[31] Spencer D. Albright, *The American Ballot,* American Council on Public Affairs (1942).

been found to circumvent the law. Assistance to illiterate and incapacitated voters may be provided, and this may be abused by party workers. The "endless chain" is where an official ballot is taken from the polling place, marked by a party worker, and given to a voter before he goes into the polls. The voter deposits the marked ballot, gets a new ballot, and delivers this to the party worker after leaving the polling place. The worker marks this ballot and gives it to the next customer or rather vendor—for this procedure is used in selling votes. This practice has been checked by the use of numbered ballots. Likewise the voter may mark his ballot so as the party worker who is also an election officer may see it as proof of "voting right." Fraud in vote counting has long plagued municipal elections. Where there is a strong party machine, there may be found most highly developed methods for fraudulent voting and counting of votes. If the election officers at the polls are party workers, they can make the counting of the ballots a farce. They hand in the number of votes that are required and forget the ballots. Ballots are often changed by election officers. Sometimes, if the voter votes "the wrong way" a cross is surreptitiously placed in another box as the ballot is opened and then the ballot is thrown out because of error. Sometimes fraud is patently obvious as when more votes for a candidate are reported than there are registered in that district, or when a candidate gets all or almost all of the votes and his opponents none or only a token number. Indicating the possibilities of fraudulent voting in large cities, as high as forty per cent of total votes were found fraudulent by a field investigation of the 1926 Chicago primary.[32]

The voting machine has been gradually replacing the ballot in urban areas. Its proponents say that it eliminates some of the most flagrant types of election frauds. Spoiling of ballots is impossible with the voting machine, as is the "endless chain" practice. Counting errors can be ruled out and reporting errors minimized. The machine, moveover, makes the count almost immediately available after the close of the polls and therefore eliminates the temptation to alter the returns if certain candidates need a boost. But party workers

[32] Key, *Politics, Parties and Pressure Groups,* third edition (1952), p. 647.

are ingenious. Voting machines have been placed where the voting
can be seen by the party worker, the machinery can be jammed so
that a party worker repairman can enter the booth and see how
the elector votes, and there still can be collusion on the part of
election officials.

According to Professor Key, the Automatic Voting Machine Corporation estimated that in the 1944 presidential campaign, 14,000,-
000 votes, or 29 per cent of the total were cast by machine, and
that voting machines were used in 3,500 cities and towns in twenty-
one states.[33]

Voting in Local Elections

Voters take less interest in local elections than in those for state
and national officers. In many states, local elections are held in
different years or in different months of the year than national and
state elections in order that local and state and national issues are
not confused in the voters' minds. Undoubtedly national and state
issues predominate when local elections are held at the same time,
and the influence of straight party voting is felt.

James K. Pollock (University of Michigan) estimated that during
the 1920's voting in city elections in Ann Arbor, Michigan, amounted
to only about one-third of that in presidential elections, and in the
municipal primaries only one-fifth. Voting in state elections was
midway between presidential and local elections in voter turnout.[34]

In a study made of the voting behavior in the forty-five cities of
Los Angeles, California, Lawrence W. O'Rourke found that apathy
on the part of citizens towards the election process was more prevalent at the municipal elections than at those of the state and national
levels. For a seventeen year average (1935–52), the turnout in state

[33] *Ibid.*, p. 657. According to *The Book of the States, 1954–55*, p. 82, Idaho,
Mississippi, North Dakota, South Dakota, Vermont and Wyoming are the states
that have no legislation authorizing voting machines; in Kansas and Utah
voting machine legislation was repealed, and in Maine such legislation is inoperative.

[34] James K. Pollock, *Voting Behavior: A Case Study,* University of Michigan
(1939).

and national elections was 77 per cent of the registered electorate, while in municipal elections it was only 41 per cent. The range in state and national elections was from 68 to 87 per cent; in municipal elections, from 10 to 61 per cent. The inference was made that many who vote consistently in national and state elections, never vote in municipal elections.[35]

While there is no comprehensive study of such differentials, it is generally agreed that municipal elections draw many fewer voters than those for state and national offices. In spite of the emphasis in many quarters about home rule and local self-government, the citizens do not take their local responsibilities seriously enough. However, when fully aroused the citizens will come out of hiding in great numbers and when they do, it does not augur well for the party organization in power for heavy local votes are generally to turn out those who are in power. The American electorate is inclined to vote *against* rather than *for*. Organization leaders always hope for a light vote when in power for they know that the hard core of party voters will have more chance to predominate.

Professors Merriam and Gosnell made an extended study of nonvoting during the 1920's in Chicago. They found that half the nonvoters gave as their reason for nonvoting just plain indifference and inertia. A quarter of them gave illness and physical difficulties as the reason. Disbelief in voting, especially women voting, and administration and legal difficulties constituted the remainder.[36]

Professor Cortez Ewing (University of Oklahoma) found that nonvoting in the southern states increased at a spectacular rate when constitution provisions were adopted setting up such qualifications as payment of poll taxes, literacy and others adopted during the last two decades of the 19th century so that Negroes could be legally kept away from the polls.[37]

[35] Lawrence W. O'Rourke, *Voting Behavior in the Forty-five Cities of Los Angeles County*, Bureau of Governmental Research, University of California, Los Angeles (1953).

[36] Charles E. Merriam and Harold F. Gosnell, *Non-voting; Causes and Methods of Control*, University of Chicago (1924).

[37] Cortez Ewing, *Primary Elections in the South: A Study in Uniparty Politics*, University of Oklahoma (1953).

Is the local vote Republican or Democratic? In 1954, the mayors of the ten largest cities of the United States were Democratic with the exception of Los Angeles which was Republican, Detroit which was nonpartisan, and Washington, D. C., in which the governing body was an appointed commission. All of the cities from eleventh to twentieth in population were either Democratic, nonpartisan, or their chief executive officer was a manager. Undoubtedly, the Republican polls better in the medium sized cities, the small towns, and the rural areas. This alignment between the urban and rural has been fairly consistent since the days of the depression. The consequences of uniform Democratic majorities in all of the larger cities in relation to national elections is obvious. Democratic mayors have been, and will be inclined to go directly to Washington when a Democratic president is in office if the state administration is in the hands of the Republicans.

POLITICAL PARTIES AND LOCAL POLITICS

While national and state politics get the biggest headlines, they rest solidly upon party organization in the localities. Local party organizations are the hewers of wood and the drawers of water. Local party workers are the ones who go from door to door fighting for votes, who call for reluctant voters and give them free rides to the polls, who beat the bushes so that political meetings featuring state and national candidates will have enthusiastic crowds, who collect money for the party, who hang up the posters with the candidates' pictures and the party slogans, and who do all of the detailed work that make political organizations tick. For every general, there are a hundred captains and a thousand enlisted men and women. The generals sometimes look the other way when the privates are at work, they don't always recognize them when they call for their just rewards, but when it is a question of bringing in the votes, they are the statesman's best friend and he knows it. Woe to the successful candidate who, once elected, forgets who put him where he is. All of which is another way of saying that American politics is built upon organization and hard work, and that it is deeply embedded in the thousands of American communities, large and small.

Ordinary Politics

Although there are many variations in local party organization, the county chairman is one of the constants. In well-organized and successful parties—that is, those that win a fair share of the elections —this personage can be considered the No. 1 local party leader. Sometimes, he is even referred to as the boss. By one way or another, he has climbed to the top of the pile. Perhaps he is a popular county officeholder who spends a great deal of time strengthening party organization in the various townships, towns, and city wards. He can do this by virtue of the fact that if his party is in power at the state capitol, his sponsorship must be obtained before any resident in his county can get a state job. Such jobs may run into the hundreds in a large county, especially if the state departments are not under civil service regulations. They include highway workers, clerical workers, inspectors, field representatives, attorneys, junior executives, accountants, and scores of other classes. The county chairman may even have something to say about federal jobs that come out of his county but, because more than ninety per cent of the federal payroll is under civil service regulations, that source is not very lucrative in jobs. Then he has many county jobs, few of which are under civil service. If he is a good county chairman, he does not handle patronage in a high-handed way: he consults his county committeemen, his local leaders, and the influential men in the party; he makes a nice division of the spoils among the various leaders and their communities.

What does this man expect in return? First of all, he wants party loyalty. When there is a primary election, he expects his job-holders to support the party ticket against all comers; in the general election, he wants action and support in getting out the vote for the party. Men and women in state and county jobs are expected to spend week-ends throughout the year, and days before the election out working for the party, and they usually do. If they don't, and some

disdain that kind of effort and get away with it, they are expected
to contribute to the party exchequer—sometimes a certain percentage of their salaries. Such contributions are of course voluntary—for
many states have laws prohibiting the "macing" of employees.
Furthermore, the Federal Hatch Act specifically and clearly prohibits political activity in the party's interest so that the county
chairman does not bank on federal employees. The county chairman
expects the state political leaders to pass legislation that will help
his county and so make life easier for him. He wants state highway,
welfare, health, and other financial aid to be forthcoming in at least
the ratio that his organization is valuable to the state organization.
The county chairman may also hold a state job himself, something
pretty good but one in which he can spend a good deal of time at
home attending to his party affairs. That is pretty near enough for
the average county chairman. He does not want the moon. He is
content with his livelihood, his power, and his politics.

At the bottom of the local organization is the precinct committeeman. He is a very humble fellow, but no political leader worth his
salt underestimates his importance. For he is the one who is expected to deliver the vote in primaries and general elections in his
little bailiwick. In highly urban areas, he has almost a full-time job.
He knows every family in his precinct, their needs, their weaknesses.
He helps the poor and the unfortunate when they need help. Perhaps a ton of coal for a poor widow, turkeys for poor families on
Thanksgiving or Christmas, bail for an unfortunate meshed up in
the law, a club house for the boys in the alley, a job for a likely
high school graduate, even a senatorial scholarship for the real
bright boy, rent money and shelter for the down-and-out. In precincts where people do not need this kind of help, perhaps he can
do something about traffic and other minor violations. He might be
able to bring his influence to bear against an increase in assessed
valuation of taxable property, against overzealous enforcement of
building regulations and such. In rural areas, the precinct committeeman is the liaison between the people and the county chairman;
there are many services a good precinct man can render his constituency no matter who they are.

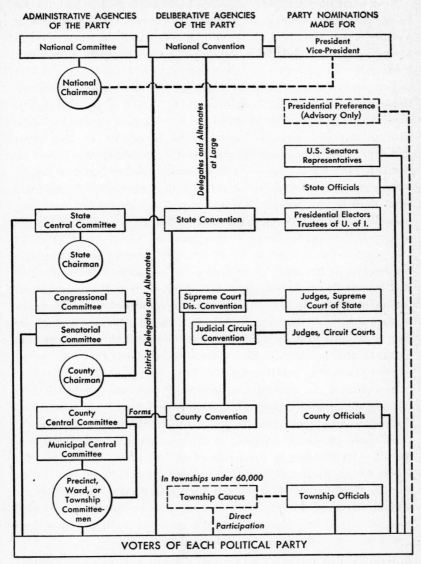

ORGANIZATION OF POLITICAL PARTIES IN ILLINOIS

Fig. 1. Organization of Political Parties in Illinois. (From *Your Business as a Voter,* University of Illinois, February 18, 1941.)

Now what does the precinct committeeman expect from those he helps? Again, he wants party loyalty. He expects his people to vote a straight party ticket in the general election and the party slate in the primary. As a Philadelphia precinct leader, quoted by Professor John Salter (University of Wisconsin) said: "I work for you 364 days a year; all I ask you to do is to work one day for me." He wants those who can, to contribute something to the party and to his work. He likes to be able to go to the ward leader, or county chairman, or city chairman—to whomever he reports on election night and say: "Here it is, chief. We carried it by hundred votes." And he wants to hear the big boy say: "Nice work, Pete, or Nate, or Bill, or Pat. I can always depend on you. I wish they were all like you." And what does he get out of all this, our precinct captain? Sometimes, only the joy of politics; perhaps some pull at the county court house or city hall when he needs it; maybe a job there—one that won't take up too much time, or be too arduous, maybe something like tax assessor or tax collector or justice of the peace or constable, one that he can do on the side for a little extra money. He doesn't want the moon either. He likes to be precinct committeeman, and he likes to earn a little on the side if there is a chance. But most of all he likes to be able to deliver his precincts because he knows his people like him, and because he likes them. Else why would anyone want to be a precinct committeeman?

In between the county chairman and precinct committee is a whole array of leaders and committees—ward, town, city, township— depending where you are. Together they make up the local party slates, hold meetings, organize campaigns, work for the party, run for office, participate in the fruits of victory where they can: jobs, favors, status, information, maybe a deal here and there. But if they lose an election, and especially if they lose a lot of them, there is nothing for them to get. All they have is hope for the future and perhaps an abiding love of the great game of politics. But it does get them out of the house at night sometimes.

"The point here is," says Professor Salter, "that all men who get elected and reelected to public office in our democracy, whether their objects are public or private, devote a substantial amount of their time and energy to paying personal attention to the constituents." [38] People like attention paid to them. They are not nearly as much interested in ideas and principles as they are in projecting themselves into personal contact with "big men" they know and can call by their first name, and on whom they can make demands no matter how trivial.

Furthermore, the political worker in large cities where there are many racial groups and much poverty is sort of an adjustor and social integrator. "It is generally conceded," says Sonya Torthal, "that the prevalence of the spoils system in the larger cities is due to the wide discrepancies between political power and distributed wealth. When the financial power is in the hands of a few and the electoral power in the hands of the many, bargaining and corruption must necessarily follow—unless, of course, those who hold the voting majority will use their numerical advantage to improve their common status." [39]

Interviewing precinct committeemen in ten rural Illinois counties including 215 precincts, Leon Weaver was impressed by the solid caliber of the men who held such positions in the party organization. "A word should be said as to the writers' impressions resulting from their personal contacts," he concludes. "Let it be noted that his respect for the rural politician was increased, not lessened, as a result of their face-to-face contacts. With but few exceptions, such politicians appear to be at least as frank, as honest, and as well intentioned as the general run of human kind." [40] Seventy-five per cent of them were farmers, clerks, salesmen, and laborers. The others were business and professional men with a few government workers. The volunteer precinct worker, who does not get pay or a job out of his political efforts fills an important role in rural party organization.

[38] John T. Salter, "Personal Attention in Politics," *American Political Science Review* (February, 1940), p. 55.

[39] Sonya Torthal, "The Small Fry and the Party Purse," *American Political Science Review* (February, 1940), p. 74.

[40] Leon Weaver, "Some Soundings in the Party System: Rural Precinct Committeemen," *American Political Science Review* (February, 1940), p. 84.

Corrupt Politics

There have been many corrupt political organizations in the United States; some still exist. More to the point, political corruption shows its head many times and in many places, anytime it gets a chance. The difference between ordinary and corrupt politics is that in the latter men devote most or all of their energies to the primary object of making money out of politics. The men who are part of the corrupt political organization—the boss, the city chairman, the county chairman, the precinct captain, the man-on-the-inside, the financier, the stooge, the hanger-on, the officeholder, the messenger, and all the others—are all out for "what they can get." And what they can get and want most is money. Persons with other ideas are soon weeded out.

How do they get it? They shake down employees in government whose jobs they sponsored; they shake down industries and businesses; they get cuts on government purchases; they sell municipal franchises; they deal out justice to whoever can pay; they organize and profit by businesses that deal in government supplies and services; and they take protection money from the underworld. An immense amount of money is available to a corrupt political organization that controls the local government in any urban and industrial area.

And here it was that the most infamous political machines in American municipal history were assembled and took their toll. After the Civil War, American cities grew like mushrooms. Immigration from foreign lands and from the American countryside and small towns swelled the population from decade to decade. Houses had to be built, streets laid out, sewerage provided, water supply increased, police and fire protection developed, schools and public buildings erected. The government that had to provide the services of city life was one inherited from the Jacksonian countryside. It was amateur, part-time, untrained, scrambled, inept. Only through the integrative efforts of a political organization and a boss could the people who wanted something from the city be guided through the governmental maze. And they paid for this guidance. Why did people come to the city anyhow? To make money, of course. Those who went into politics were just like those who went into business— they were not in it "for their health" as one boss said. But like some people in business, some carried their quest for money to extremes so much so that they became millionaires. In order to consolidate their positions, they built up tight organizations from precinct committeeman to county chairman and these were rewarded for their services according to profit accrued. The politicians spent a lot of money on their organizations. It paid handsome dividends. So it cost a lot of money to build American cities, and a lot was wasted, but the cities were built. The American city grew up in rough and ready circumstances, and became tough, but grow it did. The boss and the political machine, even when corrupt, played their part.

The corrupt political machines in American political history are legion. Almost every large city had one: the Tweed Ring of New York, the Vare gang in Philadelphia, the Thompson crowd in Chicago, the Pendergast machine in Kansas City, the Hague outfit in Jersey City, Boss Cox of Cincinnati, and many others. Some of them were exposed in the early years of the present century by the greatest of all "muckrakers," Lincoln Steffens. In his *Shame of the Cities* and his later *Autobiography,* he describes, analyzes, and philosophizes about corrupt politics in the cities of the United States as no other man has done before or since. No student of American history, government, or politics should fail to read Steffens. He and other journalistic muckrakers and reformers started a great movement that set the bosses and their machines back on their heels, a movement that was fraught with important consequences in American politics. It set the stage for the great political and administrative improvements in municipal government in the 20th century. There are still some bosses and machines in a more modern day—witness Curley of Boston, Crump of Memphis, Johnson of Atlantic City, O'Connell of Albany as recent examples—but they are not nearly as powerful, as brash, as raw as they were before 1920.

Luther Gulick, seasoned observer and veteran administrator of

municipal government, thinks that progress has been made since
the time of Steffens.[41] There is less direct thievery; better accounting
and auditing; less mugging, kidnaping, and political murder; less
franchise boodling, less raw patronage arrangements, and fewer
crooked deals. The voters are better educated; there are less vote
frauds. Mr. Gulick even thinks that the boss performs some useful
governmental functions even when building his machine and collecting graft. For example, he gives central direction to the ramshackle
city and county political structure; he makes it work, gives it discipline. In spite of inept and incompetent officials, he gives some
continuity to local government. He regulates corruption by holding
it down to tolerable limits. Likewise the political machine continues
to help the "little man" which in spite of social security he still greatly
appreciates. The boss strives to give the people what they really
want because he wants to stay in power. If it is boulevards they
want, he builds them; if it is low cost housing, he gets it; if it is
gambling and numbers, he lets them have them.

Dr. Gulick points out how cities have retrogressed, too. Government is much harder to supervise, it is more technical, and requires
much more money. There is a vast increase of "legal graft" such as
lax enforcement of regulations can bring. Civic boundaries are
more artificial because of the growth of the metropolitan areas.
Newspapers are less independent and civic morality has not been
modernized. The "shame of the cities" today is threefold: lazy
citizenship with low civic standards, lack of city pride, and failure
to look ahead. As a result, American cities still are hosts to dirt,
slums, traffic congestion, and the underworld—not a pretty picture.

Reform Politics

America was too dynamic to allow corrupt politics full sway—
even when it was busy making money and building the nation and
its cities. A strong action begets reaction, and that is what happened
in American politics. Local party offices, committees, and leaders

---

[41] Luther Gulick, "The Shame of the Cities—1946," *National Municipal Review* (January, 1947), pp. 18–25.

are to be found whether the city's political objectives are ordinary, corrupt, or reform. The difference is in the motivations of the people who occupy those places. In the average political organization, the emphasis is "just politics," a little power and a livelihood; in the corrupt organization, it is money, money, and more money; in the reform organization, the emphasis is on improvement—which is just as American as the desire for money and the love of politics for its own sake.

The reformer's stock in trade is not what favors he can bestow on all and sundry, nor ways and means of making money for himself, his friends and supporters, but it is his desire to create order out of chaos, to improve conditions, to make life better for his fellowmen. True, there are some bogus reformers, wolves in sheep's clothing, but they are not usually successful, for it is difficult to fool the American people about reformers. America from time to time takes the reformer to its heart, and gives him votes enough to "throw the rascals out." Reformers have that missionary spirit that has imbued American life from its earliest beginnings, and the average American understands this. When things get too bad, they call the reformer in. And then there is a political awakening in the city that rivals camp meeting evangelism. Thousands of workers spring up out of the wards and precincts and beg for a chance to work for a better city—and they work for nothing. Civic clubs raise money, service clubs discuss municipal problems, women's clubs wave the banners of municipal reform. The civic pride of the community wells up and overflows on all sides. Virtue has its day, and the reformers are swept into office with majorities that surprise even the most optimistic. The people have risen, have taken a hold of the offending member, tossed it out. They have used the polls to clean up the municipal mess. Perhaps the reformers have not been able to do everything they promise, their inexperience in government and politics sometimes holds them back. There is some backsliding, the people lose interest and perhaps in the next election, the political machine wins again. But make no mistake, if it does it is not the same machine. The worst members are by now liquidated, the leaders are more careful and cagey, they do not try to undo what the reformers were able to accomplish. Perhaps instead of losing the next election, the reformers consolidate their gains as they have done in Cincinnati, Kansas City, Los Angeles, Cleveland, and New York. The reformer has often been called impractical in politics, and sometimes he may be, but he has left a legacy of political and governmental institutions, methods and techniques that is gradually reforming and improving local government throughout the length and breadth of this land. These "impractical" men are responsible for improved election procedures: registration, ballot protection, voting machines, nonpartisan elections, the direct primary; for improved governmental structure: the commission and city manager plans, the strong mayor, the city administrator; for better methods: accounting and auditing, personnel administration, management science. Don't sell them short. Their accomplishments are little short of the miraculous. They are the hope of the future.

The nation can show many cities and counties where municipal reform forces carried the fight to ultimate victory at the polls and to actual reorganization of local government. *Cincinnati*, once the domain of Boss Cox and his henchmen, was known as "the worst governed city in the country." As late as 1925, it was rundown, politically corrupt. Citizen action secured adoption of the city manager plan with a council of nine elected by proportional representation. Organized as the Charter party with some liberal support, they elected six of their candidates to the council. They hired able managers including Colonel C. O. Sherrill from Washington, Dr. Clarence A. Dykstra from Los Angeles (later president of two great universities), Wilbur R. Kellogg, a local businessman, and C. A. Harrell, career city manager. Soon it became one of the best run cities. In every election, the Charter party faced stern opposition. Sometimes it lost its majority in council but the manager system remained undisturbed. It is the largest American city governed under a manager plan.

Kansas City adopted the city manager plan in 1926, and is the second largest city now under the manager plan. Here the city powers were vested in a council of nine elected on nonpartisan tickets. From 1926–40 it was under the domination of Boss Pender-

1954 ALL AMERICA CITIES AWARDS

National Municipal League and *Look Magazine* Annual awards are made to eleven cities which, in the opinion of an impartial jury, have made or are making especially noteworthy civic progress as a result of citizen action.

Chicago, Illinois (Pop. 3,740,000). Neighborhood organizations with thousands of volunteer workers sparked a far-reaching campaign to check creeping slum-blight in an area covering 56 square miles.

Decatur, Arkansas (Pop. 390). Facing total unemployment when its only industry moved away, citizens of this tiny town raised money for a new poultry-processing plant and, to attract other new businesses, voted bond issues for sewer, water, and gas lines.

Maricopa County, Arizona (Pop. 440,000). Aroused by chronic mismanagement, voters organized to elect a reform government and install a county manager. The result was elimination of waste, establishment of central purchasing, vitally needed public works.

Mexico, Missouri (Pop. 12,500). Approval at the polls of the council-manager plan of government and bond issues to install sewers, build schools, and erect a wing to the hospital were steps in a citizens' campaign to transform their "tank town" into a modern city. Volunteer groups also landscaped a large park area and built an open air theater.

Modesto, California (Pop. 35,000). Choked by boom town suburbs which paid limited taxes, the city decided that the only solution was to make Modesto so attractive that outlying areas would "beg to become a part of it." Government reform, new schools, better sewage disposal, and other citizen-inspired improvements led most of the surrounding areas to ask for annexation.

Newark, New Jersey (Pop. 446,000). A wave of citizen indignation against an entrenched, graft-ridden commission form of government produced a new charter. Initial results include a slum survey, plans for new schools, improved traffic control, and the decision of several major business firms to expand in Newark.

Pueblo, Colorado (Pop. 80,000). After 15 previous attempts, citizens finally threw out their inefficient commission government and voted for a new charter. Under its new city manager, the town tackled its chronic problems and was able to make many civic improvements without any increase in taxes.

Richfield, Minnesota (Pop. 31,756). When population increased almost ten fold in 14 years, the town was confronted with wholly inadequate facilities, including an antiquated village government. An energetic citizens' campaign resulted in a vote for an up-to-date government, a $4,000,000 sewage system, new schools, street paving, and other improvements.

Rock Island, Illinois (Pop. 50,600). Determined to crack down on extensive gambling and vice and to put their city on a sound fiscal footing, citizens won a tough battle against ward politicians and, under their new charter, elected a reform administration.

Rockville, Maryland (Pop. 13,000). Though handicapped by local laws and the "old guard," citizens of this rapidly growing Washington, D. C., suburb organized to elect a government pledged to reform. Under a new city manager, voting machines were installed, and chaotic municipal finances were straightened out.

Warren, Ohio (Pop. 52,400). Voters struck at corruption and waste by electing a mayor whose new policies brought about definite progress in ridding the city of gambling, vice, and insolvency.

gast who used the manager to get hundreds of party henchmen on
the payroll and who turned city government into a shambles. He
was finally defeated by a citizen uprising. A new council went into
office and hired a well-known manager from Saginaw, Michigan,
L. P. Cookingham, who has served with success since then.

Cambridge, Massachusetts, with a population of over 110,000 has
had a manager with both council and the school committee elected
by proportional representation since 1942. The date ended a period
of inefficiency, rising taxes, and low civic morale. Spectacular savings were made by centralized purchasing, and the use of city employees for such jobs as snow removal, refuse disposal, and street
repairs formerly given out to contractors. Recreation, police, and
health services were modernized and expanded.

Dayton, Ohio (population 260,000) was the first city of over 8,000
to adopt city manager government. Through eighteen elections,
since 1913, the manager plan has withstood any opposition and has
come through with a record of continued and serene efficiency and
service.[42]

Peoria, Illinois (population 112,000), second largest city in the
state, was governed inefficiently for many years by a 22 member
council elected by wards. Gambling, vice, protection money, and
all the rest of the paraphernalia of vice was entrenched. In 1951,
Peoria for Council-Manager (PCM) was formed and won the election for council-manager government, and it went into effect in
1953. Conditions are getting better.

Youngstown, Ohio (125,000 population) is a steel town and was
run by the rackets. It was wide open. Bookies, hoodlums, prostitutes,
gambling, and the rest of the mob plied their trades unmolested. A
reform group headed by a young Princeton graduate beat the gang
at the polls and ran them out of town. Youngstown is now an orderly
city.

Daytona Beach, Florida (30,000 population) had the problem of
gambling. The city officials did nothing. Then the citizens revived
an old law which permitted them to make personal raids on gam-

---

[42] Childs, *Civic Victories, the Story of an Unfinished Revolution* (1952). The
foregoing illustrations were drawn from various chapters in *Civic Victories*.

bling establishments which were feeding the corrupt political machine in power. Some were closed. The Civic Affairs Committee went further. It devised and worked out a fraud proof election bill and purged the voting lists which had contained thousands of sleepers. The citizens won an election and put in a reform commission, five to none. A professional manager was appointed. He immediately fired the head of the city yard, a political patronage center, and for his pains received a death threat. City employees struck but citizens manned the garbage trucks and maintained city services. The reform group started with a $138,000 deficit, soon had a $66,000 surplus. Things have improved in Daytona Beach.

In *McMinn county, Tennessee,* the political machine was driven from power after a night-long gun fight led by returning G. I.'s who could not tolerate the corrupt conditions that had been rife in the county for the past ten years. Some were hurt, no one fatally, but the fight broke up the machine which had a record of election frauds, incompetence, high expenditures, high fee collections. The County Good Government League sponsored legislation that established the county manager plan and a reformed local judicial setup.

Canton, Ohio (117,000 population) organized a Citizens Committee for Good Government in 1950 as a protest against booming vice, crime, and gambling conditions. It was a committee of six hundred drawn from all classes. In the 1951 election it elected 17 out of a 20 member council plus other elective officials and thereafter proceeded to clean up the government and the town. The new director of safety cracked down on the gambling establishments, closing 90 gambling places. The bawdy houses near City Hall were raided and closed. Canton was freed by its "Vice Center" tag by the American Social Hygiene Association after the clean-up. The motto of the Citizens Committee is: "Good government is hard to get and easy to lose." The citizens group was elected again in 1953, and only two of its original six hundred have withdrawn from the original committee. Canton, along with Daytona Beach and Peoria, was on the roll of All American Cities, 1953, an annual event, sponsored by *Look* magazine and the *National Municipal League.*

The list of cities that revolted against corrupt and crime-ridden politics can be continued indefinitely. Almost all the large cities at one time or another experienced waves of reform to offset the corruption that seeps in so quickly into local government if citizen vigilance is withdrawn. New York, Philadelphia, Boston, Jersey City, Los Angeles, New Orleans, San Francisco, Seattle, Milwaukee, Detroit, Cleveland are only a few of the larger cities that in recent years have experienced in greater or lesser degree the cleansing of reform, citizen participation, and improved government. Campaigns to improve the operation of local government are an indication that the people can act when they want to and that they know what to do when they win at the polls. Democracy is safe at home when this can happen. It is exciting, exhilarating, and good for the body politic.[43]

CIVIC ACTION AND LOCAL GOVERNMENT

The right of free elections, both primary and general, is basic to local citizenship. When elections are held regularly according to law rather than on the basis of decree from higher levels of government as they are in many other countries of the world, they constitute the foundation of municipal democracy. No matter how bad the government can become, a municipal election can clean the slate when the people so desire. The right to join political parties which try to gain control of the local government is also fundamental in American politics. But elections and political parties are not enough to answer the civic need. Without continuous citizen interest and action brought to bear upon municipal problems, American local government would be without the vigor, imagination, and will-to-accomplish that it now possesses. The citizens organized in a myriad of groups give local government its real life and bends it to the needs of the community.

Organized groups in community life are as varied as are the in-

[43] The pages of the *National Municipal Review* going back through the decades contain hundreds of stories of citizen action to produce better local government. Every student of government should spend some time browsing through the monthly issues of this publication that through the years has never dropped the banner of good government.

terests of the people; they represent occupation, religion, social life, recreation, education, mental outlook, experience, and aspirations. Through organization citizens have the means of expressing themselves and bringing their influence to bear on civic life. Community progress is a complicated process in which people organized in groups play a leading part. In fact, elections and political parties in the last analysis are only the means for making group desires and wishes into political and governmental reality.

Local Interest Groups

Business groups are well organized and directed towards their civic objectives. The chambers of commerce, the junior chambers of commerce, the manufacturing clubs, and the service clubs (Rotary, Kiwanis, Lions, and others) have as their long range program to make the community bigger and better. Their own interests will advance as do those of the community as a whole. More people mean more business, a better community will draw more people and keep more people at home. These groups, it cannot be denied, have raised the standards of community life throughout the United States. They have stood for better government—the council-manager plan received their support in many cities. They help the unfortunate— their charities are legion. They hear civic and governmental problems discussed and get civic education at their meetings. They develop a vigorous community spirit and therefore support a program for better streets, better lighting systems, better schools, better recreation. But sometimes their views are not broad enough to envision the people of the entire community. They often range themselves against such projects as low cost housing, urban redevelopment, and city planning. They oppose large increases of public expenditure for they do not want to increase their local tax obligations, and they stand against too much monkeying with assessed valuations for taxable purposes. Many of their members have their business in town but live in the suburbs, and they are inclined to evade the problems of the metropolitan area because they do not want to take responsibility for a run-down and blighted central city.

Because they belong to these mid-city associations they can influence the city government even though they live on the outside. However, all in all, these groups are influential and they have generally stood for progress.

Improvement organizations constitute another large class. Organized to work for some specific improvement or generally interested in the field of civic improvement, they include the church groups led by the clergy and dedicated laymen, educational groups such as parent-teachers associations, women's organizations such as the Federation of Women's Clubs and the League of Women Voters, civic improvement associations composed of citizens who take their civic responsibilities seriously, and neighborhood groups that watch with eagle eye developments that may affect their residential and business areas. By and large, these organizations have had a tremendous effect on municipal improvement throughout the nation during the past fifty years. It is their members who rise up and fight corrupt political machines, the underworld when it shows its head too high, and the enemies of civic progress. It is they who are chiefly responsible for local adoption of the newer instruments of democracy and improved local government. While their efforts may sometimes appear inadequate and faltering, in the long run they are deeply influential because they represent the conscience of the community.

A third arena of group action is that of *local organizations of powerful national groups* such as the American Legion, the Veterans of Foreign Wars, the Federation of Farm Bureaus, the Grange, the American Federation of Labor, and the CIO. These organizations on the local level interest themselves only incidentally in municipal problems and action but are active when their objectives and their membership are affected. The Legion and the Vets will take great interest in rooting out alleged communism in schools and other public bodies, the labor unions will bring their influence to bear on municipal action for low cost housing and urban redevelopment, the farm organizations will support demonstrations of improved farm methods and home economics, and will take a keen interest in rural schools, roads, and taxation. When the issues are clearly drawn these groups, because of their great numbers, can be most effective. They too have had a general positive impact for good in the community, although at times they may associate their narrow interests with the community as a whole.

A fourth and influential group are the *professional organizations* of doctors, attorneys, teachers, real estate salesmen, restaurateurs, barbers, beauticians, and other organized professions. Their interest in municipal affairs is also incidental but becomes sharply focused when it concerns their own livelihood. The doctors have some decided views about public health measures, the real estate agents will oppose local taxation of real estate transfers, the restaurateurs want reasonableness in restaurant hygiene regulations. Sometimes these groups can be drawn into a civic battle for improvement or against corruption but such is not their main interest.

The fifth and last general grouping of organizations influencing civic action are the so-called *social and protective associations*: the Elks, the Masons, the Moose, the Knights of Columbus, and a host of other fraternal lodges and clubs. They take great interest in civic celebrations, charities, and improvements and, although they do not usually enter the civic fray, they exercise beneficial effects on the community because of their civic pride and the help they give their needy members.

Media for Civic Action

In the American community there exist a number of media for free expression of ideas and the interchange of opinion and information. The first of these is *public discussion* which is the bulwark of our local democracy. When meetings to discuss local problems and solutions can be held without fear, the chances are that progress eventually will be made no matter how bitter and acrimonious the debate may be. The right answers will gradually come to light and will be accepted by the majority of people. There are places in the world where public discussion is forbidden and there civic freedom is no more.

Other media for civic action are the *local newspaper, radio station, and television facilities.* Through these, the people can read about and listen to ideas, arguments, and information on civic matters. The American newspaper has played a conspicuous part in the fight for civic improvement. In many communities it has led the battle against entrenched corruption. It has exposed all manner of graft and has brought many a boss and political machine to time. Perhaps in the future, radio and television will supersede the newspaper in civic affairs, but at present it is still the most influential disseminator of ideas and information. Many times civic communication facilities are biased in the direction of the ideas and interests of the ownership, but that is often counteracted by competition. Likewise the public today is better able than ever to detect the more obvious slants, and by withdrawing its support it can bring about neutrality. Newspapers have been molders of public opinion for many years. Although syndicates and national news coverage loom larger each year in the local paper, they are still of paramount local importance.

Many civic and local government problems are too complicated to be decided merely by public discussion and newspaper stories. They need detailed study and the opinion of experts. In many larger cities, this need has led to the establishment of *bureaus of municipal research* financed by private funds and governed by a committee of civic minded citizens. Staff people are hired on a full-time, permanent basis to make continuous studies of municipal government in the fields of revenue, expenditure, accounting, personnel, management, streets, welfare, and all other subjects that need study. The results of these studies are made available to the governmental officials themselves and to the public. These bureaus have done inestimable good and have more than earned the few dollars spent on them.

The research movement in local government had its origins in the civic restlessness that preceded the exposé of corrupt political machines before World War I. It was all very well for reformers to ride white chargers into the fray against civic corruption, but for the long haul there was need for accurate, continuous, and dependable information. Someone had to make the ammunition for the civic battle. The first such organization was the New York Bureau of Municipal Research established in 1907. Between 1909 and 1916, Philadelphia, Cincinnati, Chicago, Dayton, Milwaukee, Minneapolis, Toronto, Akron, Rochester, and Detroit followed suit. At one time there were thirty such bureaus in the larger American cities.[44] Smaller towns and rural communities are usually without such organization but in some states, notably Pennsylvania, tax paying organizations carry on similar functions on a county basis.

Important Civic Issues

American localities have faced many problems during the past century as the nation was becoming an urban, industrial giant. The people have invented, discussed, fought about, voted on, and finally resolved a great many issues in the process. Change has been the characteristic of community life in the United States, and change has often come from civic action.

One group of issues always facing the growing community has to do with *modern improvements.* Should the main street be paved, a new bridge built, a new school house constructed, a new city hall erected, a water system installed, a modern sewerage system put in? There are always the "pros" and the "cons." The pros are for a bigger and better community, the cons are against increased taxation which the improvement would necessitate. On such issues the "progressives" fight the "conservatives" in every locality. Sometimes one side wins, sometimes the other. In the long run, the progressives have come out on top for American communities have installed many efficient public conveniences in a short time.

Another set of issues has to do with *improvements in local government,* and it is in the urban areas that progress along these lines has been greatest. Civic minded citizens have fought for electoral reform, for changes in municipal organization, for better administrative methods. The fight is continuous and there is still much to be done. Improvement in county and township government has not

[44] Lent D. Upson, "Contributions of Citizen Research to Effective Government," *The Annals of the American Academy of Political and Social Science* (September, 1938), pp. 171–182.

been nearly as extensive as that in the urban areas. Today there is little or no movement to improve rural local government and as a result it remains as it was a century ago. The national and state governments are forced to take up the slack in rural affairs.

A third group of civic issues has to do with *racial minorities and the lower income classes*—those whom the dominant groups are prone to leave out of the civic picture. The growing American city, populated largely by immigrants from abroad and emigrants from the countryside, has included large enclaves of people from Europe settled in racial neighborhoods who have often continued to live together as they did in the old country. Americanization of these groups was one of the most important civic issues during the fifty years from 1870 until the end of World War I. Since the 1920's when European immigration was greatly reduced, this civic alignment has gradually disappeared. The public schools, the political party, and the free economic organization have done a pretty thorough Americanization job during the past two generations and the race question as between white Europeans has been at least partially solved. But the Negro question has not been solved either in the South where there has been official segregation for generations or in the North where many Negroes live in city slums. Their problems of employment, housing, relief, welfare, and crime offer a great challenge that calls for the highest type of local statesmanship.

Lower income groups tend to concentrate in urban areas and live in slums and poorer districts. Their needs in housing, welfare, relief, and all-around protection cost much more than the municipal revenue they contribute. Therefore, large scale improvement projects for these people have often been opposed by the more fortunate classes, many of which have moved away from the central city. The underprivileged classes, however, have political influence by virtue of their numbers and frequently their champions win at the polls. They then attempt to institute those measures of relief that the old city and its residents require by using general city funds mainly collected from business, industry, and the better residential areas.

Where this is not enough, federal aid is involved for the national government has been gradually moving in on urban problems.

Still another set of issues that complicate civic life are those concerned with the *central city and the suburban areas*. People have moved out of the city to enjoy fresh air, quiet, civic independence, low taxes, home ownership, and the other highly vaunted advantages of suburban life. They have not always obtained them but they deem themselves better off than in the city even if they have to commute three hours a day. Above all, they do not want to be annexed to the central city of the metropolitan area and they oppose any central city influence in their governmental lives. This problem is by no means solved and bids fair to occupy the minds of the metropolitan citizens for a generation to come.

TEN SUBJECTS FOR FURTHER STUDY

1. The "length" of the ballot in your community.
2. Restrictions on suffrage in your state.
3. Registration in your state.
4. The direct primary in your state.
5. Proportional representation in New York City.
6. The initiative and referendum on local matters in your state.
7. The New England town meeting today.
8. Nonpartisan elections in a particular state where they exist.
9. The formal party organization in your state.
10. A personality study of the county chairman of the party in power in your county.

REFERENCES

Henry J. Abraham, "One Way to Get Out the Vote," *National Municipal Review*, September 1950, pp. 395–399.

———, "What Cure for Voter Apathy," *National Municipal Review*, July 1952, pp. 346–350.

Charles A. Beard, "Political Parties in City Government," *National Municipal Review*, March 1917, pp. 201–206.

Hugh A. Bone, "Political Parties in New York City," *American Political Science Review*, April 1946, pp. 272–282.

A. C. Breckenridge, "Pre-primary Trial Dropped," *National Municipal Review*, April 1954, pp. 196–199.

William Seal Carpenter, "Reformer's Task Never Done," *National Municipal Review*, July 1952, pp. 339–345.

Richard S. Childs, "The Ballot Is Still too Long!" *National Municipal Review*, February 1946, pp. 67–70.

———, "Civic Victories in the United States," *National Municipal Review*, September 1955, pp. 398–402.

L. P. Cookingham, "Inside Story of Kansas City," *National Municipal Review*, December 1948, pp. 596–599.

Finla G. Crawford, "Operation of the Literary Test for Voters in New York," *American Political Science Review*, May 1931, pp. 342–345.

Winston W. Crouch, "Direct Legislation Laboratory," *National Municipal Review*, February 1951, pp. 81–87.

———, *The Initiative and Referendum in California* (The Haynes Foundation, 1950).

———, "The Initiative and Referendum in Cities," *American Political Science Review*, June 1943, pp. 491–504.

Harold W. Dodds, "Voter's Role in a Democracy," *National Municipal Review*, January 1947, pp. 11–17.

Harold M. Dorr, "Nomination by Money Deposit," *National Municipal Review*, June 1954, pp. 288–292.

Charles Edison, "How to Break into Politics," *National Municipal Review*, June 1947, pp. 304–309.

Justin N. Feldman, "How Tammany Holds Power," *National Municipal Review*, July 1950, pp. 330–334.

Arthur B. Gallien, "Civic Design and Democracy," Chapter V in Coleman Woodbury, ed., *The Future of Cities and Urban Redevelopment* (Chicago, 1953).

George H. Gallup, "What Makes Us So Ignorant?" *National Municipal Review*, December 1947, pp. 612–617.

Robert P. Goldman, "An Analysis of Cincinnati's Proportional Representation Elections," *American Political Science Review*, August 1930, pp. 699–710.

Harold F. Gosnell, *Negro Politicians*, University of Chicago (Chicago, 1935).

George H. Hallett, Jr., *Proportional Representation: The Key to Democracy*, National Municipal League (New York, 1940).

Joseph P. Harris, *Model Direct Primary Election System*, National Municipal League (New York, 1951), *Model Voter Registration System* (New York, 1954).

Lashley G. Harvey, "Boston's Mid-Century Revolt," *National Municipal Review*, April 1951, pp. 195–200.

Donald S. Hecock, "Long Ballot Burdens Detroit," *National Municipal Review*, July 1946, pp. 344–346.

F. C. Howe, *The City: The Hope of Democracy* (New York, 1905).

Frank Kent, *The Great Game of Politics* (New York, 1931).

Jack Kroll, "Labor's Stake in Civic Affairs," *National Municipal Review*, December 1949, pp. 542–545.

Blanche S. Lindenmayer, "Women Get the Answers," *National Municipal Review*, May 1949, pp. 232–235.

Stuart A. MacCorkle, "The Professor is a Politician," *National Municipal Review*, February 1951, pp. 76–80.

George H. McCaffrey, "Proportional Representation in New York City," *American Political Science Review*, October 1949, pp. 841–852.

C. E. Merriam and H. F. Gosnell, *Non-Voting*, University of Chicago (Chicago, 1924).

Newbold Morris, *Let the Chips Fall Where They May* (New York, 1955).

Roy V. Peel, "The Political Machine of New York City," *American Political Science Review*, August 1933, pp. 611–618.

Howard R. Penniman, *Sait's American Parties and Elections* (New York, 1948).

Jewell Cass Phillips, "Corrupt but Not Contented," *National Municipal Review*, October 1948, pp. 473–479.

Walter M. Phillips, "Let the Citizens Play a Part," *National Municipal Review*, November 1948, pp. 529–533.

Thomas R. Reid, "New Tasks for Citizens," *National Municipal Review*, December 1954, pp. 573–579.

J. T. Salter, *Boss Rule* (New York, 1935).

Waldo Schumacher, "Thirty Years of People's Rule in Oregon," *Political Science Quarterly*, June 1932, pp. 242–258.

Murray Seasongood, "The Triumph of Good Government in Cincinnati," *Annals of the American Academy of Political and Social Science*, September 1938, pp. 83–90.

John M. Selig, "San Francisco Upholds Mayor," *National Municipal Review*, October 1946, pp. 465–469.

Alfred F. Smith, "Can We Afford the Initiative," *National Municipal Review*, October 1949, pp. 437–442.

Frederick Sondern, Jr., "A City Beats the Rackets," *National Municipal Review*, October 1950, pp. 433–438.

Frank J. Sorauf, "Extra-Legal Political Parties in Wisconsin," *American Political Science Review*, September 1954, pp. 692–704.

Lincoln Steffens, *Autobiography of Lincoln Steffens* (New York, 1931).

Donald S. Strong, "The Poll Tax: The Case of Texas," *American Political Science Review*, August 1944, pp. 693–709.

Richard Wallace, "Defeat Comes to Boss Crump," *National Municipal Review*, September 1948, pp. 418–420.

Edward Weidner, "Students Investigate Politics," *National Municipal Review*, October 1947, pp. 489–493.

Belle Zeller and Hugh A. Bone, "The Repeal of P. R. in New York City—Ten Years in Retrospect," *American Political Science Review*, December 1948, pp. 1127–1148.

Chapter 7

THE FORMS OF AMERICAN
LOCAL GOVERNMENT

Form in any government depends upon offices, the points of governmental power. It is their arrangement, their functions, and their integration that determine what the form shall be. But form is not only the static arrangement of offices but their dynamic possibilities for action. Form determines what can be done and how it can be done, but it is the holders of the offices that actually are the doers.

Good men are often frustrated trying to do a good job because the form of government makes it difficult to get things done. Only a poet could have said: "For forms of government let fools contest; whate'er is best administered is best." The great Pope, however bright a star he was in the literary firmament, just could not prognosticate in 1733 about local government on this side of the ocean. Several later generations of Americans could have told him that form of government was of the essence, and that until American local government acquired sound form its progress towards efficiency, economy and effectiveness was seriously impeded. Of course, this is not to say that good government is impossible under bad forms, but it is indeed most difficult. To use an analogy, there may be some good baseball players who have awkward and clumsy playing form, but not many of them get up to or stay in the big leagues. The few that do, overcome poor form by some extraordinary gift such as speed of limb, a rifle arm, a camera eye, or just plain determination.

285

So also good government can be delivered when governmental structure is scrambled, confused, and without rhyme or reason, but then it takes extraordinary effort and ability on the part of the men and women in office.

The peculiar forms of American local government are rooted in the past. They evolved during centuries of trial and error, adjusting to the needs of the time and the political ideas of the people in each generation. The fact that the principle of separation of powers between the executive, legislative, and judicial branches of local government holds sway in the traditional forms goes back to the influence of Montesquieu, the French political thinker, on American lawmakers after the Revolution. This principle was applied to government at all three levels—national, state, and local. In colonial times and earlier in England, the local governing body of the municipal corporation was a board of aldermen in which executive, legislative, and judicial powers were united. The Montesquieu doctrine led to the separation of the mayor from that body and finally to become the strong mayor we have today in many large cities. The judicial functions were given to a separate and independent minor judiciary although in some localities the mayor and members of the council still have judicial powers usually not exercised. About the same time, the ideals of Jacksonian democracy nurtured on the frontier made a tremendous impact on local government structure. Men felt that governmental power should be rotated among citizens, that the offices should be elective and therefore close to the people, that they should be narrowly restricted by law in order to discourage arbitrary exercise of political power, and that they should be limited as to length of term. The present form of county government with its many elected offices dates back to this period. The recent development of the council-manager form of local government stems from the lessons learned in business in the early decades of this century wherein efficiency is generated with a general manager in charge of operations but responsible for policy to the board of directors.

The basic elements of the local government process are (1) the legislative or policy determination, (2) the executive or law enforcement, (3) the judicial or the application and interpretation of law, and (4) the administrative or the actual operation of government. The manner in which these elements are arranged is, for local government, spelled out in the laws of the state. The delegation of these functions to particular offices so that the best possible government results has been always one of the important political problems. The eternal quest for efficiency without sacrificing individual freedom, for economy without neglecting essential services to citizens, and for effectiveness without stultifying individual initiative has always challenged practical statesmen and political thinkers. The local political arena has offered the best opportunities in which to put to the test the various forms of government. The present vitality of American local government is the end result of vigorous experiment and of a bold, imaginative attack on community problems.

MAYOR-COUNCIL GOVERNMENT

In the mayor-council form of government, the theory is that the council is the legislative body and the mayor the executive. The practice, however, cannot be described in such simple terms for there are a great variety of combinations of these basic governmental elements. In the weak mayor government, for example, the council is strong and has the important powers of government. Conversely, in the strong mayor plan, power has been concentrated in the hands of the mayor. The inter-play between mayor and council from decade to decade has been a fascinating example of changing governmental modes and styles.

The Weak Mayor Form

The form of colonial municipal government was substantially what it was in 17th century England. The council was the chief, if not the sole, organ of the colonial borough. The mayor was a member of the council and presided over it. He was *prima inter pares,* derived social prestige from his position, but had only a few minor administrative powers. In this he differed from his English counterpart who was "lord of the town" and had broad power of appoint-

ment and administration. The colonial mayor, however, had little or
no power over appointments. Sometimes he was elected by the council as in New England but in most cases he was appointed by the
colonial governor. The council was elected by the freemen of the
borough who constituted only a small percentage of the residents
for membership in the corporation was based upon ownership of
property or other evidences of wealth or status. Even at that, it was
more democratic than in England where membership was closed,
sometimes even hereditary. The colonial council was made up of
two classes, the councilors and the aldermen. They sat together and
had the same powers except that the aldermen might act as magistrates in the borough court.

The New York City charter of 1686 provided that the members
of the common council should form a corporation under the name
of "the Mayor, Aldermen and Commonalty of Ye City of New York."
There were six aldermen and six assistants chosen annually by the
six wards in which the borough was divided. The mayor and the
recorder were to be appointed by the governor but were to sit with
the council as members. The council was authorized to make laws
and ordinances for the borough and to appoint minor officials. In
the colonial municipality the council was indeed supreme; in it was
vested all powers: legislative, executive, and judicial.[1]

After the Revolution, the impact of the New World and its ideas
made changes in the borough system of municipal government.
Separation of powers, checks and balances, and democracy were
high political principles in those days. Boston in 1822 was the first
city to make the mayor elective and by the middle of the century
its example was followed almost universally. The mayor obtained
veto power first in Baltimore in 1797, and in New York the absolute
veto in 1830. Gradually other cities followed at least with a limited
power of veto. The power of the mayor over appointments was gradually increased, and by 1850 he had become the chief, if not the
only, administrative officer of the city.

[1] William Bennett Munro, *Municipal Government and Administration* (1927),
Vol. 1, Chapters 5, 18, and 19. See also Russell M. Story, *The American
Municipal Executive* (University of Illinois, 1918).

The influence of the "federal analogy" was already noticeable in the early Baltimore charter. In this was provided a mayor and a two chambered council. The lower house was composed of two members elected annually from each of the eight wards of the city, and the upper house was made up of one elected from each ward. Each ward, moreover, chose members of an electoral college to elect the mayor. He was given power over appointments but he had to pick from a list given to him by the city council. The mayor was given authority to veto acts of council subject to repassage by a two-thirds majority. Professor Munro (Harvard University) pointed out that this was the first application of the federal principle of "checks and balances" to municipal government. "Presently," he continues, "the idea grew into an obsession; it became the cornerstone not only of national and state government, but of city government as well. Men did not stop to ask whether there was any good reason for a system of checks and balances in the subordinate areas of government. They took it for granted that if the principle was valid higher up it must be valid also lower down. At any rate the doctrine became part of the American political creed; it eventually gained recognition everywhere and determined the main channel of municipal development during the whole of the nineteenth century." [2]

For most of the century and in most municipalities, council continued to dominate city government. It carried on its administration through committees. While cities were small and administrative problems simple, the committee system was adequate but as cities grew and needs became more urgent, the committee system broke down as a method of administration. Then came a period of searching for new methods to take care of new demands: public schools, water supply, sewerage systems, police and fire protection, public health. Independent boards were established, some appointed by council, some by the mayor, some by the state governor, some were elected and some were *ex officio,* and some with all manner of combinations. There were school boards, park boards, health boards, street lighting boards, public works boards—some of which still exist today. Independent offices were also created, incumbents of which

[2] Munro, *op. cit.,* p. 93.

were elected by the people, or appointed by council, mayor, or
governor as the case might be. All in all, the council lost much of its
power during the middle decades of the 19th century. But so confused was the governmental picture, so diffused was governmental
power that it became impossible to function as an integrated organ-
ism without some over-all guidance and control. In the dark days
after the Civil War this was furnished by the boss and the political
machine in the large and growing cities. In firm control of all the
fragments of municipal authority, the boss was the man to get
action. But the price was high and the product not good enough.
All of which set the stage for the emergence of the strong mayor.

Even today the weak mayor form of local government, the common 19th century form, still describes local government in thousands
of communities. The characteristics, to summarize, are: a council
with much administrative power, operating through committees, a
mayor with little administrative power but some legislative and
judicial responsibilities, elective officials and boards taking away
some of the council's powers, and a general lack of organized leadership.

The Pennsylvania borough is a case in point. The burgess today
is an executive without any real power in administration. He appoints only a few minor officials, has nothing to do with the budget.
In charge of police activities, he can neither hire nor fire the police.
But he has a veto power and power to vote in council in case of a
tie, and can exercise some of the powers of a justice of the peace.
Council is supreme in administration which it carries on by a committee system and sometimes with an appointed manager. The law
gives the burgess general supervisory power over borough affairs
but he has no means of exercising it. As a result of the confused
pattern, in many of the almost one thousand Pennsylvania boroughs
a running fight between council and burgess is a common condition
of affairs. The result is tragic, useless fighting that consumes hours
of time and harsh words that frazzle the nerves.

In a weak mayor system, says Professor Bromage who served as
councilman in his home town of Ann Arbor, Michigan, many things
an administrator should do are done by council committees. A

weak mayor-strong council system, he says can be made to work only by an energetic mayor, hard working councilmen, and good administrators. To compensate for a lack of integrated authority all hands must pull together. If informal techniques for achieving consensus and unity fail, chaos is inevitable. And while such a system may work in more or less routine situations, when there is conflict too much time is spent to arriving at a solution. The price of a weak system is extra work, a waste of time and energy.[3]

The Strong Mayor Form

The emergence of the strong mayor in American municipalities was a gradual development taking place throughout the last half of the 19th century. It became the accepted form for the larger cities because of the need for a strong, active and honest administration in growing metropolitan communities. Here, too, the boss and the machine were more deeply entrenched and successful revolt led citizens to seek the answer to the political boss in a strong, self-sufficient, and elected mayor in whose office executive power could be concentrated and whose activities could be carried on in full view, politically speaking, of the electorate. The council having failed as an administrative body when the blue chips were down, and independent elective boards and officials having further confused the scene, this was the inevitable solution. Again the "federal analogy" played a part. The president, too, was emerging, as a strong man who could bring direction, order, and leadership out of incipient or actual governmental chaos. Lincoln, Cleveland, Roosevelt, and Wilson had their prototypes on the municipal level: Mitchel of New York, Blankenburg of Philadelphia, Tom Johnson of Cleveland, Brand Whitlock of Toledo, and a host of others captured the imagination of the public as men of leadership and destiny. They were not only executives and administrators, but were party leaders and public figures. They took the place of the invisible boss

[3] Arthur W. Bromage, "Running the City the Hard Way," *National Municipal Review* (June, 1950), pp. 283–287. Also Jewell C. Phillips, "Good Government under Old Forms," *Annals of the American Academy of Political and Social Science* (September, 1938), pp. 91–98.

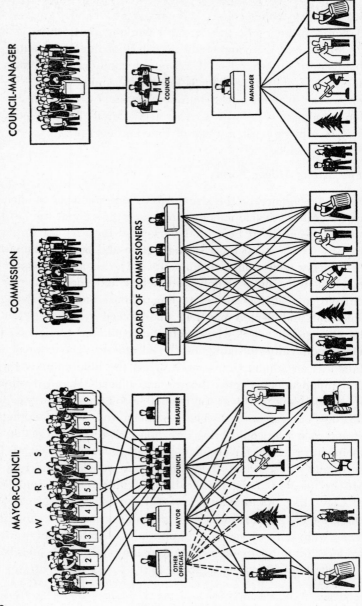

Fig. 2. Three Forms of Local Government. (By permission of the National Municipal League, New York.)

as the coordinators of a sprawling, growing government. They epitomized the spirit and pride of the city; they were "big men."

The newer charters and state laws began to give them powers comparable to the job that was waiting for them. Gradually the power to appoint heads of departments and other officials without councilmanic confirmation, to draft a municipal program for consideration of council, to veto acts of council, to draft and enforce a budget, and to direct the entire city administration was lodged in the office of the mayor. Brooklyn in 1880 was perhaps the first big city to adopt the strong mayor plan; in 1898 it was put in the Greater New York City charter. Other cities followed. Today, the strong mayor is found in most of the larger American cities and many of the smaller ones.[4]

Two chief weaknesses stand out in the strong mayor form of government. The first is that the mayor and council share both legislative and administrative powers and when they do not agree politically or on specific issues, the warfare adversely affects the operation of the government and the citizens suffer—sometimes for an extended period. Many strong mayors have taken their fight with the council, which sometimes represented the party machine, to the people. This meant headlines but seldom improved administration while the battle raged. Strong leadership or diplomacy of a high grade is always necessary to smooth the operation of a governmental machine that is founded on the principle of checks and balances.

The second weakness is that mayors, even strong leaders, are often less than top-grade administrators or just do not have the time to develop good administrative practices and procedures. The modern metropolis is a big business and needs as much expert administration as big business in industry. The average mayor cannot be everything: a party leader, a civic personage, an executive, an administrator, without some part of his responsibilities being neglected and this has usually been administration.

To offset this weakness, a number of the larger cities have set up

---

[4] Richard S. Childs, *Civic Victories, the Story of an Unfinished Revolution* (1952), p. 131.

the office of a general manager or chief administrative officer to be an assistant of the mayor and appointed by him. Beginning in San Francisco in 1932 with the appointment of a chief administrative officer, this idea has been adopted in Louisville in 1948 (consultant-administrator), Philadelphia in 1951 (managing director), New Orleans in 1953 (managing director), Boston in 1953 (director of administrative services), Newark in 1953 (business administrator), Los Angeles in 1951 (chief administrative officer), and New York City in 1954 (city administrator). The reasons for this development, Wallace Sayre (Columbia University) points out are (1) that the council-manager plan has proved unacceptable in large cities but the manager idea has been increasingly attractive; (2) that the office of mayor as the center of public leadership and government responsibility had to be preserved; and (3) the mayor-manager plan fits into the American political system in that it implements the strong executive with administrative competence.[5]

The powers of this administrator are not uniform in each case but usually include the power to appoint and remove heads of departments and agencies, to supervise city administrative operations, and to provide general advice and assistance to the mayor.

Mayor-Council Governments in the United States

The mayor-council form of government predominates in American municipalities. Of 2,527 cities over five thousand population in 1954, more than half—1,315 or 52 per cent—have mayor-council governments. This includes 16 out of 17 over 500,000 population, and 62 per cent of those between five and ten thousand.[6]

The mayor in the mayor-council form is elected directly by the people in all but a few cases where he is still elected by the council. Two-year terms are most frequent, but there are many with four. He has voting privileges (sometimes only in case of a tie) in about one-third of the cities, but is a full voting member of council in one-

---

[5] Wallace S. Sayre, "The General Manager Idea for Large Cities," *Public Administration Review* (Autumn, 1954), pp. 253–258.

[6] *The Municipal Year Book 1955*, p. 57.

tenth of the municipalities. Six out of ten mayors have some form of veto either on budget items, ordinances, or all councilmanic acts.

Councils range in membership from two to fifty, but the mean and median are seven. In cities over 100,000 the tendency is toward councils of nine to fifteen members. The two-house council, common enough in the 19th century, has all but disappeared.[7] Slightly under one-half of the cities over 5,000 population elect their mayor and council at nonpartisan elections. An equal percentage of cities elect their councilman at large and by wards, but a quarter use a combination of both. About fifty cities nominate councilmen by wards and elect them at large. Cities split about evenly in giving councilmen two and four year terms. The highest salary noted in 1954 was $12,000 but in 240 cities there was no salary.

GOVERNMENT BY BOARDS AND COMMISSIONS

By far the largest number of American local units are governed by boards and commissions. This list includes almost all counties, townships, school districts, and special districts, as well as a substantial number of cities. But there are the inevitable variations that characterize our political system. For example, boards of county commissioners and township supervisors are usually flanked by a number of "row" elective officials who share the total authority of the government. Likewise, many boards and commissions appoint a chief administrative officer such as the superintendent of schools in school districts. The council-manager form of government, treated separately below, in a strict sense belongs to this group as does the commission plan for cities. For the characteristic feature is that basic authority—both legislative and administrative—is lodged in a body of elected officials. There is no separately elected executive official such as the mayor, and there is no separation of legislative and executive powers.

[7] *Ibid.*, pp. 57–63. In 1954 the following cities still had bicameral councils: Danbury, Connecticut; Augusta and Waterville, Maine; Everett, Malden, Northampton, and Springfield, Massachusetts; and New York City.

The Commission Plan of City Government

The particular type of city government, known as the commission form, is a 20th century American invention. Historically, its first appearance was in Galveston, a result of the great tidal wave and hurricane of 1900 which wrecked the city, demolished its utilities, killed six thousand persons and left the rest of its forty thousand people homeless. Galveston had been governed by the ordinary 19th century combination of mayor, council, and independently elected officials and, while perhaps no better or worse than most of its contemporaries, it was not equal to this occasion. Faced with the emergency, the old government wrangled and got nowhere. But businessmen and merchants, who had already organized to improve the harbor, now became active and drafted a scheme of government to abolish the old form and substitute in its place a council of five with plenary municipal powers. This plan was presented to the Texas legislature and was passed in 1901. At first, the plan called for appointment of three commissioners by the governor of the state and for the election of two by the voters of the city. In fact, this commission was already at work when the state court held that the legislature had no right to authorize the governor to appoint municipal officers with powers of police jurisdiction.[8] The final plan adopted in 1903 made all five commissioners elective, four becoming heads of departments of government, and the fifth a mayor-president charged with general supervision. The four departments were: finance and revenue, water and sewerage, police and fire protection, and streets and public works. The mayor-president received an annual salary of $2,000, the others $1,200. All subordinate employees were appointed by the commission as a whole. The mayor was given no veto power but had full powers of a councilman. The old system of checks and balances, diffused authority and separation of powers was at one fell swoop relegated to limbo. The plan was an immediate success. The city was rebuilt, services improved, and taxes and debt were reduced. In five years Galveston was a new and better city, and the commission government was there to stay. Of

[8] Munro, *Municipal Government and Administration* (1927), p. 401 fn.

course, Galveston gained nationwide publicity and its new government widespread attention. The commission plan of city government was on its way to national acclaim.[9] Municipal reform organizations took the new system to their hearts. It spread to other cities, among them Des Moines in 1907.

Here some changes were made and innovations added. The result became known as the Des Moines plan. The commissioners were elected on a nonpartisan basis, and the initiative, referendum, and recall, as well as civil service reform, were added. Later charters made each elective official the full-time manager of his department. The commission form spread like wildfire, it created a veritable revolution in American municipal government. Some states made it mandatory for certain classes of cities. By 1915, four hundred and sixty-five cities were commission governed.[10]

The main advantage of the commission form of government was that all power was concentrated in the hands of a commission of five men. There could be no shifting of responsibility and fast action was possible. There was an end of checks and balances with resulting delay and confusion. Furthermore, the ordinary citizen could understand how his city government worked; it was simplicity itself. It was also the way business was run, people said, although no successful business of any size could operate if each member of the board was also a head of a department. Successful businesses hired a general manager or superintendent. But on the other hand, it tended to raise the standard of officeholders and it promoted speed and harmony in city government. It served a purpose in the American municipal picture although it proved not to be the last word in municipal reform. For after World War I, it began

[9] *Ibid.*, p. 398 fn. Between 1870 and 1891 several southern cities, New Orleans, Mobile, and Memphis had a form of commission government, but after several years abandoned it and reverted to mayor-council government. Professor Munro believes that the time for municipal reformation was then not ripe.

[10] Childs, *Civic Victories*, p. 138. The figure was reported by the secretary of the National Municipal League, but according to Mr. Childs may not have represented a full list of commission cities. The most comprehensive study of commission government is in T. S. Chang, *History and Analysis of the Commission and City Manager Plans of Municipal Government*, University of Iowa (1918).

to give ground to the even newer council-manager form of government. In fact, few cities adopted the commission form of government after 1914; and only three in the decade 1942 to 1952.

Its weaknesses as they showed up in actual practice were serious. First, the plan did not provide for unified executive power which even the strong mayor form had. Each department considered itself as an independent entity whose boss was the commissioner; in the over-all picture coordination was lacking. Second, there was no separation of policy determination from administrative action. It stood to reason that the majority of elected commissioners, although they might represent what the citizens thought and wanted, could not be classed as seasoned or trained administrators. Because of the full-time salaries often provided, the amateur citizens were tempted to run for office and when elected were forced to become administrators without any previous experience. Furthermore, the outward promise of improved government was not always matched by internal accomplishment.

The 1955 *Municipal Year Book* records that 356 cities or 14 per cent of all those in the United States over 5,000 population are governed by commissions. In three quarters of these, the mayor is elected by the people as mayor, and in the rest he is elected by city commission from the five commissioners elected. Usually there are five commissioners, but sometimes three or seven. Twenty cities over 100,000 have the commission plan. More than two-thirds of the commissions are elected on nonpartisan ballots, and in almost all cases the commissioners are elected at large with overlapping terms in about half the cities. Terms of office in half the cities are for four years, the rest two and three. Salaries range up to $10,080 but there are four cities where commissioners serve without pay.

COUNCIL-MANAGER GOVERNMENT

The commission plan for city government successfully challenged the accepted 19th century idea that municipal government should be in the image of the national government replete with checks and balances. To repeat, in the commission was lodged both executive and legislative power. Likewise the mayor was a councilman and had no veto power, and each of the commissioners were heads of departments. This was an important contribution to municipal progress, but it was soon apparent that the final answer was not the commission plan. For in it there was no provision for unified administration, and it was found wanting in that it assumed elected representatives could operate as competent administrators. It was inevitable, therefore, that the council-manager form should come into being.

Growth of Manager Government

Staunton, Virginia, in 1908, was the first city to have a city manager. The city created the office of general manager by ordinance, and Charles E. Ashburner was named to the post. The city, however, was governed by a bicameral council and a mayor, and so could not be called a council-manager government in the presently accepted sense. Lockport, New York, drafted a plan for the appointment of a city manager and presented it to the legislature in 1911 but it was not enacted into law. Sumter, South Carolina, upon passage of enabling legislation and a local referendum, put the manager plan in effect January, 1913, and a manager from "out of town" was appointed. Hickory and Morgantown, North Carolina, followed a few months later. All three towns adopted the "Lockport Plan" which was drafted by Richard S. Childs then active in the National Short Ballot Organization and since then one of the foremost promoters of council-manager government and other municipal reforms in the history of municipal progress.

The first "big city" to adopt the manager plan was Dayton, Ohio, and the occasion was the great flood which inundated the city and caused such great damage that the regular government was incapable of coping with it. Reorganization in Dayton had been started some time before the flood, and the disaster gave it new impetus. A charter commission was elected under the state home rule legislation, and a charter was drafted providing for the commission form of government plus a manager. Henry M. Waite, one-time city

engineer of Cincinnati, was engaged as city manager, and the plan
went into effect January 1, 1914. In December, 1914, the first managers' convention was held in Springfield, Ohio. There were eight
present. In 1915, the National Municipal League incorporated the
council-manager plan in its model city charter and has been promoting it ever since. The council-manager plan was on its way.[11]

The 1955 *Municipal Year Book* lists 1,275 city manager places
including six in Alaska, one in Puerto Rico, and 39 in Canada. The
number of council-manager places doubled since the end of World
War II, and bids fair to increase at a rapid pace during the next few
decades. Maine leads now with 121 places, followed by California
with 120, Texas with 105, Michigan with 96, Florida with 71 and
Virginia with 65. A total population of twenty-seven million live
under council-manager government. Forty per cent of American
cities between 10,000 and 100,000 are council-manager governed.
Only one city over 500,000 (Cincinnati) has the manager plan, but
there are nine between 250,000 and 500,000. Fifteen counties, scattered through California, Virginia, New York, North Carolina, Tennessee, Montana, Maryland, and Georgia are governed under the
manager plan.

How Council-Manager Government Works

Cities and other local units may adopt the council-manager form
of government only when state enabling legislation or home rule
provisions allow this to be done. The manager plan may then be
adopted by local ordinance or by referendum of the voters. The
most common method is by local referendum upon the basis of an
optional state law.

The accepted plan for the council-manager form of government
as adopted by the International City Managers' Association and the
National Municipal League provides the following essentials:

(1) a small council elected at large on a nonpartisan ballot;
(2) the council shall determine all municipal policies;

[11] *Ibid.,* pp. 141–152.

(3) the council shall adopt ordinances and resolutions which make these policies legally effective;

(4) the council shall levy taxes and make appropriations;

(5) the council shall appoint a trained administrator to act as its agent in carrying out its policies;

(6) the council shall not interfere with the administrative functions of the manager;

(7) the manager shall furnish the council information necessary for the council to formulate policy;

(8) the manager is held responsible for the coordination and administration of all departments under his direction;

(9) the manager appoints and may remove department heads and, subject to civil service regulations, is responsible for the selection of other administrative employees.

It is readily seen that the weaknesses of the commission form of government are here rectified. Administrative responsibility for the entire city government is centered in the hands of a professional administrator who can be hired and fired by the council at its discretion. Likewise, legislative and administrative functions are divided, the first being the prerogative of elected representatives of the people, and the second that of the professional administrator. Furthermore, the simplicity and concentration of power attained in the commission form of government are retained. In the ideal form, there are no independently elected boards, commissions, or officials dividing authority with the council. The mayor is the presiding officer of the council, the ceremonial head of the city, but in all other respects he is a member of council.

It is often difficult to divide policy making from administration. In a detailed appraisal of council-manager cities, the following functions were designated as being councilmanic: adoption of the budget, adoption of regulatory ordinances, determination of salary scale, safeguarding the financial standing of the city, awarding contracts, determining frequency of garbage collection, locating a playground, deciding on whether to give health education.

Managerial responsibilities would be such as the following:

budget making, enforcement of ordinances, designation of employees to receive salary decided on by the council, budgetary control, debt service, purchasing, layout of garbage routes, design and maintenance of playgrounds, and instruction of employees.[12]

The City Manager

Who are the city managers? What is their background? Answers to these questions go a long way in understanding the growing profession of public administration on the local level.

Of eight hundred managers studied in a 1953 survey, it was found that 82 per cent went to college and 60 per cent received bachelor or master's degrees. Only about 3 per cent did not complete at least high school. Fourteen per cent were under thirty years of age, while 27 per cent were forty-five or over. More than half began their managerial careers between thirty and forty-four. Over two hundred of the eight hundred had been in the profession more than eight years with twenty-seven having records of twenty-five years or more. Two-thirds of the managers were still serving their first city.[13]

Of 1,564 appointments of city managers between 1940 and 1949, 803 or 58 per cent came from outside the city. In 1953 this percentage had increased to 76 per cent. They came to their job on promotions from other cities (277), as former managers (177), as administrative assistants and assistant managers (69), as public administrative specialists (13), as engineers (168), as finance officers and clerks (109), as other city department heads (86), as federal, state, and county employees (171); from business and industry, (152); from engineering (51); the rest were miscellaneous or unknown.

[12] Harold A. Stone, Kathryn Stone, and Don K. Price, "Appraisal of Council-Manager Cities," Annals of the American Academy of Political and Social Science (September, 1938), pp. 50–56. The same authors, *City Manager Government in the United States—A Review after Twenty-Five Years,* 3 volumes, Public Administration Service (1940). This was the result of a three-year survey under the auspices of the Social Science Research Council.

[13] *The Municipal Year Book 1954,* p. 531. From an article in *Public Management,* January, 1953, "An Analysis of City Managers."

In recent years, there has been a growing tendency toward the appointment of men with public administration training and experience. Many of the present managers were trained by universities which offered graduate training in public administration. Many cities took on such graduates as internes with the view of apprenticeship leading to later manager appointments.

The average tenure of 105 managers leaving the service in 1953, exclusive of those with less than two years of service was 7.1 years. One had served thirty-four years, four more than twenty-five.

Managerial salaries have been increasing. The median salary for managers in cities between 250,000 and 500,000 was $20,000 in 1953; for cities between 100,000 and 250,000 it was $17,350; for cities between 50,000 and 100,000, $13,000; for cities of 25,000 to 50,000, $10,800; for cities between 10,000 and 25,000, $8,400; for cities under 10,000, from $4,800 to $7,000.

The professional organization of the managers is the International City Managers Association with headquarters at 1313 East 60th Street, Chicago, Illinois.[14]

Successes and Failures

By and large, the council-manager plan has worked well. The survey team of the Social Science Research Council concluded: "The new position of city manager provided an unprecented opportunity to administer services efficiently. The experience of the cities studied showed that the adoption of the manager form of government made it possible to arrange the divisions into a smoothly running organization, to adopt those methods which large-scale industrial enterprises had found successful, to eliminate vexing delays and to direct the entire city government at one objective—that of giving services to the citizens in accordance with the policies adopted by their representatives in council." [15]

The literature on the council-manager plan is full of testimonials

[14] *Ibid.*, pp. 529–532.
[15] Quoted in Childs, *Civic Victories, the Story of an Unfinished Revolution* (Harper and Brothers, 1952), pp. 155–156.

as to the improvements wrought under manager government. There are literally hundreds of stories about improved services, reduced debt and tax rates, far-reaching programs of planning, departmental reorganization. But these are only the more spectacular results. The more important day-by-day administration under the manager plan is bound to be smoother, more competent, and more alert. Programs have more of a chance to be planned and expertly administered.

But there have been some failures. The city manager plan has been abandoned in fifty-one communities. The reasons for failure are various: defective charters, blaming poor times on the city government, politics, old fashioned charters, and others.[16]

The manager plan has been available to Virginia counties by vote of the people under the Optional Forms Act of 1932, and five counties operate under a county manager. Among these is Henrico County with more than ten years under manager government. A department of finance was established which took over the duties of the former elective offices of treasurer and commissioner of revenue, as well as the purchase of supplies and the supervision of accounts. More efficient services at 25 per cent less cost were realized the first year. In this department, headed by a director of finance, are consolidated all the fiscal records of the county including schools. Here invoices are audited before payment, and all revenue turned in. In the first decade of Henrico's manager government, the cost of overhead in comparison to total county budget was greatly reduced, a substantial portion of the bonded indebtedness was paid off, the surplus and reserve funds were increased, and the tax rate was consistently lowered. The value of the tax dollar in terms of service was greatly increased, the people have been regularly briefed on the state of county administration. Other manager counties in Virginia showed similar improvements.[17]

In comparison with industry, public management on the local level has not kept pace in spite of the fact that local government is often the largest industry within the corporate boundaries, both in

[16] Arthur W. Bromage, *Manager Plan Abandonments,* National Municipal League (1954).

[17] George W. Spicer, "Manager Counties Evaluated," *National Municipal Review* (July, 1953), pp. 331–337.

dollar volume of expenditures and in the number of employees. There is no field of management where the demand for a single, all-knowing executive is more prevalent. The municipal manager is too often expected to know everything and do everything himself. Yet, like industry, he needs a team of management to assist him. The diversity of services requires greater management skill than most businesses. The manager is not often allowed to look for assistants outside the home town. Likewise the manager is expected to be open to all complaints of citizens and because he is unaided this takes up a great deal of time that could be put on over-all planning and organization work so desperately needed. Therefore, in most manager municipalities there should be established a management development program in order to develop men and women for positions in the high management echelons.[18]

The Appointed Executive

Many municipalities and local units have established an office to be filled by an administrative officer known variously as the chief administrative officer, business manager, or some other name indicating the headship of the administrative structure of local government. This officer is short of the status of a city or county manager. He is appointed by the governing body, is subject to its orders, and acts for it in its name in carrying out assigned administrative duties. However, instead of acting directly the chief administrative officer makes recommendations which are subject to review by the governing body. Under the theory of manager government, the manager has direct, individual authority over all the administrative affairs of the local unit. In general, the chief administrative officer is assigned his duties by the governing body on terms depending upon the particular conditions in the local unit, and he is therefore given generally more restricted powers than is the average manager.

The development of the chief administrative officer system has been recent. It received its major impetus in 1945 with the adoption

[18] International City Managers' Association, Report of Panel on "Development of Management Personnel," *Public Management* (February, 1955), pp. 29–36.

of the office by some of the larger cities as a part of the mayor-
council form, noted above. The reason for its popularity is the belief
in the manager idea without acceptance of the idea that the manager should be appointed by the governing body. In many cases,
the chief administrative officer is appointed by and works for the
mayor of the city or the chief executive officer of the local unit.
While the manager has the power of appointment of subordinate
officers, the chief administrative officer confines himself to making
recommendations. Neither does he prepare the budget. He merely
collects fiscal information for the budget which is made and adopted
by the governing body. While there is not too much real difference,
the manager holds a more formal position than does the chief administrative officer. The manager system is more rigid, the chief
administrative more flexible and informal.

Many special districts have adopted the chief administrative system in the person of the chief engineer, the chief clerk, or the business manager. Of course, school districts have for long had the
position of superintendent or principal to head up the teaching and
administrative staff of the system. Thus, the manager idea—that of
having a chief administrative officer—has developed further than
the adoption of the council-manager plan.[19]

Over-all Appraisal of City Government Forms

Today two main forms of municipal government are emerging as
best suited to American conditions of city life. They are the strong
mayor and the council-manager form of government. The weak
mayor form is being slowly superseded, but in small municipalities
it still remains a basic form of government. Its major advantage is
that it provides an executive officer elected by the people in whose
office is placed the governmental leadership of the community. Its
chief weakness is that it does not give the mayor enough power to
wield effective leadership. Most of the powers of appointment,
budget, and expenditure, and administration are in the hands of the

[19] John C. Bollens, *Appointed Executive Local Government,* Haynes Foundation (1952).

council which functions through committees. For many years, this form of government will continue to be acceptable to smaller municipalities in spite of potential conflict between the mayor and council.

The commission form of city government also is on its way out although many cities will retain this form for many years to come. It had its day and it served its purpose for it was a substitution for the confused system of the weak mayor and council government. In its early days, it stood for business rather than politics in government. It brought to city government superior personnel and concentrated all authority in three, five, or seven elected officials. It did away with invisible government election by wards, and reduced the tendency toward corruption and graft so common at the turn of the century. Its weaknesses were that it divided authority among the elected commissioners. The mayor was only one among equals and had little opportunity to exert effective political and governmental leadership. Expert administration was also lacking for the elected officials who were responsible for administration were often without training or ability along administrative lines. The system bred factionalism. Where a minority of the elected commissioners were of a different party, the majority could strip them of almost all their powers. In the commission form of government, the tendency was for each commissioner to keep his authority over personnel and purchases in his own department. As a result, centralized purchasing, the merit system, and other administrative improvements had relatively hard sledding. The over-all cost of government tended to remain higher than it should have been because of these conditions.

The council-manager form of government, because its managers are usually career administrators, gives cities a high grade quality of services. It unifies administrative authority in one office—thereby rectifying the basic weakness of both the weak mayor and commissions forms. Furthermore, the council is now strictly a legislative and policy determination body—truly a governing body because it directs the activities of the manager and may hire and fire him at will. The members of council, however, are spared the details of administration that make the job of councilman so onerous in the weak form of government. Likewise the size of the council can be adjusted to the sociological and area needs of the city. This was not possible when the small council of the commission form of government was elected at large. There is no doubt that the council-manager form of government can and does bring to American cities more economy in that the dollar can go farther because of expert administrative techniques, and develops better methods in personnel, purchasing, budgets, accounting, and all the staff services a city requires. Council-manager cities have demonstrated their superiority in administration time and again. But it has some weaknesses and harbors some dangers. It may place too much reliance on one man; council may turn too many responsibilities over to the manager. Most of the managers are under continued and insistent demands from the council, the heads of departments, and the public in general. It is a tough job under any circumstances. On the other hand, many councils may try to influence the manager in fields that are entirely administrative and when this happens there is usually trouble. No system is perfect, but the council-manager form allows the best possible combination of democracy and efficiency in local government.

The strong mayor form of government has evolved to the point that it is the accepted form of government for the largest American cities. Especially since the office of chief administrator has been added as an arm of the office of mayor. The elected mayor is, in truth, a political and governmental leader of the city, and when the office is strong in power, his position cannot be challenged. He has power to appoint and remove department heads and subordinate officials; he is the supervisor of administration and the undisputed head of the administrative departments. In carrying out his responsibilities, he can require periodic reports and make administrative changes where necessary. Legislatively he is also a leader with the veto power, the power to submit the annual budget, and the power to supervise the expenditure of money in accordance with the terms of the budget. He is the formal head of the city and is a civic leader. In fact, in his city he is like the governor of the state and the president of the United States—the all-around executive, political, and legislative leader of the community. The weaknesses of this form of government depend upon the situation in each city. Where the mayor is interested in good government, he has the power to promote improvements. When he is interested in "politics" good government may suffer. If he is a "fighting man" he may get into continual conflict with the council and then little progress can be made. If he is weak, he can be overridden or unduly influenced on all sides until he ends up as a "do-nothing" mayor. In many mayor-governed cities, administration is likely to suffer because the mayor has too many things to do and cannot concentrate on the administrative phases which are so important.

THE AMERICAN COUNTY

In spite of the fact that it has long been considered as the "dark continent of American politics" and has been tagged by some "experts" as ready for extinction and oblivion, the county has so far successfully resisted even so much as consolidation of the smaller and weaker ones into large units. One who has made a nationwide study of counties, Professor Paul W. Wager (University of North Carolina) concludes: "It is now apparent that counties are not going to be liquidated." [20] In all but a few shining examples, the county has not improved its headless and decentralized form of government or mended its poiltical ways. It is still the seat of the most concentrated local political power and of all American local units is the most wary of modern administrative techniques. But its many elective offices are eagerly sought by all classes of citizens and the "county court house" remains the symbol of 19th century Jacksonian democracy especially in the more rural areas. In urban and metropolitan regions, in fact, the county is enjoying an active renaissance for it has developed into an agency of urban government rendering municipal services to unincorporated areas and small municipalities in the metropolitan areas.

[20] Paul W. Wager, ed., *County Government across the Nation,* University of North Carolina (1950), p. 32.

The County Board

There are more than three thousand counties in the United States and these are governed, at least in part, by a board of commissioners, board of supervisors, a police jury (in Louisiana parishes), or a board by some other name. Along with this board are elective "row" offices which divide governmental responsibility with the board. Sometimes the law requires boards and other elective officials to work together in an *ex officio* capacity as when the three county

GOVERNMENT OF MERCER COUNTY, N. J.

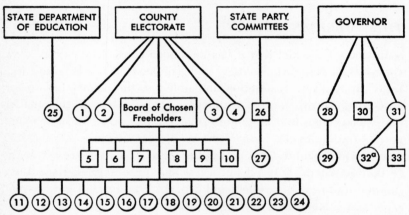

Fig. 3. Government of Mercer County, New Jersey. (From Paul W. Wager, *County Government Across the Nation*, p. 181.)

commissioners, the controller, and the head of department act as a salary board in Pennsylvania counties, but as a rule they act independently of each other thus making the county government one that has too many generals.

Generally speaking, the county board of commissioners or supervisors levies taxes, appropriates money, issues bonds and exercises the optional powers granted to it by the state legislature. In eleven states, however, the customary fiscal powers, in part or all of the counties, are lodged in another body. In Maine, New Hampshire, Massachusetts, Connecticut, and South Carolina the members of the state legislature from the county, known as the "legislative delegation," adopt the county budget, fix the tax levy, authorize the bond issues, choose appointive officials, and perform other functions. In Indiana the customary fiscal functions are carried on by the "county council" composed of seven members elected for four year terms while the elected board of commissioners carries on other functions of government. In most Tennessee counties, fiscal authority resides in the justices of the peace who together act as the county governing body. In Arkansas, Florida, Georgia, and Michigan special fiscal agencies have been established. In Florida a county budget commission is appointed by the governor. In Georgia a board of roads and revenue may be set up. In Arkansas the county court and quorum court exist side by side. The latter is made up of the justices of the peace who exercise the fiscal functions, while the county court consists solely of the county judge who has general administrative responsibilities. The size of the county governing body varies. In almost half the counties, the board is made up of three persons usually elected at large. But in 118, the functions of the governing body are carried on by one commissioner, and in 19 by two. In almost 300 counties, there are ten or more members of the governing body and in most of them, the county boards consist of the township supervisors. In another three hundred and fifty counties, the boards consist of the judicial offices of the county. Except for Oregon and Vermont, all those governed by judicial officials are in the South. Georgia provides the best example of a one-man governing body—the so-called "ordinary" in 11 counties and the commissioner of roads and revenue in 30 counties. Collateral boards for particular functions is a common arrangement in counties. Forty-five states make some provision for boards of welfare, assessments, libraries, elections, hospitals, schools, planning, highways, recreation, agriculture, personnel, penal, and finance.[21]

In New York, Michigan, and Wisconsin the township or "town" serves as the unit of representation and in these states the size of the county board of supervisors averages about twenty-five but

[21] *Ibid.*, pp. 10–15.

ranges as high as 141 in Wayne County, Michigan, in which Detroit is situated.

Government in Connecticut's eight counties consists of three commissioners chosen by the general assembly and one elective officer, the sheriff. The county commissioners appoint the county treasurer and sealer of weights and measures. In addition, the legislative delegation of the county, composed of state senators and representatives from the county, levy taxes, make appropriations, and supervise the affairs of the county.[22]

In California, the board of county supervisors consists of five members elected by districts of approximately equal population. In addition, the sheriff, district attorney, tax assessor, auditor, treasurer, superintendent of schools, and county clerk are separately elected. The grand jury, in addition to its duties in criminal justice, has certain powers of audit and investigation of the county administration.[23] In several home rule counties, county managers or chief administrative officers have been used to set up a modified executive system.

County government in West Virginia consists of a county court of three commissioners, a clerk of the county court, surveyor of lands, prosecuting attorney, sheriff, and two assessors. The court may appoint other officials such as the coroner, surveyor, and overseer of the poor.[24]

In Michigan, there is a large board of supervisors, one from each township and one or more from each city depending upon population. Elective officers include the county clerk, treasurer, sheriff, prosecuting attorney, register of deeds, drain commissioner, and coroner.[25]

In South Carolina, there are a variety of forms of county government. Most counties have a board of commissioners but in some a single commissioner acts as the chief administrator. But here, as in

[22] Max R. White, *Units of Local Government in Connecticut*, University of Connecticut (1953), pp. 5–6.

[23] Winston W. Crouch and Dean E. McHenry, *California Government*, University of California (1945), pp. 151–161.

[24] Harold J. Shamberger, *County Government and Administration in West Virginia*, West Virginia University (1952), pp. 4–5.

[25] *Study Kit on Michigan Local Government*, Institute of Public Administration, University of Michigan (1954).

Connecticut, the state legislative delegation from the county is a powerful force in that it adopts the budget, supervises the expenditures, and appoints county officers.

The Kentucky county government consists of a fiscal court composed of from three to eight magistrates, the county judge being the presiding judge although some counties have a board of commissioners in an attempt to separate the judicial from the administrative functions.[26]

While there is a variety of governmental arrangements for counties of the various states, in all there is a scattering of governmental responsibility. It is this weakness that inhibits the counties from taking a more active part in local government and as a result are losing their function to the state and to other local units. Some states have allowed counties to establish the office of county manager or chief administrative office. Others have raised the chairman of the county board, by giving him some appointments and veto power, to the status of a weak mayor. There should, however, be a complete reorganization of county government, concentrating administrative power in the hands of a small board of commissioners. The elective "row" offices should be abolished and put under the county commissioners. In most states, this would necessitate a constitutional amendment—a most difficult proceeding to say the least.[27]

The County "Row Offices"

Sharing governmental responsibility with the county board of commissioners or supervisors are a number of other elective offices. They are called "row" offices. Most of them are elected by the voters of the county, a present-day reminder of the days of Jacksonian democracy. Many state constitutions have provisions establishing these offices and requiring them to be elective. This in itself makes it most difficult to reorganize county government. In addition

[26] Bureau of the Census, *Local Government Structure in the United States*, State and Local Government Studies No. 34 (1954). This valuable pamphlet describes briefly the local government setup in each state.

[27] See Childs, *Civic Victories* (1952), Chapter 20 "Progress in County Government."

county officials are politically powerful in the state legislatures for it is the county party organizations that are responsible for the success of the legislative representatives at the polls and woe be to him who dares to suggest major legislative changes in county government. So the row offices remain and possibly will continue for a long time.

GOVERNMENT OF HARRISON COUNTY, TEXAS

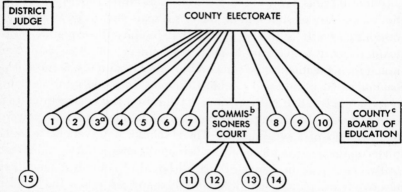

Fig. 4.   Government of Harrison County, Texas. (From Paul W. Wager, *County Government Across the Nation*, p. 564.)

The most important of the row officials are the *judges* of the county courts. They preside over the various courts within the county: civil, criminal, juvenile, probate, orphans' or whatever designations are given to them in the state law. These courts are the trial courts of the state. The only higher courts are those of appeal. The judges are usually elected but in New Jersey, Florida, Mississippi, and Massachusetts they are appointed by the governor, while in Vermont and South Carolina they are elected by legislation.[28] *Justices of the peace* are considered county judicial officials in 29 states, even when elected from smaller districts. In other states they are township and municipal officials.

In every county there is a *sheriff* who has come down through the ages as the chief executive and administrative official of the county.

[28] Fairlie and Kneier, *County Government and Administration* (1930), p. 131.

He represents the power of the state in the county. He is elected in all states except Rhode Island where he is selected by the legislature. He is the peace officer of the county and is supposed to preserve law and order but in the urban areas he has been superseded by the city police and in rural areas by the state police. Yet he is still a power to be reckoned with. In some urban counties he has developed modern police and traffic organization, while in all counties he can take measures in times of serious disturbances including the calling of a *posse comitatus* consisting of all persons in the county over fifteen years of age to aid him. This *posse comitatus,* or power of the county, is derived from ancient days but in the frontier states as the nation spread toward the West it was frequently used to control cattle rustling and to quell other forms of frontier violence. Far more important, however, is that the sheriff in these days is still the executive officer of the courts and serves writs and enforces decisions of the judges, helps to impanel juries, and is the keeper of the jail.

The *prosecuting attorney,* often called district attorney, conducts criminal prosecutions for the state within the county. It is his duty to prosecute all persons charged with crime in the minor courts, by the grand jury, and from information brought to his attention. If he is alert, watchful and fearless, he can do much to keep the criminal elements in the county under control; if he is weak, uninterested, or in league with such elements, organized crime can have a field day in his county. Many national political figures got their start in politics making a brilliant record as district attorney. In some states, counties may employ a *public defender* to give legal assistance to those charged with crime who cannot afford to hire a lawyer.

The *coroner* is another ancient county office. His chief function is to make inquests on the bodies of persons who have died by violence or under suspicious circumstances. The coroner is not usually required to be trained in medicine, and there has been considerable agitation in recent years to discontinue the office and turn the functions over to an appointed, trained medical examiner.[29] In fact,

[29] Richard S. Childs, "Rubbing Out the Coroner," *National Municipal Review* (November, 1955), pp. 494–496.

Massachusetts as early as 1877 provided for the appointment of a medical examiner by the governor in place of the elected coroner. In Rhode Island, coroners are elected by town councils. In some other states, varying practices are found chiefly making judges, justices of the peace, or county attorneys responsible for the ordinary duties of the coroner.[30]

The *clerk of the courts* is known by various names but his duty is to act as the recording agent for the various county courts. He keeps records of all court proceedings; and issues, processes, and records all actions and writs of the court. Usually elective, there may be one for each different kind of court in the county: civil, criminal, probate, or juvenile, although in many places one official takes care of all courts.

The *recorder of deeds* is in charge of public records of the county affecting title to real estate. In about half the states, this work is done by another official along with other work. In several New England states, the town clerk acts as recorder of deeds. The *register of wills*, surrogate or public administrator, administers the work of the probate or orphans' court in relation to last wills and testaments. The *county surveyor*, an important figure when the nation was expanding to the west and there were many boundary disputes, has now all but disappeared as an active county official. What functions he might have are concerned with damages and claims emanating from highway changes, and in this he is giving way to the *county engineer*, who is primarily concerned with county roads.

The county officials most concerned with finance are the members of the county board or commission, which levies all county taxes, formulates a county budget, and expends county monies. They do this, however, mainly for the functions that they carry on as a part of their own office. Many of the row offices are financially independent because they charge fees for their services to the public and pay office salaries and expenses from "their own pockets." Conditions at present are generally in a transition stage in which row officials are not any longer completely independent. Many are paid

[30] Fairlie and Kneier, *op. cit.*, pp. 150–155.

salaries from the general county fund and their accounts are audited by the county financial officials. But on the other hand the county board is by no means the prime financial authority in matters pertaining to these officials. In many of the larger counties, there is a *county controller*, who as his title indicates is the "watchdog of the treasury." He prepares budget estimates for the county board, keeps financial records, makes annual financial reports, pre-audits all expenditures and countersigns vouchers in order to make sure that the money being expended is a legal expenditure. In smaller counties, there usually is a *board of three auditors*, in place of a controller, which audits the annual accounts of county officials and agencies. While the controller is a full-time county official, the board of auditors are paid on a per diem basis and have only one duty—that of examining the annual financial reports. There is also the *county treasurer* who keeps county funds and sometimes acts as a collector of taxes and license fees for the state, the county, and the political subdivisions. He pays out county funds upon warrant drawn by the county board, or other authorized officials, and approved by the controller where there is such an official. In some states, there is a county *tax collector* who may collect county taxes only, delinquent taxes for all subdivisions only, or all local taxes. A county *board of tax assessment* sometimes acts only as the supervisory agency for locally elected tax assessors, and as the board of appeal and equalization of assessments. The *county clerk* is usually the administrative officer for the county board. He is elected in about half the states.

Other officials found in various states include two *jury commissioners* who, with the sheriff, make up panels of juries for the courts; the *county superintendent of schools*, and *county board of education*; the *road commissioner*, the *sealer of weights and measures*, the *county welfare director*, the *county manager*, and other such officials. They are usually appointed by the county board but sometimes they are elected by the voters. While elective constables are considered township officers where townships exist, in the 26 states where no townships exist, they are considered to be county officials.

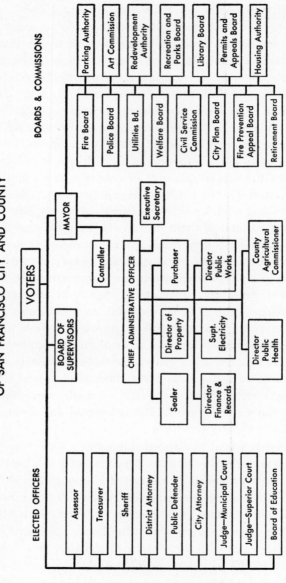

ABBREVIATED DIAGRAM OF THE GOVERNMENT
OF SAN FRANCISCO CITY AND COUNTY

Fig. 5. Government of San Francisco City and County. (By permission of Lennox L. Moak, Philadelphia Bureau of Municipal Research.)

Changes and Improvements in County Government

In spite of the fact that county government as a whole has improved little in comparison to the government of cities during the 20th century, there have been changes and improvements in individual counties that point the way towards more general betterment. There have been notable city-county consolidations—San Francisco, Denver, Baltimore, and Philadelphia, to name the more important. In six states—California (1911), Maryland (1913), Ohio (1933), Texas (1933), Missouri (1945), and Washington (1948)—county home rule has been granted to about two hundred counties. But only twelve, ten in California, one in Maryland, and one in Missouri have actually adopted home rule charters.[31] Optional legislation allowing counties a choice in the form of government by popular referendum has been enacted in a number of other states. Virginia offers the county manager and county executive plans as alternatives to the traditional forms of government; New York has a number of alternatives; and North Dakota has granted several options including a county manager plan.

It is generally agreed by expert observers that the administrative weakness of the county is the lack of a chief executive—"an individual officer charged with general oversight of an integrated administrative system." But some progress toward this goal has already been made. Fifteen counties in eight states have appointive managers recognized as such by the International City Managers' Association.[32] An even larger number of counties have administrative officers charged more or less with the general direction of county administration but without meeting the standards of a "county manager." Los Angeles county has a "chief administrative officer" and there are many counties with executive secretaries that have partial managerial powers. Some counties, such as Cook county (Chicago), have elective chief executives comparable in power to a mayor.

[31] Snider, "American County Government: A Mid-Century Review," *American Political Science Review* (March, 1952), p. 69.
[32] *The Municipal Year Book 1955*, p. 279.

Along with the development of a chief executive has come the shortening of the county ballot and the extension of the merit system, but these exist in relatively few counties. Only in New York state are counties required to have some form of the merit system.[33]

One of the most significant tendencies has been the spread of functional consolidation; that is, the cooperation of two or more local units in the performance of specific functions. This has taken place between counties, between counties and cities, and between counties and other local units within or adjacent to the county. It has been used in such functions as health, welfare, recreation, libraries, property assessment, tax collection, fire protection, civil defense, poor relief, and even jails. Such procedures have brought about joint operation without the necessity of mergers and consolidation of the local units themselves.[34]

So great have been the population shifts in the past several decades that there has been evolving what Victor Jones calls the "metropolitan county." According to the 1954 *Municipal Year Book*, there are 127 urbanized counties which account for more than one-third of the county employees and county payrolls of the entire nation. These counties provide many "municipal" services to the unincorporated areas including police protection (usually through the office of the revitalized sheriff), fire protection, street construction, garbage collection and disposal, health, housing, and other activities. While few counties report the ownership and operation of utilities, there are some instances where counties own and operate their own port facilities, sewage systems, water supply, and airports. County planning and zoning is growing in these urban counties. Many of the newer functions have been given over to special boards or commissions.[35]

If the county of the future is to retain its rightful place in the modern American governmental system, the direction of progress must be toward consolidation of city and county government in

[33] Snider, *op. cit.*, pp. 68–73.
[34] *Ibid.*, pp. 77–78.
[35] Victor Jones, "Urban Counties—Suburban or Metropolitan Governments," *Public Management* (May, 1954), pp. 98–101.

highly urbanized areas; more constitutional home rule to counties; the availability of optional forms of government for counties; provision for a chief county executive; smaller county commissions; elimination of the "row" offices and their integration under the control of the board of county commissioners or supervisors as appointed officers; the extension of the merit system among county employees; increased functional consolidation and interlocal activity; consolidation or deorganization of smaller townships and the transfer of their functions to the county; and the increase of revenue sources necessary to carry on urban services.[36]

TOWNS, TOWNSHIPS, AND SPECIAL DISTRICTS

There are more than a thousand counties outside of the six New England states which are organized into townships. These townships are mostly in rural territory but an increasing number of them are being overrun by the flight of population from the central cities into ever-widening suburbs. As the townships in metropolitan areas increase in population there is less and less disposition to form incorporated municipalities in the more congested parts as formerly was the tendency, and more and more effort to get the townships to take on urban functions. This is not an easy task for the township has a simple structure of government designed primarily for rural areas. The New England town, on the other hand, has been flexible enough to allow the development of administrative machinery consonant with the needs of their changing communities. Furthermore, it is geared to render service to both the rural and urban dweller, and thus has been preserved as a vital form of local government. On the other hand, the township has often been found wanting with the result that the county and the state as well as special districts and larger neighboring municipalities have taken care of the newer governmental needs of its inhabitants thus preserving it from the complete oblivion that its performance in many places has seemed to

[36] Snider, *op. cit.*, pp. 79–80; also H. F. Alderfer, "Design for Pennsylvania Localities," *National Municipal Review* (October, 1939), pp. 1–10.

warrant and to which it has actually gone in several states, notably Oklahoma and Iowa.

Township Government

In sixteen states outside New England, mostly in the Middle Atlantic and Midwest regions, the township exists in several forms. The central organ of township government in the northern tier of this area (New York, New Jersey, Michigan, Illinois, Wisconsin, Minnesota, Nebraska, and the Dakotas) is the township meeting which is established by law. As these states are situated due west of

TYPICAL RURAL TOWNSHIP - MICHIGAN

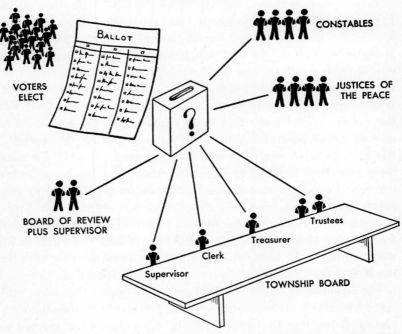

Fig. 6. Typical Rural Township—Michigan. (Reproduced by permission from *Study Kit on Michigan Local Government*, prepared by the Research Staff, Bureau of Government, Institute of Public Administration, University of Michigan, Ann Arbor, 1954.)

New England, direct democracy came from the movement of population from that section during the early 19th century. However, the annual town meeting in these states has less authority and less actual usage than in New England. Its powers are to levy taxes, pass local regulations, provide for a township hall, and elect township officials. It has been stated that attendance at these meetings is meagre compared with those of New England; in townships with five to six hundred voters only ten to twenty have been reported at such meetings, although there are, of course, many that are well attended. In the southern tier of states (Pennsylvania, Ohio, Indiana, Iowa, Kansas, and Missouri) there are no township meetings. Township officers are elected and questions are submitted for popular referendum but there is no assembly for debate and deliberation. The representative town meeting, the township board, was first introduced in Pennsylvania and was carried due west from there. The reasons for the limited development of the town meeting in those states outside New England are several. Immigrants from Europe and southern states coming to these areas had no experience in government by direct democracy and preferred the representative system. Then, too, the middle west township with its artificial square form of six miles by six miles lacked the social and economic unity of a naturally developed New England town. Moreover, in states where separate incorporated villages and cities within the township lines were made independent of township government, the township meeting was often held at out-of-the-way places not within easy reach by horse and buggy. Also the removal of villages from township government fragmented the governmental community so that what remained in the townships was hardly worth the interest of the voter. It is safe to say that in these townships, state centralization has made its greatest gains.[37]

The township, except where the town meeting exists, is a miniature of that of the county. There is usually a board and "row" offices elected by the voters. In some states, however, there is a well defined head officer—called supervisor in New York, Michigan, and

[37] Fairlie and Kneier, *County Government and Administration* (1930), pp. 458–461.

Illinois; town chairman in Wisconsin; and trustee in Indiana, Missouri, and Kansas—who may be the township representative on the county board and who may be delegated special administrative responsibilities. The office of selectman does not exist outside of New England. In Pennsylvania rural townships, there is a board of three township supervisors and other elected officers such as the tax assessor, tax collector, or justice of the peace and constable which exist side by side with the board. When the township has three hundred people per square mile, it can become a township of the first class and then it may have a larger board called board of commissioners, the members of which may be elected from wards or districts.[38]

In Kansas townships, elective offices are those of trustee, clerk, treasurer, two justices of the peace, and two constables. The trustee, clerk, and treasurer meet as the township board and also sit as the township audit board to supervise the township finances. Where there is no county road unit, these officials act also as a board of highway commissioners.[39]

The New England Town

The New England town is a type of government unique but indigenous to the soil from which it sprang. The early form approached the level of pure democracy in that basic governing power was vested in the adult male citizens qualified to vote in the annual town meeting. Here taxes were levied, appropriations made, policy determined, the officials for the coming year elected. The town meeting elected three selectmen who acted as an interim governing board and other officials including the town clerk, assessor, tax collector, treasurer, justice of the peace, constable—all of whom held office until the next town meeting. Sometimes committees on finance, schools, or streets were formed to advise the selectmen and the town meeting.

[38] Tanger, Alderfer, and McGeary, *Pennsylvania Government*, The Pennsylvania State University (1950), pp. 198–201.
[39] James W. Drury, *Township Government in Kansas*, University of Kansas (1954).

According to the town records of Boston, there were elected by the town meeting in Faneuil Hall in 1769 a total of 165 persons to 24 different town offices. These included offices that have long since vanished into the mists of historical limbo.[40]

There are a number of variations in the town meeting in existence today. One is the "limited town meeting" in which representatives from various subdivisions within the town, rather than the whole citizen body, hold the town meeting and perform its functions. This

GOVERNMENT OF GUILFORD TOWN, MAINE

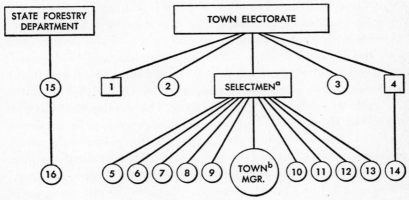

Fig. 7. Government of Guilford Town, Maine. (From Paul W. Wager, *County Government Across the Nation*, p. 58.)

has developed where population has increased to such an extent that town meetings of all citizens became an impossibility. Another variation is the addition of the town manager, appointed and responsible to the board of selectmen or the town council as the case may be. Within some towns there are village districts which have

[40] Quoted from Thomas H. Reed, *Municipal Management* (1941), pp. 42–44. The source was the *Boston Registry Department Records.* The offices were as follows: 1 town clerk, 7 selectmen, 12 overseers of the poor, 12 wardens, 16 fire wardens, 1 town treasurer, 12 constables, 12 clerks of the market, 4 collectors of taxes, 7 assessors, 1 surveyor of hemp, 16 surveyors of boards and shingles, 5 fence viewers, 2 informers of deer, 1 surveyor of boards, 5 sealers of leather, 24 cutlers of staves, 2 hogreeves, 1 hayward, 12 scavengers, 5 members of the committee of audit of treasurer and overseer of the poor, 3 purchasers of grain, 2 surveyors of wheat, and 2 assay masters.

been established by law to carry on certain functions such as fire protection, shade trees planting, care of parks, and even light plants.[41]

Special Boards and Commissions

The establishment of special boards and commissions to administer single functions of local government is a practice that began early in the 19th century as a result of the inability of municipal council committees to do a satisfactory job. Also the wish to keep certain functions "out of politics" was met by setting up independent agencies outside of city government. The state legislators began to interfere with local government by the middle of the century, and used this device for taking power out of the hands of local government and putting it in the hands of a board set up by them. In the beginning these boards were appointed by council but later the electorate was given the right to fill them. This development was considered by those guided by Jacksonian principles to be more democratic and therefore best in the long run. As the power of the mayor increased, many of these boards came under his jurisdiction and in the newer charters the functions of public works, health, sewerage, water, and lighting boards were given back to the city government to be administered by department heads appointed by him. But, of course, many boards and commissions still remain, especially in units governed by the traditional forms of government.

The most numerous and important of these are the school boards, the governing body of the school districts. In twenty-six states, school districts are independent of other units of government, but in five states there are no independent school districts and schools are entirely administered by other governments. In the other seventeen states, there is a mixed system with some independent school dis-

---

[41] Lancaster, *Government in Rural America* (1952), pp. 34–46. Also White, *Units of Local Government in Connecticut* (1953), pp. 9–10. Also Massachusetts Federation of Taxpayers, *The Town Manager Plan in Massachusetts*, revised (1951). Also John F. Sly, *Town Government in Massachusetts,* Harvard University (1930). Also Lashley G. Harvey, "The District in New Hampshire," *American Political Science Review* (December, 1948), pp. 1127–1148.

tricts and others administered by regular governments.[42] Both the educators themselves and a large share of the public support the idea of insulation from other local units. They claim the caliber of those elected to school boards is higher than in municipal councils. The elective board appoints a professionally competent educator as superintendent; the field of education has accepted the council-manager idea long before it became popular in municipal government. In eighty-five per cent of the school districts, the boards are elective, usually with three to six members. Eighty-six per cent of the boards are chosen in nonpartisan elections, and the same percentage are elected at large. About seventy-five per cent of the boards are unpaid, and the same percentage have complete control of the school budget.[43]

There is, however, substantial support, especially in political science and public administration circles, for the integration of education into the regular municipal organization. What is needed, these people say, is less units of government, and more unity of governmental planning and action on the local level. In about half of the cities with 50,000 population there are dependent school districts and investigation has shown that these have not suffered by being in the city or county orbit.

There has been a substantial increase in other *ad hoc* boards and commissions especially to administer public services and utilities which can be financed by their own revenue. Many of these were established in order to evade the financial strait-jacket in which legislatures placed local units. These boards differ from the school boards in that few, if any, are elected by the people. They are generally appointed by the governing body of the local unit which established them. It is generally conceded that in these boards, too, the quality of members is higher than in municipal councils. They represent executive and business groups that would not be interested in municipal "politics." Often because these commissions cover whole metropolitan regions rather than the central cities alone, competent men who have moved out in the suburbs can be reenlisted in

---

[42] *The Municipal Year Book 1955*, p. 18.
[43] Childs, *Civic Victories* (1952), pp. 219–220.

the work of local government in such authorities. These commissions usually do not try to administer details of administration and operation but are content to hire a manager or superintendent and put him in charge of all personnel. The council-manager idea is generally accepted in these boards.

THE COUNCIL AS GOVERNING BODY

The council has different status in different forms of government. In the weak-mayor government, council predominates although it shares some power with the elective mayor and other elective officials. In the commission form of government, it is supreme and is without any challenge to its powers. In the strong-mayor form, it takes a secondary position and the mayor is the leader if he exercises all his powers. In the council-manager form, council again comes into its own with complete legislative power and general supervision of the administration through the office of manager. In special units of local government, the boards and commissions, which are councils in fact, hold a similar position. But no matter what the form, the elective council is the key to local democracy and the bulwark of home rule. It is basic in every local government for it levies taxes, appropriates money, and declares policy. It represents the people. It is the sounding board for the public will. It translates this will into governmental action through the passage of ordinances.

There have been significant changes in municipal councils since the end of the 19th century. The two-chamber council has just about disappeared, the size of councils has been reduced, election by wards is gradually giving way to election at large, and the terms of councilmen are now generally two or four years. All these trends have had as their ultimate purpose the stabilizing of council so its members could be responsible and responsive to the will of the community. And in spite of the increase in powers of the mayors, the 20th century has also seen the office of councilman grow in power and in respect. Councils have also become more independent from political party organizations, machines, and bosses for the simple reason that their members are now of greater influence in the community than they were in the days of large, two-chambered councils, short terms, and election by wards.

Functions of Council

Council is the legislative body of the local unit; it corresponds to the state legislature and the United States Congress on the local level. As such, it adopts *local ordinances and resolutions*. These cover an area as broad as state legislation has provided. For local units are creatures of the state and can exercise only those powers specifically given to them by state law or directly implied therefrom. Professor Harvey Walker (Ohio State University) has suggested that there are three general classes of ordinances: (1) *administrative* —those that deal with the organization of the government; for example, the division of powers between departments, the establishment of salary scales for employees; and also those that provide for public works projects for the general improvement of the local unit; (2) *contractual*—those involving franchises such as grants to public utilities of the right to use public property such as streets and alleys; (3) *penal*—those that regulate the conduct of persons and are based on the general police power of the municipality to protect the health, welfare, and safety of the citizens.[44] Many such ordinances concern fields already covered by state law, but the courts have held that if the local ordinances are more severe than the laws of the state there is no conflict. But there is often confusion in the minds of the councilmen and the public. In the field of traffic control, the general tendency has been toward the adoption of a uniform system of traffic regulation throughout the state. But municipal councils often react against this in the belief that they should have the right to regulate speed limits, their own community's parking, traffic lights, and signs. In many fields of legislation there is no clear-cut line of demarcation between state and local spheres; and duplication, overlapping, and confusion often results.

[44] Harvey Walker, "The Codification and Revision of Municipal Ordinances," *Public Management* (October, 1930), pp. 516–517.

It is most important to have ordinances drawn up in proper form. This is the job for the city attorney or solicitor. If ordinances are poorly drawn, they can be questioned in the courts with the resultant delay in progress of the business at hand. An ordinance must be within the scope of state law. If it goes beyond the powers granted the local unit it is deemed *ultra vires,* and will be declared void if adjudicated in the courts. But ordinances need not be chained to every word of the state law or local charter. There is some freedom allowed by implication. In general, if the law authorizes a thing to be done, it gives the local council the right to determine the method unless this also is set down. Neither must an ordinance conflict with the state constitution, federal law, and the Constitution of the United States. Even some principles of common law apply, for ordinances must be reasonable, not oppressive; fair, not discriminatory. They shall not restrain lawful trades, or common rights, and shall not be vague and ambiguous.

Codification is described in the words of the Philadelphia Bureau of Municipal Research: "The code should be an up-to-date, logical and orderly restatement, in a single volume, of all the general ordinance law that is worth preserving. This should be accompanied by the specific repeal of every ordinance that can be repealed. The slate having thus been cleaned should be kept clean. Every proposal of a new ordinance provision should be considered in relation to the proper place of such a provision in the code. It should either become a new section in the code or amend an existing section. Constant vigilance should be exercised to prevent inconsistencies, and at frequent intervals the code should be overhauled with a view of eliminating what is out of date." [45]

Perhaps the most important function of councils is the *financing* of the local government. The power to levy taxes and raise revenue and to appropriate monies so raised, and to incur indebtedness lodges in the elective councils of local government. This holds true no matter how restrained their powers are relative to the chief

[45] Philadelphia Bureau of Municipal Research, *Citizens Business,* July 17, 1924. See also E. D. Greenman, *Codification of Ordinances,* Public Administration Service, Publication No. 6 (1928); T. F. Chrostwaite and Elizabeth Smedley, *Pennsylvania Municipal Ordinances* (1954), Chapter 1.

WARRANT FOR ANNUAL MEETING, THE STATE OF NEW HAMPSHIRE

To the inhabitants of the Township of Wilton in the County of Willsborough and State of New Hampshire qualified to vote in town affairs.

You are hereby notified to appear at the Town Hall in said Wilton on Tuesday the 11th day of March next, at nine o'clock in the forenoon to one o'clock in the afternoon to act upon the following subjects:

1. To choose all necessary Town Officers.
2. To hear the reports of town officers, agents, and committees and pass any vote relating thereto.
3. To see if the town will grant the free use of the town hall for the following purposes: . . .
4. To see if the town will vote to authorize the Selectmen to borrow money in anticipation of taxes.
5. To see what action the town will take in regard to real estate taken over by the town for non-payment of taxes.
6. To see if the town will vote to accept the budget as prepared by the Budget Committee or make any alterations relating thereto.
7. To see if the town will vote to raise and appropriate the sum of $216.00 to the Monadnock Region Association of Southern New Hampshire. . . .
8. To see if the town will authorize the Tax Collector to appoint a deputy or deputies. . . .
9. To see if the town will vote to transfer from unencumbered surplus the sum of $3000.00 for the purchase of the land and buildings of the Sullivan Blacksmith Shop, adjacent to the present Quigley Lot now owned by the town.
10. To see if the town will vote to include in the Wilton Traffic and Parking Ordinances adopted at Township Meeting March 8, 1938, an article limiting parking on Main Street proper to two hours. . . .
11. To see if the town will vote to raise and appropriate the sum of $1150.00 for a part-time extra Police Officer. . . .
12. To see if the town will vote to transfer from the present $2000.00 Capital Reserve Fund for a Veterans' Roll of Honor for World War II veterans.
13. To see if the Town will vote to raise and appropriate the sum of $2500.00 for a jail to be installed in the Town Hall.
14. To see if the Town will vote to authorize the Tax Collector to charge an additional amount of 20 cents on each Poll Tax not paid by September 1, for use of the Town, as provided by Statute.
15. To see if the Town will authorize the Selectmen to make a study of the town insurance program. . . .
16. To see if the Town will vote to appoint an airport committee. . . .
17. To see if the Town will authorize the Selectmen to use the balance of the unexpended fund for a large tractor and snow plow for equipment for the Highway Department.
18. To see what sum of money the Town will vote to raise and appropriate to defray town charges for the ensuing year. . . .
19. To transact any other business that may legally come before said meeting.

From Paul W. Wager: *County Government Across the Nation*, pp. 73–74.

executive, the administrator, the electorate, the other local officials and the state administration. State law may limit the maximum rate of tax levy and the extent of indebtedness; and it may provide for mandatory expenditures. But not one cent can be raised and not one cent spent without specific authorization by council in the form of an ordinance. While it is true that the mayor or chief administrator may prepare the annual budget and enforce it on the administrative departments, still it is the council that adopts it and translates it into revenue and appropriation ordinances.

Another general power of councils is that of *administration*. This varies from form to form, from place to place. Where there is no elected executive as is the case with boards of county commissioners, or no appointed chief administrator, or where either of these officials are "weak," the council, board, or commission is the administrative as well as the legislative body. It hires employees, sets salary scales, inspects work, grants licenses, and supervises the conduct of all departments and employees. Councils generally act through committees and these committees administer police, fire protection, water supply, sewage disposal, streets, and other activities. In strong-mayor and council-manager governments, in school districts with an appointive superintendent of schools, the purely administrative tasks of the councilmen are held at a minimum although there are always the duties of fixing street grades, making contracts, levying special assessments, and the carrying out of public improvements. In some form or other, these tasks devolve upon the council and take a lot of the councilmen's time. In fact, these duties are often so onerous that citizens are loath to run for office.

There is one field which a councilman cannot duck no matter how much he might like to. That is the field of *public relations*. Once elected, he is a public servant and has certain obligations that he as a private citizen did not have. He is subject to all sorts of requests for help and all sorts of complaints, most of which he cannot grant or is powerless to settle. But because he is a councilman elected by the people he acquires great importance in the eyes of the man-on-the-street or the housewife in the kitchen. The sewer has backed up in the basement, the rent cannot be paid, the street-cars are overcrowded, the cop on 21st Street arrested a man going only ten miles an hour, the neighbor's cats make the night hideous, the seventh grade holds school only half-time, the telephone company is cutting down a two-hundred-year-old oak, the city clerk is impertinent, there is interference in radio reception—these and a hundred other items are the constant problems given to the councilman by his fellow citizens. If he tries to evade his former friends and neighbors he is high-hat; if he says he will try to fix things up and does not deliver, he is incompetent; if he makes promises that are not fulfilled, he is a liar. Many times he is asked to intervene when a law has been violated, and sometimes he finds himself protecting segments of organized crime without really knowing what has happened. In a few instances, he does know what is happening and is in active league with the underworld, but such cases are few and far between. At its best, the job of councilman takes up hundreds of hours and raises havoc with the nervous system. At its worst, it becomes so intolerable that under no condition will the councilman run for reelection, at least not until he smells the smoke of the coming primary.[46]

The following list of services available to Iowa municipalities indicates the general range of councilmanic interest and responsibility. Not all these functions are mandatory but it can be assumed that they represent the sphere of action of the average city. Included are the repair and construction of streets, alleys, gutters and curbs; maintenance and cleaning of streets; lighting of streets and public places; repair and construction of sidewalks, bridges, underpasses and grade crossings; repair and construction of storm sewers and drainage systems; flood control; parking lots and other parking facilities; repair and construction of water mains; care of trees and shrubbery along public streets; construction and maintenance of garages for city vehicles; collection and disposal of garbage and refuse; repair and construction of sanitary sewers; construction and operation of sewage disposal plant; enforcement of state health laws; milk

[46] Charles E. Merriam, *Chicago* (1929), pp. 231–245. Professor Merriam (University of Chicago) was an alderman of the city of Chicago and tells about the pressing problems of the councilman and the battles of wits in the council meetings in this interesting book.

inspection; fire protection; police protection; jail maintenance; traffic signs and signals; speed signs; parks, playgrounds, and swimming pools; community centers, bands, and library; art gallery, memorial hall, and golf course; markets, ferries, docks, wharves; heating, electric, and gas works; water supply; hospitals; airports; cemeteries; and police and mayor's court.

In addition, council can in the interest of the health, welfare, and safety of its citizens prohibit and license certain industries and commercial establishments such as junk dealers, fertilizer factories, gasoline stations; certain recreational places such as dance halls, swimming pools, and theaters; certain persons such as peddlers and itinerant physicians. Council can require action on the part of property owners to get rid of nuisances to health and sanitation, can restrict the use of streets to vehicles, can regulate building construction, can develop programs of planning and zoning, housing and redevelopment, subdivision control, and city promotion. This enumeration of services and powers is illustrative only; there are many more. Without doubt, the councilman will not lose interest in his job through lack of problems and prospects for action.[47]

Councilmanic Organization and Procedure

Every council has a presiding officer. He is usually elected by the council except in commission governed cities where the mayor, also a member of council, runs for the office of mayor and by virtue of his office is the presiding officer. The president appoints the committees of council in accordance with the charter or council rules, and runs the meetings according to regular rules of order. Generally speaking, council committees are important agencies for getting things done. Committees are usually established for finance, streets, police, fire, health, and other main functions of local government. But functional committees are not always good for administration because they sometimes recommend expenditures without regard for the needs of the government as a whole.

[47] State University of Iowa, *Your Job as Councilman,* Institute of Public Affairs in cooperation with the League of Iowa Municipalities (1954).

The council expresses its will in the form of motions, resolutions, and ordinances. *Motions* relate generally to the conduct of council business, and are used to instruct officers, adopt reports, and authorize actions to go forward. *Resolutions* are less important than ordinances but it is hard to distinguish between the two. However, a resolution would be used to express sympathy, or to express the sentiment of council in matters beyond council's authority to legislate. Often resolutions are used to apply a general principle to a particular situation. An *ordinance* is the most solemn expression of the will of council. It is used on all occasions on which the council is laying down a rule that applies throughout the jurisdiction of the local government. It is used for tax levies, appropriations, bond issues, establishing a function of government, carrying on projects of improvement; in fact, an ordinance is used for the more important acts of council. Both the resolution and the ordinance are introduced in the same manner—by a member of council and in writing. Copies are filed with the clerk or secretary or presented on the floor. An ordinance calls for three readings, and three readings means on separate days, although ways have been developed to expedite this process. The best way, if short cuts are desired, is to have the first reading by title and written or printed copies furnished to members. If this is not possible, then a final reading should be at length. After the first reading, reference of the bill, as the proposal is now called, is made to administrative officers for the information necessary to decide on its merits. Also the bill is referred to a council committee. This committee will study the bill and perhaps hold hearings. Generally the report of the committee is decisive, and whatever amendments it decides to add to the original bill will be given serious consideration. Then the bill is given its second reading, and it lies over for a third reading. At the third reading, debate and amendment are possible. If council declares an emergency, and it often does, three readings can be dispensed with by a motion to suspend rules. Final reading and vote on an ordinance will be listed on the agenda for council so that members and the public will be aware of the business to come before the council. After passage, the ordinance is published in the local newspapers and is put in the ordinance book where it remains until repealed or consolidated with other ordinances. It is now the law of the local unit.[48]

In mayor-council governments, the mayor has important powers in the process of legislation. The strong mayor sends an annual message to council outlining his views on legislative needs, prepares the annual budget, and has a veto over council legislation. In some cases, these vetoes can be overridden by an ordinary majority, but in others council must muster a two-thirds or three-quarters majority. Likewise the mayor's department heads are often called to help in the preparation of legislation. Often the mayor attends meetings of the council but votes only in case of a tie.

The manager in the council-manager governments attends each meeting of council and advises it although he is not supposed to make positive recommendations on measures before the council. However, in the past two decades the manager has emerged not only in the role of a technical administrator but as a community leader who is responsible for providing the council with advice, suggestions, and even arguments for a particular course of action. The city manager and the council must work together on every problem for both have something useful to offer—the manager, the technical information; the council, knowledge of the community.[49]

The success or failure of a councilman is often based upon personality traits. Obviously, citizens will not run for this office if they lack the traits that make votes, if they do not like people, or if they fear criticism. Arthur Bromage (University of Michigan), says that "councilmen are another brand of that famous species known as the politician." He has discerned in them certain traits. They are willing to serve. They recognize names and faces. They often wish to be reelected. They like to sit tight until they estimate how to vote on a particular question. They are not averse to publicity. They take administrators with a grain of salt. They take "experts" with two grains of salt. They are themselves generalists, except in the special tech-

[48] Edwin A. Cottrell, "City Council Organization," *Public Management* (April, 1935), pp. 96–98; and Emmett L. Bennett, "Legislative Procedures in City Councils," *Public Management* (July, 1935), pp. 199–205.

[49] C. C. Ludwig, "Determining Municipal Policies," *Public Management* (July, 1954), pp. 146–150.

niques of handling fellow citizens and taxpayers. They have stamina.
They are willing to compromise.[50]

TEN SUBJECTS FOR FURTHER STUDY

1. The structure and organization of government of your home township, borough, or city.
2. The structure and organization of the government of your home county.
3. The structure and organization of the government of the city of Los Angeles.
4. The office of chief administrator in a large American city.
5. The origin of the city manager form of government.
6. County government in Kentucky.
7. City councils in three large cities.
8. The governmental organization of the Pennsylvania borough.
9. Fiorello LaGuardia, Mayor of the City of New York.
10. Mayor Tom Johnson of Cleveland.

REFERENCES

John W. Alexander and Monroe Berger, "Is the Town Meeting Finished?" *American Mercury,* August 1949, pp. 144–151.

H. F. Alderfer, "Pennsylvania Likes Managers," *National Municipal Review,* December 1946, pp. 590–592.

L. K. Andrews and Ed. E. Reid, *The Office of Mayor in Alabama,* Report No. 95, Alabama League of Municipalities (1952).

L. K. Andrews and Ed. E. Reid, *The Office of Municipal Councilman in Alabama,* Report No. 96, Alabama League of Municipalities (1952).

David S. Arnold, "Management of Small Cities," *Public Management,* September 1950, pp. 198–201.

———, "Trends in the Organization of City Government," *Public Management,* June 1951, pp. 122–125.

Stephen K. Bailey, "A Structured Interaction Pattern for Harpsichord and Kazoo," *Public Administration Review,* Summer 1954, pp. 202–204.

F. G. Bates, "Village Government in New England," *American Political Science Review* (August 1912).

John E. Bebout, "Management for Large Cities," *Public Administrative Review,* Summer, 1955, pp. 188–195.

---

[50] Arthur W. Bromage, "Ten Traits of City Councilmen," *Public Management* (April, 1951), pp. 74–77.

George W. Bemis and Nancy Basche, *Los Angeles County as an Agency of Municipal Government* (Los Angeles, 1946).

John C. Bollens and Stanley Scott, *Local Government in California,* University of California (Berkeley and Los Angeles, 1951).

John C. Bollens, Patricia W. Langdell, and Robert W. Binkley, Jr., *County Government Organization in California,* Bureau of Public Administration, University of California (Berkeley, 1947).

Arthur W. Bromage, "A Councilman's Pipe Dream," *National Municipal Review,* November 1951, pp. 524–526.

——, *American County Government* (New York, 1933).

——, *On the City Council* (Ann Arbor, Michigan, 1950).

——, "Preparing Future City Managers," *Public Management,* April 1950, pp. 74–76.

——, and others, *Recommendations on Township Government,* National Municipal League (New York, 1934).

——, "Reducing the City Council's Work Load," *Public Management,* April 1952, pp. 74–76.

Bureau of the Census, *County Boards and Commissions* (Washington, 1947).

Bureau of Government, *Study Kit on Michigan Local Government,* Institute of Public Administration, University of Michigan (Ann Arbor, Michigan, 1954).

William S. Busby, "The Small Council-Manager City," *Public Management,* July 1953, pp. 154–156.

Richard S. Childs, "It's a Habit in Dayton," *National Municipal Review,* September 1948, pp. 421–427.

City of Staunton, *The Origin of the City Manager Plan in Staunton, Virginia* (Staunton, Virginia, 1954).

James M. Collier, *County Government in New Jersey,* Bureau of Government Research, Rutgers University (Brunswick, 1952).

J. E. Dovell, *Florida's County Government,* Public Administration Clearing House, University of Florida (1952).

James W. Drury, *Township Government in Kansas,* University of Kansas, Governmental Research Center (Lawrence, Kansas, 1954).

Ernest Engelbert, "A Decade of County Government Reorganization in North Dakota," *American Political Science Review,* June 1942, pp. 508–515.

Henry J. Faeth, *The Connecticut County,* Institute of Public Service, University of Connecticut (Storrs, Connecticut, 1949).

John A. Fairlie and Charles M. Kneier, *County Government and Administration* (New York, 1930).

Jenniellen Wesley Ferguson, *City Council Organization and Procedures in Los Angeles County,* Bureau of Governmental Research, University of California (Los Angeles, 1955).

George K. Floro, "Types of City Managers," *Public Management,* October 1954, pp. 221–225.

Robert S. Ford and Claude R. Tharp, *Reorganization of Michigan's County Government,* Bureau of Government, University of Michigan (1946).

Stanley H. Friedenbaum, *Municipal Government in New Jersey,* Rutgers University (New Brunswick, 1954).

W. Brooke Graves, *State and Local Government in Mississippi,* Bureau of Public Administration, University of Mississippi (University, Mississippi, 1955).

Leslie M. Gravlin, "Hartford Likes Its New Plan," *National Municipal Review,* September 1949, pp. 382–385.

C. A. Harrell, "The City Manager as a Community Leader," *Public Management,* October 1948, pp. 290–294.

Lashley G. Harvey, "The Village District in New Hampshire," *American Political Science Review,* October 1946, pp. 962–965.

O. C. Hormell, *Maine Towns* (Brunswick, 1932).

Martha Murphy Lindegren, "Town Meetings—City Style," *National Municipal Review,* November 1952, pp. 490–495.

Stuart A. MacCorkle, "Small Manager Cities Thrive," *National Municipal Review,* March 1950, pp. 130–135.

Stuart A. MacCorkle and Dick Smith, *Texas Government* (New York, 1949).

Mavis Andree Mann, *The Structure of City Government in West Virginia,* Bureau for Government Research, West Virginia University (Morgantown, 1953).

T. B. Manny, *Rural Municipalities* (New York, 1930).

Elwyn A. Mauck, "County Pattern for the Future," *National Municipal Review,* February 1947, pp. 83–88.

M. Nelson McGeary, "Councilman Learns His Job," *National Municipal Review,* June 1954, pp. 284–287.

Joseph E. McLean, "Wedding Big-City Politics and Professional Management," a book review, *Public Administration Review,* Winter 1954, pp. 55–60.

National Municipal League, *Forms of Local Government—How Have They Worked?* (New York, 1953).

——, *Model City Charter* (New York, 1941).

——, *The Story of the Council-Manager Plan* (New York, 1952).

————, *The County-Manager Plan* (New York, 1945).

National Municipal Review, 1926–1929, a series of articles on American mayors and municipal executives.

Public Management, "An Analysis of City Managers," January 1954, pp. 5–8.

Leo C. Reithmayer, "Relations of the City Manager with Pressure Groups," *Public Management*, January 1954, pp. 2–5.

Clayton L. Ringgenberg, *Your Job as Councilman*, Institute of Public Affairs, University of Iowa (Iowa City, 1954).

Harold J. Shamberger, *County Government and Administration in West Virginia*, Bureau of Government Research, West Virginia University (1952).

Roy V. Sherman, "Forms of Municipal Government in Ohio," *American Political Science Review*, August 1932, pp. 692–695.

Clyde F. Snider, "American County Government: A Mid-Century Review," *American Political Science Review*, March 1952, pp. 66–80.

George W. Spicer, "Manager Counties Evaluated," *National Municipal Review*, July 1953, pp. 331–337.

Edwin O. Steve, "University Training for City Management," *Public Management*, January 1952, pp. 6–9.

Harold A. Stone, Don K. Price, and Kathryn H. Stone, *City Manager Government in the United States*, Public Administration Service (Chicago, 1940).

Temporary State Commission to Study the Organization Structure of the Government of the City of New York, *Four Steps to Better Government of New York City* (New York, 1954).

Paul Wager, ed., *County Government across the Nation* (Chapel Hill, 1950).

Harvey Walker, "Legislative Powers of City Councils," *Public Management*, May 1935, pp. 130–133.

Edward W. Weidner, "The Confused County Picture," *National Municipal Review*, I April 1946, pp. 166–171; II May 1946, pp. 228–232; III June 1946, pp. 288–294.

————, "A Review of the Controversy over County Executives," *Public Administrative Review*, Winter 1948, pp. 18–28.

Max R. White, *The Connecticut Town Meeting*, Institute of Public Service, University of Connecticut (Storrs, Connecticut, 1954).

Frank P. Zeidler, *A Course of Action for the City of Milwaukee for 1956 and the Following Years*, Mayor's Office, City of Milwaukee (1955).

Chapter 8

LOCAL FUNCTIONS, EXPENDITURES, AND DEBT

The first half of the 20th century witnessed substantial changes in local government. Expenditures soared, functions increased, and methods improved. Yet there was solid continuity between 1900 and 1950. Hardly any local function declined; all expanded no matter what yardstick is used: money, workers, or capital assets. Biggest · increases came in hospitals, public welfare, and business enterprises. Below average increases were in general control, highways, recreation, and sanitation. While there was a tendency for expenditures to slacken off during the two world wars and the depression, these declines were for construction and equipment rather than services.

The case of Detroit is typical of all large cities. Between 1900 and 1940, the number of functions carried on by the city grew from 140 to 256. Some of the newer functions were: literary censorship by the police department, high pressure water systems for fire protection, air pollution control, various types of clinics, traffic lights and signals, employment bureau, ambulance service, classes for handicapped children, branch libraries, and even an elephant ride.[1]

A survey of 34 cities showed that each one added a number of new expenditure items such as traffic lights, playgrounds, clinics, and police teletypes between 1915 and 1932. Nevertheless, the basic activities of education, streets, water, sewerage, garbage collection

[1] Lent D. Upson, *The Growth of a City Government,* Detroit Bureau of Governmental Research, Report No. 164 (1942).

and street cleaning, all of which had been established before 1900, were just as important in terms of money and effort after 1900 as the newer functions. The great increase of money spent was not only for new functions but for expansion of the older ones. There was wider coverage, better quality, and more specialization.[2]

It is easy to say as many do that national and state governments overshadow local government and that all local units are withering on the vine. But this is a generalization difficult to support espe-

---

LOCAL ACTIVITIES—LOCALLY FINANCED AND ADMINISTERED

1. Registration and conduct of elections.
2. Fire fighting.
3. Protective inspections including building inspection, plumbing inspection, electrical inspection, gas inspection, boiler inspection, elevator inspection, and smoke inspection.
4. Construction and maintenance of local streets and highways except those that are part of the state highway system.
5. Sewage and sewage disposal (except a few state agencies).
6. Street cleaning.
7. Garbage and waste collection and disposal.
8. Health inspections including dairy barns and milk plants, food handlers, housing abattoirs, and water supply.
9. Publicly owned, public-service enterprises including abattoirs, buslines, street railways, gas plants, water works, terminals, markets, cemeteries, and telephone systems.

Commission on Intergovernmental Relations, *Local Government* (June, 1955), pp. 18–19.

---

cially in regard to the more urban areas. Here local government is of utmost importance to the people. Without municipal services there would be no water to drink, no place to dispose of garbage and sewage, no protection against criminals, no areas of recreation, and no protection against fire. Furthermore, local government is a factor in economic progress, for it renders health and sanitation services, maintains law courts, provides education, carries on business enterprises, stimulates municipal housing, and is because of all these

[2] Solomon Fabricant, *The Trend of Government Activity in the United States since 1900*, National Bureau of Economic Research, Inc. (1952), pp. 77–82.

activities a large spender and consumer of goods. Local government, moreover, creates wealth in the form of streets and roads, buildings, and other permanent improvements. It contributes to the earning power of many people not only its employees but all classes of citizens. It meets social needs such as relief and welfare. It provides social conveniences such as street cleaning.

Let one simple example illustrate the place of local government in the lives of a city dweller. What does a citizen gain when a snowplow cleans the snow away from the front of his house? He saves time and energy that can be used for the pursuits at which he is more successful and which to him are more remunerative. Snow removal is therefore a productive endeavor and does not in the least regiment the beneficiary.[3]

Reasons for Increased Local Activity

What are the reasons for this increase in local government activity? It is well to remember first that all government activity has expanded: federal, state, and local. The causes cannot be isolated with any degree of precision. The whole nation has been changing and with it the role of government. Population has doubled in density and declined in the rate of increase. This tends to decrease the per capita costs for equipment and construction, and allows more intensive use of governmental facilities. On the other hand, the decline in the number of children per family leads to increased expenditures per child in education for better schools, longer terms, expanded recreational facilities, and broader health services. Urbanization, too, makes governmental services necessities of life. The larger the city the more money it takes to run its government. For example, the five cities of over a million population have more than twice as many police and five times as many fire department employees per capita as do municipalities of less than 5,000. For activities which are common to all municipalities, there were in 1953, 102 municipal employees for every 10,000 people in cities over a

[3] John M. Gaus, "The Regimentation of a Snowplow," *Public Management* (March, 1935), p. 65.

million as compared with 47 employees in the smaller places.[4] Advancing science and technology has had its impact on government activity. The automobile led to better roads. It made possible the continued movement out from the city into the suburbs which in turn brought demands for new and better school and other community facilities. Advances in chemistry and biology brought improvements in sewerage systems, garbage disposal, and other health services. Commercialization of agriculture with its modern mechanical equipment freed large segments of farm labor for the flight to the cities. Concentration in cities made necessary organized recreation, purified water systems, and mass transportation. Industrialization and urbanization raised the national income per capita, and higher incomes have led to new demands for services.

County Functions

Above all, the county is the district for the local administration of criminal and civil justice. The county court has general jurisdiction in both criminal and civil cases, its judges are usually elected by the voters of the county. In its judicial functions, the county is an arm of the state; it carries out state responsibilities within a local area. As a part of its judicial machinery, the county also maintains a courthouse and provides a jail. Elected officials such as the clerk of courts, the recorder of deeds, the register of wills, the prothonotary, the surrogate, the district attorney, the sheriff, the coroner, the probation officer assist the court in the administration of justice and provide the citizens specific services indicated by their titles. Although the sheriff is not nearly as important as formerly in the role of an officer of the peace, he is still the arm of the court in enforcing its writs and decisions.

Basically the county is the repository of official records of its inhabitants. All births, deaths, and marriages are recorded in its capacious files and vaults; all records of property, sales, deeds, and wills are there too. In most states, the county keeps records of the

[4] *American Municipal News,* "Big City Government More Expensive," May, 1954.

assessment of real and personal property for local tax purposes, and acts as the repository of all local tax and finance reports. Many of these records are official documents recognized by the courts in civil and criminal cases. The records of the court itself accumulated throughout the decades and in some states centuries provide a cross section of American community life that has not yet been fully exploited by the historian and social scientist.

In most states, the county has important responsibilities for the construction and maintenance of roads, especially those in the more rural areas. They have taken away the lead in local road building

MAJOR MUNICIPAL FUNCTIONS 1954

	Employees		Payrolls	
Function	Number (in Thousands)	Per Cent of Total City Employment	Amount (in Millions)	Per Cent of Total City Payrolls
Total, common municipal functions	973	68.5	$253.4	64.0
Police	189	13.3	60.0	15.1
Fire	153	10.8	40.1	10.1
Highways	113	7.9	28.9	7.3
Sanitation	105	7.4	28.6	7.2
Water supply	88	6.2	24.0	6.1
Recreation	60	4.2	14.4	3.6
General control	168	11.8	31.9	8.1
"All other"	99	7.0	25.5	6.4

From Bureau of the Census, *City Employment in 1954* (April 27, 1955), p. 3.

from the township and smaller municipalities, but in some states, notably North Carolina, Delaware, and Virginia, the state has taken away all roads from the counties and put them in the ever-growing state highways systems.

In most states, also, the county has extensive responsibilities in the field of public welfare. County almshouses or homes have housed the poor and indigent since colonial days; county foster homes take care of dependent children. The county is used for the administration of categorical relief such as mothers' assistance, aid to the blind and to dependent children under the federal social security system; and in most states is the unit for the administration of state and local public assistance in the form of money grants to indigent people.

In twelve southern states, the county school district is the local unit for the administration of schools, either all of them within the county or all except the independent school districts of the larger cities. In ten more, some county units exist. Each such county has a board of education and a superintendent. In thirty-nine other states, there is a county superintendent of schools who acts as a liaison between the state department of public instruction and the local school districts.

States in the Middle West, Far West and South give counties major responsibilities in local public health which include such functions as vital statistics, control of communicable diseases, health education, supervision of milk and food dispensing agencies, special clinics and laboratory services. In the eastern states, the towns, townships, and municipalities have usually dominated the local health scene, the state taking over health services in rural areas.

The county is the election and registration agency in most states. It supervises, administers, and pays for local, state, and national elections, and is the official repository of election returns and statistics.[5]

In recent years, counties have acquired new functions in addition to those that have been traditional throughout the years. Among these, mentioned by Professor Clyde F. Snider (University of Illinois), are those of hospitals, ambulance service, agricultural aid, conservation of natural resources, weed control, predatory animal control, fire protection, veterans services, libraries, parks, forests, playgrounds and recreational centers, planning and zoning, advertising and developmental activities, airports, housing, utility services, liquor dispensaries, harbors, markets, civilian defense activities, and regulation of amusements and liquor establishments in unin-

[5] See John A. Fairlie and Charles M. Kneier, *County Government and Administration* (New York, 1930), Chapter 12, pp. 221–239.

corporated areas. Professor Snider reports that the Milwaukee county board of supervisors, which a century ago handled 36 different services, in 1950 was responsible for more than 200, while in Los Angeles county the number of functions has increased from 22 in 1852 to 784 by the mid-thirties of the present century.[6]

The older county functions were as a rule mandatory in which the county acted as an agent of the state, while the newer ones are generally optional and can be utilized by the county upon the decision of the county board of commissioners. Many of the newer functions are a recognition of the increasing urban conditions in many regions, and not a few of them are those that have been taken from the rural townships and smaller municipalities.

Transfer of Functions to the State

One of the most significant changes in government during the first fifty years of the present century has been the generally gradual, but sometimes sudden, increase of power of state government at the expense of the local units. State centralization is a composite and intricate process of many levels and steps. It reached an apex in such states as North Carolina, Virginia and West Virginia when responsibility for local roads was entirely removed from local units of government and lodged in the state departments of highways, or where—again in North Carolina—the state took full charge of public education, although administering it through county boards of education. It goes only part way in states which take over part of a particular function. For example, most states take over public institutions of higher education leaving elementary and secondary schools to local districts; most states take over the network of major highways leaving to the municipalities, counties, and townships responsibility for local roads; most states take over public welfare institutions such as hospitals for mental health, and institutions for the handicapped, leaving general assistance to the indigent to localities. In other cases, the state divides a function between its

[6] Clyde F. Snider, "American County Government: A Mid-Century Review," *American Political Science Review* (March, 1952), pp. 66–80.

supervisory and operational elements taking over the first and leaving the second to the local units. Thus, local school districts may hire teachers, build school buildings, and maintain schools, while the state will certify the teachers, provide for their training, outline the courses of study, and regulate conditions of schooling. There are thus several levels of state centralization; taking over a function, taking over part of a function, and state supervision of a function. There are variations of all sorts within these limits.

Scarcely any state can be found without some power and responsibility in each of the main functions of local government—education, safety, sanitation, health, and public highways. But in education, for example, Professor Egger (University of Virginia) points out: "The prophets of progress have wisely refrained from tampering with the ark of the covenant. The symbols have been preserved, and the rituals carefully respected. But the substance of authority has passed out of the hands of local school boards, local governing boards, and even out of the hands of local school administrators. The means by which this end was achieved is the grant-in-aid." [7] The same can be said for other important local functions.

There are some good reasons for this trend. Local boundaries have long since been broken down by the automobile, the radio, and TV, and other appurtenances of 20th century life. Therefore, there are larger areas in which to maintain uniformity and efficient use of these modern conveniences. When one remembers the early days of the automobile when each county kept up its own system of roads, how welcome was the coming of the "state road" connecting important cities with a uniformly hard road. But local units were not only not large enough to do most modern jobs, they were so restricted by state law that they could not even do things that would be natural for them to do. Counties could construct and maintain modern rural roads but they did not have the necessary sources of revenue. The state may have taken over all of the gasoline tax and the county had to build roads with the revenues from property taxes. Neither could many local governments take advantage

[7] Rowland Egger, "Nature Over Art: No More Local Finance," *American Political Science Review* (June, 1953), pp. 461–477.

of technological advances for they were too small to maintain adequate staffs and equipment. The little townships could not hire the specialized health technician, the small village could not buy the big bulldozer.

It is extremely significant to find that state centralization proceeded more rapidly in the rural South than in any other region. Here there were never any strong local government traditions. There were few townships, the counties were never deeply rooted as administrative units, and the cities were until recently of small importance in politics. Here developed the county delegation system in which elected representatives to the legislature from each county virtually took over the supervision of county government. When new functions developed or old ones expanded, these county delegations vested the newer functions in state administrative boards and departments which they could supervise and control. These legislators, representing rural property owners, seemed happy to hand functions over to the state government and have them paid for with income and sales taxes rather than with property taxes. Shifting of tax burdens has had a major part in the movement towards state centralization.[8] But it is not only in the South that rural local institutions of government are becoming emasculated. The trend has proceeded at varying degrees all through the nation. Only in the New England states and to a lesser degree in the Middle Atlantic region has local government in rural areas remained vital. In New England, the town embodying both rural and urban areas in a natural economic and social unity has remained a bulwark of local government. Only in those states where townships and counties are strong in finance and power has rural America been able to keep some semblance of local home rule.

LOCAL EXPENDITURES

Government exists primarily for the services it renders and the functions it carries on: defense, law and order, supply of utilities and

[8] Paul W. Wager, "State Centralization in the South," *The American Annals of Political and Social Science* (January, 1940), pp. 144–150.

conveniences, regulation of economic enterprise, education, public welfare, public safety, and others. Local governments in the United States can exercise only those functions specifically delegated to them by state law or implied therefrom. But many local units do not exercise all the powers they are granted; in fact, many exercise only a few. So an accurate description of local government cannot be obtained only from an examination of the law. To understand any individual local government the functions it *actually performs* must be known. But to enumerate those is still not enough. For many functions are relatively unimportant and occupy only an infinitesimal fraction of total effort. The most accurate gauges are the amounts of money spent for the various functions and the number of people who do the work. Thus, the relative importance of each function can be assessed.

Governmental Expenditures on All Levels

In 1953, total direct governmental expenditures in the United States were $110.6 billion. Of this, $77.7 billion, or 70 per cent, was spent by the federal government; $11.5 billion or 10 per cent by the states; and $21.5 billion or 20 per cent by local governments. In

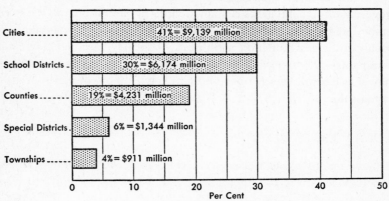

TOTAL LOCAL GOVERNMENT EXPENDITURES, 1953

Fig. 8.   Total Local Government Expenditures, 1953. (Source: Bureau of the Census, *Summary of Governmental Finances in 1953.*)

addition, the federal government gave states and local governments $2.9 billion in grants-in-aid; states gave local governments $5.4 billion in financial aid; and local government made $.2 billion in intergovernmental expenditures.[9]

Of the grand total of direct expenditures, $50.5 billion, almost half, was for national defense—all by the federal government—while $27.2 billion was expended on the national level for nondefense purposes. State and local government spending, totaled $33.0 billion. Per capita 1953 governmental total expenditures were $699, of which national defense accounted for $319 per capita, and all other public functions $380 per capita. Education came second with $64 per capita, interest on debt followed with $45 per capita, and highways $32 per capita. All other functions were considerably lower.[10]

Local Government Expenditures

Local government expenditures in 1953 were made for the following general functions: education, 35 per cent of total, highways 10 per cent, public welfare 6 per cent, water supply 5 per cent, police 5 per cent, sanitation 4 per cent, hospitals 4 per cent, and general control 4 per cent. Electric power supply, fire protection, public transit, and housing and community development each accounted for three per cent of local expenditures, while interest on debt, nonhighway transportation, health, natural resources, employees retirement, and intergovernmental expenditures each represented one or two per cent of total expenditures. The rest was for miscellaneous functions. Moneywise, education was by far the most important local function. Along with highways and public welfare, it consumed half of 1953 expenditures. Another quarter was taken for police and fire protection, water supply, sanitation health and hospitals, and general control, the latter function taking in the executive, legislative, and judicial machinery and general administrative staff. The rest of the functions are of individual minor importance in the

[9] Bureau of the Census, *Summary of Governmental Finances in 1953*, G-GF53 (October 20, 1954), p. 26.
[10] *Ibid.*, p. 1.

over-all pattern.[11] Expenditures of different classes of local units are shown in accompanying charts and tables.

In terms of money, over $6 billion in 1953, the school district is by far the most important local unit, except for cities. Education is the most important single function of local government in terms of expenditures.

CITY EXPENDITURES, 1953
Main Functions

Education	11%	$996	million
Highways	10%	947	"
Water Supply	10%	930	"
Sanitation	8%	765	"
Police	8%	752	"
Electric Power	6%	587	"
Fire Protection	6%	544	"
Public Welfare	5%	430	"
Public Transit	5%	416	"
Hospitals	4%	371	"
General Control	4%	370	"

Source: Bureau of the Census, *Survey of Governmental Finances in 1953.*

Special districts present an interesting feature of American local government in that they expend money for purposes that may have been granted to municipalities but for various reasons have been given to special districts. The greatest amount spent in 1953, $424 million or 32 per cent of total, was for housing and community development. Other public enterprises carried on by special districts were public transit, 12 per cent of total; water supply, 10 per cent; electric power supply, 10 per cent; nonhighway transportation, 7 per cent; highways, 5 per cent; and conservation of natural resources, 5 per cent; hospitals, 4 per cent; and sanitation, 4 per cent.[12]

In 1953, local governments expended $10 billion for personal services. This represents almost half of total governmental expenditures. The highest ratio, 62 per cent, was found in school districts. In all

[11] *Ibid.,* p. 26.
[12] *Ibid.,* p. 26.

other classes of local government, personal services absorbed considerably less than half of the total expenditures.[13]

In the United States as a whole, there were 197 local employees for every 10,000 population. New York was high with 264, North Carolina low with 54. Next low was Delaware with 131. North Carolina is the state that took over responsibility for all local schools and highways.[14] Accompanying tables show the distributions of personnel in the various classes of local units.

Total public expenditures in 1954 were at the same level as in 1953— $110 billion. But federal expenditures were down 4 per cent, while state and local were up 11 per cent. States spent $13 billion, local units $23.6 billion. Local units spent $1 billion more in education than in 1953, total $8.8 billion.

Bureau of the Census, *Summary of Government Finances in 1954.*

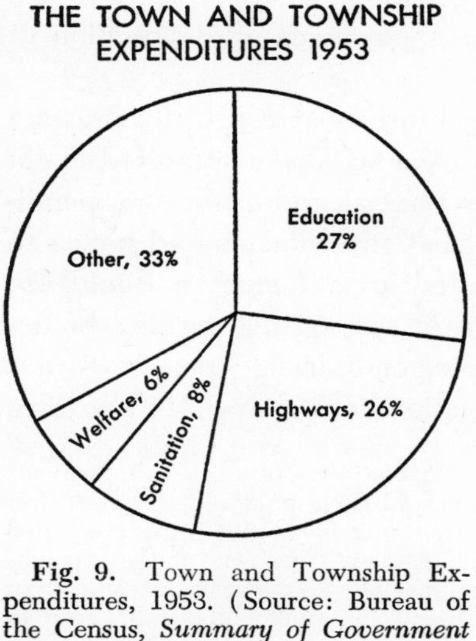

THE TOWN AND TOWNSHIP EXPENDITURES 1953

COUNTY EXPENDITURES 1953

Fig. 9. Town and Township Expenditures, 1953. (Source: Bureau of the Census, *Summary of Government Finances in 1953.*)

Fig. 10. County Expenditures, 1953. (Source: Bureau of the Census, *Summary of Governmental Finances in 1953.*)

[13] *Ibid.*, p. 27.
[14] Bureau of the Census, *State Distribution of Public Employment in 1953,* p. 15.

Mandatory Expenditures

Local government must make many expenditures which state laws or state constitutions require, and over which their governing bodies which raise the money have no discretion. These are called mandatory expenditures. According to the New York State Commission for Revision of Tax Laws, there are several classes of mandatory expenditures: (1) where the state law fixes the amount of the appropriation local units must make (judges salaries); (2) where the state confers the power to fix the amount of the appropriation upon some authority other than that which adopts the local budget (school board expenses when city council must pay for them); (3) where the state law fixes the service to be rendered but fails to specify the amount to be expended (care of dependents); (4) where the laws specify the compensation of a local officer (teachers, policemen, and firemen); (5) expenditures which become mandatory after voluntary action under general law (debt service payments after debt is incurred, pension payments after adoption of pension system).[15]

The problem of mandatory expenditures was especially pressing in the years of the depression when local taxpayers organized to get a reduction in their local tax levies through reduction of expenditures. It was then discovered that local governments had power to reduce expenditures only in a limited area. Reduction could not be brought about merely by action of the local governing bodies because state laws required certain expenditures.

The American Municipal Association in its model home rule

[15] Edward Weamer Carter, *Mandatory Expenditures of Local Governments in Pennsylvania,* University of Pennsylvania (1933), p. 28. Professor Carter (University of Pennsylvania) found that, in a year in the 1930's, in a selected number of Pennsylvania fourth-class counties only 44 per cent of the expenditures were discretionary, in fifth-class counties only 52 per cent, in counties of the sixth-class only 38 per cent, in the city and county of Philadelphia only 46 per cent, in cities of the third-class only 73 per cent, in boroughs 67 per cent, in townships of the first-class 73 per cent, in townships of the second-class, only 17 per cent, and in school districts only 10 per cent. The mandatory items included: salaries of local officers; poor relief, welfare, and prison expenditures; registration and election expenditures; court and law enforcement expenditures; education; expenditures for roads, bridges, and highways; and debt service.

amendment provides that when the legislature authorizes new
activities and functions for local units, these shall not be carried on
until either the localities vote affirmatively to accept the new functions or the legislators provide the necessary money. Organizations
of municipal and local officials such as the police and firemen are

PER CAPITA EXPENDITURES IN 12 CITIES 1953

	Police	Fire	Highways	Sanitation	Welfare	Total
New York	$12	$ 7	$11	$11	$24	$181
Chicago	11	5	11	7	5	54
Philadelphia	7	8	8	13	3	92
Los Angeles	15	8	9	9	0	66
Detroit	13	5	9	12	3	86
Baltimore	12	8	15	10	13	141
New Orleans	7	5	16	12	1	74
Long Beach	9	7	15	7	0	109
Atlantic City	16	16	14	11	2	160
York (Pa.)	5	4	4	51	0	76
Galveston	5	6	5	5	0	89
Fargo (N.D.)	6	11	11	11	0	56

Source: Bureau of the Census, *Compendium of City Government Finances in 1953.*

frequently able to get state legislation providing them with a minimum salary schedule and conditions of work which must be paid
by the local governments. This condition of affairs negates home
rule.

LOCAL GOVERNMENT DEBT

Debt is related both to expenditures and revenue. The money obtained through loans and bond issues is expended for public improvements, usually permanent ones such as buildings and streets.
But the debt must be repaid, both as to principal and interest, from
revenues that are raised from year to year. Good credit—the ability
to borrow at the best available terms—is a sound objective for every
local unit. It means that investment agencies rate the local unit as
a good financial risk: having the ability to repay in accordance with
its promises. When a local unit defaults on its principal or interest,

it is considered a bad risk and then can borrow money, if at all, only on most unfavorable conditions.

Borrowing has been an important phase in the financial development of local governments. In a vast country that has changed from a wilderness to a highly urbanized nation in the course of three centuries, the financing of improvements by the issuance of bonds based upon confidence in the future has characterized both private and public institutions. New York City incurred several loans as early as 1650, but municipal bonds began to make their appearance in the early 19th century. New York floated securities in 1812, issued its first water supply bonds in 1837. Boston in 1822 had a bonded debt of $100,000 which had increased by 1840 to $1,500,000. One of the outstanding economic characteristics of the century and a quarter between 1830 and 1955 was the rapid growth of municipal debt. It was the customary method of financing municipal improvements.[16]

In 1953, total debt of federal, state, and local governments was $300 billion. Of this:

> $266 billion or 88% was federal,
> 　 8 billion or 　3% was state,
> 　26 billion or 　9% was local.

In 1902, total debt of federal, state, and local governments was three and a third billion dollars. Of this:

> $1 billion or 35% was federal,
> ⅓ billion or 　8% was state,
> 2 billion or 57% was local.

In 1953, the per capita debt of federal, state, and local governments was $1,893. Of this:

> $1,681 was federal,
> 　50 was state,
> 　163 was local.[17]

---

[16] Paul Studenski, *Public Borrowing*, National Municipal League (1930), and A. Miller Hillhouse, *Municipal Bonds, a Century of Experience* (1936).

[17] The Tax Foundation, *Facts and Figures on Government Finance* (1954–1955), pp. 200–202.

Local total debt in 1953 was distributed as follows: [18]

Total	$25,735	million
city	13,558	million
county	2,454	million
township	434	million
school district	4,712	million
special district	4,577	million

LOCAL DEBT 1953

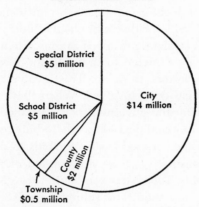

Fig. 11. Local Debt, 1953. (Source: Bureau of the Census, *Summary of Finances in 1953.*)

Annual interest on public debts in 1951 was: [19]

Total	$6,264	million or	$41	per capita
Federal	5,615	million or	36	per capita
State	130	million or	1	per capita
Local	519	million or	3	per capita
Cities Only	317	million or	1¾	per capita

Between 1940 and 1952, federal debt increased six times, state debt two times, and local debt 1⅛ times. In 1953, total debt—federal, state, and local—was 98 per cent of the national income.

[18] Bureau of the Census, *Summary of Government Finances in 1953*, p. 28.
[19] Bureau of the Census, *Government Debt in 1952*, p. 10.

Financing Local Bond Issues

Before a local unit decides to float a bond issue to procure money to construct a public improvement, its governing body and its administrative officers should make a thorough study of the problem at hand. Is there a real need for the proposed improvement? What are the alternative types of construction? How much will each cost? Which is the best of all things considered? What is the condition of the local unit's finances? How can the improvement be financed?

Once the general decisions are made, an ordinance is passed outlining the general scope of the improvement and making provision for the drawing up of plans and specifications. Engineers of the local government itself are directed to draw up the plans or an outside firm is given the contract to do so. This involves a more detailed estimate of the actual costs involved. When these plans are made, they are reviewed by the governing body. Changes are suggested, estimates revised, and final decision made to build or not to build.

An ordinance is then passed asking for bids to construct the improvement, and construction firms are notified of the decision and invited to make bids. Interested companies are given the detailed plans and at a certain time they submit bids. These bids are unopened until a formal meeting of the governing body to which the public and the interested bidders are invited. The bids are opened and the "lowest responsible" bidder awarded the contract. Let us say that this bidder agreed to construct the improvement for $1,500,000 within nine months after a contract is signed.

The next step is to get the money needed to build. It has already been decided that the entire amount should be borrowed. Before going further, it must be ascertained whether or not the local unit has the necessary borrowing power. The limits laid down by the state constitution or state law must be followed or else the indebtedness will not be recognized as legal by bond houses, the courts, or the state administrative agency which supervises local debt, and the bonds cannot be sold.

Assuming that this particular bond issue for $1,500,000 is within the local unit's debt capacity, an ordinance then is passed providing for the bond issue, and financial companies and investment houses are invited to make bids to float the issue. Conditions are laid down in the ordinance relating to the length of time the bonds should run, the kind of bonds desired, and other matters that will affect the bids. Again, the governing body holds a formal meeting at which the bids are opened, and again the "lowest responsible" bidder is awarded the bond issue. The successful bidder will be the one who offered the lowest rate of interest and the highest premium for the bonds. Before the actual money is forthcoming, many states require the bond issue to be approved by a state department which examines it to see whether all the laws regarding bond issues have been followed, whether the issue is within the limits laid down by state law, whether the bond procedure is correct, and whether the bonds are accurately drawn. When the issue is approved by the state, it often undergoes additional examination on the part of expert bond attorneys, a procedure which many investment houses require before they will buy any of the bonds. The successful bidder, usually a broker, tries to sell the bonds to banks, estates, and investment houses. Resale by the bidder to the ultimate customer is at a higher premium to cover costs, including risks, and to return a profit to the successful bidder. This margin is usually narrow. The municipal bond market is a complicated financial mosaic. It takes experts to get around it with ease.

Regular municipal bond issues are usually financed by annual tax levies separate from the regular levies. The tax levy for debt service should be sufficient to retire a certain number of bonds each year and to pay for all interest and charges during that year.

Bond issues should not exceed the expected life of the improvement; that is, all bonds should be retired before extensive obsolescence sets in. This is usually twenty to thirty years depending on the type of improvement financed. Improvements of a more temporary nature such as streets should be of only ten years duration. Experts say that it would be well for a local unit to keep its debt requirement so scheduled that at least 25 per cent of its principal is always due for retirement within a five year period.

Bonds may be divided into two classes on the basis of their

LOCAL GOVERNMENT FINANCES: 1953, 1927, 1902

(in Millions)

Item	1953	1927	1902
Total revenue	$21,007	$ 6,333	$ 914
Revenue from States	5,384	596	52
Revenue from Federal Government	300	9	4
Revenue from local sources	15,323	5,728	858
General revenue, net of			
governmental	12,687	5,298	798
Taxes	10,356	4,479	704
Property	9,010	4,360	624
Sales and gross receipts	718	25	—
Individual income	96	—	—
Corporation net income	7	—	—
License and other	523	94	80
Charges and miscellaneous	2,331	819	94
Utility and liquor stores revenue			
Liquor stores	120	—	—
Water supply system	939	247	56
Electric power system	713	111	3
Transit system	500	35	—
Gas supply system	85	10	1
Insurance trust revenue	280	27	—
Unemployment compensation	5	—	—
Employee retirement	275	27	—
Direct expenditure (by function)	21,471	6,359	959
Direct general expenditure, total	18,616	5,830	879
Education	7,756	2,017	238
Highways	2,207	1,295	171
Public welfare	1,380	111	27
Health	258	52	13
Hospitals	849	133	15
Police	919	263	50
Fire protection	598	203	40
Natural resources	173	—	—
Sanitation	908	312	51
Housing and community rede-			
velopment	628	—	—
Recreation	374	153	29
General control	864	316	118
Interest on general debt	452	337	58
Other and unallocable	1,250	474	69

LOCAL GOVERNMENT FINANCES: 1953, 1927, 1902 (*Cont.*)

Item	1953	1927	1902
Utility and liquor stores expenditures	2,559	491	80
Insurance trust expenditure	296	21	—
Total direct expenditure (by character and object)	21,471	6,359	959
Current operation	14,425	3,828	682
Capital outlay	5,058	1,864	203
Assistance and subsidies	1,057	50	5
Interest on debt (general and utility)	635	579	69
Insurance trust benefits and withdrawals	296	38	—
Exhibit: expenditure for personal services	9,868	2,680	475
Debt outstanding at end of year	25,735	12,910	1,877
Net change in outstanding debt during year	2,509	929	—

Source: Bureau of the Census, *Historical Statistics on State and Local Government Finances, 1902–1953* (Washington, D. C.), p. 21.

maturity. *Callable bonds* are those that can be called in and liquidated at any time by the issuing government before the date set for their mandatory liquidation. *Noncallable bonds* are those that mature only in the year designated in the bond. Callable bonds usually have a slightly higher interest rate because of their relative instability for long term investments. Callable bonds, however, are more desirable to the issuing unit of government because when it has a surplus of funds it can use this to liquidate debt and thereby save interest payments.

Bonds fall also in two classes as to their redemption—*serial bonds* and *sinking fund bonds*. Serial bonds are automatically redeemed at intervals stated in the bonds, usually so many each year, throughout the term of the loan. The interest on bonds outstanding are also paid each year. Serial bonds require more money in the beginning of the term than towards the end when the interest payments are reduced by the retirement of the bonds. Sinking fund bonds are all paid at the end of the term of the bond issue. Interest is paid on the whole issue each year, and certain amounts to repay the principal are put into a sinking fund, the proceeds of which can be invested in gilt-edged securities to produce some revenue to cut the cost of the interest payments. Experts say that if both systems are perfectly administered, the financial costs are practically the same. But serial bonds have been adjudged the best because their retirement is automatic and there is no problem of management with the danger that at the end of the period there will not be enough money available to retire the whole debt. A number of things can and have happened to sinking funds. Treasurers have disappeared with the funds, governing bodies have borrowed from it for "emergencies," and poor management has lost money in the course of the investment period. Many states now require serial bonds for local indebtedness. Serial bonds can be issued so that different amounts are paid off each year, depending on factors such as revenue and general economic conditions.

Special assessment bonds are those issued to pay for the costs of improving a localized benefit such as residential streets and sidewalks, water supply lines, and sewerage systems, the costs of which are paid by the abutting property owners through the issuance of municipal bonds. Sometimes these bonds are secured by the municipality and at other times by the beneficiaries' property. This property is liened in the county courthouse or city hall for the amount due for the improvement if not paid within a certain time. Then when the property is sold, the cost of the improvement, plus interest, plus charges and penalties, is taken out of the proceeds of the sale by the local unit. In fact, if the amount is not paid, the property can be sold for the amount of the debt. During the depression thousands of properties were liened and sold for delinquent special assessments as well as for delinquent taxes.

Local units should never go into debt for current operating expenses because this develops into a financially untenable situation. Current expenses should be paid through the annual budget, and not through borrowings. In some large local units, permanent improvements such as new school buildings are so numerous that if properly planned and spaced they can be systematically paid out of current funds. But smaller units must spread out their comparatively few large-scale improvements over a longer period of years.[20]

Defaults of Local Indebtedness

Bonds are considered to be in default when the principal or interest cannot be paid in accordance with promises written in the bond contract. According to Webster, a default is a "failure to pay a sum due." According to Miller Hillhouse, municipal defaults have an ancient history. He cites the 4th century B.C. Attic Maritime Association in which 10 out of 13 member city states defaulted wholly or partially on their loans made with the Delos Temple, the commercial bourse of the times. Municipal receiverships were also known among the classical Greeks. In the 5th century B.C. in the town of Assos in Ionia, situated in Asia Minor, a banker named Eubulus loaned money to a Persian official, taking as security the revenues of Assos and a neighboring town. The banker found it necessary to take over the administration of this other town in order to get his money.[21]

In the United States, the first municipal default on record was in Mobile in 1839. There were at least a thousand more during the next century. Defaults in New England were a rarity, but Bridgeport and New London, Connecticut, were among the number. Philadelphia defaulted in 1857, Pittsburgh in 1861 and again in 1877. Detroit in 1841 and Chicago in 1857 were among the earliest in the Middle West where many defaults came as a result of the issuance of local railroad aid bonds. Southern defaulting municipalities were the most numerous, a condition resulting from such causes as the carpetbaggers after the Civil War, and the Florida real estate boom of the twenties. Savannah in 1876, San Antonio in 1870, New Orleans, Nashville, and Memphis in the seventies were only a few of the examples. The new western states had defaulting cities; San

---

[20] See International City Managers' Association, *Municipal Finance Administration,* Chapter 11, "Municipal Debt Administration," third edition (1936). Also Harley L. Lutz, *Public Finance,* Chapter 23 "State and Local Debt Policies and Problems," fourth edition (1947).

[21] Hillhouse, *Municipal Bonds, a Century of Experience* (1936), p. 37.

Francisco in the eighties, for example. But the largest class of defaulters in the Far West were the irrigation districts and small local units.

The causes for defaults—the widening of the bridge between expenditures and revenues beyond a point where the gap could be bridged—were numerous. The local revenue system might have been weak and subject to shrinkage. Too much fixed overhead expense in the form of debt service might have accumulated. Heavy burdens of an emergency nature such as unemployment or a natural disaster may have caused them.[22]

The great depression in the thirties brought on still more defaults. In 1933, Carl Chatters, then executive director of the Municipal Finance Officers Association, estimated that out of a gross municipal debt of $18.5 billion, about $1.2 billion or 6.4 per cent was in default. For the whole country, 1.68 per cent of the governmental units defaulted. In Florida 44.5 per cent defaulted, in Louisiana 19 per cent, in New Jersey 15 per cent, in Tennessee 14 per cent, and in North Carolina 12 per cent. Kentucky, Alabama, Arizona, Arkansas, Ohio, Utah, and Michigan all had over two per cent of their local units in default. Eight states had no defaults: New Hampshire, Massachusetts, Connecticut, Vermont, West Virginia, Rhode Island, Delaware, and Maryland.

This unhappy debt situation stimulated scientific inquiries as to the ability of various states to support debt and the results confirmed the general conclusion that debt load is the primary cause of defaults. New Jersey, for example, ranked high in wealth, personal income, and business activity. Yet the enormous debt—$279 per capita—caused many defaults.[23]

Debt difficulties led to steps towards amelioration, adjustment, and future prevention. Federal bankruptcy laws were extended to municipalities by the Municipal Debt Adjustment Act which authorized debt adjustments to be filed with the federal court over the opposition of minority bond holders. Little use was made of this legislation and it was later declared unconstitutional. Some states

[22] *Ibid.*, pp. 236–273.
[23] Lutz, *Public Finance,* fourth edition (1947), p. 612.

authorized state aid or state assumption of local debts, others passed funding and refunding legislation. There were state receivership acts and statutes authorizing participation of local units in federal bankruptcy procedure.

Permanent measures to prevent local government defaults generally led to debt restrictions: (1) prohibition against public aid to private enterprise; (2) debt limitations fixed as a percentage of assessed value of taxable property; (3) maximum periods beyond which debt could not run; (4) requirement for referenda for all bond issues; and (5) mandates that a direct tax be levied at the time the bonded debt is incurred, and annually thereafter to pay the interest and principal of the debt. Some of these restrictions were written between 1870 and 1880 in the newer constitutions. Later, state administrative supervision over local debt was established: in New Jersey by the Municipal Finance Commission; in North Carolina by the Local Government Commission, and in Pennsylvania by the Bureau of Municipal Affairs. Finally, during the depression the United States Congress authorized the Reconstruction Finance Corporation and the Federal Emergency Administration of Public Works to extend financial aid to local units. Since the depression there has been general local prosperity and few defaults among American local units.[24]

State Limitations on Local Indebtedness

The power to borrow money by local governments is generally regulated in considerable detail by state constitutions and state laws. Limitations have grown up over a period of years, stimulated by abuses of local borrowing throughout the 19th century. Cities, counties, and school districts often plunged into debt with reckless abandon leaving future administrations and even future generations the job of paying off bonds which financed projects and operations the usefulness of which ended long before the payments of principal and interest. During the depression of the 1930's, local governments suffered severely from indebtedness created in the roaring 1920's

[24] Hillhouse, *op. cit.*, pp. 438–440.

when streets, schools, and other public improvements were built
to accommodate the needs of that post-war period.

Debt limitations are of three general types. The first deals with
the *purposes* of the bond issue. Generally, local governments are
forbidden to lend their credit to corporations or individuals. Many
cities had in the past loaned money to industrial corporations in
order to get them to locate there and thus help to build up the
economy of the community. This practice has been found by the
courts against public purpose and by experience against public interest. Other than this, local units generally have power to borrow
for any purpose for which they have jurisdiction. Most New England
counties have no power to borrow but as the county is not an important local unit in these states this prohibition is not important.

The second set of limitations concerns the *amount* of borrowing.
Usually the total amount of indebtedness allowed a local unit must
not exceed a specified proportion ranging from 2 to 10 per cent of
the assessed valuation of taxable property therein. Sometimes, different ratios are set for different classes of government, the large cities
and school districts being allowed more freedom. Frequently, local
units are allowed to borrow a certain percentage of their assessed
value by action of the governing body, but a greater percentage
when voted upon by the electorate in popular referendum. While
debt limits are logically related to assessed valuation because the
major source of local taxation is the property tax, there are a number of factors that make such arrangements unsatisfactory. Assessments themselves are in many cases not equitable as between local
units, and a uniform debt-assessment ratio for all local units has
no relation to the actual wealth of the local unit which is the basic
consideration involved in borrowing. Then, too, these ratios are
notoriously low and this keeps indebtedness far below what local
units could actually finance and what they need. Property-owners
are anxious to keep assessments low as much because it keeps down
local debt as because it keeps down local tax levies where there are
statutory tax limits.

Exceptionally low ratios of indebtedness to assessed valuations,
especially when they are made practically inflexible by constitutional

provision, have led to practices designed to evade the borrowing limits. One is the establishment of special districts or municipal "authorities" with power to issue "nondebt" revenue bonds which may be financed entirely through revenues from the projects for which the bonds were issued. In fact, revenue bonds are used increasingly by the regular units of local government when state law so provides. *The Bond Buyer* estimates that in 1955 one-third of all municipal bonds outstanding are of the revenue variety. In 1954, nearly one-half of the new issues, $3,214 million out of $6,953 million, were revenue bonds. Carl Chatters, nationally known authority on municipal finance, gives three reasons why revenue bonds are growing in use. They are used to get around the arbitrary and restrictive debt limits. The burden of debt in revenue bonds is placed upon the users of the improvement rather than on the public. Finally, they can be used by a combination of local units acting together in a special district or authority when each of them would have different debt situations that might make impossible joint action.[25]

Limitations on the amount of indebtedness have not proved entirely successful. In Illinois, Michigan, and New Jersey, for example, state legislatures have provided special local governments to take over special functions thereby evading the legal limitations. In certain cases, total local debt in New Jersey communities has risen to 30 per cent of assessed valuation, and in some Detroit suburban places it has risen to 50 per cent.[26]

The third general type of limitation is related to the *kind of bonds* that may be issued. Usually the issue may not exceed the estimated life of the improvement it is intended to finance. Some states now require serial bonds; and those that require sinking funds to liquidate the indebtedness require local units to levy a tax sufficient to cover all debt charges. Maximum interest rates, not exceeding six per cent, are sometimes provided.

[25] Carl H. Chatters, "Revenue Bonds Are Here to Stay," *Southern City* (May, 1955), p. 1.
[26] William J. Shultz and C. Lowell Harriss, *American Public Finance*, sixth edition (New York, 1954), p. 566.

State agencies are often required to check, control, or supervise local borrowing. In North Carolina, for example a local government commission approves all local bond issues. This is supposed to be the most effective system of state control. Some states, notably Indiana, Ohio, and Oklahoma, have county finance bodies which check or approve local bond issues as well as other financial actions.[27]

Revenue Bonds and Municipal Authorities

Most of the local indebtedness is in the form of general obligation bonds. These are so called because they are backed up by the taxing power of the local unit issuing the bonds. They are obligations of the local unit as a whole. On the other hand, a revenue bond is one that is issued to finance a revenue producing enterprise, and is payable exclusively, both as to principal and interest, from the revenues of that enterprise. Such bonds may be secured by a mortgage on the property and the enterprise may be taken over by the bond holders if principal and interest are in default. These bonds have no claim upon the general taxing power of the local unit which issues them. That is the chief characteristic of the revenue bond as distinguished from the general obligation bond.

Revenue bonds came into use in England in the 18th century for the financing of toll roads and bridges, but did not appear in the United States until 1897 when they were used in Spokane, Washington, to finance a water supply system. Revenue financing spread slowly until after 1921 when the Port of New York Authority was created and financed by revenue bonds. During the depression, however, revenue financing spread through all parts of the United States because of the reduction of ordinary borrowing power on the part of local units and states. By 1941, only seven states were without some authorization to local units to float revenue bonds. Projects financed by these bonds include water systems, bridges and tunnels, electric works, gas works, sewer systems, ferries, bus systems, docks, parkways, express highways, airports, stadiums, swimming pools, housing airports, school buildings, municipal buildings, and other

[27] *Ibid.,* p. 103.

revenue producing institutions.[28] Many states allow all their local units, or certain classes of them, to issue revenue bonds. Some are limited to certain kinds of projects, others include almost all kinds of public utilities.

Many states have also allowed the formation of special districts or "municipal authorities" to issue revenue bonds to finance certain types of revenue producing projects. The number of these municipal authorities, large and small, has grown at a fast rate during the past thirty years. In general, the kinds of projects constructed, maintained, and operated by these districts are those that can generate enough revenue for total financing of the projects, and those that do not do violence to the spirit of free enterprise in the community.

The concept of the municipal authority has been made a brilliant reality of local government administration by such agencies as the Port of New York Authority, the Metropolitan Water District of Southern California, the Sanitary District of Chicago, the Hartford County Metropolitan District, and others.[29] The municipal authority is a governmental agency that can operate across municipal borders. The authority device makes it possible to link together established and permanent units of local government in joint enterprise.

The municipal authority can supply urban services to large areas and large population groups which single units in a metropolitan area either cannot attempt or cannot administer with economy and efficiency. The need for modern sewage disposal in the Pittsburgh metropolitan area as the result of a state directive to eliminate stream pollution is to be met through the agency of the Allegheny County Sanitary Authority. A unified administration of harbor and transportation facilities is carried on by the Port of New York Authority. Such services could not be rendered successfully by the established local units.

The municipal authority can finance large-scale construction and operation of such utilities as water supply, sewage disposal, airports,

[28] *Municipal Finance Administration*, International City Managers' Association, pp. 266–267.

[29] Harold F. Alderfer, "Is Authority Financing the Answer?" Tax Institute, Inc., *Financing Metropolitan Government*, pp. 224–232.

transportation, parking facilities, and housing by means of borrowing on the basis of revenues derived for the particular project. The revenues so derived go exclusively for the financing of the particular project and are not diffused throughout a general municipal government to be spent for general or other purposes. Thus, the municipal authority operates in the nature of a private corporation and the public understands the direct relationship between service and charges.

The municipal authority can step into the breach in the walls of municipal finance where constitutional and statutory debt and tax levy limitations, and difficult-to-raise property assessments, make it possible for local units, large and small, to carry on expanded and new functions through regular municipal financing. While some observers see the municipal authority as a means of evading such financial restrictions on local units, the use of the authority reflects the fact that municipalities and other local units are forced to such subterfuges, if this they are, precisely because they are shackled by present state restrictions which do not take into consideration the expanded needs of the urban localities of the nation. The municipal authority is therefore a perfectly legal attempt to get out of the present financial straitjacket which states have fashioned for municipalities.

The municipal authority can provide the brand new administrative mechanism that is so necessary in solving present local government problems. Members of governing boards can be drawn from the upper executive echelons which are simply not available to regular municipal government. They can be attracted to those civic responsibilities often for the very reason that they are unpaid, that their participation is nonpolitical, and that the functioning of the authority is not hampered by the detailed and often ridiculous statutory restrictions that bind regular municipal officials. Furthermore, many of these persons live outside the confines of the central city and therefore would be ineligible for responsible municipal positions there. The municipal authority makes it possible again to utilize such persons in local civil government in a big way, and not merely as councilmen in a small residential community across city lines. Thus it has turned out that here more than in any other area of local government imaginative enterprise, flexible and elastic outlook, modern administrative methods, long-term management, stabilized policy, and aggressive functional leadership are encouraged and give great promise for future growth.

Success in municipal authority administration is not written in terms of votes, but is spelled out under the x-ray eyes of the money market where authority bonds are sold and in the profit and loss columns of financial ledgers. In the municipal authority all the sound practices of a private corporation can be utilized in the interest of the public. On the other hand, the municipal authority preserves some of the advantages of a public body because its bonds and property are not taxable, and it is generally more free from state regulation as to rates, audits and financial procedure than private utilities.

But authorities are not without dangers and disadvantages. It is generally conceded that municipal authority bonds bear a higher rate of interest than municipal bonds which are backed by the taxing power of the municipality. This differential is sometimes as high as one per cent, largely due to the fact that these bonds are "revenue" bonds, that is, amortized by revenues earned by the project that was built, and not backed by the taxing power of a local unit.

But there are some examples where the taxing power of the member municipality has indirectly been placed on the line in support of the financial structure of the authority; for example, sewer rentals may be based upon water consumption. But each municipality in the authority guarantees the collection of these sewer rentals. If the home owner does not pay the bill, municipalities must and they can enter liens on the delinquent properties. The rental is based upon data furnished by the water utilities or municipalities, which in the latter case may make lump sum annual payments and collect the sewer rentals themselves.

Municipal authorities, it must be admitted, can become deleterious instruments of local government. They are not directly responsible to the electorate or to public opinion; they are sometimes used to evade legal restrictions on local indebtedness and once the bonds are floated the projects are leased back to the municipality; they are not required to be supervised in the way municipalities of a state may be; and they are often created because of the aggressive activities of law, engineering and financial firms who hope to obtain large fees for their services. Will this condition of affairs prove an obstacle hindering more general usage of the municipal authority in metropolitan areas? Should the state provide more supervision of its financial and operational activities? True enough, any instrument of government can be abused and perhaps some municipal authorities have been used as instruments to rig local government. But, in general, they have proven themselves high grade, useful, and precise instruments of public service. Certainly state supervision is bound to increase if municipal authorities are found to be too open to malpractice, but every effort should be made to keep this at a minimum by first class administration and service on the part of authorities themselves. If the public is served well, it will support authorities against invasion and emasculation by other levels of government.

TEN SUBJECTS FOR FURTHER STUDY

1. Governmental functions of your home city, borough, or township.
2. Governmental functions of your home county.
3. The five major functions of your city, borough, or township in terms of money spent.
4. The five major functions of your county in terms of money spent.
5. The latest major bond issue of your city, borough, township, county, or school district.
6. How state laws restrict local government expenditures in your state.
7. Revenue and general obligation bonds.
8. How do state administrative agencies control local indebtedness in your state?
9. Transfer of local functions to the state in your state.
10. Local expenditures in the United States contrasted to state and federal.

REFERENCES

John C. Bollens, "When Services Get Too Big," *National Municipal Review,* November 1949, pp. 498–503.

Bureau of the Census, *City Employment in 1953* (Washington, 1954).
———, *Compendium of City Government Finances in 1953* (Washington, 1954).
———, *Historical Statistics on State and Local Governments, 1902–1953* (Washington, 1955).
———, *Local Government Finances in City Areas in 1953* (Washington, 1955).
———, *Summary of Governmental Finances in 1953* (Washington, 1954).
———, *Summary of City Government Finances in 1954* (Washington, 1955).
Carl H. Chatters and Marjorie L. Hoover, *Inventory of Governmental Activities in the United States,* Municipal Finance Officer Association (Chicago, 1947).
City of New York, *Foundation for Better Government,* First Annual Report of Mayor Robert F. Wagner to the City Council and to the People of New York (New York, 1954).
Clarence H. Elliott, "Municipal Responsibility for Cultural Activities," *Public Management,* October 1953, pp. 218–222.
Conrad H. Hammer, "Functional Realignment *vs.* County Consolidation," *National Municipal Review,* August 1932, pp. 515–518.
A. Miller Hillhouse, *Municipal Bonds: A Century of Experience* (New York, 1936).
Institute of Public Administration, *A Social Profile of Detroit: 1954,* University of Michigan (Ann Arbor, Michigan, 1954).
Lewis H. Kimmel, *Governmental Costs and Tax Levies,* The Brookings Institution (Washington, 1946).
Charles M. Kneier, "Development of Newer County Functions," *American Political Science Review,* February 1930, pp. 134–140.
Municipal Finance Officers Association, "Planning and Financing Capital Improvements," *Municipal Finance,* May 1954 (entire issue).
Municipal Finance, November 1954. Entire issue devoted to the subject of "Problems of Small and Medium-Sized Municipalities."
———, May 1949. Entire issue devoted to subject of "Revenue Bonds."
Vernon D. Northrup, "Municipal Debt Management in the United States," *Municipal Finance,* August 1955, pp. 39–47.
Clarence E. Ridley and Orin F. Nolting, *Check List on How Cities Can Cut Costs,* International City Managers' Association (Chicago, 1949).
The Tax Foundation, *Facts and Figures on Government Finance, 1954–1955* (New York, 1955).
John T. Trimble, "Revenue Bond Financing," *Municipal Finance,* August 1955, pp. 52–60.

Chapter 9

LOCAL REVENUES

In 1890, tax receipts of local governments in the United States totaled $405 million. States collected $96 million, and the federal government $365 million. Total taxes were $866 million.

In 1954, local governments raised almost $11 billion—twenty-seven times as much. But state governments raised $12 billion—one hundred and twenty-eight times as much, while the federal government raised $67 billion in taxes—one hundred and eighty-five times as much. Total taxes were $90 billion.

Thus in 1890 local governments received 47 per cent of all taxes, the state 11 per cent, and the federal government 42 per cent. In 1954, local government received 11 per cent of all taxes, the states 14 per cent, and the federal government 75 per cent.

Total taxes in 1890 came to $14.02 per capita: federal $5.91, state $1.56, and local $6.56. In 1954, total taxes rose to $572.00 per capita; the federal government took $426.65, the states, $78.17, and the local, $67.59.

In 1929, the total taxes equaled 10.7 per cent of the total national product; in 1954, they were 28 per cent of it.[1]

These tax figures etch in outline form the vast revolution in American life. Although the federal government has become super-dominant in terms of finance, all governments have grown. But while taxes are taking a large percentage of our national product, there is still 70 per cent left for other forms of economic spending.

[1] The Tax Foundation, *Facts and Figures on Government Finance* (1954–1955), pp. 116–122.

Can the nation stand this increasing drain on its pocketbook? What is its limit in tax capacity? Colin Clark, English economist, estimated the danger point of taxation at approximately 25 per cent of national income. Beyond this point, according to this expert, tax increases become inflationary and hasten economic collapse by reducing incentives to productive work and frugal management.[2]

It is frequently said that taxpayers work for the government, but they do this no more than they work for the landlord, the grocer, or the insurance company. The taxes they pay may be spent economically or extravagantly, but they purchase those services supplied to them by the government. James Arnold (Princeton Surveys) makes the point that one feature of taxation sets it apart from other expenditures— that taxes are compulsory payments. Where government would supply all human needs and where all costs were tax costs, there would be little freedom of personal choice in spending. In this sense, taxable capacity becomes that portion of the national product that the people are willing to devote to group rather than personal activities. "The answer to taxable capacity," he continues, "is, therefore, not so much a problem of how high it can become before we go broke; but rather how high taxes can become and permit us to remain free."[3]

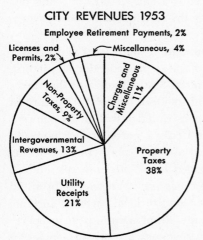

CITY REVENUES 1953

Employee Retirement Payments, 2%
Licenses and Permits, 2%
Miscellaneous, 4%
Non-Property Taxes, 9%
Charges and Miscellaneous 11%
Intergovernmental Revenues, 13%
Property Taxes 38%
Utility Receipts 21%

Fig. 12. City Revenues, 1953. (Source: Bureau of the Census, *Summary of Government Finances in 1953*.)

There is always the problem of distributing the tax burden between the three levels of government. Local governments, providing

[2] Colin Clark, "The Danger Point in Taxes," *Harper's Magazine* (December, 1950), p. 67.
[3] James A. Arnold, "State and Local Taxing Capacity," Tax Institute Inc., *Limit of Taxable Capacity*, pp. 109–125.

such services as schools, water supply, streets and roads, police and fire protection, are more able to identify their taxes as the purchase price of these services than are either the federal or state governments. Underlying this approach is the benefit theory in which taxes are viewed as service charges. But national emergencies, internal and external, come first in priority and this is why since 1916 the national government has come to the fore in its need for and ability to raise tax monies. Tax ability of local governments is seriously curtailed by legal restrictions. Federal and state government have much more legal freedom and leverage. Thus grants-in-aid are being utilized more broadly in order to rectify the restrictions in local government.

The property tax is still the foundation stone of the local tax structure. In 1933, the beginning of the depression decade, it produced more revenue within the United States than all other taxes put together—federal, state, and local. In 1941, it was still the largest revenue producer. But by 1953, it constituted less than 10 per cent of all taxes in the United States, and only 2 per cent to 3 per cent of state revenues. Still it represented about 87 per cent of local tax yields, 71 per cent of all local revenue from local sources, and 43 per cent of all local revenue.[4] But times are changing. Substantial state and federal grants-in-aid are adding to local revenue; income, sales, and other nonproperty taxes are supplementing the property tax; charges for services and utility revenues are taking a place of increasing importance in the local revenue picture.[5]

As a result of new forms of local revenue and state aid, property taxes have increased less than other sources. Viewing the total tax picture of the nation as a whole, property tax revenue only doubled in volume in the decade between 1942 and 1952, but sales and gross receipts taxes have tripled as have revenues from customs duties; corporation income taxes have quadrupled, and individual income taxes have increased eight times. Total tax revenue has quadrupled.

[4] Mabel Newcomer, *Trends in Property Taxation,* National Tax Association, Proceedings of the Forty-Sixth Annual Conference (1953), p. 49.

[5] See John R. McKinley, *Local Revenue Problems and Trends,* Bureau of Public Administration, University of California (1949).

The relative stability of property taxes has been at least partly responsible for the tremendous increase in intergovernmental revenue from the states to local units. This represents, in effect, a shifting of the cost of local functions away from property to income, sales, and corporation taxes. Is there any connection between this fact and rural domination in many state legislatures? Do the legislatures represent the real estate owners more substantially than they do other groups? May this condition of affairs also be at the bottom of the strange but tremendously powerful local opposition, reflected also in the state legislatures, that stands in the way of progress toward a more modern and stronger system of local government, a local government that would have more money to give more and better services? It has been difficult to get increased local property assessments and easier to get tremendous grants from the state for local education, highways, and welfare. If property holders fear that unpropertied majorities might control local governing bodies and thus unduly burden property (and this is often a just fear), by shackling local revenue power they make possible or encourage more state centralization and less local freedom.

Total Local Government Revenues

In 1953, American local governments raised total revenues amounting to almost $21 billion. This came from the following sources: [6]

Property taxes	$8,890 million or	43%
Intergovernmental revenues	5,685 million or	27%
Charges and miscellaneous	2,285 million or	11%
Utility revenue	2,221 million or	11%
Sales, income and other nonproperty taxes	820 million or	5%
Licenses and permits	502 million or	2%
Employee retirement payments	278 million or	1%

[6] Bureau of the Census, *Summary of Governmental Finances in 1953*, p. 25. The figure total for local intergovernmental revenue was derived by adding the amounts received by counties, cities, townships, school districts, and special districts.

Local taxes in 1942 totaled $4,624 million; in 1953, $10,356 million —more than doubling in eleven years. Property taxes were 87 per cent of all local taxes in 1953. Sales and gross receipts were 7 per cent of total; income, 1 per cent, and licenses, 5 per cent of total. Local tax collections per capita ranged from $21.86 in Arkansas to $115.03 in New York.[7]

Total government revenue in 1954 was a record high. Federal revenue rose 2 per cent, state and local 6 per cent. Property taxes were $9.6 billion, or 42 per cent of all revenue.

1953 PER CAPITA REVENUES OF SELECTED CITIES

	All General Revenue	Property Taxes	Other Taxes	Inter-governmental Revenues	Charges, etc.
New York	$198	$83	$50	$42	$ 23
Chicago	57	30	14	9	4
Philadelphia	87	30	35	4	17
Los Angeles	63	25	14	11	13
Detroit	92	55	2	22	14
Baltimore	136	66	10	47	12
New Orleans	69	19	20	15	14
Long Beach (Cal.)	185	16	6	11	151
Atlantic City	168	98	52	7	11
York (Pa.)	27	14	7	2	4
Galveston	97	23	4	1	69
Fargo (N.D.)	66	28	2	3	32

Source: Bureau of the Census, *City Government Finances in 1953.*

THE GENERAL PROPERTY TAX

What is property within the meaning of local taxation? There are two kinds: real and personal. *Real property* consists of land, buildings, and permanent improvements. *Personal property* is all other kinds: for example, clothes, furniture, jewelry, automobiles, stocks and bonds. Personal property is tangible or intangible. *Tangible* personal property includes such things as furniture and automobiles; *intangible,* stocks and bonds.

[7] The Tax Foundation, *op. cit.,* pp. 189–190.

The general property tax has always been the basic element in American local government finance. It goes back to medieval England. The American colonies used it although both assessment and levy were crude and by rule of thumb. In Connecticut, in 1676 for example, lands were assessed from 20 to 55 shillings per acre, depending on the locality. House and home lots ranged from 15 to 55 shillings. In most of the colonies, ownership of real property also constituted a qualification for voting on the theory that government should be the responsibility of those who paid the taxes, and this qualification remained in effect in some eastern and southern states until comparatively recent times.

The general property tax remained strictly a local tax until about 1840 when states began to dip into this source of revenue. In the decades after the Civil War, there was a trend toward state control of assessment either through power to equalize as between localities or by actual assessment of specialized property such as railroads. But today the main responsibility for assessment is still local, usually lodged with the county but sometimes with the city government. Locally, the property tax was used entirely by counties, towns, and townships until the middle of the 19th century. Municipal corporations, until then, existed largely from earnings from their property and services because they were considered quasi-private corporations. When these revenues proved insufficient, the legislatures were called upon to allow property taxation by municipalities for special purposes but gradually the general property tax was extended to all local units. The concept of the general property tax began to mean taxation of all property uniformly and at uniform rates.

COUNTY REVENUES 1953

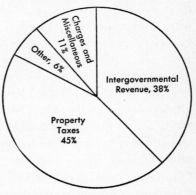

Fig. 13. County Revenues, 1953. (Source: Bureau of the Census, *Summary of Governmental Finances in 1953*.)

Two important developments began about the turn of the century. One was the separation of state and local tax sources with the general property tax tending to be the exclusive field of local taxation. The other was the classification of property for different taxing rates and purposes.

Classification of personal property was made fairly complete in Ohio when in 1932 the state departed from uniformity. Intangibles were classified separately and taxed at a uniform state-wide rate. Tangibles used in business were taxed at local rates and were classified in different categories. Machinery, equipment, and inventories of manufacturers were taxed at 50 per cent of the net book value; inventories of merchants were taxed 70 per cent of book value as were all furniture and fixtures to merchants and manufacturers. Automotive equipment was removed from the tax rolls and an "in lieu" tax substituted. Tangibles not used in business were exempted. Centralization of the administration of this system was placed in the hands of the state for all returns over $5,000 in which property was situated in more than one county. According to expert opinion, after eighteen years experience, the classification of intangibles was the most successful part of the program.[8]

The general property tax is fragmented between competing local units and there is little coordination in the interest of the local taxpayer. For example, in Illinois twenty-two local taxing units are authorized by state law to impose property taxes and units of sixteen types were known to be in existence in 1954. Residents of all areas in the state are subject to the jurisdiction of at least three units levying property taxes, and in some areas there are as many as nine to twelve units levying property taxes.[9]

[8] E. A. Cole, "Classification of Property for Tax Purposes," *Proceedings of the Forty-Third National Conference of the National Tax Association* (1950), pp. 106–112. The author thinks that most of the evils of the personal property tax system can be corrected by separate classification of tangibles and intangibles, taxation of intangibles at a statewide rate, and central administration of the larger returns.

[9] Clyde F. Snider, Gilbert Y. Steiner, and Lois Langdon, *Local Taxing Units: The Illinois Experience*. Institute of Government and Public Affairs, University of Illinois (1954). The property taxing units are: counties, township, road districts, cities-villages-incorporated towns, school districts, park districts, sanitary

Rates and burdens imposed by general property taxes vary from state to state, and from locality to locality. It was estimated by the Federal Department of Agriculture that in 1952 a total of $821 million was collected from farm real estate at the rate of $.90 per $100 of full value, or $.77 an acre. An interesting comparison is that of 1932, when the rate was $1.53 per $100 of full value, or $.46 per acre. In other words, farm real estate is taxed less in terms of value than it was two decades ago.[10]

The actual tax levy per $1,000 assessed valuation of combined city, school, and county taxes for 1954 in New York City was $38.60, in Chicago $36.16, in Philadelphia $30.25, in Los Angeles $67.40, and in Pittsburgh $44.09. The highest reported was $177.20, the lowest, $16.25. However, assessed valuation in relation to market value varies from city to city so there can be no real basis of comparison.[11]

Limitations on the General Property Tax

Local governments are not usually allowed full and unrestricted power to levy general property taxes. Provisions in state constitutions and in state laws restrict their use and guard against their abuse. The provision that *taxes must be uniform* was written into many state constitutions. Therefore, property cannot be taxed at progressive rates like those of the federal income tax. No matter how much property an individual has, it must be taxed at the same rate as the smallest holding.

Then, too, tax revenues must be *for public purpose*. The concept of public purpose goes back to the famous case brought before the United States Supreme Court in 1874.[12] The city council of Topeka,

---

districts, forest preserve districts, public health districts, fire protection districts, mosquito abatement districts, tuberculosis sanitarium districts, airport authorities, library districts, wildlife districts, river conservancy districts, water districts, street light districts, hospital districts, water service districts, water authorities, and surface water protection districts.

[10] The Tax Foundation, *Facts and Figures in Governmental Finance, 1954–1955,* p. 115.

[11] Citizens Research Council of Michigan, "Tax Rates of American Cities," *National Municipal Review* (January, 1955), pp. 14–35.

[12] Citizens' Saving and Loan Association *v.* Topeka, 20 Wallace 655 (1874).

Kansas, issued bonds to the amount of $100,000 to be donated to a bridge company as an inducement to come to the city. Later, the city refused to levy a tax to pay the interest on the bonds and the loan association which held the bonds brought suit. The court held that the tax sought to be levied was to pay a donation that was not for a public purpose, and that it was therefore unconstitutional. Courts since then have been requested many times to pass on the question of what constitutes a public purpose, but they have laid down no hard and fast definition, recognizing that it might change from time to time, from place to place. But the courts do assume that the state legislatures in granting local units the power to tax will necessarily see to it that such taxes are not levied for private gain, and therefore the courts will nullify legislation on this subject only when it is a clear violation of the principle of public purpose. Furthermore, they have held that a public purpose is what the people accept as such, and what is sanctioned by custom and usage. The courts of Maine upheld the operation of fuel yards as a public purpose, a Nebraska court the right of a city to sell gasoline and oil, the Georgia courts the establishment of a municipal ice plant. Upheld by various courts as payments for public purpose have been "necessary expenses," elections, streets, railroad aid, electric light plants, water supply, payment of interest and principal of bonds. On the other hand, courts have refused such items as entertainment of official visitors, building of theaters, prosecution of public officials, and manufacturing.[13]

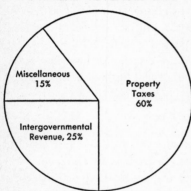

TOWNSHIP REVENUES 1953

Miscellaneous 15%

Property Taxes 60%

Intergovernmental Revenue, 25%

Fig. 14. Township Revenues, 1953. (Source: Bureau of the Census, *Summary of Governmental Finances in 1953.*)

[13] McQuillin, *The Law of Municipal Corporations,* second edition (1937), Vol. 6, pp. 337–345.

Certain types of ownership exempt property from local taxation. Constitutions or laws in most states *exempt from taxation property owned by governmental, educational, religious, and charitable institutions.* The theory behind exemption of government property was enunciated by Chief Justice Marshall when he said the power to tax involved the power to destroy. Therefore, local governments cannot levy taxes on federal property without congressional consent. But in half the states, constitutional or statutory provisions exempt all federal property from state and local taxation even when Congress may consent, but seventeen states removed such exemptions between 1945 and 1950. In the other states, federal property may be taxed when consent from Congress is forthcoming. Such consent has been given particularly in the case of lands in which the federal government holds only a proprietary title. Pressure is being brought to allow taxation of federal defense plants and installations because their removal from tax rolls has caused serious municipal stringencies. State owned property is exempt from local taxation in three-quarters of the states, while ten states permit taxation of selected property. A number of states make payments to local government "in lieu" of taxes, for example on forest lands where schools and roads are locally financed.[14]

In every state some property tax exemption is granted to religious, educational, charitable, benevolent, fraternal, literary, or scientific organizations. Such exemptions are granted upon the theory that those institutions perform functions that would, in their absence, be performed at public expense. The value of their services to the public, it is assumed, exceeds the amount the public loses from a remission of taxes. While there is no widespread disposition to remove these exemptions, many of them having been written into state constitutions, there is increasing realization of the fiscal importance of such practice. For example, exemption of property of a large university in a small town seriously burdens the taxable property of that local unit.

There are several tests on which exemptions are judged. By the

[14] Federation of Tax Administrators, *Taxation of Publicly Owned Real Estate,* Research Report No. 28 (1950).

test of *ownership* all property owned, for example, by a religious organization would be exempt no matter how the property was used. The most common test is *use*. When a religious property is exempt, the property must be used for religious purposes, not merely owned by a religious organization. Such property is not exempt if it is used for ordinary business purposes. The *use* test is the most widely accepted by the courts in deciding what properties should be exempt. The *occupancy* test is the determination whether the property is actually occupied by an institution with tax exemption privileges. Under such test the organization must actually occupy the property. Other tests are to find out whether the organization is conducting its business *for gain or profit*.

A substantial number of older educational institutions hold business and residential property free of taxes by virtue of charters which grant tax exemption to all their property and which under the famous Dartmouth College decision (Dartmouth College *v.* Woodward & Wheaton 518, 1819) are inviolable. As an example of the application of the *use* test, a Y.M.C.A. owning a building but renting part of it out as a tailor shop would be taxed only on the value assigned to the tailor shop. On the question of occupancy, a parochial school in Pennsylvania used a room just outside its assembly hall for the sale of tobacco, candy, and other light refreshments. The *occupancy* test was met, but the *use* test was not met, so this part of the building was taxable.[15]

The magnitude of exemption from property taxation of educational, religious, and philanthropic organizations is shown by the fact that in 1933 it was estimated that the total value of privately owned tax exempt property in the five states of New York, Rhode Island, Connecticut, Massachusetts, and New Jersey was $2.8 billion or 30 per cent of all tax exempt property. This amounted to 15 per cent of all property in Rhode Island and 25 per cent of all property in New York.[16] In 213 cities over 30,000 population, an average of

[15] Daugherty *v.* City of Philadelphia, 314 Pa. 298 (1934). Tax exemption of institutional property is described in: National Association of Assessing Officers, *Exemption of Institutional Real Property from Taxation*, Bulletin 23 (1939).

[16] Lucy M. Killough, Chapter 2, *Tax Exemptions*, Tax Policy League (1939), pp. 23–28.

about 18 per cent of all real property was exempt from taxation in 1952.[17]

A study of tax exempt property in Franklin county and the city of Columbus, Ohio, made in 1950 revealed that about 17 per cent of all real property was tax exempt. This meant a per capita loss of $3.85 or a millage equivalent of $3.60 per $1,000 valuation. The total tax loss was estimated at $1,500,000. The tax exempt property was distributed as follows: 28 per cent United States, 37 per cent state of Ohio, 10 per cent public schools, 8 per cent municipalities, 8 per cent churches, 3 per cent private colleges and academies, 3 per cent private charitable institutions, and 3 per cent county, township, and park districts. Total value of tax exempt property was $108 million; the number of tax exempt parcels was 1,528.[18]

Additional classes of property exempt in recent years include real property of veterans or of disabled veterans in about half the states.

All housing projects built by local housing authorities with federal assistance are exempt from local taxes. The exemptions are considered as local contributions to the projects but the United States allows "in lieu" payments to cover the cost of municipal services to these projects.

Household furnishings are fully or partially exempt from property taxation in most of the states. Arguments advanced for such exemptions are based on the difficulty of locating such property by the assessor, its relative unimportance, and the tendency to allow it to become delinquent by the taxing authorities.[19]

Many states *limit the rates* of local taxation. A few limit the amount of money to be raised by taxation. Some have maximum limits, a few have minimum limits. There are five broad types of general tax limitation: (1) tax limits which state a fixed maximum rate of tax, either on the same property or upon each governmental unit; (2) limitations which restrict the amount of the aggregate levy in terms of the amount of previous years; (3) limitations which

---

[17] Citizens Research Council of Michigan, "Tax Rates in American Cities," *National Municipal Review* (January, 1953), pp. 17–33.

[18] Citizens Research, Inc., *Real Property Tax Exemption* (June, 1951).

[19] National Association of Taxing Authorities, *Exemption of Household Furnishings from Property Taxation* (1938).

restrict the amount of revenue to be raised either per capita or aggregate sum; and (4) limitations which fix the ratio of revenues from general property taxes and revenue from other sources.[20] Such limitations are seldom the effective curbs originally sought, for the maximum levies of three units of government in which the taxable property lies, plus the extras allowed by vote of the people or by the court, makes the total levy higher than the tax levying bodies could freely go without legal limitations. The taxpayers would rise up in opposition.

SCHOOL DISTRICT REVENUES
1953

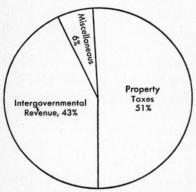

Fig. 15. School District Revenues. (Source: Bureau of the Census, *Summary of Governmental Finances in 1953.*)

Nine states had adopted *over-all tax limitations* by 1937, most of them to save real estate from mass tax delinquency and ultimate tax sale during the depression.[21] Limits on total levies ranged from one to five per cent, or from 10 to 50 mills on the dollar of assessed valuation. The chief arguments for such drastic limitations were: (1) real estate was overburdened with taxes as evidenced by a high rate of tax delinquency and tax sales during the depression because of severely reduced income from property; (2) tax on property placed an excessive burden on too small a proportion of the population—those that own property; (3) local government expenditures were extravagant and wasteful and over-all tax limitation would

[20] Rodney L. Mott and W. O. Suiter, "The Types and Extent of Existing Tax Limitations," Public Administration Service No. 36, *Property Tax Limitation Laws* (1936).

[21] The nine states were Michigan, Nevada, Indiana, New Mexico, Ohio, Oklahoma, Rhode Island, Washington, West Virginia. All but three—Rhode Island, Indiana, and Washington—had limitations written into the state constitutions. The others were by statute. See A. Miller Hillhouse and Ronald B. Welch, *Tax Limits Appraised,* Public Administration Service, Bulletin No. 55 (1937). No state has adopted over-all tax limitation since 1937.

curb such excesses; (4) over-all tax limitation would discourage borrowing and improve municipal credit; and (5) would result in more equitable assessment and bring about better allocation of governmental functions.

A study of the effects of the 20-mill over-all tax limitation constitutional amendment in West Virginia since its adoption in 1932 has led to the following conclusions: (1) a drastic reduction in the relative level of property taxes has been effected; (2) the use of indirect, consumption taxes by both the state and local governments has been increased with the result that the state now has an extremely regressive system of taxation; (3) while the aggregate of state and local taxes remained about the same, the restrictive effect on local taxes has resulted in a large scale growth of state taxes because the cost of roads and schools has been largely shifted to the state; (4) over-all tax limitation has held down local spending and hampered the performance of vital local services; (5) it has failed to bring about full-value assessments, local government reorganization, or the elimination of tax delinquency which its proponents promised; and (6) freedom of local action has been curtailed and increased centralization by the state encouraged.[22]

Because of the limitation on property taxes, the principal source of local revenue in West Virginia fell more than forty per cent— from $40 million to $23 million.[23] To make up this loss the legislature enacted gross sales taxes and a personal income tax, the latter now repealed. A state liquor monopoly system was created and thus became a chief source of state revenue. These are now the chief sources for the financing of state government, schools, and relief. Local units were granted the power to enact gross sales taxes, liquor sales taxes, and license taxes. The state increased its financial aid.

One of the main problems in the administration of an over-all tax limitation is the distribution of the millage between the various

[22] Harold J. Shamberger and James H. Thompson, *The Operation of the Tax-Limitation Amendment in West Virginia,* West Virginia University (1950).

[23] The West Virginia Commission on Interstate Cooperation and the Joint Committee on Government and Finance, *An Introductory Study of Municipal Finance on West Virginia* (1949), p. 5.

local units. In Michigan this is done by the county tax allocation board composed of three county officials and three persons appointed by the county probate judge. In May all local units of government must submit their budgets to this board to show estimated expenditures and revenues for the coming fiscal year. On the basis of this information, the board determines what tax rates are necessary, excluding the tax rate for debt service. If the board finds that the total of all tax rates required by all local units of government would exceed 15 mills—the Michigan limit—it apportions the following minimum rates: 3 mills for counties, 4 mills for school districts, and 1 mill for townships. Only eleven cities and villages voted to come under the limitation and they receive the larger share of the 15 mills although no minimum is set. The others must reserve one-tenth of one mill. The total minimum prescribed rates in most counties are 8.1 mills, and the board is allowed to allocate the remainder of the 15 mills as it seems fit. The cities and villages not under the limitation may levy rates as their governing body sees fit. Also additional taxes may be levied upon a two-thirds majority of voters.[24]

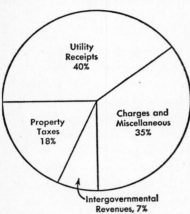

SPECIAL DISTRICT REVENUES
1953

Fig. 16.   Special District Revenues, 1953. (Source: Bureau of the Census, *Summary of Governmental Finances in 1953.*)

Another tax product of the depression was *homestead exemption.* By this means the property tax obligations of residence homesteads both rural and urban are reduced. Variations in the method have been adopted in different states. Louisiana exempted from state, parish, and special taxes all homesteads not exceeding $2,000 in

[24] Bureau of Government, University of Michigan, *Property Tax Administration* (1939), pp. 10–12.

taxable valuation and 160 acres of land. Minnesota modified the property classification system by providing for a lower percentage of value for tax purposes on the first $4,000 value of real property used by an owner of a homestead. Florida granted a $5,000 exemption on property not exceeding 160 acres in rural land and one-fourth of an acre in urban property from all taxes except special assessments. As reported by the National Association of Assessing Officers, the percentage reduction in the property base resulting from homestead exemption in 1948 ranged from 7 per cent in Wyoming to 40 per cent in Mississippi. Some states reimburse local units for losses due to homestead exemption.[25]

The property tax laws of some states, especially those in the South include *many provisions favorable to manufacturing*. Exemption of manufacturing properties is guaranteed during the initial period to induce location. Some states have preferential rates; for example, a Kentucky law provides for a combined city and school tax on whisky in storage in Louisville of $1.25 per $100 valuation, while other tangible property is subject to full state and local rates, which aggregated $2.48 per $100 in 1946. In Louisiana, plants and inventories of concerns engaged exclusively in the manufacture of waste materials are assessed only at 10 per cent of full value. Some states give permanent exemption of manufacturing machinery and inventories. South Carolina exempts for one year finished goods in the hands of manufacturers. The over-all result is that all southern states derive a larger proportion of their total state and local tax receipts from consumers than does the average state, and most of them depend more heavily on mercantile taxes. While manufacturing, as well as general economic well-being, is advancing more rapidly in the South than in the nation generally, it is the considered opinion of tax experts, that there is little, if any, correlation between tax loads

[25] Thirteen states exempted homesteads from state, or from state and local, taxes during the 1930 decade. They were Alabama, Arkansas, Florida, Georgia, Iowa, Louisiana, Minnesota, Mississippi, Oklahoma, South Dakota, Texas, West Virginia, and Wyoming. No new states have exempted homesteads since then, and some of the states have liberalized the original provisions. From Tax Institute, *Tax Policy* (February-March, 1952), p. 5. See also J. M. Leonard and Rosina Mohaupt, *Exemption of Homesteads from Taxation*, Detroit Bureau of Government Research (1937).

and their distribution, and rates of manufacturing growth. Most of the southern advance seems restricted to a few states, and some which are showing most rapid industrial development have relatively heavy tax loads.[26] In other words, taxation is not among the foremost reasons for industrial location.

A more flexible plan to limit taxation is the *Indiana* Plan. Every local tax-levying body in the state must prepare an annual budget and tax rate sufficient to meet it, and certify it to the state board of tax commissioners. On petition of any ten aggrieved taxpayers, the commission may veto any increase in the tax rate over the previous year. This plan in several variations has been adopted in several other states. Whether or not a group of state officials can make correct decisions on local levies in municipalities they have never even visited is doubtful, but it is generally agreed that in Indiana they have not abused their power.

Assessment of Property for Taxable Purposes

Assessment is the process of ascertaining the value of property for taxable purposes. First, the property must be *discovered.* This is done by the assessors who list the property in their assessment books or records. Then they must *value it for taxation*—put upon it an assessed valuation. Once this is done for all property in his district, the assessor *turns his books and records over to the county or city assessing authorities.* These agencies may *review the assessments* to see that a complete job was done according to law and to their instructions. They also *hear appeals* of aggrieved taxpayers who feel that their assessments are too high or not in line with those of their neighbors. These agencies also *equalize assessments* between various subdivisions so that the taxpayers in one unit will not pay more than their just share of taxes levied by the county or city. *These assessments are then turned over to the various taxing bodies* which take the total assessed valuation of their local unit and divide it into the amount of money they need from the property tax to

[26] James W. Martin and Glenn D. Morrow, *Taxation of Manufacturing in the South,* Bureau of Public Administration, University of Alabama (1948).

run their government for the ensuing year. The result is the *tax levy* on property for that year. For example, a city has an assessed valuation of taxable property of $250,000,000 and its council wants to raise $5,000,000 from property taxation. To get the tax levy on all property in that city, take $250,000,000 and divide it into $5,000,000. The result will be $.02, or twenty mills, on each dollar of assessed valuation.

The basic job of assessing real property is done in what might be called *primary assessment districts,* that is, those units in which the assessors actually assess property. In twenty-six states, counties are the primary assessment districts; in fifteen, townships and municipalities; and in seven there is a combination. The number of assessment districts ranges from three in Delaware to 2,587 in Minnesota.[27] *Overlapping assessment districts* exist in twenty-two states involving 6,300 units of government. For example, in Pennsylvania cities of the third class have two assessments. One is made under the supervision of the county by elected tax assessors in each ward. This was the original arrangement. But it turned out that the assessments were too low for city purposes. As there was a tax levy limitation, not enough money could be raised to balance the budgets. Legislation was enacted providing that the councils in such cities could appoint an assessor to make separate assessments for city and school purposes while the county assessment still holds for county purposes. Of course, the city assessment is nearly always much higher than the county assessment.

The assessment job in the primary districts is almost always carried on by single assessors, of which the National Association of Assessing Officers estimates there are 25,000, but in some states there are boards of assessors for the basic job. The great majority of assessors are elected and therefore more or less independent of the over-all county or city assessing authorities and the taxing bodies for whom they assess. The theory for this arrangement was that assessors ought to be close to the people. It is certainly true that assessors do not like to cross swords with their constituents. Being

[27] National Association of Assessing Officers, *Assessment Organization and Personnel* (1941), p. 5.

local residents, they are available for complaints at any time and being human they want to please their customers. Furthermore, most elected assessors have little or no training before they come into the job, and few are exposed to any after their election. Nor are they given modern equipment with which to do their work. The records of the previous assessor are turned over to them along with certain instructions from the assessing authorities, and they are directed to "go to it." What often ensues is what is known as "dining room assessment." The books from last year are laid out on the dining room table and copied into this year's book, with certain obvious changes such as new houses entered and properties destroyed taken out. But there is very little re-assessment to take care of changed property values and conditions from year to year. Even when general re-assessments are required as they are by law, the assessor does not go out and do a complete assessment. Often he is paid only a modest per diem compensation with little or no expense money for travel, and he is limited to a certain number of days far too few for the work at hand. Nor is he supervised or guided, and the result is wholly inadequate assessments. In Michigan, for example, the Rural Property Inventory Project of 1939 found that more than ten per cent of the million and a half descriptions of property on the township tax rolls were erroneous.[28]

The county or city assessing authorities, which are by law directed to supervise and administer the assessment of property for taxable purposes on the local level, do not do much better than the elected assessor. Usually, these assessment authorities are the county commissioners or the city council themselves *ex officio,* and they too are extremely sensitive to adverse public opinion. In the comparatively few places that have separate boards of assessment and revision of taxes, these are usually appointed by the assessing authorities, and in some cases, elected. They tend to do a better job because they have this single function to perform, but they too are inclined to move slowly because of the repercussions any mass alteration of

[28] Milton B. Dickerson, *State Supervision of Local Taxation and Finance in Michigan,* Michigan Agricultural Experiment Station Special Bulletin No. 327 (1944), p. 19.

assessments will have. At their worst, these supervising, review, and equalization agencies do little or nothing to improve assessment conditions. At their best, they take an active part in training the assessors, giving them complete instructions, develop new methods, put in new equipment such as property cards and tax maps, and try to get equalized tax assessments within the county or city. The general average of performance, however, is on the mediocre side.

Much real property in an urban and industrial area is so specialized that it is difficult to assess for ordinary assessors implemented only with eye, ear, and rule of thumb. Who, for example, can value a great steel manufacturing plant, a skyscraper, a big hotel? Surely only specialists and professional valuation experts. Also, there has been a tremendous and rapid accumulation of intangible property such as stocks and bonds that is difficult to discover. Likewise are many forms of tangible personal property such as jewelry, clothing, furniture, and movable machinery. As a result of difficulties with such forms of wealth, New York followed other states and in 1933 abandoned the personal property tax which for years before had been practically inoperative. There is a substantial evasion of taxation by not listing all real property or listing it at a low assessment. There is unequal and inequitable assessment of property. Smaller properties tend to receive higher valuations in relation to market value than the larger properties simply because, if for no other reason, the ordinary assessor can understand small property values better. Evidences of unequal, inequitable, excessively low assessments abound in every state, probably in almost every local unit in the nation. A study of assessment in six Pennsylvania counties made in 1926 showed that individual property assessments within single counties ranged from 9 to 133 per cent of actual sales price in urban units and from 13 to 160 per cent in rural areas, and that average ratios of assessment to sales price was as low as 26 per cent in one county and as high as 85 in another. The conclusions expressed in this study were that it is impossible to secure assessments at full value, to secure uniformity within townships and other local units, and to raise the rate of assessments as long as the present system of independently elected assessors from townships, wards, and municipalities is in effect.[29] Assessors know that their constituents will fight every substantial increase in assessed valuations with tooth and nail, even when the prospect of lower tax rates are held out as a hope for the future. They also know that if they raise assessments in their local unit while other local units in their county do not do so, their community will pay more than their just share of county taxes. When elected by their home constituency, they are rarely deaf to the appeals of their own constituency.[30]

Improving Assessments

The basic element of a sound assessment system is good personnel. It is generally agreed that better assessors can be recruited by appointment than by election. But appointment is not enough, candidates should be selected on the basis of their qualifications for the work. They should be full-time employees, compensated adequately, and protected against political changes.

The assessor's office should have modern facilities: adequate floor space, tax maps, lot and block maps depicting urban areas with accurate dimension and details, aerial maps for rural areas, and modern mechanical equipment for computing, recording, and mailing. Last but not least, assessors should follow modern administrative techniques that have been developed over the past fifty years. Standard assessment practices result in more uniform and equitable assessment as has been demonstrated in many places.

Real property cannot be assessed properly without adequate records. The characteristics of each piece of property should be placed on a separate *property card*. This contains the basic information upon which the entire assessment structure is built. Land and improvements should be separated for assessment. The proper way to discover land is to survey it, map it to scale and place all property

[29] F. P. Weaver, *Rural Taxation in Pennsylvania*, Pennsylvania Department of Agriculture Bulletin No. 437 (1926).

[30] For excellent discussions of assessment of property for taxable purposes, see Alfred G. Buehler, *Public Finance*, second edition (1940), and Joseph D. Silverherz, *The Assessment of Real Property in the United States*, State of New York, Special Report of the State Tax Commission (1936).

lines on the descriptive card. The record of ownership of each parcel of land should be contained on the basic property card. Improvements and changes in the property should be kept up-to-date.

The valuation of property is the most difficult part of the assessment process. Entirely different techniques are required to evaluate land and improvements. The first must be ascertained by comparison with market values of those recently sold in open market. The value of improvements can be found through the development of reproduction costs. The final value of a property is made by the merging of the two.

In the assessment of urban lands, a land value map should be prepared. This map shows block lines but not property boundaries. It will contain unit land values of the block in terms of the unit foot which is "a rectangular portion of urban land with a frontage of one foot and a depth equal to that of a standard lot, usually one hundred feet. Unit foot values are ascertained by securing from those who know property values a consensus on a point of high value in the area assessed and the percentages of decrease from that value in adjacent and distant blocks. For example, Block A is the center of the downtown business section and is considered to be the most valuable in the entire municipality. Block M is eight blocks to the south and in a slum area. Each block from A to M is given a certain percentage in terms of the value of Block A. Block A is, of course, 100 per cent; Block B may be 95 per cent; Block C 90 per cent; Block D 80 per cent until finally we reach Block M which may be only 25 per cent. Having the value of Block A in terms of a unit foot, it is easy to ascertain the Block M unit foot as 25 per cent of that of Block A, and to translate that into any parcel of property that exists in Block M. There are, of course, many irregularities in urban lots—corner lots, triangular lots, short lots—and formulae have been developed to take abnormalities into considerations. Rural land is usually assessed by the acre and value per acre is computed by the central assessing body on the basis of kind of land—tillable, pasture, orchard, forest or waste, and of location.

Improvements—houses, barns, apartments, and structures of all kinds—are valued by seeking their reproduction cost. This cannot be done for each structure so certain categories of buildings are made up. Usually in each category, at least one typical building is analyzed in detail, its cost computed and translated into unit cost per square foot of floor area or cubic foot. Costs for such a typical building are secured from contractors and builders, and are adjusted from year to year according to general economic conditions and prices. Physical depreciation and obsolescence are computed by means of scientific tables or by the observation of the assessor. When the cost per square or cubic foot for each category has been determined, it is easy to apply this to each particular structure by multiplying the unit cost per square or cubic foot by the number of square or cubic feet in the building. Adjustment for variations from the norm can easily be made.

For the assessment of personal property, the assessors should compile a comprehensive checklist of all persons they think have property in the district. Property tax returns are sent to these people and the taxpayers assess themselves, subject of course to personal visits by the assessor, public records, business balance sheets, federal and state income tax returns, and exchange of information between districts. Valuation of personal property should be by market value. Motor vehicles can be evaluated by such reports as the Automobile Bluebook which take into consideration year of model and depreciation. Movable machinery and equipment is counted as personal property, along with raw materials and stock in trade, goods in process of manufacture, and household furnishings and should be evaluated according to standard assessment practices.[31]

There has, of course, been gradual but continued improvement of the assessment process, especially in urban areas where "scientific" and orderly principles of assessment have been put into practice. In rural areas the improvement has not been as noticeable, perhaps because rural local units do not have as great pressure for increased revenues.

[31] The International City Managers' Association, *Municipal Finance Administration,* third edition (1946), Chapter 9. Also: National Association of Assessing Officers, *Assessing Terminology* (1937), and *Urban Land Appraisal* (1940).

LOCAL NONPROPERTY TAXES AND REVENUES

A most phenomenal development in local finances since the end of World War II has been the increased use of nonproperty taxes by local units, especially in the urban areas. This has come about not only because of the absolute need for more money but in recognition of the fact that all economic sectors of communities should contribute a share to the local coffers. While nonproperty taxes comprised only four per cent of total local government revenues in 1953, they are being adopted at a rapid pace. Already half of the cities over 10,000 population impose one or more and their number is continually growing. Best revenue producers are the income and sales taxes although they are at present confined largely to a few states. Such taxes, as well as other revenues derived from the consumer as opposed to the property owner, are especially designed to reach the "fluid population" of a municipality such as those living in suburbs, itinerant defense workers, personnel in military encampments, resort visitors, and in fact, all those who do not own real property within the community.[32]

The attitude of legislatures toward financial aid to local units seems to have veered away from increased state grants and shared taxes to a policy of allowing local units more freedom to find and develop their own sources of revenue—other than the general property tax. New York and Pennsylvania led the way with broad permissive legislation enacted in 1947.

The local permissive tax law of New York authorizes counties and municipalities to impose the following taxes: (1) a 2 per cent tax on retail sales; (2) a tax not in excess of 3 per cent on receipts from sale of food or drink in restaurants, bars, and other establishments; (3) a tax not to exceed 3 per cent on charges made for utility services; (4) a tax on alcoholic beverages not in excess of 25 per cent of the license fee prescribed by state law; (5) a tax not to exceed 5 per cent on admissions to amusements; (6) a tax on coin operated amusement devices not to exceed $25 a year per machine; (7) a tax

---

[32] Randall S. Stout and Eugene A. Myers, *"The Development of Permissive Local Legislation since 1945," Current Economic Comment* (August, 1951).

on passenger motor vehicles of $5 to $10 a year maximum; (8) a business tax on gross receipts not over three-fifths of 1 per cent; (9) and a tax on hotel rooms not to exceed 5 per cent of the rent.[33]

Pennsylvania's Act 481 permits cities, boroughs, townships, and school districts to "tax anything" not taxed by the state. But there are some limitations and exceptions. The aggregate amount of taxes annually imposed is limited to a sum equal to the amount of property taxes that could be collected under a ten-mill levy in municipalities and a fifteen-mill levy in school districts. Exemptions include manufactured goods, farm products, and natural resources. School districts may levy income taxes only on residents of the district. There are rate limitations also: $10 per person for per capita taxes, 1 per cent on earned income, 2 per cent on retail sales taxes, and 1 per cent on wholesale, 10 per cent on amusements, and 1 per cent on transfer of real estate. When two local units covering the same area impose the same tax, the combined rate may not exceed the maximum allowed by law. The local units may agree on the rate of each but if they do not agree, half is supposed to go to each. Agreements for joint collection are permitted.[34]

Under the Pennsylvania law as of April 15, 1955, a total of 2,807 local units out of an eligible 5,019—56 per cent—levied 3,719 non-property taxes. In order of adoptions, the per capita taxes led with 2,112, followed by amusement taxes with 398, income with 419, deed transfer with 336, mechanical devices with 138, trailer taxes with 182 and mercantile with 70, and with 64 others. Almost all the cities, more than half the boroughs and first-class townships, more than a third of the second-class townships, and about three-quarters of the school districts of the state participate in this taxation. During fiscal 1953, total collections were more than $42 million, excluding Philadelphia. The taxes in order of productivity were income, per capita, mercantile, deed transfer, amusement, mechanical devices, and

---

[33] Municipal Finance Officers Association, *Municipal Nonproperty Taxes,* 1951 Supplement to "Where Cities Get Their Money," p. 3.

[34] Robert A. Sigafoos, *The Pennsylvania Local Tax Law,* Pennsylvania State College, Bureau of Business Research, Bulletin No. 46 (1950). Also Elizabeth Smedley, *Legal Problems Involving Act 481,* Department of Internal Affairs, Commonwealth of Pennsylvania (1950).

trailer.[35] Another unique but highly significant development in local nonproperty taxation is collection by the state and total return to the local units. Florida provides that the local government must impose such taxes by ordinance. In Mississippi some cities are given the right to impose a sales tax which must be state collected. This latter variation is an answer to those critics who believe local administration of nonproperty taxes is bound to be less effective than the use of state facilities.

Local Income Taxes

What may be one of the most important local taxes of the future is the municipal income tax. It is of recent vintage on the local level. In 1939, Philadelphia and Washington, D. C., collected the first local income taxes levied in the United States. In 1946, Toledo adopted an income tax under Ohio's broad home rule provisions and eight other cities within the state followed suit by 1952.

In 1947, the Pennsylvania legislature passed its now famous Act 481 and by October, 1954, 403 income taxes had been levied in that state.[36] In addition to Philadelphia which was given similar power under earlier legislation, 15 Pennsylvania cities including Pittsburgh, 120 boroughs, 14 townships of the first class, and 254 school districts levy an income tax, usually at the rate of one per cent. In 1948, Louisville, Kentucky, imposed an occupational license tax, and St. Louis, Missouri, enacted its earning tax.[37]

Local income taxes, except in Washington, D. C., where unearned income is also included, are on earned income only—that is, salaries, wages, profits, and professional fees. They are usually levied on residents and nonresidents who earn income within the municipality. When a nonresident pays income tax in a city where he works,

[35] Marielle Hobart, *Act 481, State-Wide Summary,* Commonwealth of Pennsylvania, Department of Internal Affairs (April 15, 1955).

[36] Marielle Hobart, "403 Local Governments Enact Income Taxes under Act 481," Commonwealth of Pennsylvania, Department of Internal Affairs, Monthly Bulletin (November, 1954), pp. 12–14.

[37] Leon Jay Quinto, *Municipal Income Taxation in the United States,* Mayor's Committee on Management Survey, City of New York (1952), pp. 1–3.

can his residence community also levy such a tax against him? In Pennsylvania taxpayers are exempt from such double taxation by legislation which gives priority to residence communities when both tax income. Therefore, when the city of Pittsburgh enacted its income tax in 1954 there were only six local income taxes in the surrounding county of Allegheny. By October of that year, 73 had been adopted. The fringe communities in which thousands lived who worked in Pittsburgh would not have enacted this tax had not Pittsburgh done so, but they did not want the central city to get the revenue. As a result the actual usefulness of this tax—to get commuters to bear a share of the cost of city government—was partially nullified. In Philadelphia, by terms of legislation covering its income tax, the city itself has the priority of tax and therefore no communities in its metropolitan area have levied an income tax. In Toledo, a credit of 50 per cent is allowed to nonresidents if reciprocity is allowed to Toledo by their communities. In Springfield and Dayton, Ohio, residents are exempt from income tax in their home communities if they pay such a tax in outside communities from which they derive their income.

Generally the rates are one per cent, but there are a few higher and lower. They are flat rates, that is, the same rate no matter how high the income. Progressive local income taxation runs into the snag of tax uniformity provided for in many state constitutions. Collection in most jurisdictions is by withholding as with the federal income tax. The per capita yield in five of the larger cities levying a one per cent income tax in 1949 or 1950 has been as follows: Philadelphia, $14.92; Scranton, $8.87; Toledo, $19.79; Springfield, $17.63; and Louisville, $14.27.[38]

The arguments in favor of a local income tax are that (1) it provides substantial revenue; (2) it applies to nonresidents and therefore decreases the tax advantages of the suburban areas over the central city; (3) because it can develop substantial revenues, it

[38] *Ibid.*, pp. 106–114. Also: William G. Willis and William W. Boyer, Jr., "The Income Tax Puzzle in the Pittsburgh Area," *Municipal Finance* (May, 1955), pp. 140–144.

allows municipalities to do away with "nuisance" taxes having small yields; (4) the individual earner provides a share of local taxes; and (5) the administrative cost is not prohibitive.

Arguments against the local income tax are that: (1) the income tax is regressive in that it hits smaller incomes proportionately harder than large; (2) that it is another level taxing incomes and thereby further confusing the tax picture; (3) administrative problems become complicated if it is applied to nonresidents.[39]

Toledo found that the imposition of a city income tax reduced property taxes and made the city more attractive to suburbanites who also paid the income tax if they worked in the central city.[40]

The importance of the income tax as a means of getting nonresidents of the metropolitan area to help pay for the costs of central city government is shown by the fact that Philadelphia collected $5.6 million or 15 per cent of the total from nonresidents. Johnstown collected 20 per cent of the total from nonresidents, Dayton 20 per cent, Columbus 14 per cent, and Louisville 15 per cent. In places such as Scranton where communities outside the city are also allowed to impose the income tax and where residence taxing bodies have priority, the proportion collected by the central city is very low, for example, in Scranton where it is only 2.2 per cent of the total.[41]

Local Sales Taxes

New York City in 1934 was the first municipality in the United States to enact a retail sales tax. It was followed by New Orleans in 1941. Between 1945 and 1951, a total of 141 California municipali-

[39] Robert A. Blundred, "*Selecting New Income Revenue Services.*" *American Municipal Association* (March, 1951).

[40] R. T. Anderson, "Income Tax Aids Annexation," *National Municipal Review*, October, 1949, pp. 443–447; and Ronald E. Gregg, "Payroll Tax Boon to Toledo," *National Municipal Review* (April, 1949), pp. 164–166.

[41] Robert A. Sigafoos, "The Urban-Rural Fringe Population Problem and Effects of Municipal Finance," *Current Economic Comment* (November, 1952), p. 10.

ties adopted this tax. Such cities as Denver, Colorado, Atlantic City, New Jersey, and Niagara Falls also have enacted a retail sales tax. Eighty Illinois municipalities adopted a one-half of one per cent sales tax within a few months after the legislature granted them this power in 1955. This tax may be adopted by the locality without referendum and is collected by the Illinois State Department of Revenue for a 6 per cent collection cost.

Sales taxes vary in their inclusiveness and exemptions. A *retail sales tax* is one imposed only on the sale of tangible personal property at retail to the ultimate consumer. A *general sales tax* is broader, being imposed also on wholesalers and jobbers, and sometimes even on manufacturers. A *selective sales tax* applies to specific commodities such as gasoline, cigarettes, soft drinks, and other commodities. A *gross receipts tax* includes the sale of professional services as well as sales. A *"use" tax* is used to complement the sales tax and is imposed at the same rates as a sales tax on articles bought outside the city limits and is used to discourage outside purchases to get out of paying a sales tax.[42]

Sales taxes are advantageous especially to cities like Atlantic City and Niagara Falls which have large transient populations. It is the only direct way by which these people can be made to share the cost of governmental services. The tax is relatively easy to administer and costs of collection have been under five per cent of the amount collected because the burden of collection falls on the merchants themselves. A few places allow compensation to the merchant for collecting the tax. Exemptions often include food not consumed on the premises, medicines, utility service, labor, fuels, magazines, newspapers, and other items considered to be necessities of life. Rates are from one-half of one per cent to three per cent, most often one per cent. The average yield for 76 cities over 10,000 population in 1950 was $11.71 per capita.

Strong opposition to the enactment of sales taxes is usually encountered. A number of cities, notably Philadelphia, St. Louis,

[42] A. M. Hillhouse and Muriel Magelssen, *Where Cities Get Their Money*, Municipal Finance Officers Association (1945), pp. 55–56.

Miami, and Atlanta, enacted such taxes for a short time only to repeal them because of local pressures from merchants and other groups. Antagonists claim that they are more burdensome on the lower income groups but the regressivity of a particular tax depends on the number and kind of exemptions. Also it is claimed that sales taxes drive business out of town into the suburbs, and this may be true in a large metropolitan area where the central city leans heavily on outside areas for retail trade.[43]

Local Admission and Amusement Device Taxes

Admission tax rates range up to ten per cent but are usually expressed in terms of the tax on a ticket. This tax is used especially widely in localities of the states of Washington and Ohio in which the state abandoned the tax, and in Pennsylvania as a result of the "tax anything" law of 1947. In 1953, a total of 121 of the 244 cities and towns of Washington utilized this source of revenue which brought in more than $1 million. It is a tax that reaches nonresidents as well as residents, and may have had some effect on the increased popularity of "drive-ins" outside of municipal limits. But the tax is usually not excessive and is generally easy to collect. Municipal officer organizations have urged legislation to do away with the present federal tax on admissions on the theory that it is a natural one for local units.[44]

Local units in many states tax amusement devices that are mechanically operated and found in stations, stores, pool rooms, and all places where people want to congregate or wait. Idaho even taxes slot machines, Nevada and Montana gambling devices.[45] New York City imposes a 5 per cent tax on pari-mutuel race tracks receipts.

[43] Municipal Finance Officers Association, *Municipal Nonproperty Taxes,* 1951 Supplement to "Where Cities Get Their Money," p. 12.

[44] *Ibid.,* pp. 21–23, and 1953 *State Auditor's Report* of Washington.

[45] Federation of Tax Administrators, *Multiple Taxation of Amusements and Selected Utility Services, Federal, State and Local,* Research Report No. 27 (January, 1950), p. 16.

Local Cigarette and Liquor Taxes

These are in the nature of selected sales taxes but deserve special consideration. In 1951, 67 cities over ten thousand population were using a cigarette tax, and from it obtained a per capita yield of $2.99 at an average rate of two-and-a-half cents a pack. Their use in localities depends to some degree on whether or not the state imposes such a tax. It is relatively easy to collect.

Liquor is usually not taxed by local units as a commodity—only thirty-five cities over 10,000 population imposed it in 1951 but these reported an average yield of $2.37 per capita. Many municipalities benefit from the issuance of liquor licenses either by the municipality or by the state which returns the proceeds to municipalities.[46]

Local Motorists' Taxes

Municipalities tax the motorist in various ways: motor license taxes, gasoline taxes, parking meters, special trailer taxes, personal property taxes on motor vehicles, tolls, operators' licenses, and inspection fees.

Local gasoline and motor fuels taxes are specifically allowed in seven states, all southern and western, but are used most extensively in Alabama where 162 local units including 11 counties were imposing this tax in 1945. In the remaining 41 states, municipalities are either prohibited from levying gasoline taxes or the law is silent on that point. In Alabama, the municipalities have the right to levy this tax over the area included in their "police jurisdiction" which extends three miles, as the crow flies, in all directions from municipal borders.[47]

Motor vehicle license taxes were imposed in 1951 in 117 cities over ten thousand population. Most extensive use of this tax is made in Illinois where more than 250 cities use it, and Missouri, and North

---

[46] *Ibid.*, p. 24; and Hillhouse and Magelssen, *op. cit.*, pp. 63–78.
[47] Hillhouse and Magelssen, *op. cit.*, 79–83.

Carolina. Taxes are by flat amount as on the basis of weight, horse-power, value, and other common denominators. Many municipalities charge a fee for engaging in business using motor vehicles, and some impose inspection fees and operators license fees. Generally, however, these taxes are state-imposed and not within the jurisdiction of local units.

One of the newer additions to municipal revenue has been receipts from parking meters. Used first in Oklahoma City in 1935, they spread to every state in the Union. Not only did they help to ease the parking problem but they provided cities with additional revenue. Most meter companies allow cities to pay the initial costs out of the revenues and this is usually done within one year of operation. By 1950, they were being used in 1,297 cities of over five thousand population. Receipts for the month of September, 1949, averaged $6.37 per meter, and a total of more than two and a half million dollars was the "take" for the month.[48]

License Taxes

License taxes are one of the more important nonproperty revenues in municipalities. These taxes may be both for the purpose of regulating business and raising revenue. In the South, license taxes are definitely revenue measures, and in recent years a number of large cities outside the South revised their schedules for purposes of revenue rather than regulation. In the Pacific coast states, cities used the license tax device to make business which profited by large army stations in the vicinity pay their share of local government. The range of such taxes is broad; the rates are based upon various schedules: flat rates, flat rates applied to volume of sales or gross receipts, or a bracketed schedule with increasing amounts with each higher bracket.

In Pennsylvania, municipalities license and tax such subjects as

[48] *The Municipal Year Book 1950,* pp. 452–454. Also: Charles F. LeeDecker, *Parking Meters in Pennsylvania Municipalities,* Institute of Local Government, The Pennsylvania State College (1947).

amusement, auctioneers, auction sales, banks, bicycles, billboards, drays, entertainment, express companies, food, gasoline stations, junk collectors or peddlers, loud speakers, markets, meat lockers, milk—to go only part way down the alphabetical list.[49]

In Alabama, the municipal license has, in recent years, led all revenues used to finance municipal operations. In some places it accounts for as much as forty per cent of all revenue. Even in larger cities where property values are relatively higher, license taxes have a sizable place in the municipal finance picture. Its intensive use has allowed comparatively low property tax rates. The Alabama cities have almost unlimited authority in levying business license taxes. The courts have held, however, that the license tax must be reasonable and not confiscatory; it should be uniform for all items in the same class. The courts have upheld license taxes on interstate commerce carriers loading and unloading within the city. They have upheld licenses to tax itinerant merchants higher than resident merchants.[50]

The famous Green River, Wyoming, ordinance which prohibited solicitors, peddlers, and itinerant merchants from going upon the premises of private residences for the purpose of either peddling or soliciting without having been requested or invited to do so by the occupants was copied by hundreds of municipalities desiring to protect the home town merchants during the depression years. This ordinance was upheld by a federal court as to the sale of brushes [51] and by the United States Supreme Court as to the solicitation of magazine subscriptions.[52] The Supreme Court held that this type of ordinance does not violate the due process clause of the Fourteenth Amendment of the United States Constitution, the interstate commerce clause or the guarantee of freedom of speech and the press.[53]

[49] Thelma J. Showalter, *Municipal Licensing Practice in Pennsylvania,* Commonwealth of Pennsylvania, Department of Internal Affairs.

[50] Ed. E. Reid, *Municipal License Tax Administration in Alabama,* Information Report No. 103, Alabama League of Municipalities (1953).

[51] Town of Green River v. Fuller Brush Company, 65F, 2nd 112 (1933).

[52] Breard v. City of Alexander, 341 W. S. 622 (1951).

[53] T. F. Chrostwaite and Elizabeth Smedley, *Pennsylvania Municipal Ordinances* (1954), pp. 341–349.

Local Taxes on Private Utilities and Municipal Utility Service Charges

Local taxes on privately owned public utilities are numerous, lucrative, and take on a variety of forms. They include (1) licenses for doing business levied on the basis of gross receipts or as a flat amount, (2) franchises for the privilege of doing business on the streets, also by flat rate or on gross receipts, (3) taxes on the sales of utility services, (4) or licenses for each meter, telephone, car, or other equipment, (5) rentals of poll and conduits, or (6) taxes on amount of production. The gross receipts tax is most common; almost three hundred cities over 10,000 population were using this tax in 1951.[54]

A municipal utility is an enterprise carried on by a local government by which a service is made available to residents who pay for it on the basis of use. Generally, the term is used for enterprises that also might be furnished by private corporations under public regulation. Such utilities are considered to be public necessities and are therefore public in character.

The 1954 *Municipal Year Book* reported that nearly all of the almost 2,500 cities of the United States over 5,000 population owned one or more public utilities. Of the total, 74 per cent reported ownership of water supply systems; 49 per cent had sewage treatment works; 21 per cent owned their own airports and an additional 300 leased them to private or governmental agencies; and 20 per cent had electric generation or distribution systems. Other types of utilities, less numerous, included incinerators for rubbish and garbage, municipal auditoriums, street railways, bus systems, and gas utilities.[55]

Eleven per cent of all local government revenue in 1953 was from the operation of public utilities; in cities the average was 21. From the financial point of view, public utility operation raises certain questions. Shall the utility be operated so as to render service to the

[54] Hillhouse and Magelssen, *Where Cities Get Their Money*, Municipal Finance Officers Association (1945), pp. 120–141.
[55] *The Municipal Year Book 1954*, pp. 79–80.

inhabitants at as low rates as are possible consonant with solvency, or shall a surplus be developed which will be turned over to the general fund and thus reduce the tax burden? The prevailing answer, not always followed, is that the rates should be in accordance with the cost of the service and that utilities should be self-supporting, not either subsidized by or subsidizing general municipal government.

Municipal liquor stores are found in a number of states, notably Minnesota, Wisconsin, and the Dakotas. In 1952, 360 out of 805 cities and villages in Minnesota operated municipal liquor stores under a system of state control. Authorized in 1934, as an alternative to the licensing of private vendors, the power is optional and is only for cities under 10,000 population. In 1952, they grossed $33 million with $5 million net income to the cities.[56]

Charges for municipal and local services are taking a more important position in finance with each passing year. Charges most common are for garbage and refuse collection, for fire protection outside municipal boundaries, for sewer rentals, and assessments for special purposes.

Most cities charge sewer rentals on the basis of water consumption and the charge is often put on the water bill. Others charge by the number and type of plumbing fixtures, sewer connections, or type of property. Garbage and refuse collection are paid for on the basis of annual rates or number of stops. Fire protection for outside areas outside municipal boundaries is paid usually by the local unit served. It may be on an annual basis flat rate or a rate per hour for men and equipment. The list of services and their charges might be greatly expanded. The point is that many services, once paid from general municipal funds, are now charged those who receive the service.

Fees in Local Government

In the early days of the Republic, most local officials giving direct services to the people were reimbursed for their time and efforts in

[56] C. C. Ludwig, "Liquor Sales Aid to Cities," *National Municipal Review* (November, 1953), pp. 497–501.

public office by fees paid by those who received the services. This was especially common in county, town, and township government. For example, a recorder of deeds might receive a dollar for each deed he recorded, a sheriff seventy-five cents for each notice he delivered, a coroner five dollars for each body he viewed. The theory was that public officials should receive reimbursement according to what they were called on to do, rather than a fixed salary whether or not they might earn it. In these cases, public officials were generally part-time and carried on public duties only as a side-line. The fees chargeable were fixed by state law and could be used also to pay any deputies and clerks that might be needed for the office. Thus the taxpayers were not burdened directly with the cost of such services.

Gradually the fee system has been abandoned in local government. In many instances, the work of the office grew so extensive that the fees brought in far more than an ordinary salary. Fee offices were sought after as especially luscious political plums for deputies and clerks could do most of the work on a modest salary paid by the fee officer who would pocket the rest of the revenue, often very sizable in proportion to his burden of the work. The fee system is criticized also because it causes fee officers to consider their office as personal property, because their offices are not under any fiscal control, because exorbitant compensation can be concealed especially in extravagant expense accounts, and because it leads to a condition of affairs where there is unequal pay for equal work. Where law enforcement officers, such as justices of the peace and constables, are paid by fees their dispensation of justice is often influenced by the desire to get as much as possible from either the defendants or from the county or state which pays for cases which are dismissed. Likewise, the fee system does not offer incentives to officials to prevent the commission of crime.

But the fee system has not altogether disappeared. Most states still have some local officials still receiving fees for their services. In 34 states, however, the payment of salaries for county officials is specifically provided for. In six states the major county officers are paid by fees with no control other than maximum limits of a general nature.[57] These are all northern states. In Pennsylvania, fees are used for reimbursement of county officials in the smallest counties. In many states, the minor judiciary and constables are paid on a fee basis.

INTERGOVERNMENTAL REVENUES

After the general property tax, intergovernmental revenues have become the most important source of local finances in the United States. In 1953, almost a third of local revenue came from the federal, state, and other local governments. Of this, $5.4 billion was from the states, $309 million from the federal government, and $336 million from other local governments. In turn, local governments distributed $500 million to state governments and other local governments, leaving a net local intergovernmental revenue of $5.5 billion. State aid to local governments in 1953 was nearly half as much as total direct state expenditures.[58]

The drastic increase of intergovernmental revenues in recent years is an indication of the need for adjustments in the national-state-local tax system to cope with the changes in American life. For example, federal aid to states has been used to stimulate states to carry on certain functions deemed to be of national interest but in the sphere of the states according to our traditional division of powers; and to bring about more equality and uniformity among the states in services to the people. These federal grants to the states are an attempt to expand national activity without changing the constitutional pattern of powers between the national and state governments. Grants from the federal to local governments, small as they are in comparison to federal to state grants, indicate the same trend, and point to the future when federal grants made directly to local units, especially urban units, will be much greater in volume and

[57] Kentucky Legislature Council, *The Fee System as a Method of Compensating County Officials,* pp. 1–19, 31–36. States which still have the fee system as a method of compensating major county officials are Alabama, Arkansas, Kentucky, Maryland, Missouri, and North Carolina. From p. 33.

[58] Bureau of the Census, *Summary of Governmental Finances in 1953* (October, 1954), pp. 6–7, 10–11.

scope than at present. Urgent problems of national interest such as defense from atomic attack, unemployment relief, welfare and health services must be cooperatively attacked by both federal and urban governments. This will require increased federal aid and supervision.

Increasing state aid to local units is another sign of the times. Local revenues have not been sufficient to meet local needs; local governments are shackled by outmoded constitutional provisions and state laws. State aid supplements local revenue, equalizes opportunities and services in various parts of the state, and stimulates local activities. On the other hand, it has been accused of "freezing" the local pattern that would not be able to survive without state aid, of allowing state departments to dictate to local officials and thereby reducing home rule and self-government.

Federal Aid to Local Units

Direct federal grants to local governments in 1953 amounted to $309 million, of which $220 was for education.[59] This was mostly for assistance in school operation and construction in defense areas, and for the school lunch program.

According to the American Municipal Association, federal appropriations for 1955 to both state and local government which was of interest and concern to municipalities included $22 million for airports, $175 million for urban highways, $70 million aid for school construction in defense areas, $1.5 million for interest-free loans for advance planning for public works, $2 million for public facility loans for municipalities under 25,000 unable to secure private financing, $1 million for urban planning grants, $48 million for civilian defense, $39 million for capital grants for slum clearance, $10 million for disaster relief loans, $96 million for federal aid for hospital construction, $13 million for general health assistance, $6 million for tuberculosis control, $3 million for venereal disease control, $4.3 million for communicable disease control, $68 million for federal aid to the school lunch program, $1 million for water pollution control,

[59] *Ibid.*, p. 31.

and $.5 million for air pollution control. In addition, funds for the construction of 35,000 units of public housing were appropriated, and a revolving fund of $250 million to aid in financing projects for civilian defense was made available. AMA estimated that federally collected, locally shared revenues comprised about eight per cent of the budgets of local governments.[60]

Federal aid to states can have some important indirect effects on local government. As is shown in the case of South Carolina, a number of functions once local have become state functions as a result of federal grants-in-aid. In all those functions for which substantial portions of total costs are borne by federal grants, the state has taken over total or almost total responsibility. In the case of highways, little if any county highway work is done. The county health officer is a state official. County boards of welfare are appointed by the county's delegation to the state legislature with approval of the state board of welfare. Thus, there is a steady movement away from the local to the state level in terms of finance and administrative control.[61]

Another most important development is the tendency for urban units of government to turn directly to the federal government, rather than to the states, for assistance. This has been encouraged, since the depression, by the federal government itself in such fields as housing, airports, assistance in federally impacted areas, and civil defense and bids fair to make federal-local channels deeper and more permanent each year.

State Aid to Local Units

State governments paid out $5.4 billion out of a total of almost $17 billion expenditures to local government in grants, shared taxes, payment for services, and other forms of fiscal aid in 1953. This amounted to $34.75 per capita.

[60] American Municipal Association, *National Legislative Bulletin* (January 18, 1955).

[61] Governmental Affairs Institute, *Impact of Federal Grants-in-Aid of South Carolina,* report submitted to Commission on Intergovernmental Relations (1954), pp. 13–14.

The funds were spent for the following major functions: [62]

Education	$2,740,000	or 51%
Public Welfare	981,000	or 18%
Highways	803,000	or 15%
Health and Hospitals	130,000	or 2%

In addition, smaller allocations were made for public safety, non-highway transportation, housing and community redevelopment, natural resources, general control and other functions. These funds were distributed as follows:

School districts	$2,294,000	or 43%
Counties	1,592,000	or 30%
Cities	948,000	or 18%
Towns and townships	101,460	or 2%
Special districts	22,000	
Combined and unallocable	425,000	or 7%

Intergovernmental expenditures of states to local units for 1953 were almost seven per cent higher than in 1952, and those for 1952 were almost eight per cent higher than 1951, indicating the rapidly increasing volume of state aid. The 1953 amount was $1 billion higher than that of 1950. In 1952, great variations existed in the states: from $5.45 per capita in New Hampshire to $73.67 in California.[63]

State aid to local units is in the form of grants and shared taxes. Grants are usually given with some strings attached: the money must be spent for such-and-such a purpose under such-and-such conditions prescribed either in the law or by state administrative departments. Sometimes, the local government must match the state aid. Shared taxes are usually without any conditions handed down by the state; local units are by law given part of specific state-collected taxes and that is the end of it. In either case, the local units are at the mercy of the state legislature which may change its mind

[62] Bureau of the Census, *Compendium of State Government Finances in 1953* (1954), pp. 28–29.
[63] Bureau of the Census, *State Payments to Local Governments in 1952* (1954).

every session. Likewise economic conditions cause alterations in the volume of state aid, so that in any case state aid is not a stabilized element of local budgets.

Analyzing the expenditures from states to local units for 1952 several interesting facts stand out. (1) In ten states, 40 per cent or more of general state expenditures was intergovernmental: six of these were midwestern; (2) in the ten lowest states, twenty per cent or less of state expenditures went for intergovernmental expenditures; (3) in twenty-one states the percentage of intergovernmental expenditures to general expenditures increased from 1942 to 1952; (4) eleven states had per capita intergovernmental expenditures of $40 or more; thirteen states had less than $20 per capita intergovernmental expenditures. While no generalizations relating to regional characteristics can be made, the South, the Far West, and the New England states seem to be experiencing the most ferment and extremism in this phase of finance.

Several examples of the state patterns for 1952 illustrate the variety and scope of state aid to local units. Alabama paid counties for the care of some prisoners; made public welfare payments directly to individuals and not through local units of government; gave school districts $77 million from sales, income, tobacco, and other lesser excise taxes; gave counties $24 million for highway purposes from motor fuels taxes; paid cities and counties $4 million for health and hospitals, partly from federal funds; gave cities and counties over $5 million for general purposes from corporation, alcohol, and general sales taxes.

Massachusetts gave to cities and towns $100 million for old age assistance, aid to dependent children and general relief, part of which came from federal funds; gave $28 million to cities and towns for education, $6 million for highways, $2 million for veterans housing, and $1 million for health, hospitals, and aeronautics; gave cities and towns $44 million for general purposes from corporation, individual income, and public service license taxes.

Ohio gave counties and cities $26 million for categorical assistance in public welfare, partly from federal funds; about $12 million to cities and counties for general relief purposes; about $12 million dollars from public utilities gross receipts taxes for public welfare purposes; gave $96 million to school districts for education; gave cities, towns, and townships $75 million from motor user taxes for highways; gave $5 million to counties and cities for health and hospitals; gave $38 million dollars from the sales tax to local units for general purposes, and $8 million from alcohol license taxes; gave $1½ million to cities for police and firemen's pensions.[64]

The New York system of grants to local government, known as the Moore Plan, inaugurated in 1946, blazed a new trail in state-local fiscal relations. Briefly, the novel features are these: (1) discontinuance of six state-collected taxes shared with local governments; (2) establishment in their place of annual per capita grants to all classes of municipalities; (3) tapering off provisions so that the shift from shared-tax to per capita grants would not upset the financial balance in local units; (4) division of the state executive budget and the state general fund into two parts: local assistance and state purposes; (5) establishment of two reserve funds to help stabilize the state's revenues, the money to come from any excess of revenues in one year over a norm determined in advance for state and local expenditures. This program did not aim to increase state aid, but to enable localities to count upon a fixed amount of money from the state regardless of the cyclical sensitivity of the state's tax system. It was the first state program to provide grants-in-aid for general governmental purposes.[65]

Intergovernmental Revenue among Local Units

Local governments make grants, share taxes, and pay for services among themselves. The 1953 total was $336 million, more than two-thirds of it for education, $22 million in highways, $26 million in

---

[64] *Ibid.* This important document contains the detailed grants-in-aid and shared taxes for each state by amount, formula, and receiving units of government.

[65] David M. Blank, "Reform of State-Local Fiscal Relations in New York," I and II, *National Tax Journal* (December, 1950), pp. 326–347; and (March, 1951), pp. 77–91.

health and hospitals, and $1 million in public welfare. Payments of school districts to adjacent school districts for the payment of tuition and transportation charges for pupils, grants from counties to townships for highway purposes, payments of outlying municipalities to the central cities for fire protection, police protection and police radio service are examples of this kind of transaction.

The Need for Fiscal Coordination

Fiscal relations between national, state, and local governments call for greater coordination. Tax money, no matter on what level of government it is collected, comes from the pockets of the taxpayers. It is to be spent for the public good. There have been some suggestions that all tax monies should be collected at the national level and distributed to state and local units. But such a course would inevitably lead to fiscal centralization so common today in many other nations. To keep free and relatively strong, states and local units must have their own tax resources and have the power to use them as their governing bodies see fit. On the other hand, duplication of taxes, inequitable assessments, intergovernmental confusion, unreasonable levies, and other faults of our present tax system if allowed to get out of hand will lead to energetic action by organized citizen groups to achieve simplification even if it means concentration of power at the higher levels of government.

Some of the proposals that have been brought forward to achieve the needed coordination and at the same time strengthen the local financial system are the following:

(1) the abandonment of the federal amusement tax to local units;

(2) the return of at least one cent of the federal gasoline tax to the states;

(3) the payment by the federal government of all added costs placed on local units by military and defense activities;

(4) the payment of local taxes on property engaged in defense work by federal government;

(5) increased federal aid for urban streets and highways; for low rental housing, urban redevelopment, and slum clearance projects;

and for municipal airports which are a part of the national airport system;

(6) states should provide local units with adequate shares of state taxes and state grants, especially in the fields of education, highways, and public welfare;

(7) states should allow local units to impose broad-based and other nonproperty taxes;

(8) local units should assess taxable real and personal property more equitably and scientifically for this tax is still the most productive in local finance;

(9) local units should impose nonproperty taxes, and make reasonable charges for services to residents so as to reduce the burden on real property;

(10) local units that are too small and too weak to provide modern services should merge and consolidate with their neighbors into larger and more efficient units;

(11) local units should have exclusive use of property and per capita taxes, and leave state exclusive use of motor user taxes, general sales taxes, and taxes on corporate capital;

(12) the establishment of a permanent national commission on intergovernmental relations to work continuously to achieve better coordination in public finance and administration.[66]

TEN SUBJECTS FOR FURTHER STUDY

1. Revenues of your city, borough, or township.
2. Revenues of your county.
3. The assessment of real property in your county.
4. Exemption of real property from taxation in your state.
5. Limits of local taxation in your state.
6. Exemption of industrial property from local and state taxes in the South.
7. Nonproperty local taxes in New York.
8. Local income taxes in Pennsylvania.
9. Local sales taxes in California.
10. Local license taxes in Alabama.

[66] See *Report of the Pennsylvania Commission on Intergovernmental Relations,* Commonwealth of Pennsylvania (January, 1955), Chapter 5, "Our Local Governments Must Be Considered."

REFERENCES

Paul E. Alyea, *Revenues of Small Alabama Cities,* Bureau of Business Research and Bureau of Public Administration, University of Alabama (1951).

Rosalind G. Baldwin, "Property Tax Updated," *National Municipal Review,* November 1955, pp. 512–514.

Kenneth E. Beasley, *Attitudes of Labor toward City Government,* Special Report no. 9, Governmental Research Center, University of Kansas (Lawrence, Kansas, 1954).

A. E. Buck, *Municipal Finance* (New York, 1926).

Alfred Buehler, *Public Finance,* 3rd ed. (New York, 1948).

Bureau of the Census, *State and Local Governmental Revenue* (Washington, 1954).

——, *State Payments to Local Governments in 1952* (Washington, 1954).

Edward W. Carter and Edward B. Shils, "Philadelphia's Earned Income Tax," *American Political Science Review,* April 1940, pp. 311–316.

Citizens Research Council of Michigan, "Tax Rates of U. S. Cities," *National Municipal Review,* January 1955, pp. 14–35.

Commission on Intergovernmental Affairs, *Payments in Lieu of Taxes and Shared Revenues* (U. S. Printing Office, June 1955).

Commission on Intergovernmental Relations, *The Administrative and Fiscal Impact of Federal Grants-in-Aid* (U. S. Printing Office, June 1955).

Committee on Intergovernmental Fiscal Relations, *Federal, State, and Local Government Fiscal Relations* (U. S. Printing Office, Washington, 1943).

M. M. Davidson and W. K. Schmelzle, "Equalization of Property Tax Assessments in California," *National Tax Journal,* September 1950, pp. 221–232.

Lawrence Durisch, "Attracting Industry to Cities," *National Municipal Review,* May 1953, pp. 224–226.

Roger A. Freeman, "What Ails the Property Tax," *National Municipal Review,* November 1955, pp. 506–511.

Robert L. Funk, "Municipal Nonproperty Taxes," *The Municipal Year Book 1955,* pp. 210–213.

R. M. Haig and C. Shoup, *The Financial Problem of the City of New York,* Mayor's Committee on Management Survey (New York, 1952).

Charles A. Hild, "Shopping Centers and Their Assessment," *The Assessors Newsletter,* April 1955, Institute of Local Government, The Pennsylvania State University.

A. M. Hillhouse and Carl H. Chatters, *Tax-Reverted Properties in Urban Areas,* Public Administration Service (Chicago, 1942).

A. M. Hillhouse and Ronald B. Welch, *Tax Limits Appraised,* Public Administration Service (Chicago, 1937).

A. M. Hillhouse and Muriel Magelssen, *Where Cities Get Their Money,* Municipal Finance Officers Association of the United States and Canada (Chicago, 1945).

The International City Managers' Association, *Municipal Finance Administration,* Third Edition (Chicago, 1946).

John R. Kerstetter, *Local Government's Share of State-Collected Highway Funds and Revenues,* American Municipal Association (Washington, 1955).

S. E. Leland, *The Classified Property Tax in the United States* (Boston, 1928).

J. M. Leonard and Rosina Mohaupt, *Exemption of Homesteads from Taxation,* Detroit Bureau of Governmental Research, Report No. 144 (Detroit, 1937).

James W. Martin and Glenn D. Morrow, *Taxation of Manufacturing in the South,* Bureau of Public Administration, University of Alabama (University, Alabama, 1948).

Municipal Finance Officer Association of the United States and Canada, *Municipal Nonproperty Taxes,* 1956 Supplement to *Where Cities Get Their Money* (Chicago, 1956).

E. A. Myers and R. S. Stout, "Recent Trends in Property Tax Equalization," *National Tax Journal,* June 1950, pp. 179–186.

National Association of Assessing Officers, *Assessment Administration* (Chicago, 1954).

——, *Exempting of Institutional Real Property from Taxation,* Bulletin No. 23 (Chicago, 1939).

National Municipal League, *Model Real Property Tax Collection Law* (New York, 1954).

Mabel Newcomer, "The Decline of the General Property Tax," *National Tax Journal,* March 1953, pp. 38–51.

Leon Jay Quinto, *Municipal Income Taxation in the United States,* Mayor's Committee on Management Survey of the City of New York (New York, 1952).

Lloyd Bernard Raisty, *Homestead Exemption Problems in Georgia,* Institute for the Study of Georgia Problems, Pamphlet No. 2 (1939).

William D. Ross, *Louisiana Industrial Tax Exemption Program,* Division of Research, College of Commerce, Louisiana State University (Baton Rouge, 1953).

Robert K. Sawyer, "Commuters Aid City Comeback," *National Municipal Review,* June 1950, pp. 273–277.

William J. Shultz and C. Lowell Harriss, *American Public Finance* (New York, 1954).

Robert A. Sigafoos, "The Urban-Rural Fringe Population Problem and Effects on Municipal Finance," *Current Economic Comment,* November 1952, pp. 3–17.

————, *The Municipal Income Tax,* Public Administration Service (1955).

Clyde F. Snider, Gilbert Y. Steiner, and Lois Langdon, *Local Taxing Units: The Illinois Experience,* Institute of Government and Public Affairs, University of Illinois (Urbana, 1954).

Paul Studenski, "Alternatives to Grants-in-Aid," *Federal-State-Local Tax Correlation,* Tax Institute (Princeton, New Jersey, 1954).

The West Virginia Commission on Interstate Cooperation, *An Introductory Study of County Finance in West Virginia* (1950).

Chapter 10

ADMINISTRATIVE MANAGEMENT

What is administration? What is its place in local government? What is it supposed to do? What ends does it achieve?

Woodrow Wilson wrote in 1887 that American political thought in the 19th century was concerned almost exclusively with problems of constitutionality, sovereignty and popular power. "The question, how law could be administered with enlightenment, with speed, and without friction, was put aside as a practical detail which clerks could arrange after doctors agreed on principles."[1] Today, however, administration has emerged in full panoply and has taken a commanding position at all levels of government.

Administration, in relation to law making, is the implementation of public will as expressed in law. It is not concerned so much as to *what* should be done, but how it should be done so as to get the best results. In short, administration does the job; it gets things done.

How does administration do the job? Luther Gulick lists its functions: planning, organization, staffing, direction, coordination, reporting, and budgeting.[2] These functions are carried out by the

[1] Woodrow Wilson, "The Study of Administration," *Political Science Quarterly,* June, 1887. Quoted in Institute for Training in Municipal Administration, *The American City and Its Government* (1937), p. 331.

[2] Luther Gulick and L. Urwick, editors, *Papers on the Science of Administration*, Institute of Public Administration (1939), p. 13. The word POSDCORB, formed from the first letters of each of the functions listed, was coined as a means to remember the functions in their proper order.

chief executive, the chief administrative officer, or the governing body as the case may be. Programs must be *planned*, administrative agencies *organized*, *staff* set up, their activity *directed*, *coordination* between various agencies achieved, *reports* on progress made, and finances *budgeted*.

Administrative Principles

Certain general principles relating to administrative organization have evolved as the result of experience.

(1) *There must be a division of labor*. Departments and agencies can be set upon the basis of purpose, process, persons or things dealt with, and place. A fire department is organized on the basis of purpose—to protect people and property against fire. A legal department is established on the basis of process—legal relations and problems are analyzed. A department of assistance is organized on the basis of persons dealt with—all those needing relief. Precinct stations of a police department are established on the basis of place. In most local units, departments are organized on the basis of purpose and process. Within each department, too, there is a division of labor: the central core of management, skilled workers such as policemen or firemen, peculiar to the particular department, and trained workers such as secretarial staff, common to all departments.

(2) *There is a need for specialization and coordination*. The larger the organization, the more specialized is the division of labor, and the greater the need for coordination. Here is a good place to introduce the terms *line*, *staff*, and *auxiliary*. A line function is a service to the people—police protection, traffic control, and water supply, for example. These are the reasons for government's existence. A staff function is one that helps line departments do a better job—research, advising, planning, and investigation. An auxiliary function is one that helps maintain line agencies as working units—budgeting, accounting, personnel, and purchasing. An auxiliary function is often described as a "housekeeping" function. In small units, of course, staff and auxiliary functions may be carried on by the

chief administrative officer, but as the agencies grow larger there develops specialization and one of the chief problems of organization is to arrange line, staff and auxiliary personnel in an effective working unit. Staff and auxiliary functions carried on within each department cannot be as expert as those rendered by a special department specializing in such service for all departments of a unit of government, except where each department itself is of a size to demand the full time efforts of such personnel.

(3) *Authority and responsibility must be definite.* Every employee in the administrative organization should know "who's who" and how he or she is to fit in the general pattern. There must be a chain of command that extends from the newest file clerk up to the chief executive or administrator. Likewise, each person must know the limits of his own responsibility and the extent of his duties. These things in mind, it is much easier to keep an organization going with the minimum of friction. The coordinating authority at the top operates downward through the hierarchy of offices into every nook and crevice of the administrative organization thus developing a unity of command throughout the whole. Each employee should have one boss. Having more than one creates confusion and organizational weakness. Also, where there is responsibility, there should be commensurate authority. If a man is head of the department, his subordinates should not be encouraged to "go over his head" to the official next higher in the hierarchy.

(4) *There is a limit to the span of control.* Span of control is described as the limit in the number of subordinates who can be effectively supervised by one official. The number depends on the kind of work done. For example, one officer can handle more personnel when they are doing exactly the same kind of routine work, whereas in case they have different duties fewer can be effectually supervised and directed. V. A. Graicunas, a Swiss writer on administration, believes that four or five subordinates (except in the case of routine workers) are the largest numbers that should be allowed at each level of the hierarchy. He points out that the single, group and cross relationships that the head should develop in order

to get the best possible results take a lot of time, effort, and planning.[3]

A century ago local government was fragmented and decentralized within itself. There were many independent officers, boards and commissions each carrying out duties given to them by law without the benefit of unity of direction and coordination. Each was law unto itself. As a result, the political party directed by the boss and implemented by the machine entrenched itself deeply in the mazes of local government. The combination developed a sort of unity and coordination but too often the ultimate aim was for spoils rather than service. When the abuses became too great, the people revolted and threw off the yoke. Then they began to look about for forms and principles of government that would correct the condition that made these things possible.

Reformers of local government took a page out of industrial organization that in the early years after the Civil War began to streamline its organization and procedure in the quest for greater efficiency and greater profits. They saw that industry achieved internal coordination and leadership by setting up a hierarchy of personnel, the head of which was the superintendent or manager who could give orders that were transmitted smoothly down through the departments, bureaus, divisions, and sections. In turn, he could receive reports about operations from the bottom up through the ranks. Where things were not working properly, he could send assistance or rectify conditions. The over-all effect was a unified process—effective, efficient, and economical.

With this example in mind, the reformers attempted to simplify local government by consolidating its unrelated parts into a manageable organization. The commission form of government united all functions of city government into five departments each headed by an elective official, one of whom was the mayor. Bicameral and

[3] Stuart A. MacCorkle, *Municipal Administration* (1942), pp. 11–33. Also see: Dimock and Dimock, *Public Administration* (1953), Chapter 5, "Organization," pp. 103–142; and International City Managers' Association, *Municipal Finance Administration*, third edition (1946), Chapter 3, "Organization for Finance Administration" and *Municipal Personnel Administration*, fourth edition (1947).

unwieldy legislative bodies gradually disappeared from the scene replaced by the smaller body that could sit round a table and discuss problems without recourse to oratory. Independent boards and commissions were merged into regular departments headed by a director responsible to a chief executive or administrator. All along the line local government became more simple in its structure and organization. At the same time, reformers accepted the principle of a chief executive officer. In the larger cities, the mayor was given larger powers over administration and legislation. He became the leader of the government in fact as well as in name. Realizing that an elective mayor and an elective council did not always work smoothly together, they discovered a form of government that was capable of a perfectly smooth flow of administrative authority and direction. This was the council-manager form which has gained great popularity during the past forty years and today holds a place of front rank in local government. Within present forms of local government, there are still many points of obstruction to the smooth flow of authority and direction but the tendency has been toward its centralization in the hands of a chief executive or chief administrator, the latter responsible to the elected governing body. The objective is better government, quicker service, and more for the tax dollar.

The county and township, as well as the New England town and the small municipality, were much less affected by modern tendencies to integrate administration into a smooth flowing process from elected governing body, to the chief administrator, to the heads of departments, and finally down to the employees on the front line of government service. Especially in counties, in spite of the increase of their responsibilities in the growing urban and industrial areas, was it found difficult to inculcate the idea of integrated administration. Here there were many constitutionally established row officers sharing governmental power between themselves which no legislature could do much about. In a smaller way, the townships were fully as decentralized but there were only sixteen states with townships and in these townships powers were being gradually pruned down to rural roads and little else. Even here they were subject to greater and greater state control, and lost more and more road responsibility either to the state department of highways or the county. The smaller municipalities and the New England town, however, slow as they were to accept the modern tendencies, were less inflexible because of greater powers of home rule given to municipalities or, as in the case of the New England town, the ability of the structure of government to adapt itself to the idea of the chief administrator.

Measuring Municipal Activities

For many years after the exposé of civic corruption and inefficiency in the first decade of the century, it was enough to say that a local government was honest. A number of techniques were devised and applied throughout local government to insure honesty. Among them was the audit, the restraints on procedure and action set up by law, standard financial practice for accounting, budgeting and purchasing, and others. But the science of administration has gone beyond this. Government must not only be honest, it must be efficient. To find out how efficient government was or could be, new techniques had to be fashioned, and new standards of measurement developed. The need for such exploration was indicated by the mounting expenditures of local government, particularly in larger cities. In private business, management is judged by its profit and loss column, but public business is not operated for profit. Other criteria for appraising governmental activities have to be found.

How can this be done? First, a system of values or objectives must be set up. Second, it must be determined to what extent these values or objectives are being attained. What are these values or objectives? One of the most used and abused is the tax rate. Can the municipal efficiency be measured by relative taxes? City A has a general property tax rate of 20 mills, and City B of 25 mills. Is City A therefore better managed? City A may assess its taxable property at 60 per cent of market value, and City B at 40 per cent. To get the same relative revenue City B must have a higher tax rate. Furthermore, City A may have other sources of revenue like a one per cent sales tax which swells its coffers so that the property tax rate can be lower.

If tax rates are not a gauge for measurement of efficiency, how about expenditures? City A spends annually $40 per capita for municipal services; City B $60. Is City A a better governed city? City B spends money for parks and playground; City A spends nothing in this field. City B spends $10 per capita on debt service for the construction of a modern network of streets and bridges. City A gets by with repairs on an outmoded street system in which traffic is intolerably congested. Which has the better government? Gross expenditures do not tell the story.

But suppose expenditures are broken down into specific things bought? How much for personal services—salaries and wages, for example? Now we are getting somewhere. Can we further refine personal services in terms of effort—man-hours? Does it mean anything to say the police department expended 10,000 man-hours last year? Very well, but what did that 10,000 man-hours produce? What is the performance? Can it be measured? There were 15,000 miles of beat patrolled—we can get that from the records; there were 580 arrests made and 1,000 sets of fingerprints taken. Well, at last, here is something real and tangible. But what does it mean? Is the objective of a police department just to patrol a beat, make an arrest, and take a set of fingerprints? Does it mean anything to say the police department made 580 arrests last year if they only made 400 this year? Maybe, maybe not. There are other factors to take into consideration. This year there may be more employment and less crime. Does it mean anything to say that this year 18,000 miles of beat were patrolled as against 15,000 last year? Maybe, maybe not. This year two auto patrols were added to the force. We must proceed further. *How well was this work done?* Could more miles have been patrolled per man-hour with better organization or equipment? Or even more important, *did the work done help to accomplish the purpose and attain the objectives of the department?* This is more difficult to ascertain. What are the objectives of a police department? To make arrests? To convict those arrested? To lower the crime rate? To prevent crime? To run rackets and organized crime out of town?

All those are desirable but not all are measurable—though some are. "The appraisal of administration can take place only after the objectives of administration have been defined in measurable and comparable terms," say Ridley and Simon, pioneers in the field of measurement of municipal activities.[4]

But how efficient is the administration? What is efficiency? It is described as follows: "The efficiency of administration is measured by the ratio of the effects actually obtained with the available resources to the maximum effects possible with the available resources."[5] In other words, is it getting the most out of effort expended? This is the general logic behind the search for measurements of efficiency in local government. Let us see what applications have been made in several specific activities.

The final criterion of fire department adequacy and efficiency is fire loss. Standards for measurement of such loss are: (1) loss per $1,000 valuation of property; (2) loss per fire; and (3) number of fires per capita, or per $1,000 valuation. These units can be set against cost data of fire departments when and if they can be developed; and relative efficiency can then be measured.[6]

In public works, the measurement technique best suited is that of cost accounting. This has been defined as "the process of searching out and recording all the elements of expense incurred to attain a purpose, to carry on an activity or operation, to complete a unit of work, or to do a specific job.[7] Cost includes four elements: personal service, equipment, material and supplies, and overhead costs. Unit costs can be obtained by dividing the over-all cost by the number of units of work. The performance unit for street cleaning is the "cleaning mile." How much is the cost per cleaning mile? The unit for measuring the adequacy of street cleaning is "the average number of cubic yards of dirt lying on a curb mile of pavement" when cleaned. The adequacy of refuse collection would include the

[4] Clarence E. Ridley and Herbert A. Simon, *Measuring Municipal Activities,* second edition (1943), pp. 2–3.
[5] *Ibid.,* p. 3.
[6] *Ibid.,* pp. 10–14.
[7] International City Managers' Association, *Municipal Finance Administration,* third edition (1948), p. 142.

frequency of refuse collection and the completeness of service. The measure of performance would be the tons of refuse collected divided by the total cost. In sewage disposal, the cost unit is the operating cost per million gallons of sewage treated and so on.[8] The science of measurement of municipal activities has still a long way to go before it can be considered to be mature. Methods need to be more highly refined in order to become meaningful, and basic data has to become more available. Nevertheless, progress is being made in various fields towards developing measurable units of adequacy and performance of local administration.

PERSONNEL ADMINISTRATION

In January, 1955, there were 3,665,000 public employees in local governments of the United States. Of these, 1,393,000 were school employees and 2,272,000 were employees of cities, counties, towns, townships, and special districts.[9] Local nonschool employees in 1900 numbered 317,000, while school employees—state and local—totaled 467,000.[10] In a little more than a half century, local nonschool employees increased six times, and local school employees three times in number.

The rapid increase of public personnel rolls at all levels of government during the first half of the 20th century resulted in the development of a body of principles and knowledge that has for its objective the increased competence of local personnel. In colonial days and in the first decades of national existence, public employment was of a relatively high quality. From England had come the belief that only the propertied classes should hold government positions. Public office was the duty and the prerogative of the "better" classes. As political parties became more active, public offices began to be looked upon as the fruits of political victory. The democratic impulse broke down property barriers for voting and holding office. "To the victors belong the spoils" was the battle-cry of the new

[8] Ridley and Simon, *op. cit.*, pp. 21–25.
[9] Bureau of the Census, *Public Employment in January, 1955.*
[10] Soloman Fabricant, *The Trend of Government Activity in the United States since 1900,* National Bureau of Economic Research, Inc. (1952), p. 29.

regime that came to full flower in the administration of President Jackson elected in 1828 for the first of his two terms. Election rather than appointment, short terms, and rotation of office were applications of the theory which accepted the spoils system as basic in democratic government. Jackson himself said in his first annual message to Congress:

There are, perhaps, few men who can for any great length of time enjoy office and power without being more or less under the influence of feelings unfavorable to the faithful discharge of their public duties. Their integrity may be proof against improper considerations immediately addressed to themselves, but they are apt to acquire a habit of looking with indifference upon the public interests and of tolerating conduct from which an unpracticed man would revolt. Office is considered a species of

STATE AND LOCAL GOVERNMENT EMPLOYMENT JANUARY, 1955

Type of Government	Employees, January 1955		Per Cent Increase from January 1954 ("—" = decrease)
	Number (in Thousands)	Per Cent	
State governments	1,207	24.8	6.5
Local governments:			
Cities	1,403	28.8	3.2
Counties	580	11.9	6.0
School Districts	1,393	28.6	5.7
Other	288	5.9	−2.0
All local governments	3,665	75.2	4.1
Total, state, and local governments	4,872	100.0	4.8

From Bureau of the Census, *Public Employment in January, 1955* (April 15, 1955).

property, and government rather as a means of promoting individual interests than as an instrument created solely for the service of the people. Corruption in some and in others a perversion of correct feelings and principles divert government from its legitimate ends, and make it an engine for the support of the few at the expense of the many. The duties of all public officers are, or at least admit of being made, so plain and simple that men of intelligence may readily qualify themselves for their performance; and I cannot but believe that more is lost by the mere continuance of men in office than is generally gained by their experience. . . .

In a country where offices are created solely for the benefit of the people no one man has more intrinsic right to official station than another. Offices were not established to give support to particular men at the public expense. No individual wrong is, therefore, done by removal, since neither appointment to nor continuance in office is a right.[11]

All during the 19th century, the spoils system flourished in national, state and local governments. Political parties were nourished by the system of patronage. Instances of abuse piled so high that reaction was bound to set in. In 1883, the United States Congress passed the Pendleton Act which placed the first group of federal employees under the merit system. In 1883 also, New York state passed a constitutional amendment requiring that merit and fitness govern appointments in all civil governments of the state, and a number of New York cities passed civil service ordinances during the following year. From that time until World War I there was a growing and insistent demand for reform and the merit principle was extended in the national government, to a few of the states, and to many of the larger cities. In 1900 there were 85 civil service commissions in the cities of the nation, and by 1954, there were 845 cities over 10,000 population covered by civil service.[12]

Many reform organizations worked vigorously for the merit system during that period. They took full advantage of the exposés conducted by Lincoln Steffens and the other "muckrakers" who brought to public attention the low state of public employment under the spoils system in big cities. But while merit as a principle in making appointments to government service is still gaining ground, many areas are still untouched and spoils holds sway. While the national government, the larger cities, and the schools operate predominately on the merit system, in many states, in most counties, in many smaller cities, towns, and townships, there is yet a long way to go.[13]

[11] Quoted in Leonard D. White, *Introduction to the Study of Public Administration*, revised edition (1939), p. 280.

[12] *The Municipal Year Book 1954*, p. 176.

[13] Carl Joachim Friedrich, "The Rise and Decline of the Spoils Tradition," *The Annals of the American Academy of Political and Social Science* (January, 1937), pp. 10–16. The entire issue of January, 1937, is devoted to the subject: "Improved Personnel in Government Service."

The Elective Officers

In the national and state governments there are few elective officials: members of Congress and state legislatures, the chief executives, lesser state administrative officials, and sometimes the state judiciary. Altogether, they number less than one-thousandth of one per cent of total national and state personnel.

But on the local level, things are different. Here there are hundreds of thousands of elective officials: city councilmen, county commissioners, township supervisors, school directors, members of boards of special districts, mayors, burgesses, assessors, tax collectors, county clerks, registers of wills, recorders of deeds, surrogates, prothonotaries, justices of the peace, constables, and a host of others. In many of the smaller local units, all or nearly all officials are elective, an appointed officer or full-time employee is a rarity. This harks back to the day when almost all local government officials were part-time and amateur, when citizens thought of government as a side-line, often an onerous but necessary civic duty. This is still the condition of affairs in rural areas and in the small towns of the nation. Here government is still close to the people in the Jacksonian sense.

The elective official is usually an amateur—he or she does not often depend upon government service for a career and a livelihood. But amateurs are a most nourishing ingredient in American politics and government. The amateur is often highly competent in his own chosen profession and brings to government a keen mind and a broad experience in community life. He may not know the technical aspects of municipal accounting but he does know the financial verities of life. He may not know how to build a street, but he knows what kind of traffic problems his city has and he is anxious to find modern solutions. Elected for the first time, he brings a fresh point of view and a helpful departure from the old ways of doing things, especially if they are not considered presently adequate. He keeps government human—that is, geared to the needs of the community and the people of the community. There are thousands of examples, too, where amateurs have led the crusade for better government and it is they, more than any other group, who are responsible for the improved American municipal government of the 20th century.

From Spoils to Career Service

Slowly but surely, personnel practices in our local governments have improved, but improvement has been sporadic and uneven. It has taken several trends—towards greater security for local employees, towards recruitment and promotion on the basis of merit, and towards the evolution of a career service. The separate elements of this movement may be distinguished:

(1) competitive examinations for appointment and promotion;

(2) protection from removal on account of politics;

(3) bipartisan personnel administration;

(4) institution of modern personnel practices;

(5) pre-service and in-service training for the public service;

(6) better pay, conditions of work, and retirement benefits; and

(7) professionalization of public service into a career.

TEN LARGEST CITY GOVERNMENT EMPLOYERS

City	Employees in October 1954	Payroll for October 1954 (in Thousands)
New York City	237,988	$85,526
Los Angeles	31,616	12,730
Chicago	31,538	12,950
Detroit	28,070	11,914
Philadelphia	26,985	8,669
Boston	22,462	6,597
Washington, D. C.	22,014	7,427
Baltimore	21,982	6,800
Cleveland	15,936	5,339
San Francisco	15,022	5,852

From the Bureau of the Census, *City Employment in 1954* (April 27, 1955), p. 2.

The obstacles to the establishment of a career service in local government are many. *Local residence restrictions* require that young men and women interested in making a career in local government must find their opportunities in their own local communities, and if they make good there it is difficult for them to advance to better positions in other communities. There are noteworthy exceptions to this. The city manager profession, getting stronger each year, has advanced largely because its members take positions in municipalities in which they do not live, and are free to change positions when greater opportunity offers. To a lesser degree, this applies to city planners, finance officers, public health administrators and other government specialists. In fact, a growing number of cities have in recent years removed residence requirements for selected jobs. And of course, school teachers and administrators from the "outside" have for a long time been accepted in American communities. Even more serious is an attitude in the government itself that *does not encourage transfer of personnel* between departments. Thus, the emergence of a group of qualified administrators able in several sectors of local government is inhibited, to the detriment of general administrative competence and improvement. *Low standards of educational and age qualifications* tend to bring into local service personnel who do not have the educational background needed to grow in the work even though they can pass examinations that are framed to reduce the importance of college education specializing in public administration. Willingness to open local employment to all age levels, commendable too from the viewpoint of democracy, attracts into local service many older people who may have acquired some technical knowledge and so can qualify for the job better than the neophyte, but it does not en-

TOTAL LOCAL EMPLOYEES
OCTOBER, 1953

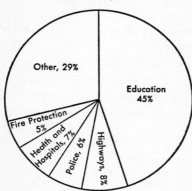

Fig. 17. Total Local Employees, October, 1953. (Source: Bureau of the Census, *Summary of Governmental Finances in 1953.*)

courage young people to enter the service as a career and who, in the long run, will prove more valuable.

Another obstacle is the *low salary schedules* for administrative officials in American local governments. While lower grades of service compare favorably with those in private industry, the higher grades are consistently lower. Thus, young men and women, aspiring to technical and administrative position, are constantly being lured into private employ or into the federal government where higher salaries, more security and more opportunity for advancement prevail. In times of depression, moreover, when any position is in demand, local employment has often been tinged with the *"charity" concept*. Even in normal times, charity has often been an element in placing people in local jobs. Heart-warming as it is from the humanistic point of view, it does hold back progress towards a career service.

Taking local government as a whole, the greatest obstacle to a career service is still the *spoils philosophy of personnel*. Key officials elected by the people who have the power to appoint subordinate officials and employees without restraints of civil service laws or regulations do so mainly in the traditional manner of rewarding party followers and friends. In many cases, however, it is not so much party as personal friendship that controls. For party organization on the local level is not always strong enough to dictate appointments to elected officials. Sometimes, the county or city organization does exercise control over appointments, but usually it is not "tight" enough to make its demands stick. The elective officers think of themselves as party leaders and it is only rarely that the "boss" in the background can pull the strings against the wishes of a bonafide elected official of his own party. Where the spoils philosophy reigns, there is little interest in the adoption of modern personnel practices. Local government service has little or no prestige in the community. In fact, it is precisely in places where the spoils system has gone overboard and to extremes that modern personnel practices have gained a foothold. The people reacted against abuses, rose up in their electoral majesty, and "threw the rascals out." On the other hand, where spoils are contained within reasonable limits and where political leaders know that good government is good politics, there is little or no opposition generated by the public to spoils as such.[14]

The evolution from spoils to career service and the transitional problems in a large city are illustrated in the case of Philadelphia. The new charter of 1951 ended councilmanic control over personnel. The civic service commission established by the 1919 charter was appointed by city council and responsible to it, but in 1952 it was replaced by a personnel system under an independent civil service commission. The mayor appoints this commission but he must appoint from a list of names submitted to him by a civil service panel, the members of which are prescribed in the charter. The members of the commission are appointed for six-year overlapping terms. The personnel director is appointed by the commission. Thus personnel, unlike budget responsibility, is not clearly within the executive power. The new charter places emphasis on the prevention of patronage abuses by restraining the executive and administrative officials in their powers over appointments. As a result, these officials are frustrated by rigid requirements and delays. The formalized personnel process places obstacles in the way of work programs for which department heads are held responsible by the mayor and council. The object of personnel policy, therefore, is to *control* rather than to *service.* And so Philadelphia, according to the report of a survey agency, had a personnel agency that succeeded in establishing the merit system, which was "a significant and praiseworthy achievement" but did not yet have a modern system of personnel management which is "essential for such a large employer." To achieve this, it was recommended, the city should move forward from the presently established merit system, based on restrictive personnel controls, to a new and higher level of *positive personnel administration* geared to the management needs of an efficient and dynamic city government. Also recommended was the integration of the personnel function into the general executive management of

[14] See International City Managers' Association, *A Career Service in Local Government* (1937).

city government under the direction of the mayor, the elimination of red-tape, and active assistance to administrative officials in solving their personnel problems.[15]

The Personnel System

Every local government has personnel problems. Employees must be recruited, selected, and supervised. In those units which operate without benefit of a merit system, the regularly elected officials or chief administrative officers "hire and fire" the employees without any formal rules or restrictions. In smaller units, the appointed personnel is at a minimum. Local governments are put under the *merit system* either by compulsory state law, city charters, or by local ordinances establishing it for all or for selected groups of local employees. Being under a merit system means that employees are selected and promoted on the basis of fitness for the job at hand, and protected from the ravages of politics.

The merit system is generally administered by a *civil service commission* appointed by the council, commission, or chief executive. This commission and its staff recruits and tests applicants for jobs, but the executive officials—the mayor, the department heads, the commission, and even sometimes the council—appoint employees from a list submitted to them by the commission. In recent years there has been a trend away from the independent civil service commission to a *single-headed personnel agency* responsible to the chief executive.

Progress toward the realization of the merit system has been made through independent civil service commissions for the emphasis of such agencies has been upon protection of employee selection from political pressures. However, positive personnel practices can be developed better by a single-headed agency directly under the chief executive. The Model City Charter of the National Municipal League provides for a professional administrator appointed by the city manager, and a personnel board of three appointed by the coun-

[15] Institute of Local and State Government, *Report on Philadelphia Personnel Administration,* University of Pennsylvania (1954), pp. 1–8.

cil for staggered six-year terms. The latter is held to be better for quasi-judicial (hearings on appeals) and quasi-legislative functions (rule-making) involved in personnel.

A good personnel system includes a series of steps by which employees are recruited, tested, selected and retained in the service of an organization.

The first essential is a *classification of positions.* By this is meant that all positions are described as to their duties, responsibilities, and other characteristics. Then the jobs are put into classes according to their similarity, and uniform pay schedules are applied. Thus, when filling positions it is possible for both the applicant and the personnel agency to understand the nature of the position to be filled and its compensation. Each position carries a title: stenographer, senior secretary, health inspector, patrolman, administrative assistant, junior accountant, and so on. A city of fifty thousand will have fifty to seventy kinds of positions described in the classification plan. Within each position is a minimum and maximum salary range, based on experience, seniority, competence, and other factors.

Recruitment and testing of candidates for local government service is the most important function of civil service commissioners and personnel agencies. Announcements of positions with the time and place of examinations must be published and distributed. Too often this is done perfunctorily without any effort to make the positions sound attractive. Most local units have not yet begun to follow the federal practice in making positive efforts to recruit those particularly fitted for and interested in governmental service.

Testing for fitness is generally done by examination. The test may be written, oral, or on the basis of physical examination, or a combination of one or more types. When a number of positions of the same kind such as stenographer are to be filled, the examination is usually written and given to assembled groups. When the position is single, such as the director of public health, and calls for highly selective qualifications, an oral examination is used and weight is given to previous experience, articles, and other evidences of accomplishment. Examinations in American local governments generally are made up to test the applicant's fitness for the particular job at hand, rather than for qualities that would indicate future possibilities in the government service.

Since the end of World War I, veterans of the United States military services have been given preference if they seek jobs that come under civil service examinations. This preference is usually in the form of five percentage points added to his examination grade, and ten points for a disabled veteran. In California, veterans who are candidates for the job of policeman or watchman are not only given five and ten percentage points but if they pass the minimum requirements they go to the head of the list.

Not all local employees come under the merit system even where one exists. Those that do are said to be classified; those that do not, unclassified. The latter generally include a few of the top appointive officials that like the mayor's secretary are considered to be personal appointees, and those who do the more routine jobs such as day laborers, janitors, and cleaning women. In some jurisdictions, only a few selected groups of positions such as police and firemen come under the merit system. Such legislation has been enacted because of the lobbying efforts of their statewide organizations. Temporary and provisional appointments, which can be filled without examination, are made by the appointing officers in accordance with laws or ordinances.

Certification and appointment is the next step after examination. The examinations having been graded, each applicant who makes the minimum grade, usually 70 per cent, is put on the eligible list in the order of his grade. When a vacancy exists in a department for a particular job under the merit system, the department head notifies the personnel agency, which submits to him several names, usually the top three, for the job. The appointing officer must choose from this list. Sometimes, only the name of the one with the highest grade is submitted, and in some cases as many as the five highest. If none of these accepts, the personnel agency submits the next highest in the eligible list. Where no more persons remain on the eligible lists, temporary appointments are made. Eligible lists of candidates are kept for one or two years, and then examinations are again held for the position. It is necessary that these lists be kept up-to-date in order that vacancies may be filled with a minimum of delay.

Once a person is appointed to a particular job under the merit system, he or she is on *probation* for a period usually lasting six months. No department is compelled to retain an employee who does not have the ability to do the work even though he passed an examination, or who has no interest in doing a good job, or has personality traits that make it impossible to adjust himself to his work or the others in the organization. In actual practice, few probationers are dismissed, the usual practice is to make the appointment permanent. Some laws make dismissal automatic at the end of the probationary period, unless the appointing officer makes a positive report that the employee is capable and worthy of a permanent berth.

A good personnel system will include a systematic plan for measuring employee performance. This is done through *service ratings* that represent a continuous assembling of data that bear on the employee's record. Competence, cooperation, industry, punctuality, output, and other qualities and factors are measured. Such ratings are used in making promotions, transfers, salary increases, layoffs, and removals. They aid immeasurably in building morale on the part of the better employees.

Conditions of work are as important in local government as they are in other employment. If these are too far out of line with private industry or with those in other levels of government, the best personnel will not be attracted to local service, nor will they stay. Hours of work, vacation time, sick leave, compensation, opportunity for advancement, protection against arbitrary dismissal, and other conditions that make jobs attractive are important elements of a good personnel policy. Some groups of employees such as police and fire personnel have statewide organizations strong enough to bring pressure to bear on state legislatures to have favorable conditions of work for themselves written into the law. In many jurisdictions, local employees are members of local branches of nationally organized unions and local union representatives deal with governing bodies on questions relating to pay and conditions of work. While the right to strike is denied local employees in many states, union pressures are often instrumental in bringing about improvements in working conditions.

In-service training is an important element in personnel management. Training not only keeps employees in touch with the latest developments in particular fields, but it provides the basic occupational education which is so often lacking. For most local employees never had any pre-service training for the work they do. A variety of training methods should be available in the in-service program: course work, lectures, inspections, demonstrations, laboratory, conferences, institutes, short courses, correspondence courses, and supervised research. Manuals, visual aids, and planned programs of study support the work of the instructors who may be senior officials and employees or outside experts. The beneficial results of in-service training have often been demonstrated. One city with an intensive police training program found that its traffic injury index had been dropping, the proportion of crimes cleared by arrest had increased, and the proportion of arrests followed by conviction had increased. All other factors having remained stable, this indicated that the improvement was brought about as a result of the training. In a state where there was a statewide program of training for fire fighters, fire losses dropped twenty per cent after five years of such training.

In these days, social security is demanded by all classes of workers and municipal employees are no exception. Many local units have *retirement programs* financed jointly by contributions from the local units and from the employees themselves. Many of these, organized as they are on a small scale, are not strong enough to meet the obligations imposed upon them by the retirement of members and thus become insolvent. They must either be bailed out by the local unit itself, or else collapse. Because of the complicated nature of retirement financing, it is unwise for a small local unit to establish its own retirement system. Sometimes it is better to handle pensions through an insurance company on an annuity program. Several states have a statewide municipal employees retirement system administered by the state retirement board. Recent federal legislation has made it possible for local officials and employees to be covered by social security with or without local retirement systems.[16]

Personnel in Counties

Although there has been some improvement in county personnel practices during the past fifty years, it can safely be said that examples of progress are few and far between. One authority says that "some ninety per cent of the country's counties still lack even the form, to say nothing of the substance, of a merit system." [17] A few within the remaining ten per cent have their own civil service commissions, but more are served by state personnel agencies. But while ten states authorize a state agency to assist in local personnel, there is little demand for such services when they are not mandatory.[18] Only in New York is every county required to have some form of a merit system. The state constitution has since 1895 provided that appointments and promotions in the civil service of all divisions of the state "shall be made according to merit and fitness to be ascertained, as far as practicable, by examinations, which, so far as practicable, shall be competitive." The New York state personnel agency assists the most populous counties and prescribes rules and regulations to put the merit system proviso into effect.[19]

[16] See Clay Morris Ross, *A Survey of Public Personnel Legislation and Administrative Regulations,* Bureau of Public Administration, University of Virginia (1940). Also: International City Managers' Association, *Municipal Personnel Administration,* fourth edition (1947); William E. Mosher, J. Donald Kingsley and Glenn O. Stahl, *Public Personnel Administration* (1950); Public Administration Service, *Personnel Programs for Smaller Cities* (1939); Civil Service Assembly, *Position-Classification in the Public Service* (1941), and *Merit System Installation* (1941). Also: International City Managers' Association, *The City's Role in Strikes* (1937); Bureau of Municipal Research, *Fringe Benefits in Municipal Employment,* University of Oregon (1954); Robert H. McManus, "Group Insurance for Municipal Employees," *Municipal Finance* (November, 1954), pp. 66–69; Municipal Finance Officers Association, "Retirement Planning for Small Municipalities" (1948).

[17] Snider, "American County Government: A Mid-Century Review," *American Political Science Review* (March, 1952), p. 72.

[18] Wager, *County Government across the Nation* (Chapel Hill, North Carolina, 1950), p. 30. The states are New York, Massachusetts, Rhode Island, California, Minnesota, Tennessee, Wisconsin, Maryland, New Jersey, and Ohio.

[19] Fairlie and Kneier, *County Government and Administration* (1930), p. 205.

In Massachusetts the services of the state civil service commission are available to towns. In the other eight states, state services are generally available on the option of local units, usually on a fee basis.

In other states, what was said in 1913 by the secretary of the National Civil Service Reform League unfortunately still describes the situation in the vast majority of the more than three thousand American counties: "The management of county charitable institutions, the important and difficult work in county legal offices and the administration of county public works, all calling for trained expert services, are commonly conducted by political appointees, chosen because of their political beliefs and activities but poorly qualified to do their work. County jails, workhouses, and other corrections and charitable institutions are badly kept and mismanaged, and the wards of the community are ill treated or not treated at all. The clerical service in county offices is frequently inefficient, the business of the county clerk's and county register's offices is poorly conducted, and records are kept at the best in a haphazard, accidental fashion which is expensive alike to the county and to the individual citizen in his business affairs. Meanwhile, the service of the county is the property of the political party which happens to be in power and supports a small army of political hangers-on who form the nucleus of the political spoils machine. In the service of a great and important administrative division of the state, in other words, the evils of the spoils system are allowed to continue unabated." [20]

Several qualifications to this bleak picture should be made. Under the terms of the Federal Social Security Act, county welfare and health employees that administer federally aided programs are required to come under some sort of merit system approved by federal authorities and usually supervised by a state agency. Moreover, in some city-county consolidations, a joint civil service agency operates under modern procedures and organization. In some special fields

[20] Robert W. Belcher, "The Merit System and the County Civil Service," 47 *Annals of the American Academy of Political and Social Science,* 101 (1913). Quoted in Fairlie and Kneier, *op. cit.,* p. 204.

such as assessment, records, health, and welfare in-service training for employees and modern equipment for offices have increased efficiency. As mentioned previously, a small number of counties have adopted the county manager or county executive plan. The elective row offices in the smaller counties have led to the extensive use of the part-time official, who gets to the office a few hours a day or week, collects his salary or fees, and allows the daily routine of the office to be handled by a competent deputy or secretary generally poorly paid in comparison to what the do-little-or-nothing incumbent gets. In some states, small offices like these are being combined and placed in the hands of one full-time official.

The pension system in American counties has spread in recent years. A number of states require pensions for county officials and employees, but many of the pension systems are not fiscally solvent and need pump priming in order to continue to exist. Some states, notably Wisconsin, have developed a statewide municipal and local employees retirement system either in connection with or independent of the state employees retirement, and in this way it is possible to establish a sound pension system which most small local units could not have themselves. Since 1950, local employees have been allowed to join the federal social security system and many of the counties supplement their own retirement payments with social security thus making available better protection at lower cost.

Personnel Practices in Cities over 10,000

According to the 1954 *Municipal Year Book*, personnel administration in a typical city over 10,000 in 1953 included one or more 3-member civil service boards appointed by the mayor or council, with jurisdiction over all employees. These boards, made up of lay people, were responsible for recruiting and examining applicants, certifying them for appointment, hearing appeals from suspension, dismissal and other administrative actions.

Of the total number of 1,347 cities over 10,000, 845 reported being under the merit system. Of these, 50 per cent covered all employees, while the rest only selected groups such as police and fire. All eighteen cities over 500,000 operated under the merit system, only one covering less than all employees. Many smaller cities were without the merit system—317 or 38 per cent of those between 10,000 and 25,000.

Laws in several states require cities to provide the merit system for certain groups of employees. In Iowa and Ohio all cities must have a 3-member civil service commission. New York has the proviso that cities must have their own or may use the county civil service commission. They may also appoint a full-time personnel director. In New Jersey cities may operate under the civil service commission which provides statewide recruitment, examination, certification, classification, and specific rules. In Massachusetts, all cities over 100,000 must and all others may come under the state civil service commission. The mayor and city council appoint civil service commissions in about an equal number of cities, while city managers appoint them in a few cases.

In addition to civil service commissions which represent the traditional merit system pattern, 144 cities have full-time personnel officers, appointed either by the city council or the mayor. Almost 500 cities handle personnel matters through department heads, while in almost the same number the mayor is the chief personnel authority.

In the typical city over 10,000, city employees have a work week of forty hours or less, with Saturdays off or with a skeleton staff. Employees get two weeks vacation time and from 12 to 15 days of sick leave with pay annually. Group hospitalization insurance is available, and employees are covered by a local or state-administered retirement plan. Some employees are members of a national labor union and some are affiliated with other employee organizations such as the Fraternal Order of Police and the State Firemen's Association.

About half of the cities engage in some type of in-service training, most of them in police, fire, public works, recreation, and utilities. Some cities take advantage of outside aid in training given by the International City Managers' Association, the Federal Bureau of In-

vestigation, state public service programs under vocational education, and university and college courses for local officials.

Almost all of the cities over 10,000 have retirement systems covering all employees. Local systems are found in 752 cities, state administered systems in 727, and 412 come under federal social security
alone or in combination with regular retirement programs. Almost
all states have signed agreements with the Federal Social Security
Board and have passed enabling legislation making social security
for local employees possible on the option of the local unit and the
members of local retirement systems.

Of the 1,347 cities over 10,000, 65 per cent have employees in one
or more of the national organizations for public employees. Of
these, 365 cities have employees in the American Federation of
State, County and Municipal Employees and over 600 cities have
members in the International Association of Fire Fighters. Both of
these organizations are affiliated with the American Federation of
Labor, while the CIO Government and Civic Employees Organizing
Committee is in 99 cities. Some 350 cities have employee organizations unaffiliated with national unions.[21]

Professionalization in the Public Service

The growth of professional organizations of public servants is a
phenomenon of utmost importance in local administration. It means
that specific services in local government are continuously being
improved by the joint efforts of the fraternity of trained personnel
working in the field. The members of these organizations not only
improve the services they render to the public but they aim to improve their own status in the governmental system and to increase
their own knowledge and competence.

Among the more important professional organizations of local
officials and employees are: International Association of Chiefs of
Police, Fraternal Order of Police, International Association of Fire
Chiefs, International Association of Fire Fighters, Municipal Finance

---

[21] *The Municipal Year Book 1954,* pp. 173–183.

Officers Association, International City Managers' Association, National Association of Assessing Officers, Institute of Traffic Engineers, American Public Health Association, American Society for Public Administration, National Institute of Municipal Clerks, American Society of Planning Officials, and National Institute of Municipal Law Officers.

The *Municipal Year Book* for 1936 described the objectives of such organizations as follows: (1) an organized body of knowledge available to its members; (2) the establishment of standards of competence for entrance and promotion in the service; (3) the development of training opportunities for its members; (4) a well-developed sense of the dignity and worth of public service; (5) a deep feeling of obligation to serve the public; and (6) a code of ethical conduct the violation of which by any member will bar him from the profession.

York Willbern (University of Alabama) points out the advantages of professionalization in the public service. It tends to promote respect and recognition for technical expertness in government. It facilitiates communications and the spread of new developments in a particular function or service. It provides an "in-group" loyalty and encourages "the instinct of workmanship." It produces a group concern for minimum standards, both in technical performance and ethical standards.

But there are certain disadvantages, some of them not so obvious as the advantages. The welfare of the professional group sometimes competes with the welfare of the people served. Professionalization insulates the group from political control in the public interest as well as from political favoritism. Sometimes the separatism of the professional group increases the difficulty of achieving the coordination and integration of governmental functions as a whole. Various professions try to get themselves free from over-all control. All they ask is for the government to supply the money for them to carry on the work.[22]

[22] York Willbern, "Professionalization in the Public Service: Too Little or Too Much?" *Public Administration Review* (Winter, 1954), pp. 13–21.

FINANCIAL ADMINISTRATION

In most local units financial organization is decentralized. In cities, appropriations and tax levies are adopted by the council. In a strong mayor form of government, the mayor has power to prepare and enforce the budget which must be adopted by council. There may be independently elected finance officers such as controller and treasurer, while others such as purchasing agent and assessor may be appointed by the mayor. In commission governed cities, a director of finance is one of the elected commissioners and he may, or may not, have all the financial functions in his office. Sometimes, both a controller and treasurer are elected while the assessor and purchasing agent, if any, may be appointed by the entire council. In council-manager government, the manager has under him a department of finance and in this department all of the financial functions such as accounting, purchasing, budgeting, assessing, and collecting are lodged. In counties, decentralization reaches the limit as most all of the officials are elected, and each may purchase, budget, account and report for his agency almost the way he wishes. The treasurer, controller, and even the chief clerk are sometimes elected. In school districts, finance officers are appointed by the board as they are in special districts. In towns and townships, they sometimes are appointed by the governing body and sometimes elected.

Centralized financial administration is found more frequently in strong mayor and council-manager government. Here a unified department of finance can be established, and in it can be lodged all the functions of finance.

In the Model City Charter of the National Municipal League a department of finance headed by a director appointed by the manager is proposed. This department contains bureaus of accounts, budget, taxation and assessments, purchasing, and treasury. The independent audit is made by an auditor or a firm of certified public accountants appointed by and responsible to the city council.[23]

[23] International City Managers' Association, *Municipal Finance Administration,* third edition (1946). Chapter 3, "Organization for Finance Administration," pp. 37–61.

Budgeting

A budget is an estimate of proposed expenditures and a plan to raise the money to pay them. Applied to local government, this is an annual document that is prepared and adopted before the beginning of the fiscal year. On it depends the actual operation of the government for the ensuing year and the rate of taxes levied. The objective of the budget is to merge necessary expenditures with possible revenues into a unified financial plan so that there will be enough money to do the things the governing body determines should be done.

A standard budget consists first of all of a *summary of expenditures and revenues,* showing the budget as a whole. This is accompanied by an *explanation of the main items* which will provide an over-all fiscal picture of the local government. The second part of the budget is made up of the *detailed schedules* with proposed expenditures for each department, function and activity, as well as estimated revenues from each source. Included also may be a list of salaries paid, a debt statement, the departmental work programs, and other data that may aid in understanding the fiscal problems of the local government. The third part of the budget is composed of drafts of the *appropriation, revenue and borrowing ordinances* that are necessary to put the budget into effect.

The budget is usually prepared by the chief executive in strong mayor-council governments. Where the municipality is large enough, the mayor may have a budget officer as a member of his staff. In commission government, the budget is drafted by the director of finance or by the controller under the direction of the council itself. In council-manager governments, the budget is the responsibility of the manager. Where there is a chief administrative officer, a director of finance, or even a chief clerk, the budget as far as its preliminary preparation is concerned usually falls on him. In some local units, where there is no such official, budgeting is done by the governing body itself, and is prepared by the finance or budget committee. The executive budget is now the most popular and is most acceptable by good administrative standards, but this is a recent innovation. At one time, all financial planning was in the hands of the legislative body which was responsible for levying taxes and spending money.

The first step in the budgetary process is the *preparation of expenditure and revenue estimates.* Forms for expenditure budgeting are sent to the spending agencies—the departments, commissions, and other divisions of the government. The revenue estimates are prepared by the revenue collection agency, the treasurer or the controller. Expenditure forms are designed to elicit the following information: the actual expenditures of the previous year, appropriations for the current year, estimated expenditures for the current year, and departmental requests for the coming year. These items are requested for the detailed items of expenditures depending on the *classification of expenditures* adopted for budget purposes. Expenditures may be classified in the budget according to function, activity, organizational unit, character, and object. The National Committee on Municipal Accounting recommends classification by function and activity because a budget on this basis is more comprehensible to the public.

The modern name for this approach is *performance budgeting.* The goal of performance budgeting is to prepare and interpret the financial data in terms of service and activity programs, rather than in terms of objects of disbursements such as personal services, supplies, and equipment. To get "on a performance basis" has its difficulties because it has been assumed that *cost accounting* is a prerequisite of performance budgeting. However, cost accounting is applicable only to such productive activities as square yards of street construction, lineal mile for ice and snow removal, number of tons for waste removal, and lineal mile for street cleaning. In such cases, all the costs can be brought into focus in terms of cost per unit. But there are alternatives to cost accounting where production can be put in terms of man-hours. The man-hour approach differs from cost accounting in that personnel requirements only, rather than all cost factors, are made the basis of program estimates. Under this system two items are required: measures of productive output, and measures of employee time. Thus, for example, if thirty thousand units of work are performed requiring 10,440 man-hours, it takes .35 man-hours per unit. In the coming year, if it is estimated that 35,000 units of work are required in this particular activity, the total man-hours needed will be 12,250 man-hours. On the basis of 2,088 man-hours per year per employee, one more person will be required for the growing work load. For nonmeasurable activities, a ratio-of-personnel, for example, 15 per cent of total personnel to be supervisory, can be used.[24]

Most budgets, however, are prepared on the basis of the organization unit because it shows what each department spends. Classification by character indicates whether the item is for current expense, fixed charges, capital outlay, or debt redemption. Classification by object shows what is purchased for the expenditures: personal services, contractual services, equipment or supplies. Many budgets have a combination of classifications so that in budgeting for police protection, for example, it can be shown how much is for salaries or equipment as well as for the different functions. Sometimes each department is requested to provide a *work program* which shows the amount and type of work and activity planned for the amount requested in the budget. Revenue estimates are calculated on the basis of previous years' receipts, proposed increases or decreases in tax levies, business conditions, and other factors.

When the budget officer receives all the estimates, he holds meetings with the department heads to allow them to justify what they ask for. He may revise according to the total program, over-all budget needs, and general financial conditions. After the budget officer assembles the revised estimates, he submits them to the chief executive who may in turn make further revisions. Then he prepares his message to the council and submits both the message and the budget itself. Council may consider it in committee of the whole or give it to its finance committee. The council generally confers with the chief administrator, the budget officer, and the department

[24] Frank Sherwood, "Some Non-cost Accounting Approaches to Performance Budgeting," *Public Management* (January, 1954), pp. 9–12. Also: Samuel M. Roberts, "Trend toward Performance Budgeting," *Public Management,* October, 1952; Catheryn Seckler-Hudson, "Performance Budgeting in Government," *Society for Advancement of Management.*

heads, holding hearings to which the public is invited. While there usually is ample publicity about the new budget in the newspapers and other media of communication, the public is not much interested unless tax rates are increased, or some large scale new expenditure is planned. When the budget is finally agreed upon, it is adopted in the form of appropriation and tax levy ordinances.[25]

Budgetary Control

The adoption of a budget is only half the battle. It must be enforced throughout the entire year or it is of no consequence, merely a scrap of paper. After its adoption it is given back to the budget officer and it is his duty to provide the budgetary control and administration. First, there must be an *allotment system* for all expenditures so that they are spaced out for the twelve months and budget deficiencies do not develop. The allotment must take into consideration seasonal or fluctuating activity and be integrated into the work programs of the departments.

After allotments are made, it is up to the fiscal officers to hold the department heads to these allotments and this they do with the aid of *budget accounting*. Under this procedure, requisitions for more than the allotted money cannot be made except by special permission of the chief administrator. An appropriation and expenditures ledger is used to keep track of expenditures in relation to allotments. There must be periodic reports to determine the condition of the appropriations and funds. These are supplemented by audits of expenditures, work done, and supplies purchased. There are times when budget changes are made necessary during the fiscal year. There may be an emergency requiring extraordinary expenditures not planned for in the budget, and other changing conditions might arise. If changes in the ordinance are necessary, legislative action is involved; otherwise transfers can be made by the chief executive or

[25] *Municipal Finance Administration, op. cit.,* Chapter 4, "Municipal Budget-Making," pp. 62–88. Also: National Committee on Municipal Accounting, *A Standard Classification of Municipal Revenues and Expenditures,* Bulletin 9, Municipal Finance Officers Association (1939); A. E. Buck, *Budgeting for Small Cities,* Municipal Administration Service (1931).

budget authority. These changes can be made by simple transfer from one item to another. Sometimes there must be reductions all around if the revenues do not meet expectations. But all such changes should be made only for good and sound reasons.[26]

Municipal Accounting

Municipal accounting provides for the recording of financial information so that it can be utilized by municipal officials to manage the affairs of the local unit. It is the tool to determine whether the financial plan set up in the budget is being carried out. According to the National Committee on Municipal Accounting, there are general principles that can be used to guide municipal accounting.

(1) All accounts should be under the direction of one official.

(2) Accounting should be on a double-entry basis.

(3) Accounts should be classified into funds.

(4) The accrual basis should be used in accounting for revenues and expenditures.

(5) Periodic independent audits should be made.

(6) Financial reports should be prepared periodically.

In local units the official in charge of accounting is usually called the *controller*. He is usually elected on the theory that he should be independent of both the spending and the tax levying authorities and should represent the public as the "watchdog of the treasury." However, most controllers are not elected on the basis of their qualifications for accountancy and therefore the local unit must often rely on the competence of their subordinates. Usually some one person takes charge of the technical aspects of the work, while the controller has over-all direction of the department. The office of controller keeps all controlling records of the municipality, pre-audits all expenditures and sees to it that no payment is made without its written approval. It sees to it that there is enough money left in the budget to pay each particular expenditure and that it has

[26] *Municipal Finance Administration, op. cit.,* Chapter 5, "Budget Administration and Expenditure Control." Also: Carl H. Chatters and Irving Tenner, *Municipal and Governmental Accounting* (1940).

been made in accordance with law. The controller is also responsible for the preparation of all financial reports of the local unit.

In the accrual system of accounting, recommended for municipal accounts, emphasis is laid upon the period in which the transaction has occurred. Under the accrual basis, revenues are accounted for when earned, or in the case of taxes, when billed, and expenditures are accounted for when the liability has been incurred. In the cash basis of accounting, revenues are accounted for when received in cash, and expenditures only when they are actually paid. Under the accrual system it is possible to get a more accurate picture of finances in a set of a particular period of time, preferably the year.

In municipal accounting the double-entry system should be used. This system assumes that each transaction has a twofold aspect— the debit and the credit side. An entry into one side must be followed by a corresponding entry on the other, and always the total of one should balance the total of the other. Financial transactions are recorded in two steps: the journal entry and the posting of them in the proper ledger account. All financial reports are prepared from the ledgers.

In municipal accounting there are usually several funds. A fund is a sum of money set aside for the handling of particular functions. The National Committee on Municipal Accounting has recommended the use of the following funds: (1) *the general fund,* all normal revenues and expenditures not marked for a particular purpose; (2) *special funds,* those that are ear-marked for particular purposes; (3) *bond funds,* those which account for the receipts and expenditures of bonds issued by the local unit; (4) *sinking funds,* used to retire the principal of bonds issues; (5) *trust and agency funds,* those for money or property held by the municipality in trust or as custodian; (6) *special assessment funds,* those to finance improvements from special assessments levied against benefited property; (7) *working capital funds,* for particular services within the local unit; and (8) utility funds, used to finance particular revenue producing utilities.

A municipal balance sheet shows the local unit's financial condition at any particular time. It lists assets, offset by liabilities, reserves and surplus. In understanding the changing condition of finances, the factors that caused changes between two balance sheets must be analyzed.

In accounting for revenues, the budgetary estimate of revenues needed to balance the budget must be replaced gradually by actual revenues. All revenues due the local unit should be recorded and action taken to obtain them. In accounting for expenditures, it must be insured that they are made according to law, that what they buy represents value received for the expenditure, and that they are authorized by the proper authorities.[27]

Cost Accounting

The use of cost accounting in municipal finance has been growing. It is the recording of expense so that it will be possible to develop costs of particular units of work of particular jobs. First, a distribution of direct and indirect expense must be made to arrive at an accurate total cost. The four basic local costs are labor, equipment, materials and supplies, and overhead charges. Standard work units are then established in various activities. Examples are the cleaning mile, the tone of refuse collected, the gallon of sewage treated, patient days in a hospital, interviews in employment service, and tests made. When standard work units have been established, unit costs may be determined by dividing the number of work units into the total expense of a particular operation. Future work programs can be based upon these unit costs.

The value of cost accounting is that it protects against loss, waste and inefficiency. It provides data for policy determination because accurate estimates of costs per project can more readily be found. It also allows more correct pricing of services and rates, better budg-

[27] *Municipal Finance Administration, op. cit.,* Chapter 6, "Municipal Accounting," pp. 111–141. Also: Lloyd Morey and Orval W. Diehl, *Municipal Accounting* (1942); J. W. Oliver, "Getting the Most from Machine Accounting," *Municipal Finance* (November, 1954), pp. 79–83; Joseph M. Lowery, "The National Committee on Governmental Accounting," *Municipal Finance* (February, 1951), pp. 120–123.

etary control over expenditures, and better knowledge of personal performance on the job. Finally, it is a means of reporting to the public, in understandable terms, the activities of local government.[28]

Financial Reporting

Financial reports are statements which set forth the financial condition of the local unit. They should be made either by the chief financial official or the chief administrator, and may be made to the chief executive, the council, and to the public. The most important of these is the *annual financial report*. There are two types: one, the complete financial report with detailed financial data; the second, prepared especially for the public to give a briefer and more concise picture. The latter type attempts to show what the local inhabitants are getting for their money and the general condition of local finances. The public report, in addition to a round-up of financial figures, should contain such information as: (1) expenditures for each activity and their per cent of total expenditures; (2) revenues produced for each activity; (3) unit costs for each activity, if available; and (4) per capita costs when they are meaningful. It should also contain a description of the duties of each agency or department of government, a brief outline of its activities during the past year, and plans for the future. Charts and other illustrative material add to the interest of the report to the citizens.

The complete financial report should contain the summarized balance sheet for each fund, the budget and its relation to actual expenditures, the revenue and expense statement showing revenues by source and expenditures by activities, with an analysis of surplus or deficit, the condition of local indebtedness, and facts relating to assessment, levy and collection of taxes.

About half the states require some state administrative supervision over local financial reports. Some require uniform reports so that

---

[28] *Municipal Finance Administration, op. cit.*, Chapter 7, "Cost Accounting," pp. 142–161.

comparable statistics can be developed and others offer advice and assistance in preparing the reports.[29]

The Audit of Local Finances

There are two kinds of audits performed on local finances. The first is the current audit by the controller or chief finance officer. It is called the *pre-audit* since it is made prior to the payment of claims and bills. It also takes care of the daily, weekly, or monthly checking of revenues and receipts. This kind of audit serves as the basis of final entries in the controller's accounts and is the only valid method of accounting control.

The other kind of audit is the *post-audit*. This is done after the financial transactions for the year have been completed. This should be done by a source independent of the controller or the administration in general. In an independent audit it is necessary for the auditor to check and verify the accounts, vouchers and other documents, and to report his findings to the council. The independent audit should be done by an auditor appointed by council, by a firm of certified public accountants appointed by council, or by a state agency. In thirty states, the state audits municipal accounts. In many local units, there is no independent audit because the controller or director of finance does this work. But an independent audit cannot be obtained by the officer who performs the current audit because this would merely be a review of his own work and decisions.

The Model City Charter recommends an independent audit of all accounts of the local government by qualified public accountants, selected by the council, "who have no personal interest directly or

[29] *Municipal Finance Administration, op. cit.,* Chapter 8, "Financial Reporting," pp. 162–191. Also: Carl H. Chatters, *Accounting Manual for Small Cities,* Municipal Finance Officers' Association (1933); and Clarence E. Ridley and Herbert A. Simon, *Specifications for the Annual Municipal Report,* International City Managers' Association (1939), and *A Checklist of Suggested Items for the Annual Municipal Report* (1940); Wylie Kilpatrick, *State Supervision of Local Budgeting,* National Municipal League (1939); William H. Sherman, "Reports to Taxpayers and Reports to Management," *Municipal Finance* (November, 1954), pp. 101–103.

indirectly in the financial affairs of the city government or of any of its officers." The ideal auditor, according to G. F. Shirras, is "one who asks every question that may be expected from an intelligent taxpayer bent on getting the best value for his money." [30]

Tax Collection

As property taxes are the most substantial of local revenues, their collection should be prompt and efficient. In many cases, however, it is done in a slip-shod manner. Where the tax collector is elected, and this is the case in many local units, especially smaller cities and rural areas, he is often a tax receiver rather than a tax collector. In other words, he takes what comes to him and allows the rest go into delinquency. In many states, he is still paid by a percentage of taxes collected so that taxes difficult to collect do not repay him for the extra effort he must put forth to get them. But in some local units—such as one-industry towns or coal mining rural townships, where almost the entire tax is paid by one property owner—the tax collector, if paid on a percentage basis, has the most lucrative of all local government plums. Going to the post office to receive the check for taxes from this company, he may "earn" fifteen or twenty thousand dollars. In the larger cities, however, the tax collector, usually the city treasurer, is appointed and paid on a salary basis.

The basic information upon which a property tax bill is made is the assessed worth of a property as evaluated by the assessor. From this is prepared the tax roll on which the tax is calculated by taking the assessed valuation and multiplying it by the tax levy. For example, Citizen A has property assessed at $4,500. The city tax levy is 15 mills, the school district 35 mills, and the county 10 mills. Assuming all these taxes are collected by the same tax collector, he would extend the taxes due on a bill and send them to the property owner. The total tax bill would be 60 mills, or $60 for each $1,000 assessed valuation. The total, in this case, would amount to $270.00;

[30] G. F. Shirras, *The Science of Public Finance*, p. 609. See also: *Municipal Finance Administration, op. cit.*, pp. 53–33; and Lutz, *Public Finance*, fourth edition (1947), pp. 676–678.

and this would be allocated in the following proportions: to the city, $67.50; to the school district, $157.50; and to the county, $45.00. On the bill would be specified a date when the payment was due, and sometimes discount might be offered on taxes paid before the due date. After the date due, the taxes would be payable at par for a certain period usually a year. After that penalty and interest would be added for another year, and then the delinquent property might be liened for the amount of the tax. This means that a record of the tax owed is made in court, and after another lapse of time may be sold for taxes. The owner might redeem the property by paying the interest and penalties, but if not they might be finally sold, and proceeds divided among the local units having tax claims against the property. In recent years, installment paying of taxes has come into vogue, usually on a quarterly basis. In some states, banks act as tax receivers and tax payments can be mailed. During the depression of the 1930's thousands of properties became delinquent and state legislatures passed legislation to abate many of the ordinary penalties of tax delinquency. Interest and penalties were abated, time for payment extended, and tax sales held up.

Revenues other than taxes on real property are usually collected by appointed officials or elected treasurers of the local unit. They are rarely given to the elected tax collectors. This applies generally to fines for traffic violations, license fees, parking meter receipts, utility charges, revenues from services, and revenues from other taxes such as sales and income.[31]

The Custody of Funds

The custodian of funds in local governments is the treasurer. Very often he is an elective official. During the 19th century when municipalities and local units were operated without the benefit of modern financial management and protection, large sums of money were lost because of defalcation and loose handling. The depositories for

[31] *Municipal Finance Administration, op. cit.,* pp. 234–252. Also: Carl H. Chatters, *The Enforcement of Real Estate Tax Liens* (1928); E. A. Danby, "Tax and Other Revenue Collection Procedures," *Municipal Finance* (November, 1954), pp. 84–86.

local funds are banks, and they should be selected on the basis of their financial soundness. Very often, local funds are divided between the banks in the jurisdiction, and this has been done so that no irreparable loss will come from the failure of one particular bank. Banks are supposed to give security for deposits. This should be collateral that can be cashed within six months if the depository bank should close its doors. The amount of the collateral should be at least 10 per cent in excess of the amount deposited. All securities of the municipality should also be in the custody of the treasurer.

Local officials who handle money are usually under some kind of bond. This is to guarantee public monies against human weakness and the various pressures and problems incident to the job at hand. Not many public officials go wrong, one surety company estimates only one per cent of their seven million persons in all classes of responsibility, including public officials, betrayed their trust, and that the rate of public officials is no higher than those in private capacities. Until recent times, public officials were bonded by responsible persons whom they knew, but this method is rapidly losing ground to large financial corporations organized to write fidelity and surety bonds on a strictly business basis.

An official bond has two purposes: (1) to protect the local unit against monetary loss by public officials, and (2) to guarantee faithful performance of duty on the part of the official or employee bonded. "Faithful performance" bonds, while much more costly than ordinary surety bonds, are not worth much more than surety bonds because the courts have strictly construed their limitations. Recovery comes largely when losses are from theft, defalcation, or fraud. Few companies pay anything for inability to collect taxes. Generally it is agreed by experts that official bonds should be paid out of public monies, that official bonds should be limited to positions in which the official or employee handles money or valuable things, that official bonds should be written to cover the position rather than the person, that the purchase of official bonds should be on a competitive and an annual basis, and that the bond should not be excessive but should cover the amount of financial responsibility of the official or employee.[32]

Purchasing

Until recent decades, local governments purchased supplies and equipment without regard to scientific principles. Buying was done by department heads, often in small quantities, and frequently at retail prices. There was little attempt at standardization of specifications, testing and inspection, or wholesale purchasing. This is still the case in thousands of local units, especially the smaller ones. Following the lead of industry, some of the cities and larger local units have embarked on a program of centralized purchasing carried on by a purchasing agent who is a full-time appointive officer usually under the supervision of the chief finance officer, the chief executive or administrative officer.

The chief advantages of centralized purchasing are that group purchasing leads to lower prices because of the larger quantities bought. Firms are anxious to compete for this kind of business and are willing to shave prices. Purchasing departments usually take advantage of discounts for prompt payment. Furthermore, a list of qualified vendors can be established thus preventing unreliable vendors from bidding and delivering, if successful, shoddy merchandise. Standards can be adopted thus reducing the number of articles used for the same purpose. Standard specifications make the bidding process more efficient. Centralized inspection and testing keeps down the amount of inferior merchandise. Experts say that the cost of purchasing is less than one per cent of the amount of goods purchased and that by efficient methods of purchasing, from 10 to 15 per cent of the amount of annual purchases can be saved.

[32] *Municipal Finance Administration, op. cit.*, pp. 252–255f., and 391–394. Also: Mayo Fesler, "A Sound Policy for Bonding City Officials," *Public Management,* February, 1934; and Hilliard B. Wilson, *Municipal Insurance Practices,* American Municipal Association (1939).

Purchasing procedure begins with the preparation of a requisition by the using department, signed by the department head. The requisition is sent to the purchasing agent. The purchasing agent tries to get wide competition because this leads to lower prices. Most states have laws requiring that all purchases over a certain amount, perhaps three or five hundred dollars, be advertised in order to secure bids. For small purchases, bids can be sought by phone, but others should come through the mail through the use of request-for-quotation forms. These are sent out to card lists of bonafide vendors. Some local units require that quotations for bidding be accompanied by a certified check from the vendor as a guarantee the vendor will accept the order if awarded to him. After the bids are opened, they are tabulated and the purchase is awarded to the "lowest responsible bidder." Many local units like to give preference to local vendors but this practice should be limited to instances when the price, quality and service are equal. For purchases over a certain amount, contracts are required which are guaranteed by surety. For smaller purchases and emergency orders, using departments may be allowed to purchase without going through the purchasing agent and the regular procedure.

Upon receipt of the goods, there should be records made by the purchasing agent and notification to the using department. On some purchases it is necessary to establish inspection and tests. The National Bureau of Standards will make tests for other governmental agencies for a small fee, and here local units can get expert service.[33]

County Financial Administration

While the foregoing elements of the financial process apply to all local units of government, it must be emphasized that the greatest progress towards modernization has been made in municipalities where there is a strong executive, a chief administrative officer, or

[33] *Municipal Finance Administration, op cit.,* Chapter 13, "Purchasing and Storing," pp. 328–353. Also: Russell Forbes and others, *Purchasing for Small Cities,* Public Administrative Service (1951); Frank H. Whelan, "Economical Buying Methods for Governmental Units," *Municipal Finance* (November, 1954), pp. 75–78.

a manager. Improved procedures in finance generally tend to follow improved administration. Counties, being sadly deficient in modern administrative organization, have comparatively few shining examples of good financial organization and practice. Not that there have not been improvements here and there, but in general the fact that there is no central executive office with control over the entire administration makes it impossible to develop systematic budgeting, and modern accounting. Budgets, to be sure, may be prepared but they are paper presentations from the various independent offices rather than the culmination of an integrated administrative process. Few counties have centralized their purchasing, the row offices continue to buy materials and supplies in piecemeal fashion and largely at retail prices. Where there is a full-time controller, pre-auditing of expenditures, uniform accounting, post-audit of books and other financial activities may be carried on in a modern and effective manner, although the fact that the controller is elective tends to make his office political rather than administrative, and independent rather than a part of an integrated process. In smaller counties, where only post-auditing of annual accounts is done by elected officials paid on a per diem basis, the result is negative at its best. At its worst only cursory and meaningless examinations of accounts are made. In many states, annual budget and financial report forms are prescribed by a supervisory state department, and the use of these have proved a means of getting increased uniformity of accounting. "In general," Professor Snider (University of Illinois) states, "county auditing appears to be most satisfactory in those states where the task is performed by the auditing staff of a state administrative agency. State auditors are in a position to advise and assist inexperienced local officers in matters of bookkeeping procedure, and regular state audits afford a strong deterrent to malpractice." [34]

An extreme example of financial decentralization is afforded by *South Carolina* where the counties are dependent to a very great extent upon the action of the general assembly. Each year the legis-

[34] Snider, "American County Government: A Mid-Century Review," *American Political Science Review* (March, 1952), p. 77.

lature passes 46 county supply bills, one for each county in the state. The county legislative delegations, composed of the one senator and the representatives of the lower house who are elected from the county, meet in the counties before the legislative session. They survey the probable income available and hear requests for appropriations from the several officers and agencies of the county. Based on this information, the county supply bills are drafted by the delegations and presented to the legislature. Every county supply bill can be vetoed by the senator from the county because the bills must be passed by both houses and each county defers to the others in a sort of legislative courtesy.[35]

Another example of decentralization is found in Oklahoma. The county governing board has three commissioners. It appropriates money and levies taxes, subject to the approval of the excise board. The county excise board has three members appointed for two year terms. One is appointed by the Oklahoma tax commission, one by the district judge or judges, and one by the county commissioners. The board meets on the first Monday in July to allocate the 15 mill constitutional tax levy among local governmental units—county, city, town, and school district. This board must follow statutory provisions regarding the number of mills which must go to the various subdivisions and sometimes only has discretion as to one of the 15 mills. The exise board also checks all local budgets. This board acts also as the board of equalization of assessments. The state equalization board upon the recommendation of the state tax commission can increase or decrease the assessments by class of property and the action is applicable to the whole county. The county board of commissioners may audit any accounts of all officials handling county money. It determines the pay and number of deputies within the law. It may construct certain buildings only with the consent of the voters.[36]

In California, a different arrangement exists. Here the board of supervisors has three general fields of governmental power: (1) as

[35] Wager, *County Government across the Nation* (Chapel Hill, North Carolina 1950), p. 425.
[36] Wager, *op. cit.*, pp. 579–581.

a governing body for all county affairs including such areas as the sheriff's office, roads, hospital and charities; (2) as an *ex-officio* governing body for certain special districts; and (3) as fiscal agents for other governing boards: for example, they raise but do not spend monies for the school districts. In comparatively recent years, the board of supervisors has been given power to control all county salaries and to prepare the budget for all county departments. The auditor tabulates and classifies the budget items and makes a report on the financing possibilities of the submitted programs. After hearings and deliberation of the county board the budget is adopted. Some counties submit work programs along with the budgets. The California system more nearly approaches a system of integrated fiscal management not only in the county and for all its officials but for allied local boards covering the same areas as well.[37]

TEN SUBJECTS FOR FURTHER STUDY

1. Local government employees serving your community.
2. The elective officials of your city, borough, or township, and of your county and school district.
3. Merit provisions for local officials and employees in your state.
4. The procedure of budget making in your city or county.
5. Tax collection in your community.
6. Cost accounting in local government.
7. Analysis of the annual financial report of your city or county.
8. Centralized purchasing.
9. The powers of a chief financial officer in a big city government.
10. Municipal work programming and budgeting.

REFERENCES

C. A. Adams, "Employee Service Reports in Smaller Cities," *Public Management,* March 1940, pp. 67–70.

L. K. Andrews and Ed. E. Reid, *Municipal License Tax Administration,* Alabama League of Municipalities, Report No. 103 (1954).

[37] County Supervisors Association of California, *County Government in California,* Bureau of Governmental Research, University of California, Los Angeles, pp. 32–36.

The Annals of the American Academy of Political and Social Science, January 1937. Entire issue devoted to the subject: "Improved Personnel in Government Service."

Ruth Bruton, "Microfilm or Be Swamped," *The American City,* March 1955, p. 127.

A. E. Buck, *Budgeting for Small Cities,* Municipal Administration Service (New York, 1931).

James C. Charlesworth, *Governmental Administration* (New York, 1951).

Civil Service Assembly of the United States, *Employee Relations in the Public Service* (Chicago, 1942).

———, *Employee Training in the Public Service* (Chicago, 1941).

———, *Placement and Probation in the Public Service* (Chicago, 1946).

———, *Position Classification in the Public Service* (Chicago, 1941).

Robert Connery, "A Laboratory Method for Teaching Public Administration," *American Political Science Review,* February 1948, pp.68–74.

Winston W. Crouch and Judith Jamison, *The Job of a Civil Service Commissioner,* Civil Service Assembly (Chicago, 1955).

———, *The Work of Civil Service Commissions,* Civil Service Assembly (Chicago, 1955).

Robert T. Daland, *A Brief Survey of Municipal Auditing Practices in Alabama,* Bureau of Public Administration, University of Alabama (1954).

Martin L. Faust, "Providing Security for Public Deposits," *Municipal Finance,* August 1934, pp. 18–22.

Herman Feldman, "Public Employees and Unions," *National Municipal Review,* April 1946, pp. 161–165.

Russell Forbes, *Governmental Purchasing* (New York, 1929).

———, *Purchasing for Small Cities,* Public Administration Service (Chicago, 1951).

George A. Graham, *Education for Public Administration,* Public Administration Service (Chicago, 1941).

W. Brooke Graves, *Public Administration in a Democratic Society* (Boston, 1950).

Luther Gulick, "The Goals of Management," *Public Management,* January 1955, pp. 2–6.

W. G. Hamilton, "Relationship of the Independent Auditor to the Municipality," *Municipal Finance,* August 1955, pp. 18–24.

The International City Managers' Association, *A Career Service in Local Government* (Chicago, 1937).

———, *The City's Role in Strikes.* A series of articles from the February and April 1937 issues of *Public Management.*

————, *Municipal Personnel Administration,* Fourth Edition (Chicago, 1947).

————, *The Technique of Municipal Administration* (Chicago, 1947),

Edith B. Kidney, *Fringe Benefits for Salaried Employees in Government and Industry,* Civil Service Assembly (Chicago, 1954).

James D. Kitchen, *Cooperative Governmental Purchasing,* Bureau of Governmental Research, University of California (Los Angeles, 1935).

George M. Link, "Centralized Financial Control," *National Municipal Review,* February 1946, pp. 71–76.

Stuart MacCorkle, *Municipal Administration* (New York, 1942).

Leifur Magnusson, *Government and Union-Employer Relations,* Public Administration Service, No. 39 (Chicago, 1945).

Joseph E. McLean (ed.), *The Public Service and University Education* (Princeton, 1949).

William E. Mosher, Donald Kingsley, and Glenn O. Stahl, *Public Personnel Administration* (New York, 1950).

Municipal Finance Officers Association of the United States and Canada, *Coordinating Local Retirement Systems with Federal Social Security,* Special Bulletin (Chicago, 1955).

————, *Retirement Planning for Small Municipalities,* Special Bulletin (Chicago, 1948).

————, *Performance Budgeting and Unit Cost Accounting for Governmental Units* (Chicago, 1954).

————, *Administrative Uses of Performance Budgets* (Chicago, 1954).

National Municipal League, *The Model Real Property Tax Collection Law* (New York, 1954).

Orin F. Nolting, *How Municipal Fire Defense Affects Insurance Rates,* International City Managers' Association (Chicago, 1939).

————, *Management Methods in City Government,* International City Managers' Association (Chicago, 1942).

John A. Perkins, "Preparation of the Local Budget," *American Political Science Review,* October 1946, pp. 949–958.

J. M. Pfiffner, *Municipal Administration* (New York, 1940).

Public Administration Service, *Merit System Installation,* Pamphlet No. 77 (1941).

Thomas H. Reed, *Municipal Management* (New York, 1941).

Charles S. Rhyne, *Labor Unions and Municipal Employee Law,* National Institute of Municipal Law Officers (Washington, 1946).

Clarence E. Ridley and Herbert A. Simon, *Measuring Municipal Activities,* International City Managers' Association (1943).

Richard Ruddell, *Cities and Their Records in the Modern Era,* American Municipal Association (Washington, 1955).

Stanley Scott, Joseph D. Lubin, and Robert J. McNeill, *Public Services in Unincorporated Communities,* Bureau of Public Administration, University of California (Berkeley, 1953).

John F. Sly, H. F. Alderfer, and Victor D. Brannon, "Watchdogs of Local Finance," *National Municipal Review,* July 1947, pp. 384–388.

John E. Swanson and Francis A. Mishell, *Public Employee Retirement in Texas,* Institute of Public Affairs, University of Texas (Austin, 1955).

William G. Torpey, *Public Personnel Management* (New York, 1953).

Harvey Walker, *Public Administration in the United States* (New York, 1937).

Leonard D. White, *Introduction to the Study of Public Administration,* Fourth edition (New York, 1955).

York Willbern, "Losing the Human Touch," *National Municipal Review,* October 1950, pp. 439–444.

———, "Professionalization in the Public Service: Too Little or Too Much?" *Public Administration Review,* Winter 1954, pp. 13–21.

Hilliard B. Wilson, *Municipal Insurance Costs and Practices,* American Municipal Association (Chicago, 1939).

Frank P. Zeidler, "The Administrator and Public Policy," *Public Administration Review,* Summer, 1954, pp. 180–182.

Chapter 11

POLICE AND
CRIMINAL JUSTICE

The administration of criminal justice is essentially a local function, but during the last fifty years both national and state governments have taken upon themselves increasing responsibilities in this field. The Federal Bureau of Investigation hunts down and prosecutes violators of national laws many of which aim to bring about federal impact on crime in general and not only in relation to violation of federal regulations on specific subjects. While the FBI spearheads the joint national-state-local fight against organized crime, other federal agencies including the Secret Service and the Narcotics Bureau of the Treasury Department and the Post Office Department, are concerned with crime. All states have established state police systems of one kind or another to assist local authorities to preserve law and order. Their activities are especially directed towards regulating automobile traffic on state highways and acting as a police force for the rural areas of the state. But they also provide police services in cases that require statewide search and action. On the local level, there are forty thousand law enforcement agencies in city, county, and township. As Bruce Smith, a foremost authority on police organization in the United States, aptly says, "There is therefore no such thing in the United States as a police system, nor even a set of police systems within any reasonably accurate sense of the term. Our so-called systems are mere collections of police units having some similarity of authority, organization, or jurisdiction; but they lack any systematic relationship to each other." [1]

While violations of national law are handled by federal officers and tried in the federal courts, most criminal offenses are defined by state law and these are dealt with by state and local enforcement officials. The states, except for the limited activity of state police, have left the responsibility for law enforcement to local officials, and while the courts are established by state law they are local in that they are found in every county and civil subdivision, and many of the judges and other officials are elected by the local electorate and paid from local funds.

Briefly, it might be well to review the procedure involved in the administration of criminal justice. First, a criminal act is committed, and it is reported to the police by a person who makes a statement or complaint that the crime was done by a known person who is named. A *warrant* is issued for his arrest. "John Doe" warrants are available to officers when the person is unknown so as to allow them to pick up suspects. If the crime is committed in the presence of an officer or a citizen, the arrest may be made *on sight*. The alleged offender is brought before a member of the minor judiciary such as a justice of the peace, a police magistrate, or even a mayor or burgess in states where they still have judicial powers, and given a preliminary hearing, at which the person arrested is charged. If the justice thinks the evidence justifies holding the accused for trial, he is put into jail or allowed freedom on *bail* pending action by the *trial court,* usually known as the county court, which has jurisdiction over all crimes. In case the criminal action was minor such as a traffic violation or disorderly conduct the justice of the peace holds a *summary trial,* in which the case is heard and determined by the justice who can dismiss the case, fine the culprit, or send him to the local "lock-up" or "hoosegow" for a short jail sentence. If the case is not minor, an *indictment* is presented by the prosecuting or district attorney, usually an elective official of the county, to the *grand jury*

[1] Bruce Smith, *Police Systems in the United States,* revised edition (Harper & Brothers, 1949), p. 22.

which decides whether the accused shall be held for trial, and if so, returns a *true bill*. The grand jury may also initiate its own inquiries into situations that may bring persons to trial, or the district attorney may draw up an *information* and present it directly to the trial court. Then comes the *arraignment* where the accused is given the opportunity to plead guilty or not guilty. If the plea is guilty, the judge sentences. If the plea is "not guilty," the *trial by jury* is held. If the jury finds the person not guilty, he is released and cannot again be tried for the same crime. If the jury finds him guilty, he is sentenced by the judge according to the limits imposed by state law. If the sentence is imprisonment, the convicted person is incarcerated in a state penitentiary or a county jail from which on good behavior he may be released or put on *parole* before his full sentence is served. Or the court may put him on *probation,* not sending him to prison but putting him under supervision in an attempt to achieve rehabilitation without jail sentence.

Crime in the United States

It is generally agreed that crime in the United States is a social problem of front rank. Crime is becoming more baffling and better organized as our great metropolitan areas develop, as rapid transportation allows criminals to escape more easily across the boundaries of local jurisdictions, and as the increase of wealth brings more valuable things in the open. Crime in the United States is a greater problem than in the older countries of Western Europe. It may be that this condition is the result of general social and economic instability and unrest that is characteristic of a new, vigorous nation. Be that as it may, it is of staggering proportions. Bruce Smith estimates that larcenies approach one million annually, burglaries one-third of a million, auto thefts about 200,000, while homicide, rape, assault with gun and knife, and robbery account for 80,000 crimes of major seriousness. These figures, large as they are, do not include felonies and misdemeanors such as embezzlement, fraud, forgery, counterfeiting, violation of narcotic and liquor laws, gambling, motor vehicle violations, and many others that are heavy burdens on police agencies but may not seriously undermine community life.[2]

Urban crime rates are generally higher than those in rural areas. This may be explained by the congested manner of living, the anonymity of the large floating population, and the temptation to commit crimes that come from the display of valuable goods. Larceny is four times as great in urban than in rural places. For murder, manslaughter, negligent homicide (motor vehicle fatalities), and rape, the rural crime rate equals the urban. Larger cities have higher crime rates. So do states south of the Mason-Dixon line and west of the Rockies. Aggravated crimes are lower in winter and higher in summer. Crimes against property are higher in winter, traffic accidents are higher in early fall and winter. The days of most crime are Saturday and Sunday.

About 80 per cent of reportable crimes against the person are cleared by police action, but only 40 per cent of robberies, 30 to 35 per cent of burglaries, 30 per cent of auto thefts, and 20 to 25 per cent of miscellaneous larcenies. Between 55 to 65 per cent of the defendants are convicted for crimes against the persons, about 70 to 85 per cent of the defendants in cases of robbery, burglary, motor theft, and larceny. An astounding 10 per cent of the entire population is arrested or summoned by the police each year. Five-sixths of these are for traffic violations, drunkenness, and disorderly conduct. Men outnumber women in being arrested by 12 to 1. The ages from 18 to 30 mark the crest of criminal activity, the high peak being from 19 to 25 years with a marked falling off after 35 years of age. Youth is high in robbery but low in assaults, narcotics, fraud, embezzlement, liquor violations, nonsupport, drunken driving, and gambling. One-fourth of those dealt with for robbery are youths.

The rates of crime for native born whites is double that of foreign born whites, and that of Negroes is six times that of foreign born whites. Excessive criminality on the part of the second generation aliens is generally accepted as fact but not easily proved. The rate is low when people live in foreign colonies, and higher as they mix,

[2] *Ibid.*, p. 32.

leaving the possibility that crime may relate to contacts with delinquency and to a conflict of standards of living. The arrest rate for Negroes is highest of all racial groups, they show especially high proclivities toward homicide, assault, drunkenness, gambling, and concealed weapons. But no matter what the statistics show, police know that communities with a large proportion of Negroes, foreign-born, and persons of foreign parentage elements are troublesome from the viewpoint of law and order. Recidivists, those arrested and fingerprinted before, make up about 55 per cent of the arrests. Repeaters are highest in narcotics violations, forgery, counterfeiting, embezzlement, fraud, and robbery. More than 400,000 annual repeaters are distributed throughout all levels of crime.

No one actually knows how much crime costs the nation, but some estimates run as high as $15 billion. The average value of property stolen per case is $750 in auto theft, $200 in robbery, $125 in burglary, and $60 in small larceny. "Fences," those who traffic in stolen property, take a large toll from the seller of stolen goods. The youth who steals not for a regular livelihood but in order to have money for conspicuous spending is a most common offender. Nine out of every ten stolen autos are returned, but only about one-fourth of other property.[3]

Major crime reached an all-time high in the United States in 1953. The urban and rural crimes per 100,000 population were as follows:[4]

	Urban	Rural
Murder; nonnegligent manslaughter	2.35	2.34
Manslaughter by negligence	1.72	2.52
Rape	5.76	6.22
Robbery	30.1	9.1
Aggravated Assault	40.4	18.2
Burglary	200.5	99.5
Larceny	477.6	136.8
Auto Theft	96.1	29.8

The Pacific states had the highest crime rate for robbery, burglary, larceny, and auto theft. Alabama, Kentucky, Mississippi, and Ten-

[3] *Ibid.*, pp. 34–57.
[4] *Municipal Year Book 1954*, p. 423.

nessee exceeded all others in murder. The New England states ranked lowest in all crime rates.

Uniform Crime Reports are the basic and primary source of data concerning crimes and police operations in the United States today, its territories and possessions. They are collected, assembled, and analyzed by the Federal Bureau of Investigation from local police departments. The International Association of Chiefs of Police with the aid of a Committee on Uniform Crime Records cooperated in the development of a new classification of offenses and a general organization of this service which began in 1930.

Rural Peace Officers

Officers for keeping the peace in rural areas are the sheriff and the constable who have come down through the years from earliest England. While in England sheriffs have become little more than court officers, and the constable has disappeared altogether, those officers were important in the 19th century in rural America, especially in the frontier regions, although whenever urban conditions prevailed they gave way to the more highly organized uniformed police agencies. In America, central control over these officers was eliminated as they became elective. Being elective officials naturally brought them in politics and thus it has become difficult to trim their powers because of their influence with the county political machines and the legislators.

The sheriff is found in all counties within the United States and is, except for a very few instances, an elective official. In fact, many state constitutions require his election. He is thus an independent official, subject to no superior officer, although his duties are usually prescribed in detail by statute. He needs no particular qualifications that might apply to the job of maintaining law and order. A study of the office made in Indiana in 1935 showed the typical sheriff to be "a married man, forty-eight years of age; he did not attend school beyond the eighth grade; his previous occupation was farming; he has been a sheriff not more than three years; he did not have any previous law enforcement experience. His annual salary is approximately $1,700 a year and he is certain he will lose his job if the political party in power is defeated." [5]

But there are many counties in which the sheriff is well compensated. While he may or may not receive a basic salary, he relies heavily upon fees he receives for the performance of nearly every official act. These fees are prescribed by state law. His most important duties being to act as an officer of the county court both in its civil and criminal capacities, he serves writs and processes, executes court decrees, serves election notices, attends courts, keeps the county jail, feeds the prisoners, and has many other duties not directly connected with law enforcement. He receives a liberal allowance for transporting prisoners from county jail to state penitentiaries or from their place of capture to the county jail. In the more populous counties, his salary may range as high as $15,000 annually, but the total take of his office has in some instances reached $100,000. However, where fees are collected the sheriff is obligated to pay from them the costs of his office including the salaries of deputies and clerks. The office of sheriff is still considered to be one of the most lucrative of local offices in most localities.

As a police officer, the sheriff has not, in most counties, kept pace with modern conditions. His period of greatness in the United States was in the frontier days when he spearheaded the fight against lawless elements that came into the new country. His fame still is preserved in moving pictures and comic books. Here he is a two-gun man, a hard rider, a dedicated enemy of the cattle and horse thief, the stage hold-up man, and all the other variegated threats to law and order that flourished on the American frontier. But those days are gone, perhaps forever. He has been left behind, even in the West, by the FBI, the state police, and the city police departments. Nevertheless, he still has the powers of a police officer, and can call together a *posse comitatus* from among the citizenry to pursue wrongdoers. This power is used today only in emergencies. "Viewed as a police agency," says Bruce Smith, "the office is little more than

[5] Quoted in Lane Lancaster, *Government in Rural America*, revised edition (Copyright 1952, D. Van Nostrand Company, Inc.), p. 164, from *Report of the Indiana State Committee on Governmental Economy* (1935), p. 390.

a monument to a historic past." [6] However, in many areas the sheriff is still the most important police office with an almost impossible job to do considering his lack of trained personnel and modern facilities. In some counties, notably the urban counties in which vast hordes of people have migrated over city lines into unincorporated areas, the sheriff's office has been transformed into a modern police department with uniformed officers, traffic regulation equipment, radio cars, records, and all the other appurtenances needed to control crime.

Whereas the sheriff is a county officer, the constable is a peace officer of township, town, borough, and even city wards. Like the sheriff, his law enforcement activities today are few and insignificant. If he does anything at all, he serves writs, processes, and election notices as an agent of the justice of the peace or board of elections. He is an elected official, but in many jurisdictions no one runs for the office. He is paid entirely from fees, except in a very few places, and these fees, unlike those of the sheriff, are not numerous or large. Constables, therefore, have other occupations and act as constables only as a sideline. It was concluded in a survey made in the state of Delaware that "in the age of the telephone and the automobile the office is an anachronism, a historical relic." [7] However, it was not many years ago that the constable acted as the law enforcement officer in most of the small towns and villages of the nation, and even in the early days of the automobile regulated traffic within their jurisdictions. Often, it is true, they raised the ire of motorists caught in their toils and ultimately the organized antagonism of motor clubs. Now, even there the uniformed policeman has taken their place. In some states, the peace officer of small towns and villages is called the marshal. Whatever the name of the village and small town peace officer, many of whom are elected by the people, they are nonprofessional police officers and carry out their duties on an amateur, part-time basis.

[6] *Illinois Crime Survey* (1927), p. 338–339.
[7] C. C. Maxey, *County Administration,* p. 25. See also Raymond Moley, "The Sheriff and the Constable," *The Annals of the American Academy of Political and Social Science* (November, 1929), p. 31.

County police forces have been been established in some of the more populous areas. Sometimes these consist of uniformed police as a part of the sheriff's office, for example in Hamilton county, Ohio, in the area around Cincinnati, and Monroe county, New York, around Rochester. More ambitious is the arrangement in Los Angeles county which has a population of a half million in its unincorporated sections. Here the sheriff heads a staff of deputies and constabulary numbering six hundred with local stations and modern paraphernalia of criminal investigation, records, communication, laboratories, and police science. Special county police forces appointed sometimes by a county board, and sometimes by the governor on the recommendation of the members of the state legislature from the county in question, exist in South Carolina. In Kentucky and Virginia there are some county police patrols appointed by the judge. In Nassau County, New York, adjacent to New York City, the county police unit consists of six hundred and fifty officers and men, and serves a population of one-half million. With the advent of this county police force, the sheriff, constables, and the state police were relieved of police duties in this area. Another type of county police are the parkway police such as are found policing parkways and boulevards of the country around New York City.

Another type of county enforcement officer are the detectives of the district attorney or county prosecutor. Still another are the county "vigilantes" used chiefly in the Middle West during the wave of bank robberies in the 1920's. These were volunteer guards in banks who were given firearms and authority to act in case of a bank hold-up. These were patterned after the vigilante organizations of the 19th century in the cattle country of the West. Such county police units cannot be supported by the average county. On the other hand, metropolitan areas are larger than counties in many cases, and therefore some form of regional cooperation would be more practicable. In the Cincinnati metropolitan areas there are 147 police agencies, each independent of the other but overlapping to some degree. In the Boston area there are 40 cities and towns each with its own police agency; in the Chicago area there are 350 such agencies.[8]

During the past forty years, there has been a phenomenal growth of state police agencies and state highway patrols. In 1914, there were only four states with police agencies: Texas, Pennsylvania, Massachusetts, and Connecticut, the latter two limited in scope. Today, there is a state police agency of some kind in every state in the Union. According to a survey of the International Association of Chiefs of Police, 25 states had state police units invested with general powers in criminal and traffic cases. State police evolution has followed the changing pattern of rural life. The movement to the suburbs has brought large segments of population to semi-rural areas policed only by state police departments. Looking forward into the future, there may be planned dispersion of vital industries outside heavily populated areas to protect them from the threat of atomic attack. This will bring new population and new problems of crime to the urban fringe. The first state police forces and highway patrols were established to maintain law and order in labor conflicts and strikes and later to police state highways. Now they are general law enforcement officers in rural areas, succeeding the sheriff-constable combination.[9]

Urban Police Agencies

According to Chief John M. Gleason of Greenwich, Connecticut, "The attack on crime, accidents and traffic congestion, juvenile delinquency, and other important phases of police operation is the same in cities of two million as in towns of 50,000. There is simply a difference in the extent and sometimes the degree of application of fundamentals generally accepted. But this point must be stressed: the smaller the community, the more personal the entire operation

[8] Smith, *Police Systems in the United States,* revised edition (1949), pp. 75–119.

[9] Edward J. Hickey, "Trends in Rural Police Protection," *The Annals of the American Academy of Political and Social Science* (January, 1954), pp. 22–30. This entire issue is devoted to the subject: "New Goals in Police Management."

becomes." [10] Chief Gleason points out that many smaller police departments have a defeatist attitude and complain that they do not have the resources to do a good job. But there are many central services available to the small city including those of the identification bureau, crime laboratory, and statistics sections of the Federal Bureau of Investigation, and those of the various identification, radio and teletype, motor vehicle bureaus of the state police. Furthermore, in metropolitan areas the services of the central city police department are available; and cooperation with state and national agencies and neighboring units make available modern police communication to all departments, large or small. The National System of Identification of Criminals and Uniform Crime Reporting also links each department to the state and national networks of police agencies. In some aspects, small cities have certain advantages; more personal contacts with citizens, more intimate knowledge of the criminally inclined, better use of motor patrols, and better integration of the police force itself. One of the drawbacks in small jurisdictions is the residence requirement for policemen. "Many a fine police career has come from an out-of-town farm," says Chief Gleason.

In the many localities where there is only one policeman appointed by the mayor or council, there is no problem of organization. This officer is the community's sole representative of law and order and his activities cover the whole range of police work within his abilities and the need. In larger towns and smaller cities where there is a force of eight or ten men, there develops what Bruce Smith calls *subdivision by levels of activity*, that is, higher ranks (chief of police, lieutenant, sergeant) direct the lower ranks (patrolmen). As cities grow, specialization develops—subdivision by kinds of activity. There may be division of duties into headquarters desk duty, patrol and investigation, and traffic regulation. The headquarters group handles communications including police telephone, radio and teletype, records and police blotters, police lock-up and tem-

[10] John M. Gleason, "Policing the Smaller Cities," *Annals* (January, 1954), pp. 14–21.

porary custody of persons held for questioning and preliminary hearing. In larger cities and jurisdictions, there is a further development in supervision: the chief of police; the captains and lieutenants in charge of major activities and groups such as records, patrol, detectives, and traffic; and lieutenants in charge of several platoons of patrolmen. Then comes the time when the police force becomes so large that it has to be *subdivision by areas of activity* and various police districts are established throughout the city. Over the entire patrol force of the city is the inspector, with captains in charge of each district, and lieutenants in charge of each platoon within the district.

In New York City, the patrol force is divided into 84 precincts or police districts. Each is headed by a police captain, who reports to one of 16 division inspectors, who are supervised by five deputy chief inspectors, who are responsible to the chief inspector, who is the immediate subordinate of the police commissioner of New York City. Such arrangements apply also to the detective division, traffic division, and crime prevention division. New York City, with 20,000 on the police force, is unique in its need for decentralized organization. It takes into consideration that the "span of control" of a police administrator must be severely limited or else slipshod and undisciplined police work results. To have eighty-four precinct captains report to the police commissioner would make an impossible situation.

The Chicago police department as reorganized in 1932 set up a director of personnel, chief of traffic, chief of patrol force, chief of detectives, departmental secretary, and the director of the bureau of information and statistics, all reporting directly to the commissioner of police. Each one of these administrators was in charge of a special bureau. Chicago has about 8,500 paid employees.

The police department of the city of Greenwich, Connecticut, serves a municipality of about 40,000 people and an area of 48 square miles. It is almost exclusively a residential town, suburban to New York City. Many of the crimes common to larger and industrial communities are almost unknown in Greenwich, and the major police problems are the control of traffic, the protection of property, and the enforcement of minor regulations of the city. But Greenwich because it is a wealthy community near New York and has many residents who are away from their houses for long periods of time, is particularly susceptible to burglaries. Likewise the city is old and the streets are haphazard and narrow so traffic control is a vital service. The basic organization of the police department are the four divisions: detective, traffic, patrol, and records. Berkeley, California, is a university town, mostly residential. It has well over 100,000 population. The police department is divided into ten divisions: personnel and training, radio, patrol, traffic, reserve, pound, detective, vice, juvenile, and records and jail.[11]

In Wichita, Kansas, the police staff numbers 240. Six captains and a personnel director report to the chief of police. These captains are in charge of the following divisions: crime prevention, traffic, patrol, detective, records, and vice.[12]

The Los Angeles police department is governed by a five-man board of police commissioners, appointed for five years by the mayor and approved by the city council. This board controls the policies of the police department and appoints a chief of police. The following bureaus have been established: personnel and training, technical services, administration, traffic, patrol, corrections, and detective. About 5,400 employees are in the police department.

The 1952 annual report of the Los Angeles police department describes the average police officer as thirty-five years old who has served the city for seven years. He is married and has at least one child of school age. A high school graduate, the chances are even that he has a college education or is presently working to attain a degree. He is a veteran of military service. Out of thirty-three applicants, he was the only one who successfully passed a battery of civil service examinations and a six-month probationary period to become a policeman. He will vie against two thousand fellow officers when he takes another civil service examination in an effort to rise to the rank of sergeant. The average police officer takes home

[11] The International City Managers' Association, *Municipal Police Administration* (Chicago, 1950), pp. 77–86.

[12] Smith, *op. cit.,* Chapter 8, "Organization," pp. 233–271.

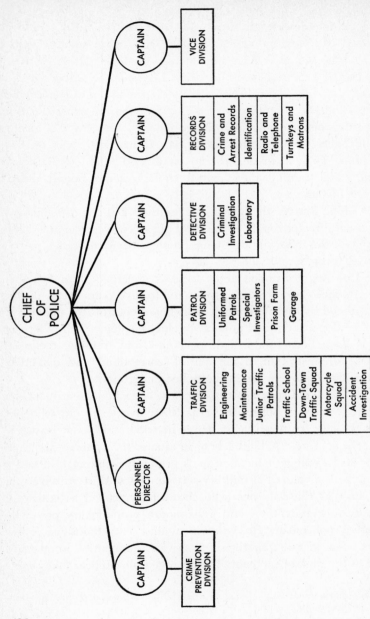

Fig. 18. Organization of the Wichita, Kansas, Police Department. (From Bruce Smith, *Police Systems in the United States*, p. 244.)

approximately $164.15 twice a month, out of which he purchases his uniforms, guns, ammunition, and other equipment. He has a thirty per cent chance of being injured on duty during the year, but he will receive city care for his injuries. Unlike most citizens, his private as well as his public life will be closely regulated but the possibilities are only .004 that he will be found guilty of dishonesty, use of excessive force or abuse of civil rights. In event that he violates the law either while on or off duty, he will be subject to action by the criminal courts, in addition to a police trial board. If he survives odds of better than 100 to 1 and becomes a captain of police, his semi-monthly take-home pay will average $249.96. As a division commander, he may be responsible for the protection of the lives and property of up to one-third million persons.[13]

The urban areas of the United States embrace almost 100 million people and these are protected by 120,000 policemen. The largest single force is New York City with 20,000. For cities over 250,000 population, two and one-third police employees per thousand population is average; but in cities under that figure the ratio is lower, down to one and a third per thousand in smaller cities and large villages. Five-sixths of our cities and towns are below 25,000 population. The average strength of the police department is eight per municipality.

The entrance salary for patrolmen salaries in cities over 10,000 in 1954 ranged from $1,770 to $5,070, the median being $3,350 to $3,900. Maximum salaries were $5,830. Salaries of police chiefs ranged from $2,690 to $18,000.[14] The almost constant increase in police salaries was brought about by the rising cost of living, the need for attracting recruits of superior quality, a desire to retain experienced policemen, and a recognition by politicians of the city employee vote.[15] Recent years have brought a shorter work week, forty to forty-four hours, to most policemen. In virtually all departments, the standard workday is now eight hours. In 952 cities which spent a total of $58 million on police in 1953, more than 90% was for

[13] Los Angeles Police Department, *1952 Annual Report,* pp. 2–10
[14] *The Municipal Year Book 1955,* p. 410.
[15] Bruce Smith, Jr., "The Policeman's Hire," *The Annals* (January, 1954), pp. 119–126.

wages and salaries. Police expenditures per capita averaged $6.77 in cities between 10,000 and 25,000; but in cities over 500,000 they were $11.72.[16]

Police departments are established to carry out certain primary duties in the community. They maintain law and order by persuasion and if necessary by force. Their basic purposes are to prevent crime, to suppress criminal activity, to apprehend criminals, to preserve the peace, to regulate conduct, and to protect life and property. *Patrol activities* are carried on by uniformed police and include moving about a "beat" and observing conditions, controlling public gatherings, inspecting business and commercial establishments after closing hours, answering calls in any kind of emergency such as robbery, accidents, and fire; settling minor complaints, investigating on the spot, preserving physical evidence of crime, arresting offenders, preparing reports, and testifying in court. A patrolman should be able to give first aid, should know his beat and the people in it, and be ready for anything. The most common and oldest patrol is the foot patrol. In recent years, however, automobile patrol has been becoming standard. The auto patrol covers a greater area at less expense, can overtake offenders in automobiles, can respond to emergency calls with speed, and with a two-way radio can keep in constant touch with headquarters. The automobile also allows the patrol to carry extra equipment and heavier firearms. Foot patrols are still necessary for such functions as the inspection of business places. It is generally agreed that a one-man auto patrol is preferable to a two-man patrol. It gives greater patrol coverage for the same number of men, it is safer for the police, and has been found to be more efficient.

Police must *investigate crimes*. The requirements of criminal investigation in medium and large cities demand that there be a detective division whose members are not in uniform. Most crimes are solved by intelligence, hard work, and information. A detective seeks "the facts," analyzes them, and tries to use them to apprehend the offender and solve the crime. A modern police department is equipped with many scientific and technical aids: chemistry, micros-

[16] *The Municipal Year Book 1955,* p. 412.

copy, photography, medical knowledge, impression casts, criminal records, fingerprinting, lie detectors, and even psychiatry. Auxiliary to the larger police forces is a corps of specialists who are brought into cases which require expert assistance.

The enforcement of laws relating to gambling, prostitution, narcotics, and liquor is known as *vice control*. Vice operations are often highly organized because of the large potential profits in such illicit activities. As the televised investigations of the United States Senate conducted in 1950 and 1951 by the Kefauver Committee indicated, organized vice crosses local, state, and even national boundaries and cooperation of law enforcement agencies at all levels is necessary to control the operations of the "underworld." Because of rapid transit and communications, vice in Chicago or Detroit cannot be controlled solely by the police departments in those cities. The tremendous profits of vice are used to corrupt the government and enforcement officials where possible. When the underworld has partners in government itself, suppression of organized crime is almost an impossibility and an electoral revolution at the polls is often necessary to "clean up the mess." For many years, organized crime has been a major factor in political and governmental life in many cities, and in all larger places is a problem of significant proportions. Vice squads which specialize in various forms of vice control are common in larger cities, but the efforts of patrolmen and detectives are always basic. The Kefauver Committee reported that there was evidence of corruption and connivance with organized crime in state and local government, and was present in four different forms: (1) direct bribe or protection payments; (2) political influence to protect criminal activities; (3) law enforcement officials found with unusual and unexplained wealth; and (4) law enforcement officials participating directly in organized crime.[17]

The national concern with *juvenile delinquency* has focused attention on another general task of the local police department. In most states, a juvenile for the purposes of criminal prosecution is

[17] *National Municipal Review* (July, 1951), "Crime Up to States and Cities," pp. 254–359, being excerpts from *Third Interim Report of the Special Committee to Investigate Organized Crime in Interstate Commerce, United States Senate.*

under 17 or 18 years of age and may receive special treatment in the courts, the object being rehabilitation rather than punishment. Many police departments have established juvenile delinquency bureaus to help communitywide campaigns to control this growing menace. For juvenile delinquency is more than a police problem, it is a community problem and the cooperation of schools, welfare agencies, health agencies, and others are needed. The role of the police in the prevention of juvenile delinquency is to keep watch

---

CITY DEPARTMENT OF POLICE AT WORK

An over-all view of the work of a department of police in a large city is furnished by the 1954 report of the police commissioner of the city of Philadelphia. The department had 4,569 uniformed and plain-clothed police men and women, 638 school crossing guards, and 1,062 reserves. The statistical record for 1953 was as follows: 259 manslaughters and murders, 93% cleared up by arrest; 2,948 robberies, 33% cleared up by arrests; 2,198 aggravated assaults, 86% cleared up by arrests; 444 statutory offenses, 61% cleared up by arrests; 12,256 burglaries, 17% cleared up by arrests; 16,602 larcenies, 15% cleared up by arrests; 4,549 autos stolen, 32% cleared up by arrests and 75% of the cars returned; 84,722 arrests for all other felonies and misdemeanors. The police service budget amounted to $22.6 million, of which $21 million was for personal services. Incidentally, 15,763 sick persons were assisted by the police; 1,658 residents left their doors unlocked; 2,216 dogs bit people and police stepped in; 1,468 people were accidentally hurt and police assisted; and 393 persons attempted suicide and police went to their aid, saving many of them.

From "Today's World" in *The Philadelphia Inquirer* (March 24, 1955), p. 3.

---

and report on conditions that constitute a danger to the community, to investigate offenses committed by juveniles and offenses committed by adults on juveniles, to help organize healthful juvenile activities in the community, and to help in the adjustment of a pre-delinquent or delinquent youngster. Members of the juvenile delinquency bureau should be qualified to specialize in juvenile problems rather than in regular police work.

Traffic regulation is the most important single function of police departments today in terms of manpower and money expended. The traffic problem is broader than police supervision. Police agencies are only part of vast network involved in traffic control. The President's Highway Safety Conference projected three fields of action. These were engineering, education, and enforcement which were expanded in eight major areas of activity: laws and ordinances, accident records, education, enforcement, engineering, motor vehicle administration, organized public support, and public information. The President's Highway Safety Conference defines traffic supervision of the police. First, it involves *directing traffic*—answering questions, telling motorists and pedestrians what to do, and making emergency rules for the flow of traffic. Second, it means *investigating accidents*—giving first aid, protecting the scene from pile-ups, finding out what happened, and reporting facts and conclusions to headquarters. Third, it includes *traffic enforcement*—detecting and remedying defects in driver behavior and equipment, starting appropriate action to prevent traffic congestion from such defects, and helping in the trial and punishment of traffic violators.[18]

The Court System

Once the offender is apprehended and arrested by police or other law enforcement officers, he is brought before the courts for trial. The first level of courts is known as the minor judiciary, the members of which are variously known as justices of the peace, magistrates, recorders, aldermen, and others. These courts are not courts of record and the judges are not trained in the law. Generally their jurisdiction is limited to cases wherein the maximum sentence is thirty days or $100 or $200 fine. State law provides for the precise areas in which these courts may act. They are elected by the people of townships, boroughs, villages, and sometimes wards of cities. For the most part they are part-time dispensers of justice and are paid by fees derived from the cases they hear. In larger cities, these justices may be on a salary basis, may be trained in the law, and work full-time at their duties.

These minor courts have two general responsibilities. First, they hear and determine minor criminal cases. Their precise jurisdiction

[18] International City Managers' Association, *Municipal Police Administration* (1950), pp. 285–286.

in this regard is outlined in state law. Such cases include traffic violations, violations of local ordinances, and breaches of the peace such as being drunk and disorderly, and other criminal actions in which the fine is not higher than one or two hundred dollars. Sometimes, penalties imposed may include a limited jail sentence. Always the defendant has the right to appeal his sentence to the higher court.

Second, the minor courts are empowered to hold preliminary hearings in cases of more serious crimes. At these hearings, only the evidence or testimony against the accused may be presented. At this stage, lawyers often advise their clients to say nothing. After the judge hears the case, he may dismiss it for want of evidence and the person arrested may go free. Or he may hold him for trial, either by sending him to jail or allowing him to go free by putting up bail as a guarantee that he will not leave the jurisdiction before he is slated for trial.

While the system of minor courts was fairly adequate for the rural and small town conditions of the 19th century, they are totally outmoded for the judicial business in industrial, urban, and congested areas. Many of them do little or no business. In fact, in many jurisdictions no persons can be found to run for the office. In a study made in Michigan in 1932, it was found that in six counties having 290 justices of the peace, 269 did no business at all. The other 21 justices did all the business in those counties outside of the cities.[19]

A study in Pennsylvania revealed that only 71 per cent of the total number of justices elected in the six-year period ending 1939 were actually commissioned. The average age for the justices in office in 1940 was 50, and their average term of office was slightly over six years, which is the length of one term. Justices came from many occupations: laborer or unskilled workers, 17 per cent; farmers, 12 per cent; skilled laborers, 11 per cent; merchants, 8 per cent;

---

[19] Maxine Boord Virtue, "Improving the Structure of the Courts," *The Annals of the American Academy of Political and Social Science* (May, 1953), p. 142. This entire issue is devoted to the topic: "Judicial Administration and Common Man."

clerks, 7 per cent; real estate and insurance, 6 per cent; and those who listed as their occupations "justice of the peace," 21 per cent. Also there were retired persons, housewives, salesmen, and others.

Out of 27,000 cases heard by justices in 60 Pennsylvania counties in 1940, 25 per cent were offenses against property, 18 per cent offenses against persons, 16 per cent motor vehicle violations, 13 per cent offenses against public peace, 11 per cent offenses against public policy, economy, and health; 10 per cent involved family relationships; 4 per cent offenses against public morals and decency; and 2 per cent were unclassified. From questionnaires received from about 300 justices, 7 per cent had no formal education, 42 per cent went as far as grammar school, 25 per cent finished high school, and 25 per cent went for some period to college or business school. From the same questionnaires, 20 per cent of the justices said that they devoted full time to their judicial duties, 14 per cent about half-time, and the rest indicated that they were concerned only occasionally with their judicial duties. Most of the justices had relatively few cases, the average justice had only about 20 cases a year, and 23 per cent had no cases at all in 1940, while 29 per cent had ten or less.[20]

Many criticisms have been leveled at the justice of the peace system. One of the cardinal defects is the fee system, although most states still cling to it.[21] The fee system is criticized because it causes delays and adjournments, allowing justices to earn unwarranted fees, because it encourages fee splitting with the arresting officers, because justices hold court when their compensation depends upon fees from convictions, and because the income is low and uncertain to the point that there is no incentive for capable men to aspire to the office. Frequently the charge has been made that justices are

[20] Pennsylvania Bar Association and Institute of Local Government, The Pennsylvania State College, *Survey of the Minor Judiciary in Pennsylvania* (1942).

[21] Among the states to abandon the fee system completely are Arizona, Nevada, Florida, and Virginia, while Louisiana and South Carolina have abandoned it for criminal cases.

not completely impartial. The initials J. P. are said to mean "justice for the plaintiff," according to some critics. Arresting officers usually have a choice of justices before whom they can bring their cases, and they are likely to evade those justices who do not see things their way. A study of Mississippi justices' courts revealed in 98 per cent of the cases judgments were rendered in favor of the plaintiff.[22] A study of 25,000 cases in Tennessee revealed that 98 per cent of the cases in the justices' courts were decided in favor of the plaintiffs.[23] The same situation was found in Michigan, New York, and Illinois, although in Ohio the defendants in criminal cases were successful in 21% of them. In the present fee system, a justice is at the mercy of the plaintiffs and the arresting officers for his revenue and must satisfy them if he expects future business. Other defects of the justice of the peace system are that incumbents lack legal training, and that there is no supervision, and that the records of the office are inadequate. But there are also advantages. The justices of the peace courts, are courts of the people. They are not overburdened with legal technicalities and at their best reflect the opinion and will of the community which elects them. Regardless of the quality of justice dispensed, justices' courts are speedy, accessible, and can be reached at hours when no other court is open. And they are low in cost, a survey in Tennessee revealed an average of $3.55 a court case, and surveys in other states reveal relative low costs per case.

Proposals for reform and changes in the justice of the peace system cover a wide range. They include outright abolition of the justices and a transfer of their duties to full-time salaried judges trained in the law in a district court larger in size than a township, under the supervision of the general trial court of the county. They include also proposals for a reduction in the number and a consolidation of the work in fewer offices, the abolition of fees for annual salaries, in-service training of justices, stripping them from their power as trial judges, and closer supervision of their work by the county courts. Radical changes are difficult because in all but a few

[22] P. S. Sikes, "Judicial Administration in Mississippi," *Mississippi Law Journal* (December, 1933), pp. 109–132.

[23] T. L. Howard, "The Justice of the Peace System in Tennessee," *Tennessee Law Review* (December, 1934), pp. 6–8.

states the justices are constitutional officers. Furthermore, they are politically influential in state legislatures and have been able to combat successfully many attempts to change their prerogatives and manner of doing things.

Whatever usefulness the office has in rural areas, it has proven inadequate in urban and metropolitan places because of the complexity of criminal justice and the concentration of population. Untrained, part-time, fee-paid justices simply cannot do the work required. Many of the city magistrates are full-time, trained in the law, and on a salary basis. Furthermore, new and special types of courts have been established to take care of the heavy load in a more practical and efficient way than the ordinary justices' courts. A notable example is the municipal court of Philadelphia established by the state legislature in 1913. The court consists of a president judge and one associate judge for each 200,000 population elected by the people for ten-year terms. They are paid by salary, are learned in the law, and are clothed not only with the powers of the justice of the peace, but in addition have broader powers. The court has five divisions: civil, criminal, juvenile, domestic relations, and misdemeanants. The criminal jurisdiction of the municipal court extends in all criminal actions and suits for penalties, except in the trial of indictments for the major and graver crimes. It has exclusive jurisdiction in all proceedings concerning neglected, delinquent, and dependent children under 18 years of age, except in case of murder. It has exclusive jurisdiction also over cases of desertion and nonsupport. The misdemeanants division is concerned with trials of charges of disorderly conduct, drunkenness, and other such matters. It is sometimes known as the "morals court" of Philadelphia. The municipal court in Philadelphia is an example of an attempt to bring the legal machinery of a great city to a point where it is able to meet the complicated problems of criminal justice under urban conditions. It occupies a middle ground between the lower justices courts, called magistrates in Philadelphia, and the trial courts of quarter sessions. Emphasis is laid on informal procedures to attain adjustment and rehabilitation. It is a unified system in which legal justice and social problems are brought into focus as they apply to individuals charged with crime.[24] In many cities, there are special juvenile, traffic, morals, and other courts in which trained judges and staff attempt to administer justice in speedy and fair procedures.

After arrest and the preliminary hearing by a justice of the peace or magistrate comes the next step in the process of criminal justice. This is the indictment or accusation by information. If a grand jury is functioning, the case is brought to its attention by the prosecuting officer in a secret session in which testimony in behalf of the accused is not heard. The grand jury is a body of from seven to twenty-three persons taken from the body of citizens by the process of nomination and drawing by lot. They consider the evidence against the accused and if this evidence, if uncontradicted, would result in conviction, the grand jury hands down a "true bill." If a true bill is found, the accused is scheduled for trial in the next session of the court. This ancient method of indictment has been challenged in about half the states by the method of information which is brought to the trial court directly by the prosecuting attorney upon oath on the basis of evidence received from private persons or law enforcement officers. It sets the machinery of trial in motion. But in all cases the grand jury may be used as an alternative method. Conceded that the process of information may ultimately supersede the grand jury as a routine method of accusation, the grand jury as representative of the community can still be called by the judge or by petition of residents and may open up investigation of crime without any specific charge. The Kefauver Committee said: "The grand jury is the traditional organ of law enforcement charged with the responsibility of uncovering corruption in government and misfeasance and nonfeasance in office of public officials."

The prosecuting attorney, known variously as prosecutor, state's attorney, or district attorney, is usually a county official elected by the people and paid in most states from county funds. Outside of the judge he is the most important unit in the process of law enforcement. He decides who shall be prosecuted by the state and brought

[24] Tanger, Alderfer, and McGeary, *Pennsylvania Government, State and Local* (1950), pp. 141–157.

to trial. Even where the grand jury acts, it takes his recommendations to a great extent for he has the staff of deputies and detectives
to collect and assemble evidence in the case. Furthermore, he conducts the trial against the accused and is responsible to a great degree as to the outcome in terms of conviction, dismissal, or compromise. The office is often sought by younger members of the bar
who view it as a stepping stone to higher political or judicial preferment. This office has provided such preferment for hundreds of
important political leaders including Governor Dewey of New York,
Senator Hiram Johnson of California, Senator Robert La Follette
and his son Phil of Wisconsin, and Governor Earl Warren of California. A study of 767 lawyer governors and members of Congress
shows that forty-two per cent had been prosecuting attorneys most
of them holding the office at the beginning of their political
careers.[25]

The trial court in all states is the most important institution of
criminal justice. Here the accused stands trial, the prosecutor presents evidence designed to convict him, the accused person's lawyer
strives to prove his innocence of the charge, the judge presides over
the battle of wits and enforces legal rules and regulations according
to law, the jury of twelve decide on the guilt of the accused, and the
judge sentences according to law. The trial is an exceedingly complicated procedure and important trials may run for weeks and
months. As Judge Curtis Bok says: "The courts were once the country's greatest theatre. People came from miles around and hung on
every syllable as the lawyers talked for days. Happy was he who
could sit in the jury box and be directly thundered at." [26] The right
of trial by jury exists in the Constitution of the United States and in
the constitutions of the states, and stems directly from the common
law of England. Any politician who would attempt to abolish it
would last only as long as his next election. But jury trials are becoming of less importance. In certain states, juries are used infre-

[25] J. A. Fairlie and C. M. Kneier, *County Government and Administration*
(1930), p. 252.

[26] Curtis Bok, "The Jury System in America," *Annals* (May, 1953), pp.
92–93.

quently. The jury is now used mostly in criminal cases, and 75 to 80 per cent of civil cases using jury are accident cases.[27] As long as the people retain the *right* of trial by jury, if they desire it, it is possible to explore avenues for the improvement of procedure in the trial court. Grand and coroner's juries seem to have reached the end of their usefulness. Some observers feel that majority verdicts of trial juries, rather than unanimous verdicts, should be possible. The rules of evidence should be liberalized.

The judge of the county court, whatever happens to be the name of the court in a particular state, is the apex of the local system of law enforcement. Most judges are elected by the people but, in certain states, some are appointed by the governor or the legislature. Raymond Moley says: "Considering what the sovereign democracy compels its judges to suffer, it is served better than it deserves. American state trial judges are, in spite of unfortunate exceptions, a hopeful group of public servants. The observer, as he goes from state to state, comes to recognize that, in character and common sense, judges are the best of those in public life." [28]

Other local officials have to do with law enforcement and criminal justice. The coroner, a county official usually elected by the people, inquires into the causes of death of a violent or suspicious character, or where the deceased had no medical attention before death. If he suspects foul play, he may summon a jury, seize evidence, and aid in the apprehension of the criminal. Often coroners are paid by fees. Often, too, they have no medical qualifications and cannot live up to the responsibilities of their office especially where the crime rate is high. A good coroner should be to some degree at least a medico-legal expert. Abolition of the coroner and substitution of a trained medical examiner has been put forward as a needed reform. In some states, the powers of coroner have been given to the prosecuting attorney. In some states, counties may have public defenders who take cases in behalf of persons charged with crime who cannot afford to hire a lawyer.

[27] *Ibid.,* p. 92.
[28] Raymond Moley, *Our Criminal Courts* (G. P. Putnam's, 1930), pp. 256–257.

There are usually a number of court officers such as the clerk of courts, prothonotary, surrogate, register of wills, sheriff, jury commissioners, court criers, bailiffs, probation and parole officers, sheriff, prison warden, and others who carry on various functions connected with court, sometimes along with other local administrative duties. Some of these officials are elective by the people of the county, others are appointed by the judges of the court or the county commissioners.

When an accused person charged with crime is convicted by the jury and sentenced by the judge, he must carry out the terms of his sentence. Local units of government are charged only with maintenance of city jails and lock-ups used for "overnight guests" awaiting hearing or summary trial in the morning, or for short term offenders convicted of summary and minor charges. The county jail is a more formidable institution usually under the supervision of the sheriff or county jail warden. Its inmates are usually those persons convicted of crimes tried in the county courts but whose terms are not usually longer than ninety days. Sentences for more serious crimes are served in state penitentiaries and, if convicted in federal courts, in United States penitentiaries. The Federal Bureau of Prisons since 1930 has inspected local prisons and jails to determine their fitness for short sentence or held-for-trial federal prisoners. Out of 3,000 prisons inspected, full approval was granted to only 435 and emergency approval for another 365. Less than one per cent rated above 70 on a scale of 100, and not one 90 or more. "Most jails even today contaminate and degrade those confined in them," the bureau reports. "This is inevitable since most of them are squalid and filthy; they are steeped in primitive retributive traditions; they lack adequate facilities to segregate offenders of various types, ages, and degrees of criminality; they permit most inmates, sentenced as well as unsentenced, to remain completely idle a greater part of the time; and they are usually operated by persons who are without qualifications for their tasks." [29]

Many offenders convicted of less serious crimes are given sus-

---

[29] Quoted in Lane Lancaster, *Government in Rural America,* revised edition (1952), p. 202; from *Federal Prisons* (1948), pp. 48–49.

pended sentences, with or without probation. If probation is granted, the offender reports regularly to probation officers supervised by the court while taking his regular place in society. In state and federal prisons, a convicted and imprisoned person may be released under parole supervision before his full sentence is served. Also pardons may be granted, a person with pardon receives full freedom.

Law Enforcement Can Be Improved

Much of the blame for the unsatisfactory condition of law enforcement can be placed upon the constantly changing conditions of American life. Mass immigration, industrialization, urbanization, world wars, international responsibilities, new inventions have kept the nation in a state of flux, and sometimes jitters, during the first half of the 20th century. In fact, American institutions have never been stabilized; they have always been dynamic. As a result, large segments of American population were often off-balance, maladjusted, and insecure. Many people lived lives that were unsettled, subject to terrific stresses and strain. It is small wonder, then, that our crime rate in the United States is high compared with European nations that are much more "set in their ways." High crime rates are characteristic of our kind of society.

But the people of the nation have it in their power to improve conditions; in fact, improvements in organization and technique have been continuously adopted and applied. The challenge of organized crime has brought a counter-challenge, the conflict between good and evil has been going on since the turn of the century. The fight against crime enlists the enthusiasm of citizens and technicians alike. As organized crime rears its head above the everyday scene, there are men and women, organizations and institutions ready to take it on without fear of consequences.

Observers, critics, and experts have studied the American situation and come up with some answers. Many of them are long-term, involving political and economic improvements—effort toward elimination of slums, the mitigation of the evil effects of poverty, the attempt to bring more security into American life. Others have to do with governmental organization and techniques of administration. Of the latter, brief mention is made of a few of the suggestions:

(1) Small police forces, independent, ill-equipped, and untrained, must give way to larger regional units, especially in metropolitan areas.

(2) The elective sheriff, coroner, and constable must be relieved of their law enforcement responsibilities.

(3) Police officers must be trained both before and after entering service. They should be protected against political dismissals.

(4) All police agencies should be equipped with modern equipment, and should take advantage of specialized services and leadership offered by state and national law enforcement agencies.

(5) State police organization, having become recognized law enforcement agencies along state highways and in rural areas, should be constantly strengthened for these responsibilities.

(6) Centralization of police authority at the national and state levels must be opposed, but it is necessary to develop greater cooperation on all three levels. Some state supervision to achieve uniformity in law enforcement policies and methods appears to be needed.

(7) Rates of pay and economic security for law enforcement officers must be on a par with those in business and industry, and in recognition of their special duties.

(8) The minor judiciary must be better trained and equipped for its job of administering criminal justice in localities.

(9) The court system within the state as a whole should be better integrated in order to speed the work of law enforcement, eliminate costly duplication, and raise the morale of law enforcement agencies.

(10) There must be a unified court system in metropolitan areas designed to attain specialization and integration of all institutions within the metropolitan community.[30]

[30] See *Senate Special Committee to Investigate Organized Crime in Interstate Commerce,* Final Report made August 31, 1951. This was the Kefauver Committee which televised its hearings. Also: American Bar Association, *Report of the Commission on Organized Crime* (1951).

TEN SUBJECTS FOR FURTHER STUDY

1. Crime rates in your state.
2. Uniform crime reporting.
3. The organization of the police department in the largest city in your state.
4. The English sheriff—past and present.
5. The minor judiciary in your state.
6. The municipal court of Philadelphia.
7. The state police and local police in your state.
8. State and national organizations of municipal police.
9. The county coroner.
10. The board of police commissioners in Los Angeles.

REFERENCES

The Annals of the American Academy of Political and Social Science, *Crime in the United States,* entire issue, September 1941.

———, *New Goals in Police Management,* entire issue, January 1954.

———, *Judicial Administration and the Common Man,* entire issue, May, 1953.

Children's Bureau, U. S. Department of Health, Education, and Welfare, *Police Services for Juveniles* (Washington, 1954).

Richard S. Childs, "First Civil Service Sheriff," *National Municipal Review,* June 1948, pp. 293–297.

———, "Rubbing Out the Coroners," *National Municipal Review,* November 1950, pp. 494–496.

Jerome Frank, "Something's Wrong with Our Jury System," *Collier's,* December 9, 1950, pp. 28–29, 64–66.

Louis E. Goodman, "In Defense of Our Jury System," *Collier's,* April 21, 1951, pp. 24–25, 45–48.

The International City Managers' Association, *Municipal Police Administration,* fourth edition (Chicago, 1954).

Institute of Public Administration, *The New York Police Survey* (New York, 1952).

International Association of Chiefs of Police, *Police Unions and Other Police Organizations* (Washington, 1944).

John J. Kelley, "Equipping and Using a Mobile Crime Laboratory," Federal Bureau of Investigation, *FBI Law Enforcement Bulletin,* May 1955, pp. 12–15.

V. A. Leonard, *Police Organization and Management* (Brooklyn, 1951).

D. E. J. MacNamera, "American Police Administration at Mid-Century," *Public Administration Review,* Summer 1950, pp. 181–189.

Arthur C. Millspaugh, *Local Democracy and Crime Control,* The Brookings Institution (Baltimore, 1936).

Raymond Moley, *Our Criminal Courts* (New York, 1930).

National Municipal League, *Coroners in 1953* (New York, 1954).

——, *Model State Medico-Legal Investigative System* (New York, 1954).

Pennsylvania Bar Association and Institute of Local Government, The Pennsylvania State University, *Survey of the Minor Judiciary in Pennsylvania* (State College, 1942).

Virgil W. Peterson, *Gambling: Should It Be Legalized?* (Springfield, Illinois, 1951).

Public Charities Association, *The Court and Correctional System of the State of Pennsylvania* (Philadelphia, 1949).

Bruce Smith, *Police Systems in the United States* (New York, 1949).

Ralph R. Temple, "What Ails County Justice," *National Municipal Review,* July 1947, pp. 376–381.

B. Clyde Vedder, *The Juvenile Offender* (Garden City, New York, 1954).

August Vollmer, *The Criminal* (New York, 1949).

——, *The Police and Modern Society,* University of California (Berkeley, 1936).

O. W. Wilson, *Distribution of Police Patrol Force,* Public Administration Service, No. 74 (Chicago, 1941).

——, *Police Administration* (New York, 1950).

——, "Put the Cop Back on the Beat," *Public Management,* June 1955, pp. 121–125.

——, "Police Administration Developments in 1954," *The Municipal Year Book 1955,* pp. 403–431.

Chapter 12

TRAFFIC CONTROL

The United States has been described as a "nation on wheels." By the end of 1954, there were more than 58 million motor vehicle registrations, of which almost 10 million were trucks. This is an increase of 66 per cent over the World War II peak. Traffic deaths in 1954 reached 36,300; nonfatal injuries totaled 1,250,000; total economic losses were estimated at more than $4 billion. The death rate of 6.5 per 100 million vehicle miles traveled was an all-time low—one sign of improvement in the traffic situation. The United Bureau of Public Roads estimates that motor vehicle registrations will be 81 million by 1965, and that 814 billion miles will be traveled in that year.[1]

In 1953, an aggregate of $5.5 billion was spent for highway purposes by all levels of government. Two-thirds of this amount was for construction. Yet it is generally agreed that tremendous amounts of money must still be spent in order to modernize the nation's road and street system. The importance of doing this was highlighted by President Eisenhower's bold $101 billion road construction proposal made in 1955 to Congress which called for a ten-year, joint national-state-local program of road construction.

Traffic control, therefore, is a function of extraordinary importance

[1] Franklin M. Kreml, "Traffic Administration—Developments in 1954," *The Municipal Year Book 1955*, p. 535. In 1954, traffic deaths figures were announced at 36,300 by the National Safety Council. This is a 5 per cent reduction over 1953 and compares favorably with the 1941 all-time high of 39,969. The number of motor vehicles on the streets and roads jumped from 35 million in 1941 to 58 million in 1954. Vehicle miles traveled increased from 333 billion in 1941 to 557 billion in 1954.

to American life. In urban areas, it is almost entirely locally administered but guided by state law and regulations. In rural areas, it has become almost entirely a state function carried on by state police or highway patrols. It is significant that the trend in traffic accidents has been slowly shifting from urban to rural areas. In urban areas, the problem is one of traffic accident prevention and traffic facilitation, while in rural areas the major problem is still that of traffic safety.[2]

Traffic safety is a national problem of major proportions today. Although the national government has little or no legal responsibility in this field, it has recognized its importance and is trying to coordinate the efforts of state and local governments as well as those of private agencies such as national automobile and safety organizations. Such conferences as the President's Highway Safety Conference have spotlighted for national attention the problems of highway safety and the possibilities for joint effort through an Action Program.[3]

Traffic experts have evolved a comprehensive program to improve traffic control and to increase traffic safety. It is based upon the three E's—engineering, education, and enforcement—and embraces eight areas: laws and ordinances, accident records, education, enforcement, engineering, motor vehicle administration, organized public support, and public information. Responsibility for traffic safety must be allocated between states and local units, between police and other official agencies, and between official agencies and private organizations. No one agency can do all that is needed. It is a task requiring a high degree of cooperation and coordination.

Laws and Ordinances

Ever since the advent of the motor vehicle during the first years of the present century, states have been trying to legislate a body of law that will control automotive traffic. State motor vehicle codes and local ordinances regulate in detail the manner in which motor

[2] *The Book of the States 1954–55*, p. 276.
[3] President's Highway Safety Conference, *Priorities in the Action Program*.

vehicles can be driven, the persons allowed to drive, their driving qualifications, the condition of their motor vehicles, traffic signs and signals, speed limits and their enforcement, the duties of police officers in traffic, and a host of other vehicular items. Of course, each state has the right to make its own laws, and within the restrictions of state law each municipality may pass traffic ordinaries to apply within its borders. In the beginning of traffic regulation, there was a minimum of uniformity between states and between municipalities within states. Drivers were often confused and safety was jeopardized by the variegated regulations and their enforcement. In order to stimulate uniformity of traffic regulation throughout the nation, the National Committee on Uniform Traffic Laws and Ordinances, composed of experts from all areas of traffic activity, developed the Uniform Vehicle Code for states and the Model Traffic Ordinance for municipalities. Gradually the states are comparing their own motor vehicle code to the Uniform Code and bringing them into conformity with one or more of the five acts: (I) administration, registration, and certificate of title; (II) driver licensing; (III) financial liability; (IV) safety responsibility; and (V) rule of the road. Many municipalities have adopted the whole or parts of the Model Traffic Ordinance.

Frank Kreml (Northwestern University), nationally recognized traffic expert, says: "Adoption of the Uniform Vehicle Code has been quite general. We have, in fact, a substantial degree of uniformity, particularly in rules of the road (Act V of the Code), throughout the United States. The Model Traffic Ordinance has been widely adopted by municipalities. Among the states, rules of the road differ mainly in legal speed limits. . . . Much sharper differences between the several states in sizes, weights, loads, and the related vehicle licensing laws place a real burden upon enforcement and have deep economic implications. Suffice it to say that a closer approach to uniformity in this important area is essential to the sound development of highway transportation. Failure of most of our states to meet the driver licensing standards of Act II of the Uniform Vehicle Code is a real impediment to safety. The issue is not lack of uniformity, but rather the enactment of substandard legislation, which, in fact, amounts to no driver licensing of the quality intended by the National Committee on Uniform Traffic Laws and Ordinances. This places an unreasonable burden of enforcement upon the police and the courts." [4] The Council of State Government says: "The public is and has been overwhelmingly in favor of more uniform traffic laws, but action to attain uniformity has been lagging." It stresses the need to require city ordinances on traffic to conform to state and national standards. Within almost all the states, committees on traffic, leagues of municipalities, and other organizations are working towards such conformity so that uniform regulation in the near future will be the rule rather than the exception.

Accident Records

In order to improve traffic conditions, the recording and analysis of traffic accidents is basic. Accident investigation is conducted to find out what caused the accident, to secure evidence of traffic law violations leading to the accident, and to obtain pertinent engineering and statistical data about the accident. Only when the facts of traffic accidents are known can constructive action be taken to eliminate the causes. Unfortunately, accident investigation and records in most municipalities and states have not kept up with increase of traffic accidents. It is not enough to report accidents, police need to be trained to report them with accuracy and to analyze them. In larger police departments this is a job for a traffic division in which traffic experts can operate, but in smaller jurisdictions such work must be carried on by regular police personnel. Among the elements of a good accident record program are *standard forms* for reporting accidents, *standard monthly summaries,* files that include reports on the basis of location, and *spot maps* of all accidents. The analysis should be continuous to ascertain the high accident locations and the action that should be taken to eliminate the causes. Sometimes, this means better street lighting, improved traffic routing, different signs and signals, more enforcement of speed regulations, or any other

[4] Franklin M. Kreml, *Traffic Law Enforcement,* Traffic Institute, Northwestern University (1952), pp. 10–11.

action. In this way, and in this way only, can the accident rate be reduced.

Traffic Education

During the school year 1953–54, more than ten thousand high schools enrolled 835,000 pupils in driver education courses, while 248 colleges offered some type of traffic education to prepare teachers for future safety work in high schools. Dealers provided 7,300 automobiles for behind-the-wheel instruction. Most state departments of education had staff members stimulating and organizing this type of instruction for teen-agers about ready to apply for their driver's licenses. In addition to driver training, schools are interested in teaching pedestrian and bicycle safety. Safety patrols guard hazardous school crossings.[5]

Traffic education is not only carried on in the schools but is an integral part of the work of traffic police and community organizations. The object is to develop safe driving habits for all drivers and safe walking habits for pedestrians. One recent development that has proved successful is the school for traffic violators. The District of Columbia operates such a school under the supervision of the metropolitan police department. The judges of the municipal court, which has jurisdiction over traffic cases, refers the violator to the school if he is deemed to have been careless or ignorant, and if he appears to be cooperative. Final disposition of his case is postponed for a month and in the meantime he is placed on probation. He then signs up to attend this school for three two-hour sessions on successive Friday nights or Saturday mornings. The violator is told that his final sentence may depend in some measure upon his progress in the class as reflected in the final examination. A final lecture is devoted to courtesy, attitude, and self-discipline as important to good driving.[6]

Community organization is necessary to educate the public in

[5] *The Municipal Year Book 1955*, p. 437.

[6] George D. Neilson, "Firm Traffic Enforcement," *Traffic Quarterly* (April, 1952), pp. 196–202. By courtesy of the *Traffic Quarterly* and the Eno Foundation.

traffic safety. A traffic commission composed of citizens known to be civic minded and interested in the problem of traffic safety, and official representatives of all organizations interested in traffic safety, are found in many communities. The Model Traffic Ordinance says: "It shall be the duty of the traffic commission, and to this end it shall have the authority within the limits of the funds at its disposal, to coordinate traffic matters, to carry on educational activities in traffic matters, and to recommend to the legislative body of the city and to the city traffic engineer, the chief of the traffic division, and other city officials ways and means for improving traffic conditions and the administration and enforcement of traffic regulations." Local safety councils acting as champions of the traffic safety movement are also useful community agencies. They disseminate information, conduct meetings, stimulate action on particular traffic problems, and develop civic unity on traffic measures.[7]

Traffic Enforcement

Judge George Neilson of the municipal court of the District of Columbia says: "If more drivers were punished for violations, there would be fewer accidents. The certainty of the punishment is the important thing. It is perhaps the most vital step in effective handling of the traffic enforcement problem. Drivers who take chances on escaping punishment are encouraged in their careless tendencies by the belief that the odds favor them. As long as the operator believes his chances of being punished, even if he is caught, are slight, he is likely to continue his irresponsible driving. He realizes in the first place he must be apprehended by the police, and by the law of averages it will be impossible for the latter to catch up with him every time. If, and when, they do, the penalty will be a small money fine. So, he reasons, why not take a chance? Of course, this attitude is the result of fallacious reasoning. It overlooks the tragic but nevertheless real fact that the life the driver sooner or later is likely to take may be his own. Every time he violates a traffic law, espe-

---

[7] The International City Managers' Association, *Municipal Police Administration,* fourth edition, pp. 324–326.

THE LOUISVILLE TRAFFIC ORGANIZATION

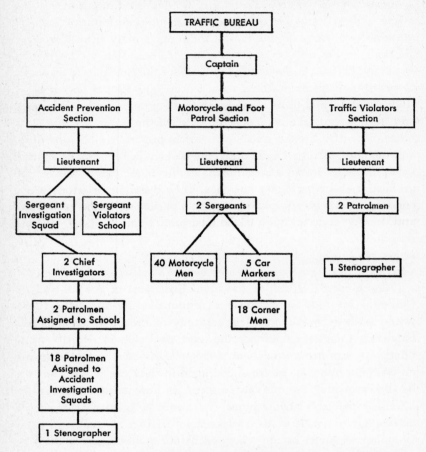

Fig. 19. The Louisville, Kentucky, Traffic Organization. (From International Association of Chiefs of Police and Northwestern University Traffic Safety Institute, *Accident Prevention Bureaus in Municipal Police Departments*, p. 30.)

cially one of those in the category causing most of our highway accidents, he moves one step nearer to his own injury or complete destruction." [8]

[8] Neilson, *op cit.*, pp. 193–194.

Traffic enforcement is largely the responsibility of the police and the courts. One of the basic problems in police organization is the amount of specialization needed for traffic enforcement. Obviously in smaller local units the regular uniformed police must function as traffic officers as well as general police officers. In fact, a growing percentage of the time of the average police officer is being taken up with traffic problems. But as the size of the local unit increases, the volume of traffic and congestion also increase. There are many traffic authorities who believe that specialization in traffic is as necessary as it is in criminal investigation, and that a special traffic division and special traffic officer are required as much as a separate bureau of investigation and detectives. There appears to be no formula by which to determine when a full-scale traffic division is necessary. When the job is big enough and when efficiency can be improved thereby a traffic division should be established no matter what the size of the municipality. The most simple specialization is where the uniformed general police officer handles traffic on the streets as a part of his regular duties, while in headquarters there may be a part-time or full-time police officer concerned with traffic statistics, records, planning, and investigation. In most places the answer has been to insist that the traffic policeman is also a general police officer, although his energies are devoted mostly to traffic, and that general police officers should also have some responsibilities in traffic control. But as the municipality becomes larger, more specialization both in staff and line police officers in the field of traffic appears to be the natural development. Frank Kreml concludes: "Training of the general uniformed forces in most of our city police departments today is such that it would be contrary to the public interest to place this added responsibility (traffic) in their hands. Enforcement quantity and quality would deteriorate rapidly. In most city police departments, the problems of securing adequate reporting and investigating of incidents assigned to the uniformed forces, adequate performance of patrol duties, maintenance of discipline, and similar problems, are still of major administrative concern. With fundamental training and routine supervision essential to the solution of these elemental problems still in the developmental stage, we cannot hope that the much more complicated problems of traffic supervision can yet be turned over to the general uniformed forces with promise of good results. A relatively high degree of police traffic specialization is still required, and probably will be for many years." [9]

The duties of the traffic division where such exists include the keeping of accident and violation records, traffic analysis and direction, traffic patrol and enforcement, and accident investigation. For general traffic patrol, automobiles give the mobility desired. There have been so many injuries from motorcycles that many departments have given them up.

There has been a steady increase in in-service training of police officers in the field of traffic. Led by the Traffic Institute of Northwestern University, many universities and colleges including Harvard, Yale, Purdue, Penn State, and others have been giving specialized traffic courses for police officers. Subjects included in such courses are accident investigation, court procedure, driver training, enforcement, education, engineering, traffic laws, and ordinances. The collective and beneficent results of such efforts over the past three decades have been significant and cumulative. Today, the usefulness of specialized traffic training is generally recognized.[10]

There are four main phases of traffic enforcement. The first is *apprehension,* essentially a police function. It includes all actions in observing, detecting, and preventing violations of traffic law as well as taking appropriate action be it arrest or mere warning to the offender. But it is clear that all violations cannot be spotted or all places covered. This would involve thousands more officers than are available. Therefore, the guiding principle of *selective enforcement* has been evolved. This means that enforcement measures are planned with specific objectives rather than being at random or haphazard. "Selective enforcement," states the Enforcement Report of the 1949 President's Highway Safety Conference, "is enforcement which is proportional to traffic accidents with respect to time, place,

[9] Kreml, *op. cit.,* pp. 15–16.
[10] Shelby Gallien, "Effective Police Traffic Training," *Traffic Quarterly* (October, 1953), pp. 531–539.

and type of violation." From accident records, spot maps and violation data, the traffic administrator finds out what are the hot spots
of traffic trouble, and organizes his enforcement program to reduce
that trouble. He assigns his men to carry out the plan for enforcement as evolved from the analysis of the data. Arrest of violators are
thus made with regard to the volume and type of violation causing
most of the accidents.

Prosecution of traffic violations is carried on by the police themselves in minor cases brought before the minor judiciary. Here are
heard cases involving speeding, failure to stop at stop signs or signals, illegal parking, and other violations of a less serious nature. In
order to get conviction, the police officer must make a clear case.
Many a case has been lost by ineptness in handling the evidence
and facts. Naturally, no one should be allowed the use of the "fix"
for nothing undermines the authority of the police and the courts
so much than preferential treatment for political or monetary reasons. In more serious cases involving the trial courts, the police must
be good witnesses and good reporters. Facts must hold up against
adverse witnesses. In such cases, the prosecutor, usually the district
attorney is in charge of the prosecution by the state. He must work
closely with the police officers involved so that the best use of the
evidence is made, and should use every effort to get cases considered
promptly and expeditiously.

The third step is *adjudication* and this involves the courts. Both
minor court justices and trial court judges should have an understanding of the problems of selective enforcement. Special traffic
courts and violations bureaus are now found in many cities. They
have been established to handle traffic cases only. The violation
bureaus process cases without court trial where the defendant ad-
mits his guilt. These agencies are handling more cases every year,
and the traffic judges hear and determine many traffic cases by
devoting only a few minutes to each case. This often nullifies the
work of the police and makes the public resentful of the hurried
process of justice. For as long as minor traffic violations are considered criminal actions every defendant should have his day in
court. It is the considered opinion of some traffic experts that only

the more serious traffic violations should be considered as criminal offenses to be tried under established rules of criminal procedure. The minor ones could be settled in a violations bureau if guilt were admitted; or if the defendant did not want to plead guilty he could be heard before a referee or hearing commissioner under the jurisdiction of the traffic court with a right to appeal to a trial judge. Minor offenses should not be answerable in the violations bureau but before the referee or hearing commissioner with the right to appeal.[11]

The fourth step in traffic enforcement is *penalization* and this is the responsibility of the court. Upon conviction, the judge applies the law which places penalties upon the defendant. The more serious traffic violations are automobile homicide, driving while intoxicated, leaving the scene of the accident, and reckless driving. In order to stop the present highway slaughter, says Judge Neilson, "a firm policy must be adopted and this means jailing the drunken, reckless, and hit-and-run driver." [12] But for minor infractions or for those defendants with long records of safe driving, different treatment may be in order. Many corrective measures are available that cannot be classed as punishment. One of these is the violators school in which offenders are given driver training. Another is the psychological clinic in which the driver's defects are studied and corrected. In both such cases, suspended sentences or probation are utilized and final sentence depends to some degree upon the defendant's reactions and attitudes. For voluntary compliance and improvement are the objectives sought. Another measure is placing restrictions on the driver's license. Ordinary penalization includes money fines, court costs, bail forfeitures, and jail sentence. But municipalities should prevent any public impression that traffic violators are brought in to replenish the public treasury, or worse yet, to add to the fees of the justice or magistrate hearing the case.[13]

But it is a fact that when traffic enforcement increases, traffic accidents go down. Detroit in 1937 had 335 fatal motor accidents.

---

[11] Kreml, *op. cit.*, pp. 22–23.
[12] Neilson, *op. cit.*, p. 199.
[13] *Municipal Police Administration, op. cit.*, pp. 312–318.

The city inaugurated a traffic supervision program and the next year fatalities were reduced to 196, a drop of 41 per cent. Los Angeles in 1941 had 518 fatalities. The city put on a similar program, and the next year there were only 320 fatalities, a reduction of 38 per cent. Seattle in 1945 had 109 fatal accidents. The city inaugurated a program of traffic enforcement with the result that the next year there were only 80 traffic deaths, a reduction of 26 per cent. "Enforcement has been in the vanguard of the attack that has produced a reduction of over 50 per cent in the fatality rate the past 15 years," Kreml says. Enforcement, however, does not only mean arrest, trial, and penalties. It is most effective when these procedures are combined with the intelligent and wide use of admonitions, written warnings, instruction to pedestrians and drivers, examination of drivers apparently deficient in skills for driving, training of careless and negligent drivers, and their supervision under probation officers.[14]

Traffic Engineering

Most of the streets and roads of the nation were laid out before the coming of the automobile and motor truck. The pattern was adequate for the "horse-and-buggy" days but to a great extent is responsible for the congestion found today in urban areas, especially in the downtown sections of our older cities. Traffic engineering deals with planning for and improving street and highway traffic from the physical standpoint, and with the movement of vehicles and persons called traffic flow, for the storage of vehicles by curb or off-street parking, and for loading and unloading passengers and merchandise. The traffic engineer, a newcomer to local government, must be interested in the construction of any new bridge or street in a city. He will not, of course, have anything to do with the construction itself but should advise the architects and engineers on such matters as location, width of roadway, connecting traffic facilities, signs and markings, the grades, parking, and all other elements of the bridge or street which will affect the flow of traffic. He is interested in any improvement that will improve traffic con-

[14] Kreml, *op. cit.*, pp. 3–5.

ditions and traffic flow. He is also concerned with the behavior of human beings when they are drivers and pedestrians in order to know how they act in relation to different traffic conditions. He conducts research on traffic flow, congestion, parking, hazards, and accidents. The traffic engineer is really the general manager of the street transportation system rather than merely an engineer concerned with painting signs and installing traffic lights.

The Action Program of the President's Highway Safety Conference stresses the need for full-time traffic engineers in all cities larger than 50,000 population. Most of the large cities have traffic engineers and traffic engineering bureaus, but the medium sized cities still rely on the city engineer to take care of traffic engineering. The application of the science of traffic engineering has yielded impressive results in thousands of communities, large and small. Wilmington, Delaware, suffered from excessive congestion due to double and even triple parking caused by warehouses and merchandising distributing centers along two adjacent parallel streets on the edge of the business district. There was a high accident rate especially among pedestrians, and strict enforcement of parking regulations did not help. Both streets were converted into one-way streets, and traffic signals were retimed to handle one-way traffic smoothly. The results exceeded expectations. Traffic flow increased, accidents were reduced 50 per cent in one year, and the public was pleased. All this cost $175 for the installation of one-way signs. In Buffalo, New York, many railroad viaducts overpassing city streets were found to be locations of high accident frequency. Most of these viaducts had piers in the center of the roadway marked only with two small red lights about four feet above the pavement. Motorists said they sometimes mistook these lights for taillights of other moving vehicles. The remedy included the installation of three amber signals on the center pier facing each approach, two of which were always flashing. The center piers were also painted with black and white diagonal stripes. The subsequent reduction of accidents was almost one hundred per cent at the cost of $266. South Bend, Indiana, relocated its bus loading zone away from the intersections thus increasing traffic flow and decreasing accidents. Nashville, Tennessee, placed

four-way stops at a dangerous intersection where visability was restricted by existing buildings. Result: 70 per cent reduction of accidents at the cost of $34. Shreveport, Louisiana, moved its trolley
coach loading zones away from center street locations to mid-block
sections at curbs with the result that congestion was reduced and
accidents eliminated.[15]

Traffic engineering on both state and local levels has been responsible for the improvements made in traffic signals and signs so
that they conform more closely with drivers' sensory, physical, and
psychological requirements. Signs and signals have become more
standardized and more legible.[16]

Traffic engineers are becoming increasingly aware of their responsibilities in the event large masses of people and vehicles must
be moved in case of emergency, namely enemy atomic attack. Emergency traffic plans must take into consideration the existing street
system and establish through-traffic routes to the open countryside
and to air, water, and rail connections. Direct, all around access and
egress to the devastated area must be provided. Independent escape
ways for refugees from the devastated area must be available. Civil
defense authorities have utilized a traffic engineering department
in their plans for emergency evacuation.[17]

Another traffic engineering problem is that of the school crossing
hazard. Ever increasing traffic on streets creates real and imaginary
fears on the part of parents for the safety of their children and they
harass public officials with demands for signs, traffic signals, adult
crossing guards, underpasses, and other safety devices whether they
are really needed or not. Public officials are put on the spot. They
must make some decision and it should be based upon study. A safe
condition at a school crossing might be defined as a condition in
which an approaching vehicle is far enough from a pedestrian crosswalk to permit a child or group of children at the curb to analyze

[15] Robert J. Allen, "Correcting Traffic Difficulties," *Traffic Quarterly* (October, 1953), pp. 479–497.
[16] A. R. Lauer, "Psychological Factors in Effective Traffic Control Devices,"
Traffic Quarterly (January, 1951), pp. 86–95.
[17] Charles G. Gonter, "Moving Traffic in Time of Disaster," *Traffic Quarterly*
(January, 1952), pp. 5–10.

the hazard and walk across the street before the vehicle reaches them. This can be ascertained by surveys which include information about the critical pavement width, the pedestrian walking velocity, the additional pedestrian clearance time, the vehicular velocity, the pedestrian perception and reaction time, and the crosswalk blockade. Formulas can be evolved from these facts, and traffic signals and other safety devices may be adjusted to them.[18]

In addition to the more common traffic signals and school patrol systems, many cities are beginning to use ladies to guard school crossings at appropriate hours. These ladies live in the neighborhood, are given a uniform and instruction, and are paid on an hourly basis. This has proved to be more economical than utilizing regular policemen for this service.

The Parking Problem

The parking problem is an indication that the use of the automobile within the traditional urban pattern of streets, especially in business sections, has not been satisfactory. In fact, it is the very opposite and is causing grave concern not only to people who are hunting places to park but to those whose economic interests are tied up in business and central city properties. The problem is universal, not only in the central business districts of cities, but also in business sections of suburban and neighborhood areas. Parking facilities or the lack of them determine to a large extent where patrons will go to buy commodities and to do business. If the present demand for parking space is great, in the future it will be greater for there are an increasing number of automobiles on the streets each year, and there is an absolute limit, sometimes already reached, of parking spaces in many business sections. It is estimated by the National Automobile Dealers' Association that there were 400,000 too few parking spaces in 1955, and this might rise to 800,000 by 1960 if vigorous action is not taken to make up this deficit.

The economic effects of this problem in downtown areas are

[18] Robert D. Dier, "A Study of a School Crossing Hazard," *Traffic Quarterly* (January, 1952), pp. 102–115.

already painfully apparent. It is speeding the decentralization of cities and accounts for much of the boom in suburban and fringe communities. It is partly responsible for the wholesale exodus of residences, businesses, and industries to the outlying sections of metropolitan areas. Baltimore's central business section suffered a $60 million, or 34 per cent, decline in assessed valuation between 1931 and 1945. Philadelphia's assessment went down from $512 million in 1936 to $364 million in 1946; Rochester, New York, lost $43 million in sixteen years before 1946; Worcester, Massachusetts, lost $63 million, or 20 per cent, in the period between 1930 and 1945; and St. Petersburg, Florida, gave up $26 million, or 29 per cent in the same period.[19] It is the same all over the nation. Often, complicating matters still more, cities are building expressways into the central areas that have tremendous capacities for moving traffic fast, but when the vehicles are debouched downtown there are no spaces for parking. Some experts believe that automobiles must be prohibited from coming into the central cities and that mass transportation facilities must be utilized within the most congested areas. Thus, commuters and shoppers could drive into the outlying sections of the city, park their cars at a small charge, and ride into the center of town on rapid transportation facilities. But the tentative experiments in this direction have not yet proven popular; people want to use their automobiles. Statistical evidence of this trend is that United States municipalities show a continued decreasing revenue and passenger volume of passengers carried by transit lines. In 1954 transit lines carried 12,386,000,000 passengers, a decrease of 10 per cent since 1953. The 1953 traffic was down 8 per cent from 1952. Since World War II mass transit operations have ceased in more than two dozen municipalities. If people cannot find parking places where they have been used to going, they will hunt other places. So the quest for parking space has been intensive; on it hinges success or failure for many businesses. In the new suburban regions, the problem is similar, for those areas that cannot provide convenient parking facilities will lose trade and suffer economic loss in spite of the

---

[19] Ben Solomon, *Parking*, The American Municipal Association (April, 1951), p. 2.

fact that they are far from the central city. Even in neighborhoods, people will not walk to stores. Curb parking is not sufficient, and therefore off-street parking must be made available.

Various means have been used to provide off-street parking in American cities. In downtown and already blighted areas close to the central business districts, many obsolete buildings have been torn down and the lots used for parking. Most of these have been operated privately with charges at the rate of what the traffic will bear. Many municipalities have gone into the off-street parking business, utilizing public lands or lots that have reverted to the city for delinquent taxes. By the end of 1954, 685 cities out of 1,219 of over 10,000 population owned and operated a total of 2,179 city-owned lots, an average of three to a city. Of these, 345 were metered, 31 charged for parking with an attendant, and 291 allowed free parking.[20]

While the supply of off-street parking facilities operated by commercial firms has greatly increased in recent years, it has not met the demand. The old-time parking garage has construction and operating costs that make rates too high for the ordinary motorist. The newer parking garages with ramps and open-air levels are often better placed with regard to location, and offer excellent service but they, too, have rates too high for the regular commuter and shopper. Commercial parking lots more nearly meet the demand for low-cost, convenient facilities but many of them are off the beaten track, not conveniently located for late-night return, are not maintained adequately and are sometimes at the mercy of auto-thieves. Nevertheless most of these lots are used to capacity. However, greatly expanding facilities of this kind will probably not be available in the future. Two alternative solutions to the parking problem exist. One is to let things go their natural course and allow decentralization of larger cities to continue apace and the problem of business and shopping location in smaller cities and suburban areas to work itself out. The other alternative is to realize that parking is a public problem and have cities and local units take on responsibility to provide for it in order to preserve the existing property

[20] *The Municipal Year Book 1955*, pp. 440–447.

values of the area. More than half of the states have in recent years given municipalities power to construct, maintain, operate, and finance off-street parking facilities. Some states, notably Pennsylvania, California, and Connecticut, have given *ad hoc* local units such as municipal authorities, parking districts, or redevelopment agencies power to construct and maintain parking facilities and to finance them through bonds payable from the revenues of the facility.[21]

Kansas City, Missouri, is constructing a central business district parking terminal to accommodate 1,800 cars with a magnificent approach from a new freeway to the heart of the city. This is a project of federal, state, city, and private business cooperation. The Kansas City Master Plan called for a system of radial expressways centering in the downtown area and connecting it with the residential and other commercial and suburban areas throughout the metropolitan region. A survey conducted in 1953 indicated a deficiency of about 2,000 parking spaces in the 69-block cordon area. The city officials have long been cognizant of the need to stabilize and reclaim the central business district as a unit of highest economic importance within the metropolitan area. The problem was, of course, how to secure the finances necessary for a large off-street parking project. Title 1 of the 1949 Federal Housing Act made available federal aid for slum clearance and urban redevelopment and provided for the resale of cleared land to private developers. It was found that this area qualified and work was begun. The Downtown Redevelopment Corporation was established and financed by citizens to construct and operate the project which, upon completion in 1956, will have multi-level garages and surface parking. It is a bold and imaginative approach to the problem of mid-city deterioration as well as to that of parking.[22]

In Baltimore, Maryland, the transit company leased a lot one and

---

[21] James C. Yocum and Joan P. Whipple, *Municipal Provision of Parking Facilities—State Laws and City Projects,* Bureau of Business Research, Ohio State University (1946). Also see: Orin F. Nolting and Paul Opperman, *The Parking Problem in Central Business Districts,* Public Administration Service (1938).

[22] L. P. Cookingham, *Kansas City, Missouri, Clears Slums for Central Business District Parking Terminal,* American Municipal Association, September, 1954.

a third miles from the center of the business section for parking lot purposes. It had a capacity of 208 cars, and was improved for $10,000. The company provides busses every five minutes at peak period time and every seven and a half minutes at other times to the central district. The lot averages about three hundred parkers a day, most of whom use the bus into the central district. This is another type of solution tried in a number of cities.[23]

Parking Meters

The parking meter became popular with local government officials almost overnight. The first installation of this invention by Carl Magee was in Oklahoma City in 1935. By January, 1952, it was estimated that there were approximately 1,113,000 parking meters in more than 2,800 localities in the United States, bringing in a gross annual revenue of $76 million. This appears to be just the beginning for only 16 per cent of the urbanized areas of the nation had parking meters as of that date. However, it must be related that one state, North Dakota, outlawed parking meters by referendum of the people although by a narrow majority, and a few cities have removed them after installation, but it is generally agreed that this gadget is no longer an insignificant mechanism to extract painlessly pennies and nickels from motorists, but is an important institution of traffic regulation.

The parking meter is a mechanical clock device which aids the police officer in determining when a car is parked over the legal limit. It is operated by depositing a coin, either a penny or a nickel, in a slot which allows the car to park for a limited time, usually at the rate of five cents an hour. There are two types of meters: automatic and manual. In the automatic, the insertion of the coin sets the clock in motion, and in the manual this is done by a hand crank. More than half of the present meters are automatic. The great bulk of parking meters are found in the commercial sections where there is the largest parking demand.

[23] Yocum and Whipple, *op. cit.*, p. 68.

There are a number of different arrangements for the purchase of parking meters. The most common one is where the company retains ownership of the meters until paid by the municipality from the revenue of the meters. Thus, there is no capital investment. The estimated average annual revenue per meter was in 1951 about $70. Generally the larger the population of the local unit, the greater the revenue. In the same year, it was estimated that $16 million was collected for parking meter violations, about 20 per cent of the gross collections from the meters themselves. The average collections from parking meter fines per meter was about $12. The average price per parking meter has dropped from $69 in 1945 to $61 in 1951—this in a period when everything else has increased in price.

There is an increasing tendency to integrate curb and off-street parking facilities into one system. Many off-street parking lots have been acquired from curb meter revenues. Commercial advertising on parking meters, in spite of its questionable legality and taste, seems to be gaining momentum.

It has been found that parking meters do effectively reduce overtime parking at the curb, increase parking turnover, and assist generally in the enforcement of parking regulations.

About 23 per cent of gross parking meter revenue in 1951 went toward the parking meter program which included amortization of parking meters, police enforcement, meter repair and maintenance, collection of meter revenue; while 42 per cent went for general municipal purposes including the general fund, the police department, and other miscellaneous purposes. Another 20 per cent went for off-street parking, traffic control and other such purposes, while the remaining 15 per cent was not indicated in the reports made by the municipalities.[24]

While parking meters make the enforcement of parking regulations easier, and reduce the obstructions to shoppers looking for

[24] David R. Levin, *Parking Meters, a Study of Their Number, Revenue and Use*, Highway Research Board Bulletin 81 (Washington, 1954). This contains the findings and conclusions of the first comprehensive factual survey of parking meters.

parking space, they still do not provide more curb space for parking and therefore, despite the golden flow of pennies and nickels, they are not the ultimate answer to the parking problem.[25]

THE AMERICAN MUNICIPAL ASSOCIATION 1954 TRAFFIC POLICY STATEMENTS

The uniform distribution of America's 58 million vehicles over the entire highway mileage of the nation would present no great problem. However, measured by gasoline consumption and traffic counts, approximately one-half of all the motor traffic is concentrated on city streets. These streets constitute only 10 per cent of the nation's highway mileage. How can urban communities effectively handle 50 per cent of the nation's motor traffic on 10 per cent of the nation's highway mileage and, at the same time, provide parking spaces for millions of motor vehicles? This is the traffic, transit, and parking problem confronting American cities.

The solution will be found in a combination of (1) making the greatest use of existing facilities, (2) providing adequate off-street parking, (3) most efficient use of public transit, (4) a program of modern traffic ways with comprehensive planning for future development.

Traffic

The first step in achieving maximum effectiveness of existing streets is for each municipality to concern itself as a matter of public policy with effectively organizing and administering a modern program of traffic engineering. Responsibility for efficient traffic engineering should be definitely fixed by each municipality, with the administrative official reporting directly to the chief administrative officer of the municipality. Each city should make a complete analysis of existing facilities and prepare a program to insure maximum traffic carrying potentials on existing streets. Skillful traffic engineer-

---

[25] Solomon, *op. cit.*, p. 14. Also see Charles F. LeeDecker, *Parking Meters in Pennsylvania Municipalities,* Institute of Local Government, Pennsylvania State University (1943).

ing principles and recommendations should receive the support of governing bodies in the light of the general public good. Municipal officials should display courage in meeting this important problem.

Municipal traffic engineers, planners, and finance officers must be called upon by the governing body to provide plans for a modern system of traffic ways. Determination must be made, in the light of traffic demand, where new arteries of travel should be constructed, so that municipalities can build an integrated system of traffic ways, limited access freeways, and service roads. The financing of such improvements should bear a relationship to the use. On all but residential and local service streets, the state and federal governments must bear their proportionate share of the cost. It is the responsibility of the governing bodies of all levels of government to provide the means by which the program can be realized.

Once the proper administrative organization for traffic engineering is established by a municipality, the minimum program for such an agency would be to make an exhaustive study of:

a. The most effective use of existing streets, including the pairing of streets for one-way traffic, elimination of inefficient curb parking, elimination of unnecessary turning movements, channelization, truck routes, and properly designed and installed traffic control signals.

b. The extent of the need for new traffic ways, with recommended locations and costs and suggested means of financing. This study should, of course, project these needs for several years in the future.

c. The extent of the need, over and above existing permanent facilities, for off-street parking and the location of areas that are, or can be, made available for additional off-street parking.

d. Blighted areas that would qualify for federal aid under the federal-state program of land clearance for urban renewal and redevelopment, which might properly include provision for off-street parking.

Parking

The American Municipal Association regards as academic the question of whether or not the municipality shall be engaged in off-street parking activities. It must be so engaged. The primary responsibility for solving the parking problem rests with the municipality. This is so because of public need and demand. The provisions of parking places off-the-street, in the motor age, has come to be regarded as a legitimate, expected, and necessary public municipal service. For the welfare, safety, and convenience of its citizens, and to insure its own future existence, each municipality must accept the responsibility for definite action which will result in the furnishing of adequate, permanent parking facilities at reasonable rates.

With full factual data furnished by the traffic engineering agency, the city government should determine basic parking policies and delineate the areas which will be left to private enterprise. The municipality must also determine which public controls shall be imposed on parking rate schedules and other phases of private parking operation.

The municipality should determine policy with respect to the requirement of a fixed amount of parking facilities in connection with construction of new multiple housing units and buildings designed for public assemblage.

The municipality should also develop and put into effect an adequate over-all citywide parking plan and program that will cover both curb and off-street parking. This program must be designed for at least a ten or fifteen year period. The governing body of each municipality should, where possible, consider the enactment of legislation to enable private business to provide parking facilities or to adapt for local needs the parking programs successfully instituted by both public and private agencies in other cities.

Much of the future value of the downtown central business district of each municipality is dependent upon provision of sufficient parking for the vehicles of the people who come downtown.

Transit

The aims of the public transportation operators and the municipal government in providing rapid, efficient, economical mass transit in municipalities should be identical. Municipalities should encourage the greater use of mass transportation. Streets can serve many more people via mass transit than via private automobiles. The loss of public transit service in 120 municipalities during the past 10 years has created a hardship on those who must depend on public transportation. The municipality should formulate policies of street design and traffic control features so as to expedite the operations of transit vehicles in any new construction program. Engineering improvements can be accomplished in most municipalities which will facilitate and speed up transit service.

TEN SUBJECTS FOR FURTHER STUDY

1. The traffic accident rates in your state.
2. The President's Highway Safety Conference.
3. The Uniform Vehicle Code.
4. Driver education in your state.
5. Modern urban traffic courts.
6. The organization of a traffic division in the police department of the largest city in your state.
7. Traffic engineering.
8. Off-street parking.
9. Parking meters.
10. In-service training for traffic police.

REFERENCES

Shelby Gallien, "Effective Police Traffic Training," *Traffic Quarterly,* October 1953, pp. 531–539.

Norman Hebden, *Effective Administration in State-City Highway Activity,* Yale Bureau of Highway Traffic (New Haven, Connecticut, 1951).

Charles S. LeCraw, Jr., and Wilbur S. Smith, *Municipal Regulation of Parking Lots,* Eno Foundation for Highway Traffic Control (Saugatuck, Connecticut, 1949).

David R. Levin, *Parking Meters: Their Number, Revenue and Use* (Chicago, 1954).

Robert B. Mitchell and Chester Rapkin, *Urban Traffic, a Function of Land Use,* Columbia University (New York, 1954).

National Safety Council, *Accident Facts: 1954* (Chicago, 1954).

Miner B. Phillipps and Irving Tenner, *Financing Municipal Off-Street Parking Facilities,* Municipal Finance Officers Association (Chicago, 1948).

President's Highway Safety Conference, *Priorities in the Action Program* (Washington, 1951).

John L. Sullivan, "Three Parking Lots for 750 Cars at $363 per Stall," *The American City*, January 1952, pp. 133–135.

Traffic Engineering Functions and Administration, Public Administration Service (Chicago, 1948).

William J. Watkins, "Relationship between Downtown Automobile Parking Conditions and Retail-Business Decentralization," Part 3: *Parking As a Factor in Business*, Highway Research Board (Washington, 1953).

Chapter 13

FIRE PROTECTION

Fire protection does not only include fighting fires that are started, but also trying to prevent fires from starting, keeping loss of life and property to a minimum in case fire does start, confining the fire to the place of origin so that it does not spread, and extinguishing it. Fire prevention, in the long run, is just as important as fire fighting. Although not as dramatic, it pays off in lowered fire losses and greater safety.

Fire caused 12,550 deaths in the United States and Canada in 1954, according to the National Fire Protection Association. Property damage in the United States was estimated at $1,099,500,000. During the year there were 55 major aircraft fire accidents causing the loss of 240 lives and nearly $70 million property damage. In 1953 occurred the largest industrial fire loss on record at the General Motors Corporation fire at Livonia, Michigan, estimated at $110,000,000.[1] The total fire cost in a community is not only the value of the property destroyed, but also the cost of fire protection, the cost of insurance premiums in excess of losses paid, fire prevention costs such as safety devices required by ordinances, loss of life, personal injury, and losses due to disruption of business. Some of these items are not measurable in terms of money.

Fire losses in the United States are far greater than they are in Europe in spite of the fact that more is spent on fire protection. American mechanical equipment is without peer and more people

[1] *The Municipal Year Book 1955*, p. 359, and *The Municipal Year Book 1954*, p. 378.

are trained for fire fighting. High losses in the United States as contrasted to Europe are due to a number of factors. There are higher
values in property; more buildings are made of wood. In the United
States, there is little emphasis upon the fixing of responsibility for
negligence whereas in Europe the causes of each fire are pains-
takingly sought and responsibility once fixed leads to payment of
costs and damages by the person or persons responsible. Likewise,
measures for the prevention of fire are more highly developed in
Europe.

Major fire hazards include lumber yards in which lumber is
crowded in a small space, is readily ignited, burns rapidly, and
spreads quickly. Vast amounts of water are needed to control such
fires. Bulk oil storage stations from which fuel oil and gasoline are
distributed to retail filling stations and home are hazards and should
not be allowed in congested places. Piers and wharves are the scenes
of many big fires because of the concentration of goods. Cities like
New Orleans and Los Angeles have equipped their wharf property
with automatic sprinklers. Public buildings such as schools, hospitals, and institutions are hazards because of the concentration of
people and property values. Fire resistant building construction has
improved conditions in such buildings but not to the point where
they can be said to be fireproof. The central mercantile area of a
city is a top hazard because of the concentration of buildings, many
of them old and not well kept. Group fires may spread through
blocks and become sweeping conflagrations. Mercantile property
has the poorest fire record, especially the smaller retail stores that
have no adequate private fire protection such as a sprinkler system.
Fires also have been known to be started on such property by
owners who seek insurance payments to get them out of financial
stringency. Buildings with "multiple occupancy" are the source of
serious fire losses. There may be stores on the street level, shops and
club rooms above, small apartments scattered through the building
and perhaps small manufacturing enterprises on top floors. Causes
for fire in such places are many, and loss from water damage is
usually great. Some fires are started by persons with malicious inten-
tions. Arson or incendiarism are responsible for a substantial per-

centage of annual fire loss. It is estimated that perhaps half of the big fires in cities must be classified as incendiary or from unknown causes.

CAUSES OF FIRES IN BUILDINGS

(Tabulation of One Year's Record in a Typical City)

Cause		Number
Fire started in rubbish in and around buildings		62
Sparks on wooden shingle roofs		40
Chimneys burning out (chimney fires)		33
Electrical causes		31
Wiring (mostly extension cords)	18	
Overheated motors	8	
Electric irons	3	
Other electrical fires	2	
Flammable liquids		24
Cleaning with gasoline	6	
Other gasoline fires	12	
Oil burners	2	
Kerosene lamps and stoves	2	
Other flammable liquid fires	2	
Defective chimneys or fireplaces		21
Defectively installed heating apparatus		20
Matches		16
Children playing with matches	11	
Using matches in closets	5	
Smoking		13
Awning fires	5	
Cigarette ignited furniture	5	
Smoking in bed	3	
Hot ashes		8
Food or grease on stove		8
Miscellaneous other known causes		40
Suspicious		5
Unknown		59
Total fires in buildings		380

From The International City Managers' Association: *Municipal Fire Administration*, p. 16.

The best fire record is held by high class industrial property because of the private fire protective devices installed and the constant supervision and care given the property. Hotels have been the scenes of bad fires with severe loss of life and property. It is most difficult to control smoking in bed which is the known cause of many fires, and to control fires because of the drafts through the elevator systems. Dwellings are responsible for two-thirds the fires in buildings, but only one-third of the fire losses. It is generally held that the automatic sprinkler system is the best means of protection against fires in buildings. By this means, water is piped to points near the ceilings of every room and concealed space in the building. In case of fire, water is discharged directly on the fire through a head or nozzle controlled by a fusible plug, and alarm is given. The best municipal fire department cannot do the work of an automatic sprinkler. Fire fighting by firemen demands that someone discover the fire, turn in the alarm, which brings the men and equipment to direct the hose streams through smoke and flame often obstructed by smoke. Losses in sprinklered buildings, it is estimated, are not more than 10 per cent of losses in nonsprinklered buildings.[2]

Walter Y. Kimball, engineer of the National Fire Protection Association, describes some of the recent improvements in fire-fighting apparatus. "Where 60 men were needed to apply a 250 gallon per minute stream with the hand engine, and a dozen men supplied perhaps an average of 300 gallons per minute with the steamer, a well-trained pump crew of 4 men can put a 700 gallon per minute fog nozzle to work in a matter of seconds if the department has kept up to date in new equipment and operating techniques. Unfortunately, however, few departments can be really classed as progressive and up to date in all phases of operation.

"Not only has the ability of the fire company to throw water been stepped up but the extinguishing effectiveness of fog or spray streams properly applied is many times the old solid stream of water that wrecked everything in its path. A solid stream presents little surface area for heat absorption. Most of the water strikes a wall and runs off causing heavy water damage in the process. The spray stream on the other hand offers hundreds of square feet of surface area of the individual water drops. These absorb heat and quickly turn to steam. The heat absorption in turning heat into steam is some 7 times that required to raise the liquid water to the boiling point.

[2] The International City Managers' Association, *Municipal Fire Administration*, fifth edition (1950), pp. 9–14.

Also when turned into steam the water expands in volume some 1,650 times, not only smothering the fire but purging the area of heat, smoke, and other products of combustion.

"The modern, informed fire chief judges the effectiveness of his attack by observing the amount of steam generated. When the fire is out it is not unusual to find the fire area almost dry except for small amounts of condensation. The so-called 'indirect attack' is where the water fog is directed into heated areas not in direct contact with the stream of water from the fog nozzles.

"A number of big cities have proven the effectiveness of big fog nozzles on big fires. Memphis has jumbo fog nozzles mounted on all its salvage rigs and Chief Klinck reports that his big fires are knocked down in 15 minutes or less compared with hours of fire fighting under former methods which resulted in total property loss in many instances." [3]

Fire Protection in Small Towns and Rural Areas

The most common fire protection organization in American small towns and rural areas is the volunteer fire department. In some places, there is a skeleton force of paid firemen or drivers which provides the nucleus for a large force of volunteer firemen drawn from the ranks of the male citizenry. There are more than 15,000 volunteer fire companies in the United States and Canada. Originally all local and municipal fire companies were volunteer and only toward the end of the 19th century did the paid, full-time fire company become the common mode of organization in the larger cities. Philadelphia is the original home of the pioneer volunteer fire company, the first one being established in 1735. The Commonwealth of Pennsylvania, along with the states of Delaware, Maryland, and parts of New York, New Jersey, Virginia, and West Virginia lean heavily on the volunteer system. Reading with 14 companies and Harrisburg, both close to the 100,000 mark in population are largely volunteer with a small echelon of paid apparatus operators and offi-

[3] Talk given at the 1954 Annual Conference of the Government Research Association, Shawness-on-the-Delaware, Pennsylvania.

cers, and in Pennsylvania as a whole there are more than 1,700 active volunteer fire companies with about 250,000 members including 80,000 active fire fighters.[4]

These volunteer companies not only are fire fighting units, but are social institutions as well and most of them have club rooms and recreation facilities in the "fire house." Having as members large numbers of citizens from all walks of life including a goodly share of young men, these companies are an important community force and are responsible for many improvements other than fire protection in the locality. They take an inordinate pride in their equipment, spending huge sums of money for the newest and most modern fire apparatus kept bright and shining at all times. Furthermore, many of these volunteer companies engage in programs of in-service training in fire fighting and prevention given by state departments of education, universities, and other organizations.

The volunteer company is usually organized as an independent corporation or nonprofit organization under state law, and is responsible only in part to the local government. In some cases, the local government buys part of the apparatus and supplies, or audits their accounts, or supervises the purchases, or enters into mutual aid agreements, or contracts for fire protection outside the borders of the municipality, or reports fire statistics, or appoints the paid members of the company. The company itself operates under its own charters and by-laws, has its own organization, and elects its own officers including the chief and the drivers. Money for volunteer fire companies may be raised from a variety of sources: taxes, municipal appropriations, proceeds from bazaars, bingo, carnivals and other community events, contributions from merchants, membership dues, and even revenues from state-collected taxes such as that on premiums of fire insurance companies.

Strictly rural areas—outside the boundaries of municipalities—often have little or no organized fire protection, and when fire breaks out must rely on their own efforts and those of their neighbors. A common event in the countryside in past years was the burn-

---

[4] Elizabeth Smedley, *Local Fire Administration in Pennsylvania,* Department of Internal Affairs, Commonwealth of Pennsylvania, p. 8.

ing of a barn full of hay, straw, and other combustible material, but with the coming of the machine age on the farm and the passing of the horses and other beasts of burden, this kind of fire hazard is going the way of the great hay barn along railroad sidings that a generation ago was the assembly point for hay and straw for the big city barns and stables. Many rural farms are too far from the nearest fire company to get any protection, but some are near enough to municipalities to be served by their fire companies. Sometimes, this service is given free as a community service: farmers shop in town, the town protects the farmer in case of fire. The only reward for such service is perhaps a dinner for the firemen or a contribution to the company after a fire. Other times, this service is on a more businesslike basis with rates to be paid for the use of apparatus and men, payable by the township in which the farmer lives or by the actual beneficiary. Sometimes the outlying sections buy a piece of equipment for the fire company. Often too the township pays an annual fee for this service under an intermunicipal agreement. In some states, rural fire departments can be organized to serve the farm areas. These are usually organized around and stationed at an unincorporated village.[5] In states where rural townships exist, mostly in the middle Atlantic and midwestern regions, they are allowed by law to organize fire departments which may be financed from tax money. In New England, the town has power to organize fire companies within and outside the urban settlements within their jurisdiction. Some counties, notably Los Angeles which has the third largest fire department on the Pacific coast, have fire departments.[6]

City Fire Departments

Almost all cities over 10,000 and many between 5,000 and 10,000 have full-time paid fire departments. The average city over 10,000

[5] The states are: California, Illinois, Maryland, New York, Oregon, Rhode Island, Texas, and Washington. See National Fire Protection Association, *Volunteer Fire Departments for Rural and Small Community Service* (1947).

[6] James Trump and Morton Kroll, *County Administered Fire Protection,* Bureau of Governmental Research, University of California (1951).

had 1.31 full-time fire department employees per 1,000 population
in 1955. Entrance salaries ranged from $2,077 to $5,070, maximum
salaries between $2,077 and $5,980. Fire chiefs ranged in salary
from $2,700 to $15,500. As to organization, in 427 cities over 25,000
reporting, the fire chief is appointed by the city manager in 173
places, by the mayor in 101, by the city council in 66, by a fire and
safety board in 45, and by a fire and safety commissioner in 39.[7]

In Boston, the fire commissioner is appointed by the mayor for a
four year term. He has direct supervision over headquarters, the
fire alarm and electrical inspection divisions, the medical examiner,
and the chaplains. His executive officer is the chief of the department who is responsible for the fire fighting force, and the fire prevention and maintenance divisions. The fire fighting force is in three
divisions, two with 4 and one with 6 districts. A deputy chief is in
charge of each division on each shift, a district chief is in charge
of each district on each shift. The number of companies in each
district is from 4 to 12, with a total of 51 engine companies, 34
ladder companies, 3 rescue squad companies, 3 fire boats, 3 lighting
plant companies and 2 water tower companies. There are about
2,500 full-time employees. Plans for top-level reorganization in 1954
called for the establishment of three new top positions with the new
rank of assistant chief to head operations, fire prevention, and personnel and training. The chief should be put under civil service, it
was recommended, and the policy making power on fire problems
would be given to the director of health and safety. The span of
control of the chief of department would be reduced from 17 deputy
chiefs and a superintendent of maintenance reporting directly to
the chief to three senior deputy chiefs for the three districts and the
three assistant chiefs.[8]

The Philadelphia fire department has about 3,000 full-time employees. It is headed by a fire commissioner who is appointed by the
head of the department of public safety. Directly under the fire commissioner are the fire training school, the administrative services
division, the personnel division, and the fire marshal's office. There
are two deputy commissioners—one for fire prevention and the other

[7] *The Municipal Year Book 1955*, pp. 363–375.
[8] Boston Municipal Research Bureau, *Survey of Boston's Fire Department*
(January, 1954), pp. 13–19.

for fire fighting. Under the fire fighting deputy, there are two fire fighting divisions, a repair and service section, a marine division, and a reserve fire force.[9]

The typical fire department for a city of 200,000 population has the fire chief appointed by the mayor or city manager. Under him are staff offices for research, records, public relations, medical services, and maintenance of equipment. Also under him is the assistant chief in charge of the bureau of fire prevention, the assistant chief in charge of the training school, the superintendent of the fire alarm system, and the assistant chief, assisted by three district chiefs, in charge of 16 fire stations including sixteen engine or hose companies and seven ladder companies, as required by the National Board Grading Schedule.[10]

Expenditures of the fire departments of 18 cities over 500,000 population on a per capita and a square mile basis in 1952 were as follows: [11]

Cities over 500,000 in Order of Population	Fire Department Expenditures, 1952	Expenditures per Person	Expenditures per Sq. Mile
New York	$55,679,000	$ 7.06	$176,700
Chicago	16,364,000	4.52	78,863
Philadelphia	13,068,000	6.31	102,736
Los Angeles	13,459,000	6.83	29,849
Detroit	9,318,000	5.04	66,748
Baltimore	6,546,000	6.89	83,177
Cleveland	5,592,000	6.11	74,560
St. Louis	4,318,000	5.04	70,787
Washington, D. C.	5,101,000	6.36	83,078
Boston	10,408,000	12.99	217,741
San Francisco	8,529,000	11.01	191,233
Pittsburgh	4,298,000	6.35	79,299
Milwaukee	4,383,000	6.88	84,942
Houston	3,350,000	5.62	20,937
Buffalo	4,451,000	7.67	112,969
New Orleans	2,878,000	5.05	14,433
Minneapolis	2,658,000	5.09	49,405
Cincinnati	3,293,000	6.53	43,848

[9] Philadelphia Fire Department, *A Period of Progress* (1954), p. 3.

[10] *Municipal Fire Administration,* International City Managers' Association, fifth edition (1950), p. 68.

[11] *Survey of Boston's Fire Department, op. cit.,* p. 5.

An analysis of the causes of 380 fires in buildings as tabulated in a typical city for one year revealed that 62 fires started in rubbish in and around buildings, 40 from sparks on wooden shingle roofs, 33 were chimney fires; 31 started from electrical deficiencies mostly from wiring in extension cords, 24 from flammable liquids, 21 from defective chimneys or fireplaces, 20 from defectively installed heating apparatus, 16 from matches, 13 from smoking, 8 from hot ashes, 8 from food or grease from stove, and 104 from miscellaneous known and unknown causes.[12]

The number of actual fires and the average loss per building indicates to some extent the work load of the fire department and the degree of fire extinguishment effected as well as the seriousness of the fire involved. The following data are for 16 cities over 500,000 population in 1952: [13]

	No. of Building Fires per 1,000 Pop.	Average Loss per Building Fire
New York	3.1	$1,112
Chicago	5.3	475
Philadelphia	3.2	1,784
Los Angeles	4.7	202
Detroit	3.5	145
Baltimore	6.0	607
Cleveland	3.2	1,107
St. Louis	4.0	330
Washington, D. C.	3.7	652
Boston	5.6	590
Milwaukee	2.4	1,485
Houston	4.5	1,069
Buffalo	2.3	1,751
New Orleans	3.1	591
Minneapolis	7.2	521
Cincinnati	4.1	640

[12] *Municipal Fire Administration, op. cit.,* p. 16.
[13] Data from *Municipal Year Book 1953* and *Quarterly of the National Fire Protection Association,* April, 1953, as quoted in *Survey of Boston's Fire Department, op. cit.,* p. 7.

Fire Defenses and Insurance Rates

It is obvious that there should be a close relationship between the quality and quantity of community facilities for fire fighting and prevention, and the actual cost of fire insurance to the property owners of the community.

The premium rates charged by fire insurance companies for fire insurance are based partly upon the fire protection provided by the local unit. The National Board of Fire Underwriters has developed a grading schedule which contains standards by which local conditions are measured. Local units are analyzed and measured by rating engineers according to their standards by means of *deficiency points*. The local unit with a small number of deficiency points is rated high and therefore its insurance rates are lower than one with a large number of deficiency points. The total number of deficiency points is 5,000 and they are distributed over seven major items as follows:

	Relative Values	*Per Cent of Total*
1. Water Supply	1,700	34
2. Fire Department	1,500	30
3. Fire Alarm	550	11
4. Police	50	1
5. Building Laws	200	4
6. Fire Prevention	300	6
7. Structural conditions	700	14
Total	5,000	100

Localities are divided into ten classes. Class 1 has from 0 to 500 points of deficiency; Class 2 from 500 to 1,000 points and from there on in 500 point jumps to Class 10 which has from 4,501 to 5,000 deficiency points. Each of the seven items measured provides also a basis for classification. For example, the fire department having a total of 1,500 points has ten steps of classification each with a range of 150 points. Therefore, a municipality can know how its fire department stands and can take action for improvement, but it is the sum total deficiency points that determine the final classification and the insurance rates. Deficiency points may also be assessed for "climatic conditions" and "divergence between water supply and fire department." The National Board Grading Schedule is used in all states but Texas where fire defenses are graded by the rating engineers of the Texas State Fire Insurance Department rather than by the engineers of the National Board of Fire Underwriters. The general items are similar but rates are directly determined in dollars and cents.

In rating water supply of a local unit, thirty-two items are surveyed and weighed. They include conditions relating to employees, organization, handling of alarms, source of water supply, pumping stations, installation of water mains, gate valves, and hydrants. Fire departments are rated on the basis of the number and quality of officers, operators, apparatus, hose, fire stations, discipline, drills, training, methods, records, building inspections, and other factors. For local units with no organized fire departments, no credit is given even when they have apparatus and a full deficiency of 1,500 will be applied.[14]

The final fire insurance class ratings of cities in the United States over 500,00 population in 1955 was Chicago 3, Philadelphia 4, Los Angeles 3, Detroit 2, Baltimore 2, Cleveland 4, St. Louis 3, Washington 2, Boston 2, San Francisco 2, Pittsburgh 4, Milwaukee 2, Houston 4, Buffalo 3, New Orleans 4, Minneapolis 3, and Cincinnati 2. New York was ungraded. Only four cities in the nation—Los Angeles, Detroit, Washington, and Milwaukee—ranked in Class 1 for fire departments. Cities over 25,000 generally classed higher than cities between 10,000 and 25,000.[15]

In 1953, of 503 cities of over 25,000, there were none in Class 1, 29 in Class 2, 122 in Class 3, 157 in Class 4, 121 in Class 5, 62 in Class 6, 12 in Class 7, and none in Classes 8, 9, and 10. The great

---

[14] National Board of Fire Underwriters, *Standard Schedule for Grading Cities and Towns of the United States with References to their Fire Defenses and Physical Conditions* (1942). The original schedule was adopted in 1916, and revisions were made in 1930 and 1942.

[15] *The Municipal Year Book 1955*, pp. 373, 376–377.

majority of cities from 10,000 to 25,000 population were in Classes 5 and 6.

Fire Fighting Apparatus and Equipment

Fire fighting equipment in the United States is continually improving in effectiveness. The basic unit is the triple combination *pumper truck* carrying hose in three or more sizes in total amounts of 1,800 feet or more; a pump capable of drafting water from static or open sources and of increasing pressure from hydrants or from a water tank on the apparatus and throwing water on the fire at a rate of from 500 to 1,000 gallons a minute; a water tank of sufficient capacity to control small fires; and a selection of ladders and other tools and appliances such as masks, first aid fire extinguishers, and salvage covers. The second most common type of fire fighting unit is the *ladder truck*. There are two main types: a pumper-ladder combination, and an aerial ladder raised by mechanical devices. Ladder trucks are for two purposes: life-saving and facilitating fire-fighting operations. They are needed to provide access to upper stories or roofs and to provide a footing from which firemen may direct streams. In addition, ladder-men can let smoke out of buildings by ventilation and can protect property against water damage. Depending on the size and type of municipality, there are many items of specialized equipment such as water towers and other heavy stream devices, fog nozzles, brush fire trucks, salvage wagons, squad wagons, rescue trucks, lighting and power units, fireboats, and foam extinguishers. The engine company with the pumper and ladder trucks make up the basic fire fighting team, and the trucks are usually housed together.

Adequate coverage for the whole area is of utmost importance. The number and placement of fire stations determines the length of run by the apparatus. To guarantee quick response of apparatus to fires, no part of the local unit should be more than three miles from an engine company. As property values and congestion increase, this should be cut down to one and a half to two miles, or even one mile in central areas with multi-storied and minor mercantile sections. Special hazard districts should be no more than three-quarters of a mile away. Where there is heavy traffic congestion, one-half mile is a standard distance. Ladder companies may be more widely spread. The National Board of Fire Underwriters set a minimum standard of seven men to man pumper or ladder trucks in high-value districts, 6 men per ladder company in an ordinary district, and 5 men per pumper company in an ordinary district. Under-manning of trucks is rated as a major deficiency, for fire fighting is strenuous and dangerous work which cannot be effectively performed by undermanned companies.

A working fire alarm system is an important part of fire defenses. In small communities, it is usually a siren or a horn calling the volunteer firemen. A municipal fire alarm system consists of street boxes from which alarms can be sent to headquarters, and also wire circuits to notify substations immediately upon receiving the alarm. Pulling a hook off at the street box identifies the location, and this signal is automatically sent to the substations. Many fire alarms come over the telephone, and radio is now coming into widespread use.

Selection and Training of Personnel

In order to have adequate fire protection, it is necessary to have good personnel. In volunteer companies, the problem of morale and training depends almost entirely on the members and the leadership they themselves recognize and develop. In paid fire departments, good conditions of work are essential as about 90 per cent of all expenditures are for personnel. Positions in the department should be *classified* to the end that those with the same duties receive relatively the same pay, and that the uniform qualifications be used in recruiting new members. A standard *compensation* plan should be in force. Personnel should be selected on *merit by examinations* and promoted the same way. Recruits should be given a complete *in-service training* program, and older personnel should have refresher and specialized courses from time to time. *Service ratings* should be available to measure performance. *Conditions of work:* vacations, sick leave, hours of work, transfers, should be standard and in line with those in industry. A sound *retirement* system should be adopted by the local unit in order to guarantee security in old age. Discipline should be fair and uniform.

The qualifications of a good fireman include physical health, strength, and agility as well as some mechanical aptitude as his duties involve working with tools, equipment, and apparatus. The prospective fireman should be the cooperative type because of the importance of teamwork and should be able to understand and follow directions. He should be between 18 and 27 at the time of selection, should have at least two years of high school, and some experience working with mechanics' tools. Examinations should include physical check, written tests, performance test, and oral interview.[16]

Fire Prevention

Most fires could have been prevented with proper regulations and enforcement. Usually reform in fire regulation comes after calamity. The Iroquois Theater disaster in Chicago in 1903 caused many cities to adopt requirements for safer exits, fire resistant curtains, and automatic sprinklers in public places. After Salem, Massachusetts, was devastated in 1914 by a conflagration because of wooden-shingle roofs, hundreds of communities adopted ordinances against such roofs. The loss of 125 lives in the Cleveland Clinic fire in 1929 led many cities to regulate the storage of nitrocellulose x-ray film. The hotel fires in Chicago and Atlantic City in 1946 led to new ordinances designed to prevent such fires.[17]

There are state laws and local ordinances the purpose of which is fire prevention. They relate to building regulations, the handling of

[16] Public Administration Service, *The Selection of Fire Fighters* (1940), pp. 4–5.
[17] *Municipal Fire Administration, op. cit.,* p. 316.

flammable, hazardous materials such as explosives and gasoline, and the prohibition of conditions such as the dumping of oil wastes that might lead to fires. Building codes specify the kind of materials that may be used, means of egress, ventilation, electric installations, and other such subjects. The technical standards used in building and fire prevention codes and ordinances are usually adopted on the basis of recommendations of national or state bodies such as the National Board of Fire Underwriters that specialize in the development of fire prevention measures. Such codes are often adopted *in toto* as the National Electrical Code which was devised by the Electrical Section of the National Fire Protection Association and generally adopted throughout the United States and Canada. Zoning and planning ordinances also aid in fire prevention. For example, they may call for the segregation and isolation of occupancies of buildings that are hazardous.

Fire prevention regulations are enforced by inspection on the part of state and local officials as an exercise of "police power" of government, that is, the right to regulate persons and property in behalf of the general welfare, health, and safety of the people. Inspections are carried on by the fire department both to prevent fires and to familiarize the firemen with the layout of the buildings and general area. Most fire departments divide the locality into districts for inspection purposes and fire department personnel are sent to take stock of and record the "target" hazards and other properties that need inspection. These inspections cover rubbish burners, incinerators, vacant lot hazards, storage of flammable materials, fire doors, installation of heating devices, condition of chimneys, fire extinguishers, and other such items. In most cities, this work is done in a fire prevention bureau in the fire department. This bureau also issues licenses to store hazardous materials in order to guarantee proper regulation.

It is most necessary to get public cooperation and general education in fire prevention. In many places, local fire prevention committees conduct special educational programs. Most states also have fire marshals who sponsor all kinds of fire prevention activities. They investigate and prosecute arson, collect statistics, and conduct educational campaigns.[18]

Civil Defense

The atomic age has brought the threat of war, conflagration, and destruction to every American community. Americans have reacted to this threat with characteristic speed by organizing a nationwide system of civil defense. Each community of any size has a civil defense organization guided and to some extent financed by national and state civil defense agencies.

Some of the conditions visualized in case of atomic attack on an urban place include a large devastated area, hundreds of fires, reduced water pressure and supply, roads blocked by debris, gas mains broken; thousands of people dead, buried alive, and injured; water and food supply contaminated; panic, looting, lack of housing, and homeless masses. Only by planning, organizing, and training can such a disaster be met with any degree of effectiveness.

The civilian defense organization of a locality includes the director appointed by the chief executive of the local government and various deputy directors in charge of specialized activities of civil defense. These include communication services such as air raid warning and aircraft observation, medical aid and health services, warden and plant protection services; radiological, chemical, and special weapon defense; fire, police, and mobile services; engineering including rescue and public utilities; transportation, feeding, and evacuation of refugees; and public information and education.

Mayor Frank P. Zeidler, city of Milwaukee, testified before the subcommittee on Civil Defense of the Senate Armed Forces Committee on March 9, 1955: "The nature of the threat has increased so tremendously in the past year that it is almost beyond the power of words to describe the conditions that exist in the field of potential

---

[18] *Ibid.*, pp. 316–364. See also: The President's Conference on Fire Prevention, *Report of Committee on Fire Fighting Services*, and *Action Program* (May 6–8), 1947.

destruction that can be effected by atomic, biological or chemical weapons.

"As you know, if you were to measure the strength of energy released by an atomic bomb such as was released over Hiroshima, you would measure it in 20,000 tons of TNT released. This is called in the parlance of the scientist the X bomb. Today it is possible theoretically to release power from hydrogen bombs many hundreds of times the power released over Hiroshima. Some authorities say the latest hydrogen bomb released has the power of 750 X, and they are now talking about the release of energy in terms of 1,000 X.

"The President of the United States in 1953 in a meeting of mayors said that there are now atomic weapons twenty-five times the size of the Hiroshima weapon, and there are hydrogen weapons that are in the range of many megatons. A megaton is in terms of millions of tons of explosive power. The lethal fireball of the first hydrogen bomb that was exploded was said to be 3¼ miles in diameter, and one of the most recent was 5 miles in diameter. In addition a new factor has increased the danger of poisoning from radioactivity. The danger of poisoning from radioactive ash caught in a down-draft position is anywhere from 100 to 200 miles down wind, covering an area of 7,000 square miles, and you may suffer in a few hours from lethal radioactivity. . . .

"The Civil Defense Administration in making an estimate of the condition in 1955 has estimated that if this country were to suffer an attack from a hostile source, that attack would be air-borne, and many of the American cities could be destroyed, or at least partially destroyed, with resultant casualties of many millions of people if the people did not move to some other location. Those who have had major catastrophes which involved hundreds of people in their community know how the sources of salvation are saturated with that kind of a situation. And when we talk in millions, not thousands, it is almost beyond comprehension to understand what is going on in this particular problem.

"In order to help solve this problem the Civil Defense Administration has now advocated a policy of evacution of target cities, and some of the cities in the United States have practiced evacuation programs.

"Recently in my city the Federal Civil Defense Administration released an official study, prepared by Northwestern University and a consultant from Connecticut, of how long it would take to evacuate 1,010,000 people from the potential target surrounding metropolitan Milwaukee. With present facilities it would take seven hours. In view of the fact that we may not have more than a 2-hour warning system, you can see what an enormous problem this poses."

Conclusions of Commission on Intergovernmental Relations on Civil Defense

In a staff report on "Civil Defense and Urban Vulnerability" submitted to the Commission on Intergovernmental Relations, a number of conclusions relating to civil defense were made:

1. Intergovernmental responsibilities for civil defense are presently inappropriately defined and assigned. The states and local units were made responsible for a function over which they had no real part in policy formulation or technical leadership and for which they are becoming unwilling to bear the preponderant financial burden.

2. The political and financial support of the civil defense function has deteriorated since 1952 at both the state and local levels, but mostly at the state level.

3. Critical target areas have been more inclined to take active civil defense measures than have the states.

4. Intergovernmental responsibilities in respect to preattack planning should differ from postattack operations, but a shift to the latter should not change the basic intergovernmental relationships.

5. Intergovernmental financial responsibility for civil defense has been improperly assigned.

6. Intergovernmental relationship patterns are too rigid.

7. The reduction of urban vulnerability to enemy attack is a press-

ing national problem but with strong elements of state and local responsibility.

Certain recommendations made in this report were: (1) that Congress reallocate responsibility from a primary state and local responsibility to a joint responsibility of national, state, and local governments; (2) that Congress should liberalize national financial participation in state and critical area costs, and restrict national financial participation in state and local expenditures for equipment; (3) that national participation should be on a state plan rather than on the basis of projects and items; and that to be eligible for national assistance the state or critical target area should submit a plan that followed the Federal Civil Defense Administration requirements; (4) that national assistance should be through the states with certain exceptions, that population of the state and target areas be the basis for financial allocation, and that matching continue on a fifty-fifty basis; (5) that direct relations between the critical target cities and the national government be authorized where the target areas cross state lines and where the state has failed to take positive action; and (6) national civil defense agencies should secure direct participation of municipal officers in national civil defense planning.[19]

TEN SUBJECTS FOR FURTHER STUDY

1. Fire losses in your state.
2. Modern fire fighting machinery.
3. The volunteer fire company.
4. Fire protection in rural and suburban areas.
5. The organization of the fire department of the largest city in your state.
6. Fire defenses and insurance rates in your community.
7. In-service training of fire personnel.
8. Civil defense and fire protection.
9. Major fire hazards in your community.
10. Fire prevention programs.

[19] Commission on Intergovernmental Relations, *Civil Defense and Urban Vulnerability* (June, 1955), pp. 1–4.

REFERENCES

Bulletin of the Atomic Scientists, September 1951, pp. 244–284, devoted to the subject of "Defense Through Decentralization."

Commission on Intergovernmental Relations, *Civil Defense and Urban Vulnerability* (U. S. Printing Office, June 1955).

James R. Donoghue, *Intergovernmental Cooperation in Fire Protection in the Los Angeles Area,* Bureau of Governmental Research, University of California (Los Angeles, 1943).

Federal Civil Defense Administration, *Clearance and Restoration of Streets and Highways in Civil Defense Emergencies* (Washington, 1954).

————, *Annual Statistical Report,* June 30, 1955 (Battle Creek, Michigan).

The International City Managers' Association, *Municipal Fire Administration,* fifth edition (Chicago, 1950).

Eugenia Gravatt Kimmel, *Fire Protection Outside Municipal Boundaries in Pennsylvania,* Institute of Local Government, The Pennsylvania State University (State College, 1945).

Warren Y. Kimball, "Use of Man Power at Large Fires," *Public Management,* June 1946, pp. 162–167.

National Board of Fire Underwriters, *Standard Schedule for Grading Cities and Towns in the United States* (New York, 1942).

National Fire Protection Association, *Volunteer Fire Departments* (Boston, 1952).

H. G. Pope, "Organization of Fire and Police Services in Small Cities," *Public Management,* May 1951, pp. 98–104.

The President's Conference on Fire Prevention, *Report of Committee on Fire-Fighting Services* (Washington, 1947).

Public Administration Service, *The Selection of Fire Fighters,* No. 68 (Chicago, 1940).

James Trump and Morton Kroll, *County Administered Fire Protection,* Bureau of Governmental Research, University of California (Berkeley, 1951).

U. S. Department of Agriculture, *Fire Departments for Rural Communities; How to Organize and Operate Them* (Washington, 1954).

Chapter 14

PUBLIC WORKS
AND UTILITIES

The term public works covers a broad field of activity in local government. If there is any bond of unity, it is that public works activities call to a greater or lesser degree for personnel trained in engineering. Likewise public works are concerned with the installation, construction, operation, and maintenance of physical plant and equipment used to service the needs of the people of the community. For example, sewage disposal is a health problem but the construction of a sewage disposal plant requires an engineer and not a medical officer.

Among the activities that can be put in the public works category are: street design, improvement and maintenance; street cleaning; construction and maintenance of sidewalks; street lighting; traffic control signs, signals, and painted lines; street name signs; house numbering; bridge design, construction, and maintenance; sewer design, construction, and maintenance; sewage disposal; refuse collection and disposal; water supply; electric utilities; public buildings and grounds; airports; auditoriums, parks, and playgrounds; and others.

In most of the larger local units of government, there is a public works department. In smaller municipalities and local units where there is no separate public works department, the city engineer or specific officials named by local ordinance carry on public works activities. The state constitutions and laws generally give local units the power to provide facilities for all the services they are authorized to render.

In cities with public works departments, the complexity of organization is in relation to the size of the city and the variety of tasks to be done. For example in cities under 10,000, the director of public works or the city engineer mans the department which may be divided into the following bureaus: streets, sewers, utilities, refuse, standards, and public property, or a combination of them. The director or the engineer will probably make all the plans and surveys for routine improvement, and he will direct foremen to carry on the work in each bureau. In cities between 10,000 and 100,000 population, the organization will be slightly more complex with a staff officer who might be called the office engineer in charge of plans and drawings while the head of the department will do more general supervision and over-all planning. The heads of bureaus will likely be engineers rather than foremen and the latter will continue to be in charge of the work units. When population reaches 100,000 to 500,000, the auxiliary and staff functions will expand. Under the director of public works, there may be an office engineer in charge of research, design, inspection, and cost accounting, and a works engineer in charge of the line bureaus such as streets, sewers, utilities, refuse, standards, and public property. In cities over 500,000 each line bureau is further divided into divisions as for example the sewers bureau will have divisions for storm, sanitary, and sewage disposal, and these in turn may have construction and maintenance districts in various parts of the city. Under the director of public works will be a chief engineer and he will direct the work of the office and work engineers, thus allowing the director of public works the time to concentrate upon the larger aspects of departmental work and policy.[1]

More than $5 billion dollars out of a total of $21 billion was spent by local government in 1953 on capital outlay. This included $4.2 billion for land and existing structures, and $.5 billion for equipment. This is the highest amount spent for local public works ever recorded

[1] The International City Managers' Association, *Municipal Public Works Administration*, third edition (1946), pp. 1–16, 297–300.

by the United States census. In 1946 the amount was only $.9 billion. In 1927, it was higher than any year before 1948—$1.9 billion. In 1902, it was $.2 billion.[2]

OWNERSHIP AND OPERATION OF UTILITIES
(Cities Over 5,000)

Type of Utility	Number	Percentage Reporting
Auditorium	409	17
Bus or Trolley Bus	38	2
Electric Generation and Distribution	289	12
Electric Distribution Only	210	9
Gas Manufacturing and Distribution	43	2
Gas Distribution Only	68	3
Incinerator	420	17
Port Facilities	78	3
Street Railway	8	0
Sewage Treatment Plant	1,209	49
Slaughter House	26	1
Water Supply and Distribution	1,662	68
Water Supply Distribution Only	145	6
Airport	512	21
Cities Having None	297	12
Cities Not Reporting	80	3

From The International City Managers' Association: *The Municipal Year Book 1955*, p. 64.

Local Streets and Roads

Total highway mileage in the United States in 1953 was 3,366,190 miles. Of this, a little over 640,000 miles, or 19 per cent were under state control. About 90,000, mostly national forest and Indian reservation roads, were under federal control. The rest, almost 80 per cent, or 2,636,000 miles was under local control. This included the following:

County roads	1,710,516	miles
Town and township roads	563,189	"
Other local roads	48,307	"
Total rural roads	2,322,012	"
Total municipal streets	314,650	"
Total under local control	2,636,662	" [3]

[2] Bureau of the Census, *Historical Statistics on State and Local Government Finances, 1902–1953* (1955), p. 21.

[3] The President's Advisory Committee on a National Highway Program, *A Ten-Year National Highway Program, a Report to the President* (January, 1955), pp. 38–39.

Of the total highways in the United States, 2,160,000 miles are surfaced and 1,205,000 are nonsurfaced. Most of the nonsurfaced highways are of rural mileage under local control.[4] In 1953, local governments in the United States spent $2,207 million for highways. In 1940, the total was only $780 million; in 1902, it was $171 million.[5]

State payments to local governments as highway aid totaled $803 million in 1953. In 1940, it was $332 million; in 1902, only $2 million.[6] State aid is in two forms: sharing of highway-user revenues and grants for highway purposes. Thirty-four states share with their local governments highway-user revenues. Eleven states restrict their sharing to counties alone.[7] Nineteen states also share some of their highway-user revenues through the device of state grants, while five others reimburse local units for highway work on a contractual basis.[8]

The location, design, construction, improvement, and maintenance of local streets and roads is the largest public works program of local government. The design and construction of a street depends on a number of factors: what kind of traffic it will carry, how heavy the traffic will be, what will its relation be to the arterial street plan, and what type of land use is bordering it.

Many local streets and roads, especially in rural areas and small towns, are unpaved except for applications of stone, gravel, cinder, and slag. These necessitate constant maintenance. Some method of treating the natural soil to satisfy minimum pavement needs where traffic is light and infrequent has been sought for many years. There are three general types of low-cost surfaces in which mineral material such as shale, gravel, sandy soil, or crushed rock is treated with asphaltic oil or similar material. *Surface mix* consists of applications of bituminous material to the surface of the street and covering it with fine crushed stone or gravel. *Road mix* is where the bituminous

---

[4] *Ibid.*, pp. 40–41.
[5] Bureau of the Census, *Historical Statistics*, p. 21.
[6] *Ibid.*, p. 19.
[7] John R. Kerstetter, *Local Government's Share of State-Collected Highway Funds and Revenues*, American Municipal Association (January, 1955), p. 37. The states are: Florida, Kentucky, Louisiana, Minnesota, Mississippi, New Mexico, New York, North Dakota, Pennsylvania, South Dakota, and Texas.
[8] *Ibid.*, p. 40.

and other materials are mixed on the street by means of power graders or discs. *Plant mix* is where the bituminous and mineral materials are mixed in a plant and hauled in to be spread on the surface and rolled. As automobile traffic increases, the demand for "hard" roads increases and the mileage of paved streets expands.

There are a number of common types of paving in general use. *Sheet asphalt* is the name given to a smooth "black-top" wearing surface, made from a mechanical mixture of sand, limestone, and asphalt. This type of road has three layers: (1) the wearing surface; (2) the binder course; and (3) the cement concrete base. Sheet asphalt has demonstrated its ability to carry large volumes of heavy city traffic. The street must be laid hot but it can be used even over a somewhat rough base. It is a high-type pavement. *Bituminous concrete* is also black-top, but of coarser texture than sheet asphalt. It is made of graded broken stone, and sand, bonded together with asphalt or tar. *Portland cement concrete* has been used extensively for pavement surfaces. *Waterbound macadam* is a pavement composed of stone or similar material broken into irregular fragments and compacted by a roller, and bound together by stone, dust, and water. It is low in initial cost but requires constant maintenance where there is heavy traffic. *Bituminous macadam* is one in which the binder is asphalt or tar spread over the surface and allowed to percolate in it, usually before rolling. *Brick and stone blocks* were once used extensively and are still economical for heavy traffic industrial and commercial streets. They are high in cost and when worn are not smooth for riding, but they need a minimum of maintenance.

Important factors in the design of modern streets and roads are the determination of width in order to take care of traffic, requirements for parking which would assume that street surfaces are for circulation of traffic rather than for storage of cars, safety conditions such as physical separation of traffic, street grades, the drainage structure, the placement of sidewalks, and the use of alleys. Maintenance and repair are constant functions for the public works department. Street cleaning and snow removal are done by men and

machinery in various combinations. For the modern heavy automobile traffic in the city and country both are needed.

Road construction and maintenance in rural areas throughout the
United States is basically a county function. However, this is shared
increasingly by the state. In fact, in Delaware, North Carolina, Virginia, and West Virginia, the state has taken over all roads and
relieved the county of any such responsibilities. Pennsylvania, too,
has added substantial mileage to its state system by taking over
county roads, but townships still retain control over almost 50,000
miles of rural roads. The township is losing out in the road function
throughout the United States simply because it is too small in our
motor age to do a technically competent and economical job. Where
the county is not relieving the township of this function, the state
inevitably will do so in whole or in part. Theoretically, it is the
county that is the ideal highway unit for building and maintaining
rural and secondary roads. Generally, it is large enough to develop
an organization that has modern equipment and trained personnel.
The state departments of highways logically should have the important task of constructing and maintaining the major and primary
systems of state highways, and not be bothered by the secondary
system.

Dodge County in Wisconsin can be cited as having a typical
county road responsibility. Its highway department, in terms of
persons employed and money expended, is the most important single
agency of its county government. The governing body of the county
is a board of 67 supervisors elected from towns, villages, and cities
within the county. This board elects a county highway committee
empowered to look after road construction and maintenance. The
committee is composed of five of the board of supervisors and they
are paid a per diem rate and expenses for their work on the committee. The board of county supervisors nearly always accepts their
recommendations. The board of supervisors also elects a county
highway commissioner who has charge of the road operations and
directs the work of the 145 employees (in 1948) who are chosen
by the highway committee and the commissioner under a board

resolution. Maintenance is carried on by 16 patrolmen and their maintenance crews working in all sections of the county. Construction projects not done by a contractor are given to the chief engineer and then built by the construction engineer and his crews. Rural public highways in Wisconsin are composed of state trunk highways, county trunk highways, and town roads. Dodge county, however, has legally designated a portion of its town road system as a "county aid highway system," and has assumed full responsibility for construction, maintenance, and snow removal on these roads. In Dodge county in 1948, there were 1,722 miles of rural public highways. Of these 1,209 miles were town roads, 287 of which have been incorporated into the county aid highway system. The state trunk system had 238 miles in Dodge county of which all but 11 miles were concrete or blacktop. The county trunk system was 275 miles of which 19 miles were concrete, 35 were bituminous, and 105 gravel. The county aid system uses gravel almost entirely. The State Department of Highways engages the Dodge county highway department to remove snow from the state highways in the county at standard rates fixed for the entire state. Most of the towns also engage the county department to construct, maintain, and remove snow on some of their roads. The county trunk lines are financed by the county property tax and state aid. The county aid highways are financed largely by the county property tax. County disbursements for highways in 1947 ran well over a million dollars. In addition to the county and state mileage, cities, and villages have 118 miles of road within the county.[9]

Street Lighting

Street lighting is considered to be a most important element in traffic safety. The National Safety Council reported as follows: "Traffic hazards and accident severity begin to increase at an alarming rate at sundown. The fatal accident rate per mile of travel is

[9] Paul W. Wager, ed., *County Government across the Nation* (Chapel Hill, North Carolina, 1950), pp. 299–301. The Wisconsin section was written by Fred A. Clarenback, University of Wisconsin.

three times as high at night as during the day. Pedestrian accidents, primarily adults, constitute a relatively high proportion of night accidents in urban areas. Half the pedestrian deaths occur between 6 p.m. and midnight." Improved lighting systems have actually reduced accident rates in many places. Street lighting is now down to a science where it can be ascertained what type and intensity of illumination is necessary for the type of street and traffic. Adequate street lighting is also a deterrent to crime. It is on the poorly lighted streets that assaults and hold-ups by hoodlums and gangs are likely to occur.[10] Recent developments in street lighting include mercury-vapor, fluorescent-mercury, and fluorescent street lights. The new 700-watt fluorescent-mercury lamp introduced in 1953 reportedly produces two and one-half times more white light and gives 300 per cent longer life than an incandescent street light—without increasing power costs. Structurally it is said to be a light within a light. An inner mercury tube gives off a brilliant blue-green light and in addition ultra-violet rays. The invisible rays excite the phosphorus coating on the outer bulb, making it fluorescent red. The combination of the blue-green hues with the red produces the white light of high intensity.[11] Perhaps the most important recent development in street lighting has been the fluorescent luminare. An outstanding feature of this type of lighting is the comfortable even quality of illumination with virtually no glare. Fluorescent street lighting results in a quality of illumination that far surpasses anything else available at present. "It will be the traffic safety lighting of the future," says one expert.[12]

Municipal Waterworks

The first public water system in the United States was constructed in Boston in 1652. There was a reservoir twelve feet square to which water was conveyed from neighboring springs through wooden pipes. This water supply was used both for domestic and fire pro-

---

[10] *Municipal Public Works Administration, op. cit.*, 17–103.
[11] *The Municipal Year Book 1954*, p. 334.
[12] C. K. Fulton, "Future Glimpsed in Present Street Illumination," *The American City* (March, 1955), pp. 155–156.

tection purposes. The second water system in the United States was in Shaefferstown, Lebanon county, Pennsylvania, and dated sometime before 1750. From a large spring near the town the water flowed by gravity through pipes into large uncovered troughs along the main street. The system was given to the community by the terms of Mr. Shaeffer's will. Each property owner on the main street was to be a stockholder and pay ten cents annually for each member of the family. Other residents, not residing on the main street but using the water, were to pay twenty cents for each member of the family. The first municipally owned waterworks was constructed in Winchester, Virginia, in 1799. At the turn of the century there were 14 public water supply systems in the United States, all but one privately owned.[13]

The Municipal Year Book of 1952 reports that 74 per cent of all cities over 5,000 reported municipal ownership of water supply and distribution systems. Of all the utilities owned by American municipalities, waterworks are the most numerous.[14] According to the American Water Works Association, there was in 1946 a total of 12,800 waterworks in the United States, of which 9,350 or 73 per cent, were municipally owned.

Water supply needs in a community are threefold: (1) there should be an adequate supply for home, business, and industrial use; (2) there should be adequate pressure and supply for fire fighting; and (3) the cost should be reasonable. Water supply is the most common of municipally owned utilities. There are several methods of administering water utilities. Some municipalities have independent water boards or commissions which construct, operate, and finance the community's waterworks. These include "water authorities" or special districts which have jurisdiction over water supply and are financed entirely by the revenues from the utility. In smaller municipalities, water is frequently administered by a committee of the council which supervises the waterworks operator or engineer and his staff. In larger cities, there is sometimes a department of

[13] John H. Ferguson and Charles F. LeeDecker, *Municipally Owned Waterworks in Pennsylvania,* Institute of Local Government, Pennsylvania State University (1948), pp. 1–10.

[14] *The Municipal Year Book 1953,* pp. 52–53.

water supply, the head of which is appointed by the mayor or the city manager. Sometimes, an elective head of public works carries this responsibility.

The practice of charging all classes of users rates for water supply on the basis of the amount used is common. Large users are often given lower rates for use in quantity. Many communities are still unmetered and users are charged a flat rate irrespective of the amount of water used. Likewise, householders and owners of business properties are billed for the installation of connections. Revenues are set to the point where they can pay for the operating costs and the debt service. Surpluses are usually set aside for extensions to the system, but sometimes they are transferred to general municipal funds and used to keep the tax rates lower. This practice is regarded as unsound because it taxes water-users higher than other classes of citizens for general government purposes. Many municipalities serve residents and institutions outside corporation limits. In some cases, the rates are the same as to those within the municipality; in others, an increase of twenty-five per cent or so is placed on the bill. The latter practice is recommended for if the nonresidents get water at the same price as residents there is no reason for them to be annexed and therefore it will be impossible to expand the municipality into the built-up sections "outside of town." As an example, water rates of the city of Cincinnati range from $1.50 to $90 a month depending upon the size of meter. Rates outside the city are generally double what they are inside city lines.[15]

There are many problems to be met in supplying water. Health considerations are of utmost importance. If the source is exposed to pollution there must be chlorination and purification. More and more cities are adding fluoride to their water supply in order to reduce tooth decay—although there is still some opposition against this program. The importance of water supply is no place better dramatized than in the case of Los Angeles. Faced with severe drought from 1893 to 1903 which brought the city close to actual danger, it became apparent that the local resources of the Los Angeles river basin were not adequate for the growing population.

[15] *The American City*, "Modern Water Rates" (March, 1955), p. 135.

From 1905 to 1913 the city's financial, legal, and engineering resources were devoted to acquiring water rights and to the construction of an aqueduct system to bring 400 cubic feet a second from the High Sierras 223 miles away. But still there was not enough water. In 1927 the Metropolitan Water District was established by the state legislature. The Colorado river, three hundred miles away, became a new source and through the Hoover Dam is now making available tremendous water and electric power resources to southern California cities. Looking into the future, experts say more water will be needed if the Los Angeles area is to keep up its phenomenal growth. They are looking for it as far as the Columbia River eight hundred miles away.[16]

Sewage Disposal

Sewage is carried from residences, places of business, industrial establishments, and other institutions to a sewage disposal plant or other suitable places of disposal by a system of drains, sewers, and pumps called the sewerage system. It is almost entirely a gravity flow system continuing through the lines to its ultimate disposal place which is lower than the place of its source. In some communities, the storm and sanitary sewers are combined, in others they are separate. The former disposes of all rain water, the latter all sewage. The advantage of a combination system is that only one set of expensive sewerage installations is needed. On the other hand, difficulties in separation arise when sewage treatment is undertaken. There is difficulty in cleaning sewers in dry periods, and there is danger of backflow of contaminated water into cellars through house connections in time of severe rainstorms. The general trend is away from combined systems.

There are two general methods of sewage disposal. One is to empty it into rivers or natural bodies of water which can effectively take care of small amounts without endangering health in the area.

[16] Richard Bigger and James D. Kitchen, *How the Cities Grew*, Bureau of Governmental Research, University of California, Los Angeles (1952), pp. 18–22.

For the basis of all modern sewage disposal practices is the oxidation of the organic matter through bacterial action. Where population becomes concentrated, nature cannot do the job adequately and pollution of streams is the result. Ninety-nine per cent plus of sewage is water. Only a very small part is made up of solids in suspension, floating materials in solution, and sewage germs. But these are the elements that make trouble and provide the hazards to health and are responsible for typhoid fever, dysentery, and other intestinal diseases. When sewage is discharged into rivers, streams, and other bodies of water, it contaminates sources of water supply, impairs bathing beaches, injures aquatic life, and generally impairs life in the vicinity. Most of the streams that pass through or near our great industrial and population centers are intolerably contaminated to the point that many states have insisted that municipalities and industries refrain from polluting public waters and establish sewage treatment works.

There are three commonly used sewage treatment processes. The *tank treatment,* sometimes called primary treatment, is to remove the solids in suspension from the sewage, to render these solids inoffensive through decomposition, and to dispose of them by burning, by using them as fertilizer, or by some other means. Such installations as settling and digestion tanks, Imhoff tanks, septic tanks, sludge draining beds, sludge filters, screens, grit chambers, and oil skimming devices are the equipment used to do this job. *Oxidation* processes aim at oxidation of the organic material in solution or after it is taken from the tank through the agency of bacteria or other organisms. *Sterilization or disinfection* aims to kill whatever germs that are left, and chlorine is the germicide most commonly used.[17]

The cost of sewerage and sewage disposal is generally passed on to the householder. As to the sewerage system installation, there are special assessments against the abutting property for sewer construction, fees charges for sewer connections, and special taxes for sewerage facilities. These are charged to the property and may be paid by installments or rentals with a lien on the property until the full amount of the levy is paid. Sewerage facilities are expensive

[17] *Municipal Public Works Administration, op. cit.,* pp. 145–180.

items and often run to $1,000 for an average house and lot. Sewage
service charges are periodic charges to the users of the sewer system
based upon the extent of use. Two principal bases are used for
charging the residential customer for sewage disposal service. One is
water consumption and the bill is usually made for a definite percentage of the water rate. The other is by flat rate on some unit
either plumbing fixtures, sewer connections, or front foot of property.
In some cities, sewer meters are used for industrial establishments
that have special problems. Domestic charges range from an average
of 57 to 81 cents a month depending upon the size of the city. Per
capita revenue from sewage service charges ranges from an average
of $2.50 to $3.25 a year depending upon the size of the municipality.[18]

The American Public Works Association asked 130 cities what the
three most objectionable types of industrial wastes known to be
discharged into their sewer systems were. Their replies were ranked
in this order: dairy wastes, meat packing and rendering, metals and
metal plating, food processing, cannery, oils and oil products, chemical, poultry, textile, garages and gas stations, dye and dry cleaning,
breweries, laundries, tanneries, paper, biological, tobacco, paint,
glass, photographical, and restaurants. A total of 49 cities said that
industrial wastes make up more than 25 per cent of their total sewage
treatment load. Fifteen of those said such wastes constitute more
than 50 per cent of their total loads.

More than 255 United States cities of over 5,000 population make
industries pay for discharging industrial waste material into municipal sewers. Nearly one-third of the 255 cities reporting charges said
they had adopted them since 1950. Generally, the charge is based
on how much water an industry uses, but 41 have flat charges and
32 base their charge on both quantity of waste discharged and the
kind or quality of waste. For example, a firm that disposed of a
corrosive waste harmful to the sewer system might be charged more
than others even though their volume of waste is larger.[19]

[18] *The Municipal Year Book 1954*, pp. 339–340.
[19] American Public Works Association, *Industrial Waste Disposal Charges in
Cities over 5,000 Population* (1955).

Refuse Collection and Disposal

Refuse collection and disposal consists of the collection at each household, business property, or institution of solid wastes; their transportation to a disposal site; and their ultimate disposal so that nuisances will not be created. Refuse includes garbage, rubbish, ashes, street refuse, dead animals, abandoned automobiles, and industrial refuse.[20] Garbage is collected at least once a week, and in some areas more often. Ashes and rubbish are collected not more than once a week and sometimes less. As a general rule garbage is collected separately, as are rubbish and ashes. Various kinds of receptacles are required of the householder and regular routes and crews are used for the collection. Sanitary trucks, especially for garbage, are generally used in order to reduce the health menace.

Refuse disposal is accomplished by a variety of methods depending on the circumstances and conditions involved in each particular problem. In the more urban areas, these problems are becoming more difficult to solve. *Land fill* or dumping on land is almost universally used for rubbish and ashes. When it is used for garbage, as it often is, it becomes a health menace. The place becomes a breeding place for insects, germs, and rats. However, in this way much swamp land has been made useful. *Barging refuse into sea* has been carried on by many cities along the shore line but here the danger is that tides and currents bring the refuse in-shore to have it land on beaches and create a nuisance. New York City did this from 1890 to 1930 but after the currents drove the refuse onto the New Jersey shores, protests were lodged with the result that finally the United States Supreme Court ended the practice in 1934. *Feeding of garbage to hogs* is employed by many municipalities. Garbage is sold to farmers for fifty cents to a dollar a ton. Some large cities like St. Louis and Los Angeles use this method, and while many hog farms are carelessly managed and become health menaces, they can be administered with care and safety. The United States Bureau of Public Health has warned for many years that feeding garbage to hogs has caused a great increase in the disease of trichinosis. It

[20] *Municipal Public Works Administration, op. cit.,* pp. 104–109.

claimed that the incidence of the disease reached serious proportions in those areas of the country—the West Coast and New England—where hog feeding was common. Some states have prohibited hog feeding and there is no doubt that it is a dangerous practice and will gradually be abandoned. *Reduction* of garbage in order to retrieve the grease content has been widely utilized. New York City used this process and for some years made a profit from two plants which processed annually 100,000 tons of garbage. Rising costs, however, made it impractical and it was abandoned. *Burial of refuse* is practiced in many local units. It is placed on the ground and plowed under immediately. Usually it is not practicable because of the amount of land that is needed which requires expensive hauling for long distances from the city. *Fermentation* is a newer method just in the experimental stages. Garbage is placed in trays, heat is applied, and the bacterial action is stimulated. After thirty-five days, the garbage is dried and resembles humus while the liquids have been drained off. *Garbage grinding* at home and in food establishments, after which it is discharged in the sewage system, is expensive and it is relatively difficult to obtain general acceptance of the practice. But when it is collected by the city and ground at special plants near trunk sewers, or ground at sewage disposal plants and added to the sewage there, it shows some possibilities. In Canton, Ohio, the addition of garbage made the sewage treatment plant virtually independent of outside power requirements. Gas production, resulting from the digestion of garbage with the sewage solids supplies power to all the pumping and air blown equipment, producing 375,000 cubic feet of gas per day double the production without the garbage.[21] The most spectacular newcomer to the field of sanitation in recent years has been the *sanitary-fill* method. Refuse is deposited in a trench 3 or 4 feet deep and 12 to 20 feet wide. It is thoroughly compacted to a depth of 6 to 10 feet—and covered quickly with dirt from the next adjacent trench. The only equipment needed is a drag line shovel and a bulldozer. This method has been

[21] Gerald F. Johnson, "Ground Garbage Boosts Sewage Treatment," *The American City* (February, 1955), pp. 97–99.

pronounced sanitary and safe by the United States Public Health Service. It is low in cost, no segregation of material is required, and there is no investment in a plant. Its drawback is that it requires eight or ten acres for each one hundred thousand persons and thus might not be practicable for large cities. *Incineration* is one of the most common methods used. Refuse is hauled to incinerators close to the city, and destroyed in furnaces. Improved incinerators have reduced odor and eliminated gases so that they can be operated near enough to eliminate long truck hauls.[22]

There are three methods used for the collection of refuse. The municipality may handle it through its own departmental employees. The municipality may also pay a contractor for doing the collection work. Householders themselves may individually pay collectors or private operating agencies. If the municipality operates the service, it may be paid from the general fund or by service charges.

The 1954 *Municipal Year Book* reports that of 1,050 cities of over 10,000 reporting, in 647 garbage was collected by the city, in 306 by contract, and in 97 by private enterprise. Ashes were collected by the city in 556 municipalities, by contract in 134, and by private persons in 203. Rubbish was collected by the city in 658 cities, by contract in 152, and by private persons in 176.

In 1,003 cities of over 10,000 population reporting on garbage disposal methods, the open dump system was used by 207, incineration by 190, sanitary land fill by 466, hog feeding of cooked garbage by 156, hog feeding of uncooked garbage by 92, and grinding at the sewage plant by 18. Open dump and sanitary land fill were used by most cities to dispose of ashes and rubbish.[23]

Airports

Airports have long since been accepted as a municipal utility. Private enterprise has been inadequate to care for airport facilities

[22] Casimir A. Rogers, "Sanitary Fills and Incinerators," *The American City* (March, 1955), pp. 114–115.
[23] *The Municipal Year Book 1954*, pp. 344–345.

necessary for the majority of urban communities. Likewise, many public aspects call for public control and support. It was soon recognized that it was desirable to have a national airport program which called for national planning and federal support. Before 1933, there had been no state or federal participation in airport development. In 1920, there were 271 civil airports, of which 145 were municipal. Cities were beginning to think of their place on the air map of the country. The Air Commerce Act of 1926 indicated that the federal government should designate airways and should supply air navigation facilities *except airports*. This policy continued until the Civil Aeronautics Act of 1938, although federal participation in airport construction under work relief programs of the depression was substantial—almost $400 million being expended in this manner. The shift from commercial to municipal ownership and operation of airports that began around 1930 has continued ever since. In 1938, the Civil Aeronautics Act established the Civil Aeronautics Authority (CAA) and extensive surveys were made which resulted in a report to Congress recommending federal aid for airport development. During the war years, the federal government through CAA expended $350 million for the development of military landing areas in the United States, and over 500 of the military airport facilities constructed during the war were turned over to cities, counties, and states for airport use.

The Federal Airport Act of 1946 is the basis for present federal interest in airports. It calls for the development of a "nationwide system of public airports" to meet the present and future needs of civil aeronautics. Projects for which federal aid is requested must meet with the approval of the CAA standards for location, layout, grading, paving, drainage, and lighting, and all work must be approved by CAA representatives. Federal appropriations should be matched on a fifty-fifty basis, 75 per cent of the federal share to be apportioned to the states on the basis of area and population. The act authorized an appropriation of $500 million over a period of seven years at a rate not to exceed $100 million a year. By the end of fiscal 1953 almost $200 million had been used for airport grants-in-aid, a sum which represented 2,355 projects at 1,160 civil airports. In the 1953 National Airport Plan of the Department of Commerce, 2,060 airports were listed as needed. Federal appropriations, since then have been seriously curtailed. President Eisenhower recommended a token figure of $11 million to confirm federal interest for the 1956 budget, and $22 million was made available for 1955. The assumption is that cities and local units can finance their own airports without extensive federal aid.

During 1952, United States domestic and international scheduled airlines carried 27 million passengers, equivalent to one-sixth of the population of the United States. They flew 16 billion passenger miles, a gain of 18 per cent over 1951. In 1953, domestic scheduled airlines accounted for 55 per cent of the first class travel market, flying 15 billion miles in contrast to the rail-pullman 10 million miles. In 1932 airline passenger traffic was only 1 per cent of pullman passenger traffic. About 171 million pounds of mail were carried in 1952 as against 270,000 pounds in 1926. In addition, the growth of business flying during the last decade has been impressive. Well over 5,000 business corporations and firms operate their own planes. The growth of civil aviation has been truly phenomenal. It will continue to expand and increase.

It is essential that an effective national transport system cannot tolerate conflicting airport design standards. An airport of destination must be able to handle traffic from an airport of origin. In order that there be a continuous and safe flow of persons, mail, and cargo between all points in the United States and from foreign countries there must be uniformity in airport site selection, runways, taxiways and aprons, terminal buildings, flight obstruction prohibitions, lighting, and other conditions. Therefore, it is obvious that there should be federal-local cooperation in a national airport program, and there is need for federal aid as well as for uniform regulation of civil aeronautics.[24]

---

[24] United States Government Printing Office, *The National Airport Program*, Report of the Airport Panel of the Transportation Council of the Department of Commerce on the Growth of the United States Airport System (1954).

Municipalities own and operate the major airports of the nation. These are vital to the defense and the progress of the nation. A national system of airports is required for national defense, business convenience, and public transportation. The present system of airports is an example of federal-municipal cooperation, an augury of things to come in other public activities within a foreseeable future. American cities have now had enough experience to know that most airports will not bring a profit to the city. Not more than five per cent of the airports do operate at a profit. The function is governmental in its broadest sense, not proprietary.

Municipally Owned Electric Utilities

Lighting with electricity started around 1880. Public and private ownership of electric plants developed together. By 1902 there were 2,805 privately owned stations as compared with 815 publicly owned. After the first World War, private companies consolidated into larger systems while publicly owned plants remained small and independent. By 1947, commercial plants had 87 per cent of the customers and took in more than $3 billion in revenue while the municipal plants had less than $400,000,000.[25]

Almost 500 cities over 5,000 population have municipally owned electric utilities. A very few counties, special districts, and other local units also supply electricity to customers in their vicinities. Electric utilities are managed by utility boards in 134 cities. The boards are appointed by council in more than half the cities, and appointed by mayors or city managers in the others. Some few are elected. But in most of the cities, electric utilities are directly under the control of council or the mayor or city manager who appoint the superintendent. Many of the cities have no generating plants but purchase electricity and then distribute it in their localities.[26]

Although the great majority of publicly owned systems are in the

[25] John H. Ferguson and Charles F. LeeDecker, *Municipally Owned Electric Utilities in Pennsylvania,* Institute of Local Government, The Pennsylvania State University (1951), pp. 1–3.
[26] *The Municipal Year Book 1952,* pp. 349–359.

smaller municipalities, there are some large cities which own and operate in whole or in part their electric utilities. Examples are Seattle and Tacoma, Washington; Los Angeles and Pasedena, California; Colorado Springs, Colorado; Detroit, Michigan (public lighting and street railway power); Cleveland, Ohio; Jacksonville, Florida; Kansas City, Kansas; and a number of others. In Ontario, Canada, more than nine hundred local units including Toronto are united in one large publicly owned power system governed by the Hydro-Electric Power Commission.

There is no more controversial subject in the field of local government than that involving public or private ownership of electric utilities. The chief advantages claimed for private ownership are: (1) greater freedom of initiative; (2) territorial flexibility (not restricted by municipal boundaries); (3) the incentive of profit which induces economy and efficiency; (4) freedom of association with other utilities which brings financial and technical advantages that municipal utilities do not have; (5) freedom from debt limits and other governmental regulation which makes for more business-like operation; and (6) freedom from politics and civil service red-tape which makes operation more efficient.[27]

On the other hand, the Public Ownership League of America is quite enthusiastic and outspoken in favor of municipal ownership. This organization claims that the experience of 3,020 communities owning electric utilities has demonstrated that: (1) municipal ownership requires less capital; (2) that money can be borrowed at a lower rate of interest; (3) that municipal ownership gradually eliminates capital charges by paying off on their debt each year; (4) that municipal ownership avoids overcapitalization; (5) that municipalities can get service at cost; and (6) that municipal plants can serve their customers at lower rates.[28]

The general objectives of municipal ownership as outlined by Delos Wilcox are: (1) to give adequate service at reasonable rates

[27] Delos F. Wilcox, *The Administration of Municipally Owned Utilities* (1931), p. 6.

[28] Carl D. Thompson, *Own Your Own*, Public Ownership League of America, Bulletin No. 40 (1944).

to the individual customers; (2) to expand utility service for the greatest common good; (3) to limit and distribute the cost of utility service so as to impose the minimum of hardship and confer the maximum of benefit on the consumers; (4) to remove from public life influences of private interests exploiting public service for profit; (5) to eliminate the expense of public regulation; and (6) to escape the dangers of private monopoly in public service.[29]

Auditoriums

Municipal auditoriums are perhaps an outgrowth of the New England town hall which was a focal point of community activity from the earliest colonial days. But the municipal auditorium of the present day is a comparatively recent development. Only 11 out of the 166 city auditoriums studied by the Public Administration Service in 1950 were completed before 1900. Municipal auditoriums became more numerous after World War I when many were built as memorials to the war dead. The depression also added to the number as WPA and PWA projects put men to work and at the same time increased civic properties. Of the auditoriums throughout the nation, only one-third are privately owned and operated. A city auditorium is usually a handsome structure accommodating thousands of persons, and used for the staging of concerts, circuses, ice shows, expositions, conventions, operas, and theatricals.

The auditorium is managed by a manager appointed by the mayor, or separate auditorium board, or by the department head under which the auditorium is placed, or by the mayor or city manager directly, or by the city council or its committee. Salaries of managers range from $1,500 to $8,500 a year. Most auditoriums are operated to pay expenses only or to be a community service maintained partly from tax funds. They are considered to be excellent community facilities and aid local business in that they bring conventions and meetings to the city.[30]

[29] Wilcox, *op. cit.*, p. 80. See also Frederick L. Bird, *The Management of Small Municipal Lighting Plants* (1932), pp. 122–123.

[30] Farrell G. H. Symons, *Municipal Auditoriums,* Public Administration Service (1950).

Regulation, Inspection, and Licensing

As cities grew and as modern conveniences became standard equipment for urban and rural living alike, the task of regulating and inspecting various conditions, services, and items by local government increased. Such regulation and inspection are essential to the life, health, and safety of the people and have long been upheld by the courts as a proper exercise of the police power of the state and its subdivisions. In general, state laws are mandatory, other times optional. Local ordinances apply these grants to power to the specific needs of the community, and local officials are given power to enforce them.

The chronological development of city inspection services is illustrated by Lent Upson in the case of Detroit. They are: control of weights and measures, and fire prevention (1824); sanitary patrol (1867); inspection of public structures (1874); inspection of paving construction (1877); inspection of food and meats (1879); inspection of milk (1887); approval of plans and construction of all buildings (1885); inspection of plumbing (1894); inspection of boilers and electric wiring (1896); inspection of sewer construction (1900); smoke inspection (1902); sanitary inspection (1909); inspection of elevators and signs (1911); inspection of inflammables (1915); inspection of swimming pools (1915); inspection of refrigeration (1916); inspection of food-handlers (1918); inspection of maternity hospitals (1913); inspection of day nurseries (1922); inspection of oil burners (1925); inspection of explosives, Negro housing, hairdressers, and cosmeticians (1926); inspection of retail liquor establishments (1933); inspection of mattress factories (1935); inspection of substandard dwellings (1941).[31]

There are, therefore, in any large city a host of food inspectors, sanitary inspectors, building inspectors, elevator inspectors, plumbing inspectors, smoke inspectors, weights and measures inspectors, fire inspectors, electrical inspectors and others depending upon the size of the municipality and the scope of its responsibilities. These may be lodged in a number of departments depending upon the

[31] Lent D. Upson, *The Growth of a City Government* (1942), pp. 13–22.

organizational setup of the city; they may be under the merit system or not, again depending upon the municipality; expenses are met in full or in part by charges and fees.[32]

Inspection service may be good or bad. When it is good, the welfare of the people is enhanced for such is the delicate balance of modern life, especially in congested urban areas, that good inspection is necessary to insure normal safety. When the inspection is poor, epidemics, disastrous fires, and accidents may occur. Sometimes, political parties utilize inspectional services to place "deserving vote getters" in modest positions. Sometimes, inspectors are willing to overlook conditions for extra emoluments, but the public is aroused only when things get out of hand. When the general administration is good, the inspection services are usually good.

The licensing of privately operated amusements such as billiard parlors, amusement parks, theaters, dance halls, night clubs, taverns, bars, and the like is for the dual purpose of raising revenue and for regulation from the viewpoint of safety, law and order, cleanliness and morals. Amusement places of low repute are often watched by the police with especial interest because they harbor many of the criminally inclined and less desirable elements of the population. They are especially vulnerable as places that are prone to activities involving the numbers, horse betting, and other forms of gambling and activity prohibited by city ordinances or state laws. Licenses to hold parades and public meetings are also issued in order to assure law and order, although the right to meet and parade is generally regarded as available to any organization provided that public safety is adequately protected. Merchants, business establishments, and itinerant peddlers and salesmen are also licensed by many municipalities.

Public Works Organization and Procedure

As an example of public works organization in a large city, the Department of Public Works in New York City operates and main-

[32] Edna Trull, *The Administration of Regulatory Inspectional Services in American Cities,* Municipal Administration Service (1932).

tains water works, sewage treatment works, incinerators, court buildings, firehouses, a fireboat, parking field, and other structures. The old Brooklyn Bridge dedicated in 1883 was modernized at a cost of $7 million. The department is responsible for cleaning, maintaining, and operating 61 public buildings scattered through the five boroughs of the city. As of December 31, 1954, there were 4,247 employees in the department, and all but 213 provisional appointments were under civil service. The divisions of the department are buildings, bridges, sewage disposal, building management, engineering services, motor vehicles, shops, contract procedure, and administration, each headed by a director. The commissioner of public works, appointed by the mayor is in charge of the department.[33]

A city of 10,000 population or less will have a department headed either by the city engineer or a director of public works, and will have the following typical divisions: streets and sewers, utilities, refuse, standards, and public property. As the city becomes larger, staff functions such as cost accounting, design, research, and inspection may be added.[34]

The preparation of an *annual work program* for services and activities to be carried on during the coming year is indispensable for the preparation of budget estimates and for the administration of the department of public works during the year. There must be a forecast of the nature, cost, amount, and time of work to be done for each public works activity. This will include the preparation of unit cost standards for each of the activities and operations. Separate schedules must be worked out for street cleaning, waste collection, street repairs, property maintenance, and other activities. Unit cost standards are calculated from last year's records or from the elements that are estimated to be included in a unit of work such as the "street cleaning mile," the "ton of garbage collection," the "ton of incineration," the "cubic yard of spreading ashes," or the "square yard of concrete street repairs." Then detailed plans for each specific project falling under the jurisdiction of the department must

[33] City of New York, Department of Public Works, *1954 Annual Report.*
[34] *Municipal Public Works Administration,* The International City Managers' Association, third edition (1946), pp. 297–298.

be made, detailed expenditures must be calculated, and later summarized in a general program. After council takes action and makes the changes it desires, the program then can be executed within the limits of the funds that are provided. Monthly allotments may be made and seasonal programming undertaken with monthly and quarterly reports and reviews.[35]

Work of public works departments is carried on by local personnel or by private contractors. In large cities, and in smaller under certain circumstances, it is feasible for local employees to carry on the work of constructing or maintaining public works. This is called *force account* operation. But the general practice is for local units to carry on most of their major construction by contract. Provided that fair and competitive bidding can be expected this is usually considered safer and more economical. The profit motive tends to produce efficient management, the contractor takes the risks, the contracting firm has a trained personnel built up and is experienced in the kind of construction undertaken. Under contract procedure, bids are advertised, bidders are checked for qualifications, bids are opened in public at a specified hour and the "lowest responsible" bidder is awarded the contract. A surety or performance bond is required of the successful bidder. As the work progresses and is completed the municipality must inspect the work and see to it that the provisions of the contract are carried out. The entire process of construction by contract is a complicated process rigorously regulated by law for the past is strewn with thousands of cases in which contractors have taken advantage of the local unit because of carelessness, ignorance, neglect, and even collusion on the part of local employees.

TEN SUBJECTS FOR FURTHER STUDY

1. The mileage of highways, streets, and roads in your state.
2. State aid to local units for highway purposes in your state.
3. Modern street lighting.
4. Water supply problems in your state.
5. The sanitary-fill method of garbage and refuse disposal.
6. Municipal airports in your state.

[35] *Ibid.*, pp. 344–359.

7. Municipally owned electric utilities in your state.
8. House numbering.
9. A modern sewage treatment and disposal plant.
10. Organization for public works in your city.

REFERENCES

The American City Magazine, Modern Water Rates and Sewer Service Charges (New York, 1949).

American Public Works Association, *An Analysis of Sanitary-Fill Operations and Refuse Collection Problems* (Chicago, 1948).

———, *Refuse Collection and Disposal Practices* (Chicago, 1950).

Automotive Safety Foundation, *Highway Facts* (Washington, 1952).

H. E. Babbit, *Sewerage and Sewage Treatment* (New York, 1947).

Gilbert R. Barnhart, *Local Development and Enforcement of Housing Codes,* Housing and Home Finance Agency (Washington, 1953).

John Bauer and Peter Costello, *Public Organization of Electric Power* (New York, 1949).

Blanche Davis Blank, "Licenses Can Be Policemen," *National Municipal Review,* February 1948, pp. 73–76.

Chamber of Commerce of the United States, *Better Roads for Our Growing Nation* (Washington, 1955).

Warner O. Chapman and Oliver P. Field, *Indiana Licensing Law,* Bureau of Government Research, Department of Government, Indiana University (Bloomington, 1953).

Commission on Intergovernmental Relations, *Federal Aid to Airports* (U. S. Printing Office, June 1955).

———, *Federal Aid to Highway* (U. S. Printing Office, June 1955).

———, *Natural Resources and Conservation* (U. S. Printing Office, June 1955).

John B. Dawson, "Legal Aspects and Historical Background of Public Power," *The Daily Bond Buyer,* Special Convention Issue, Part One (November 28, 1955), pp. 28–30.

Federal Power Commission, *Statistics of Publicly Owned Electric Utilities,* issued annually (Washington).

Robert H. Gregory, *Municipal Electric Utilities in Texas,* Bureau of Municipal Research, University of Texas (Austin, 1942).

W. Earle Hawkins and J. Howard Wenner, "World's Most Powerful Street Lights," *The American City,* July 1954, p. 145.

Housing and Home Finance Agency, *Building Regulations Systems in the United States* (Washington, 1951).

The International City Managers' Association, *Municipal Public Works Administration,* third edition (Chicago, 1946).

H. S. Nonneman, "You Must Have a Street-Lighting Plan," *The American City,* January 1954, pp. 135–139.

John F. Porter, "Good Streets Cost Less," *The American City,* December 1953, pp. 100–101.

The President's Advisory Committee on a National Highway Program, *A Ten-Year Highway Program* (Washington, 1955).

Herbert W. Stevens and James B. Lambeth, "Raleigh Classifies Its Streets," *The American City,* August 1952, pp. 90–91.

Donald C. Stone, *The Management of Municipal Public Works,* Public Administration Service (Chicago, 1939).

Irving Tenner, *Financial Administration of Municipal Utilities,* Public Administration Service (Chicago, 1947).

John R. Thoman, *Statistical Summary of Sewage Works in the United States,* Federal Security Agency, Supplement (April 1950).

Edna Trull, *The Administration of Regulatory Inspectional Services in American Cities,* Municipal Administration Service (New York, 1932).

H. W. Tyler, "Seattle's 333 Miles of 20,000-Lumen Mercuries," *The American City,* January 1952, pp. 127–129.

U. S. Public Health Service and the American Public Works Association, *Refuse Collection and Disposal for the Small Community* (Chicago, 1953).

United States Senate, *The National Airport Program,* Report of the Airport Panel (Washington, 1954).

Delos F. Wilcox, *The Administration of Municipally Owned Utilities,* Municipal Administration Service (New York, 1931).

Chapter 15

PUBLIC HEALTH
AND WELFARE

Public Health

Public health, in its broadest outline is a function in which federal, state, and local governments have a joint responsibility. At one time, health was not a governmental function at all. It was deemed a private responsibility, an affair between doctor and family, or at the most one in which voluntary civic or religious organizations might take a hand in providing hospital facilities or help for the indigent. Then, local government gradually assumed specific functions and the state took on supervisory interest as well as some special activities. Federal interest came last in the form of grants-in-aid in specific fields of public health.

It is now generally conceded by professional public health people and by local government officials as well that local government should be responsible for the delivery of the primary public health services. The American Health Association has stated, as a result of a long-time survey, that the six basic functions of a local health department should be:

1. Vital statistics, or the recording, tabulation, interpretation, and publication of the essential facts of births, deaths, and reportable diseases;

2. Control of communicable diseases, including tuberculosis, the venereal diseases, malaria, and hookworm disease;

3. Environmental sanitation, including supervision of milk and milk products, food processing and public eating places, and maintenance of sanitary conditions of employment;

4. Public health laboratory services;

5. Hygiene-maternity, infancy, and childhood, including supervision of the health of the school child;

6. Health education of the general public so far as not covered by the functions of the departments of education.

Furthermore, the association declared that each local public health unit should contain at least 50,000 persons so that it could finance a staff composed of one full-time professionally trained and experienced medical health officer, a full-time public health or sanitary engineer, a sanitarian of nonprofessional grade, ten public health nurses, one of a supervisory grade, and three persons for clerical work. The association also considered that such a minimum public health program could be procured at the cost of approximately $1 per capita, but that costs up to $2.50 per capita might be needed for an optimum local health service. It was assumed that in such a unit consultant, advisory, and other services would be available from voluntary local health and medical associations and from state departments of health.

The association suggested also that for the United States as a whole there should be 1,197 local public health units; and as the result of a detailed state-by-state check came up with the following distribution: 318 single county units, 821 multi-county units, 36 county-district units, and 22 city units. Such a unit should be governed by a board of health of five or seven members appointed by the executives of local government of the area included in the unit, and selected from among persons with professional or civic interest. As matters actually stand, there are approximately 18,500 local government units, outside of school districts responsible for school health, that render local public health services. One-third of the entire population of the nation lives in communities where local health services have either not been undertaken at all or are under part-time, untrained, and inexperienced health officers. This conclusion is supported in general by the United States Public Health

Service. In many of the New England and Middle Atlantic states, most of the towns, townships, villages, and cities have their own board of health and health officers. But the large majority of these are too small to give efficient service with the result that state departments have taken on major public health responsibilities. In the South and the western states, the county has been the local unit. But, of course, many of the counties are much smaller in population than the American Health Association's suggested standard of 50,000 population and because of their small size they, too, are unable to furnish a modern program of public health services.[1]

In the year 1953, amounts spent for public health services in the United States totaled $280 million. Of this, $117 million was expended by the states, $103 million by local units, and $4 million by private agencies; while $56 million was from federal funds distributed to the states, some of which filtered down to local units. Federal funds were distributed for the following specific purposes and programs: general health, venereal diseases, tuberculosis control, cancer, mental health, heart disease control, industrial waste studies, and hospital surveys and planning.[2]

The *county of Jefferson* in which the city of *Birmingham, Alabama,* is situated has a public health program administered by a state-local agency on a countywide basis. This has been in effect since 1917 at which time the area was recovering from a serious typhoid epidemic, a disease from which the city of Birmingham suffered the highest death rate in the country. On the recommendation of a public health doctor from the United States Public Health Service a unified city-county health department was established. Under the provisions of state law, the county board of health is composed of five physicians elected by the Jefferson County Medical Society, and an *ex officio* member, the president of the county commission. One physician member is elected each year for a five-year

[1] The Commonwealth Fund, *Local Health Units for the Nation,* a report by Dr. Haven Emerson, Chairman of the Subcommittee on Local Health Units, Committee on Administrative Practice, American Public Health Association (1945), pp. 1–5. Also see Public Health Service, *Public Health Areas and Hospital Facilities* (1950).

[2] Commission on Intergovernmental Relations, *Federal Aid to Public Health* (June, 1955), p. 39.

term. The board has sole authority, except for the state board of health, for public health in the county, and all enforcement of health regulations is done in its name. In fact, state law forbids any municipality to establish a health department. The powers of the county health board as outlined in state law include: the enforcement of all state health laws and county health regulations; the investigation of outbreaks of diseases; the abatement of nuisances; the supervision of sanitary conditions; and the election of a county health officer. The health officer is elected for a period not less than three years and is subject to the approval of the county personnel board and the state board of health. He is the chief executive officer of the board of health. The total personnel in 1946 was 309 located in the following bureaus: administration (7), records and vital statistics (9), laboratories (18), health education (4), food and dairy inspection (25), sanitation (16), communicable diseases (6), dental hygiene (6), child hygiene and public health nursing (104), Bessemer branch office (9), and Slossfield maternity service (104). The Federal Social Security Act of 1935 encouraged the establishment of health centers. Outstanding success is attributed to them in raising the standards of health for the least fortunate segments of society and the development of community health associations. In 1945, expenditures for health amounted to $1.00 per capita, more than half of which went for child hygiene and public health nursing. Twelve per cent went for food and dairy inspection. The remaining 20 per cent was divided between sanitation, laboratories, education, records, communicable disease control, and administration. With a countywide health unit, health services can be provided for the smaller municipalities which otherwise could not be made available without outside help. The county unit makes it possible to have one strong administrative agency rather than several poorly equipped and manned. City-county health consolidation in Jefferson county has been a success.[3]

The federal government has spent large amounts in the various states for hospitals. As of September, 1954, a total of 2,336 projects

[3] Weldon Cooper, *Metropolitan County—A Survey of Government in the Birmingham Area,* Bureau of Public Administration, University of Alabama (1949).

involving 112,000 beds at a cost of $1.9 billion of which the federal government contributed $361 million, or 34 per cent, was carried on under the Hill-Burton program through which federal aid was given to localities on the basis of a series of formulae involving need, facilities, and local matching. Of the total, 73 per cent of all projects were for general hospitals in combination with public health centers; 18 per cent were for public health centers; the remaining 9 per cent were for mental, tuberculosis, and chronic disease hospitals. New facilities amounted to 59 per cent of the projects; alterations and additions to existing facilities claimed the rest. The majority of the new general hospitals were built in communities not having any hospitals before. Over half of the approved projects were in the southern states. Most of the new hospitals are small with less than one hundred beds. The remaining national need for hospital facilities is 812,000 beds.[4]

A study committee report to the Commission on Intergovernmental Affairs contains certain conclusions and recommendations relating to federal aid to states and local units in the field of health. The federal government has "proper responsibility" to participate in public health by means of grants-in-aid, subject to important limitations. The primary responsibility for meeting health problems, however, should be vested in the individual, the states, and the local communities. Federal grants-in-aid should supplement, not supplant, local effort. In 1943, the ratio of state and local expenditures to federal expenditures in public health was 1.9 to 1, while in 1953 it was 3.8 to 1, thus indicating that federal effort stimulated local action to a remarkable degree. The objective of equalization is valid for grants-in-aid programs, but local need is uppermost. Federal grants should be considered of limited duration and should be used mainly to stimulate local effort. Exceptions to this would be in research, national defense, and emergency public health services. Matching should be a part of the federal aid program but should not be inflexible. In general, says the committee, the present grants-in-aid for health should be continued at the present level, about $57 million out of a total of $280 million spent for such programs in 1953.

[4] *Federal Aid to Public Health, op. cit.*, p. 48.

Commenting on the Hill-Burton construction of hospitals, the committee believes it was in the public interest and that substantial construction of health facilities was made in areas where it was desperately needed. Research in the health sciences should be stimulated by federal grants to educational and hospital institutions throughout the nation rather than by the expansion of federal agencies in such work. Likewise grants should be made to assist local training in the field of public health.[5]

Actual expenditures for public health by local units are illustrated by a study of the American Public Health Association for more than 200 communities in 1947–48. Local funds spent by health departments ranged from six cents per capita to $2.28; the median was fifty cents. Total funds, including state and federal aid, spent by local units for public health ranged from $.14 to $4.48, with a median of $1.05 in the larger communities. Instead of the $1.00 per capita health expenditures which seemed fairly adequate to experts some years ago, it is now considered that this figure should be between $1.50 and $2.00 per capita. Voluntary private organizations add substantially to the amount spent for public health in local areas.[6]

Of full-time local health departments serving cities of more than 10,000 population in 1949, more than half of the local health departments finance the major part of their health activities from local funds. Only 109 received the major part of their health funds from state and federal sources.[7]

The work of the New York City department of health illustrates the volume and scope of local health services in a big city. In 1954, the city had 75 child health stations which treated 142,000 children. It operated 24 district health centers, 1,100 public parochial school clinics, and a number of clinics for special diseases which treated more than 250,000 children or gave them medical examinations. In order to control tuberculosis, 314,000 persons were chest x-rayed. Almost 4,400 persons were examined for cancer. There were 202,000

[5] Commission on Intergovernmental Relations, *Federal Aid to Public Health* (June, 1955), pp. 1–13.
[6] *The Municipal Year Book 1950*, pp. 293–297.
[7] *Ibid.*, pp. 303–304.

food and drug examinations, and over a million pounds of food and drugs were condemned. A total of 215,000 sanitary inspections were made. The city had 33 hospital institutions with 20,000 beds; the average daily patient census was over 18,000.[8]

Public Recreation

Recreation has always been an important segment of life. The more highly organized a society becomes, the more complicated are the facilities of recreation. The ancient Greeks had their athletic games at Olympia, Delphi, Athens, and other city states. The Romans had their great baths. The medieval barons had their jousts and hunts. In the early days of our nation, however, there was little organized recreation—there was the forest to subdue and the land to clear. The energies of early American settlers were largely absorbed in work. Many people felt it was beneath them to play when there was so much serious work to be done. It was not until after the Civil War, when cities began to grow large, that organized sports became popular. As urbanization continued they grew more varied and more available to all the people.

The rise of recreation as a public function of local government came only after cities had become so crowded and congested that children had to be taken off the street for safety. Playgrounds multiplied slowly because in large cities little open spaces had been left. American life changed in many respects during the first fifty years of the present century. Due to the machine age, household work has been reduced. Children have fewer chores to do, so do adults, and the problem of organizing leisure time becomes serious. The speed of modern life, especially in urban areas, makes for nervous tension and pressure for which human beings are not prepared. Nervous ailments and psychopathic conditions are increasing with each year. The crowding, noisy, fast-moving, nerve-wracking,

[8] New York City, *Foundations for Better Government,* First Annual Report of Mayor Robert F. Wagner to the City Council and to the People of New York City (1954), pp. 41–48.

heartless and impersonal life in big cities is too much for many people. Recreation once a luxury has become a necessity.

Federal and state governments have made some contribution to the field of recreation in the form of parks and playgrounds in their forest preserves. Counties have laid out parks, built swimming pools, and provided other facilities, especially in urban areas. But the municipalities furnish the bulk of public recreation. For in spite of the fact that both commercial and civic agencies offer recreation and sports to the dwellers of the city, municipally organized recreation affords a large percentage of the people their only opportunity for wholesome forms of fun and play. The many thousands that cannot afford golf, swimming, tennis, and other forms of recreation that cost more than nominal sums are the customers for municipal programs. Only through public efforts can adequate lands be acquired for parks and playgrounds through eminent domain, subdivision control, and city planning. Municipal recreation is democratic and inclusive, it is comparatively inexpensive, and it takes into consideration all ages, races, and occupation groups.

The event that is generally regarded as marking the beginning of the playground movement was the opening of a sand garden in Boston in 1885. A large sand pile was placed in front of the Children's Mission on Parmenter Street by the Massachusetts Emergency and Hygiene Association, and each day for the first two months an average of fifteen children played in the sand. By 1887, ten centers were opened. The movement spread to other cities. In 1892 in connection with the famous Hull House in Chicago, a well equipped model playground for small children and older ones was opened. In 1889 the Boston park department converted a ten-acre tract in a congested section along the Charles River into an open air gymnasium for boys and men, and two years later one was established for girls and women. The South Park playgrounds and centers, opened in 1905, exerted a great influence on the playground and recreation movement. "The most notable civic achievement of any American city," said Theodore Roosevelt. The National Playground Association of America later the National Recreation Association was formed in 1906 and since then has disseminated information about organized recreation and has done much to bring about public acceptance of municipal support for playgrounds and recreation centers. During the depression, the need for recreation for the masses of unemployed became acute, and large sums were spent for projects in every American city.

The types of recreation areas in a typical city include the *play lot* or block playground. A space of 2,500 to 5,000 square feet is deemed large enough and it should be situated in the middle of a block so that children do not have to cross the street to reach it. It takes the place of a backyard in the ordinary home and is for small children. The *neighborhood playground* is intended to supply recreation for the people of the neighborhood. It serves primarily children of school age, and is often located in the schoolyard or adjacent to it. The *playfield* is for young people and adults and should have 12 to 30 acres of land. It has space and equipment for athletic games and contests, and should include an area in which four playgrounds are located. The *recreation park* should be away from the congested areas of the city, a place for picnics, athletic games, day camping, and water sports. Then there are *special recreation spots* such as golf courses, swimming beaches, bathing pools, and a stadium. The *landscape park* right in the central congested sections affords peace and quiet to those who seek it; the *reservation* is an area for hiking and camping. The *parkway* is for pleasure driving and is a road running through an elongated park. A *recreation building* should be available for each 20,000 people.

How much space should be devoted to recreation? The National Recreation Association states that there should be an acre of park and recreation space for each one hundred people, and further that an acre of playground space and another acre of playfield space should be the standard for every eight hundred people. Some experts have estimated that one-tenth of the city's area should be set off for recreation purposes. Therefore, in the average city of 100,000 people, there should be 1,000 acres devoted to recreation. These would take care of 20 neighborhood playgrounds, 4 playfields, 2 playfield parks, 1 athletic field, 1 golf course, 6 neighborhood parks, 2 large recreation parks, and 1 reservation.[9]

New York City has 27,000 acres of parks and 627 playgrounds. It was estimated that in one year 170 million persons took park in various activities at the park facilities. Parks, beaches, and swimming pools attracted 61 million people, active sports another 23 million. A million used the golf links and tennis courts. Three-quarters of a million people used the bridle and bicycle paths, one-half million the ice and roller skating rinks. Outdoor concerts and dances are scheduled during the summer months.[10]

Recreation organization in a city of 100,000 people is illustrated in the case of *Austin, Texas.* Here the superintendent of recreation is directly responsible to the city manager. There is no park department, parks being maintained by the engineering department and operated by the recreation department. An advisory park and recreation board of eleven members appointed by the mayor advises city officials in planning and developing a recreation program. There are nine divisions, each with a chief: athletics, playground-community centers, golf courses, maintenance, war recreation program for military personnel, Negro division, swimming resort, music, and administration, besides an assistant superintendent of recreation.

In *Cincinnati, Ohio,* the public recreation commission of five members is appointed by the mayor (three members), by the board of education (one member), and by the park board (one member). It operates properties totaling a thousand acres including school grounds. School recreation areas are maintained jointly by the city and the school district. The director of recreation is in charge and he is assisted by supervisors in different fields of activities. Supervisors head the divisions of nature camping, special activities, girls' activities, recreation fields, playgrounds, music, and tennis. Staff services include personnel, accounting, maintenance, and construction.

[9] The International City Managers' Association, *Municipal Recreation Administration* (1945), pp. 73–79.

[10] *1954 Annual Report,* New York City, *op. cit.,* pp. 63–64.

Reading, Pennsylvania, typifies the smaller city. The mayor appoints a board, two of which must be members of the board of education. The year-round program is administered by the recreation superintendent and four supervisors in charge of special fields. The city bureau of parks and public property maintains the parks of the city. There is a playground federation composed of thirty neighboring associations, thus making a metropolitan program for the entire community.[11]

Three hundred million local tax dollars were spent in the United States for play and leisure facilities and services in 1954. Voters approved an additional 30 million dollars in bond issues and special levies for parks and playgrounds. An analysis of trends in community recreation by the National Recreation Association indicates that the great boom in municipally operated recreation and park services which began after World War II continued strong through 1954. There is every indication that it will go on for some years ahead. One city manager in a Wisconsin city recently noted that community recreation is the fastest growing municipal service today.

The number of recreation departments under full-time leadership has more than tripled in the past fourteen years. Seventy-two municipalities established new departments for the first time in 1954. Most of these were small cities. Nearly half of the 2,438 communities with 5,000 or more population now have full-time recreation leadership. Next to new playgrounds, swimming pools headed the list of new park and playground facilities in 1954.[12]

Air Pollution

Economic losses in the United States from air pollution, according to the Stanford Research Institute, amount to at least $1.5 billion per year. This is roughly $10 per person for extra costs in cleaning, painting, laundry, damage to merchandise and buildings. While air pollution control has only recently been recognized as a local government function, the American Municipal Association reports that

---

[11] *Municipal Recreation Administration, op. cit.,* pp. 324–334.
[12] *National Recreation Association,* News Release.

almost all cities over 25,000 population have established some kind of air pollution control. Industry itself, it is estimated, has spent at least $1 billion to clear up its share of air pollution in the five year period beginning in 1950. The cities of St. Louis and Pittsburgh are outstanding examples of the manner in which local government and industry can team together to bring about lasting results.

Principal causes for air pollution are industry, motor vehicles, private coal burning homes, apartment incinerators, and the like. The increase in industrial production and the consequent metropolitan growth in recent years has intensified the problem. Industrial demands for power have gone up enormously in the past generation. In 1930, the production of electrical energy for industrial purposes consumed 40 million tons of coal, 9 million barrels of oil, and 120 billion cubic feet of gas. By 1952 these figures had climbed to 107 million tons of coal, 67 million barrels of oil, and 921 billion cubic feet of gas. The millions of tons of combustion products now being poured into the air by smoke stacks, chimneys, and exhaust pipes stagger the imagination.[13]

The United States Public Health Service made a survey of air pollution control in the state of New York. They found that almost half of the urban communities and a third of the rural communities have air pollution problems they would like to have corrected. In a substantial number of local units, the sources of air pollution are outside their jurisdiction. About half of the urban communities and most of the rural communities had no air pollution or smoke-control ordinances. In only 8 out of the 455 communities having smoke pollution problems is personnel employed full time to cope with them. In a few others the county health departments give this function some attention. Regional air pollution control agencies, such as the one in the San Francisco Bay area, point the way to more effective control where whole metropolitan and industrial areas can be brought under one act of control.[14]

Three and a half years of study of the problem in Los Angeles

[13] G. E. Pendray, *Management Aspects of Air Pollution*, The American Society of Mechanical Engineers, Paper 55–APC–13, March 1, 1955.

[14] A. C. Stern, *Air Pollution Control—Administrative Needs and Patterns*, The American Society of Mechanical Engineers, Paper 55–APC–15, March 1, 1955.

county indicate that the present known results of "smog"—reduced visibility, eye and throat irritations, damage to crops, and other nuisances—arise from more than 50 different substances released in the air.[15]

The Department of Air Pollution Control of New York City is responsible not only for smoke control and abatement, but for the control of other kinds of air pollution. The job is most difficult and complex because in a single year New York City consumes 13 million tons of coal, over 3 billion gallons of fuel oil, and over 1 billion gallons of gasoline for motor vehicles. In addition, 400,000 tons of refuse are burned in the 10,000 incinerators of multiple dwelling buildings. Another big factor is the smoke of 12,000 ships, mostly oil driven, which use the port each year. The department has 30 inspectors who examine installations and enforce air pollution ordinances. As a part of city-industry cooperation, 1954 commitments made by industry to abate air pollution whittled $16 million as a result of all the effort. Laboratory tests indicate that New York air is becoming cleaner. The soot-fall in the city has decreased in the past decade thereby saving millions of dollars in cleaner buildings, reduced depreciation, and lower laundry bills.[16]

Public Welfare

The term "public welfare" is not a precise one. At one period, it may mean a closely related group of activities pertaining to assistance for the needy; at another time, it may be a broader field including organized effort to combat unemployment, delinquency, crime, and the whole range of social evils. It may vary from state to state, from city to city, and from county to county. Generally speaking, it might be described as "the helping hand of the state," the state in this case meaning government as a whole—federal, state, and local. Specifically, it can be said to include all governmental activities for the prevention and treatment of dependency, neglect, delinquency, crime, and physical and mental handicaps. It includes programs of

---

[15] *The Municipal Year Book 1953*, p. 313.
[16] *1954 Annual Report*, New York City, *op. cit.*, pp. 56–57.

public assistance such as poor relief, unemployment relief (both direct and work), disaster relief, assistance to special groups such as the aged, dependent children, the blind, the physically handicapped, and the disabled veterans. It includes services to physically and mentally handicapped, and to delinquent children; and the administration of state and local institutions for the poor, the delinquent, and the handicapped.[17]

Public welfare is dynamic in another sense. Once it was entirely local, based upon the heritage of the Elizabethan poor laws which came with the early settlers in colonial times. Its first manifestation was the county or town poorhouse or home where all sorts of people not able to care for themselves were placed. Often these were, even until recent times, places in which the poor, the aged, the sick, the mentally deficient, and even the criminal elements were cared for by local authorities. The latter part of the 19th century saw the advance of knowledge and understanding in the treatment of individuals who needed community assistance. Public welfare was broken into specialized segments each calling for a different approach and treatment. Specialized state institutions for the mentally handicapped, the criminally inclined, the youthful delinquent began to be established. Outdoor relief began to supplement institutional care in local areas and departments of public welfare in counties and cities displaced the old poor boards. It was recognized that such groups as the blind, the aged, the mothers, the widows with minor children could hold their normal place in the community if they received some financial assistance.

The responsibility for mass unemployment, until the depression of the thirties, was given to private welfare organizations and local poor agencies supplementing family responsibility where it was deficient. But the immense volume of depression unemployment and need for relief brought both the state and the national governments into the public welfare field in a big way. At first the national government provided aid to states and local units for the maintenance of adequate relief standards and services. Then it provided work relief wherein money for public works was granted or loaned to

[17] Marietta Stevenson, *Public Welfare Administration* (1938), pp. 1–4.

PROPORTION OF POPULATION RECEIVING ASSISTANCE
(RECIPIENT RATES), BY STATE, JUNE 1954 [a]

States (Ranked by 1951–53 Income per Capita)	Old-Age Assistance [b]	Aid to Dependent Children [c]	States (Ranked by 1951–53 Income per Capita)	Old-Age Assistance [b]	Aid to Dependent Children [c]
U.S. average	184	28	Iowa	147	18
			Minnesota	177	18
Delaware	57	24	Arizona	257	40
Nevada	206	1 [d]	Utah	197	26
Connecticut	83	17	Texas	374	20
New York	75	28	Idaho	181	20
Illinois	119	21	South Dakota	182	28
New Jersey	46	9	Vermont	161	20
California	258	39	Florida	236	54
Ohio	133	14	Maine	128	31
Michigan	148	20	Virginia	71	19
Washington	255	26	New Mexico	318	57
Maryland	59	22	North Dakota	157	16
Massachusetts	181	20	Oklahoma	440	44
Pennsylvania	61	21	West Virginia	166	60
Indiana	97	15	Louisiana	578	44
Montana	165	26	Georgia	389	24
Oregon	135	18	Tennessee	253	43
Rhode Island	111	33	Kentucky	217	38
Wyoming	199	12	North Carolina	198	29
Wisconsin	135	17	South Carolina	325	23
Colorado	376	33	Alabama	277	35
Missouri	299	40	Arkansas	311	28
New Hampshire	108	16	Mississippi	387	43
Kansas	165	17	District of Columbia	46	34
Nebraska	130	14			

[a] Includes recipients receiving only vendor payments for medical care.

[b] Recipients of old-age assistance per 1,000 population aged 65 and over; based on population estimated by the Bureau of Public Assistance as of June 1954.

[c] Children receiving aid to dependent children per 1,000 population under age 18; based on population estimated by the Bureau of Public Assistance as of June 1954.

[d] Program in Nevada administered without Federal participation.

Source: Department of Health, Education, and Welfare, *Social Security Bulletin* (September 1954), p. 31. From Commission on Intergovernmental Relations, *Federal Aid to Welfare* (June, 1955), p. 92.

states and local units provided they would hire unemployed and pay them standard wages—enough to keep them and their families on a subsistence basis in their own homes. In 1935, a permanent federal program was established. The federal government divided relief recipients into employables and nonemployables. For the employables, the federal government provided a works program. As to the unemployables, federal grants to states were made for the relief of certain categorical groups. Aid to the aged, to dependent children, to the blind, to the permanently and totally disabled, and for child welfare services was given to the states on a matching basis under the 1935 Social Security Act. In addition, the Old Age and Survivors Insurance Program administered solely by the national government, and the Unemployment Compensation Program administered by the states under national standards and financed from nationally collected employers contributions have put the federal government into the public welfare and social security picture as a major partner. General assistance and relief of the indigent was made entirely a state responsibility which it might share with the local units in any way it wished. Thus in Pennsylvania direct relief or public assistance to the needy is financed and administered entirely by the state through its department of public assistance and their county boards of public assistance within the framework of the department. The county commissioners administer county homes for the indigent, and aid the state in administering categorical relief financed jointly by federal, state, and local contributions. Such aid must be administered under plans approved by the Social Security Agency of the federal government. In about a third of the states, local government bears the entire burden of general assistance or direct relief. In thirty others, the state and local governments share the costs and administration.

As of October, 1954, almost five million persons received aid under the welfare programs classified under the Social Security Act as public assistance. By far the largest number of these categories were the aged totaling two and a half million. The average monthly payment for old age assistance was $51.53 including medical care. Amounts available differ from state to state, and the range was from $28.08 in Mississippi to $82.86 in Connecticut. Aid to dependent children was given to more than a million and a half children of almost 600,000 families. Average amount received per month by recipients was $23.93 amounting to $85.92 per family. Blind assistance was given to almost a hundred thousand persons, the average monthly amount being $56.22. Aid to the permanently and totally disabled was given to more than two hundred thousand persons at the average rate of $54.40 per month. Federal funds were available also for about 273,000 children in institutions, foster homes, or in their own homes. About 310,000 cases at the rate of $54.47 a case received general assistance grants from state and local governments, the federal government not sharing in this form of assistance.[18]

With regard to federal financial assistance in the field of welfare, a study committee report to the Commission on Intergovernmental Relations contained a number of recommendations for future policy. It agreed that there was a clear national interest in welfare, specifically the provision of opportunity to receive economic aid needed for maintenance including aid for medical care for the jobless, unemployable people; for children who otherwise would be deprived of parental care and who are separated from their families; for the disabled including the blind; and for the aged. Also the federal government has an interest in providing the mentally and physically disabled to receive services needed to make them fit for employment or less dependent upon others for public support. The major purposes of federal assistance, it was recognized, are to equalize among states the financial burden of providing an adequate welfare program, and to help support minimum standards. Federal funds should be made available in one comprehensive welfare program rather than in categorical units as is the case at present. Federal administrative effort in the welfare program should be restricted to that of research, special studies, compilation of statistical data, development of standards consultation, advice, audit, and reviews. Federal controls over state and local action should be confined to developing a stated formula for making available federal funds to states. Federal funds should be used only for purposes stated in federal

[18] *The Municipal Year Book 1955*, pp. 318–320.

law, available only on a matching basis. They should be used to audit state expenditures of federal funds, to approve a state plan for the administration of financial aid, and to require states to have minimum standards of administration of such funds including the merit system for employees in public welfare administration.[19]

The most important single element in local welfare administration are the *case workers*. These persons make available the facilities of the local welfare agencies and of the community at large to families and individuals who need and are eligible to receive public assistance in one or more of its many forms. Case workers must have a social outlook and professional training. Trained in social service, they bring relief on an individual basis, ascertain the circumstances of each client, continue to maintain contact, and grant relief in accordance with the need within the limits allowed by law or regulation. Case work, according to those who favor the administration of public welfare through professional personnel, is justified for reasons of public economy, protection to the community, and humanity. Only through trained social workers can there be adequate investigation of need and the proper utilization of available resources. They visit families and homes, and find out the conditions that cause indigency, delinquency, and crime. They understand what the effects of poverty are upon families and their children, and try to mitigate these effects by continuous and judicious use of assistance, knowledge, and understanding. There has been criticism of the social worker from the standpoint of the expenditures for personnel and the alleged high rate of relief and assistance grants and services administered by them. It does not help the situation, some say, to "coddle" relief clients. Nevertheless, professional social workers are being used in increasing numbers wherever there are groups that need the ministrations of public welfare. It is a profession that is finding increasing respect and usefulness in the industrial and urban world in which we are living.

New York City's department of welfare in 1954 gave assistance to 311,000 persons, some in their homes and some in institutions, in

---

[19] Commission on Intergovernmental Relations, *Federal Aid to Welfare* (June 1955), pp. 5–9.

ten different programs. Annual expenditures totaled $221 million. The cost was shared about equally between the federal government, the state of New York, and the city government. In that year, on December 31, there were 191,000 who filed unemployment compensation claims, a rough gauge of economic conditions. About 52,000 received old age assistance; about 29,000 received relief because of permanent disability. Many of the disabled persons are rehabilitated by various city welfare agencies and returned to work. About 140,000 persons received aid for dependent children given largely to those whose fathers could not or would not support them.[20]

In forty states, county boards of welfare can be established to handle welfare activities. In counties as a whole throughout the nation, public welfare, including assistance of all kinds, is the largest item of expenditure but a large share of the money for it comes from federal and state governments in the form of grants. Thus the county has developed into a state-local-national agency in the field of welfare. It is part state because it must adhere to state regulations when carrying out state welfare activities and spending state money. It is local when carrying out local responsibilities and spending county money. When it carries on welfare activities under the Federal Social Security Act it must abide by federal regulations relating to merit system for employees and the prohibition against political activity by employees.

Mercer County in New Jersey in which Trenton, the state capital, is situated, has a population of over 200,000 and can be considered an urban county. The governing body of the county is the board of chosen freeholders composed of seven members elected for overlapping terms of three years. The county board of welfare consists of seven members, five of whom are appointed by the board of freeholders, while the freeholders also delegate two of their number to be on the board. Unless the county adjuster, appointed by the county judge is made director of welfare, he is *ex officio* a member of the board. The county board of welfare appoints the director of welfare and other personnel, but they must qualify under the merit system, and appointments must be approved by the state division of

[20] *1954 Annual Report,* New York City, *op. cit.,* pp. 49–50.

old-age assistance and the state civil service commission. The welfare program is not integrated. The State Department of Institutions and Agencies is responsible for old-age assistance; the State Commission for the Blind is responsible for aid to the blind; the State Board of Child Welfare administers assistance to children. The county board of welfare administers the old-age assistance program and through its staff investigates cases, determines eligibility, and estimates the amount of need. This program is administered under state regulations. The federal, state, and local governments share the costs. The State Board of Child Welfare has two divisions—home life assistance and foster home care. The state is responsible for all investigations and recommends the amount of assistance to be given. The county referee reviews this action and makes his recommendation to the county board. Federal, state, and county governments split the costs 50–25–25 per cent. Foster care is a responsibility of the state board, and the county board performs no functions in this field but does split the costs with the state. Aid to the needy blind is administered through the county welfare board, and the federal government and the county share the financial costs. General relief is the responsibility of the state and the municipalities. The municipalities have a director of welfare sometimes referred to as the overseer of the poor. The responsibilities of the state are administered through the division of municipal aid of the Department of Economic Development. The state may make suggestions but the municipality has the final word. If the municipality elects to accept state financial aid, it must abide by state regulations in the administration of the relief. The aid varies between 40 and 60 per cent.[21]

TEN SUBJECTS FOR FURTHER STUDY

1. The local units providing health services in your state.
2. Expenditures for health in your city.
3. The organization of public health work in your community.
4. Recreation areas in your city.
5. The attack on pollution in Pittsburgh.

[21] Wager, *County Government across the Nation* (Chapel Hill, North Carolina, 1950), pp. 187–188.

6. Public welfare organization and services in your city.
7. Health education in the public schools.
8. Los Angeles attacks smog.
9. Public assistance in your state.
10. Local organization against unemployment.

REFERENCES

Bureau of Public Assistance, *Characteristics of State Public Assistance Plans; Old Age Assistance, Aid to the Blind, Aid to Dependent Children, Aid to Permanently and Totally Disabled,* Social Security Administration (Washington, 1953).

George D. Butler, *Introduction to Community Recreation* (New York, 1940).

———, *Recreation Areas—Their Design and Equipment,* National Recreation Association (New York, 1946).

———, *Standards for Municipal Recreation Areas,* National Recreation Association (New York, 1948).

Commission on Intergovernmental Affairs, *Federal Aid to Public Health* (U. S. Printing Office, June 1955).

———, *Natural Disaster Relief* (U. S. Printing Office, June 1955).

———, *Federal Aid to Welfare* (U.S. Printing Office, June 1955).

L. P. Cookingham, "A Plan to Meet Disaster," *National Municipal Review,* February 1952, pp. 74–79.

Robert T. Daland, *Government and Health,* Bureau of Public Administration (University of Alabama, 1955).

Howard G. Danford, *Recreation in the American Community* (New York, 1953).

Victor M. Ehlers and E. W. Steel, *Municipal and Rural Sanitation* (New York, 1950).

Haven Emerson and Martha Luginbuhl, *Local Health Units for the Nation,* The Commonwealth Fund (New York, 1945).

Governmental Affairs Foundation, Inc., *Trends and Relationships in Public Assistance in the United States* (September 1954).

Governmental Research Center, *The Social Worker's Role in Mental Health,* University of Kansas (Lawrence, 1954).

Ira V. Hiscock, *Community Health Organization* (Cambridge, Massachusetts, 1950).

———, "Public Health Developments of 1954," *The Municipal Year Book 1955,* pp. 325–329.

Fred K. Hoehler, "Public Welfare and Health, 1900–1950," *State Government,* June 1950, pp. 129–133, 142.

William T. Ingram, "Control of Community Sanitation," *Public Management,* October 1949, pp. 266–268.

The International City Managers' Association, *Municipal Recreation Administration,* second edition (Chicago, 1945).

Robert S. Lewis, *Health Administration on Third Class Cities in Pennsylvania,* Institute of Local Government, The Pennsylvania State University (State College, 1938).

Martha Luginbuhl, "Local Responsibility for Public Health," *Public Administration Review,* Winter 1946, pp. 30–41.

Wayne McMillen, *Community Organization for Social Welfare,* University of Chicago (Chicago, 1945).

Arthur C. Millspaugh, *Public Welfare Organization,* The Brookings Institution (Baltimore, 1935).

Margaret G. Morden and Richard Bigger, *Cooperative Health Administration in Metropolitan Los Angeles,* Bureau of Governmental Research, University of California (Los Angeles, 1949).

James E. Pate, *Recreation as a Function of Government in Virginia* (Richmond, 1953).

Public Health Service, *Report of Local Health Resources, 1952* (Washington, 1954).

Wilson G. Smillie, *Public Health Administration in the United States* (New York, 1947).

Marshall Stalley, "Horizons Beyond the Smoke," *National Municipal Review,* November 1947, pp. 558–564.

Maurice E. Trout, "Cleaning Up the Restaurants," *National Municipal Review,* July 1949, pp. 335–338.

U. S. Public Health Service, *Distribution of Health Services in the Structure of State Government, 1950,* Washington, 1952.

R. Clyde White, *Administration of Public Welfare* (Chicago, 1950).

Chapter 16

PLANNING AND BUILDING
THE FUTURE CITY

The American city is a dynamic entity. In a century of growth it has developed from a small town into a metropolis. It is still growing and changing. Its population is bursting out of its municipal boundaries. The automobile and rapid transit facilities have allowed it to extend miles out into the once rural areas just as the elevator and the steel structure skyscrapers created the congestion in the center that characterized cities a generation ago.

All during the 19th century cities grew with little or no planning or design except the exigencies and needs of the moment which were largely attuned to the development of the economy of the growing nation. While there were some instances of planning for a city at its beginnings, for example, that of William Penn for Philadelphia as exemplified by the width of the two intersecting main streets, Market and Broad, and in the case of Washington, D. C. where the French L'Enfant laid out a plan of streets around a central hub, the average American city just grew, street by street, avenue by avenue, usually under the pressure of the real estate salesmen and the building contractor. As a result, most cities are found wanting not only from the viewpoint of modern needs which could not be foreseen, but also because they were jerry-built, poorly conceived, quick-to-deteriorate, uncomfortable, dull, and uneconomical.

One is shocked by the realization that most European cities are planned, built, and maintained better. The dread disease of blight is now in full attack on every American city that is fifty years old or more. It is a challenge that must receive serious attention if the big investment in the central city areas is to be saved. The problems of the periphery in which communities have sprung up almost overnight are hardly yet realized. The vague but horrible threat of atomic attack has temporarily immobilized efforts to seek more permanent solutions to traffic, industrial location, housing, school construction, and other pressing matters.

This is not to say that there has been no action in the field of city planning—far from it. It is merely to record that city growth has far outstripped any concerted effort to plan ahead. The first wave of city planning in the United States came from the Chicago World's Fair in 1893 when men and women from all over saw the possibilities of an orderly arrangement of monumental buildings, parks, and streets as laid out in the fair grounds now occupied by Chicago University. From Chicago, too, came the classic utterance of Daniel Burnham who was engaged in making the impressive plans now in full flower along the Lake Michigan waterfront. He said: "Make no little plans; they have no magic to stir men's blood and probably themselves will not be realized. Make big plans; aim high in hope and work, remembering that a noble logical diagram once recorded will never die, but long after we are gone will be a living thing, asserting itself with ever growing insistency. Remember that our sons and grandsons are going to do things that will stagger us. Let your watchword be order and your beacon beauty." This was the basis of the famous Chicago Plan and its rudiments were put in manual form and used as a textbook for the Chicago schools.

All over the nation the idea of the *city beautiful* expressed itself in civic buildings, civic centers, parks, street planting, artistic lamp posts, and other forms of civic art. *Park areas* became especially popular. Cities had grown up without open spaces to provide relief from the sometimes intolerable congestion. Children had no place to play except in the street. Frederick L. Olmstead, Sr., who planned the development of Central Park in New York in 1875, ushered in the park era. Since then, no self-respecting city or town wants to be without park or outdoor recreation facilities. The conditions of big city tenements toward the end of the 19th century led to *tenement laws* that attempted to ameliorate the terrible living conditions of congested slum areas. The advent of the automobile led to modern street planning including street widening, one-way streets, boulevards, limited access highways, and downtown off-street parking facilities. The downtown congestion brought about *zoning* with its usage, height, and area restrictions to limit overcrowding.

WHAT'S NEXT FOR AMERICAN CITIES

Luther Gulick, first "city administrator" of the city of New York (1954), looks ahead to the American city of 1960. He sees more population . . . more young folks in school . . . more people with leisure . . . more suburbs with more shopping and entertainment centers . . . more automobiles and congestion . . . more public housing and slum clearance . . . more wealth per capita. Cities will have to expand their schools . . . extend their public health functions . . . develop their hospitals . . . modernize their downtown areas . . . improve the parks and playgrounds . . . achieve new street layouts. To do all this taxes on real estate will rise by 25 to 50 per cent . . . other types of levies will increase . . . federal aid will increase . . . local debt will hit all time highs . . . intermunicipal cooperation will increase . . . the council-manager plan will continue to spread . . . but the problems of metropolitan government, local-state relations, and local revenues will not yet be solved.

From *The American City,* December, 1949.

At the beginning of the present century, Ebenezer Howard, an Englishman, wrote about garden cities in which new cities of six thousand acres were to be built with residences, parks, farms, industries, and business—all in functional proportion and with limited population. Such a city was Letchworth, first garden city in England, built in 1903, thirty-two miles from London. These garden cities had great influence in the development of high class residential suburbs in the United States after World War I. Examples are Kingsport, Tennessee; Longview, Washington; Fairfield, Alabama; and Hershey, Pennsylvania, founded by industries; others such as Roland Park in Baltimore, Maryland; the Country Club District of Kansas City, Missouri; Shaker Heights of Cleveland, Ohio; Forest

Hills Gardens in Long Island, New York; and the Palos Verdes Estates of California were developed by real estate groups. During the depression of the thirties, the federal government built such communities as Greenbelt, Maryland; Norris, Tennessee; Green Hills, Ohio; and Greendale, Wisconsin. *Subdivision control*, brought on by the tremendous expansion in the outlying parts of the metropolitan areas, was imposed so that these new sections did not immediately fall into the same errors that cities were trying to correct in the older parts of town. Gradually there evolved the idea of the *comprehensive plan* in which all the physical elements of the city or community were involved. Included were not only streets, parks, and civic centers, but also water supply, housing, industrial sites, traffic control—in fact the entire city. But it soon became evident that a *master plan* could not be static, that it could not be made realistic for any particular period of time. The city needed continuous planning in terms both of time and of space. So evolved the *metropolitan area plan*.[1]

Even now the impact of the automobile, jet air travel, and atomic power indicate that the American city has not yet reached its ultimate design. The express highway that links cities together by rapid automotive transportation is just coming into its own. Its effects on metropolitan development are hardly yet discernible but they are bound to be substantial.

Take the case of Yonkers, New York. The Buffalo-New York City Thruway is going through the city of Yonkers just north of New York City. Twenty-five million vehicles will race through Yonkers every year. This will cause profound consequences, according to Harrison E. Salisbury of the *New York Times*.[2] Taxable property with an assessed valuation of $2,500,000 will be displaced. The cost for the three miles of thruway will total almost $18 million, making it one of the most expensive bits of road construction in history. While there is no aroused civic challenge to the six-lane highway

---

[1] The International City Managers' Association, *Local Planning Administration* (1948), pp. 1–6.

[2] *New York Times*, April 21, 1955.

laid right through the principal business street of the city, there are signs that the highway will sever the unity of the city forever. The fundamental problem which Yonkers is contending as far as the thruway is concerned, says Mr. Salisbury, is "the twenty-first century phenomenon that Oswald Spengler calls 'Megalopolis.' Megalopolis was Spengler's projection of the 'barracks city' of the future. The American Megalopolis of the twenty-first century is clearly going to be barracks-plus-wheels. Already Yonkers is far along the pathway toward becoming merely a dormitory annex, a traffic corridor and a minor shopping service and relaxation center for the multimillions of Megalopolis—much farther than is realized by some of the Getty Square men who still measure the seasons by the run of shad up the Hudson and the seasonal coming and going of the Hudson River Day liners.

"But the Yonkers future, like that of many another town and city that geography has made satellite to the Big City and the Big Highway, is not an inexorable fate that must be accepted with the resignation of a Buddha. There are choices Yonkers can make. By aggressive attack, many natural obstacles such as lack of lateral communications can be overcome. Past neglect rather than current disinterest lies more at the heart of the school problem. Economic shifts can be treated as opportunities for the new rather than penal sentences for the old. . . . The fact is that Yonkers can, to a great extent, pick the kind of future it would have—within the periphery of Megalopolis. But it must make the choice quickly. The twenty-first century permits no backward glimpses. And it must pursue its objective vigorously and in intelligent accord with the majority interests of its citizens. Better communities do not grow untended like wild roses along a county lane. Even the best gardens can become seedy with neglect. And few flower beds would not be improved by new seed strains and the latest biochemical aids."

Spengler himself took a dim view of the modern city. He sees its transformation into its ultimate form of the future. "Now the old mature cities with their Gothic nucleus of cathedral, townhalls, and high-gabled streets, with their old walls, towers and gates, ringed about by the Baroque growth of brighter and more elegant patricians' houses, palaces, and hall-churches, begin to overflow in all directions in formless masses, to eat into the decaying countryside with their multiplied barrack-tenements and utility buildings, and to destroy the noble aspect of the old time by clearances and re-buildings. Looking down from one of the old towers upon the sea of houses, we perceive in this petrification of a historic being the exact epoch that marks the end of organic growth and the beginning of an inorganic and therefore unrestrained process of massing without limit. And now, too, appears that artificial, mathematical, utterly land-alien product of a pure intellectual satisfaction in the appropriate, the city of the city-architect. In all civilizations alike, these cities aim at the chessboard form, which is the symbol of soullessness. Regular rectangle blocks astounded Heroditus in Babylon and Cortez in Tenochitlan. In the Classical world, the series of 'abstract' cities begins with Thurii, which was planned by Hippodamus of Miletus in 441. Priene, whose chessboard scheme entirely ignores the ups and downs of the site, Rhodes, and Alexandria follow, and become in turn models for innumerable provincial cities of the Imperial Age. The Islamic architects laid out Baghdad from 762, and the giant city of Samarra a century later, according to plan. In the West-European and American world the lay-out of Washington in 1791 is the first big example. There can be no doubt that the world-cities of the Han period in China and the Maurys dynasty in India possessed this same geometric pattern. Even now the world-cities of the Western Civilization are far from having reached the peak of their development. I see, long after A.D. 2000, cities laid out for ten to twenty million inhabitants, spread over enormous areas of countryside, with buildings that will dwarf the biggest of today's and notions of traffic and communication that we should regard as fantastic to the point of madness." [3] Oswald Spengler, the German school master, wrote this during World War I. Now forty years later what he said gains more reality each year.

[3] Oswald Spengler, *The Decline of the West*, Vol. 2 (Alfred A. Knopf, Inc., 1928), pp. 100–101.

Local Planning

Planning for a city, a county, or a metropolitan area must be based upon facts which can be collected and made known. These facts must then be assembled and analyzed. What is the *population* of the community? What kind of people live in it? Is the population increasing? Why? How do these people earn their living? Where do they live? How are they housed? What are the *physical character-istics* of the community? What is the pattern of land use? What about streets, traffic, transportation facilities, natural resources? What about the *economic make-up*: the industries, commercial establishments, volume of business, unemployment, trade area, migration of industry and labor? What of *public services and finances*: what do local governments do, what is the cost, how is the revenue raised, what needs to be done? The *social problems* are also important: education, recreation, crime, delinquency, health and welfare activities. Facts can be obtained by surveys, research, and studies—not necessarily carried on in one comprehensive project but rather continuously and upon a variety of segments of community life. They can be projected in charts, tables, maps, and other media in order to be understood in relation to each other by the community as a whole. *Land use studies* are especially indispensable to community planning. How the land area is being utilized must be known before plans for the future can be made. In a land use study an inventory of all parcels of land and the uses to which they are put (residential, commercial, industrial, public) is made. Maps are drawn to indicate the character, condition, height, and occupancy of all basic structures and buildings and their yard spaces.

Most cities grew on the basis of economic forces. For example, an industry developed in the area because of natural resources, location in relation to transportation facilities, or a number of other reasons. People moved in the community to work in the industry. Increase in population gave rise to more business establishments and was reflected in new housing, schools, parks, and other facilities. The pattern of community growth in the average locality was to a large extent based upon its industry; business and residences clustered in areas where there were industrial opportunities. But often such natural arrangements were not entirely satisfactory from the viewpoint of living conditions, community facilities, the street and transportation network, and even for industrial development itself. Short-sighted policies resulted in maladjustment, expensive community overhead costs, blighted areas, and economic disintegration. While economics did screen out industries that did not pan out financially, the community itself was often left with a residue of mistakes that indicated the need for conscious planning for the future. Naturally, most cities and communities today cannot be made over by planning, but they can be adjusted to new conditions and the future can be charted more accurately when intelligent thought and study are made. Furthermore, communities can be made more desirable to industry, business, and residents if progressive measures are taken to insure modern and harmonious development.

The first major step is a *plan for land uses* of the community. It simply does not pay to allow industry, business, and residences to mingle together without any control. Land values under such conditions deteriorate once their primary economic uses are fulfilled. The community plan should lay out residential, industrial, business, and recreational areas, and when this is translated by *zoning* into actuality it will have a great deal to do with where people will live, how they will commute to work, and where they will shop. The city plan will also be concerned with *public services*: water supply, electric power, gas, busses, trolleys, streets, public buildings, and parks. These must be developed to serve the best needs of the people. Land use and community facilities must be merged in the master plan which will be balanced, as to present conditions and future needs, between the financial resources of the community and the demands of its people.

The implementation of the master plan into reality is never complete but it is accomplished in part in a variety of ways. *Advice* is given to local officials in the preparation of plans for particular public facilities. Where should they be located? What are the pros-

PERCENTAGE DISTRIBUTION OF LAND BY TYPE OF USE

Cuyahoga County and the City of Cleveland

	County Total	*U r b a n* Central	Outer	Total	Sub-urban	Rural
Total Land Area	100.0%	100.0%	100.0%	100.0%	100.0%	100.0%
Total "Developed" Area	26.4	67.4	66.3	66.7	31.6	11.9
Residential	13.6	31.6	45.9	40.7	16.8	4.0
Stores & Offices	.9	5.7	2.5	3.6	.7	.1
Industrial	3.0	20.5	5.1	10.0	3.8	.4
Outdoor Business & Activity	.6	.2	.3	.3	1.9	.2
Cemetery	.7	1.6	2.0	1.9	.5	.4
Recreational	6.7	4.9	8.1	6.9	6.8	6.5
Institutional	.9	2.9	2.4	2.6	1.1	.3
Streets & R. R. (est.)	8.5	19.2	18.2	18.3	11.4	4.1
Vacant (est.)	65.0	13.4	15.5	15.0	57.0	84.0

Source: Regional Planning Commission, *Our Citified County* (1954).

pects for increased population which they would service? *Regulation* includes zoning, control of subdivision design, building codes, and other ordinances prepared by the planning agency, passed by the governing body, and administered by certain municipal departments of government. *Education* is necessary to raise the sights of the citizens to the possibilities of taking public action to get better housing, better traffic conditions, better land use—and therefore enhancing the worth of the community and the welfare of its citizens.

Local governments receive powers to plan through enabling acts passed by the state legislature. Such legislation exists in almost every state. Cities in nearly all states, counties in many, and regional areas in some are empowered to establish planning agencies. The local ordinance, within the limits of the enabling act, provides for the composition of the planning agency, its procedures and powers. The 1955 *Municipal Year Book* reveals that 86 per cent of all cities reporting on this question have planning agencies, but that only 29 per cent of them employ a staff of one or more persons. *City and*

ORGANIZATION CHART FOR PLANNING THE SMALL CITY

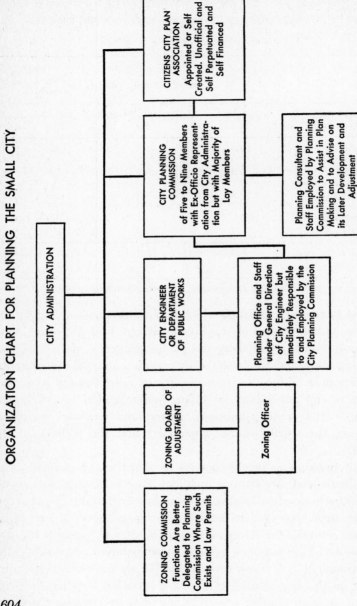

Fig. 20. Organization Chart for Planning the Small City. (From Russell Van Nest Black, *Planning for the Small American City*, Public Administration Service No. 87, p. 11.)

county planning commissions are usually composed of a board of lay citizens serving without pay, appointed by the mayor or county commissioners, together with certain *ex officio* membership. In many cases they have the power only to advise but not to administer. In other cases, council can pass ordinances on some planning subjects after approval or recommendation of the planning board. In this way, actions of the governing body can be related to the master or comprehensive plan. Typical powers are: (1) preparation and adoption of a master plan; (2) preparation and adoption of platting regulations, and approval of land subdivision plats; (3) preparation of a zoning ordinance; (4) preparation of an urban redevelopment program; (5) preparation of a mapped street plan and an official map; (6) reporting to chief executive and legislative body of the local unit on planning problems referred to it; (7) preparation of reports, surveys, and studies on any general planning problem. In order to do its work, a staff is needed. Many municipalities have planning boards without budgets to employ competent staff personnel and in such cases planning is merely a "paper" function or at the most advisory. It is recommended that a planning agency for a city or county of fifty thousand population should have a permanent planning staff consisting of an experienced city planner, a draftsman, and a stenographer. One with 500,000 population might well have a permanent staff of from fifteen to twenty members.[4]

According to Robert A. Walker, an authority on local planning, urban planning agencies have so far fallen short of their potential usefulness. They have been set up as independent, unpaid boards at the periphery of the administrative structure of local government, not well integrated with the other phases of government, and their activities have been largely restricted to the physical aspects of planning rather than the social and economic. Most of the members are business executives, realtors, architects, and engineers. Persons identified with labor, social welfare, and education are rarely found on these commissions. The original pioneers in planning have passed on. The successors too often lack their enthusiasm, imagination, and

[4] International City Managers' Association, *Local Planning Administration* (1948), pp. 35–38.

general interest. Mr. Walker thinks that planning is a staff function and should be attached to the executive office instead of being off in a corner as a commission. Planning agencies are handicapped when they do not have a full-time executive head, and the ordinary planning staff, where there is one, is inadequate.[5]

The function of planning is gradually extending across municipal and county boundaries in metropolitan areas and regions. In 1954, Arkansas, Maine, Indiana, and Massachusetts were added to the list of states whose legislatures provided for the establishment of planning commissions on a regional basis. The Indiana law requires the establishment of a metropolitan planning commission for Marion county and the city of Indianapolis, and transfers city, county, and town planning functions to the new commission. Metropolitan planning action has recently been taken in such areas as Denver (The Inter-County Regional Planning Commission of four contiguous counties), and Monroe county, Michigan, which became a member of the Detroit Planning Commission.

A few illustrations will indicate the actual activities of local planning commissions and agencies:

In *Westchester county, New York,* the Department of Planning conducted a survey on how residents feel about new parkways, shopping centers, office buildings, and other such developments in their neighborhoods both before and after completion. The study also measured the effects of these improvements on surrounding property values.[6] In *San Benito, Texas,* a "pilot plan" was developed. This was not as detailed as a master plan but it gave the citizens and civic groups an idea of the over-all problems of the community. Later a master plan was drawn for specific areas.[7] In *Davenport, Iowa,* progress in planning has been made since the City Planning Commission was established in 1946. It is composed of 17 members, including the school board, park board, levee commission, real estate board members, engineers, architects, businessmen, the mayor, an

[5] Robert A. Walker, *The Planning Function in Urban Government* (Chicago, 1941), pp. 329–337.

[6] *The American City* (March, 1955), page 175.

[7] *The American City* (November, 1952), pp. 102–104.

alderman, and the city attorney.[8] In *Easton, Pennsylvania,* an Easton
Area Regional Planning Commission composed of representatives of
the city of Easton, three boroughs, and three townships was established in 1951 and has made progress in developing zoning ordinances, extending sewer services, and developing traffic, parking,
and redevelopment planning in all of the communities concerned.[9]
In *Pasadena, California,* the Planning Commission surveyed 197
blocks of the poorest housing, launched an inspection program, and
ordered repairs, demolition, or rebuilding of several thousand
dwellings. Good public relations, the use of existing personnel, and
the enforcement of existing ordinances, and freedom from state or
federal aid made this a workable local program.[10] In *Greenwich, Connecticut,* the Planning Commission studied the relationship of different land uses to tax income and cost of municipal
services. This study was useful in determining the proper future
balance between profitable and unprofitable uses in planning increased developments. It was shown, for example, that two-family
houses and apartment houses do not return enough in taxes to equal
the cost of municipal services, but that vacant land, single family
houses, and industries yield more in taxes than is expended on them
in services.[11] In *Milwaukee, Wisconsin,* an ordinance was passed
designed to discourage long-term investments in areas scheduled
for future purchases for public improvements. Included in this
program for planning public improvements are (1) a detailed capital
improvement budget which programs timing and costs of future
projects; (2) a map showing properties needed for the capital
program; and (3) procedure for referring building permit applications to the city council when the application involves properties
scheduled for future improvements. The council either withholds
the permit or grants it with a warning that the property will be
taken for future improvements and that long-term investments are
not advised. Such areas are placed into four classes depending on

[8] *The American City* (January, 1954), pp. 98–100.
[9] *The American City* (May, 1954), pp. 154–155.
[10] *The American City* (July, 1954), pp. 116–117.
[11] *The American City* (May, 1955), p. 117.

the time when improvements are contemplated, i.e., first two budget years, next two, projects specifically contemplated or otherwise included in the capital program, and projects included in final planning.[12]

Zoning

Zoning is the division of the community into districts for the purpose of regulating the *use of the land and buildings* in each district in accordance with the desired character of the district, for the purpose of regulating *the height and bulk of buildings, the proportion of the lot that can be covered by them,* and *the density of population.* Zoning is deemed an exercise of the police power of the state for the purpose of promoting the health, safety, morals, and general welfare of the community. Zoning should not be considered as a means to exclude undesirable uses from a community or a district by excluding laundries, garbage disposal plants, or other essential services even though their effects may be disagreeable. Nor is it used for racial segregation. Furthermore, it cannot be retroactive. Uses contrary to the zoning ordinance which were established prior to the ordinance are termed *nonconforming uses,* and sometimes provisions are made to allow their gradual discontinuance without unreasonable burden upon the property owners. Nor is zoning undertaken to promote civic beauty although in the long run this is sometimes accomplished and is always desirable. Zoning is a tool for the planner; through zoning, streets and utilities can be planned to meet the needs of ascertainable kinds and numbers of population, and to afford better and more economical police and fire protection. Its real value is to bring about better neighborhood development and more efficient provision of public services. It protects the home owner from an invasion of his neighborhood by harmful business and industry. It assures more space and light in crowded areas, and keeps down congestion and overcrowding. Cities rarely have powers to zone outside city lines but zoning is needed in the suburban areas to bring order out of the chaos of un-

[12] *The American City* (May, 1955), p. 116.

planned settlement. A comprehensive zoning ordinance adopted jointly by suburban units would be highly desirable in fringe areas. Many counties have developed zoning for areas outside the larger municipalities for just this purpose. Rural zoning has also proven a useful tool in preventing the growth of scattering settlements in areas that should be entirely forest or recreation. In this way, money for roads and schools which serve only a few people can be saved.

Regulation of the use of land and buildings by means of a zoning ordinance is by establishing different types of use districts and designating what uses may be permitted in each. The customary use districts are residential, business, and industrial, but there may be several grades in one or more of these divisions. In *residential* use districts there may be as many as four subdistricts, single-family residences, two-family residences, four-family residences, and apartment houses residence districts. In such districts, no use other than residential is allowed. Business and industry are excluded. In *business* use districts, commercial uses as well as residences are allowed. There are two kinds of business districts—the central, downtown area and the neighborhood shopping districts. *Industrial* districts may be divided into light industry, heavy industry, and unrestricted districts. In heavy industry areas, so-called nuisance or dangerous industries such as chemical plants, oil refineries, blast furnaces, fertilizer plants, fireworks factories, and the like are allowed. In many industrial areas, residential uses are disallowed.

Regulation of building heights is designed to reduce congestion and to preserve light and air for city areas. There are usually from three to six height districts, and height regulations are expressed in terms of the maximum number of feet or stories permitted in relation to street width. In central business districts of larger cities, building setbacks at certain levels may be provided and this has resulted in the indigenous and entirely modern American skyscraper architecture since the first such regulations went into effect in New York City early in the present century. Typical regulations for single or two family residence districts limit the height to 35 feet or two and a half stories. In apartment house districts, three to seven stories may be the limit or the total floor area may not exceed 275

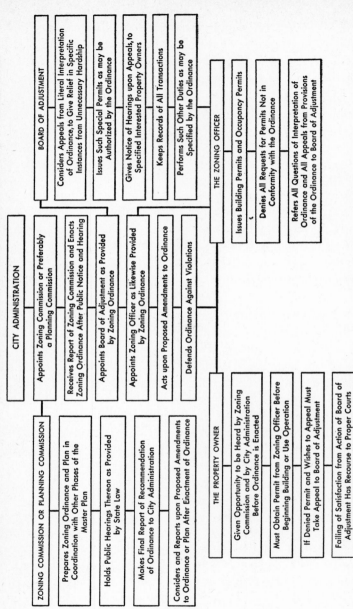

Fig. 21. Procedure for Making and Administering Zoning Ordinances and Plans in Small Cities. (From Russell Van Nest Black, *Planning for the Small American City*, Public Administration Service, No. 87, p. 66.)

per cent of the areas of the lot. In central business areas, the height may be not more than the width of the street before setbacks must be made. Usually the height before setback is not more than twelve stories. Area regulations include the maximum permitted density of population, the percentage of lot that may be built upon, the minimum size of front, rear, and side yards; and the minimum size of courts.

The zoning ordinance includes the zoning regulations and zoning districts and is prepared either by the planning agency or by a specially appointed zoning commission. Information is assembled, tentative maps are made, hearings are held, and finally the zoning map and ordinance are ready for the city council to approve. Once adopted the zoning ordinance is enforced by the building commissioner, city engineer, or the officer who issues the building permits. The application for a building permit usually contains an application for a certification of occupancy that will permit the use of the completed building for its designated purpose. Zoning ordinances permit an appeal from a negative decision on the part of the city to issue a permit to a board of zoning appeals or adjustment. The function of this board is to decide appeals from the decision of the building permit officer, and to hear and decide cases of special exception, and to grant variances from the strict letter of the law if they believe that enforcement would cause a needless hardship.[13]

The 1955 *Municipal Year Book* reports that virtually all cities in the United States of over 10,000 population have comprehensive zoning ordinances. More than sixty per cent of the cities have revised their zoning laws since 1946. Of more than six hundred cities reporting, the median sized lot allowed for single family residences was 5,000 square feet, and the median minimum frontage was fifty feet. Lexington, Massachusetts, had the highest minimum with 15,000 square feet and a frontage of 125 feet. About two hundred and fifty cities reported that their ordinances required the gradual elimination of nonconforming uses such as junk yards, auto-wrecking yards, nonconforming structures, and billboards.[14]

---

[13] *The American City* (May, 1955), pp. 218–247.
[14] *The American City* (May, 1955), p. 31.

Subdivision Control

As a city or urban settlement expands, unoccupied land is built up. During the past century there has been a tremendous urban expansion into the countryside around almost every city, and this process is continuing during the mid-century decades at an accelerated pace. Most of this expansion, especially in earlier years, was unplanned and unregulated. A real estate agent or a private individual undertook to get control of large parcels of land in likely locations and to subdivide them into building lots and sell them to the public. Many of these subdivisions were located in unsuitable areas where perhaps land was low and swampy and subjected to spring floods. In other cases, streets, pavements, water supply, and other utilities were not provided for with the result that the owners found themselves saddled with properties they could not afford to improve.

In many municipalities, there were premature and excessive land subdivisions with the result that there were acres and acres of weed-grown vacant property stretching out for blocks at the edge of town which represented a loss to the owner, the subdivider, and the local government. Special assessment bonds may have been used to finance the improvements and when these areas were not built up the city which made the improvements had to take over the lots for nonpayment of these costs on the part of the property owner. Where there are subdivisions with only a few scattered houses within a municipality there is an unwarranted increase in the costs of public services which have to be paid by the other residents of the city.

During the depression of the thirties many towns were financially drained by excessive subdivisions. Niles township, in the Chicago area, had in 1928 a population of 9,000 and enough vacant lots for a population of 190,000. In 1938, the state of New Jersey was reported to have enough vacant lots to take care of a population of four million, as many people as the state had at that time. In Detroit and its environs in 1935 there were enough vacant lots to take care of three million people. The real reason for excessive subdivision is the chance that a great deal of money can be made by buying farm land and converting it into building lots. Naturally, the owner or real estate promoter wants to spend as little as possible and make as much as possible on the transaction, and frequently he has made a lot of money but often in the end the property buyer and the local government have paid a big price for excessive subdivision. Subdivisions have been carried out to make a maximum of profit but often without technical skill and knowledge of the ways to get the most out of the land for both the developer and buyer as well. Modern, well-conceived plans can be more attractive than the ordinary gridiron pattern and therefore bring a better price and increase permanent land values.

State legislatures give cities and local units the right to regulate land subdivisions through the power to withhold the privilege of public records from subdivision plats that do not meet the required standards. If the plat is not recorded, lots within it may be sold only by "metes and bounds" descriptions of their boundary lines. This makes building lots more difficult to sell. It would probably be unconstitutional to prohibit the sale of lots that were not approved by the municipality because this would violate the right of an individual to dispose of his property. State enabling acts generally give the power to approve subdivisions to city or local planning boards or commissions, or permit the governing body of the local unit to delegate this function to them. Obviously, a planning agency should approve subdivisions because they become a part of the city plan and should conform to standards relating to street width, open spaces, utilities, and other factors.

In checking and approving land subdivisions, the planning agency is concerned with the layout and width of streets, the length and depth of blocks, the width and depth of lots, the provision for open spaces for parks and recreation areas, the provision of water and sewerage, and other such matters. The procedure followed begins with the filing of a preliminary plan to the planning agency by the subdivider. Platting regulation developed by the planning agency should be furnished beforehand so that the subdivider can make his preliminary plans to meet the requirements. Then the plans are reviewed by the planning agency and other municipal officials, such

PROCEDURE IN THE CONTROL OF LAND SUBDIVISION

CITY ADMINISTRATION

- Grants Authority to Planning Commission by Ordinance
- Accepts Dedicated Areas Shown on Final Plat After Approval by Planning Commission

LAND DEVELOPER

- Submits Preliminary Plat Map to Planning Commission in Form and Containing Information as Required by the Rules and Regulations of the Planning Commission
- Prepares Final Plat Map in Accordance with Conditions of Approval of Preliminary Plat Map
- Obtains Planning Commissions Approval of Final Plat Map
- Has Final Plat Map Made Matter of Record at County Court House
- Usually Requests Municipal Administration to Accept Dedicated Areas Such as Streets and Parks
- Proceeds with Sale of Lots by Reference to Recorded Plat and Lot Numbers

CITY PLANNING COMMISSION

- Adopts Policy and Rules and Regulations
- Requires Submission of Preliminary Plat for Consideration and Approval
- Approves Preliminary Plat as to Form
- Requires Submission of Final Record Plat and Checks for Conformity to Approved Preliminary Plat
- Approves and Endorses Final Plat Map

COUNTY RECORDER OR CORRESPONDING OFFICIAL

- Records Plat Maps Approved by Planning Commission
- Refuses to Record Unapproved Plat Maps

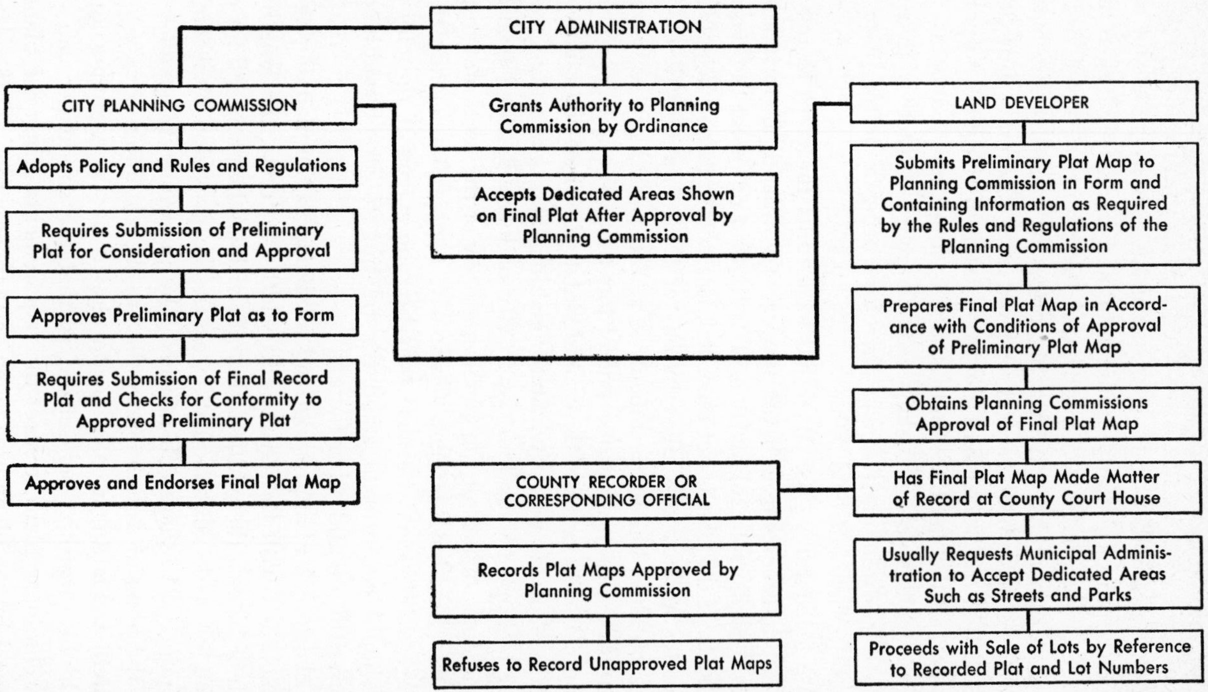

Fig. 22. Procedure in the Control of Land Subdivision. (From Russell Van Nest Black, *Planning for the Small American City,* Public Administration Service, No. 87, p. 58.)

as the street commissioner and city engineer, to see if the plans follow the general requirements for streets and utilities. Hearings may be held by the planning agency so that abutting owners may have a chance to discuss the layout. Then follows adjustments, if deemed necessary, and preliminary approval. When building is about to start, the proper permits may be issued by the building officers of the municipality.

Today most of the cities have reached their limits as far as building is concerned, and most of the real estate development is outside city boundaries. In fact, half of the increase of population in the United States between 1940 and 1950 was in the suburbs, and the movement of residences towards the periphery of the metropolitan areas still goes on. Many states have authorized their cities to exercise land subdivision regulation outside city lines, in some cases as much as ten miles out. Five miles, however, is the recommended distance. In many states, also, county planning commissions have been given the right to regulate subdivisions in unincorporated areas. Laws usually make provision for adjustments where two jurisdictions having platting authority overlap.

In order to insure that subdividers obey platting regulations, a variety of means of enforcement have been developed. City enabling acts normally prohibit the county recorder of deeds from recording an unapproved plat. Other methods include the licensing of real estate dealers and making it unlawful for him to sell unplatted and unrecorded subdivision lots. Real estate developers sometimes try to evade the installation of services such as water and utilities in order that they need not entail that extra expense. Likewise, they try to utilize every square inch of the development for salable lots and not provide for open spaces that will help to make living conditions better for the residents.[15]

Blighted Areas

During the past several decades, the term "blighted areas" has forced its way into the American public mind. Many American cities

[15] *Local Planning Administration, op. cit.,* pp. 248–267.

are now more than a century old and older portions have been allowed to deteriorate to the point where they have become civic liabilities. The old city as we have known it is rapidly becoming a thing of the past. Central cities are losing population. Outlying areas are developing sometimes at terrific speed. In either case, blighted areas develop in the central city, from neglect; in the outlying areas from mushroom growth without adequate planning.

Between 1910 and 1930, the borough of Manhattan in New York City lost a half million population. The cities of Chicago, Philadelphia, Detroit, Cleveland, St. Louis, and Boston either actually lost population during recent decades or experienced little or no increase in comparison to the early decades of the century. Los Angeles gained tremendously, but this city has the largest area of any American city. Other cities would not have lost but gained had they the boundaries of the surrounding metropolitan and urbanized territories. For the real cities, which are the metropolitan areas, are not losing but are gaining population. America is becoming a highly urbanized nation and this applies to all sections irrespective of age or location. The new concept of the "fluid city" where workers commute great distances from home to work is taking shape in reality. Central cities are becoming less congested, but blighted areas remain in the wake of the exodus.[16]

What are blighted areas? Two basic characteristics are substandardness and stagnation or deterioration. Substandardness, as defined by Allen A. Twitchell, is basically a condition in which the area falls below officially adopted or generally accepted requirements of fitness for the purpose for which it is being used.[17] "Quite commonly," he says, "in urban areas, substandardness can be identified in buildings—their design, equipment, structural soundness, repair, and maintenance; in land subdivision and layout—size and shape of lots, coverage, density, and sometimes even the amount and allocation of

---

[16] Tax Institute, Inc., *The Disintegration of American Cities*, from *Tax Policy*, June–July, 1947.

[17] Jones and Twitchell, "Measuring the Quality of Housing in Planning for Urban Redevelopment," Part I, Coleman Woodbury, ed., *Urban Redevelopment: Problems and Practices* (Copyright 1953 by the University of Chicago), pp. 10–15.

areas for new and expanding uses; in community facilities and services—water, sewer, schools, recreation, transportation, etc.; and in location—nearness to obnoxious uses, accessibility to other districts that a particular area serves or from which people and goods regularly go back and forth. When a district is markedly substandard in some or all of these respects, it is usually, but not always, blighted." In addition to this, if an area is not improving or is actually deteriorating, it can be termed blighted. Once an area begins to go downhill, it usually keeps on going in that direction. Generally a blighted area becomes a public liability—that is, it collects taxes from that area far less than the city spends on it for police and fire protection and other municipal services. Perhaps, as Twitchell says, this concept of economic liability is open to some doubt because almost every section of a city, except the high class residential and business and industrial areas, has spent upon it for public services an amount in excess of revenues produced but not all of these are blighted. In fact, residents of low and middle class-income residential districts often work in other areas and add to the production of wealth and to the municipal income in those areas. Likewise, how about the loss of energy and time to people living in the suburbs and traveling two hours a day to and from work?

Another name for blighted residential districts is "slum." But there are commercial and industrial sections, too, that are blighted. Furthermore, blighted areas are not only built-up areas; arrested and deteriorating subdivision areas often qualify as blighted. Blighted areas are caused by three major factors: poverty, land speculation, and the nuisances created when inappropriate types of activities are permitted in a residential area. Excessive densities and overcrowding help to produce unhealthy living conditions—lack of air and light, recreation facilities, living space, individual and family privacy; excessive noise, dirt, and air pollution; delinquency, crime, and family maladjustments produced by poor conditions; accident, noise, and dirt factors due to heavy traffic; high prices of land because of concentrated usage which slows up any improvement short of public activity; disproportionate per capita costs of municipal services; threatened economic strangulation of central urban areas because of high costs of public and private services; and actual moving of population without lessening of the service costs.[18]

Public Housing

Municipal and local governments, because of the general recognition that poor housing is a detriment to the community, are empowered by state law to stimulate better housing conditions. They may enact construction and maintenance regulations aimed at the worst abuses that are fire and health hazards; they may plan and zone to keep blight from the newly developed parts of the community. But going it alone, municipalities and local units have not made much of a dent on the intolerable housing conditions that characterize certain sections of almost every urban community. The problem is just too big. During the depression years, the United States government interested itself in low-cost housing for low-income groups, and at the same time their projects provided work for the unemployed. The federal government by loans and grants and by actual operation itself stimulated action in the low-cost housing field.

The first major federal legislation on housing was the Housing Act of 1937 which established the United States Housing Authority and authorized it to loan money to public housing agencies. The object of this legislation was to aid state and local governments to clear slums and to provide for low-income groups who could not afford the rents which would have to be paid if private enterprise financed the construction and the operation. The sum of $800 million was appropriated but the initiative had to be taken by local housing authorities. These authorities were created by the municipalities on the basis of state enabling legislation and they were given the power to borrow money, build housing, and rent such housing to families that came under the requirements made by the federal government. Once the projects of the local housing authorities were approved by USHA, the national government made loans up to 90 per cent of the cost of the project at a low rate of interest. Direct subsidies

[18] *Ibid.*, p. 203.

at ten per cent of the shelter rent were also provided. To be eligible for participation in this housing program and to help to reduce rentals, local governments had to raise contributions at least one-fifth of the federal subsidies in the form of cash, tax exemption, or tax remission. The Housing Act of 1949, and its amendments, authorized additional loans and capital grants totaling $1.5 billion for slum clearance and for the construction and operation of 810,000 addition units of low rent housing over a period of six years. Nathan Straus estimates that eighty per cent of the cost of public housing is met by the tenants, while twenty per cent is met by local and national subsidies. The national subsidy is in the form of the difference between what the annual cost of the housing project is and what the tenants can afford to pay. Local subsidies are usually in the form of tax exemption. National annual subsidies are limited to 3½ per cent of the total cost of the project and are payable for 40 years.[19]

State participation in local housing is largely that of permitting local units to participate in housing activities and in particular in federal housing projects. As of 1953, forty-three of the forty-eight states allowed localities to participate in federal housing programs for low-income families. As a result some 1,000 localities had more than 450,000 units of low-rent housing either completed or on the way. However, ten states made available direct state aid.[20]

Slum Clearance, Urban Redevelopment, and Urban Renewal

Closely connected with the program of low-cost public housing, which since 1952 has been substantially reduced in volume as far as federal aid is concerned, is the whole problem of slum clearance, urban redevelopment, and urban renewal. These concepts are com-

[19] Nathan Straus, *Two-Thirds of a Nation* (1952), p. 203. According to Mr. Straus, twenty per cent of the people of the United States live in slums or substandard housing. This means they lack most of the "modern conveniences" now deemed necessary in American houses. The National Association of Housing Officials estimated a need for more than 17 million houses for the ten year period ending in 1960.

[20] *The Book of the States, 1954–55*, pp. 353–355. These states are California, Connecticut, Illinois, Massachusetts, New Hampshire, New Jersey, New York, Ohio, Pennsylvania, and Wisconsin.

paratively new to municipal government; it might be said that they received their greatest stimulus from the Federal Housing Acts of 1949 and 1954. The general idea is that blighted areas can be improved; in fact, that they must be improved in order to keep the tremendous investment that has been made in our central cities and in order to preserve the whole metropolitan area from deterioration and chaos. Furthermore, in view of the atomic threat, fire hazards that surround the cental city core must be eliminated. The improvement of present blight conditions, therefore, is not a luxury that we cannot afford; it is a necessity without which we will be vulnerable to internal and external dangers of fearsome proportions.

Slum clearance means the clearing of slum areas by tearing down old buildings and structures, and the building of new housing on the same site. *Urban redevelopment* is a broader term. It includes all the activities designed to do away with the major forms of physical blight in cities and to bring about changes in urban structure and institutions contributing to a more favorable environment for a healthy life for all urban dwellers.[21] Indicated treatment in urban redevelopment runs from drastic clearance to mild conservation and adjustment. The heaviest responsibilities for redevelopment, in spite of federal assistance, lies with the local officials and civic organizations themselves. The former carry on the action in a program, and the latter must help to mold public opinion for an understanding of the problem of urban blight and the ways it can be attacked. Under the redevelopment section of the Act of 1949, Title I, federal assistance can be given for the following types of projects: redevelopment of residential slums or blighted areas for any locally approved use; (2) redevelopment of blighted commer-

---

[21] Woodbury, *op. cit.*, p. vii. The difference between "clearance" and "conservation" indicates the range of activity that might be applied to blighted areas. Clearance is the demolition or removal of all or nearly all of the buildings from an area—often accompanied by a new site layout and underground utilities. "Conservation" means measures to maintain or to improve the quality of residential districts without excessive clearance—it would include repair and modernization of buildings, demolition of scattered buildings of poor quality, provision of better recreational and open space, re-zoning, sometimes closing and dead-ending minor streets to prevent heavy traffic from going through the residential area, providing off-street parking facilities, and making available more adequate school and other facilities. *Ibid.*, p. 6 fn.

cial and industrial areas for residential use; (3) residential redevelopment of predominantly open land with blight such as that of the dead or arrested subdivision; and (4) residential development of essentially open land needed for sound community growth. Loans and grants were available on the first three; loans only for the fourth.[22]

Urban renewal is the Eisenhower administration's term for the prevention and elimination of urban decay. To slum clearance and urban redevelopment under the 1949 Housing Act, urban renewal as provided in the 1954 Housing Act adds the concept of conservation and rehabilitation in treating decayed areas. For an acceptable urban renewal program, the federal government requires interest and action from the city. The locality must demonstrate that it has a workable program for the elimination of slums and blight. This means that the city must have done or must plan to do a number of things. If interested in financial aid from the federal government, it must submit a report to the Housing and Home Finance Agency showing that the city government has or can supply the following: (1) adequate codes and ordinances covering minimum housing standards; (2) a general plan for the community; (3) identification of bad housing conditions and a plan of action to remedy them; (4) an administrative organization to administer housing codes; (5) provision for the additional funds necessary for enforcement and planning; (6) a recognition of the problem of rehousing families displaced because of urban renewal activities; (7) evidence of community understanding and participation in the urban renewal program.

An urban renewal project under 1954 legislation is of the same general pattern as an urban redevelopment project under the 1949 Housing Act. The federal government agrees to pay two-thirds of the net cost of the undertaking and the locality must put up one-third. This one-third, however, does not need to be in direct appropriations but may include public improvements—schools, streets, playgrounds, and other facilities. But the 1954 Housing Act is broader in that it allows the locality to treat larger areas and provide

[22] *Ibid.*, p. 9.

improvements other than clearance and rebuilding. In addition, financial assistance to private owners is possible. Private houses in renewal areas may be eligible for substantial loans for major rehabilitation work through a special mortgage insurance fund.[23]

J. Frederick Dewhurst, writing on urban redevelopment for the Twentieth Century Fund, estimates the total cost of complete urban redevelopment in the United States as follows: "The entire urban housing replacement, rehabilitation and redevelopment program can now be summarized. With a completely centralized redevelopment program, it would cost $85.5 billion to eliminate all our urban residential slums and blighted areas and to provide every family living in urban areas in 1950 with at least a minimum standard dwelling in a satisfactory neighborhood." He goes on to say that other improvements are needed: high speed traffic arteries, interurban terminals, airports, renovated public utilities, more and better schools, hospitals, and other facilities. "Main Street needs to have its face lifted," he says. And he points out the great strides that have been made in cities like Chicago and Pittsburgh to show what can be done. This echoes the older generation: "Make no little plans. . . ." [24]

The Rising Suburbs

In the 168 standard metropolitan areas as delineated by the Bureau of the Census in 1950, central cities had 58 per cent of the population while the suburbs had 42 per cent. Over the past thirty years, the proportion of population has steadily shifted in favor of the suburban areas and the same tendency will to all appearances continue in the foreseeable future. Suburban areas account for large proportions of new housing. Some of the housing projects, notably Levittown, both on Long Island, New York, and in Bucks county, outside Philadelphia, are on a grand scale and attract residents from the central city by the thousands. But suburban housing often leaves

[23] William L. Slayton, "Urban Renewal—a Program for Cities," *Public Management* (April, 1955), pp. 74–77.
[24] J. Frederick Dewhurst, "Urban Redevelopment, a Second Chance and What It May Cost," *The American City* (May, 1955), pp. 138, 191–192.

something to be desired. Its defects are poor location, inadequate size, inadequate facilities—water supply, sewage disposal, and schools. Poor location, a result of urban sprawl, leads to difficulty in transportation to the central city. Utility and facility deficiencies are the result of fast growth coupled with inadequate financial resources on the part of local governments. While there has been a slow increase of industrial workers in suburbia since 1930, and a faster increase in commercial establishments, local governments in these suburban regions are too fragmented and too small to do the urban job of providing services for their rising number of residents even though the gap between central city tax rates and those of the fringe are rapidly closing.[25]

The core problem for suburbia lies in the fact that many of the local units on the fringe are strictly or almost entirely residential areas, many of them middle-income, some even low income. It is pretty well settled that middle and low priced residential properties cannot raise enough general property tax money to provide the kind of urban services needed in suburban towns. For example, it has been shown that in Greenwich, Connecticut, two-family and apartment houses, stores and offices do not return enough in taxes to equal the cost of providing them with municipal services. On the other hand, vacant land, single-family houses, and industries pay more into the town treasury than Greenwich expends to service them.[26]

This is further substantiated by a study made by the Urban Land Institute in 1951. Of the seven cities over 50,000 which had a record of allocations of property taxes to specific expenditures revealed that residential land use produced a deficit. "This means," the report says, "that the municipalities do not collect from the residential areas as much as it costs to provide public services. This deficit must be made up from other land uses. . . . In each of these reporting cities, the commercial and industrial areas show a profit to the city. The surplus comes from the fact that these users pay more in

[25] Coleman Woodbury, "Suburbanization and Suburbia," *American Journal of Public Health* (January, 1955), pp. 1–9.
[26] *The American City*, "Planning Study Shows Municipal Costs for Different Land Uses" (May, 1955), p. 117.

property taxes than it costs the city to provide services to the area." [27] Similar results were found from a study in three towns in Connecticut.[28] This simply goes to show that in some way the wealth of a larger metropolitan area must be pooled in order that residential suburbs will be able to exist without the deterioration that comes from strangulated finances. Either there must be some kind of federation or consolidation so as to include in each local unit property that gives more in taxes than it receives in services, or increased state aid or state services must fill the gap. If this problem is not solved, the next generation will see blighted areas in the suburbs even more extensive than they are now in the central cities.

TEN SUBJECTS FOR FURTHER STUDY

1. The Chicago Plan.
2. Zoning districts in your city.
3. Outline of a planning survey for your community.
4. Land use sketch of a ten block area in your neighborhood.
5. Modern subdivision control.
6. The need for public housing in your community.
7. Zoning in New York City for the regulation of height and bulk of buildings.
8. Parkways.
9. Urban renewal under the 1954 Housing Act.
10. The master plan for your community.

REFERENCES

Annals of the American Academy of Political and Social Science, November 1945. Entire issue devoted to the subject of "Building the Future City."

Edward M. Bassett, *Zoning; the Laws, Administration, and Court Decisions during the First Twenty Years,* Russell Sage Foundation (New York, 1940).

Catherine Bauer, "Redevelopment: A Misfit in the Fifties," Chapter I in Coleman Woodbury, ed., *The Future of Cities and Urban Development* (Chicago, 1953).

[27] Max S. Wehrly and S. Ross McKeever, *Urban Land Use and Property Taxation,* Technical Bulletin No. 18, Urban Land Institute (1952), p. 7.

[28] Belden H. Schaffer, *Small Homes and Community Growth,* Institute of Public Service, University of Connecticut (1954).

R. V. Black, *Planning for the Small American City,* Public Administration Service (Chicago, 1944).

Henry Bruere, "Goals for the Modern City," *National Municipal Review,* December 1951, pp. 566–573.

Miles L. Colean, *Renewing Our Cities* (New York, 1953).

P. H. Covnick, *The Results of Premature Subdivision* (New York, 1937).

The International City Managers' Association, *Local Planning Administration,* second edition (Chicago, 1948).

Victor Jones, "Metropolitan Studies," a book review, *Public Administration Review,* Winter 1953, pp. 57–63.

Harold W. Lautner, *Subdivision Regulations: An Analysis of Land Subdivision Control Practices,* Public Administration Service (Chicago, 1941).

Stuart A. MacCorkle, *The Texas City, Its Power to Zone,* Institute of Public Affairs, The University of Texas (September, 1955).

Harold V. Miller, *Mr. Planning Commissioner* (Chicago, 1954).

Lewis Mumford, *The Culture of Cities* (New York, 1938).

———, *City Development* (New York, 1945).

National Association of Real Estate Boards, *Blueprint for Neighborhood Conservation* (Washington, 1953).

National Municipal League, *Model State and Regional Planning Laws,* Introduction by Coleman Woodbury (New York, 1954).

National Resources Committee, *Our Cities: Their Role in the National Economy* (Washington, 1937).

———, *Urban Government* (Washington, 1939).

Regional Plan Association, Inc., *Metropolis in the Making: The Next Twenty-five Years in the New York Metropolitan Region* (New York, 1955).

Donald Robinson, "Slum Clearance Pays Off," *National Municipal Review,* October 1955, pp. 461–465.

Eliel Saarinen, *The City: Its Growth; Its Decay; Its Future* (New York, 1943).

Leonard A. Salter, "County Zoning and Post-War Problems," *State Government,* October 1945.

Belden H. Schaffer, *Small Homes and Community Growth,* The Institute of Public Service, University of Connecticut (Storrs, 1954).

Alfred Steinberg, "Pittsburgh, a New City," *National Municipal Review,* March 1955, pp. 126–131.

Robert A. Walker, *Planning Function in Urban Government,* University of Chicago (Chicago, 1950).

Coleman Woodbury, ed., *The Future of Cities and Urban Redevelopment,* Urban Redevelopment Study (Chicago, 1953).

————, *Urban Redevelopment: Problems and Practices,* Urban Redevelopment Study (Chicago, 1953).

Coleman Woodbury and Frank Cliffe, "Industrial Location and Urban Redevelopment," Part II in Coleman Woodbury, ed., *The Future of Cities and Urban Redevelopment* (Chicago, 1953).

Chapter 17

THE PUBLIC SCHOOLS

The American public school system is fundamental to the American way of life. Originally based upon the cultural heritage of the early English colonists, it was quickly molded to American conditions and ideas. In turn, it vitally influenced the development of American democracy and was a chief catalyst in molding diverse elements into a unified nation. The central core of the public school system is the "common school." It is available to all of the young of the community regardless of class, creed, or color. Moreover, it is free to all, supported by public funds derived from taxation. It is controlled by elected representatives of the whole community rather than by religious, economic, political, or professional groups. Its ultimate aim is to train for responsible citizenship in an atmosphere of liberty, freedom, and equality, and to fit the youth of the nation to make their way in life.

Two basic ideas dominated education in the 17th century England when the first settlers came to American shores. One was the tradition of *philanthropy* which asserted the right and duty of individual families to provide through private means for the education of their children. The community was responsible only for the education of the poor and indigent. Opposed to this was the Calvinist doctrine of *collectivism* which placed in the hands of civil government the responsibility for the education of all. The idea of philanthropy became firmly rooted in the agrarian society of the South and to a lesser extent in the middle colonies and continued to dominate educational policy there for decades after the Revolution. The collectivist doctrine was just as strongly grounded in New England where the school law, as early as 1647 in Massachusetts, placed on the various towns the responsibility for educating the young in the rudiments of knowledge. Both reflected the Christian assumption of education for all. But the one was attuned to a class conscious society, the other to one in which the community had responsibilities for all the people. The New England concept took root in the Northwest territories where public grants of land were set aside for education. The Ordinance of 1785 carried a provision reserving each sixteenth section of a township for the maintenance of public schools.

The evolution of the public school system during the early 19th century was influenced by the spread of democratic thinking which affected all aspects of American life. If all people were to be granted citizenship and the right of suffrage, they should be educated to the task. The new voice of labor in the growing cities joined in the demand for public education for their children as a means of bolstering their agitation for equality. Immigration from foreign countries made necessary the absorption of American ideals by the children of the newly arrived if not by the immigrants themselves. By 1850, public support for education was generally accepted. Every state had established some sort of school fund and all but Arkansas had permitted taxation for public education. Likewise, public control of education had taken firm root. The states adopted general education policies and objectives, and provided for over-all supervision and some measure of financial support. But the local communities had the responsibility to establish, maintain and govern the schools of the locality. By mid-century, ninety per cent of all pupils were enrolled in public schools. In the northeast states great progress was made, and in the South the old philanthropic doctrine remained strong. While the three R's were basic, other subjects such as history, grammar, and geography were gradually added. After great and long controversy, religious education by sectarian teaching was barred.[1]

---

[1] Lawrence A. Cremin, *The American Common School* (1951). This is a brilliant analysis of early American ideas that were basic in the establishment of the present public school system.

Local School Districts

Public education is a state function. State constitutions and state laws prescribe the general outline of the public school system and its objectives, but the actual administration is left to local school districts or local units of government. In 1954, according to the United States Census, there were 59,631 school districts besides those state and local governments which carried on school functions in the states of Maryland, Massachusetts, North Carolina, Rhode Island, and Virginia.[2] The mixed system, where there are some school districts and some school systems that are administered by the local governments themselves, is found in 17 additional states. Where local governments carry on the school functions, the municipal-school relationship is much closer than in independent school districts where the school system is governed wholly by an elected board of directors. While in most of these municipalities, there is an elected board of education, in some places these are appointed by the mayor, the city council, the courts, or even the legislature. St. Paul, Minnesota, and Chattanooga, Tennessee, have no boards of education; one of the city councilmen is appointed as commissioner of education. Sometimes, the mayor or some other official of the city is *ex officio* a member of the school board and, in a large number of cities, city treasurers act as treasurers of the school board. Sometimes, budget estimates and tax levies of school boards are subject to review by municipal authorities. In many cities, the schools and the city carry out joint programs in traffic education, health, libraries, and other activities.[3]

[2] Bureau of the Census, *School Districts in the United States in 1954,* Release March 21, 1955. Public school systems other than school districts in 1952 totaled 2,409. These were municipalities, townships, and counties which carried on all or part of the school functions in 22 states. Among these were Pennsylvania with 254 joint schools maintained by two or more basic school district governments.

The number of "administrative units" in 1954–55 as estimated by the National Education Association was 60,416. In 1933, a total of 127,244 administrative units were reported. The difference represents a decline of 52.5 per cent in 22 years.

[3] Nelson B. Henry and Jerome G. Kerwin, *Schools and City Government* (Chicago, 1938).

There are several main types of school districts. The *common school* district is one that is created only for school purposes and has a board or official with basic powers of control over its operation. Common school districts exist in 27 states.[4] The town or township school district is found in the six New England states and in three others where the school district is coterminous with the township.[5] In New England, the town is the unit of government and is designated the local unit for school purposes. It elects a board of school directors at its annual school election or town meeting. While the towns may levy the taxes for school support, the school boards carry out the school functions given to them by state law. In other states the township may be the school district or the school district may be coterminous with the township. The county school district, found in twelve states, may either include all schools within the county or all schools except the independent school districts of cities and other municipalities. Each county has a board of education and a superintendent. The county school district is usually fiscally independent of the county government although certain county officers such as the treasurer or the tax collector may be assigned duties in relation to schools.[6] Independent city school districts are found in common school, township, and county district states. Sometimes these are entirely separate from the city government with school boards elected by the voters, and sometimes they are merged with the city government, the school boards appointed by the mayor or council. They are called "independent" because they do not come under the supervision of the county superintendent of schools in

[4] The National Commission on School District Reorganization, *Your School District* (1948), pp. 49, 263. The common school states are Arizona, Arkansas, California, Colorado, Delaware, Idaho, Illinois, Iowa, Kansas, Michigan, Minnesota, Mississippi, Missouri, Montana, Nebraska, Nevada, New York, North Dakota, Oregon, South Carolina, Ohio, Oklahoma, South Dakota, Texas, Washington, Wisconsin, and Wyoming.

[5] *Ibid.*, pp. 49, 260. States having town or township systems of schools are Connecticut, Indiana, Maine, Massachusetts, New Hampshire, New Jersey, Pennsylvania, Rhode Island, Vermont.

[6] *Ibid.*, pp. 50, 261–262. County unit states are Alabama, Florida, Georgia, Kentucky, Louisiana, Maryland, New Mexico, North Carolina, Tennessee, Utah, Virginia, and West Virginia. In addition, nine other states have some county units. They are Arkansas, California, Minnesota, Nebraska, New Jersey, North Dakota, Oregon, South Dakota, and Texas.

NUMBER OF SCHOOL DISTRICT GOVERNMENTS IN 1952 AND 1954; AND NUMBER OF OTHER SCHOOL SYSTEMS IN 1952

State	Number of School Districts		Other Public School Systems 1952 [a]	State	Number of School Districts		Other Public School Systems 1952 [a]
	1954	1952			1954	1952	
United States total	59,631	67,346	2,409	Montana	1,222	1,287	—
Alabama	111	108	—	Nebraska	6,113	6,392	—
Arizona	257	270	[b] 7	Nevada	153	166	[g] 12
Arkansas	422	422	—	New Hampshire	226	228	9
California	1,966	2,010	—	New Jersey	482	481	73
Colorado	[c] 1,156	1,352	—	New Mexico	100	106	—
Connecticut	[c] 3	3	168	New York	2,682	2,915	6
Delaware	15	15	[d] 2	North Carolina	—	—	172
District of Columbia	—	—	1	North Dakota	2,102	2,079	—
Florida	67	67	—	Ohio	1,327	1,465	—
Georgia	203	187	—	Oklahoma	1,869	2,100	[h] 77
Idaho	207	305	—	Oregon	[e] 794	1,071	—
Illinois	2,557	3,484	—	Pennsylvania	2,490	2,506	[i] 254
Indiana	1,077	1,115	—	Rhode Island	—	—	39
Iowa	[c] 4,477	4,653	—	South Carolina	103	49	—
Kansas	3,592	3,984	—	South Dakota	3,388	3,399	(j)
Kentucky	224	232	—	Tennessee	13	13	137
Louisiana	67	67	—	Texas	2,035	2,479	17
Maine	[e] 5	4	482	Utah	40	40	—
Maryland	—	—	24	Vermont	18	20	245
Massachusetts	—	—	354	Virginia	—	—	127
Michigan	4,313	4,845	—	Washington	517	545	—
Minnesota	4,996	6,227	16	West Virginia	55	55	—
Mississippi	87	93	[f] 82	Wisconsin	[e] 4,591	5,298	105
Missouri	3,204	4,891	—	Wyoming	305	318	—

[a] Counties, municipalities, or townships in which all or part of the school system is operated by the county, municipality, or township government.

[b] Counties operating "county accommodation schools."

[c] For the 1952–53 school year.

[d] State Board Unit Schools and City of Wilmington.

[e] For the 1954–55 school year.

[f] Number of county governments; each county government administers numerous subordinate school units or districts. (See text.)

[g] Number of county governments operating "county high schools."

[h] Number of county governments; each county government administers the "separate" schools in "dependent" school districts within its jurisdiction.

[i] Joint schools maintained by two or more basic school district governments.

[j] In three counties the county governments administer schools for certain "unorganized territories" within their jurisdiction.

From Bureau of the Census, *School Districts in the United States in 1954* (March 21, 1955).

states where this official exercises supervisory powers over rural schools. In some states, notably California and Illinois, there are high school districts established to provide only secondary educational facilities. Subdivisions of these basic units are found in some states: attendance units, the area from which pupils attend a single school; subdistricts, in which there may be advisory committeemen to the county board of education; and fiscal subdistricts established to raise money for educational purposes in those districts.

One of the most important movements in the field of local government in recent decades has been the consolidation of local school districts. Especially since the end of World War II have great strides been made. In 1942, there were 108,579 school districts in the United States; by 1952, the number had been reduced to 67,346, a reduction of thirty-eight per cent, and by 1954, the number was 59,631.[7]

A number of factors are responsible for this trend. The cost per pupil in small schools is higher. It was found that in Iowa urban school districts averaged about 30 pupils per teacher, rural districts only 18. Teachers in urban districts received almost twice as much salary and it can be assumed were the better qualified. But the cost of urban schools exceeded the cost of rural schools only about 10 per cent per pupil, and much greater educational opportunities were offered. The Regents' Inquiry in New York state showed that the cost of education per pupil rose as the number of pupils per teacher dropped. A study in Idaho showed that schools having fewer than 50 pupils cost on an average of 53 per cent more per pupil than schools with 300 pupils. In the state of Washington in high schools having fewer than 50 pupils the cost was 67 per cent higher than in those with more than 150 pupils, and the cost per pupil decreased until enrollments reached 1,500.[8]

But in 1947–48, there were still more than 75,000 one-teacher schools. Iowa, Minnesota, Missouri, Nebraska, and Wisconsin had more than 4,000 such schools each. In these states and in Illinois and the Dakotas, 75 or more per cent of all elementary schools were

[7] *School Districts in the United States in 1954, op. cit.* Between 1952 and 1954, Illinois reduced its number by 927, Michigan by 582, Minnesota by 1,231, Missouri by 1,687, Texas by 444, and Wisconsin by 707.

[8] *Your School District, op. cit.,* pp. 89–90.

of the one-teacher type. On the other hand, there were fourteen states in which one-teacher schools were 25 per cent or less of the total number of elementary schools.[9] In high school enrollment per school, New Jersey lead with 90 per cent of its high schools having 300 or more pupils, the size that it is generally agreed can provide a comprehensive program at reasonable cost. Other states with more than half of their high schools over 300 include Rhode Island, Connecticut, California, Delaware, and Pennsylvania.

Small schools cannot offer the broad and comprehensive educational program that is now regarded to be in line with modern standards. Among the new and expanded features and services deemed economically available only in larger units are high schools, kindergartens, competitive athletics, adult education, education for handicapped children, vocational education, and guidance counseling.

Far-reaching social and economic changes in American life have made the ordinary small and independent one-room school hopelessly out of date, even though all agree that it had many virtues and provided the basic education for the great majority of Americans during the first century and a half of national existence. In fact, it is still the basic educational institution in most of rural America. One of these changes is the marked decline of children of school age in farming areas brought about by the decrease in size of farm families, the migration of people to urban and suburban places, and the increase in the size of farms. The one-room school is too expensive and inadequate under these rapidly changing conditions. The differences between rural and urban life have decreased to such an extent that the same type of educational opportunities including longer terms and more years of schooling, and the "enrichment" of the curriculum are sought by both urban and rural people. Furthermore, the hard road and the motor vehicle have made possible the establishment of larger districts through the agency of the school bus. Thus has social community been enlarged. It is now

[9] These are in order of percentage: Massachusetts (7.3%), Utah, Rhode Island, New Jersey, Washington, Ohio, Connecticut, Indiana, Maryland, North Carolina, Texas, Arizona, California, and New Hampshire (24.7%). See Council of State Governments, *The Forty-Eight State School Systems* (1948), pp. 56–57.

the town and its rural neighborhoods; there are fewer isolated and independent rural communities.

The National Commission on School Reorganization has established a set of standards on the basis of which each administrative school unit should have at least 1,200 pupils between the ages of 6 and 18, and if possible as many as 10,000. If the number falls much below 10,000, the unit should be made a part of an intermediary school unit which would supply certain services not available in the basic unit. A minimum enrollment of 1,200 would require forty classroom teachers if one teacher is provided for each thirty pupils. No elementary school should have less than 175 pupils with seven teachers; no junior or senior high school less than 300 pupils with 12 teachers. Elementary pupils should not travel more than 45 minutes each way from home to school, and high school students not more than one hour.[10]

As of 1948, only three states—Louisiana, Maryland, and West Virginia—had no districts employing fewer than forty teachers, and only in nine other states, all in the South where the county unit prevails, and in Nevada did the majority of districts meet this requirement. In thirty-one states, less than 10 per cent of the districts employed forty or more teachers. But consolidation has made much headway since 1948. For example, the United States Office of Education reports that in 1953 in eight states 552 reorganized districts replaced 8,424 former districts, notably in Illinois where one new district replaced 21.6 old districts.

The trend towards larger units of school administration has led to a variety of school district organizations. Little change has come in the city schools districts, except in some of the smaller cities and boroughs that have merged in joint school districts with those in outlying areas to create a larger unit either for high school only or for all grades. These districts have usually more than one attendance area for elementary school children. Common school districts have consolidated into community districts maintaining a high school and an elementary school in the community center and several elementary schools in outlying neighborhoods. A town or

[10] *Your School District, op. cit.,* p. 131.

township unit also may contain several schools within its borders and still be coterminous with the political subdivision. There are also intermediate units which provide special services to the local districts including supervision of teaching in many one-room districts, and instruction and services in special areas such as music and health.[11]

The governing body of the local school district is the board of school directors. This body adopts the policies for the operation of the school system, appoints the superintendent, appoints other members of the teaching staff and other employees on the recommendation of the superintendent, levies taxes, appropriates money, incurs indebtedness, and generally supervises the administration of the schools. The number of members in boards ranges from three to twenty-one, five being most common. Most of the boards are popularly elected but there are some interesting exceptions. In 1955, the NEA estimated that there were 234,000 school board members in the nation.[12]

The superintendent of schools is the chief executive and administrative officer of the local school system. Usually selected by the board of education, he is responsible to them for the administration of the school system. His professional qualifications are generally expressed in terms of training and experience in the field of education. In 1955, the number of school superintendents was estimated by NEA at 15,000.

Virginia is one of the states which operates under the county unit school district. The organization of Albermarle *county* is illustrative.

[11] *Ibid.*, pp. 127–128. Consolidation and joint districts have been stimulated by state financial aid for new buildings, for bonuses to close one-room schools, and other inducements. Generally speaking, the teaching profession led the campaign for consolidation of school districts in the various states.

[12] In Georgia, the county boards of education are appointed by the grand jury; in Maryland, by the governor; in North Carolina, by the state legislature; in Virginia, by a school trustees electoral board which is in turn appointed by the circuit judges of the state courts; in South Carolina, by the state board of education; in New Mexico, by the state superintendent, the chairman of the board of county commissioners, and the district judge; and in Tennessee, by the county courts. In most of the states, city school board members are elected by the people, but in some they are appointed by the mayor or city council. *Ibid.*, pp. 61–62.

Its population is about 25,000, largely rural. It operates under a
county executive form of government, the governing body of which
is the county board of supervisors, one member being elected from
each of six magisterial districts of the county. The board appoints a
county executive who may act as head of one or more of the departments of county government. One of these departments is that
of education, headed by the division superintendent of schools and
including the local school board. The county school board of six
members is chosen by the county board of supervisors—one from
each of the magisterial districts—and selects the division superintendent of schools. (In most of Virginia's counties, the school board
is appointed by the school trustee electoral board which is in turn
appointed by the circuit court judge who himself is elected by the
state legislature. Under this scheme the school board bears no
responsibility to the county board of supervisors for the administration of schools.) In Albermarle county, school expenditures are
coordinated with the county budget, the preparation and execution
of which is the responsibility of the county executive. The board of
supervisors fixes the salary of the superintendent and determines all
expenses of the school board. The county department of finance
handles all school purchases and accounting. The board of county
supervisors may remove the school board and through the powers
vested in the county executive whom it hires and fires is in a position
to exercise continuous control over school finances. In this way
school matters are brought closer to the people than in most of the
other Virginia counties. The officers and teachers of the school system are chosen by the county school board upon the recommendation
of the division superintendent. As the county handles financial matters, the superintendent and county school board can concentrate on
educational administration. The school budget is prepared by the
division superintendent, approved by the school board, submitted
to the county executive, and finally adopted by the board of county
supervisors. The county's share of school revenues is derived from
a tax levy of $2.10 per $100. The total cost of education is split fairly
evenly between county and state. In the county system there are
22 white schools and 27 Negro schools. Total school enrollment is

about five thousand pupils with 176 teachers and a total budget of well over one-half million dollars a year.[13]

The County Superintendent of Schools

In the early days of the Republic, public education was a local institution but when free schools were mandated by law during the first half of the 19th century, the state took on some responsibilities for the educational system. The state superintendent of education emerged as the chief school officer of the state. It was then that the county superintendent came into being, taking an intermediate position between the state and the local school district. It was he who represented the state on the local level taking the place of any county officials who had taken on the general function of overseeing the schools within the county. These included the county judge, the land commissioner, the county clerk, and the chairman of the county board of school visitors. The first state to establish the county superintendent was Delaware in 1829, and strangely enough, along with Nevada, is the only state now without a county superintendent or rural area supervisor. Connecticut, Massachusetts, and Rhode Island are the only states that never had a school official representing the county as a whole, for the New England states and New York have what is known as *supervisory unions* in which two or more districts join to form a supervisory unit. In the thirty-nine other states, there are between 3,300 and 3,400 county superintendents. They are of two kinds: the county intermediate superintendent in which the superintendent acts as an intermediary between the state and local districts (27 states), and county superintendents of the 12 county unit states in which the county superintendent is the active head of the entire county school system in the same capacity as the superintendent of city or consolidated schools. Most of the latter type are south of the Ohio River and east of the Mississippi River.

[13] Paul W. Wager, ed., *County Government across the Nation* (Chapel Hill, North Carolina, 1950), pp. 368–369. The chapter on Virginia was prepared by Dr. George W. Spicer, Department of Political Science, University of Virginia.

In those states in which the county superintendent acts as an intermediary between the state and the local districts, the functions of the office include record keeping and reporting in order to see that local units adhere to state law and conversely that they receive their rightful state subsidies. The superintendent takes the lead in working for progressive measures such as jointure and consolidation, the installation of new programs of study, and the improvement of buildings and equipment. Generally also he supervises the instruction in those places where one-room schools still exist. He also takes on new duties and functions which can be administered on a countywide scale. Actually, the county superintendent of schools acts as the leader of the rural school system where there is no consolidation of districts.[14]

The Teachers

In 1954–55, the United States Office of Education estimated a total of 1,126,561 members of public school instructional staffs. This includes 690,000 elementary school teachers, 376,000 secondary school teachers, and 60,000 principals and supervisors. During the three years preceding, elementary school teachers increased by 63,000 and secondary school teachers by 47,000. While in 1939–40, there were few classroom teachers that did not hold "regular" certificates, it was estimated that there would be more than 80,000 emergency classroom teachers in 1954–55. Total turnover is about 90,000 a year, while 75,000 drop out of teaching. One-third of these leave because of marriage and family reasons and 15 per cent for age and disability. Others go to other states, to more lucrative employment, or leave for miscellaneous reasons.[15] The Research Division of NEA showed that teacher-education institutions produced 95,565 persons in 1953–54 qualified in their respective states for teaching certificates. If, as it is assumed, 40 per cent of this number or 38,000

[14] National Education Association, *The County Superintendent of Schools in the United States,* Yearbook (February, 1950), pp. 28–53.

[15] National Education Association, *Advance Estimates of Public Elementary and Secondary Schools for the School Year 1954–55* (issued November, 1954), pp. 2–5.

MINIMUM, MAXIMUM, AND MEDIAN SALARIES, CLASSROOM TEACHERS

(Cities Over 100,000 Population)
By Degree and by Region
School Year 1954–55

	South	Northeast	North Central	West	All Cities Reporting
Bachelor's Degree					
Minimum					
Low	$2,400	$2,700	$3,000	$3,120	
High	3,440	3,700	3,862	3,940	
Median	2,845	3,000	3,325	3,500	$3,115
Maximum					
Low	3,391	4,200	4,600	4,700	
High	5,400	6,750	6,020	6,000	
Median	4,325	5,310	5,500	5,510	5,190
Master's Degree					
Minimum					
Low	2,600	2,700	3,200	3,342	
High	4,016	3,700	4,102	4,150	
Median	3,125	3,200	3,500	3,800	3,400
Maximum					
Low	3,804	4,400	5,025	4,880	
High	5,792	7,000	6,260	6,590	
Median	4,840	5,555	5,700	6,000	5,450
Doctor's Degree					
Minimum					
Low	3,000	3,100	3,200	3,450	
High	4,450	5,400	4,000	4,632	
Median	3,412	3,430	3,827	4,016	3,600
Maximum					
Low	4,650	4,760	5,325	5,060	
High	5,800	7,300	6,650	7,278	
Median	5,000	5,900	6,050	6,600	5,805

From The Tax Foundation, *School Teachers' Salaries in Large Cities* (New York, 1955), p. 24.

go into teaching, then a gap of 135,000 exists between that number and the estimated 173,000 actually needed. Part of this need is met by the employment of 80,500 emergency teachers; the remainder of the need is not met except by enlarging classes or other improvisation.[16]

[16] National Education Association, "The 1954 Teacher Supply and Demand," *Journal of Teacher Education*, March, 1954.

One of the primary objects of state and local school administration is to provide well-qualified teachers. Most states have not only set up standards for teacher certification but have also recognized or have established institutions to train teachers in accordance with those standards. Legislation relating to teacher tenure, minimum salaries and increments, and retirement has been adopted by most states. Four years of college education for a certificate to teach in high school, including from nine to forty-two hours of professional courses in education are generally required. New York and Washington require five years of college, and California requires a bachelor's degree plus 18 semester hours of graduate work. In most of the states, requirements for a certificate to teach in elementary schools are lower, usually one or two years of college with a certain number of professional courses in education, although in 17 states four years of college are required. Of more than 850,000 teachers from all the forty-eight states reported in 1948, 48 per cent had bachelor's degrees, 14 per cent had master's degrees or higher, 38 per cent had less than four years of college, and 3 per cent had no college preparation. More than half the California teachers held master's or higher degrees but no other state approached this record. In eight states, 70 or more per cent of the teachers held bachelor's degrees.[17] On the other hand, 30 per cent or more of the teachers in seven states had less than two years of college.[18] Teachers with less than two years of college preparation are usually found in small rural elementary schools.

Teachers salaries are increasing slowly and a little faster than prices, but these gains are offset by higher taxes and the fact that earnings in other professions are increasing at a faster rate. Like all public employment, teachers salaries are not flexible enough to supply and demand. The average salary for all instructional personnel in the United States in 1954–55 was $3,932. In terms of

[17] Arizona, Oklahoma, Texas, California, Utah, Nevada, North Carolina, and Florida. *The Forty-Eight State School Systems,* p. 210.

[18] Iowa, Mississippi, South Dakota, North Dakota, Nebraska, Kansas, and Massachusetts. Only New Jersey and West Virginia had the distinction of employing no teachers with less than two years of college preparation. Other states with less than three per cent in this class are Oklahoma, Arizona, Delaware, Pennsylvania, Maryland, and Nevada. *Ibid.,* pp. 72–73.

1935–1939 dollars this amounts to $2,050. Elementary classroom teachers averaged $3,614, secondary teachers $4,194. Twelve per cent of all teachers received less than $2,500; while 22 per cent received $4,500 or more. In 1939, the salary of teachers was slightly higher than that of the general average, today it is about the same. Highest state average salary for elementary school teachers was New York at $4,700, lowest was Mississippi at $1,880. Highest state average for secondary school teachers was New York at $5,375, lowest was Mississippi at $2,400.[19]

In 1953, beginning teachers with two years of college preparation were in most states being offered salaries from $2,400 to $2,900, while those with four years were starting at salaries from $3,100 to $3,900. California had a minimum salary from $3,000 to $3,400; Nevada, $3,200; New Mexico, $3,200; Wisconsin, $2,600; Ohio, $2,500; while many other states had a $2,400 minimum. The National Education Association called for a minimum salary of $3,600 in place of its 1949 standard of $2,400. It was reported by the National Citizens Committee for the Public Schools that major corporations offered new college graduates starting salaries that were higher than the average salaries paid to public school teachers.[20]

The Pupils

In the school year, 1954–55, the United States Office of Education estimated that there were a total of 30,673,800 public school enrollments. These were divided between 24,091,000 elementary pupils and 6,582,300 secondary pupils. California and New York each had almost two and one-half million, while Illinois, Michigan, North Carolina, Ohio, Pennsylvania, and Texas each had more than a million. As compared with the school year 1953–54, there were significant changes showing the dynamic character of school population in the 1950 decade. There was an increase of 1,263,000 pupils, of 43,000 instructional staff, of $487 million in current expenditures, and an increase of 5 per cent in average salary of instructional staff.

[19] *Advance Estimates, op. cit.,* pp. 5–6, 16.
[20] *The Municipal Year Book 1954,* pp. 491–492.

The accelerated growth of pupil enrollments has caused a shortage of buildings and qualified teachers, which during the past eight years were critical on the elementary level and are now producing serious problems in secondary schools.[21] It is estimated that by 1959–60 there will more than 36 million pupils in public schools. This increase represents the first major influx of students since after World War I for there was relative stability of school population during the 1930's and the 1940's. The NEA estimates the elementary classroom shortage of the nation in 1955 at 70,000, using 30 pupils as a unit. All but a few states also reported shortages in secondary facilities.

According to educational authorities, the coverage of the school age population given by public schools is still far from complete. Somewhat under half of those who enter as high school freshmen drop out before completion of four years of secondary training. Other gaps include children of migratory workers and handicapped or exceptional children requiring special provisions not usually available in the poorer school systems. Likewise, the problem of designing a high school curriculum where only one out of four high school graduates goes to college and the other three need technical education to enter the job market has not yet been fully resolved. More and more emphasis has been given to the problems of the community in order to provide an answer to that problem.[22]

The United States Office of Education made a study in 1949 of curriculum changes in secondary schools since 1934. "For the most part," the report says, "the changes are in the direction of more functional education. They represent efforts to meet life needs of increasingly diverse bodies of pupils." The study found that the largest enrollments were in health, safety, physical education, English, and the social studies. Many general courses such as general science and general mathematics had increased their enrollments at the expense of specific subjects such as physics, algebra, and

[21] Research Division, National Educational Association of the United States, *Advance Estimates of Public Elementary and Secondary Schools for the Year 1954–55* (issued November, 1954), pp. 1, 7. In addition, there were estimated to be 4,300,000 pupils enrolled in nonpublic schools.

[22] *Advance Estimates, op. cit.*, p. 238.

geometry. The outstanding percentage increases between 1934 and 1949 were in physical education, typewriting, and general mathematics. Subjects taught in 1949 but not in 1934 in fifteen or more states were conservation, consumer buying, safety education, driver education, home management, fundamentals of electricity, radio speaking, and aeronautics. In 1934, a total of 206 subjects were offered; in 1949, 274. Of these, 111 in 1934 and 194 in 1949 were taught in fifteen or more states.[23]

For many years, there has been an appreciable difference between city and rural schools. In 1951, the United States Office of Education published the results of a study of these differences. The conclusions were stated as follows: "The indices presented, both financial and non-financial, show the public elementary and secondary schools in city systems to be on the average somewhat better than those in rural systems. Urban schools pay higher salaries to their teachers; they spend more per pupil for education; and they have a longer school term. All these factors suggest more adequate educational services. The slightly smaller pupil-teacher ratio in the rural schools indicates smaller schools rather than higher educational standards. Rural schools, however, are improving; the differences between rural and urban schools are gradually decreasing in such important items as teachers salaries and per pupil expenditures. In some states the rural areas present a more favorable picture than the urban areas in other states, since large differences among the states still prevail.[24]

Public School Financing

Current expenses for schools in the year 1954–55 as estimated by NEA exceeds $7 billion. Add to this $2.3 for capital outlay, and the grand total is $9.3.

In the year 1952–53, the total expenditure was estimated at $6.6, representing roughly 2.3 per cent of the national income put at

[23] The Tax Foundation, Inc., *Public School Financing 1930–1954* (1954), p. 9.

[24] Rose Marie Smith, *Education in Rural and City School Systems,* United States Office of Education, Circular No. 329 (November, 1951), p. 5.

RESOURCES AND EFFORT FOR SCHOOLS, 1950–51

[Disposable income ª per child 5–17 years of age, current expenditures per pupil in average daily attendance in public schools 1950–51 and expenditures as per cent of income.]

State	ª Disposable Income 1950 (millions)	Children 5–17 July 1, 1950 (thousands)	Income per Child	Current Expenditure per Pupil in Average Daily Attendance, 1950–51	
				In Dollars	In Per Cent of Income per Child
Total all States	$196,980	30,697	$6,417	$224	3.49
Alabama	2,412	783	3,080	126	4.09
Arizona	846	182	4,648	254	5.46
Arkansas	1,493	484	3,085	117	3.79
California	16,640	1,871	8,894	277	3.11
Colorado	1,658	272	6,096	233	3.82
Connecticut	3,165	356	8,890	265	2.98
Delaware	503	62	8,113	290	3.57
D. C.	1,899	114	16,658	266	1.60
Florida	3,097	548	5,651	196	3.47
Georgia	3,177	840	3,782	133	3.52
Idaho	691	141	4,901	209	4.26
Illinois	13,679	1,573	8,696	281	3.23
Indiana	5,268	794	6,635	248	3.74
Iowa	3,443	538	6,400	248	3.88
Kansas	2,359	383	6,159	228	3.70
Kentucky	2,485	714	3,480	135	3.88
Louisiana	2,618	643	4,072	228	5.60
Maine	993	196	5,066	166	3.28
Maryland	3,001	461	6,510	222	3.41
Massachusetts	6,794	840	8,088	251	3.10
Michigan	9,139	1,308	6,987	247	3.54
Minnesota	3,654	618	5,913	251	4.24
Mississippi	1,451	573	2,532	93	3.67
Missouri	5,071	766	6,620	190	2.87
Montana	855	127	6,732	276	4.10
Nebraska	1,810	266	6,805	235	3.45
Nevada	266	30	8,867	260	2.93
New Hampshire	626	103	6,078	237	3.90

ª Disposable income means income payments to individuals less federal individual income taxes.

From Commission on Intergovernmental Relations, *Federal Responsibility in the Field of Education* (June, 1955), p. 137.

RESOURCES AND EFFORT FOR SCHOOLS, 1950–51 (*Cont.*)

State	*ᵃ Disposable Income 1950 (millions)*	*Children 5–17 July 1, 1950 (thousands)*	*Income per Child*	*Current Expenditure per Pupil in Average Daily Attendance, 1950–51*	
				In Dollars	*In Per Cent of Income per Child*
New Jersey	6,931	838	8,271	301	3.64
New Mexico	709	177	4,006	238	5.94
New York	25,390	2,522	10,067	328	3.26
North Carolina	3,610	1,030	3,505	155	4.42
North Dakota	741	148	5,007	235	4.69
Ohio	11,381	1,514	7,517	202	2.69
Oklahoma	2,200	508	4,331	211	4.87
Oregon	2,086	300	6,953	282	4.06
Pennsylvania	14,653	2,034	7,204	246	3.41
Rhode Island	1,093	139	7,863	261	3.32
South Carolina	1,647	576	2,859	132	4.62
South Dakota	789	145	5,441	239	4.39
Tennessee	2,963	772	3,838	138	3.60
Texas	8,848	1,704	5,192	215	4.14
Utah	820	171	4,795	183	3.82
Vermont	407	81	5,025	223	4.44
Virginia	3,262	735	4,438	157	3.54
Washington	3,525	454	7,764	258	3.32
West Virginia	1,965	499	3,938	158	4.01
Wisconsin	4,524	701	6,454	252	3.90
Wyoming	400	63	6,349	281	4.43

$225 billion, and $1,639 per capita.[25] Of the total local income for public schools estimated in 1954–55 of $8.4 billion, 38 per cent came from state sources. The range of state aid was from 4.1 per cent in New Hampshire to 85 per cent in Delaware. Federal aid is estimated at $200 million.

The estimated expenditure per pupil in 1954–55 is $261.68. This compares with $88 in 1939–40. But in terms of the pre-war dollar, the 1954–55 figure is $136.43, a gain in purchasing power of only 55 per cent.[26]

[25] *Advance Estimates, op. cit.,* p. 20; and *The Book of the States 1954–55, op. cit.,* p. 237.
[26] *Advance Estimates, op. cit.,* pp. 8–9.

Between 1930 and 1946, school revenues from state sources tripled, and from 1946 to 1951 they more than doubled. Local sources provided only 13 per cent more revenue in 1946 than in 1930, but from 1946 to 1951 they increased 73 per cent. Local revenues for schools have not quite doubled between 1930 and 1951, but receipts from state sources have increased about seven times. Local support of schools has decreased from 83 per cent of total revenue receipts in 1931 to 57 per cent in 1951. On the other hand, state participation rose from 17 to 40 per cent during the same period. Federal aid, though not entirely absent, is still a very small percentage of the total. It is spent mostly for school lunches, vocational education, and aid to "federally impacted" school districts.

What are the reasons for the lag in local school support and the increase in state aid? First, local school districts and local units are operating under severe financial restrictions placed in the state laws. Maximum rates of tax levy are prescribed. Assessments of property for local taxation are low. Revenue from tax levies is based on assessments and indebtedness is limited to a percentage of assessed valuations in most school districts. Property tax exemptions also cut down revenues. Second, state aid recognized that fiscal capacity to support public education varies from community to community within the state, and that equalization of educational opportunity is a most desirable governmental objective. As school costs began to increase, state legislators leaned toward state aid rather than toward increasing local potentialities although in a few states notably Pennsylvania, New York, and California legislatures passed laws enabling the levy of local nonproperty taxes such as income and sales taxes to supplement property tax revenues. But the increase of school expenditures was so great that state aid has become a major item of state expenditure. In 1952, educational grants-in-aid constituted 16 per cent of total state expenditures in the United States. The range was from 1.5% in New Hampshire to 29% in New Mexico and North Carolina.[27]

State aid formulas are generally devised with four major provisions. First, the local district must levy taxes up to a certain level.

[27] *The Book of the States 1954–55*, p. 247.

Usually this is in the form of a mandatory tax levy for school purposes at a specific minimum rate on the assessed valuation of the taxable property in the district in terms of actual market value. Second, an equalization level must be established by state law. This is in the form of a certain dollar amount per pupil, per teacher, or per classroom unit. The state then pays the local school district the difference between the equalization level and the amount per unit that is yielded by the mandatory tax levy. In this way the state reimburses poorer districts at a higher ratio than comparatively more wealthy districts. Third, a flat grant per pupil or other local unit is given to each local district. This is a help to all districts irrespective of wealth and is a general relief of property owners. Fourth, special aid is granted for particular items such as school buildings, bus transportation, vocational education, kindergartens, and others.[28]

Many states have recently increased their level of state support for foundation programs, most of the additional funds going into equalization aid rather than flat grants: for example, Georgia, from $103 to $144 per pupil; Washington, from 20 to 30 cents a day per pupil; and Illinois, from $160 to $173 per pupil.

In a few states in recent years the state has acted as a lender to local school districts for the purpose of school construction. California and Arkansas are examples of states which loan money for approved school buildings. Several other states, notably Pennsylvania, Georgia, Indiana, Kentucky, and Maine, have established state school building authorities which loan money to school districts for building construction. The local district repays the authority in the form of rents, part of which are reimbursable to local districts by state aid.[29]

In recent years, extensive study and deliberation has been devoted to the problem of federal aid to education besides what is now being done in certain specialized fields and under the impact of

[28] *Ibid.*, p. 240.
[29] See *Public School Financing, 1930–1954, op. cit.* Also see Arvid J. Burke, *Financing Public Schools in the United States* (1951); United States Office of Education, *Expenditures for Education at the Midcentury* (1953) and the *Supplement* (1954).

defense production. During the past thirty years, bills proposing annual federal appropriations to aid the states in financing general elementary and secondary education have been introduced in the United States Congress, and many nationwide committees have made certain recommendations for federal assistance in the field of general education.

Proponents of federal aid have declared that the federal government is partly responsible for general education because the preservation of democracy and the national welfare depends on the existence of a high standard of education; that the present mobility of population makes education a matter of national concern; that the bestowal of citizenship upon large numbers of Negroes created a federal responsibility in the states with large Negro populations; and that the federal government is the only agency that can bring about an equitable distribution of educational opportunities. The principle of federal aid is well established in education and other fields, the proponents continue, and the Supreme Court has ruled it constitutional. Inequality exists in an appalling degree among states and localities largely on account of unequal financial ability. Even so, they say, the poorer states are making a greater effort to support education than the rich ones.

Opponents to federal aid point out that, according to the Constitution of the United States and the general governmental division of powers between states and nation, education is a state and local concern; that education is better controlled when it is local; that aid would unwisely increase federal spending when there is already in existence the highest national debt in history; and that federal aid would take away from the states and local units their real responsibility and continue legal shackles that make increased local support difficult; and that grants would increase the dangers of federal centralization and regimentation.[30]

A study committee report to the Commission on Intergovernmental Relations made a number of significant recommendations on the problem of federal financial aid for public schools. *First*, it empha-

---

[30] Charles A. Quattlebaum, *Federal Aid to Elementary and Secondary Education*, Public Administration Service (1948), pp. i–ix.

sizes the principle that adequate education for American youth is essential to the welfare of the nation and the preservation of the Republic. *Second,* it recognizes that educational costs are on the rise and that an increasing portion of the national income must be spent for education. "The question is not whether the United States can afford to spend more on education than it does now, but how the needed funds can best be raised," its report made in June, 1955, states. *Third,* education is undoubtedly an affair of the states and localities. It is as dangerous for the federal government to assume disproportionate powers in this field as it is for the states and local units to neglect them. In a free society the function of education should not be in the hands of the national government for fear of developing sterile orthodoxy and paralyzing absolutism. Moreover, the federal government cannot achieve universal educational opportunity, sought for by some through federal channels, by appropriating money to states to be distributed at their discretion. *Fourth,* the states and localities have unused tax capacity and fiscal resources available for the educational needs of the present day. *Fifth,* states should support education not only by its financial contributions but by removing the financial shackles from local school districts and by improving the machinery of local government organization, procedures, and fiscal ability.

"The general conclusion is that Federal aid is not necessary either for current operating expenses for public schools or for capital expenditures for new school facilities. Local communities and states are able to supply both in accordance with the will of their citizens," the report concludes. School lunches, however, should continue to receive federal surplus commodities, but cash contributions should be tapered off and finally abolished. Vocational education should be supported entirely by the states and localities except where national interest is clearly involved. Public libraries are a state and local responsibility, not one of the national government. But federally impacted areas should continue to receive federal assistance in the construction and operation of schools.[31]

[31] Commission on Intergovernmental Relations, *Federal Responsibility in the Field of Education* (June, 1955), pp. 5–11.

Public Libraries

There are about 7,400 public libraries in the United States. According to the American Library Association, financial support for local library service to the public in cities of 25,000 population or more should be $1.50 per capita per year for minimum or limited service, $2.25 per capita for reasonably good service, and $3 per capita for superior service. The minimum annual income recommended for a city of 25,000 is $37,500 for book purchases and current expenses to meet these financial standards. According to the United States Office of Education, in 1948, only 22 out of the 42 libraries in the largest cities met the $1.50 requirements; only three—Long Beach (Calif.), Cleveland, and Boston—met the $2.25 standard for reasonably good service, while Cleveland alone attained the $3 standard for superior service. The average current expenditures for all public libraries was 72 cents per capita.[32]

Carleton B. Joeckel divided public libraries into four classes: (1) the corporate and association libraries—these are more or less independent of city government having a self-perpetuating board of trustees and their own endowments and sources of revenue, although their revenue is often obtained from a special library tax levy; (2) school district libraries—governed by the school board or a library board appointed by the school board, the latter being preferable; (3) municipal libraries without boards—those administered directly by the city manager or some department of city government; and (4) municipal libraries with boards which may be elected or appointed as the case may be. These latter are the most numerous.[33]

Most librarians feel the way school administrators and certain other classes of public servants do—that they should be insulated more or less from city hall, that their sources of revenues should be permanent and their conditions of employment secure from the vagaries of public service in general. There are others, notably Carl Chatters, municipal finance authority, who believe that libraries

[32] Helen A. Ridgway, "Standards for Public Library Service," *The Municipal Year Book 1950*, pp. 485–486.
[33] Carleton B. Joeckel, *Government of the American Public Library*, University of Chicago (1935).

should be considered exactly like other departments of city government.[34]

New developments in public libraries have been county libraries, bookmobiles, extension divisions of state libraries, and audio-visual materials. Like so many other worth-while civic institutions, libraries never seem to have enough money to serve the community adequately.

Cultural Activities of Cities

American cities provide many cultural activities and contribute to the support of others: museums, symphony orchestras, community bands, theater groups, zoos, and aquariums, to mention the most common. When these are municipal functions they are generally under the control of semi-independent boards or commissions composed of public spirited citizens who serve without compensation. They choose a general manager and he generally hires and fires the subordinates under city rules and regulations.

The first public museum building was erected in Plymouth, Massachusetts, in 1824. The famous New York City Metropolitan Museum of Art began its distinguished career in 1871 and the city of New York agreed to provide a building for it and its maintenance. As of 1955, 257 out of the 1,233 incorporated cities, or 26 per cent, have one or more museums. About 37 per cent are government owned (98 by cities, 6 by counties, and 6 by states), and somewhat over half of their operating costs are supplied from city funds, the rest coming from endowment, gifts, and dues. Most of the museums in the larger cities are supported only in small part by city funds.

Baltimore and Denver had the first municipal bands about the turn of the century. Baltimore and Los Angeles now have bureaus of music. In San Francisco the city through its art commission presents a series of symphony concerts, and maintains a municipal chorus and band. Thirty major symphony orchestras are found in the larger American cities, many of which receive city support. None

[34] Carl H. Chatters, "Financing the Library as a Municipal Service," *The Library Quarterly* (January, 1939), pp. 1–16.

of the legitimate theaters of the United States is owned and operated municipally, but a number of cities make contributions to community theater groups.

Arboretums and botanical gardens are found in about one hundred and fifty cities. A number of cities own and operate such institutions usually under the department of parks. There are about 136 zoos in the nation, most of them publicly owned, and 80 per cent of them operated by municipal park boards and commissions.

Many cities have fine arts commissions to approve architectural designs for public buildings. Typical of the art commission is the one in Cleveland composed of 10 members appointed by the mayor and six *ex officio* members chiefly chairmen of library, planning, park, and other boards. This commission passes on any work of art placed on any city property but also gives advice with respect to design of buildings, bridges, viaducts, and other structures erected by the city or county.

Some municipalities have gone in for "higher education"—establishing and supporting junior colleges, colleges, and universities. In California cities, there are many junior colleges supported by municipal funds; and such cities as New York, Detroit, Toledo, and Cincinnati have full-fledged colleges and universities.

American cities have not given as much time, money, or supervision to the field of art as have most major European cities. In the 19th century, such activities were almost unknown in America but during the past 50 years civic interest and support has grown to substantial proportions.[35]

TEN SUBJECTS FOR FURTHER STUDY

1. School districts in your state.
2. School population in your state.
3. The public school system in the largest city in your state.
4. Reduction of one-room schools in your state.
5. Revenues of school districts in your state.
6. The functions of the county superintendent in your state.

[35] Orin F. Nolting, "Cultural Activities of Cities," *The Municipal Year Book 1955*, pp. 263–275.

7. Comparison of your state with New York in support for public schools.
8. Teachers' salaries.
9. County libraries.

REFERENCES

E. Maxwell Benton, "Better Schooling, Less Cost," *National Municipal Review*, November 1949, pp. 494–497.

Biennial Survey of Education in the United States (Washington, 1953).

Arvid J. Burke, *Financing Public Schools in the United States* (New York, 1951).

Commission on Intergovernmental Relations, *Federal Responsibility in the Field of Education* (U. S. Printing Office, June 1955).

Robert T. Daland, *Public Recreation as a Municipal Service in Alabama*, Bureau of Public Administration, University of Alabama, and Alabama League of Municipalities (Montgomery, Alabama, 1953).

Ernest A. Engelbert, "Education—a Thing Apart," *National Municipal Review*, February 1953, pp. 78–82.

Roger A. Freeman, "State Aid and the Support of Our Public Schools," *State Government*, October 1953, pp. 237–240, 252–253.

Walter H. Gaumnitz and David T. Blose, *The One-Teacher School—Its Mid-Century Status*, Office of Education, Federal Security Agency (Washington, 1950).

Harlan L. Hagman, *Administration of American Public Schools* (New York, 1951).

———, "Schools and Education—Developments in 1954," *The Municipal Year Book 1955*, pp. 459–464.

Clayton D. Hutchins and Albert B. Munse, *Expenditures for Education at the Mid-century*, and *Supplement*, Office of Education, U. S. Department of Health, Education, and Welfare (Washington, 1953).

S. Janice Kee, "Public Libraries, Developments in 1954," *The Municipal Year Book 1955*, pp. 468–472.

National Citizens Commission for the Public Schools, *Financing Public Education in the Decade Ahead* (New York, 1954).

———, *How Do We Pay for Our Schools?* (New York, 1954).

Charles A. Quattlebaum, *Federal Aid to Elementary and Secondary Education*, Public Administrative Service (Chicago, 1948).

Report of the National Commission on School District Reorganization, *Your School District* (Washington, 1948).

The Tax Foundation, Inc., *Public School Financing 1930–1954* (New York, 1954).